I0762368

INSPIRED BY NATURE

A guide to designing botanical characters

3dtotal Publishing

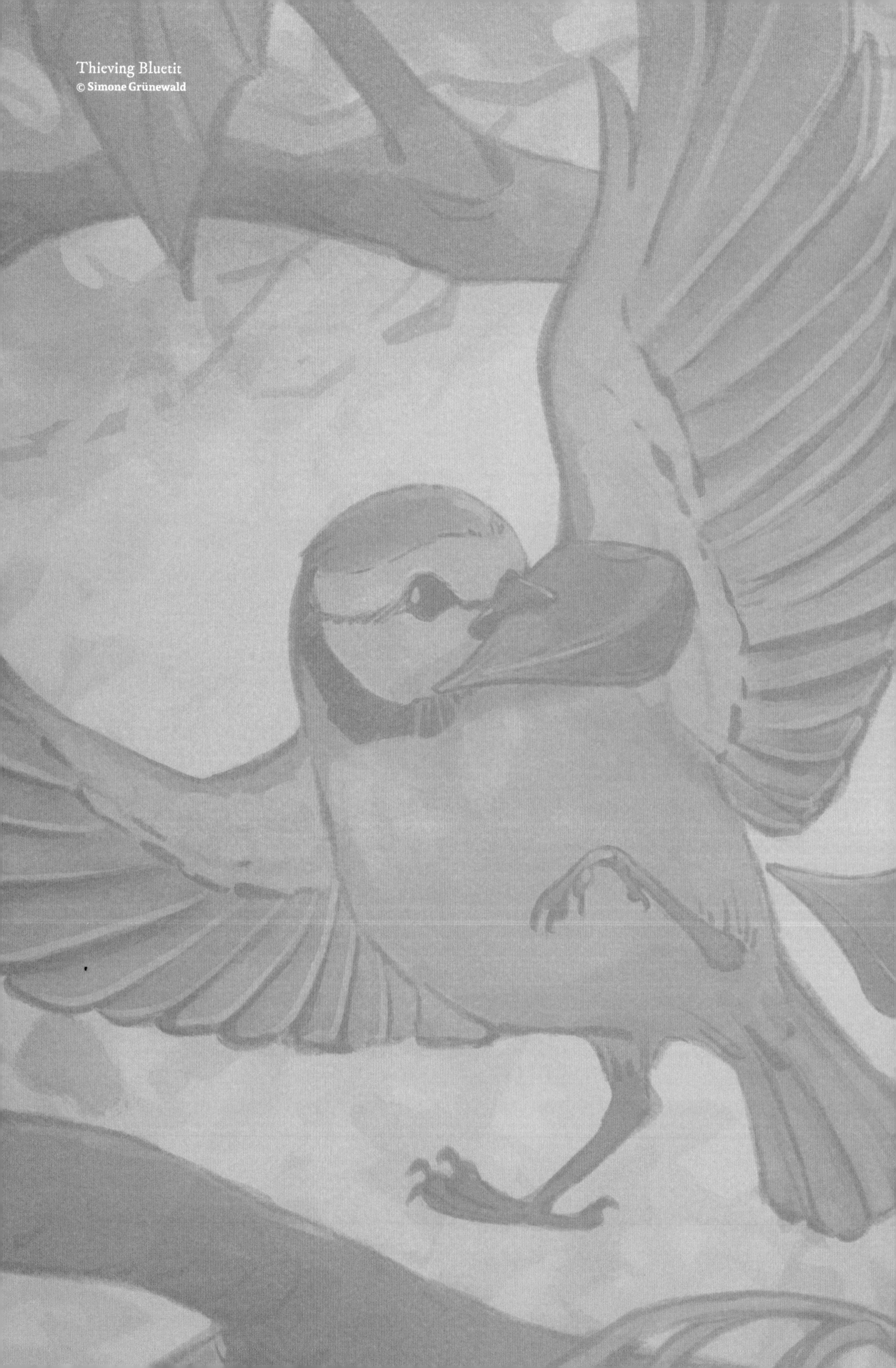

Thieving Bluetit

INSPIRED BY NATURE

A guide to designing botanical characters

3dtotalPublishing

3dtotal Publishing
Correspondence: publishing@3dtotal.com
Website: store.3dtotal.com

Every effort has been made to ensure the credits and contact information listed are present and correct. In the case of any errors that have occurred, the publisher respectfully directs readers to store.3dtotal.com/pages/information for any updated information and/or corrections.

First published in the United Kingdom, 2023, by 3dtotal Publishing.

Address: 3dtotal.com Ltd,
29 Foregate Street, Worcester,
WR1 1DS, United Kingdom.

Hard cover ISBN: 978-1-912843-84-8

Printed and bound in China
by C&C Offset Printing Co., Ltd

Visit store.3dtotal.com for a complete
list of available book titles.

Editor: Philippa Barker
Designer: Matthew Lewis
Lead Editor: Samantha Rigby
Lead Designer: Joseph Cartwright
Studio Manager: Simon Morse
Managing Director: Tom Greenway

Front of jacket artwork by Ognjen Sporin, based on designs by individual artists as listed throughout the book. Back of jacket artwork © Kacey Lynn Brown. Flap artwork © Sibylline Meynet and Corah Louise.

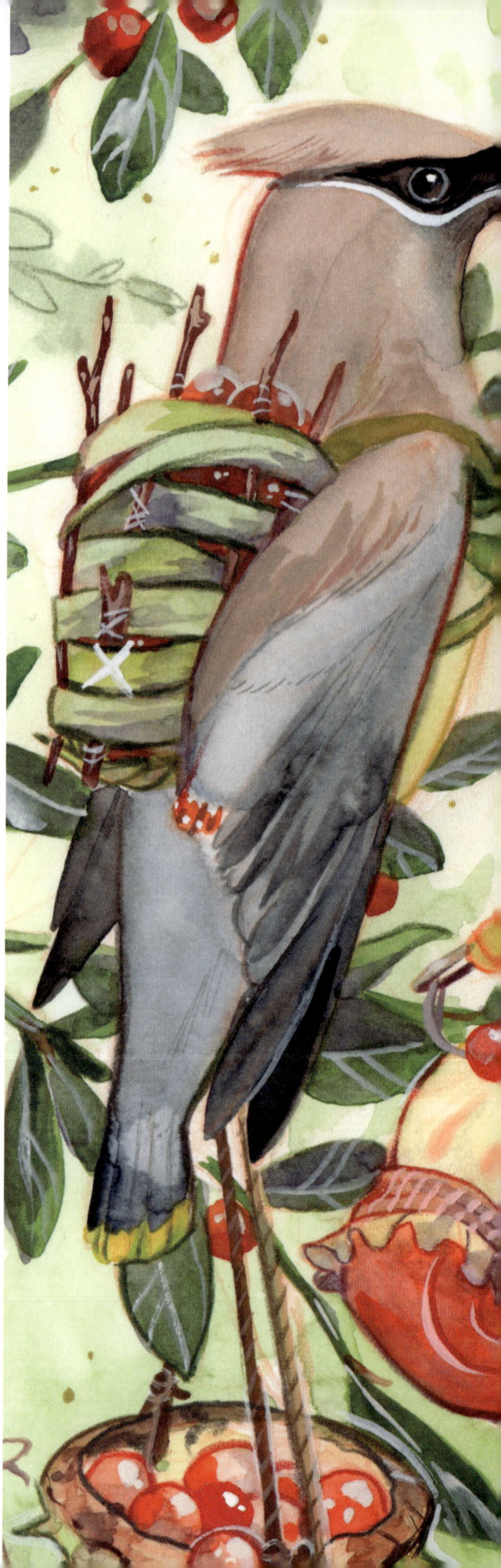

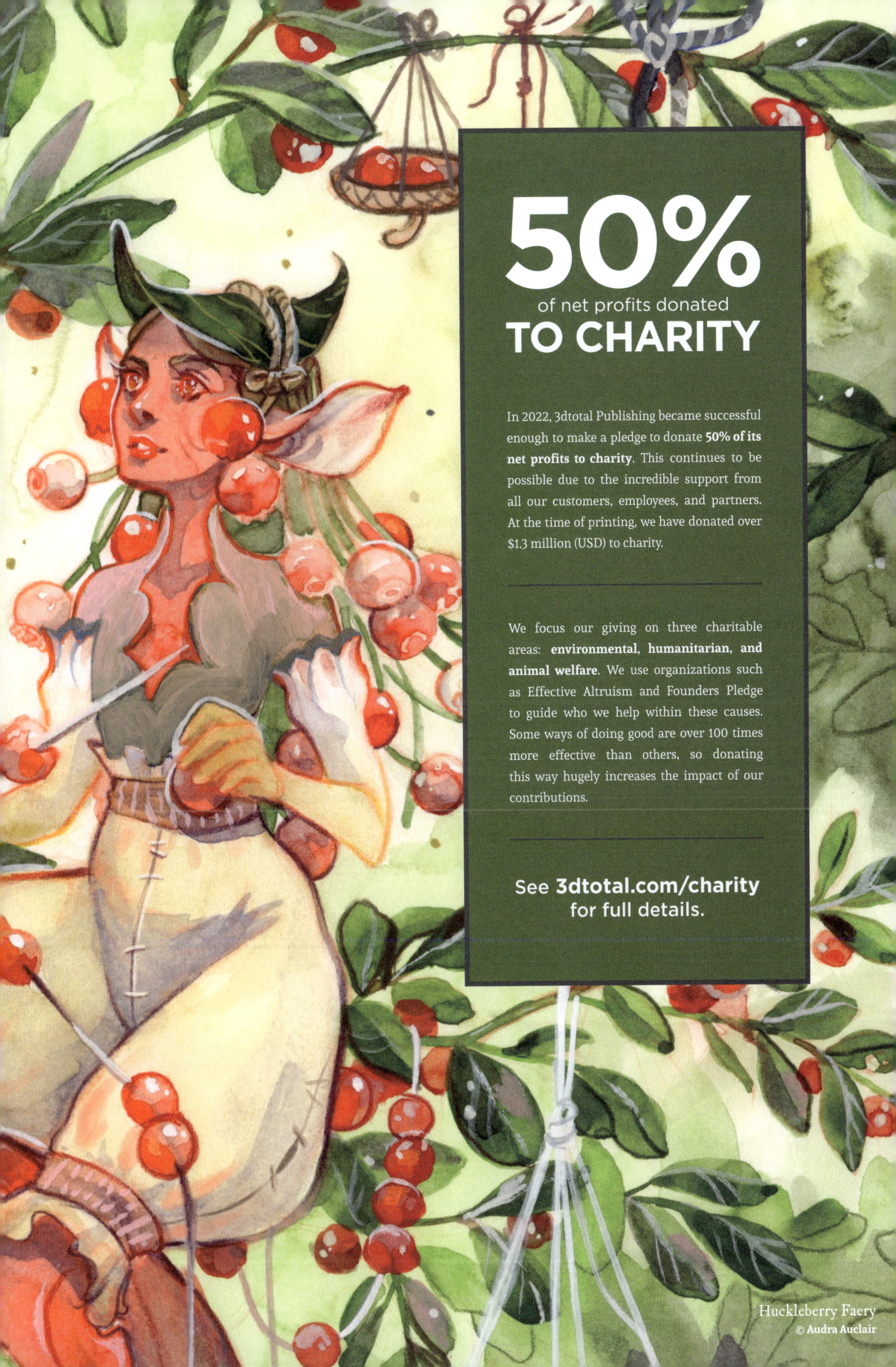
50%
of net profits donated
TO CHARITY
In 2022, 3dtotal Publishing became successful enough to make a pledge to donate **50% of its net profits to charity**. This continues to be possible due to the incredible support from all our customers, employees, and partners. At the time of printing, we have donated over $1.3 million (USD) to charity.
We focus our giving on three charitable areas: **environmental, humanitarian, and animal welfare**. We use organizations such as Effective Altruism and Founders Pledge to guide who we help within these causes. Some ways of doing good are over 100 times more effective than others, so donating this way hugely increases the impact of our contributions.
See **3dtotal.com/charity** for full details.
Huckleberry Faery
© Audra Auclair

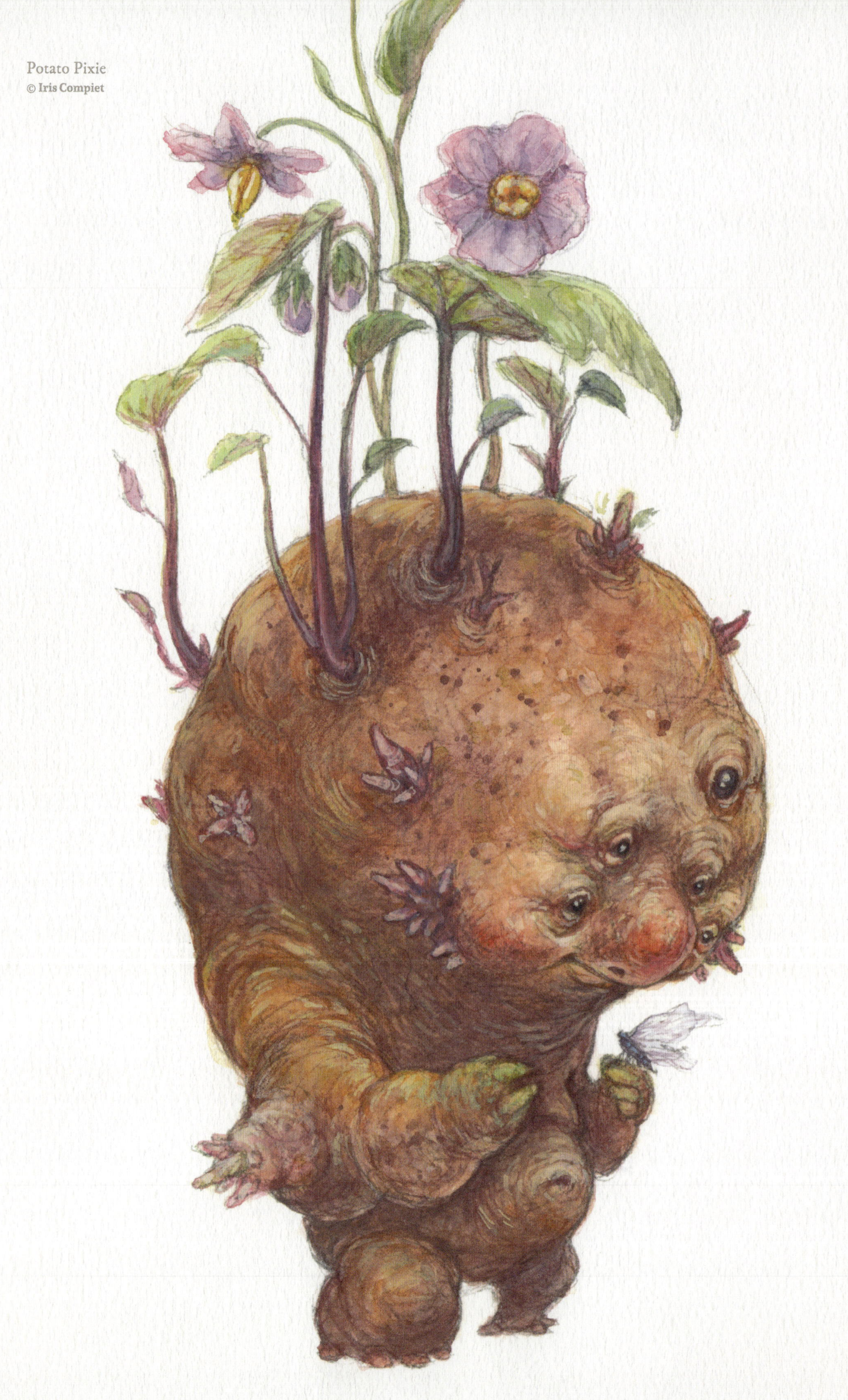

Potato Pixie
© Iris Compiet

CONTENTS

INTRODUCTION 8

TUTORIALS 12

SPRING: FOXGLOVE FAERY 14
Kacey Lynn Brown

SUMMER: CORNFLOWER GOBLIN 28
Nora Potwora

AUTUMN: BEECHNUTTER 42
Simone Grünewald

WINTER: PINECONE FAERY 56
Kiri Leonard

CARNIVOROUS: VENUS FLYTRAP CLOWN 70
Chris Hong

FUNGI: DEVIL'S TOOTH TROLL 86
Corah Louise

VINE: GRAPEVINE GOLEM 100
Ognjen Sporin

VEGETABLE: POTATO PIXIE 114
Iris Compiet

TREE: CHERRY BLOSSOM GIRL 128
Sibylline Meynet

SUCCULENT: DESERT SPIRIT 142
Ester Conceicao

FUNGI: CELESTIAL MUSHROOM GIRL 156
Feefal

TROPICAL: ORCHID ENCHANTRESS 170
Lara Georgia Carson

TREE: WILLOW-TREE GUARDIAN 184
Roma Gewska

HERB: DANDELION HERO 198
David Navarro

FUNGI: WALKING MILK CAP FAERY 212
Dominique Vassie

WETLAND: PURPLE PITCHER SPIRIT 226
Eliza Ivanova

FRUIT: HUCKLEBERRY FAERY 240
Audra Auclair

GALLERY 254

CONTRIBUTORS 290

INTRODUCTION

The natural world has been an inexhaustible source of inspiration and wonder for humankind since time immemorial, with the oldest artistic depiction of a tree in a cave painting dating as far back as 25,000 years ago. Throughout the history of art, botanical motifs are encountered and drawn from again and again. They adorn architecture and objects from the earliest Islamic period in the form of arabesques, create a rich background for millefleur tapestries of the late Middle Ages in Europe, grace the decorative wallpaper and textile designs of William Morris in the nineteenth century, and inspire the sinuous whiplash ornaments of Art Nouveau.

Botanical illustration – a unique art dedicated to depicting the form, colour, anatomy, and details of plant species – can also be traced back to antiquity, though it began to develop in earnest around the fifteenth century with the advent of herbals: books that taught the various uses of plants with illustrations accompanied by written explanations. Famous artists of the renaissance period, such as Leonardo da Vinci and Albrecht Dürer, both studied and created detailed, naturalistic drawings of plant life. Botanical art then saw its true flowering in the period between the eighteenth and nineteenth centuries, often regarded as the golden century of natural history illustration.

There is an undeniable unity and harmony in nature's innate design and its accord with the passing of the seasons, and that balance and intricacy is reflected in its visual appearance. In the imagery of plant life, a wealth of design principles are on display; plants are balanced, yet asymmetrical in shape, with pleasing form variety and natural gesture, ripe for studying and referencing. In the vastness of the various plant types and species, you can find a limitless supply of inspiration for your own creative endeavours, but it's very important to thoroughly research and gather sufficient and specific reference to enable you to take advantage of all that the natural world has to offer. In the words of Albrecht Dürer: 'Truly, art is embedded in nature; he who can extract it, has it.'*

Natural motifs can be used in various ways, so when drawing influence from plants, it's helpful to research not only their appearance, but also other qualities such as cultivation, habitat, history, and cultural context and importance. A character or creature could literally be a plant, being fully made of plant matter. Or their design could be part-plant, or simply themed around a plant in some way. Famous examples of this in pop culture include Pokémon's Bulbasaur, Marvel Comics' Groot, and DC Comics' Poison Ivy.

* *Four Books on Human Proportion* (1528) by Albrecht Dürer

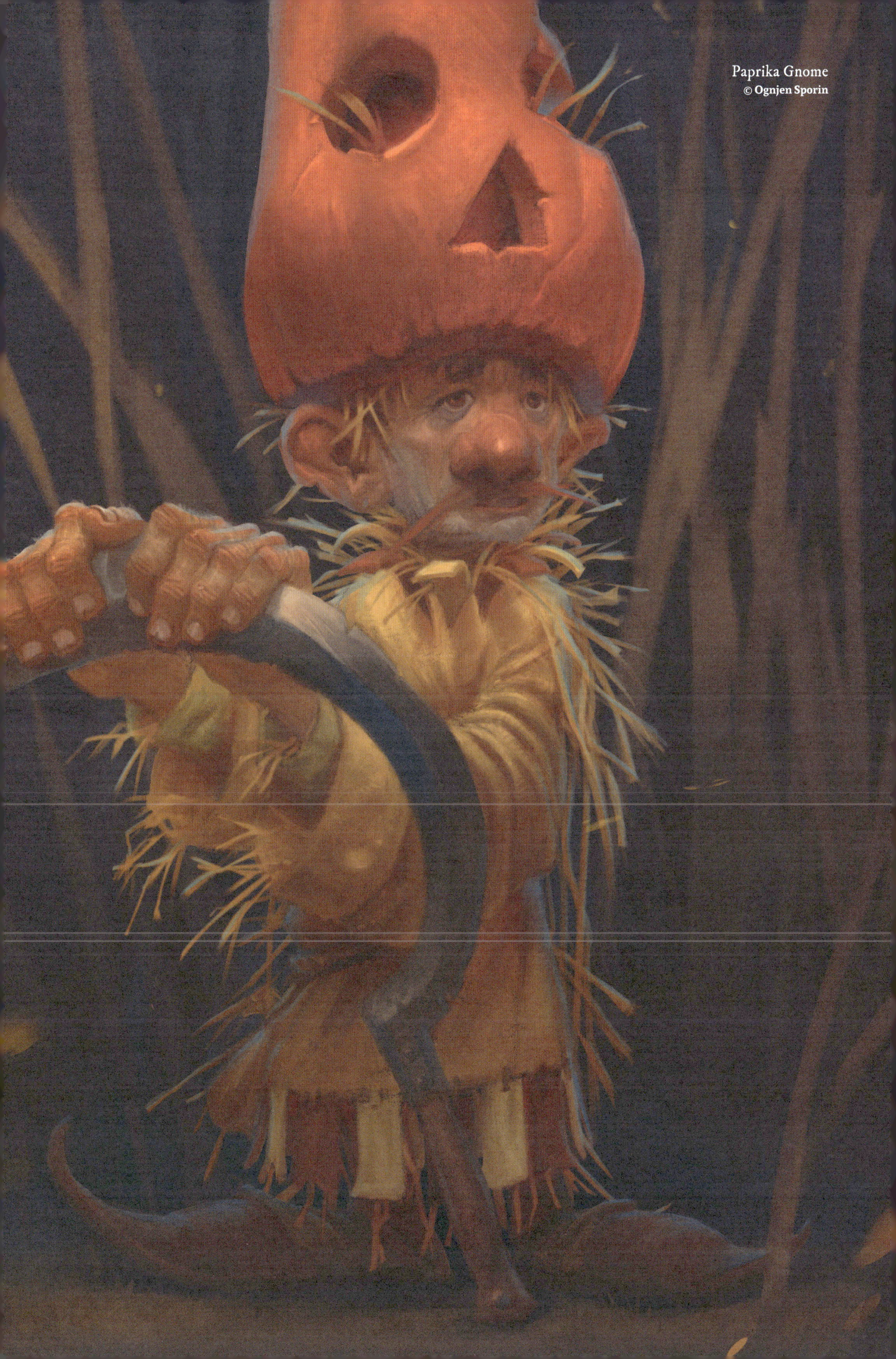
Paprika Gnome

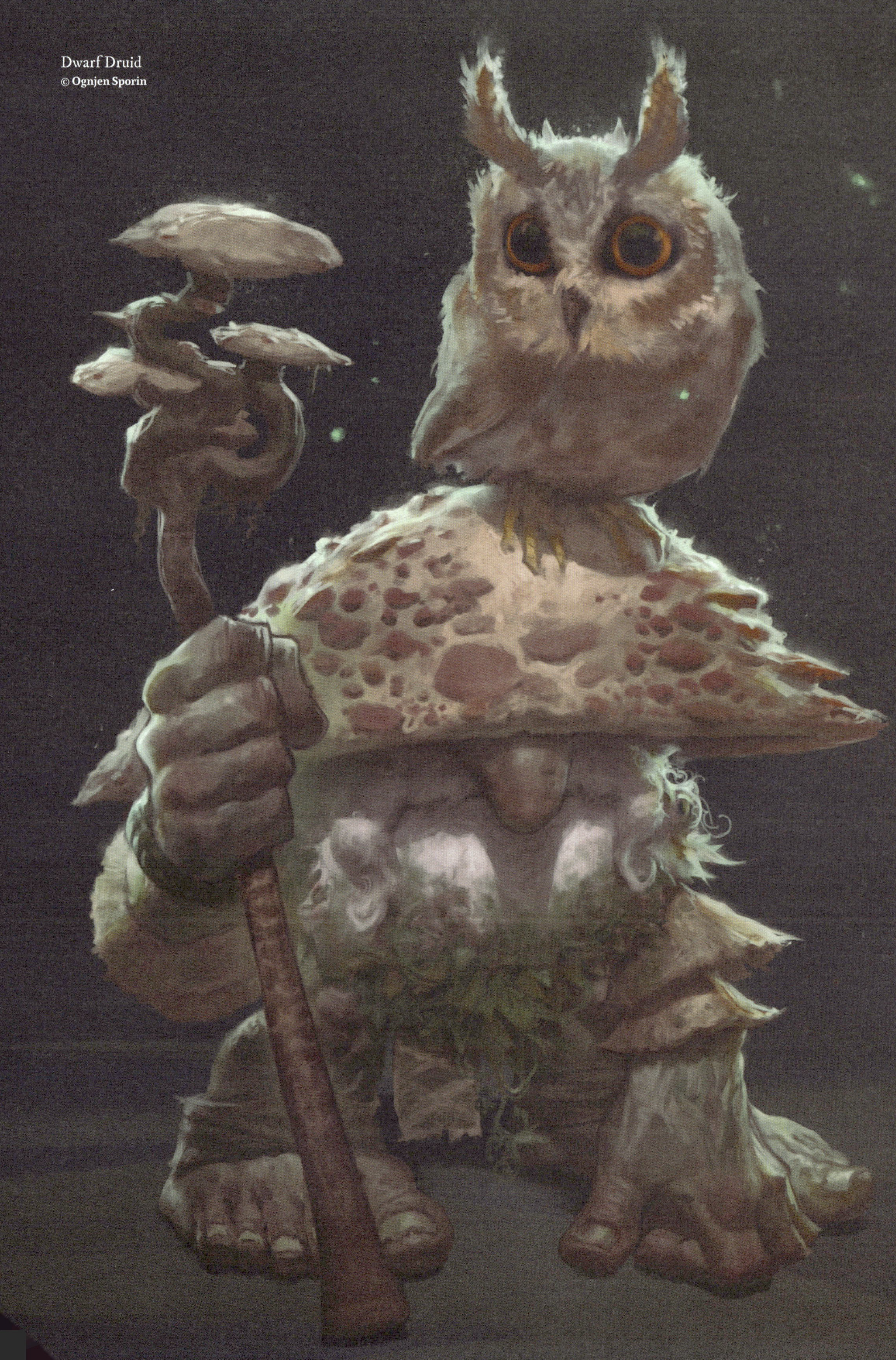

Dwarf Druid

A subtler approach might be to analyse the reference abstractly and try to somehow echo it in a graphic way. For example, instead of drawing the actual plant, you might decide to include some abstract quality of it, such as its curved shape, colour varieties, or vegetal forms, like elegance and spindliness. An iconic example of this is the design of the Mirkwood elven armour in Peter Jackson's *The Lord of the Rings* films; even though not literally depicting plants or flowers in the ornamentation, it still clearly evokes vines and stems.

Another interesting and less common use of plant motifs and themes is to consider their habitat, cultural importance, and associations. For example, holly is inextricably culturally linked to Christmas festivities, as a decoration commonly used in Europe and North America. Similarly, cherry blossoms are one of Japan's most iconic symbols, often regarded as its unofficial national flower. And certain types of mushrooms might suggest psychological exploration and extra-dimensional or shamanic themes.

Finally, mythology and symbolism can add a deeper and more esoteric layer to plant themes. At one level, a tree might be a beautiful and interesting assortment of shapes and forms, but on another, it might signify the old Norse world tree, Yggdrasil, while a fruit tree might, in a specific artistic context, also symbolize the biblical Tree of Knowledge of Good and Evil.

The tradition of botanical illustration, as well as the prevalence of nature and plant motifs that inspire art, continues into the present day, now with an unprecedented wealth of engaging styles and mediums. This book aims to showcase some of that abundance, while also providing readers with a behind-the-scenes look into how professional artists use plant life as their muse for character designs. Over the following pages, seventeen leading illustrators will design a character based on a different plant, tree, or fungi in their own distinctive styles. Step by step, they will explain their process from the planning and sketching stage, all the way through to the final rendered image, sharing valuable tips and advice throughout. There's also a gallery of botanical-themed character artwork to provide you with further inspiration for your own designs.

Whether you're only just beginning your character design journey or are seeking to develop your existing practice, following the tutorials in this book will equip you with the knowledge and skills needed to create your own unique botanical-inspired characters.

Ognjen Sporin

TUTORIALS

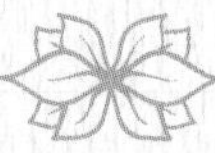

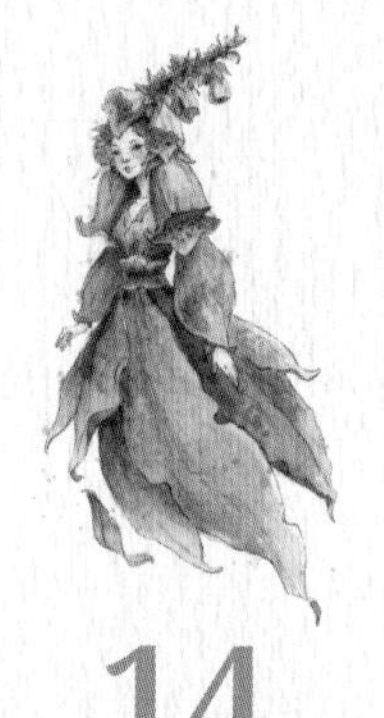

14
FOXGLOVE FAERY
Kacey Lynn Brown

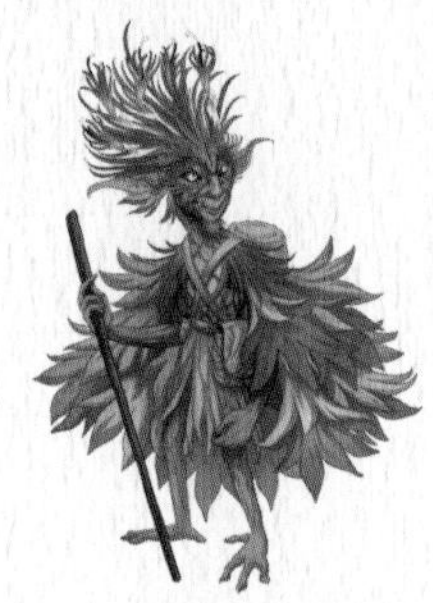

28
CORNFLOWER GOBLIN
Nora Potwora

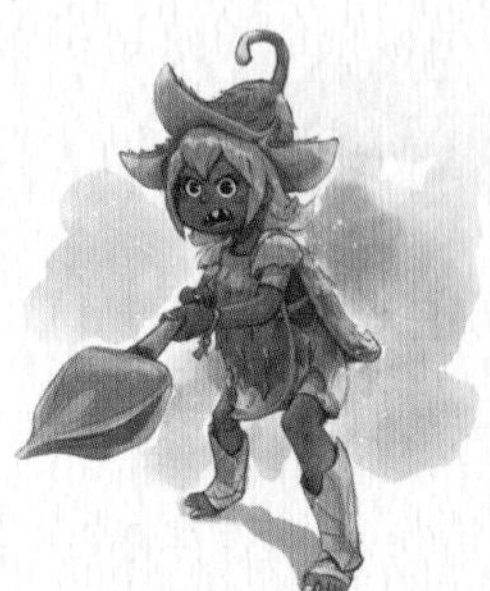

42
BEECHNUTTER
Simone Grünewald

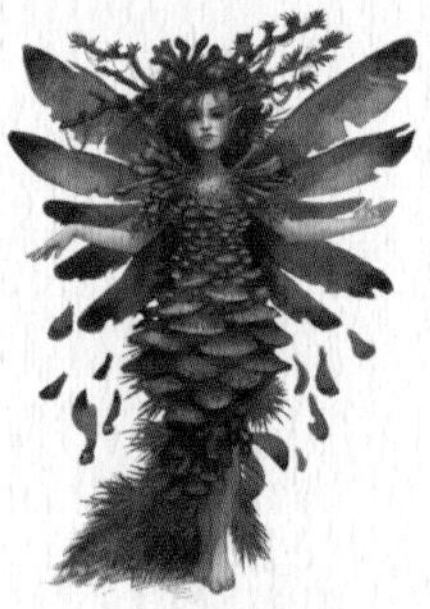

56
PINECONE FAERY
Kiri Leonard

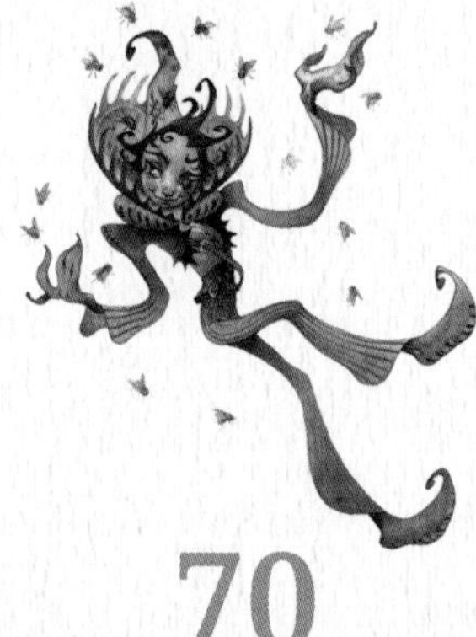

70
VENUS FLYTRAP CLOWN
Chris Hong

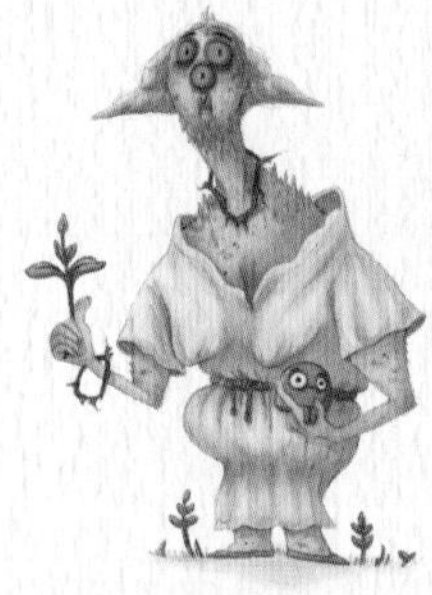

86
DEVIL'S TOOTH TROLL
Corah Louise

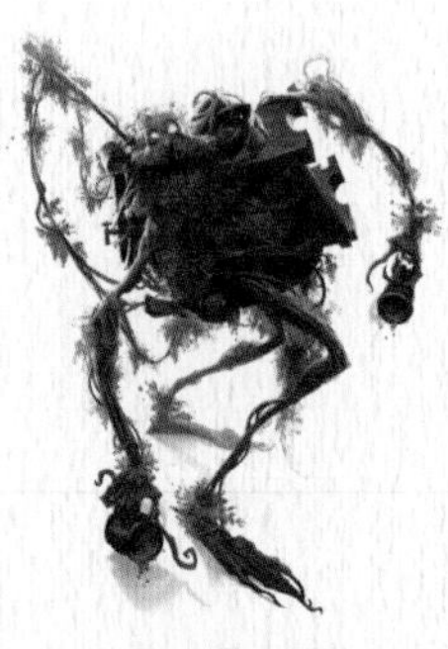

100
GRAPEVINE GOLEM
Ognjen Sporin

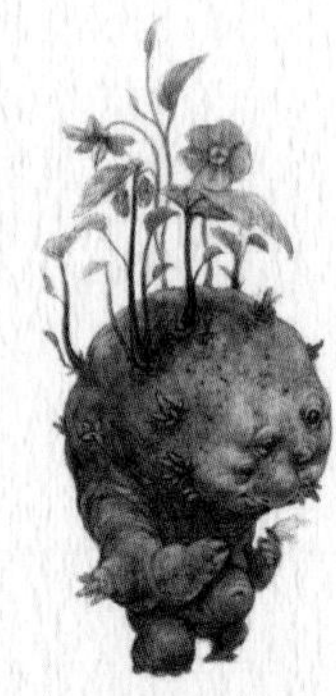

114
POTATO PIXIE
Iris Compiet

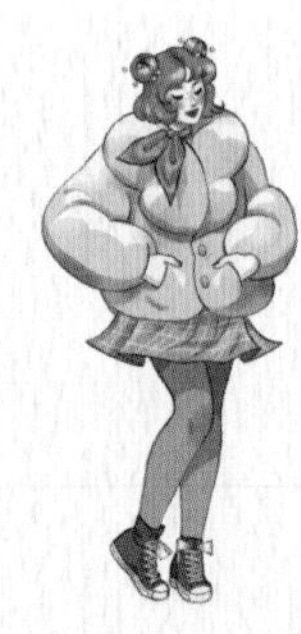

128
CHERRY BLOSSOM GIRL
Sibylline Meynet

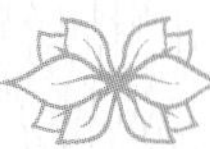

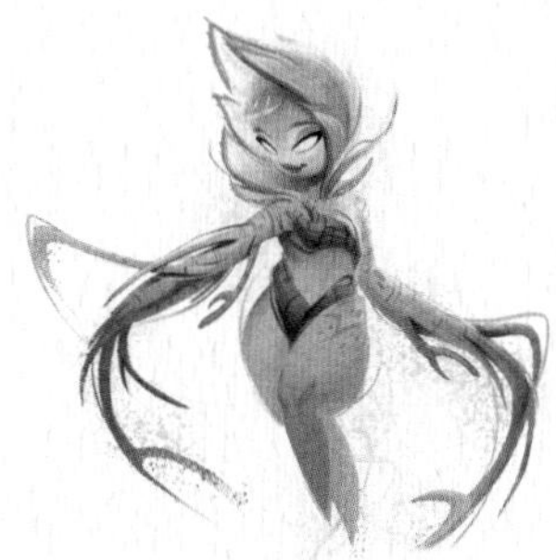

142
DESERT SPIRIT
Ester Conceicao

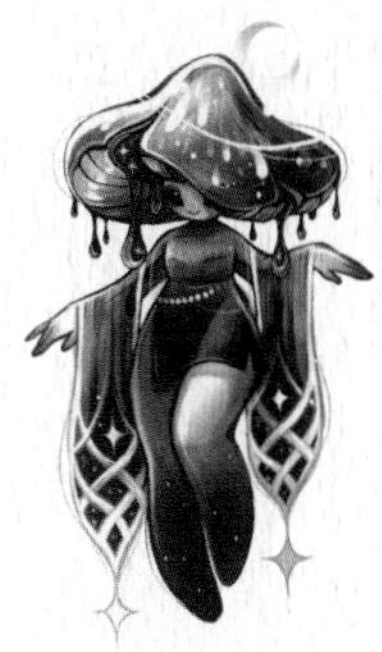

156
CELESTIAL MUSHROOM GIRL
Feefal

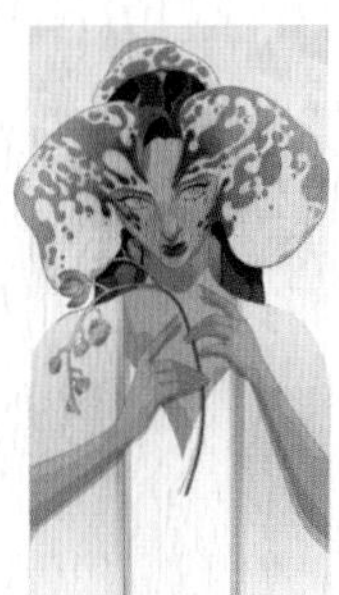

170
ORCHID ENCHANTRESS
Lara Georgia Carson

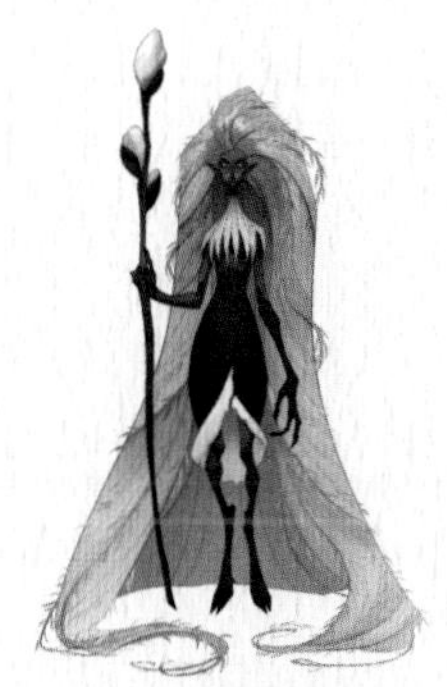

184
WILLOW-TREE GUARDIAN
Roma Gewska

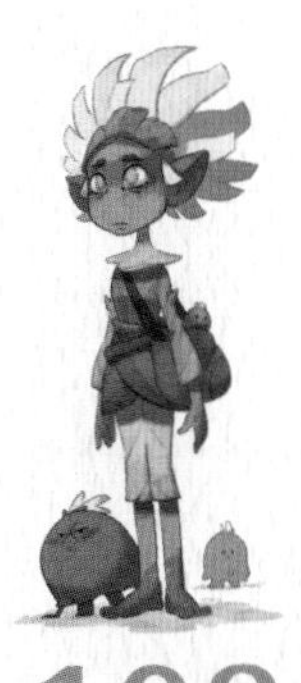

198
DANDELION HERO
David Navarro

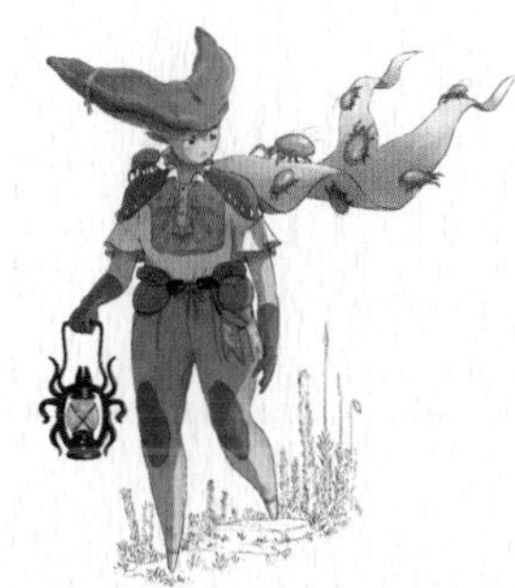

212
WALKING MILK CAP FAERY
Dominique Vassie

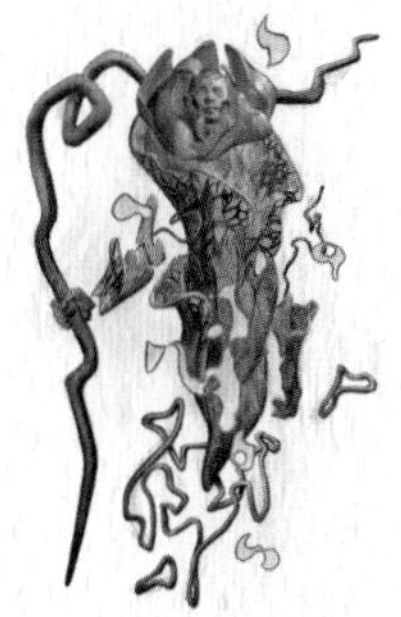

226
PURPLE PITCHER SPIRIT
Eliza Ivanova

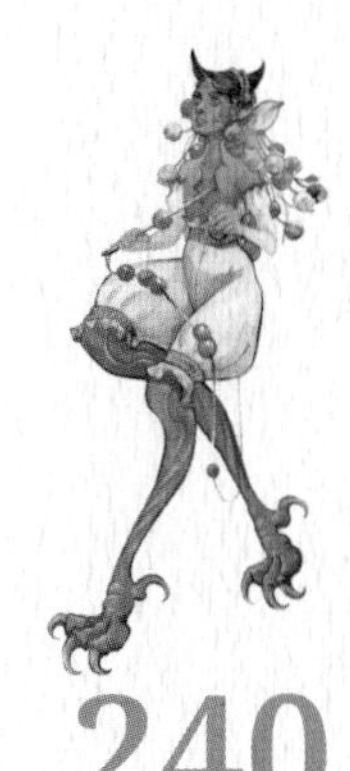

240
HUCKLEBERRY FAERY
Audra Auclair

Discover seventeen botanical-inspired character-design tutorials. Each one contains notes on the research, ideation, design, and creation of the character, leading to an eye-catching final image. Some are created using digital software, while others employ traditional tools, and some use a skilled combination of both mediums. Following each one in turn will equip you with the knowledge and ideas needed to create your own vibrant characters inspired by the wild kingdom of flora, fauna, and fungi!

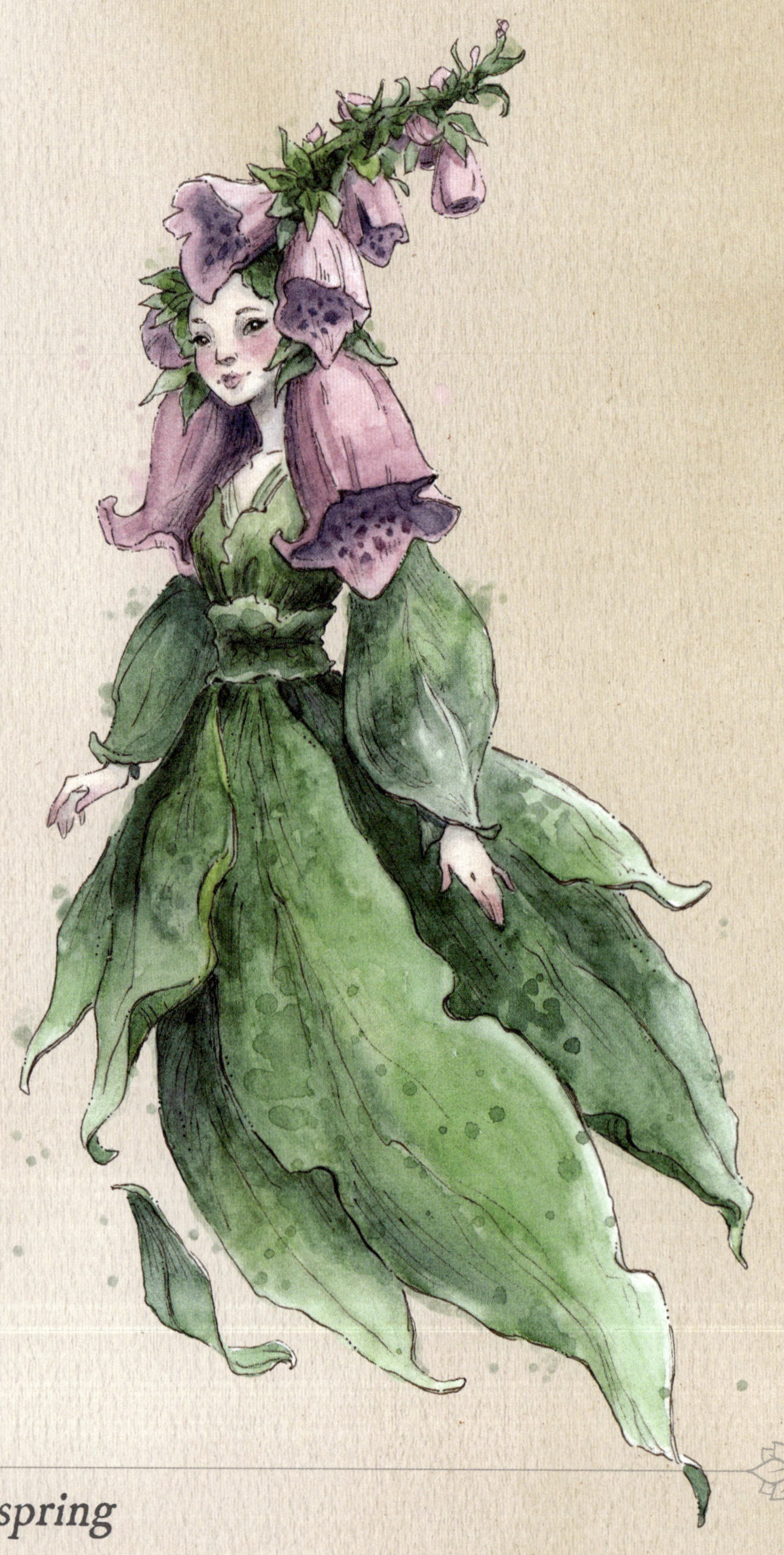

In the spring, gardens are full of an abundance of flowers. Their colour and beauty are a welcome sight after the cold, monochromatic winter, and they provide much reference material for creating interesting characters.

This tutorial will take inspiration from the springtime flower, the foxglove, using its distinctive qualities to create a whimsical faery character. Faery creatures can be found in the most ordinary of places – even a springtime flower garden – hiding just out of sight. The following pages will teach you how to identify the iconic elements of the flower and incorporate them into the faery design, in addition to demonstrating the artist's unique approach to painting with ink and watercolour.

spring

FOXGLOVE FAERY

KACEY LYNN BROWN

Final image © Kacey Lynn Brown

FINDING REFERENCE MATERIAL

The foxglove plant has a whimsical quality that lends itself to the faery aesthetic. It's also known by various other names, including goblin's gloves, witch's gloves, and dead man's bells, all of which are very intriguing. The folklore of the foxglove tells that it's a plant the faeries take great delight in and it's therefore unlucky to pick them (you should never deprive the faeries of something they love).

There is also an interesting duality to the foxglove: contact or ingestion of the plant directly is poisonous, and yet it contains a chemical that is used for the medicinal purposes of treating heart failure. Overall, it's a fascinating plant that provides much potential for a character design.

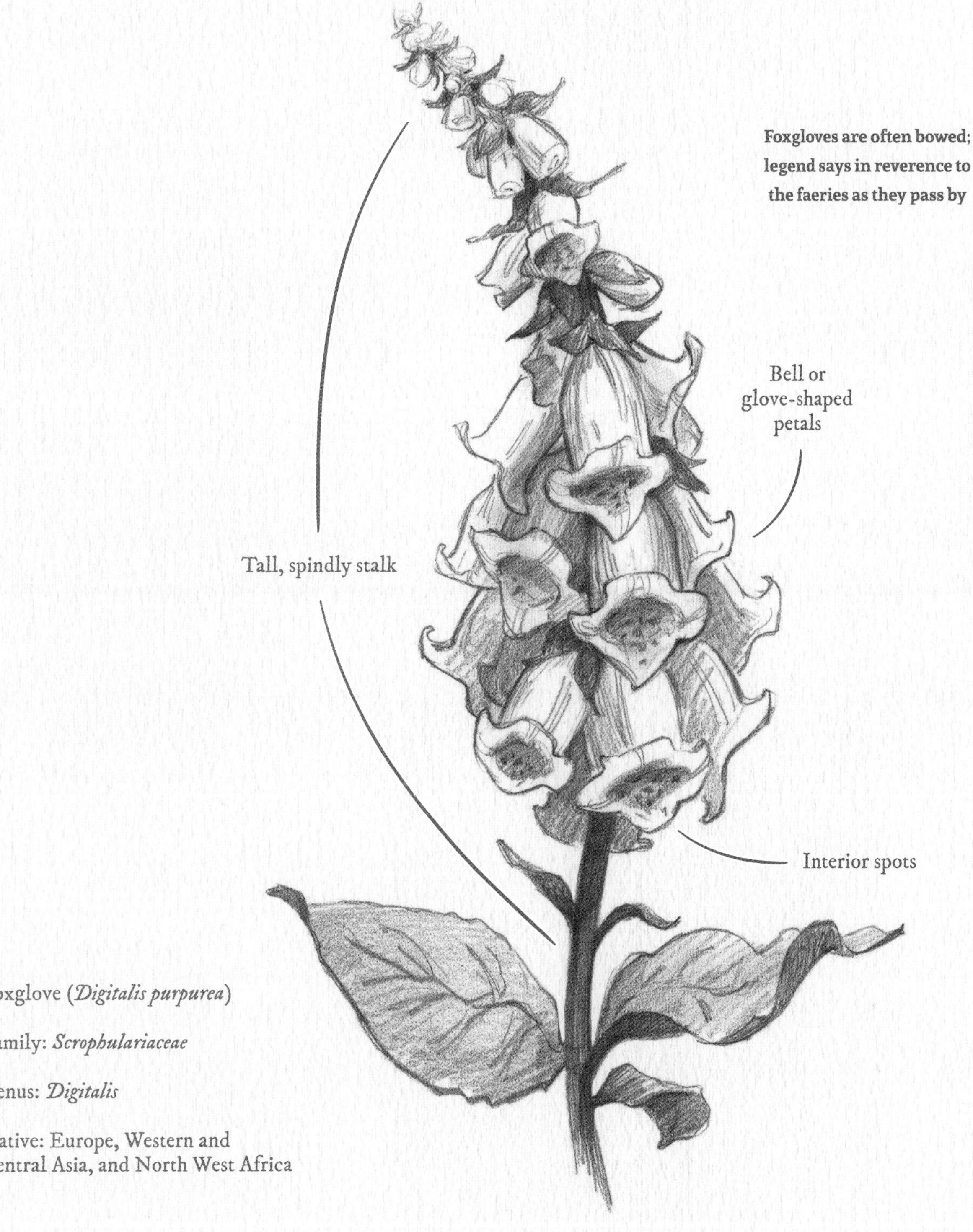

Foxglove (*Digitalis purpurea*)

Family: *Scrophulariaceae*

Genus: *Digitalis*

Native: Europe, Western and Central Asia, and North West Africa

SKETCH STUDIES

Start by sketching small studies of the foxglove plant. This is a critical first step, especially when you're referencing a subject with which you may already be familiar. We all have an idea in our head of what a certain flower looks like, but our knowledge often has many gaps. Creating studies will help you to observe all the interesting details about the flower that you may not have noticed previously. Use these sketches to practise the shapes of the flowers before you begin work on the character.

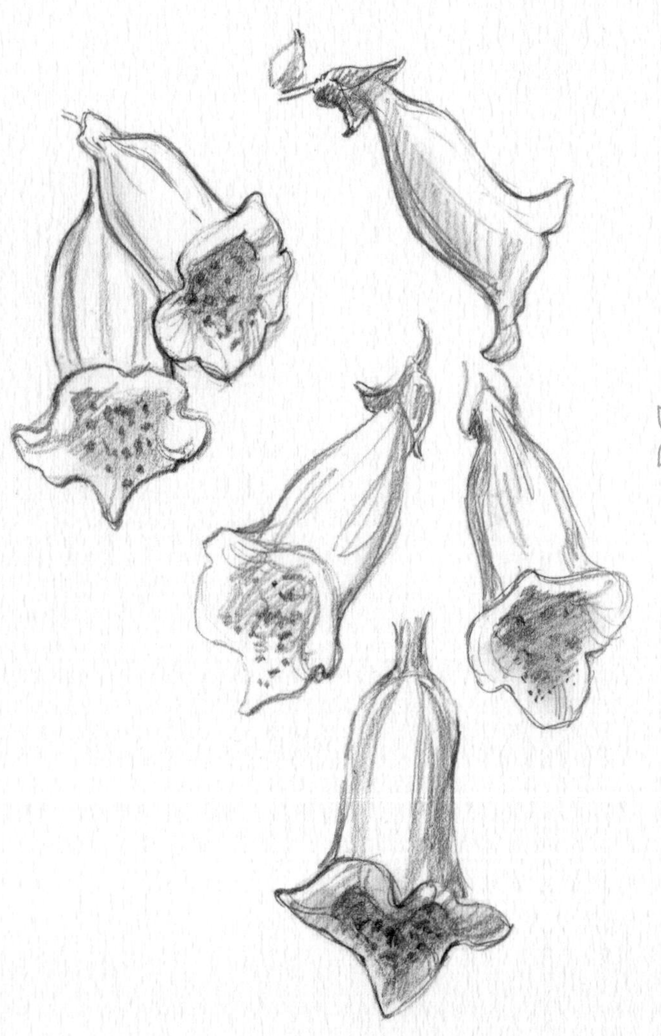

Make sure you have a good understanding of the plant before beginning your character design

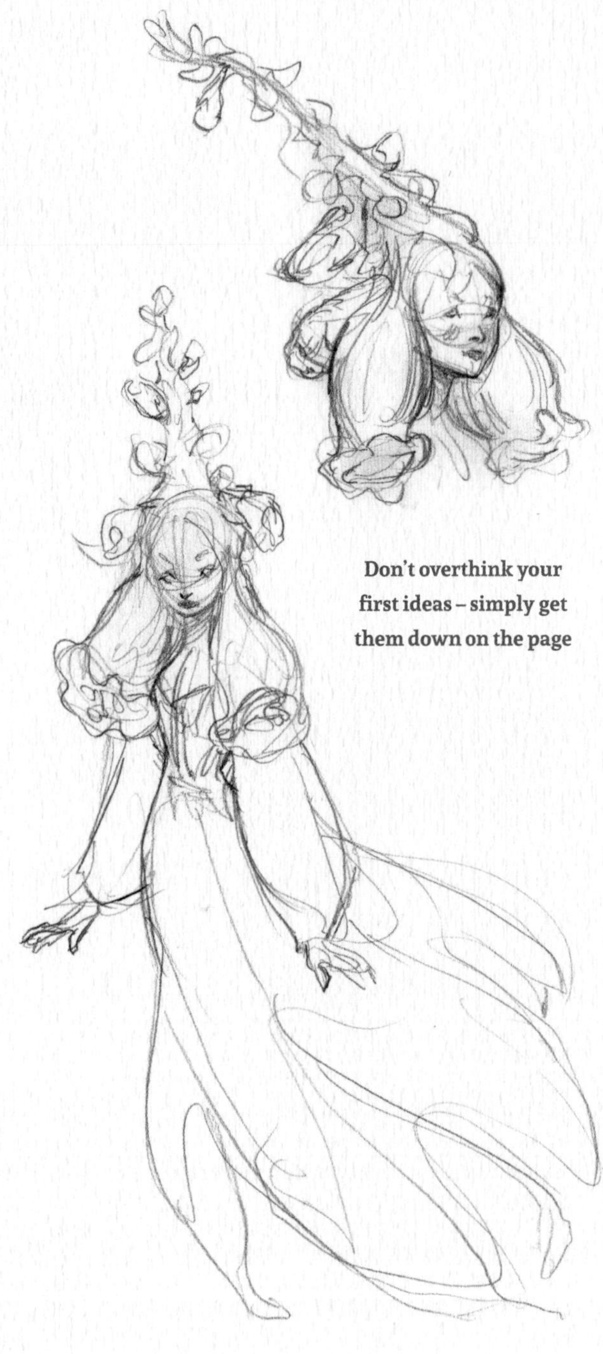

Don't overthink your first ideas – simply get them down on the page

FIRST IDEAS

Once you've created studies and are familiar with all the unique qualities of the flower, it's time to start exploring how to merge the flower's features with a human's features. The two most striking attributes of the foxglove are its tall, spindly stem and bell-shaped flowers. Start to experiment with how this might look on a character. Figure out how the flowers could fit into or sit on top of a faery's face, or lie across her body. Give yourself the freedom to create rough and somewhat unfinished drawings at this stage. All that matters is that you're generating ideas.

KEEP EXPLORING

It's impossible to draw too many variations of a design. Each drawing will refine the idea and move closer to what the design wants to be. Explore what the character might look like without the tall stalk, or if the stalk were replaced with a subtler, hat-like shape. Experiment with how the flowers interact with her head. For example, the buds could form a crown that frames her head and leads the viewer's eye to the large bell shapes of the main foxglove blooms. In these designs her face is completely surrounded by the flowers.

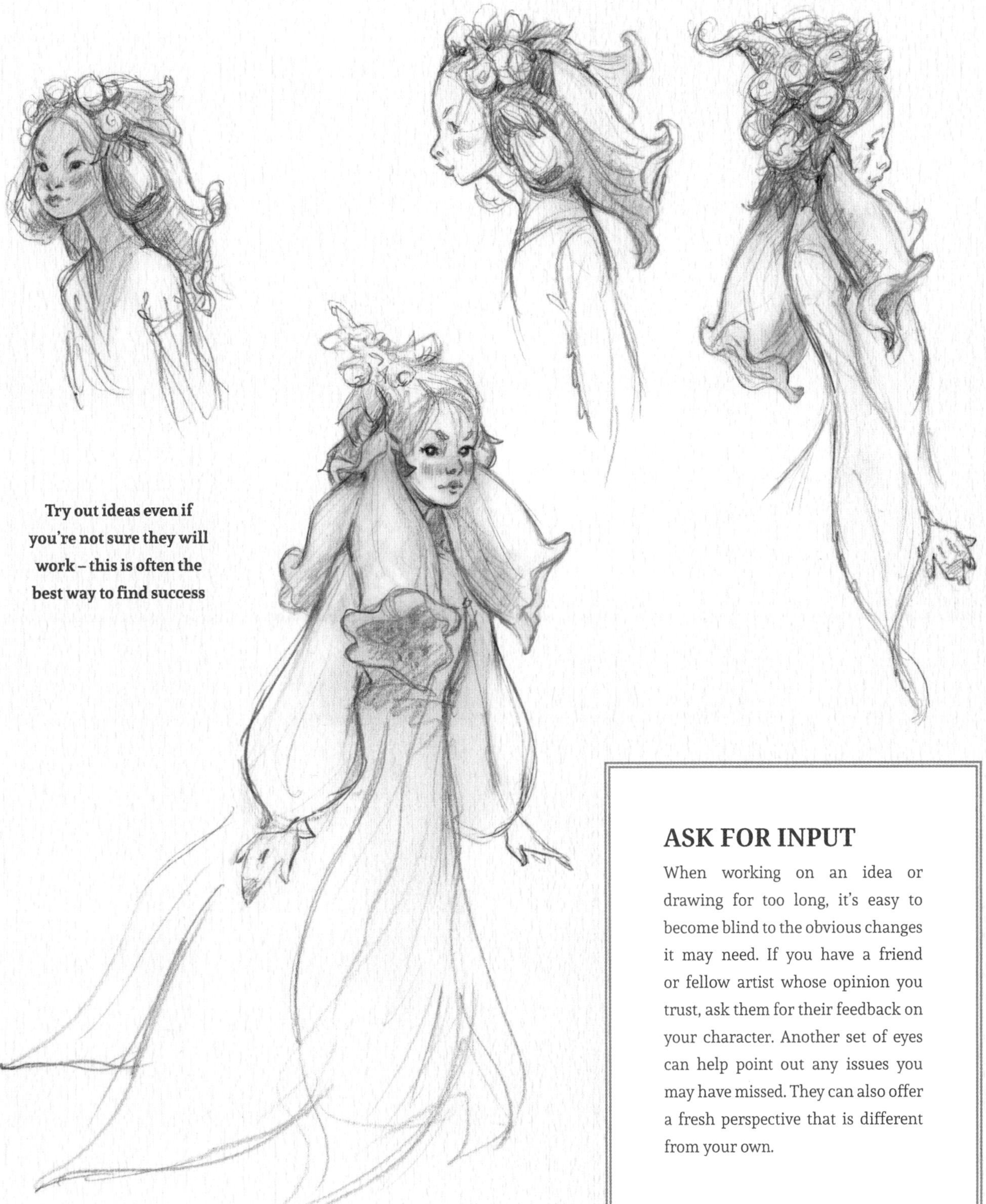

Try out ideas even if you're not sure they will work – this is often the best way to find success

ASK FOR INPUT

When working on an idea or drawing for too long, it's easy to become blind to the obvious changes it may need. If you have a friend or fellow artist whose opinion you trust, ask them for their feedback on your character. Another set of eyes can help point out any issues you may have missed. They can also offer a fresh perspective that is different from your own.

PERSONALITY

As you're sketching out ideas for your character, consider their personality. This faery will be a flower spirit and will share some of the aspects of the foxglove plant. Faeries are usually unpredictable creatures, and perhaps like the foxglove, this faery has the potential to be poisonous and healing at the same time. What mood would you find her in if you were to stumble upon her among the flowers? Would she help a lost traveller in their time of need, or turn out to be their worst nightmare? The more you understand your character, the better you will be able to capture them on the page.

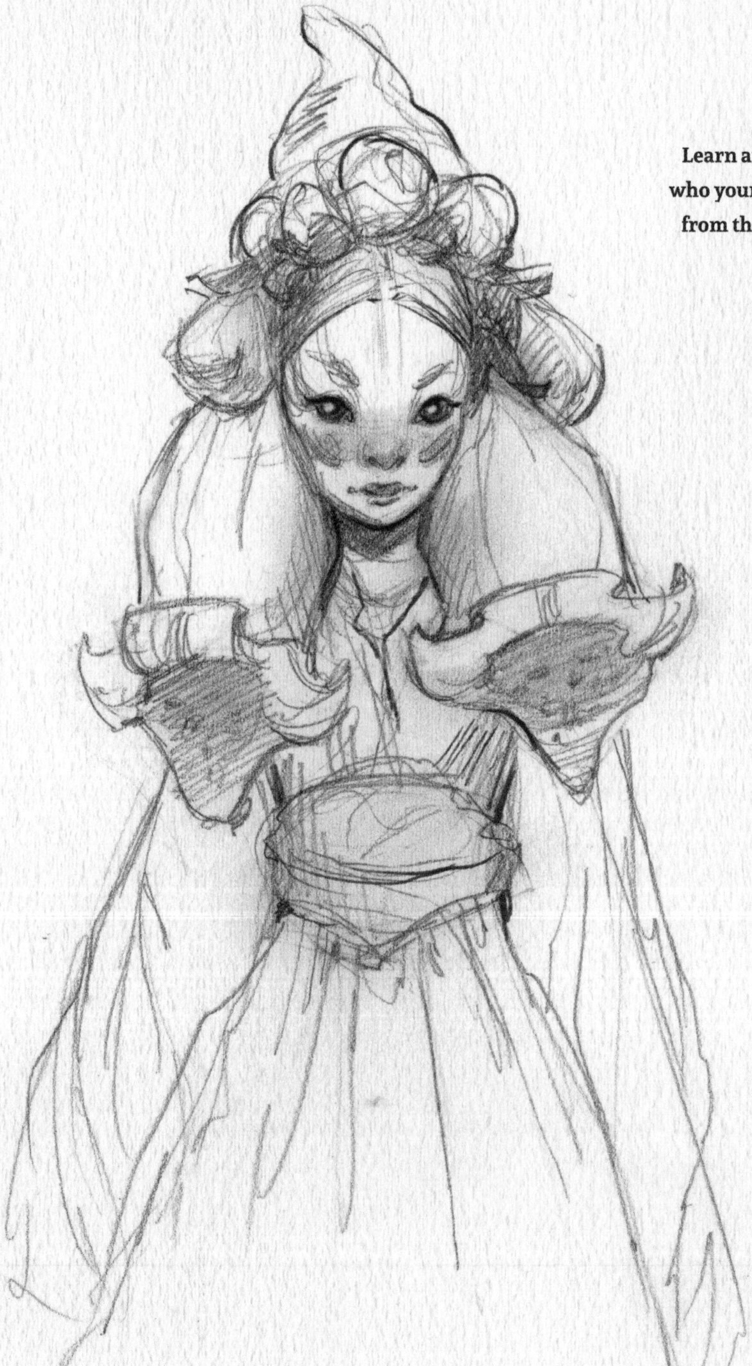

Learn and discover who your character is from the inside out

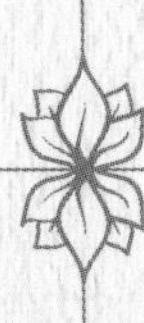

THE BIGGER PICTURE

Expand your field of vision and consider what your character's whole body might look like. Keep your sketches loose; there's no need for a finished drawing yet. Draw big leafy sleeves that repeat the general shape of the flowers. Repeating shapes can help a design to feel coherent, as long as they're balanced by some contrasting forms, such as the sharper-shaped leaves near her head. As a flower spirit she should appear light and airy as she floats through her spring garden, so try to emphasize this feeling in her pose.

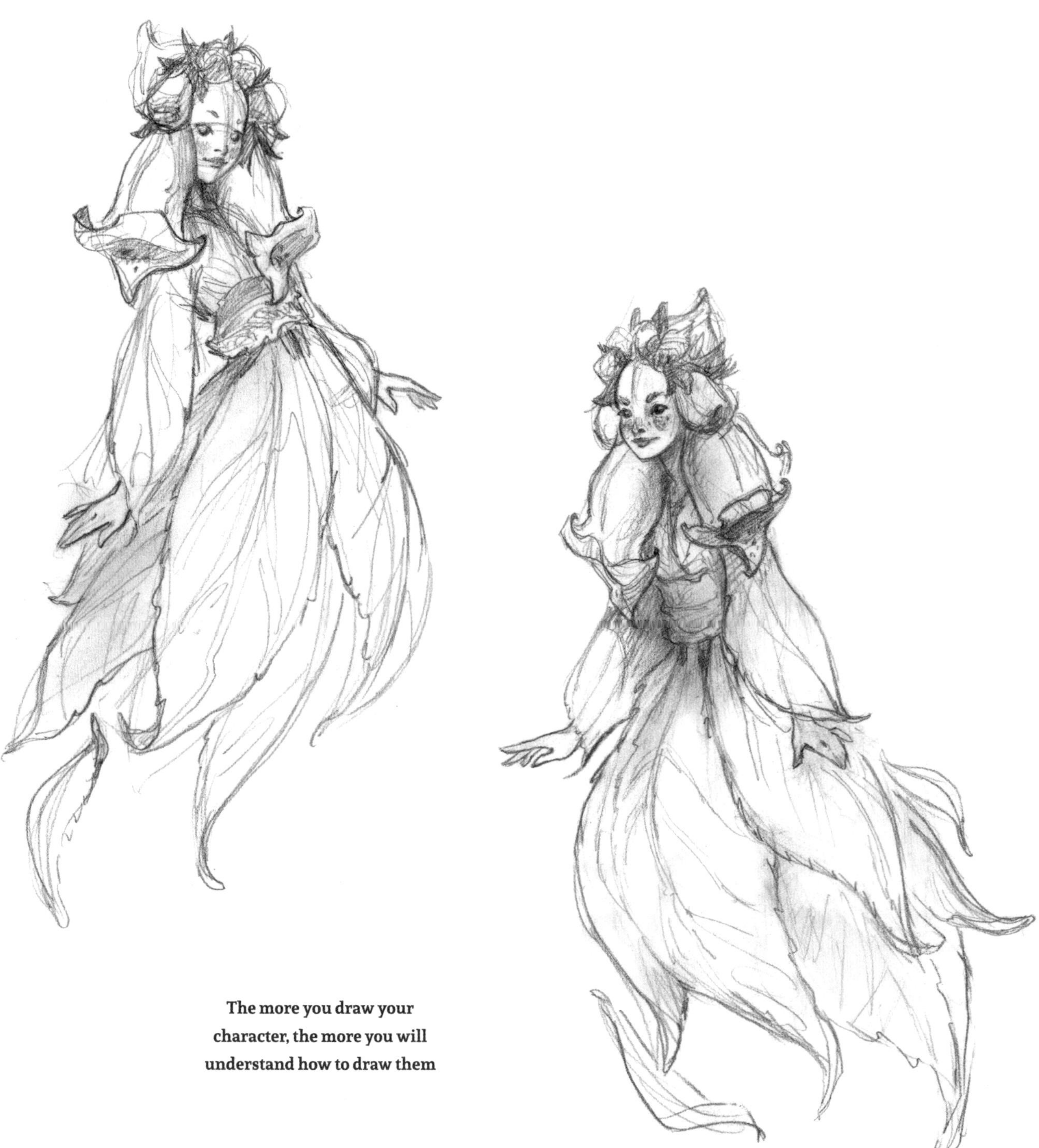

The more you draw your character, the more you will understand how to draw them

FIND THE POSE

Thumbnails are an invaluable way to find the gesture of a pose. They allow you to explore many ideas in a short amount of time. When looking for the gesture, consider how the action is carried from the top to the bottom of the character, and how the arms and legs (or dress) also respond to the action. Sketch as many thumbnails as it takes to find a pose you're happy with; one that expresses what you want to say with the character. The main goal with these thumbnails is to conjure the idea that she's floating through the air. The leaves of her dress react to her movements, giving her an ethereal quality. She is the spirit of the flowers she emulates.

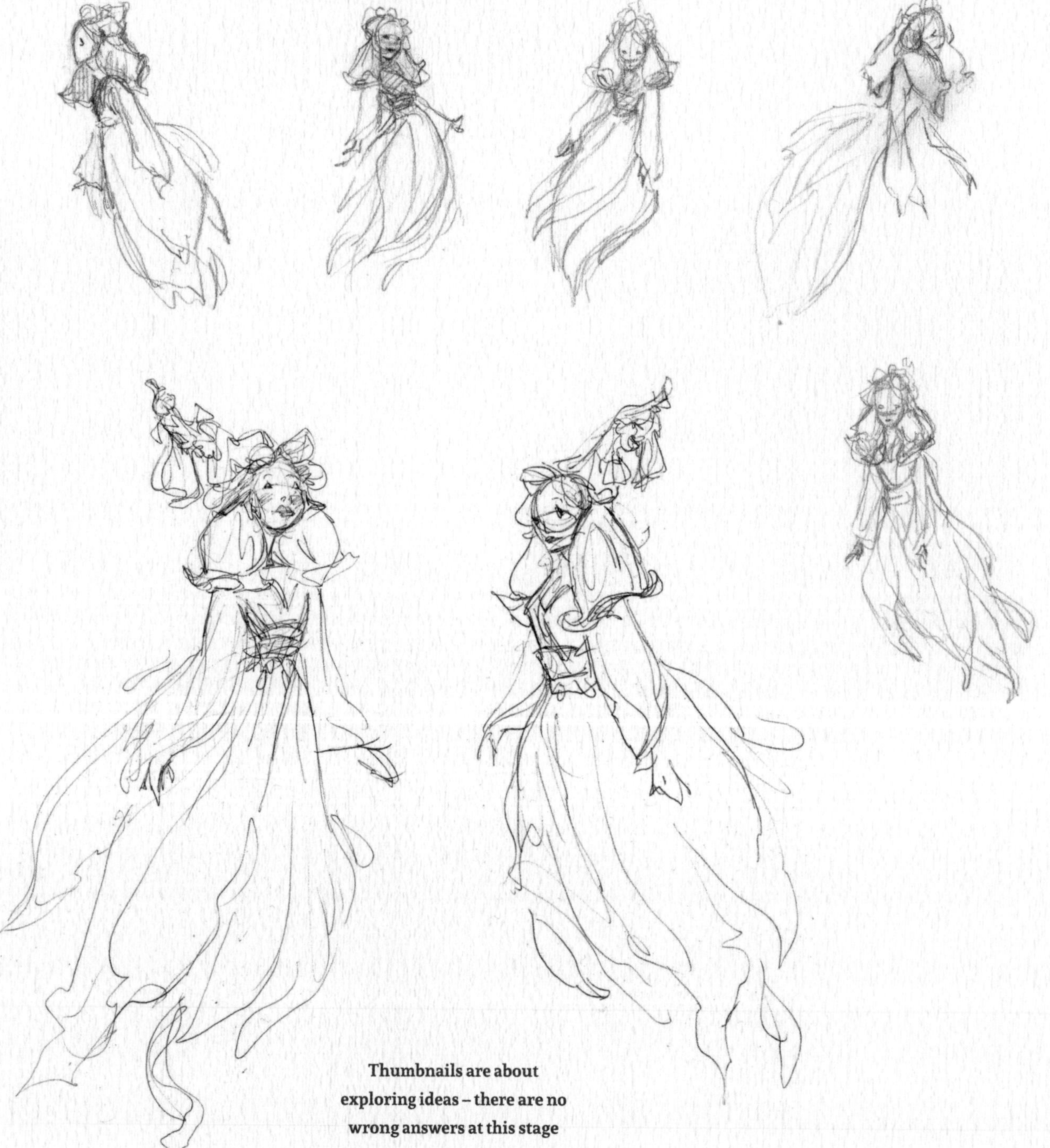

Thumbnails are about exploring ideas – there are no wrong answers at this stage

ROUGH SKETCH

Once you've found a pose you like, draw it again, but larger, paying close attention to maintaining the gesture from the thumbnail. It's ok if it's a little rough and sketchy at this stage, as you will clean it up in the next step. This faery has the foxglove's tall stalk incorporated into the design once again, as when the stalk is removed, the design feels like it's missing something. Take care to keep the pleasing arrangement of buds and flowers around her head to frame her face, along with the billowy sleeves to repeat the shapes of the large blooms.

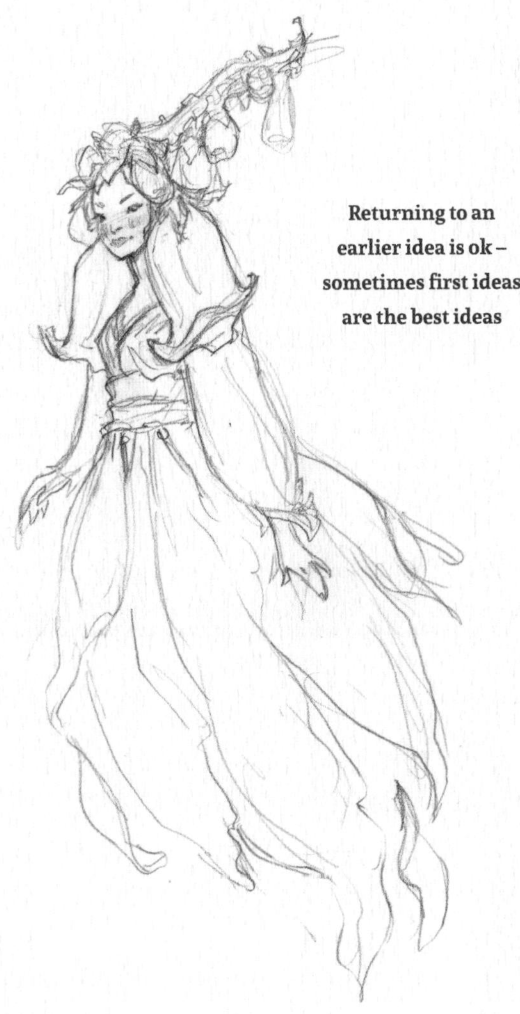

Returning to an earlier idea is ok – sometimes first ideas are the best ideas

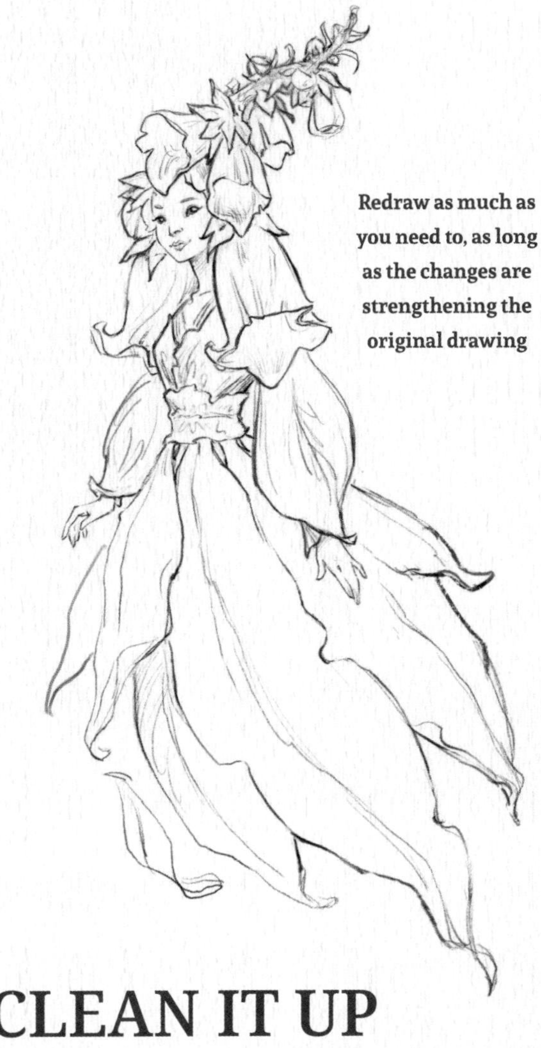

Redraw as much as you need to, as long as the changes are strengthening the original drawing

CLEAN IT UP

There will be many changes that occur between the rough sketch and final drawing, but what's important is that you keep the gesture and general big shapes intact. At this step, the goal is to correct drawing errors, reinforce the forms and construction, and to make any additional tweaks you feel promote a stronger design. Here you can adjust the character's anatomy, further defining her waist and adding a small negative space between her body and arm to ensure the silhouette reads clearly. Make the flowers more pronounced around her face and contrast their round forms with the more angular shapes of the leaves.

COMBINE MEDIUMS

Feel free to combine traditional and digital mediums. For example, you could draw your ideas out with a pencil first, then scan the sketch into the computer and open it up in Adobe Photoshop where you can make as many changes as you like. This can be a highly efficient way to improve a character sketch, as working digitally allows you to try out different ideas risk-free, as you can always return to a previous version. Photoshop also offers many tools to help you manipulate certain aspects of the drawing. Always try to work smarter, not harder.

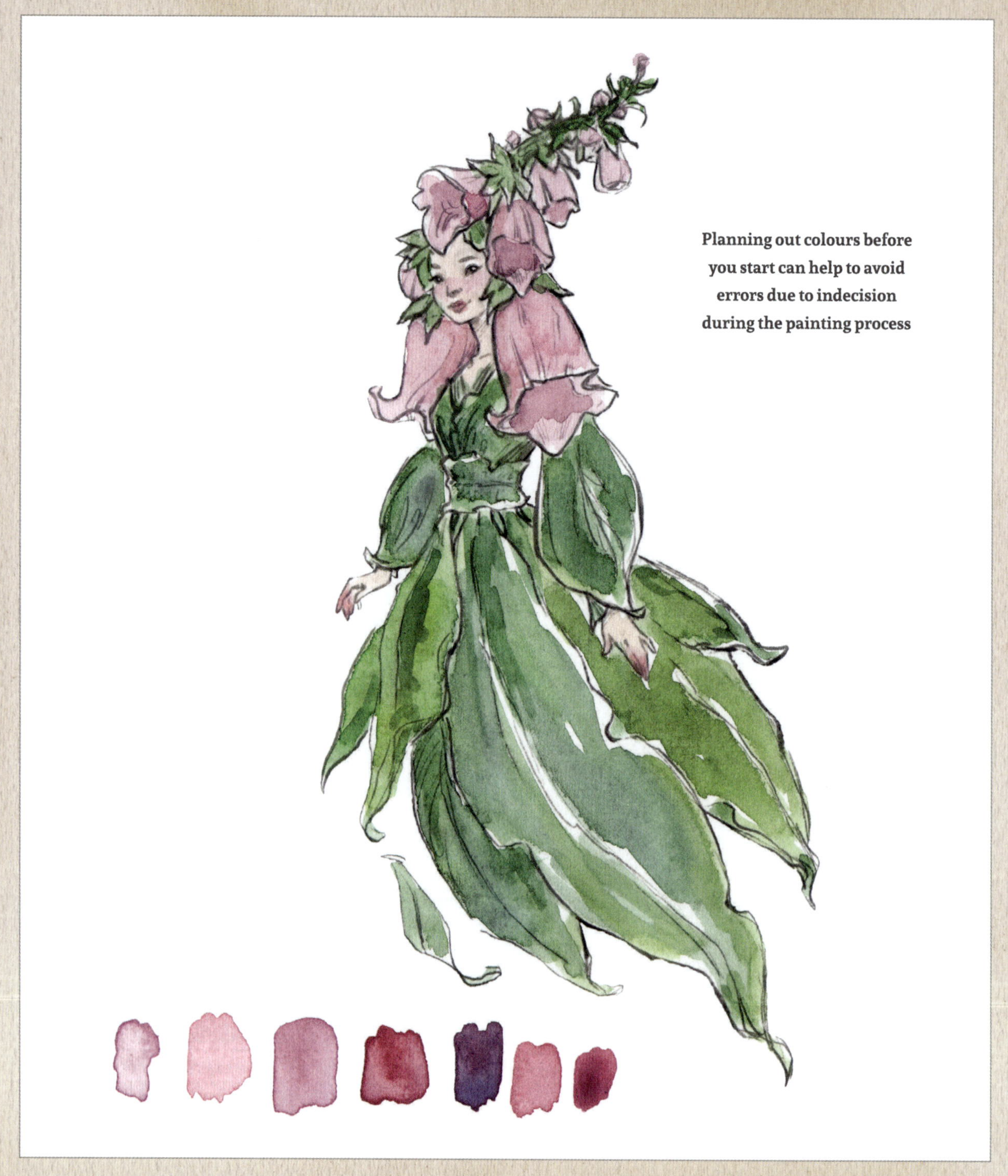

Planning out colours before you start can help to avoid errors due to indecision during the painting process

A STUDY IN COLOUR

No matter what medium you choose to create your character with, taking the time to make a colour study before you begin the painting is a very useful step. As with the thumbnails, create as many colour studies as necessary to discover what colours work best for your character. Foxgloves range from pinkish-purple to cream and yellow.

This foxglove faery will have purple flowers, as this will contrast well with the green of the leaves and draw the viewer's eye towards the character's face. When using watercolour, spend some time mixing different hues of purple to find a colour you're happy with.

INK THE LINE WORK

To create the line work you can either print your sketch with low opacity directly onto watercolour paper, or transfer the drawing to the watercolour paper by tracing via a lightbox. The line work here is created using traditional ink, but it could easily be drawn digitally as well. When inking, try to vary the line weight by making some lines thicker than others and breaking them up using small dots. This adds interest to the drawing and helps to describe the forms of the shapes. Make sure to use a pen with waterproof ink to ensure the lines won't run when you apply the watercolour in the next step.

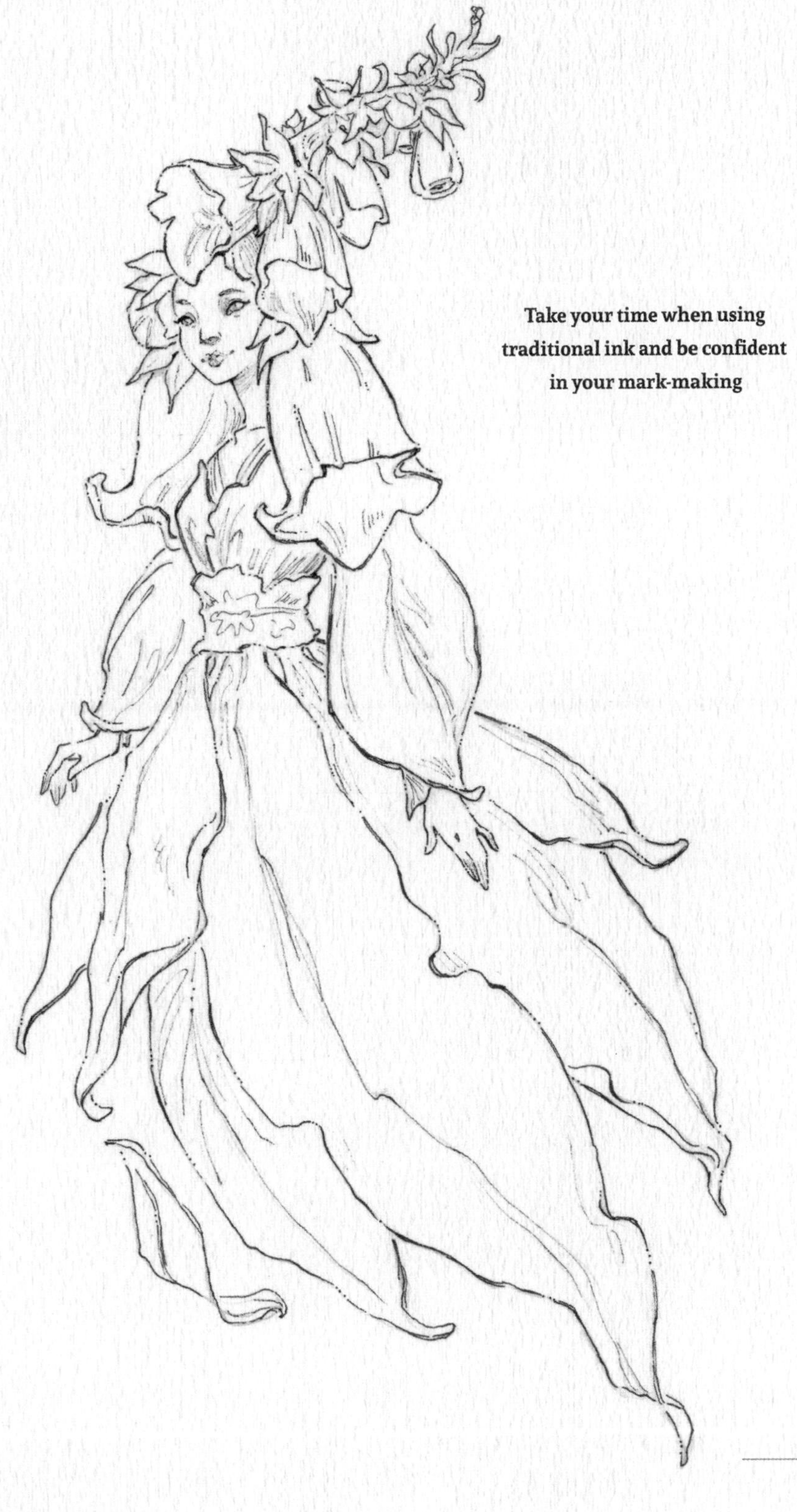

Take your time when using traditional ink and be confident in your mark-making

WASHES OF WATERCOLOUR

Start by applying watercolour to the character's face and the flowers, before moving on to the greens. This is just the first layer. The watercolour painting process involves gradually adding more details and darker values as you go. Consider the colour temperature as you apply the paint, especially in the leaves. Using both a warm green and a cool green will add variety and life to the image. For the face, use the colour of the flowers to introduce a healthy blush to her cheeks, along with some colour to the tips of her fingers, which will help to connect her face and hands to the flowers.

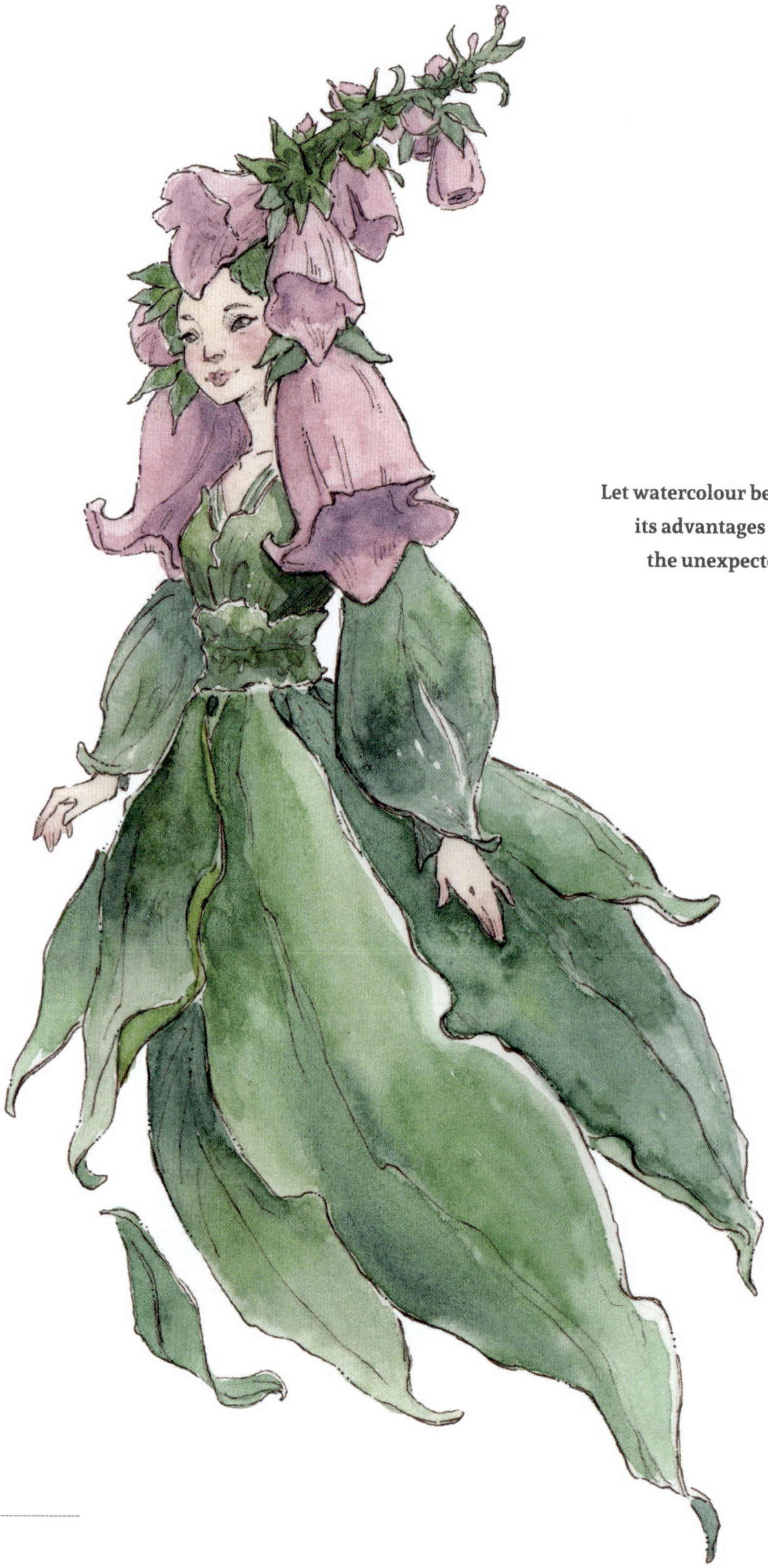

Let watercolour be watercolour – its advantages often lie in the unexpected results

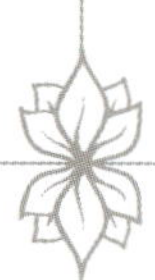

DON'T BE AFRAID TO START OVER

When you're working in a traditional medium, at some point you will most likely need to start the piece over. Mistakes happen and things often don't go as planned. While this is very frustrating, it can lead to even better results the second (or third!) time around. Be open to starting over if you know you can make a painting better. Persistence is key to creating art you can be proud of.

HANDS

Hands are just as important to your character's design as their face, so it's worth spending a little extra time to ensure you get them right. They can express something about your character's personality, or simply just carry and support the gesture. If you're not sure how to draw the hands, find a suitable reference. Look at your own hands, or ask a friend to pose for you. Sketch a few hand studies, then return to your character, using the information you have gathered to revise the drawing. It can take time, but with practice you will see an improvement in your skills.

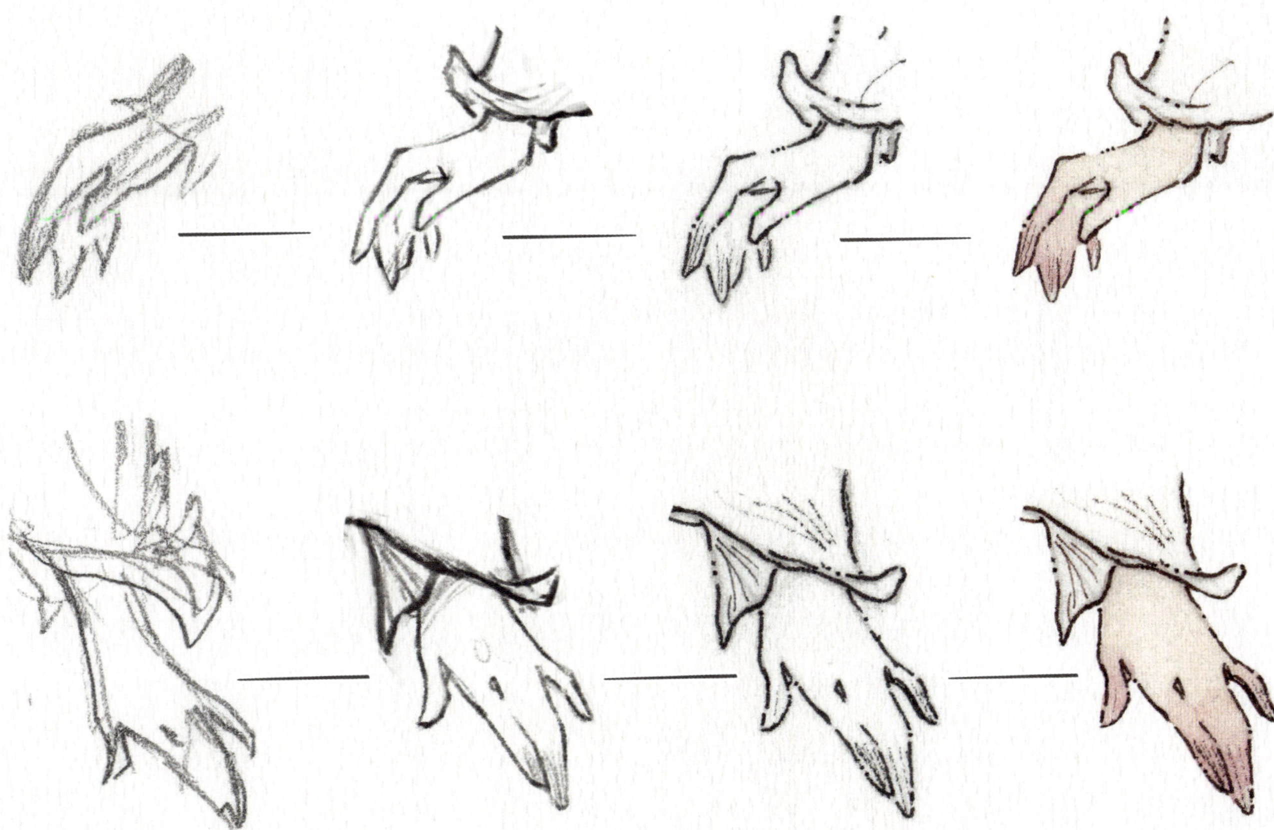

This faery's hands are as soft and delicate as foxglove petals

THE FOXGLOVE FAERY

For the final steps, paint in some darker values to bring dimension to the forms. Add small details, such as the tiny spots inside the flower petals. Introduce a few extra layers of texture by using the paintbrush to carefully splash the paint onto certain areas. Returning to the pen, add a few more defining ink lines in any areas where you feel the drawing has become somewhat lost under the paint. Finish by adding tiny white highlights to her eyes. This last little step may be the most important, as it brings the character to life. The face is the focal point of the painting, and the eyes are the focal point of the face. Take your time to paint them well to finish the design.

Bringing the plant world into your character designs will always provide a wealth of inspiration. There is something magical about finding a way to blend natural elements with human personas. Make a habit of slowing down and appreciating the flora and fauna that can be found right outside your door. When you take the time to foster the skills of observation and study, it opens up your ability to create interesting and memorable plant-inspired characters.

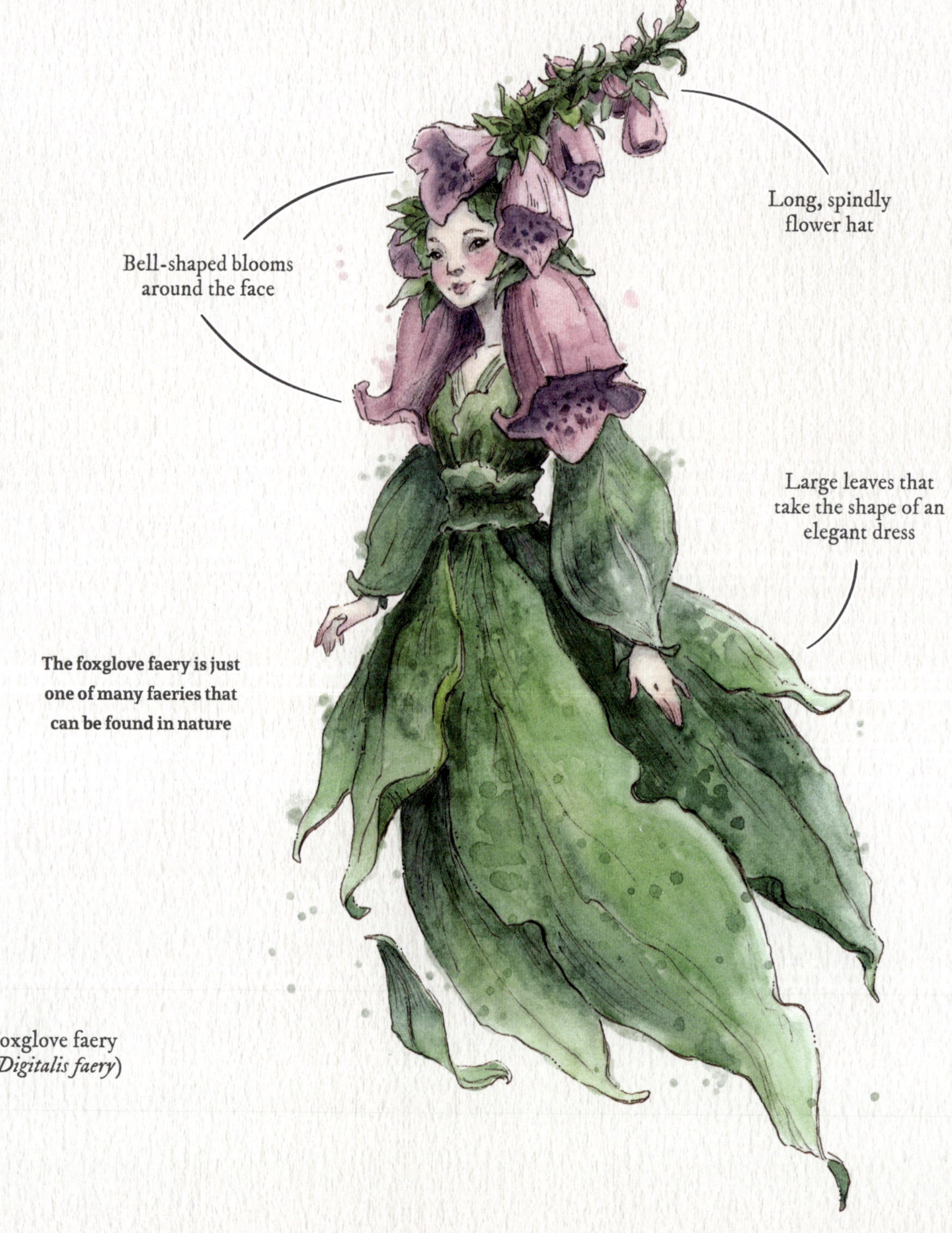

The foxglove faery is just one of many faeries that can be found in nature

Foxglove faery
(*Digitalis faery*)

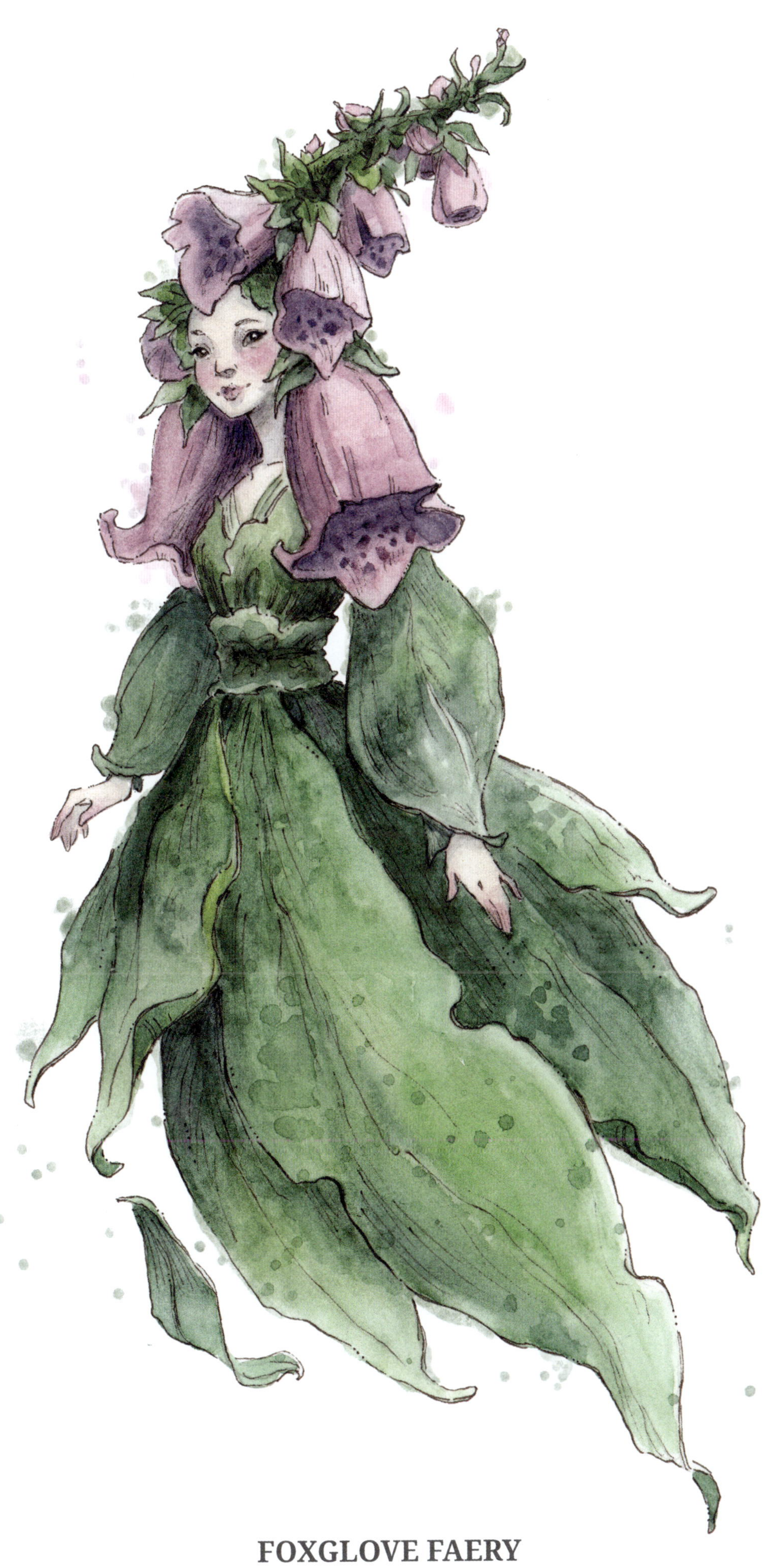

FOXGLOVE FAERY

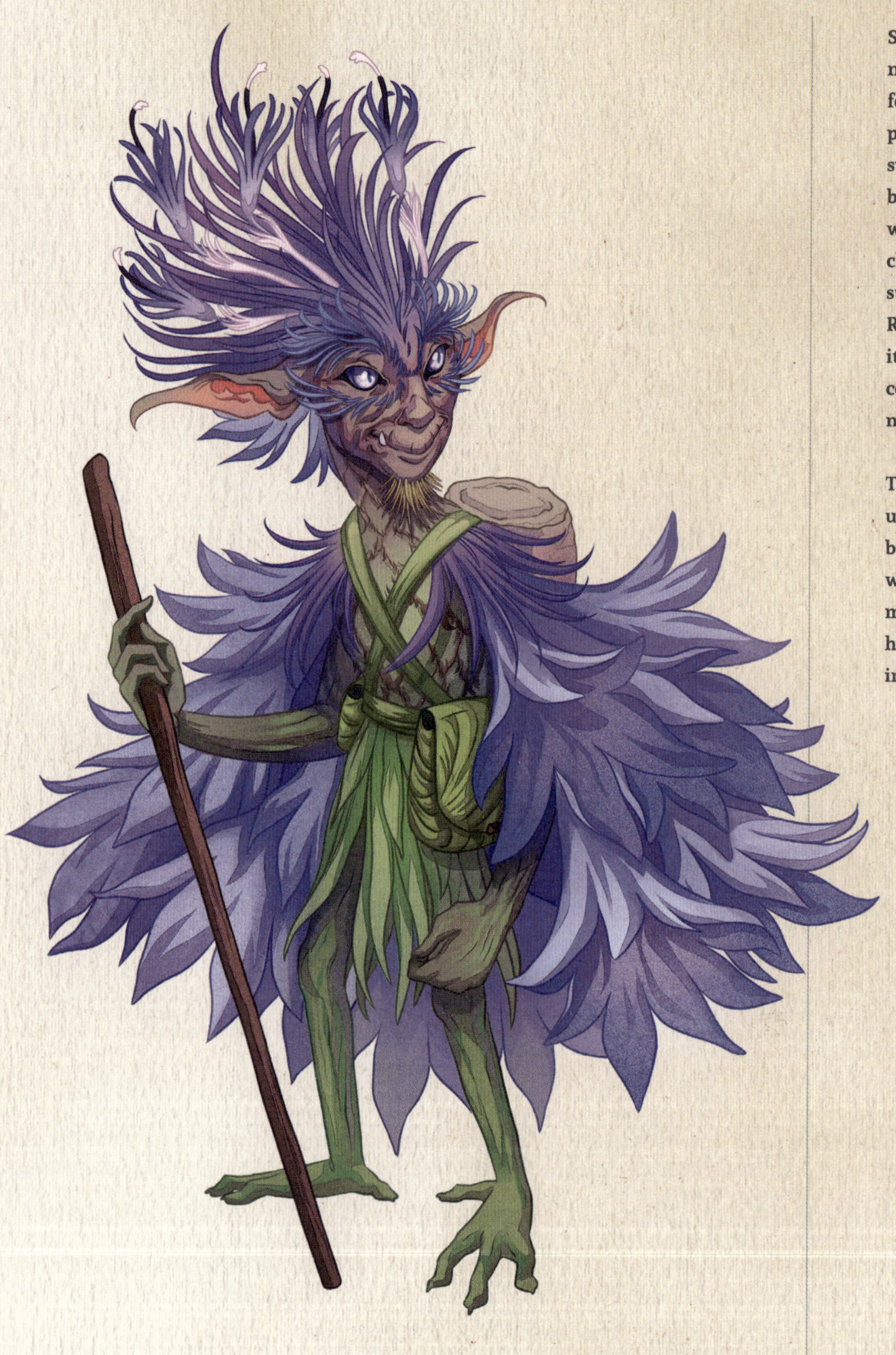

Summer is a time of year when nature displays its full wealth of forms, shapes, and colours. In the plant world, flowering is in full swing, and seeds and fruits are beginning to appear. This tutorial will teach you how to create a character based on a beautiful summer flower: the cornflower. Related to the work of pollinators, it shows the connectedness and cooperation that takes place in the natural world.

This tutorial will be completed using an iPad Pro and Procreate™, but feel free to follow along with your choice of software or materials. By the end you will have a fully realized, cornflower-inspired character.

summer

CORNFLOWER GOBLIN

NORA POTWORA

RESEARCH & REFERENCE

Proper research is crucial to create a compelling design. The most important aspect of this step is understanding the structure of the flower. Take a closer look at how it's built – the amount of detail you will discover may surprise you. Carefully inspect photos and encyclopaedic botanical art; it's even better if you can study the real flower. Sketching parts of the plant will help you to understand its structure, but you can also practise by tracing lines over photographs of the species. This will make it even easier to understand the plant's construction and draw it fully by yourself later on.

Try to determine the general shape of the flower. Is it round or pointed? Stocky or slender? Large or small and delicate? How do the petals and stalk look? Ask yourself questions as you go along, as all these details will help you to create your character.

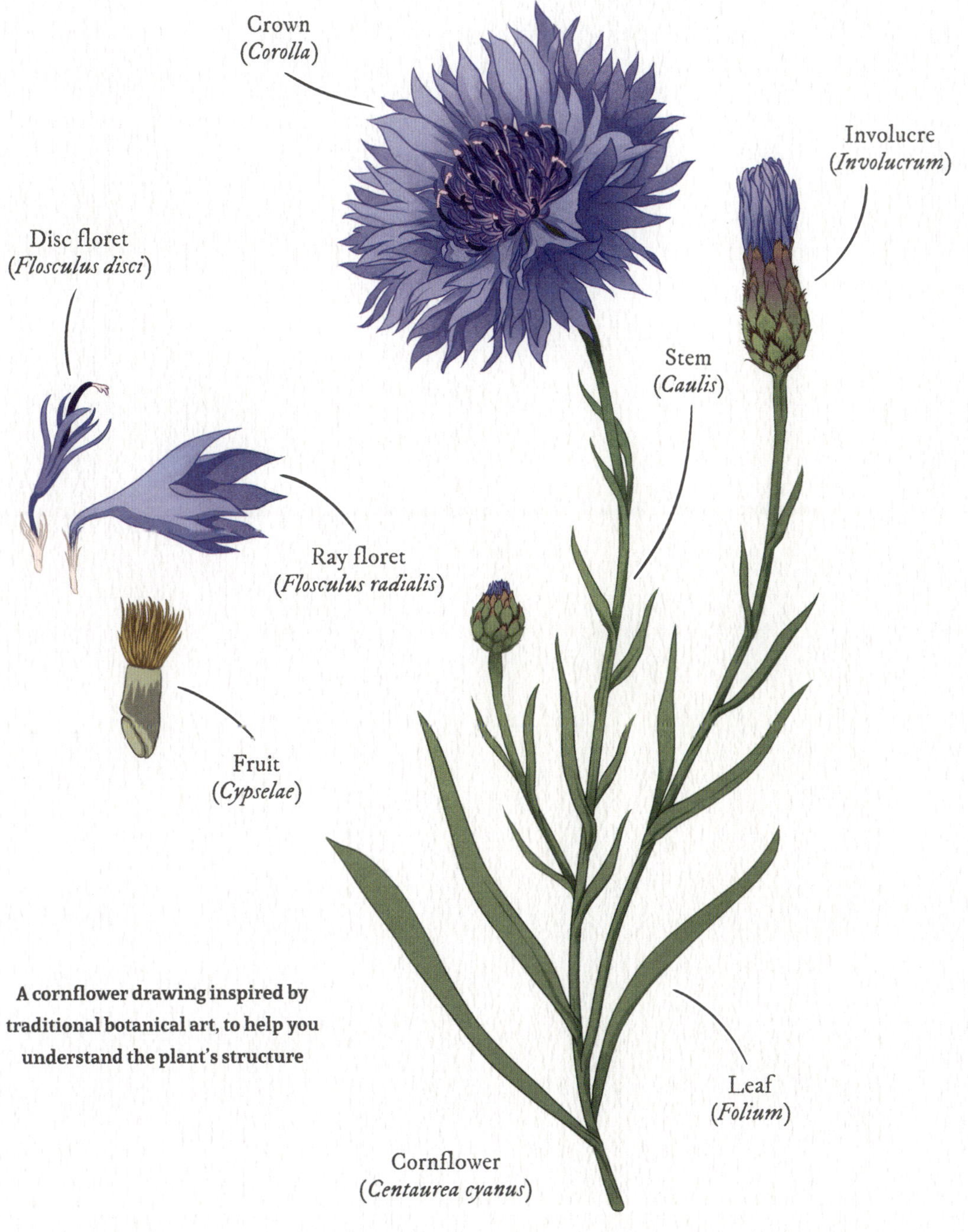

A cornflower drawing inspired by traditional botanical art, to help you understand the plant's structure

CREATE A STORY

It's important to give your character a personality and purpose. Consider their strengths and weaknesses, what they are passionate about, and what motivates them. This will help you to create a character that feels real and relatable. Even a simple outline will be helpful. The character we are going to create is a cornflower goblin named Periwinkle who lives in a meadow. He is a friendly mischief-maker who enjoys making new friends, and collects nectar and pollen to make infusions and medicines for animals and insects in need. Sometimes Periwinkle is quite lazy and he doesn't like to climb very tall flowers, so his friend and assistant, a bumblebee, helps him with collecting ingredients. This, in turn, helps to pollinate flowers.

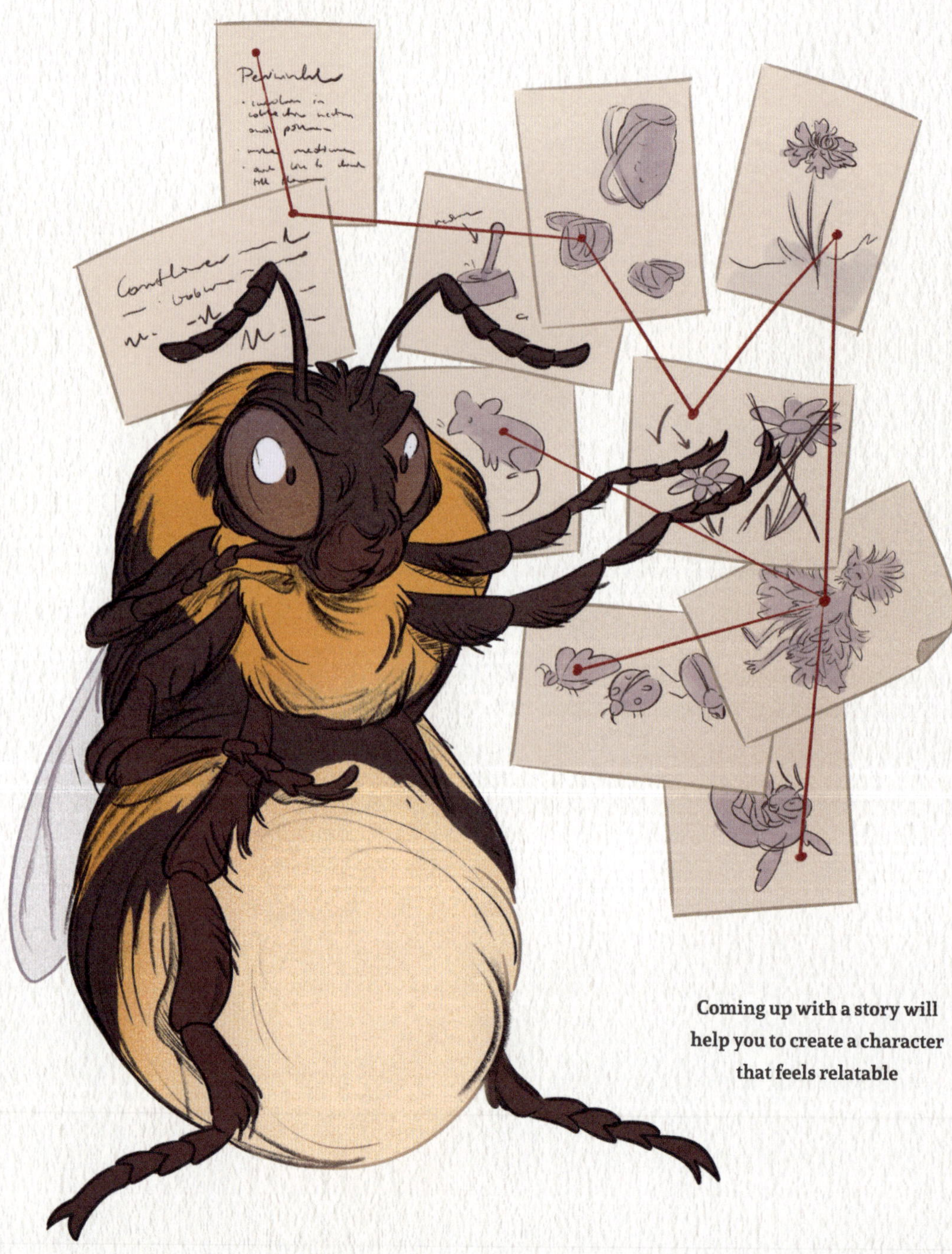

Coming up with a story will help you to create a character that feels relatable

EXPLORING SHAPES

The basic shape of your character should convey their traits and personality, while also reflecting the form of the flower. When you create a character's silhouette, always explore a few variations – the least expected shape may be the one you like the most! The cornflower is a slender plant, with a crown that at first glance is oval and wide; upon closer inspection, the crown reveals a centre made up of tiny disc florets, surrounded by spiky petals of ray florets. The plant's leaves are green and lance-shaped.

You can use flower parts as additions to the design or to create a character whose full body is based on the flower's structure – the latter approach is shown here. It helps to start designs with a simple pose, as it allows you to focus on the design without getting distracted.

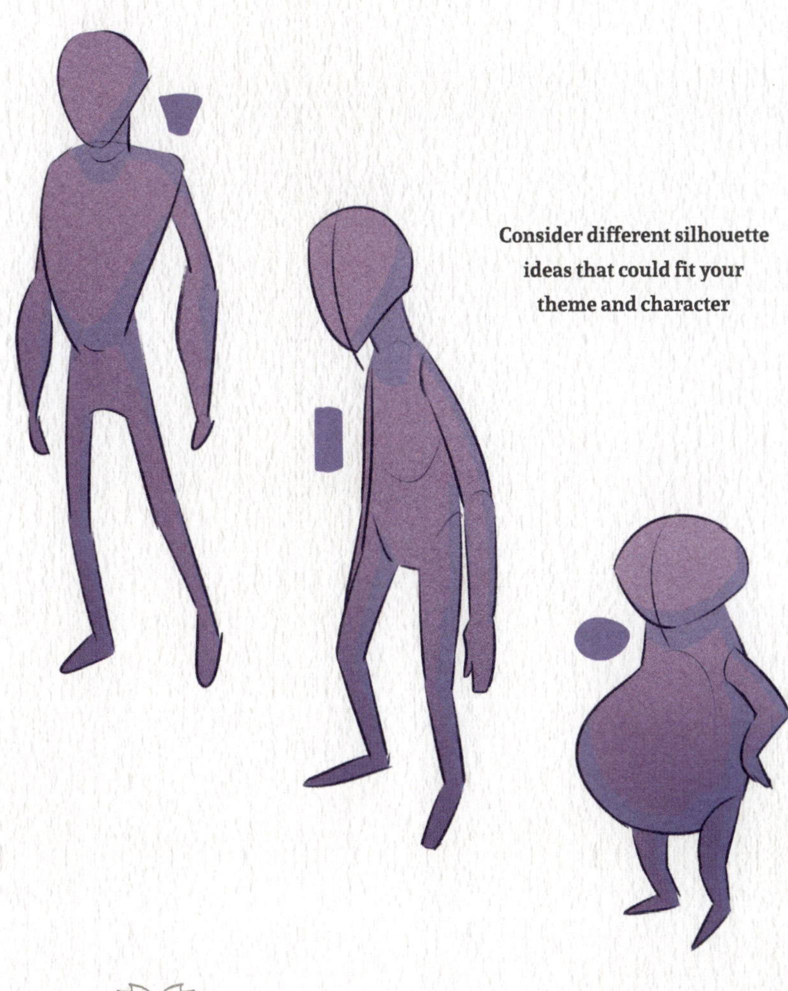

Consider different silhouette ideas that could fit your theme and character

DESIGNING THE FACE

The process of discovering the face is similar to the previous step. Try out a few different shapes for the base – not only is it great fun, but it's also an interesting exercise. Experiment with making round, square, or triangular shapes, with differently shaped noses, mouths, eyes, ears, and chins. The face should be somehow consistent with the rest of the body, but it's worth checking options that seemingly may not fit. Consider your character's disposition and how the face reflects it. During this process, think about which flower parts you would like to include in the head and face design, then try sketching them on top of your bases to check how they look.

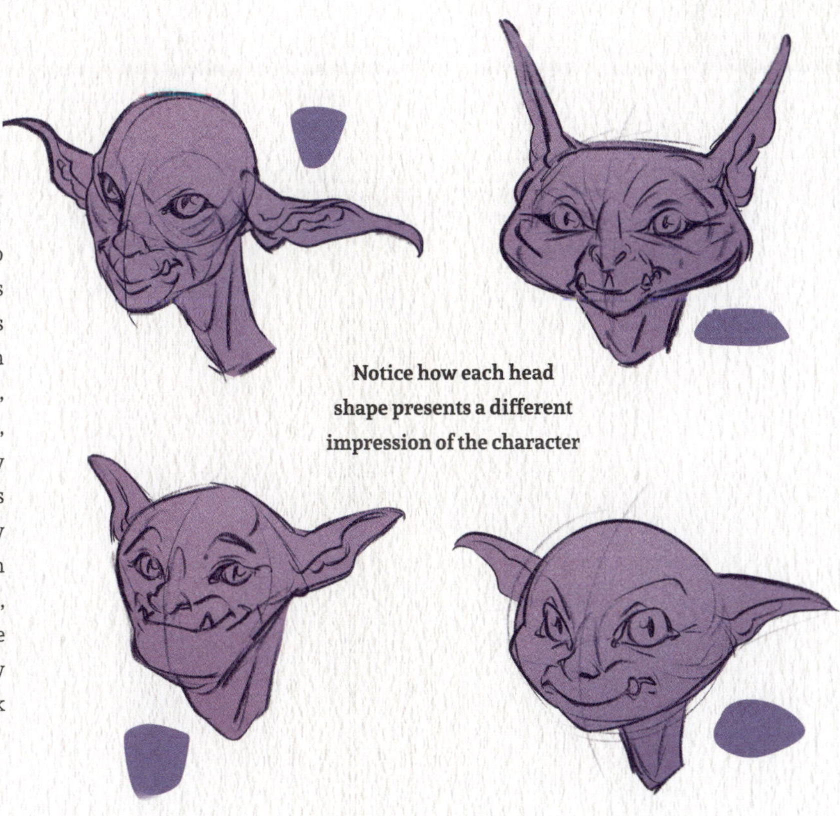

Notice how each head shape presents a different impression of the character

BUILDING UP THE DESIGN

Now it's time to put everything together, starting with your character's basic shape. In this case, a slender-looking body feels the most fitting compared to the real flower. Notice how the skinny, elongated limbs are inspired by the flower's stem. The shape of the face refers to the shape of the cornflower's petals, with slim features and triangular ears.

For the first major flower element, the most obvious idea would be to use the flower's crown as part of the character's head. It's a natural choice, because we tend to perceive this element as the plant's head. However, for a more unusual approach, you could use the flower's crown as a wide cape that grows out of the goblin's shoulders.

JUST THE BEGINNING

Remember that this is only the beginning of your character-design journey. It's easy to feel discouraged or frustrated when your initial sketches and ideas don't turn out exactly as you envisioned them or are a bit messy, but don't give up! Keep in mind that this stage is all about exploring different possibilities and finding what works best for your character. It's fine to make mistakes or to try again with a different approach.

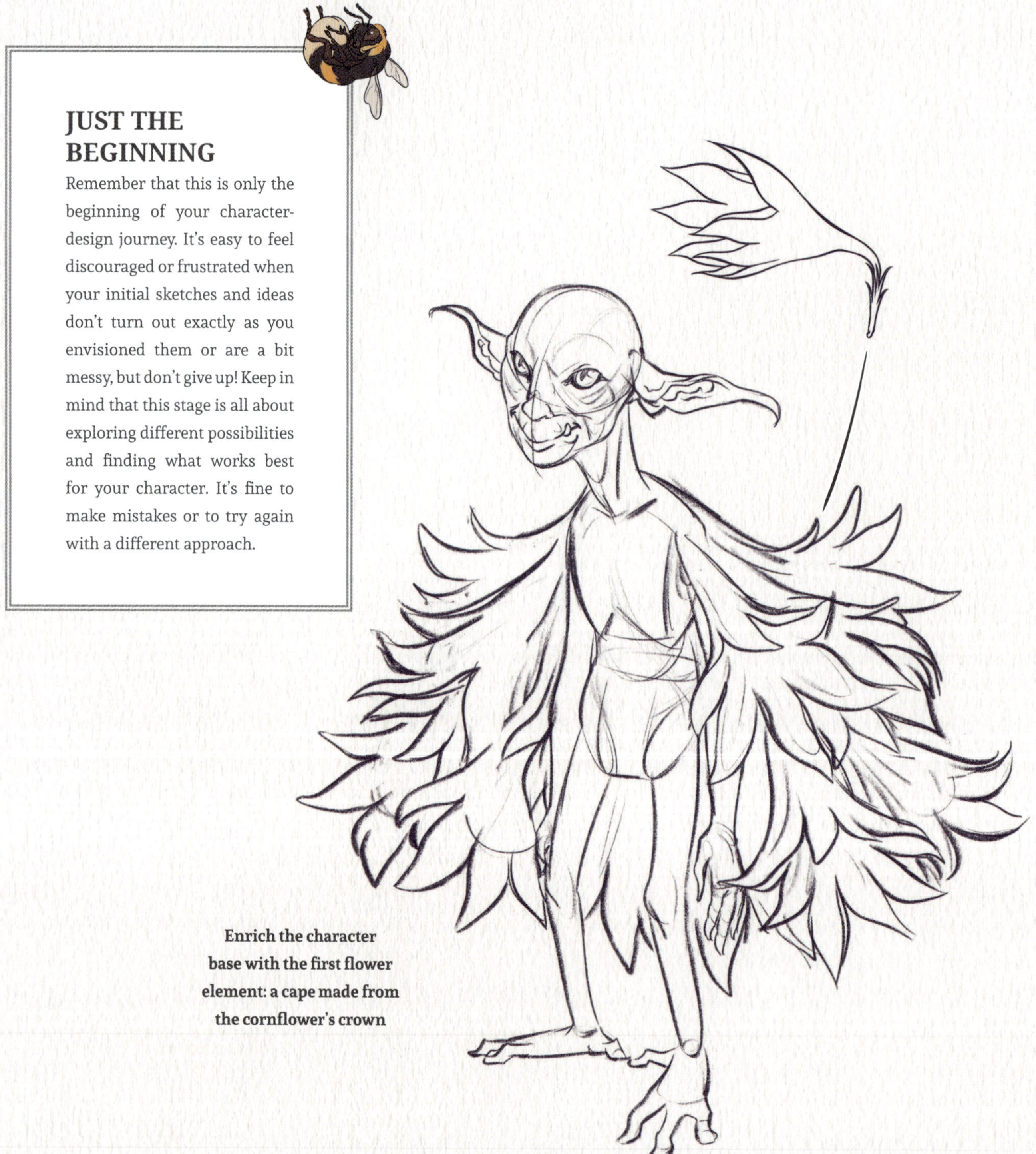

Enrich the character base with the first flower element: a cape made from the cornflower's crown

FLORAL ENHANCEMENTS

Examine your flower references and continue asking yourself which elements you can use in the design. In the cornflower's case, there are a few more elements that you can easily use to make the design more appealing. The cornflower crown has disc florets in the centre, which you can use along with the petals to create a hairstyle; at first glance, their shape resembles human hair, so this is a natural choice.

Add small petals around the eyebrow arch and cheekbones to make the face more interesting. The goblin's ornate chin detail is based on the fruit part of the cornflower. His neck, arms, and torso are covered with involucral bracts (a type of small, pointed leaf), and his waist and shoulders are covered with larger lance-shaped leaves.

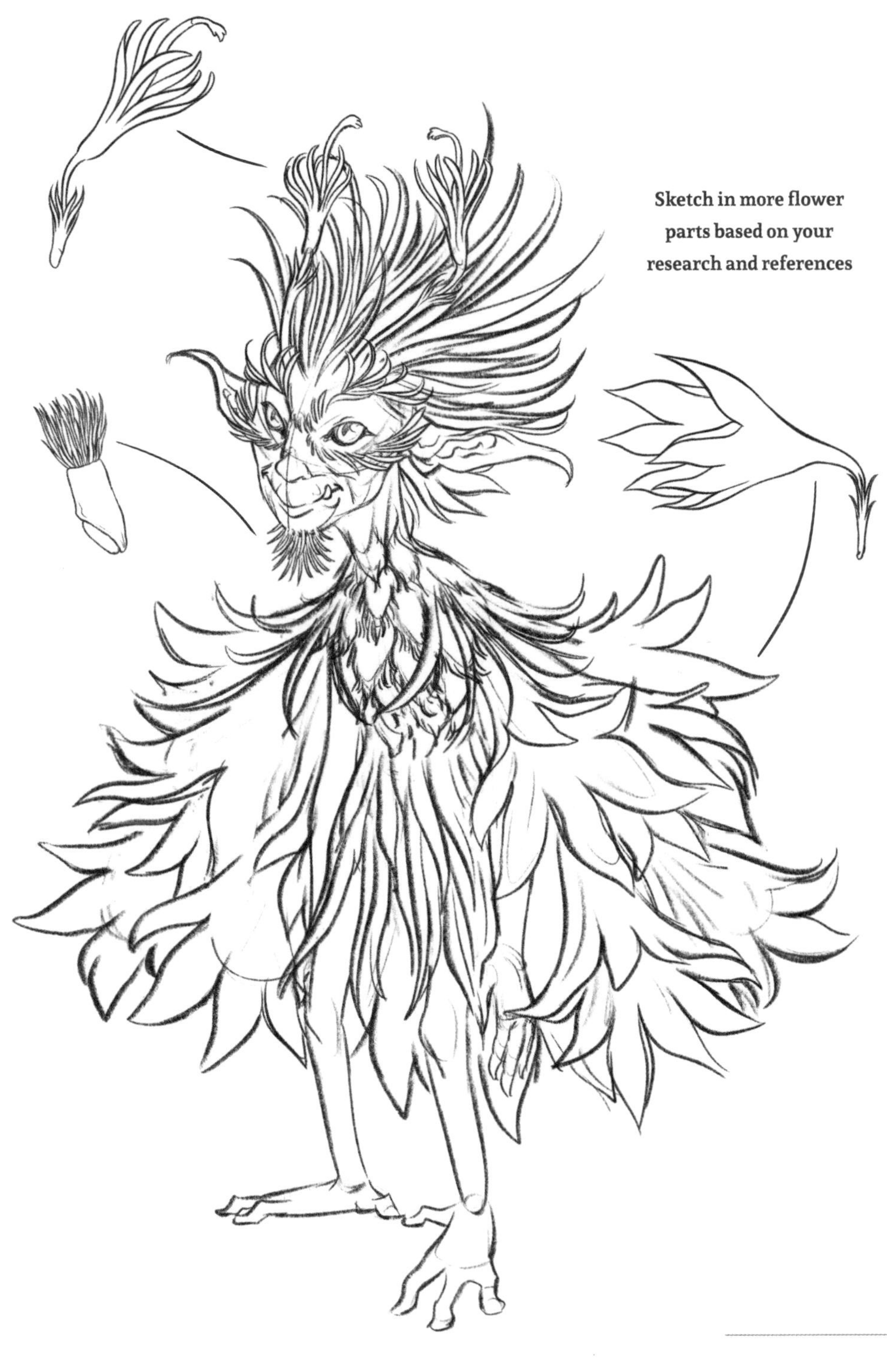

Sketch in more flower parts based on your research and references

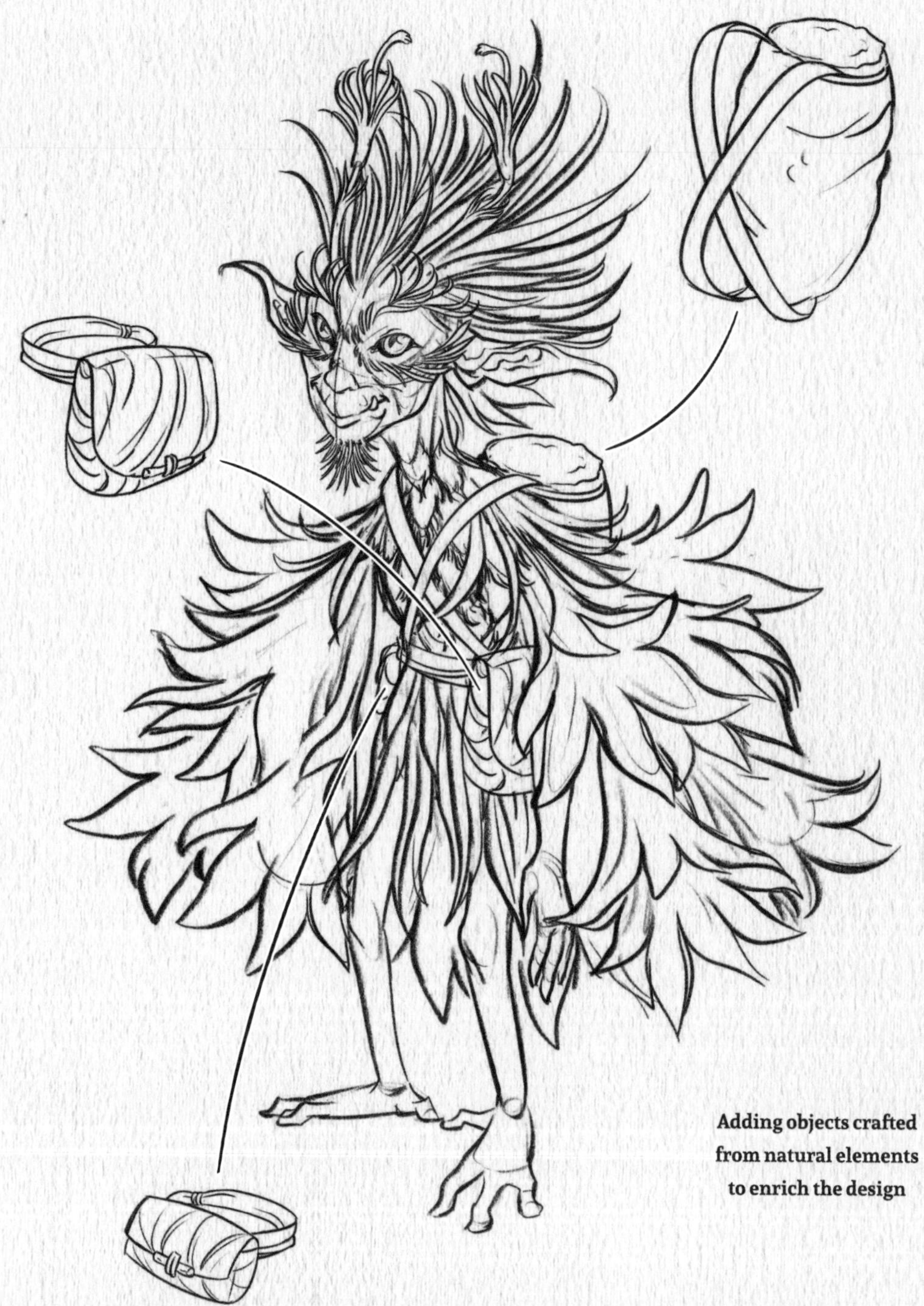

Adding objects crafted from natural elements to enrich the design

ADDING ACCESSORIES

Remember to pay attention to the details of your character's design and ensure that everything is consistent with their overall aesthetic. When you add accessories, consider the environment in which the character lives, as this can affect how the accessories should look. Periwinkle is a tiny creature who lives in a meadow; he dabbles in collecting pollen, helped by his bumblebee companion. For such tasks, he will need some accessories that will help him hold the pollen as he climbs from flower to flower, such as a basket and bags. As he is a tiny meadow-dwelling creature, his belongings could be fashioned from an abandoned insect nest, grasses, and leaves.

EVALUATING THE DESIGN

Now that you have a full initial sketch of your character, it's important to step back and evaluate the design as a whole. Ask yourself if the character's appearance and personality fit together and if they are consistent with the story you want to tell. If there are any elements that feel out of place or don't quite work, now is the best time to make changes; add or delete any elements or try to revise them with a different approach. Making corrections now will save you a lot of work in later stages. Here, the crown-cape shape has been slightly modified, and a few more disc florets have been added to the goblin's head.

KEEP AN OPEN MIND

Remember that designing is a process. It's totally normal to make mistakes or to feel overwhelmed by either the amount of ideas or the lack of them. Keep an open mind. If you're lacking ideas, try to search for inspiration both in the natural world and in other artists' work. If something in your design feels 'off' to you, try different approaches. Taking a break is also a good idea; stepping away from a project even for a short period of time can help you to approach it with new eyes and a refreshed mind.

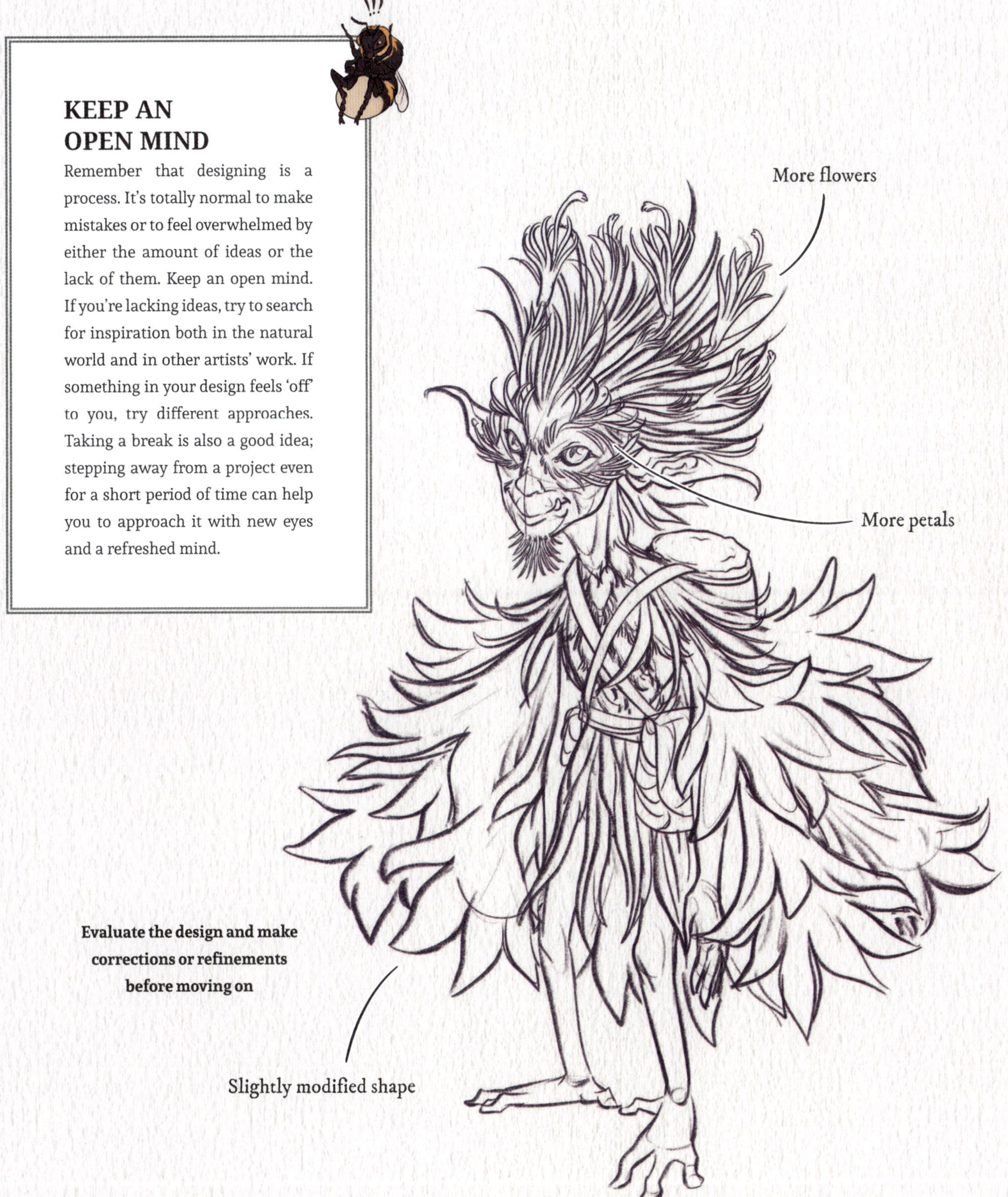

Evaluate the design and make corrections or refinements before moving on

FINAL SKETCH

Now you need to create the final sketch – a refined version of what you have created so far. If you started with a straight, standing pose, you can now redraw the character with a more dynamic one. You can make slight modifications, such as widening the leg spacing, turning the head, and changing the positions of the hands – or leave them as they are if you already have a clean, clear, expressive pose that you're happy with. In this case, giving Periwinkle a walking stick and turning his head help show his inquisitive nature.

This stage allows you to bring all the elements together into a cohesive design, so ensure that everything about the design and pose is consistent with the aesthetic and personality of your character. You may need to make some final adjustments to the proportions to ensure everything is balanced and harmonious.

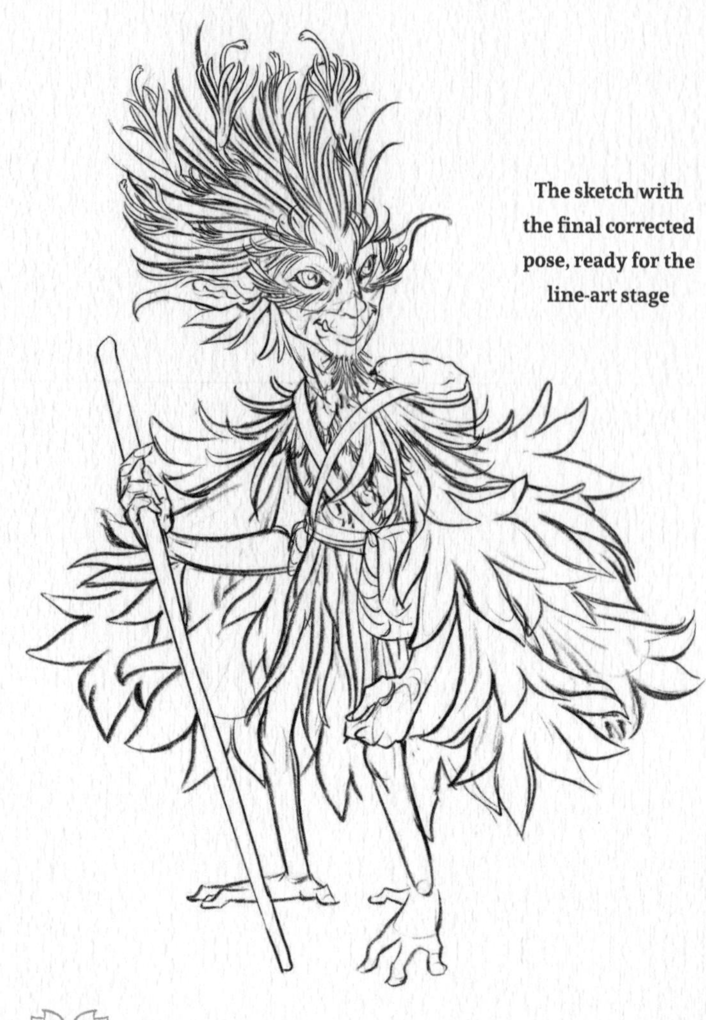

The sketch with the final corrected pose, ready for the line-art stage

LINE ART

With the design and pose sketched out, it's time to create the final outlines of your character. Trace over your final sketch on a new layer, using a harder brush to add more definition to the design. You can also modify some shapes at this stage, if needed; in this case, a few tweaks help round out the shape and layers of the crown-cape.

It's important to pay attention to the consistency of your lines; be decisive and make them well-defined. You may need to experiment with different line weights, tools, or brushes to find the most effective approach. Line art requires patience and attention to detail to achieve the desired result, so take as much time as you need and don't rush it. This stage should result in a high-quality, polished version of your character that is ready for colouring.

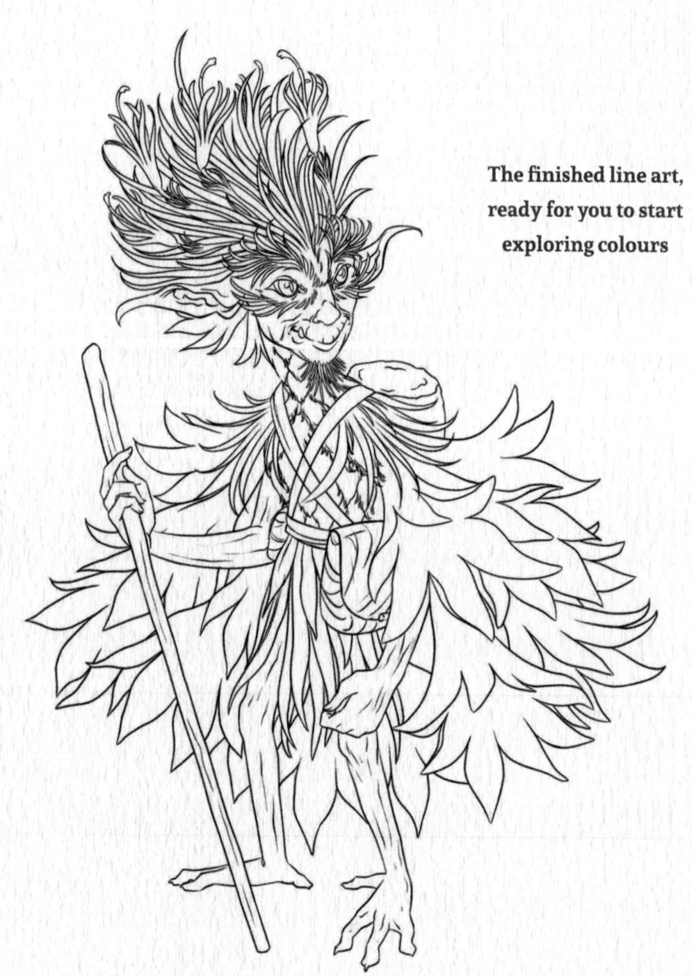

The finished line art, ready for you to start exploring colours

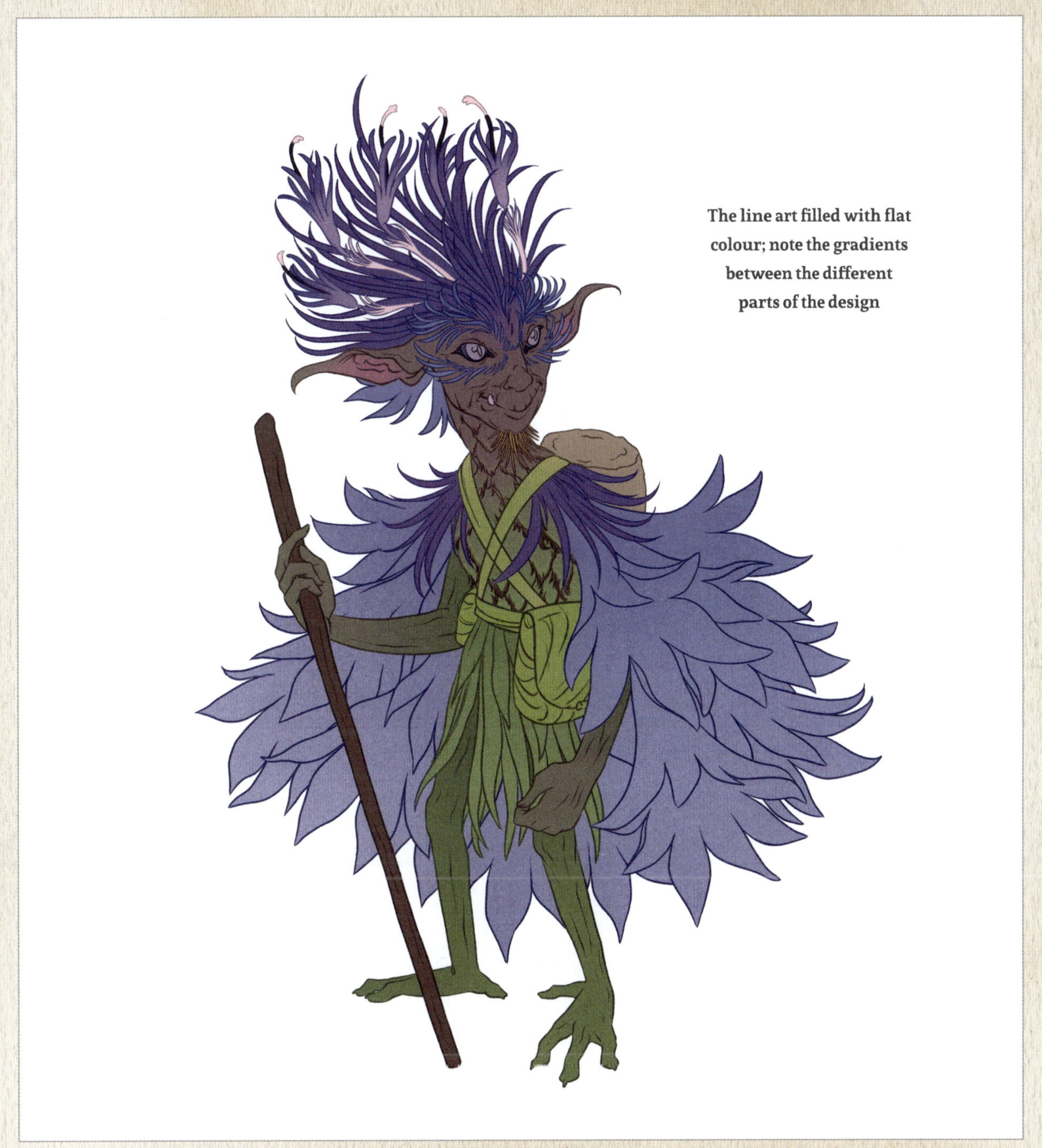

The line art filled with flat colour; note the gradients between the different parts of the design

ADDING BASE COLOURS

Now the magic can begin! Start adding colours to your character, below the line-art layer, using a colour palette based on your flower. At first glance, the cornflower has purplish-blue flowers and green stems and leaves, but upon closer inspection, you will also find subtle tones of white, brown, and pink. Remember that you can always experiment with the hues slightly – they don't need to be exactly the same as your main reference.

Fill the whole design with flat colours. Occasional soft gradients can help to create transitions between different colours and parts of the design. It can be helpful to work on separate layers for different parts of the character, such as skin, hair, and accessories. These layers will allow you to make quick colour changes and adjustments without affecting the rest of your work.

ADDING DIMENSION

The character now needs a more three-dimensional look. Paint in clean, well-defined shadows first, followed by highlights to create more depth and volume. Keep the light source in mind during this step and be conscious of how it emphasizes the character's face and body. At this stage you can also add textures and patterns, and render everything up to make a cohesive whole. Notice the texture on Periwinkle's arms and legs, for example – it's inspired by the texture of the cornflower's stem, rendered in brown and green with hints of purple cast by his cape.

Pay attention to the overall balance of your character design, ensuring that the shadows and light enhance the whole look. Some areas should be more defined and detailed, while others can be more subtle and soft. Overdone rendering will look distracting and can easily happen, especially with highly detailed characters.

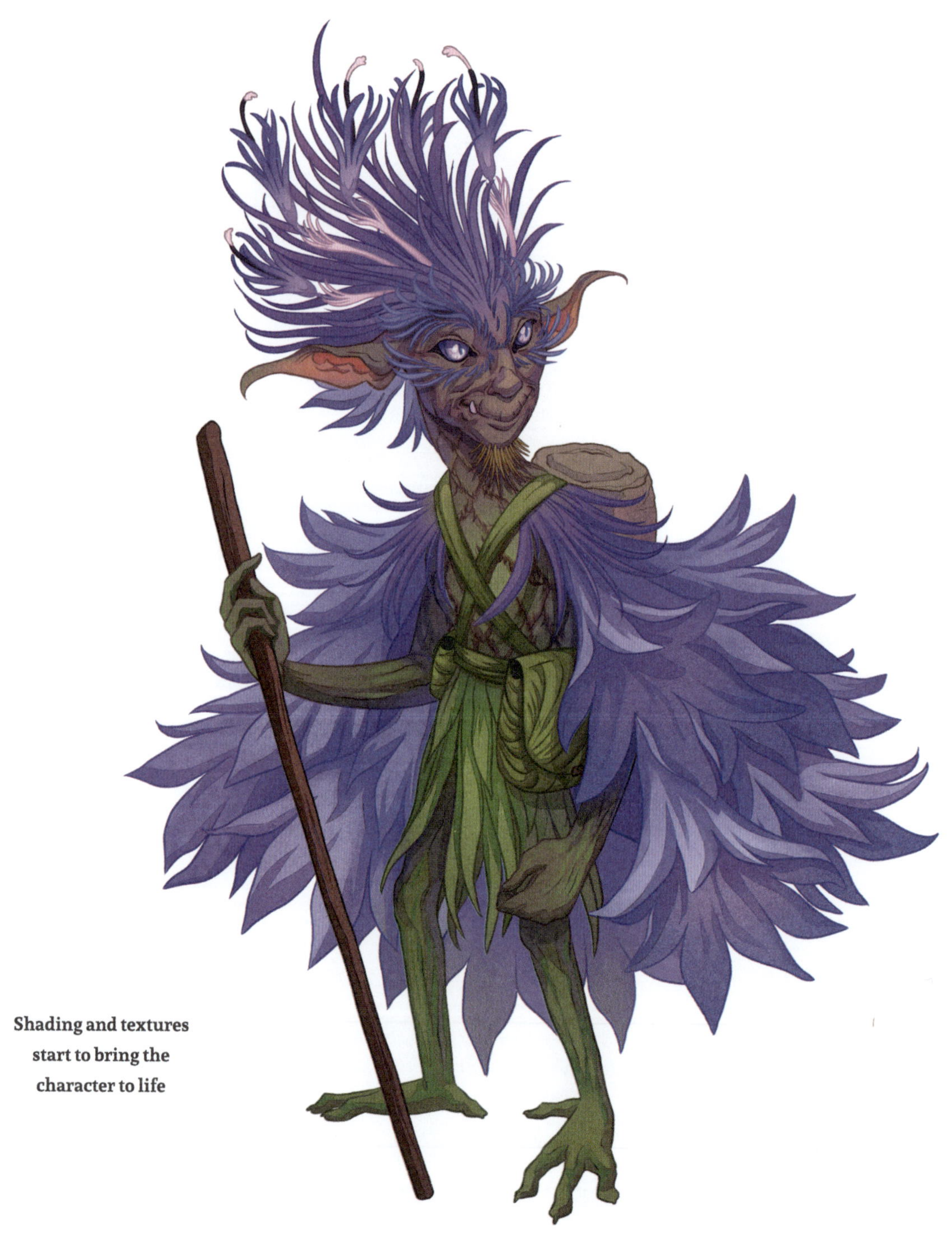

Shading and textures start to bring the character to life

CHECK THE VALUES

Always remember to inspect the values of your artwork. Perhaps something feels off, but the design's composition and anatomy are strong. If you aren't able to pinpoint the exact problem, it's highly likely that the values are weak. If you work digitally, you can check the values by overlaying a greyscale colour layer to convert the painting to black and white. If you work traditionally, you can take a photo of your image and convert that to greyscale.

Examine what you see. Is there enough contrast between the light and dark parts of the image, and the most and least important parts? If everything is too close in value, it's probably the reason for that 'off' feeling. Add stronger shadow and light, or fade back the less-important parts, and check your values once again to see the improvement.

Comparison colours and values before and after slight correction

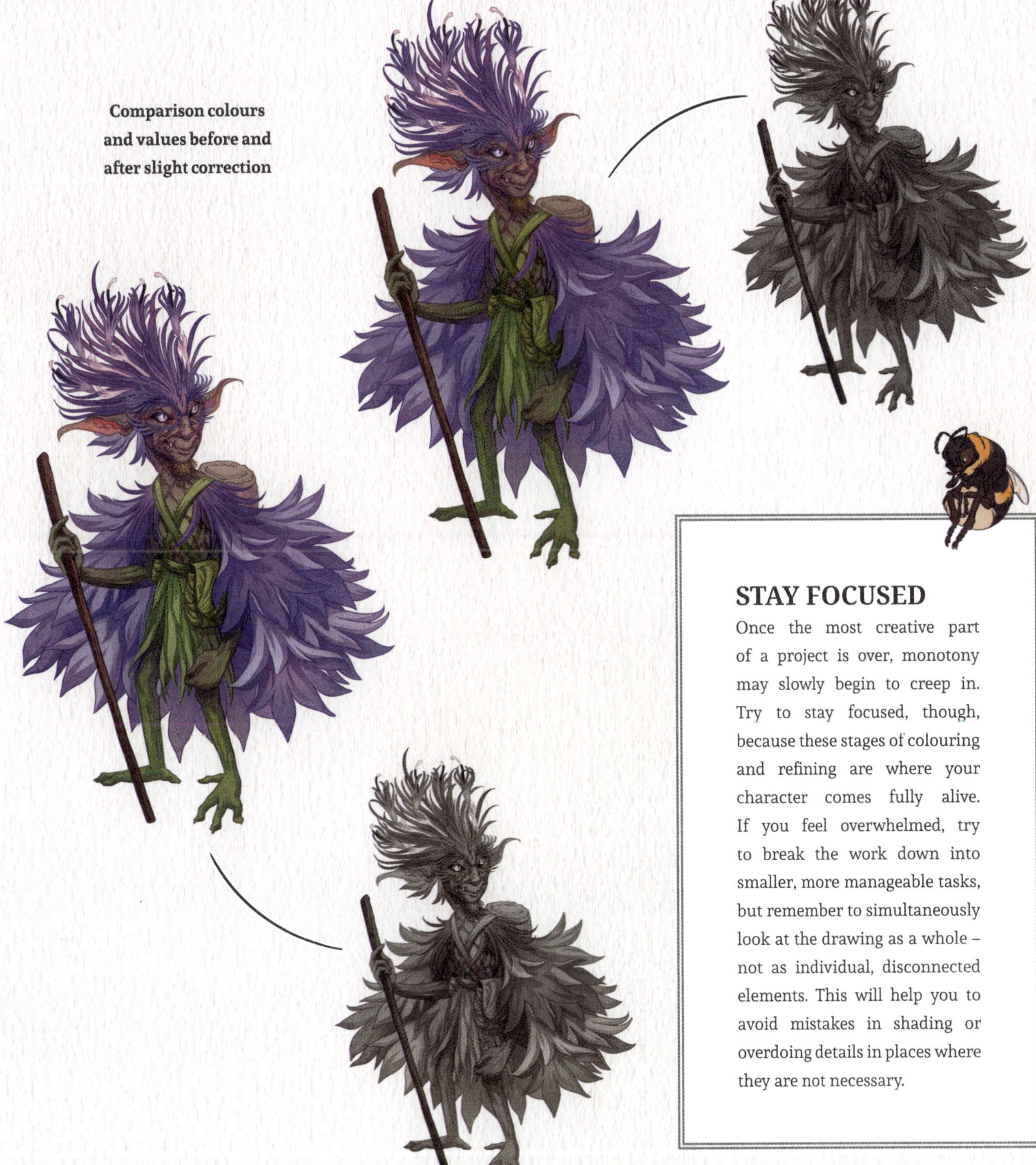

STAY FOCUSED

Once the most creative part of a project is over, monotony may slowly begin to creep in. Try to stay focused, though, because these stages of colouring and refining are where your character comes fully alive. If you feel overwhelmed, try to break the work down into smaller, more manageable tasks, but remember to simultaneously look at the drawing as a whole – not as individual, disconnected elements. This will help you to avoid mistakes in shading or overdoing details in places where they are not necessary.

FINAL TOUCHES

Study the overall composition of your design to check that all of the elements are well balanced and complement each other. Pay close attention to the details, zooming in around 40–60% to inspect each element. You can also zoom in on your plant references; they may inspire you to add some extra details that you hadn't previously considered.

Now it's time to add the smallest details, such as a glint in the character's eyes. Eyes are capable of giving life to a whole drawing.

Add more details on the body or petals if needed; such tiny details will make your character even more interesting. For example, paint some delicate veining on the flowers, but take care not to overdo these details.

You have now successfully brought your character to life, incorporating the intricate beauty of the cornflower.

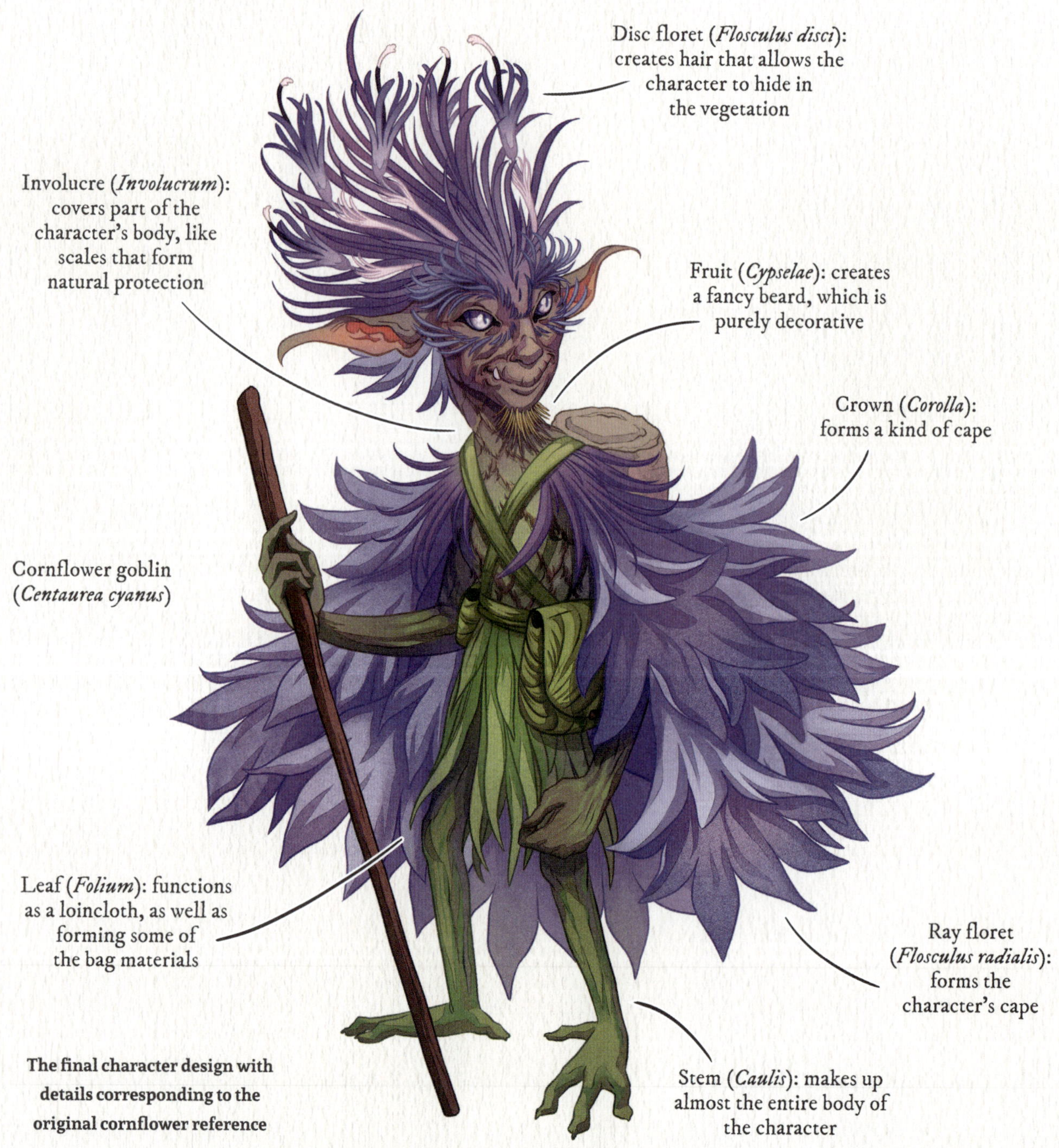

The final character design with details corresponding to the original cornflower reference

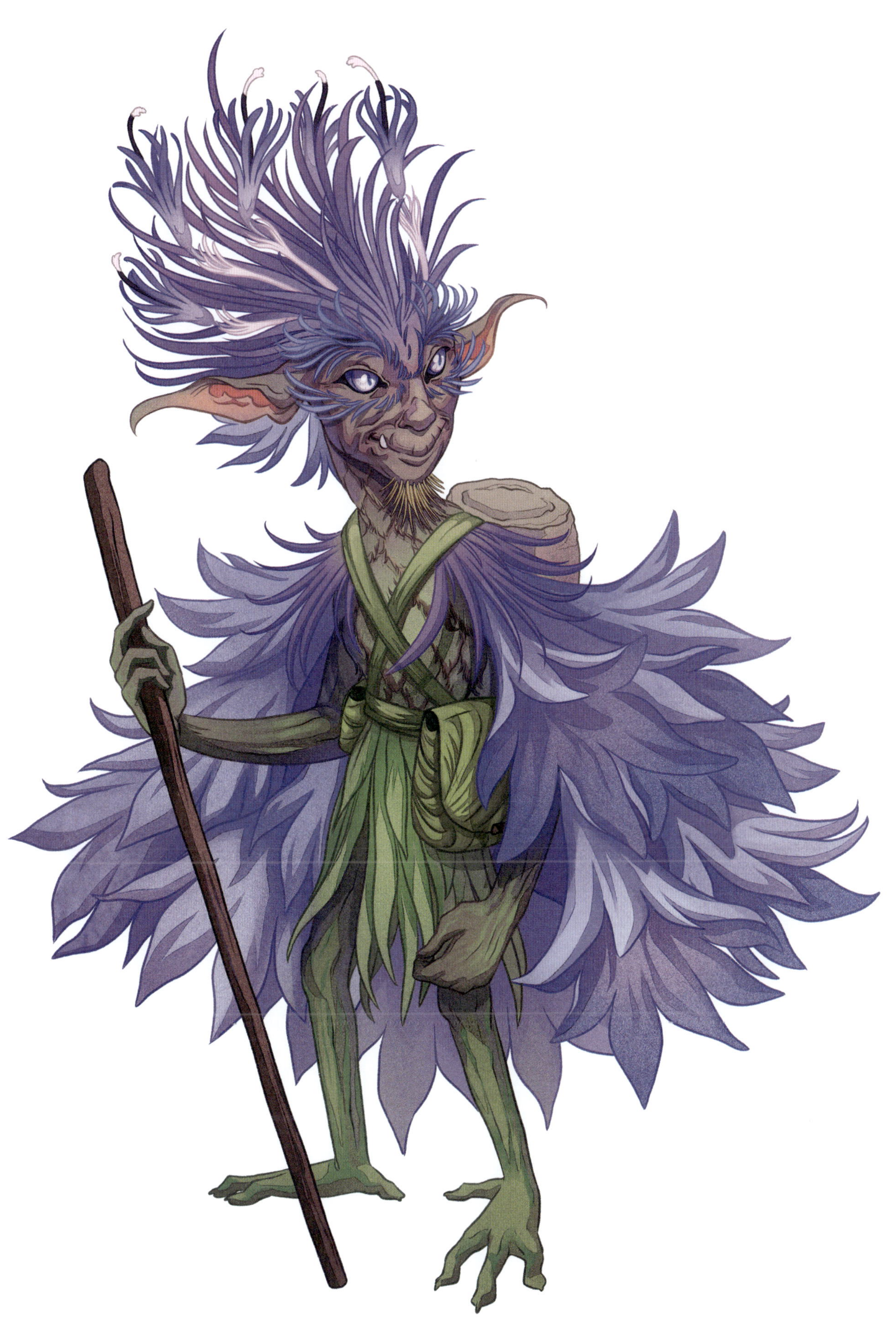

CORNFLOWER GOBLIN

Final image © Nora Potwora

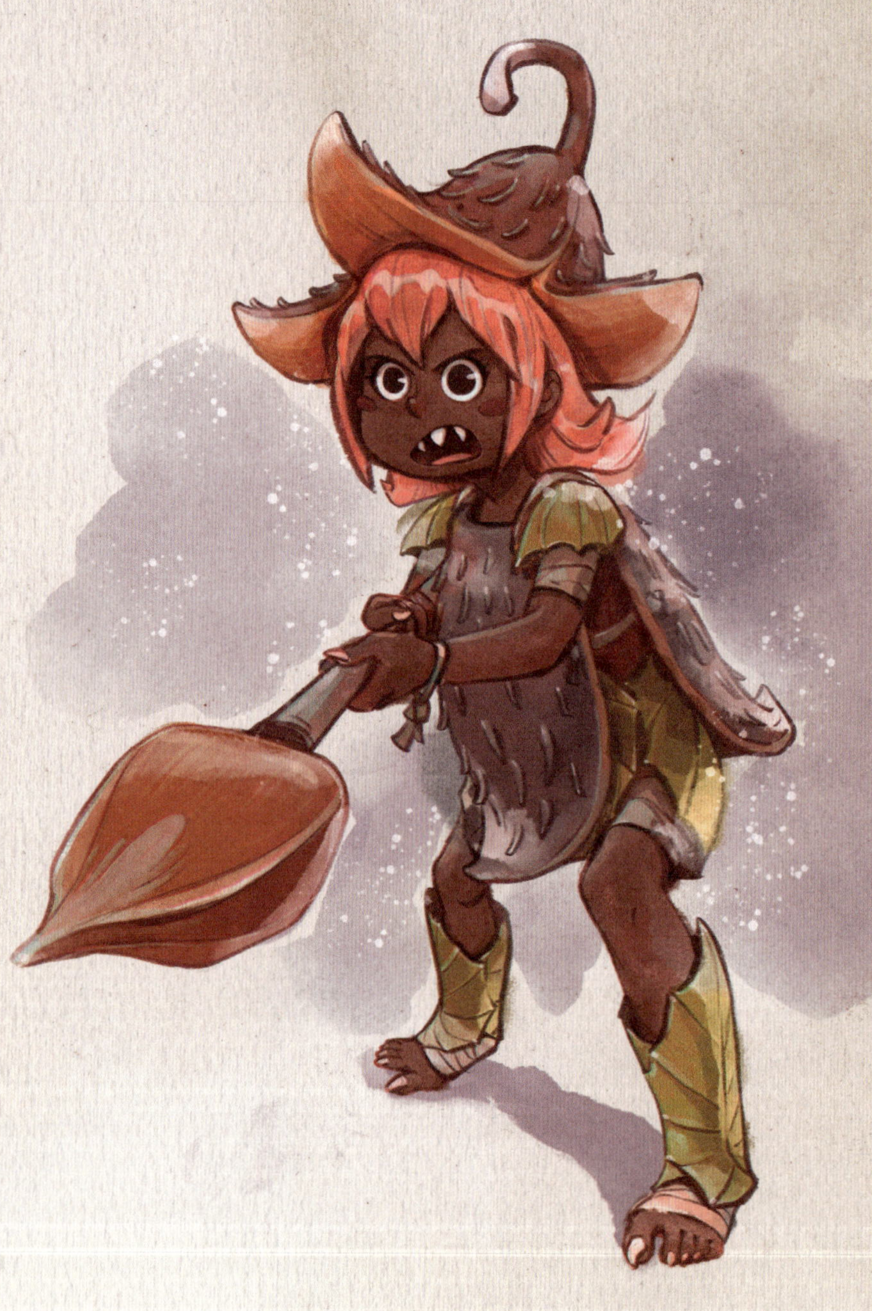

Also known as 'fall' and 'harvest time', autumn is the season when fruit, vegetables, and crops are ready to be harvested. Falling between summer and winter, it's marked by the changing colour of deciduous leaves as they prepare to shed, along with the falling of seed pods such as conkers, acorns, and beechnuts.

Over the course of this chapter you will learn how to use nature typical to the season of autumn as inspiration for a character design. It will show you how to study reference material to search out intricate details that you can then interpret and build upon through multiple sketches as you develop ideas for your character, always trying to think outside of the box.

This character will be created using Procreate, but the techniques used throughout the tutorial can be applied to other digital painting programs.

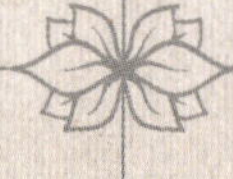

autumn

BEECHNUTTER

SIMONE GRÜNEWALD

Final image © Simone Grünewald

RESEARCH & STUDIES

When designing a character based on a plant or tree, choose one that has multiple interesting features you can draw inspiration from. Create a Pinterest board, or similar gathering of references, to collect all of your findings. Remember to explore the different life stages the plant might cycle through too.

The beech tree, specifically the European Beech, has beautiful distinctly toothed leaves that change colour but don't shed in the winter. They have edible nuts that grow in nut cupules, which are prickly on the outside but silky and smooth on the inside. They start off green and shaped like droplets when closed. When fully opened, they will turn brown, their appearance changing to resemble tiny stiff banana peels. Sketch out the various elements of the European Beech and its nut, considering how you could incorporate them into a character design.

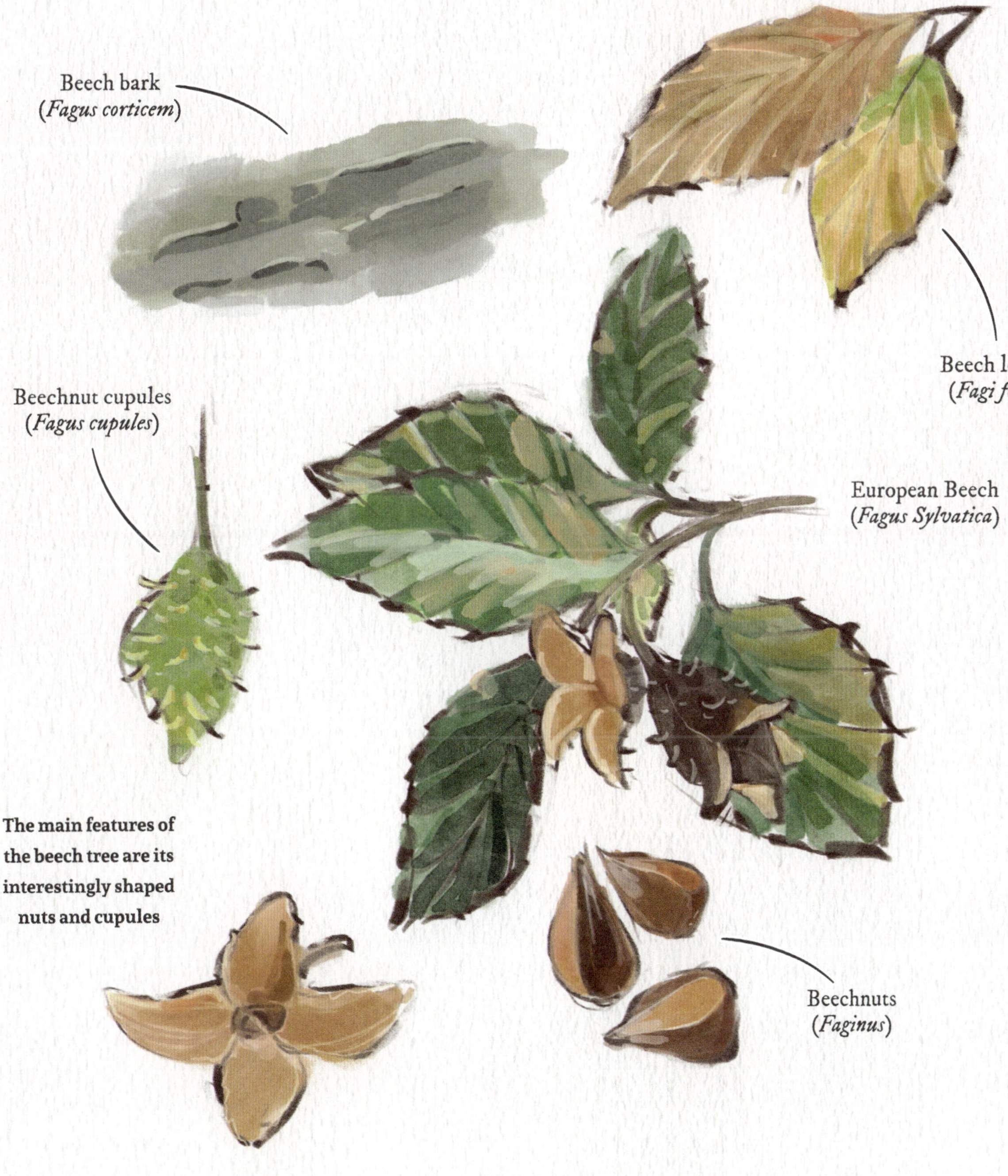

Beech bark
(*Fagus corticem*)

Beech leaves
(*Fagi folia*)

Beechnut cupules
(*Fagus cupules*)

European Beech
(*Fagus Sylvatica*)

The main features of the beech tree are its interestingly shaped nuts and cupules

Beechnuts
(*Faginus*)

INITIAL SKETCHES

Before you start sketching, decide what genre or audience you're designing for, if not already predetermined. This character will be for a children's book. With your reference material beside you, begin sketching your first idea for the character. Here the cupules could be a kind of armour; strong and defensive on the outside, but silky soft on the inside. This produces a little warrior-type humanoid character the size of a thumb. His tiny size will already partly determine the look of his design. Sketch clothing onto your character, trying to keep to the tiny scale. Think about the beechnut materials you have to work with and how they can be utilized. The nut cupules can be worn as body armour, but also as a hat. Perhaps a leaf could be worn as a cape and sleeves too. A rolled-up leaf with a droplet of water at the end could even be used as a telescope! The beechnuts themselves also look a little prickly. This is perfect for a spearhead. Their triangular shape will also work for two pointy shoes.

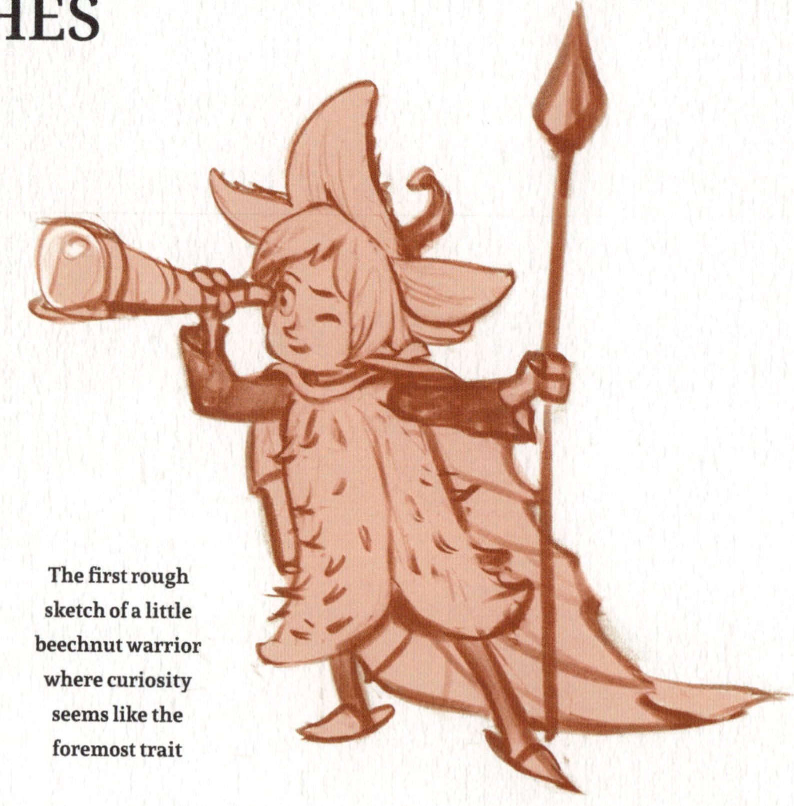

The first rough sketch of a little beechnut warrior where curiosity seems like the foremost trait

EXPLORATION

The first sketch can already hold a lot of information, but keep pushing and experimenting with the ideas, continually asking yourself questions to develop the design. What shapes work well? What kind of character is this? Are you going for default cute? Which elements do you like? The character will evolve as you continue to sketch and try out ideas, poses, and expressions.

Here the character turns into a prickly little person that has to defend its delicious beechnuts from other more powerful creatures. This implies that the character needs more of an edge to it. It may be cute, but look at those sharp teeth!

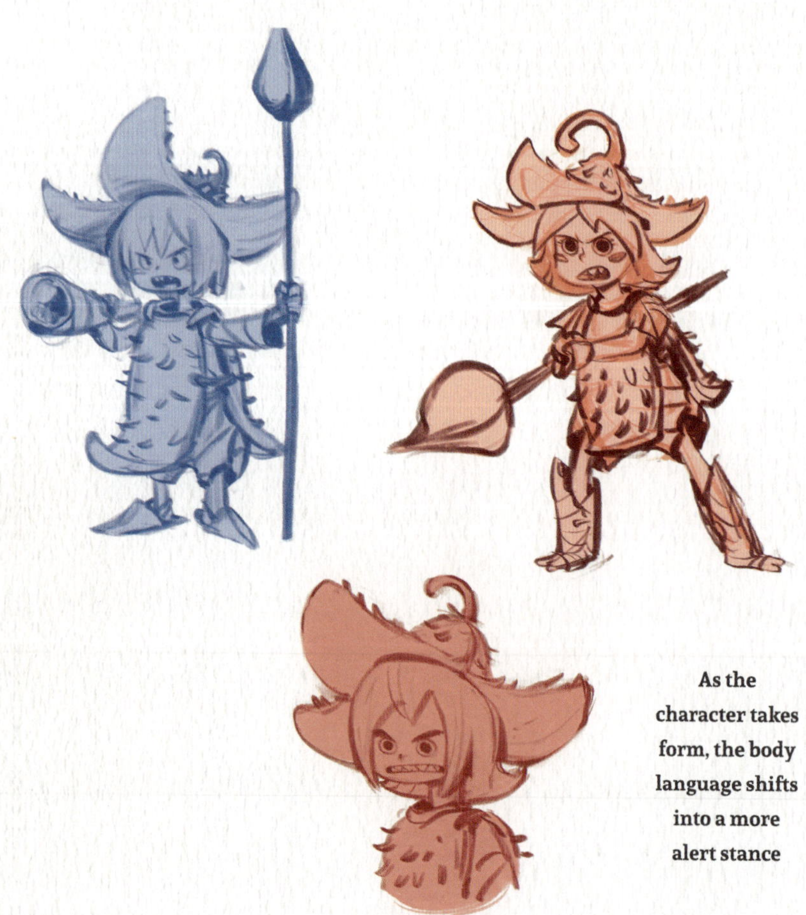

As the character takes form, the body language shifts into a more alert stance

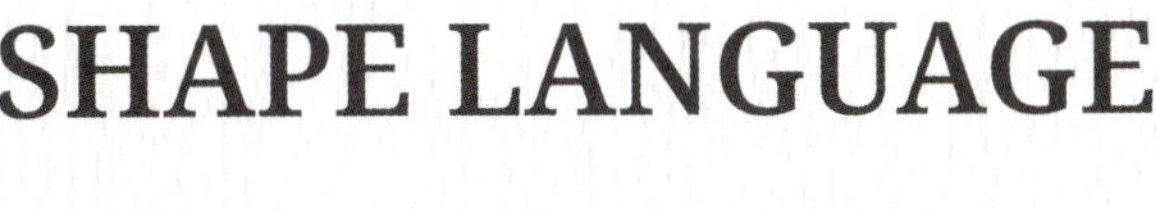

SHAPE LANGUAGE

To further underline the nature of the character, pay attention to the shape language you use. Apart from the prickly nature of the nut cupules, the other shapes don't necessarily have to be sharp-edged and angular. The hair shapes are rather hard and ridged, almost like a helmet, and end in pointy strands. Flowing curls would make the character seem softer and friendlier. The shoes and legwarmers are both fashioned out of soft leaves, but their sharp edges are exaggerated. Imagine them to be small but hard and painful, kind of like stepping on a Lego brick.

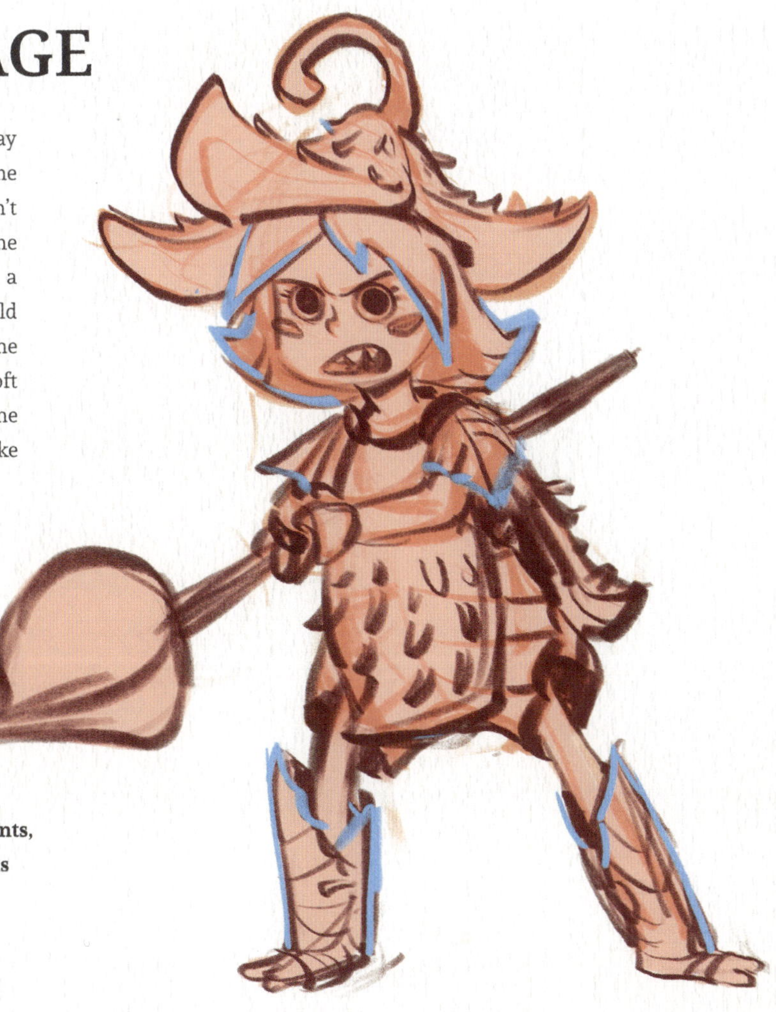

With lots of angular elements, the character is nearly as prickly as a porcupine!

EXPLORE YOUR CHARACTER'S STORY VIA THUMBNAILS

If you want to achieve further understanding of how your character acts and moves in their surroundings, sketch some thumbnails of your character in their home environment. Birds and squirrels could be the thieves this character needs to defend against. Caterpillars could be harming the tree that nourishes them, so they might be unwelcome too. The environment itself also informs the character. You could go even further and sketch out your character's living space to help you envision what they surround themselves with. As a further perk, you will have prepared ideas for illustrations.

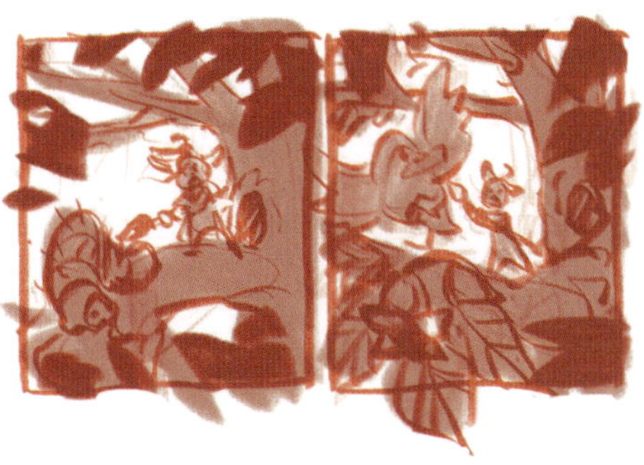

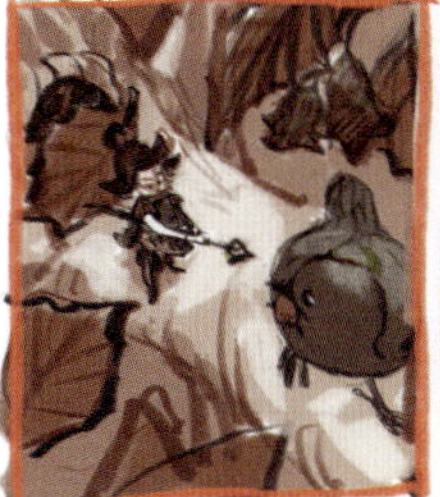

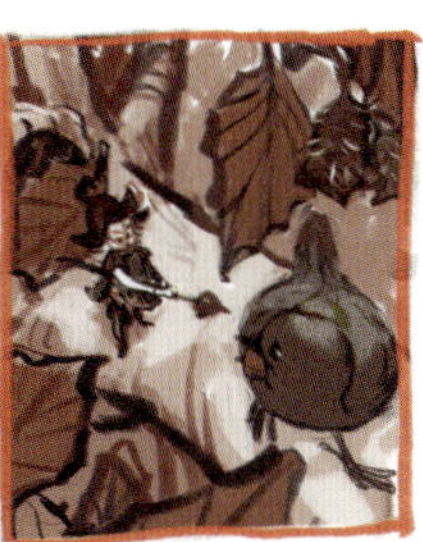

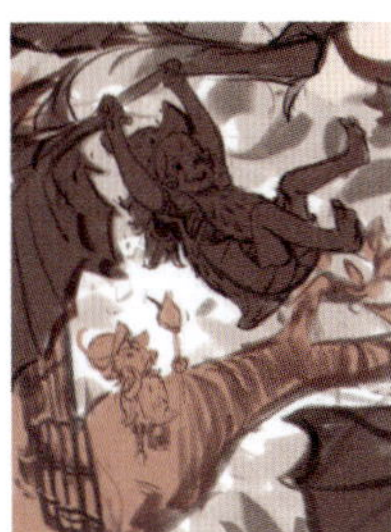

BODY PROPORTIONS & AGE

The character's proportions are rather cartoon-like from the start, befitting a children's book, but it's still useful to experiment further to see if other proportions would work any better. The long proportioned character is interesting; you could push it even further to give it really long limbs and only a protective core. But these elongated proportions don't quite serve the defensive character that in essence is a nut cupule protecting its insides.

Think about the context of your design. Is your character part of a larger group or tribe? What do elders look like? Roughly what kind of age is your character? Consider these questions before defaulting to the same age you usually draw.

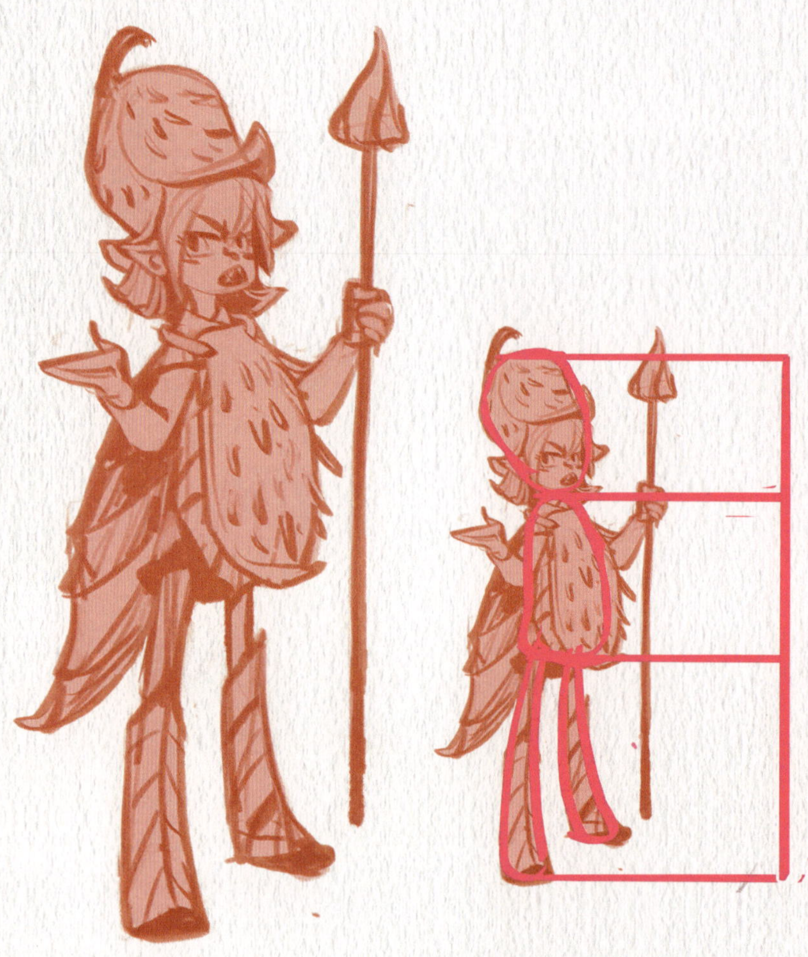

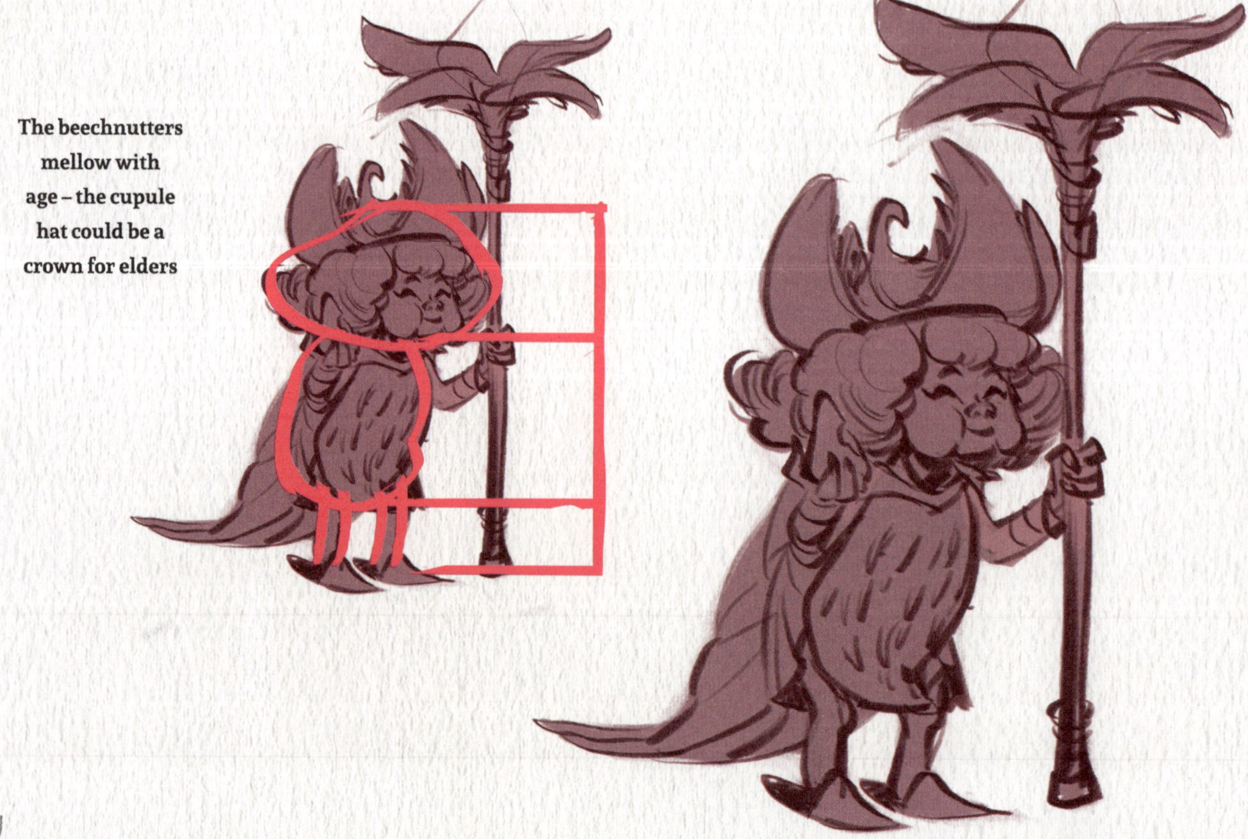

The beechnutters mellow with age – the cupule hat could be a crown for elders

FINAL SKETCH

Look over your accumulated sketches and choose the strongest to take forward. Begin to redraw and develop it. Try combining elements from several sketches or adjusting the pose. In this case, the initial sketch lacked dimension and the pose itself felt wrong. By acting the pose out yourself, you can check if it actually works.

To fix an incorrect pose, set the sketch to roughly 20% transparency and redraw the pose on a new layer on top. Once you're satisfied, you can start to draw your final sketch. Think about the dimensions of your character and how each material wraps around their different body parts when sketching their clothes and accessories.

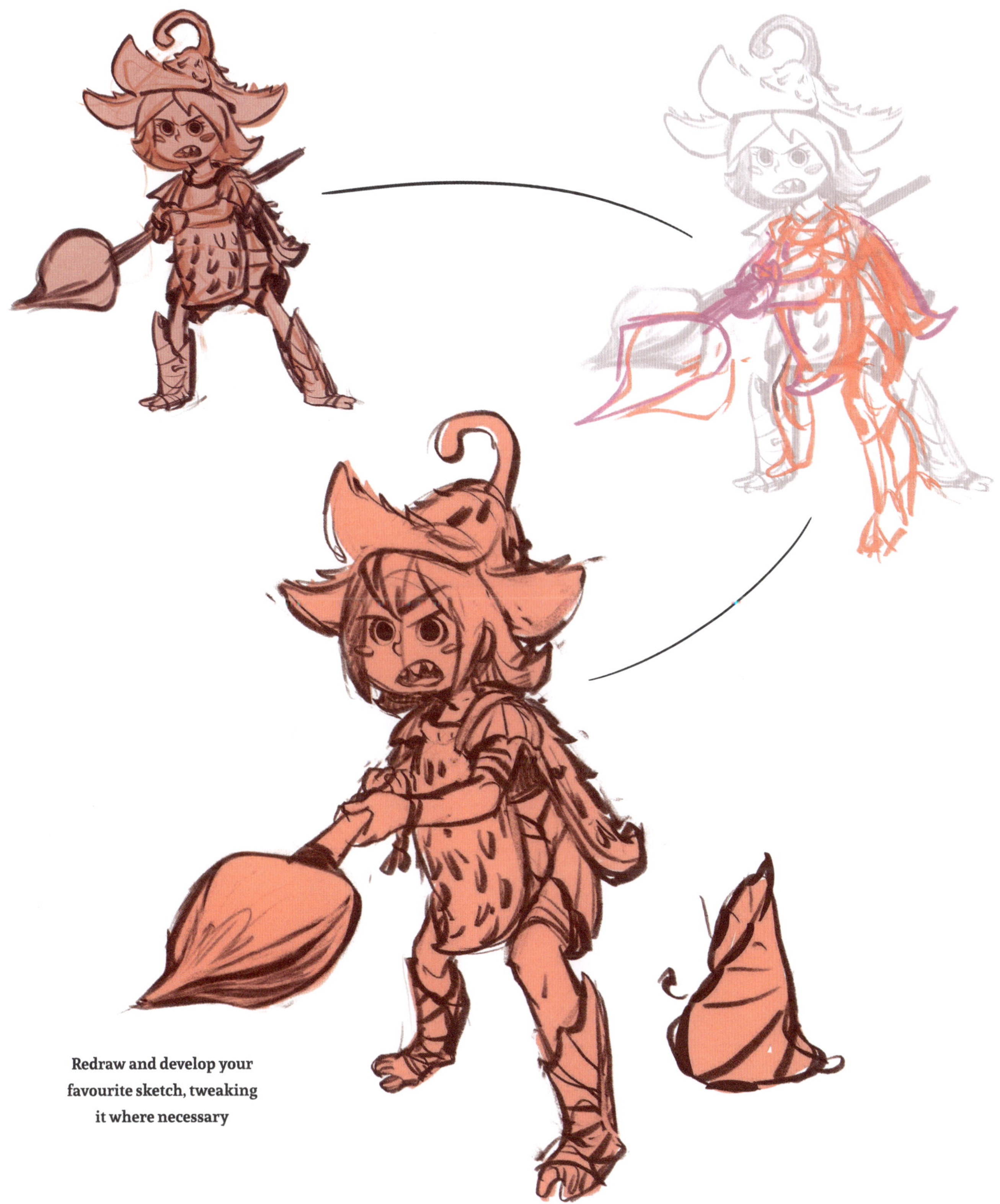

Redraw and develop your favourite sketch, tweaking it where necessary

LINE ART & BLOCK IN

To draw the line art, set your sketch to about 20% transparency to prevent you from confusing the sketch with the line art. Keeping it faint in this way will ensure your line art will still look good when the sketch below is removed. Use a brush you feel comfortable with, perhaps one with a little texture. Next, create a new layer underneath your line art and paint the silhouette of the character. This is your block-in of the character, on top of which you will stack the colours.

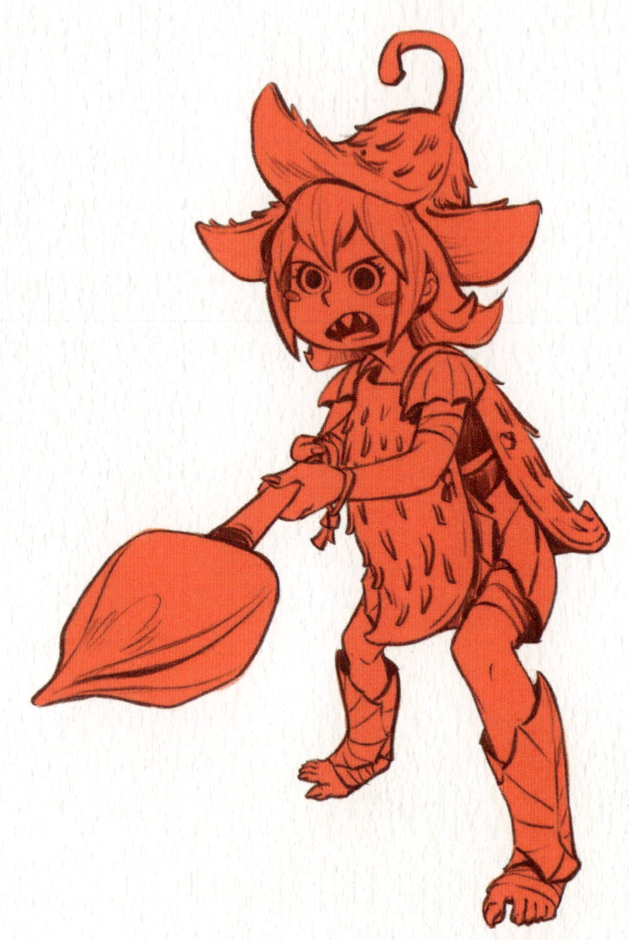

Draw your line art on a new layer, then block in your character on a layer beneath

LOCAL COLOURS

To add local colour to your character, create a new layer on top of your block-in. You could carefully paint within the character's boundaries, but this would be a little tedious. The easier option is to create a Clipping Mask. When you set a layer to Clipping Mask on top of a defined silhouette, it will only allow you to paint within its boundaries. You can also use this for multiple layers, consequently saving a lot of time as you paint your character.

When choosing colours, look back at your beechnut reference material for guidance. You may have also experimented with colour palettes in your early sketches and studies. Try to find colours that balance any you have already selected. Complementary colours are known for working well together. For example, the red of the character's hair complements the green of the beech leaves.

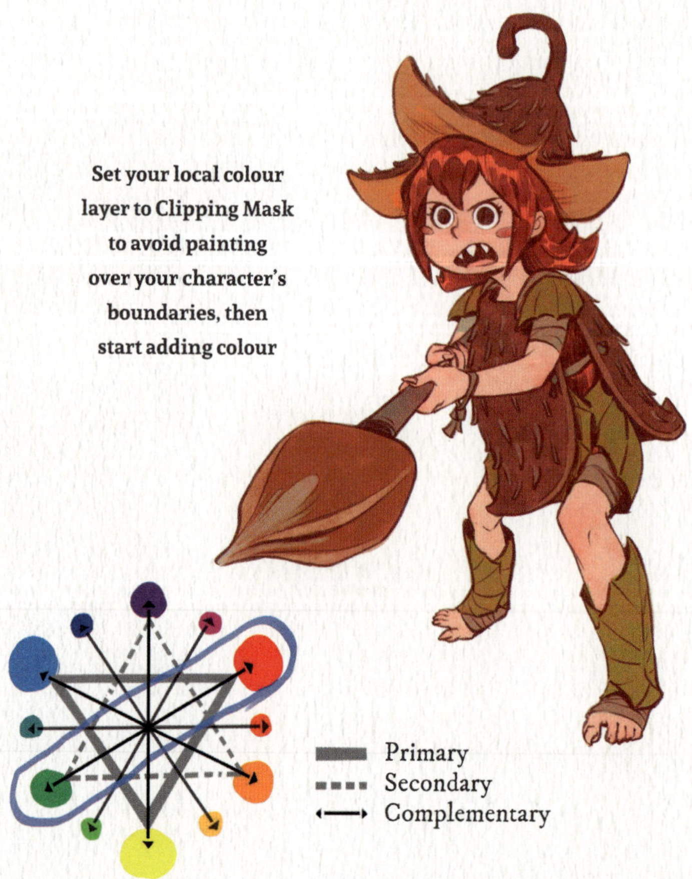

Set your local colour layer to Clipping Mask to avoid painting over your character's boundaries, then start adding colour

SHADOWS VIA THE LAYER MODE MULTIPLY

Once you've painted in your flat colours, it's time to add some shading. For a character design, it's good to use a rather neutral lighting set-up that will show off your character's colours, while also allowing for some rendering to provide dimension. To quickly achieve good-looking shadow colours, create a new layer on top of the local colour layer and set it to Clipping Mask and Multiply. Multiply mode will take the colour you paint and mix it with the colour underneath. Paint your shadows using your existing colour palette. When set to Multiply, they will automatically become darker and more saturated. Adjust the opacity to your liking. This works best with midtones.

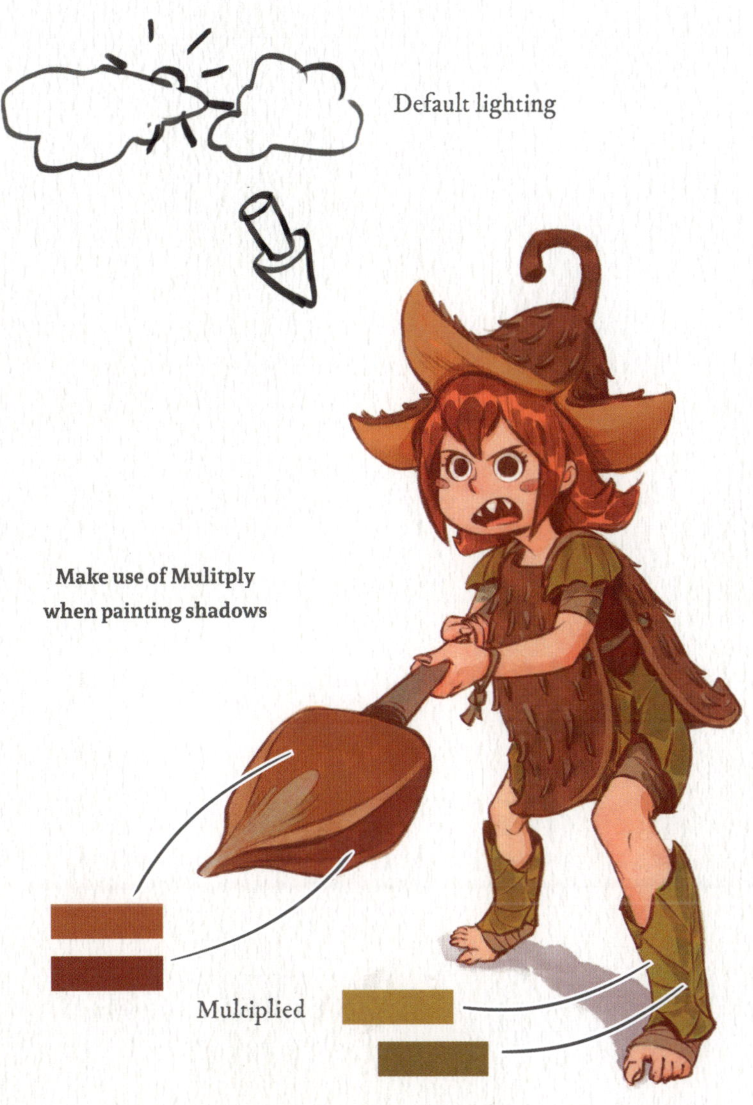

CREATE VIBRANT SHADOW COLOUR

Achieving the right colours takes practice. There is no one perfect shadow colour that will produce the correct result every time, because each hue has different characteristics. When you choose a colour that doesn't work when multiplied, you can correct it by adjusting its value and lightness/darkness.

Skin tones can be tricky. Try tweaking the hue and maybe even the saturation slightly if the shadow colour looks too dull. With enough practice, you'll soon develop a feeling for what works well. Shifting the hue slightly in the shadows is a habit to get into, especially if it isn't vibrant enough.

DIFFUSE LIGHT FROM ABOVE

Gently paint light hitting your character on the surfaces facing upwards. Reduce the opacity slightly; this light is meant to be unobtrusive, simply adding further dimension to the character. You can also add some highlights. An additional way to lighten your character is with layer effects. Copy and paste the current colours onto a new layer, clip this layer to the block-in layer on top of the others, and then set it to Screen mode. This will lighten your whole character. You can now erase the parts you want in shadow.

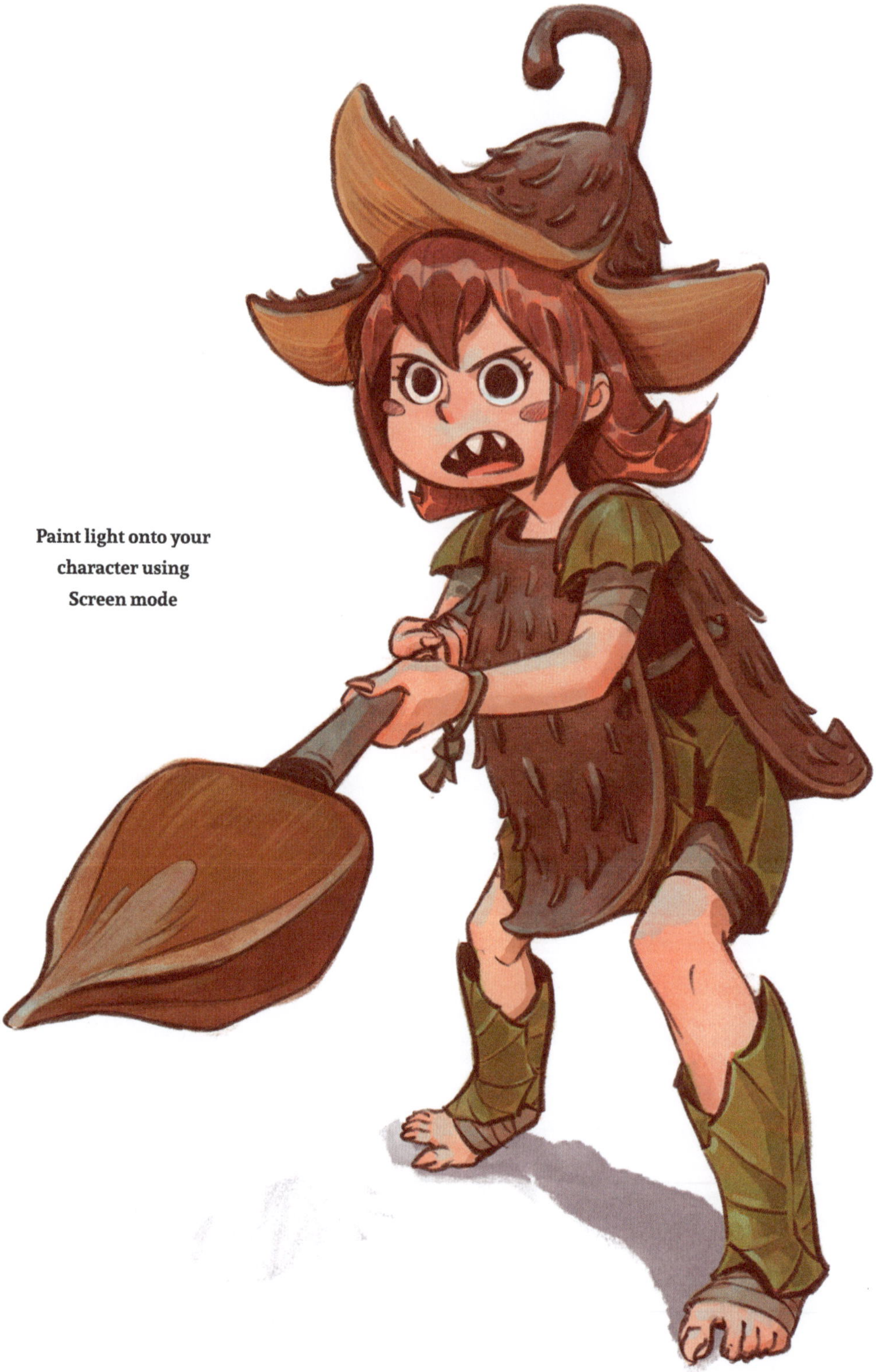

Paint light onto your character using Screen mode

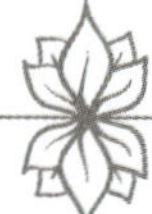

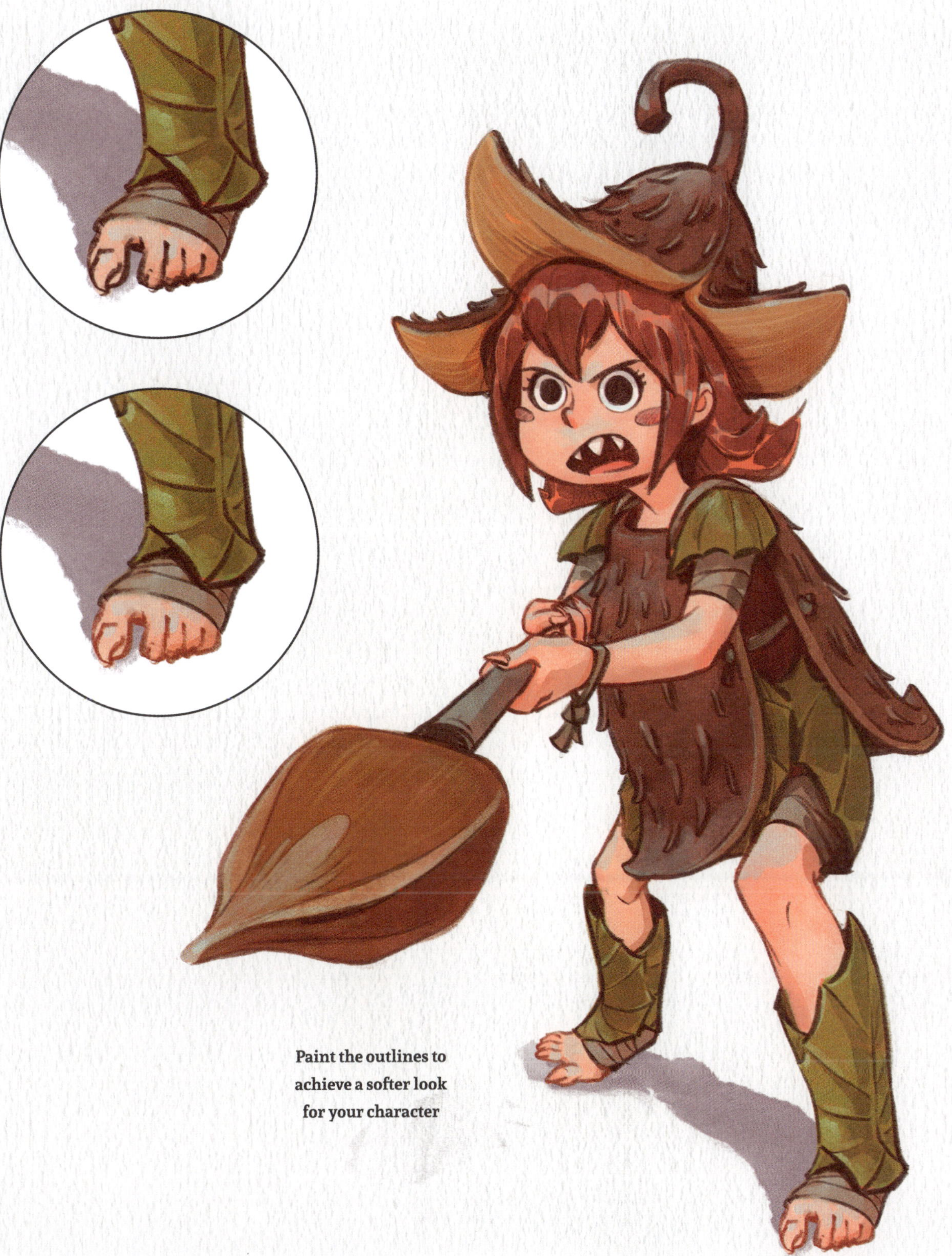

Paint the outlines to achieve a softer look for your character

COLOURED LINES

Coloured outlines aren't a necessity, but they will make the appearance softer. As the lines are on a separate layer, you can simply clip a layer on top of it and paint on top of the outlines. Finding the right colours for the outlines can be tricky. They need to be darker and more saturated than the colour they are outlining to really stand out. This character was sketched and outlined in a dark red tone, verging on brown, rather than pure black. Right from the start you know that most light to mid-value skin tones and brown earthy tones will work well. Where the reddish brown clashes, or its value is too dark, it can be tinted by painting it.

FINISHING TOUCHES

Up until now you've been adding colour information to your character, using the beechnut reference material as a guide. This last stage is reserved for additional details, corrections, and effects. Take a step back and look at your character as a whole. Evaluate where it's still lacking and consider what you need to add to finalize the design. Again, look back at your references and see if there are any additional details you can add to link it back to the beechnut.

The brushes you have used will have played a part in defining the style of the character design. At this point you may wish to add some further texture by creating a new layer and using a watercolour brush to paint some watercolour blots in the background. You can also use a watercolour detail brush to paint white on top of the outlines to enhance the organic watercolour effect.

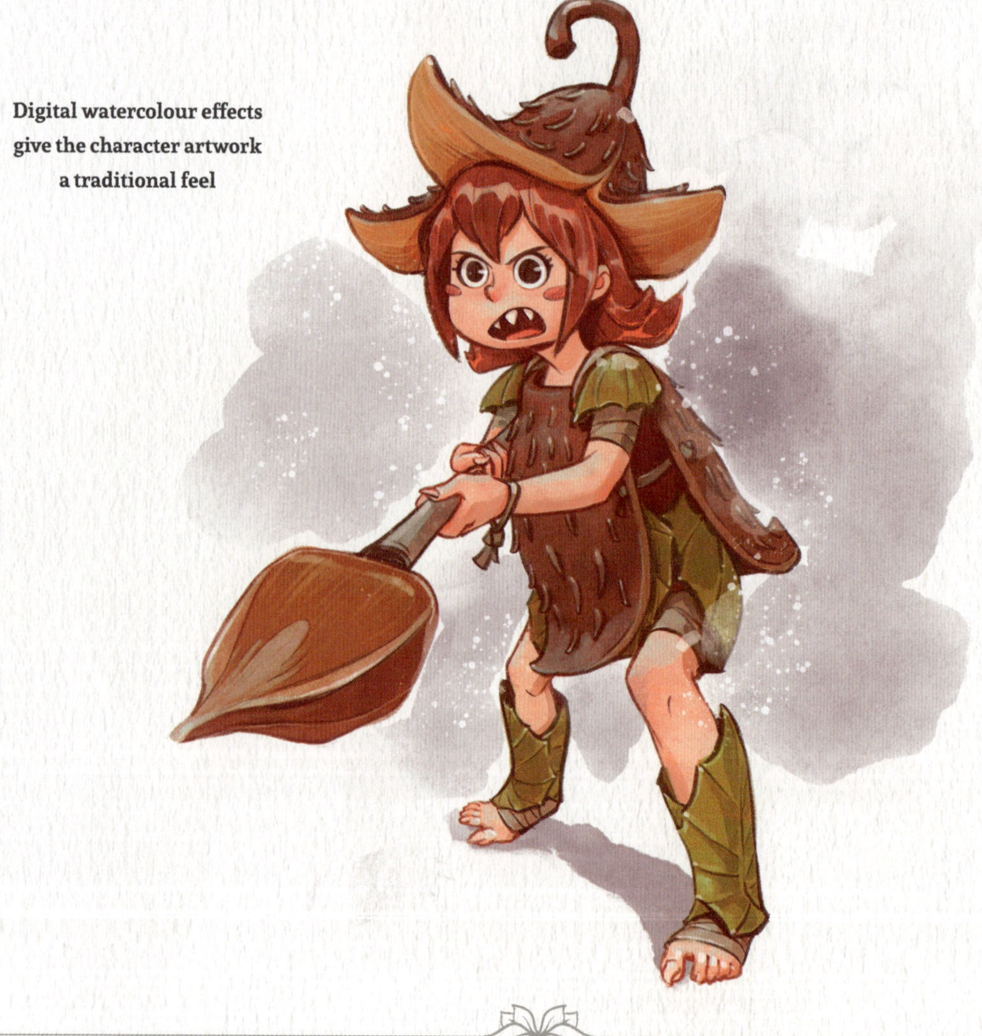

Digital watercolour effects give the character artwork a traditional feel

WATERCOLOUR BRUSHES

Max Ulichney's watercolour brushes for Procreate (The Watercolor MaxPack) provide lovely watercolour textures. They can take a little getting used to, as every stroke you paint on top of another will darken and become more saturated, behaving a little differently to normal digital brushes. The trick is to create a new layer when you want to avoid that darkening. Also, consider where you want to create edges, versus where a smooth uninterrupted brushstroke will look better.

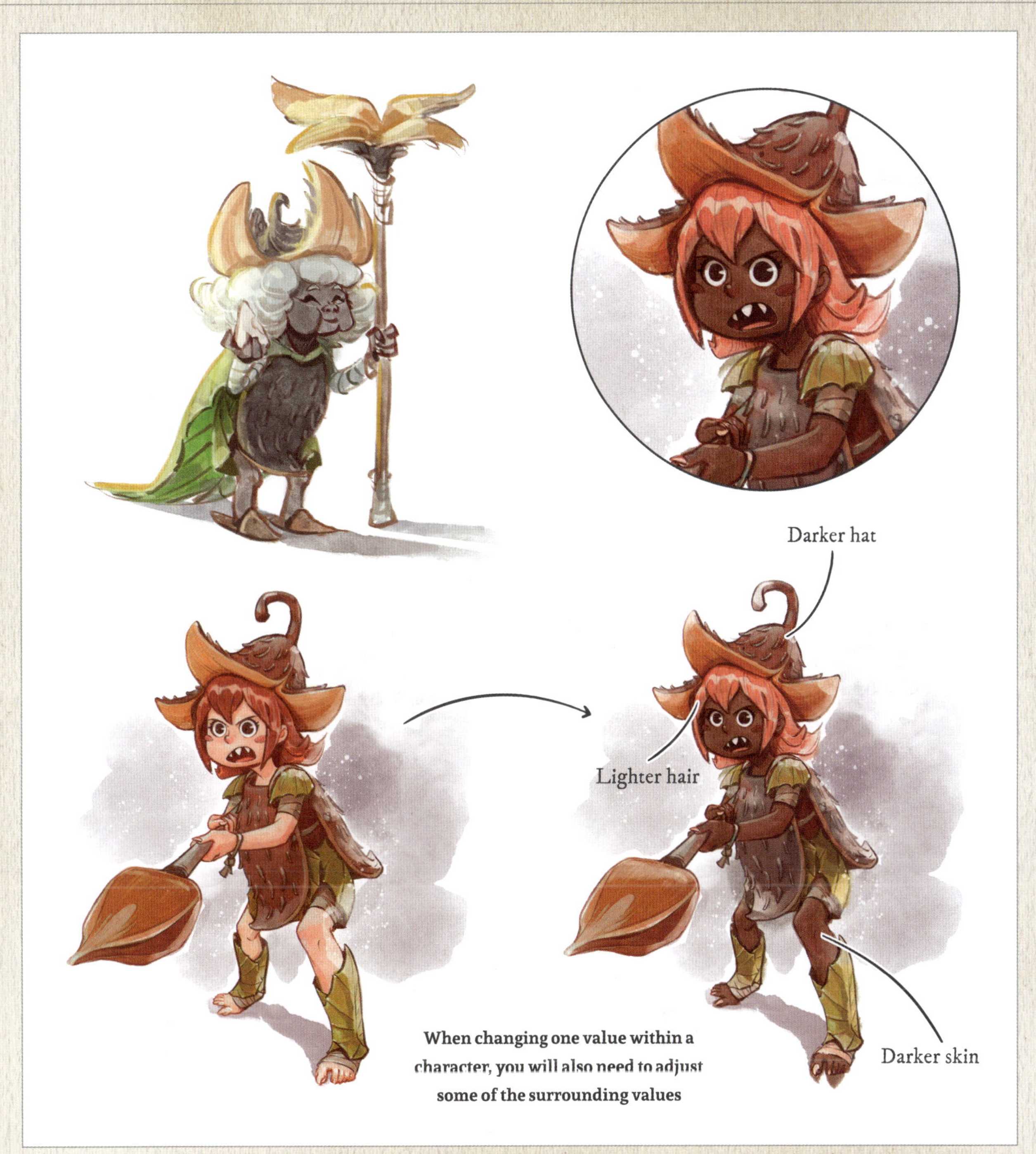

When changing one value within a character, you will also need to adjust some of the surrounding values

CHANGES VIA LAYER MODES

Remember those defaults you gravitate to without thinking? After adding some colour to the sketch of the elder beechnut when exploring the wider beechnutter world, it's decided that the beechnutters will be a darker-skinned folk. It's not uncommon to make adjustments to an illustration when it's almost finished. When painting digitally, you can use colour modes to alter colour without disrupting the original painting. When changing the value of one part, such as the skin tone, keep in mind that you will have to adjust the surrounding values too, as you will have previously balanced everything to suit the original values. Colour correction is easily achieved by painting the new colour on a new layer set to either Hue or Colour, then duplicating this layer and choosing a layer mode that will either darken or lighten the same area in order to achieve the desired value.

BEECHNUTTER

This plucky character is part of a large settlement of beechnutters, nicknamed as such by those who accidently encroach on their territory and experience their prickly nature! They ferociously defend what is theirs and don't stop until the danger is vanquished. Their young are playful and, if you listen carefully, you might be able to hear their merry laughter in the beeches on a warm day.

Inspired by the European beechnut, the nut cupules form the breastplate and helmet, while beech bark is used as string and undergarments. Beech leaves are fashioned into decorative shoulder pads and leg protectors, plus make comfy underwear, while a whole beechnut is used for a spearhead.

Every character design is a journey. Have fun as you jump from association to inspiration, plucking ideas to carry over into the design while sieving out any elements that don't ring true. Push yourself out of your comfort zone to see how you can incorporate the chosen plant into your design, transforming it into a truly unique character.

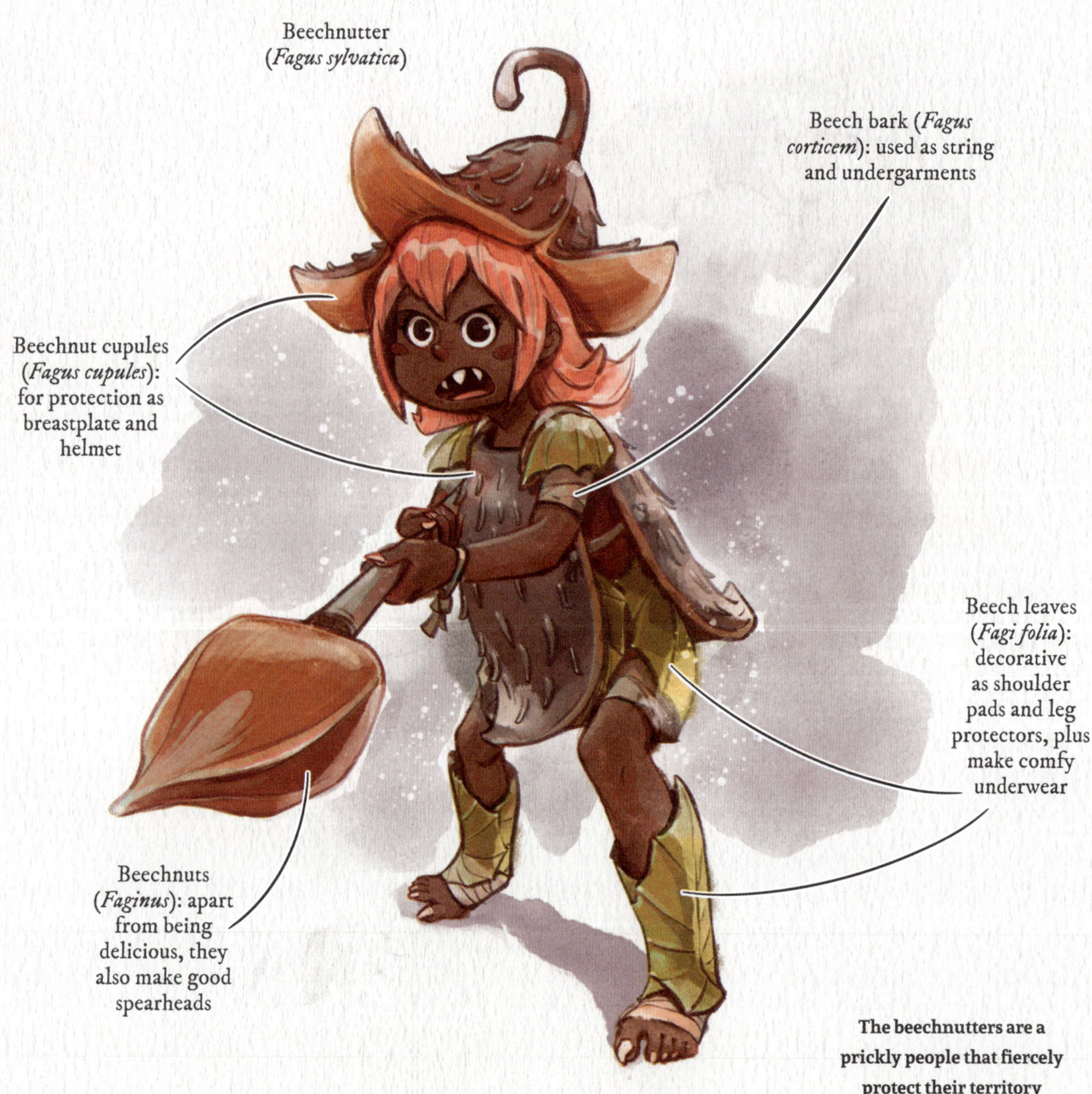

The beechnutters are a prickly people that fiercely protect their territory

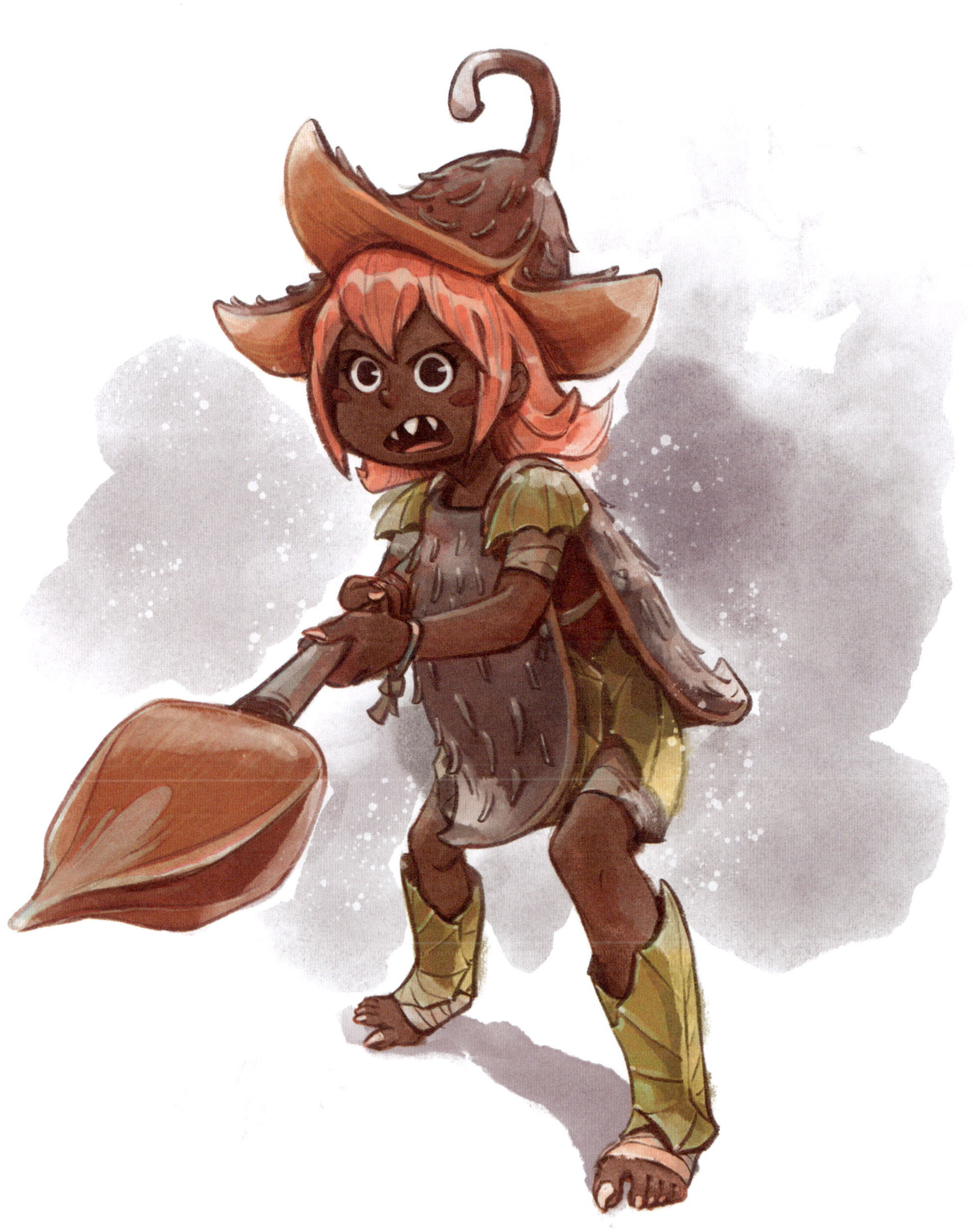

BEECHNUTTER

Final image © Simone Grünewald

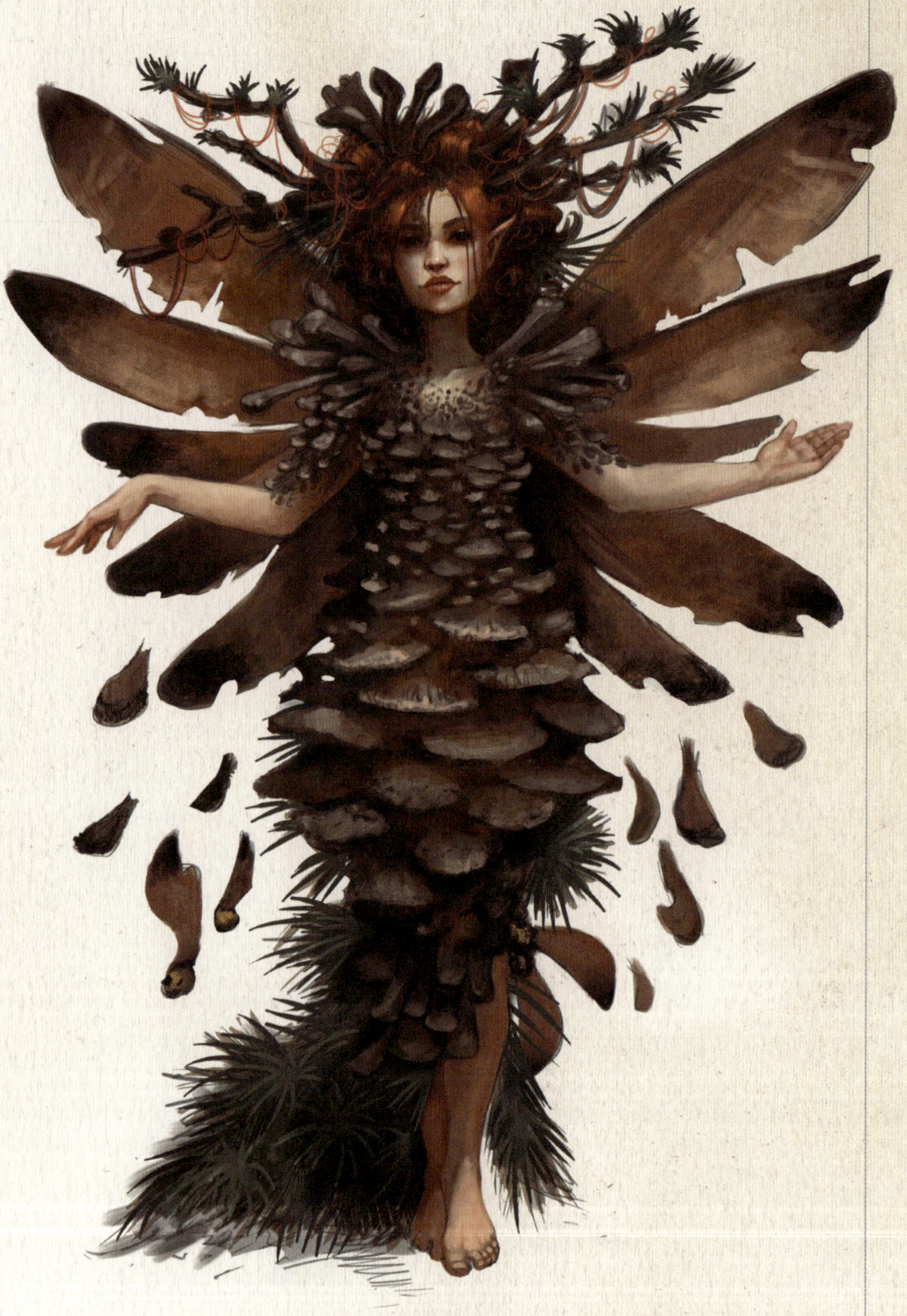

This tutorial will explore how to create a pinecone faery character using inspiration from the natural world and season of winter. A time when many plants die or rest in hibernation, winter is a season of strong shape language – bare branches, seeds, evergreens, and husks – that contrasts against the softer forms of spring and summer. Whether seen on trees or used in seasonal decoration, pinecones are often seen to embody winter and their woody scales and conical shape makes them instantly recognizable. There are also many different varieties, which makes them all the more interesting to work with. This tutorial will use Adobe Photoshop and artist Greg Rutkowski's brushset, but follow along with your preferred choice of software.

winter

PINECONE FAERY

KIRI LEONARD

Final image © Kiri Leonard

START WITH RESEARCH

Start by researching the pinecone to familiarize yourself with its anatomy. This research stage is terrific for sparking ideas as to which elements could be incorporated into the character design. Study old botanical drawings, look at photo references, and then sketch some studies yourself. Letting the shape of the pinecone flow through your hands as you study it will give you a better feel for your design once you begin combining it with the human aspect. One of the most distinctive elements of the pinecone is its scales. There are numerous innovative ways you could incorporate them into a character design, especially a faery design. The pine-seed wings could also translate well into delicate faery wings.

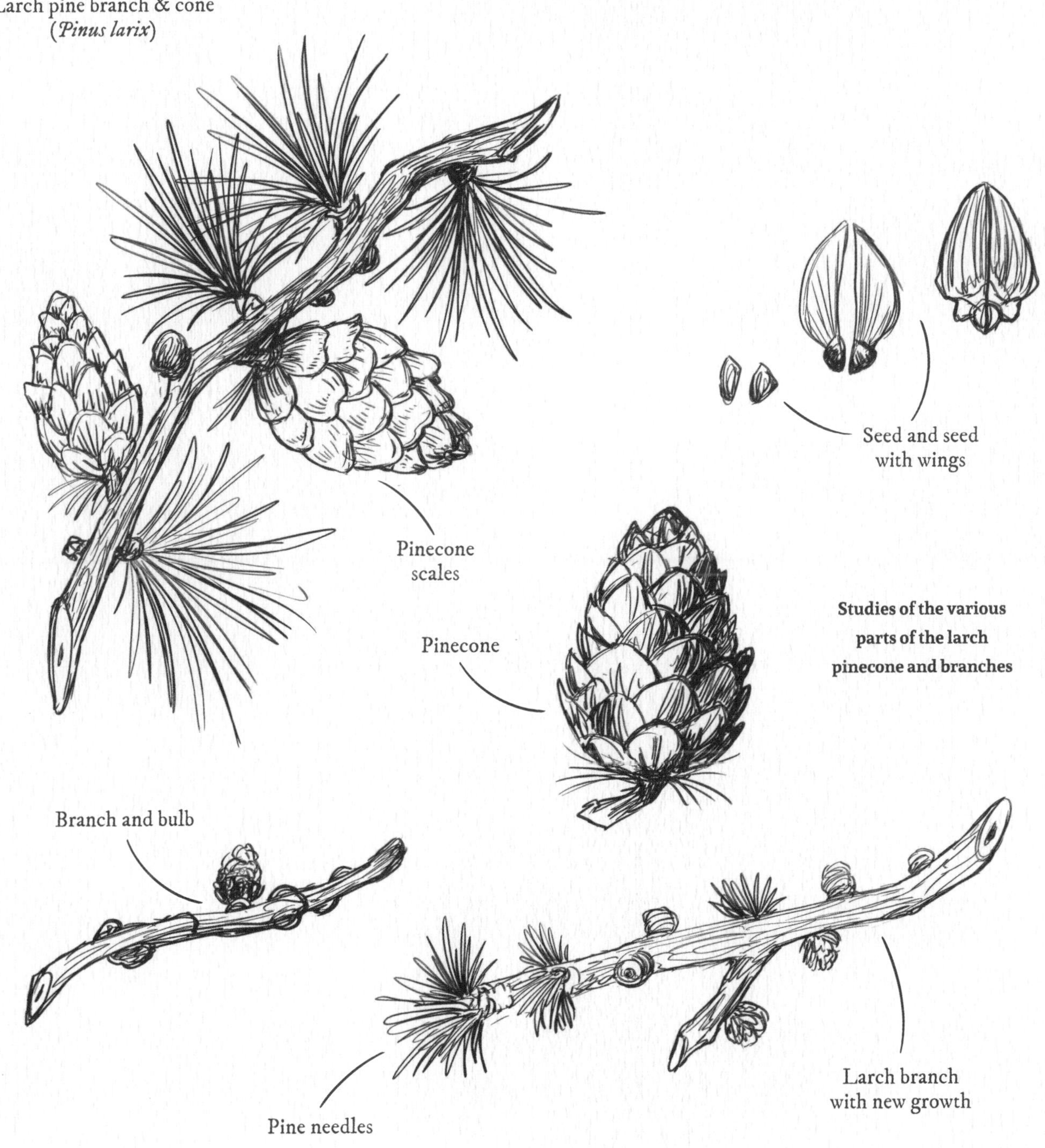

Studies of the various parts of the larch pinecone and branches

INITIAL SKETCHES

Create a series of initial sketches, loosely exploring the idea of a pinecone faery. Focus on getting your ideas down on paper as you explore various shapes, textures, and character concepts. Experiment to see how different parts of a pinecone could integrate with the anatomy of a faery creature. You can also try out different angles and compositions, which will lead into the thumbnail sketches.

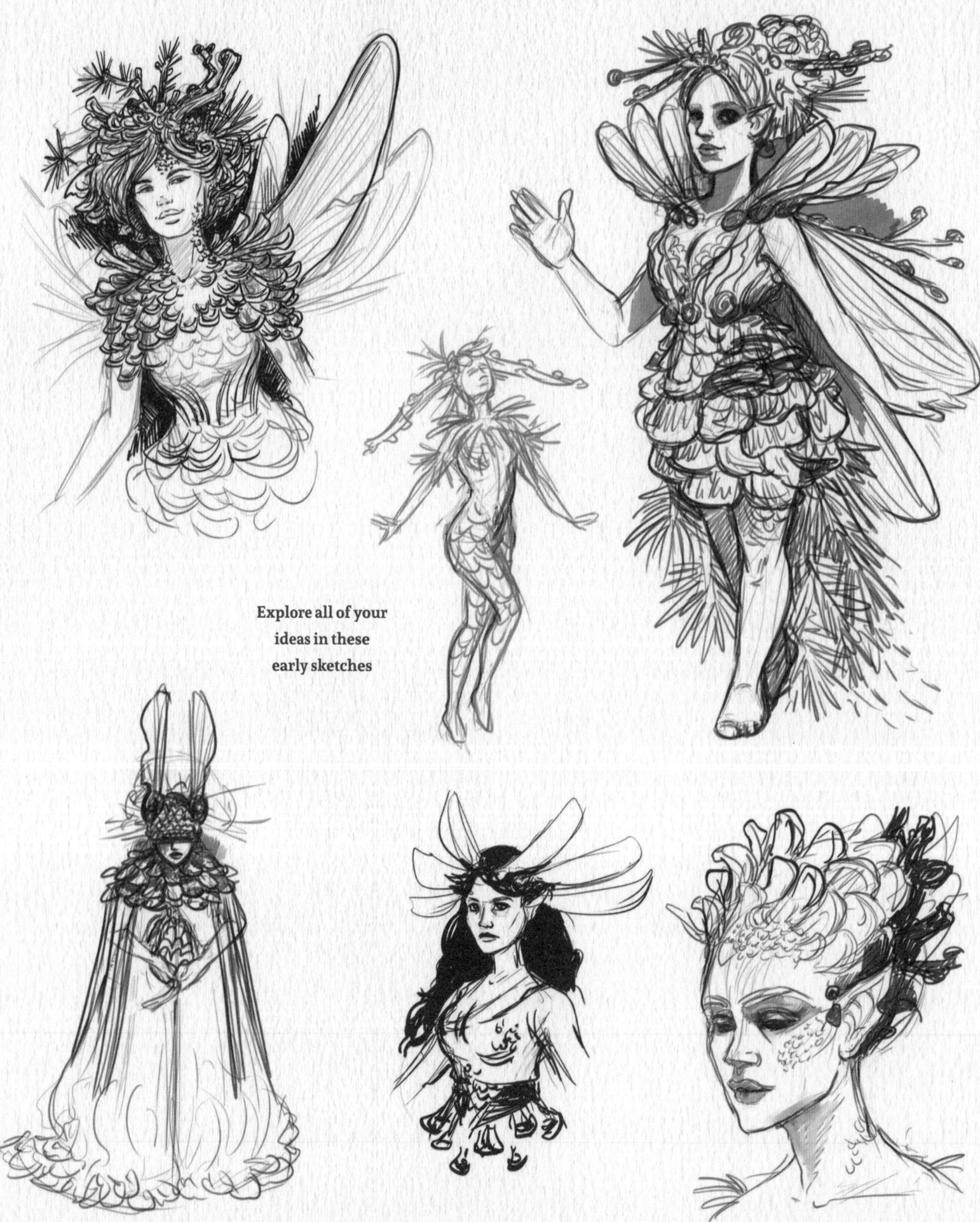

Explore all of your ideas in these early sketches

THUMBNAILS

Next, sketch out a series of rough thumbnail designs. Thumbnails allow you to explore various possibilities to help you decide which direction you wish to take. This is a good stage to start considering the composition of the image. Even though you're not creating a background for the final character, it can sometimes help to envision it as a full piece. You can also use this step to keep exploring how the overall form of the pinecone can be integrated into the character's design. Here, the first design will be taken forward and developed.

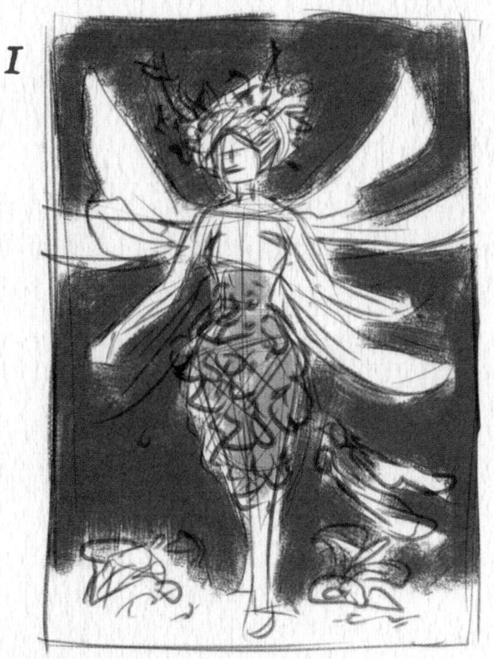

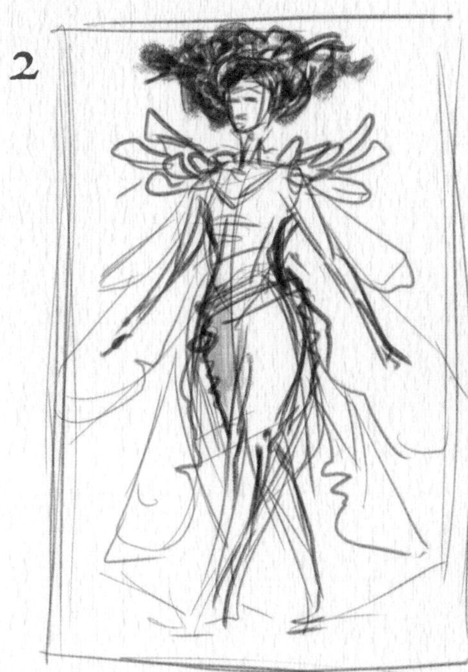

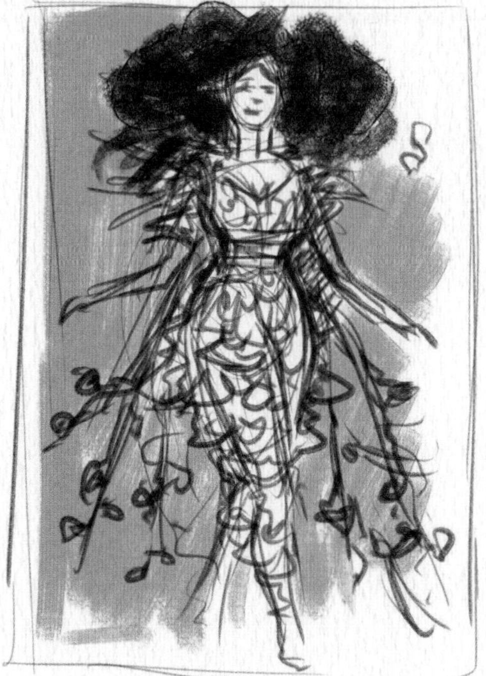

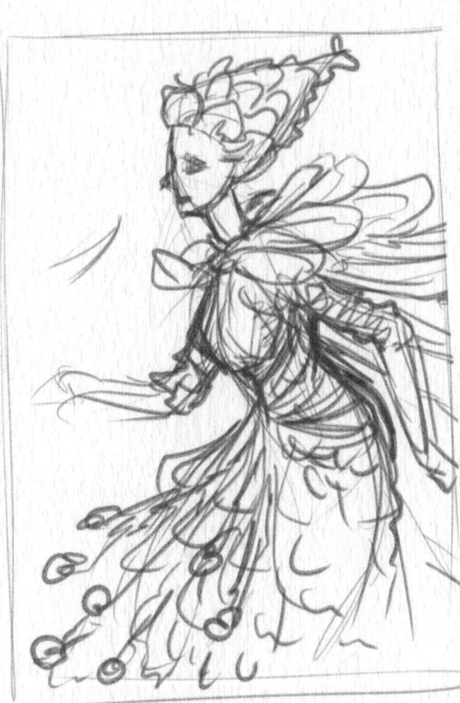

When sketching thumbnails, focus on the composition and how to frame the character – details can wait until later

STARTING THE SKETCH

Once you have your initial sketches and thumbnails, it's time to begin the first sketch of the character. Try to work loosely and organically with the drawing, allowing it room to breathe and develop following the initial composition idea of your thumbnail. Remember to refer back to your botanical studies to remind you how you could incorporate elements of the pinecone. The seed wings will work well as faery wings, and there are many interesting ways to include the woody scales too. Sketch them to form a dress, but also growing naturally from her body. Just as they sprout from the centre of the pinecone, they sprout from the faery's body also.

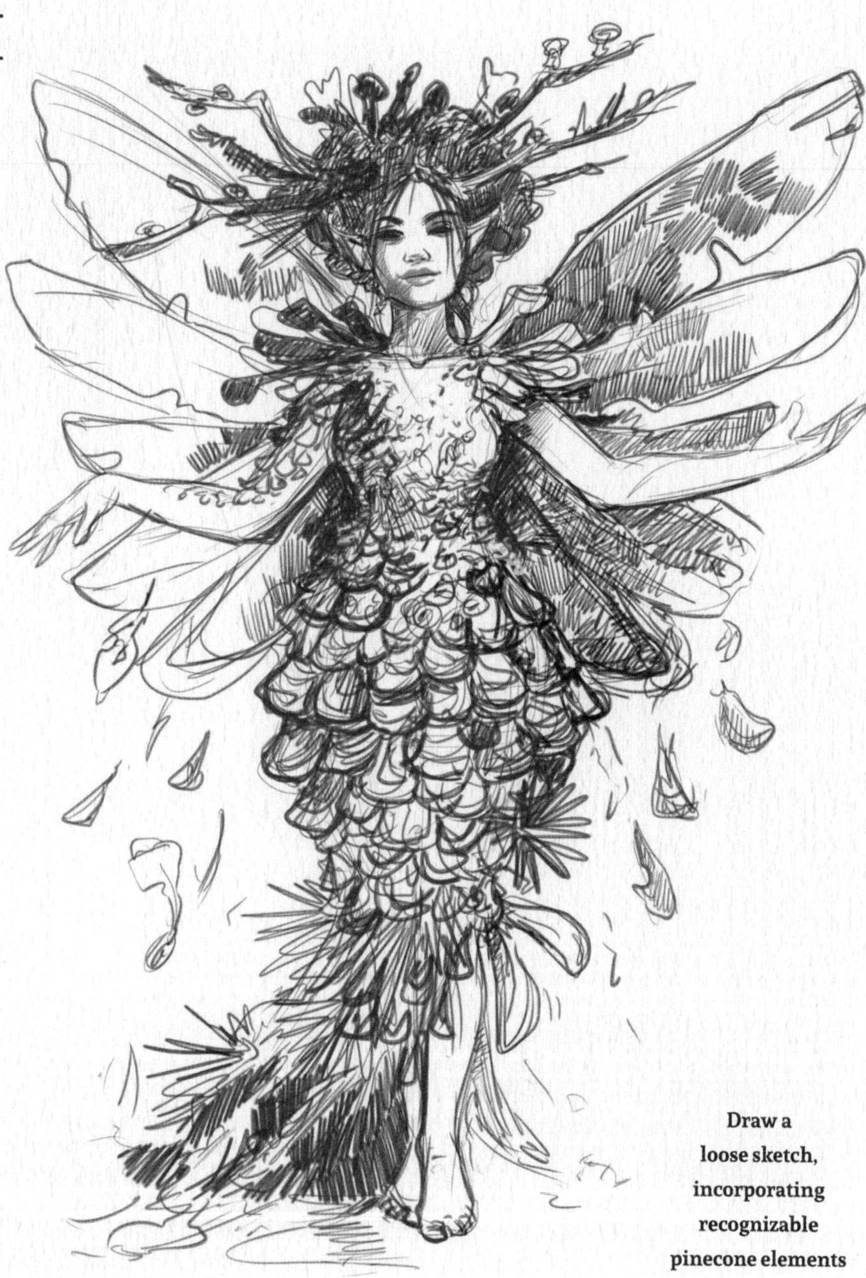

Draw a loose sketch, incorporating recognizable pinecone elements

LAYER UP

One of the great benefits of working digitally is that you can always add another layer. This provides a lot of freedom when it comes to developing both the drawing and painting, as you don't have to worry about making mistakes. Learn from your previous lines and simply draw on top, refining your drawing as you go. You will find you can explore some interesting line qualities this way.

REFINING THE ROUGH SKETCH

Once you're happy with your rough sketch, create a new layer on top. Drawing on this new layer, begin to refine the sketch and pull out some of the pinecone details. You may decide to mix up the type of pinecone scales the design includes, so it's not just larch pinecones (which have softer scales) but also a combination of harder-edged scales, as found on a conifer cone.

Depending on how this process goes, this sketch could end up as the final drawing, or it could just be another step in the process of refining the design. Enjoy yourself and don't stress over the redrawing process. Every time you redraw, it will get a little better!

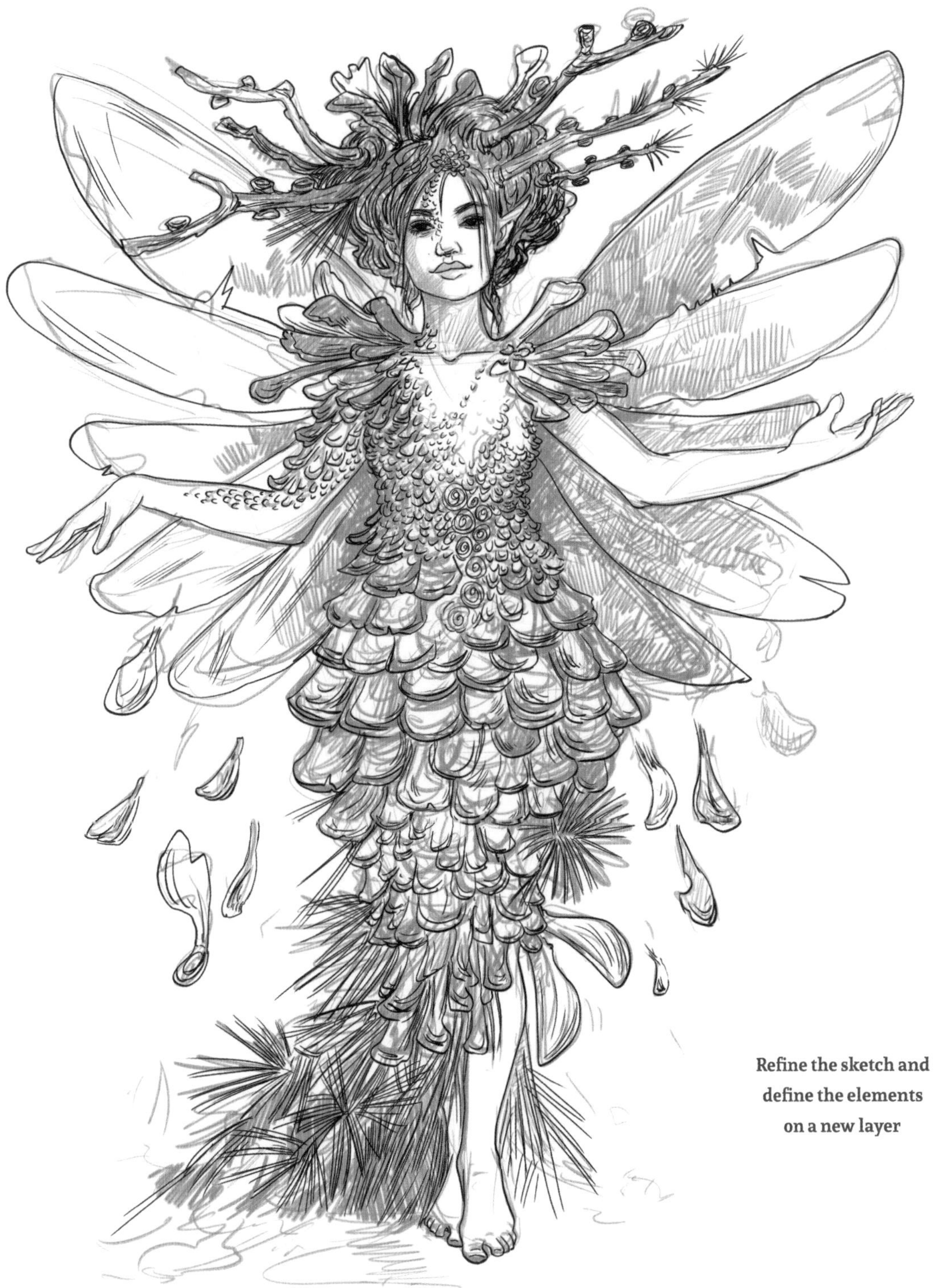

Refine the sketch and define the elements on a new layer

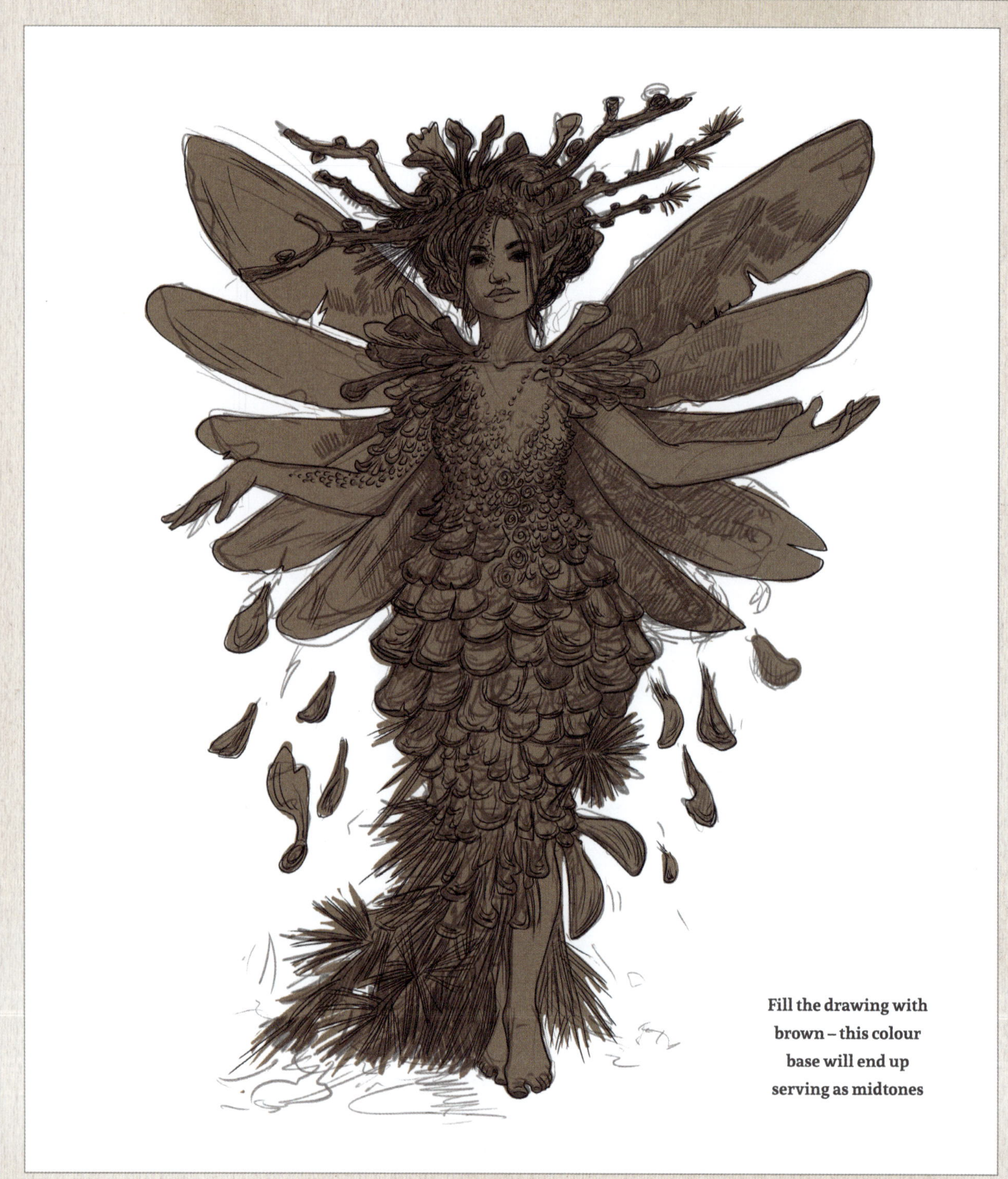

Fill the drawing with brown – this colour base will end up serving as midtones

COLOUR BASE

Once you have your final detailed sketch and a clear direction, it's time to begin with a colour base. As the character is a winter faery with pinecone elements, use brown for the base. Due to snow and frost, you might think of white as a traditional colour for winter, but it's the plant that's the essential part here. As pinecones are withered in winter, a simple, woody brown is the key colour. Create a new layer underneath the sketch and set the sketch layers to Multiply, which will make them transparent, so the lines will blend with the colours. For the initial colour, fill the whole character with the same brown tone. Colour variety will be added later in the rendering stages.

COLOUR FOUNDATION

The next step is to create a foundation for the brown winter colours. Create a new layer on top of your colour base, but still underneath the sketch layer, and set this new layer to Overlay. Next, begin to shape the character by using darker and lighter tones of grey and brown to darken and lighten areas. There's a lot of give and take in this process, and you might find that some of the initial lights and darks may change as you progress. Don't worry too much about what the final image needs to look like just yet; this is an exploration process. See what shapes and effects you can create as you experiment with lights and darks on your base colour; different shades and shadings will suggest different moods.

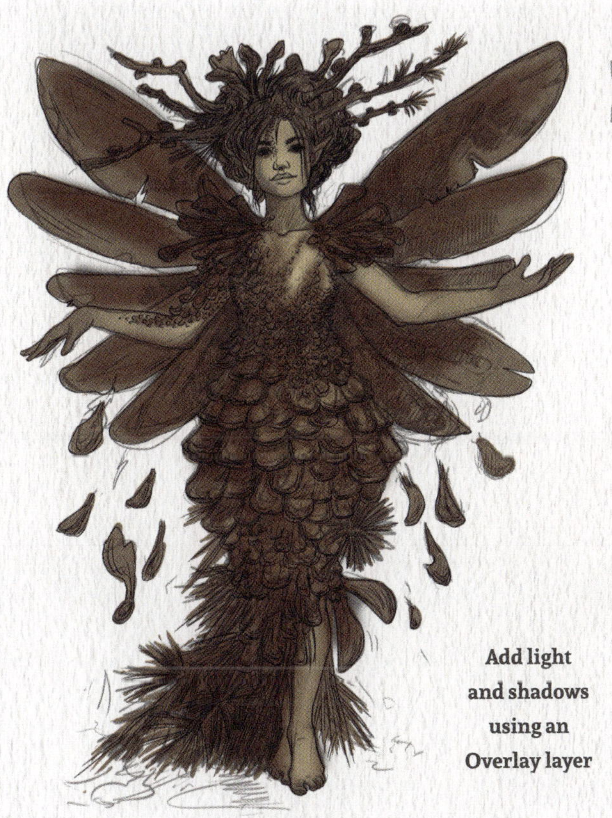

Add light and shadows using an Overlay layer

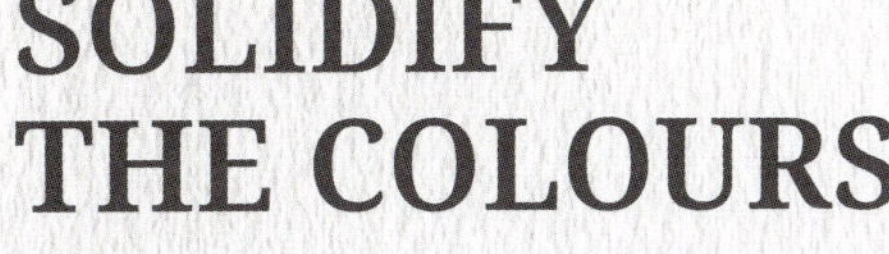

SOLIDIFY THE COLOURS

The next step is to solidify the colours. As pinecones are the inspiration and she's a winter faery, lean heavily into the earthy brown tones. The wings should differ slightly from the colours of the body to ensure they stand out, so paint them with a warmer tone, then use a darker tone for the main part of her body. At this stage she looks very withered, which is perfect for winter and pinecones. However, as she's a living creature, it would help to give her a little more life and vivacity going forward, which can be done through the use of colour.

Solidify your chosen colours – as she's a winter faery, introduce woody brown shades

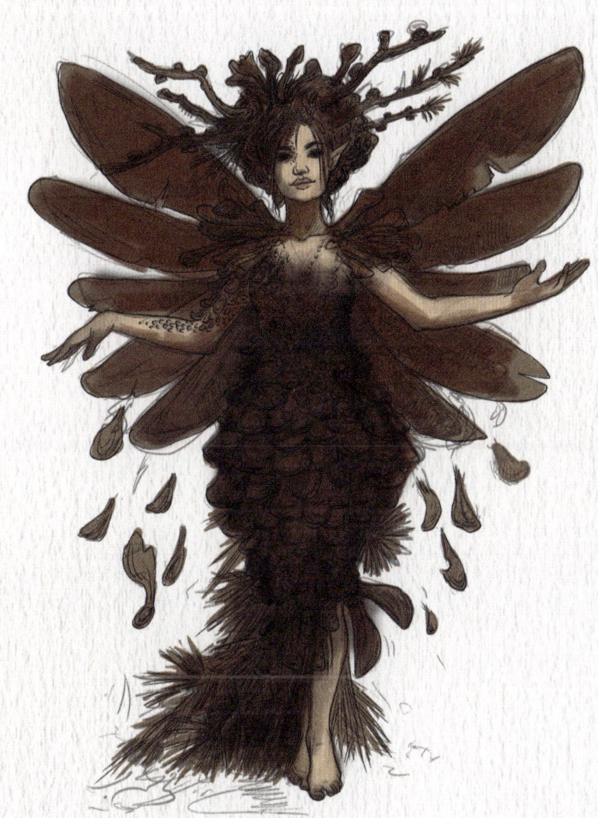

HAIR & PERSONALITY

Hair is a lot of fun, because it can be and do anything. When drawing hair for your character, try to think of sculptural ways you can explore its shape to highlight aspects of the character's personality. Since this character is a faery, consider adding various sticks and pinecone elements to her hairstyle to convey her wild, untameable nature. This will make it much more interesting than just plain hair.

FACE

It can be tempting to jump into working on the character's face right away, but it's worth waiting until some of the other elements are in place first. Once you paint in a face you like, it can help you to connect with the character and can hold your interest in the image throughout the painting process. The face will always be what viewers look at and connect with first, so it's important to get it right. This doesn't mean that every faery character has to be cute. Whatever mood, feeling, or personality you want your character to convey should be shown through the face and the expression they wear.

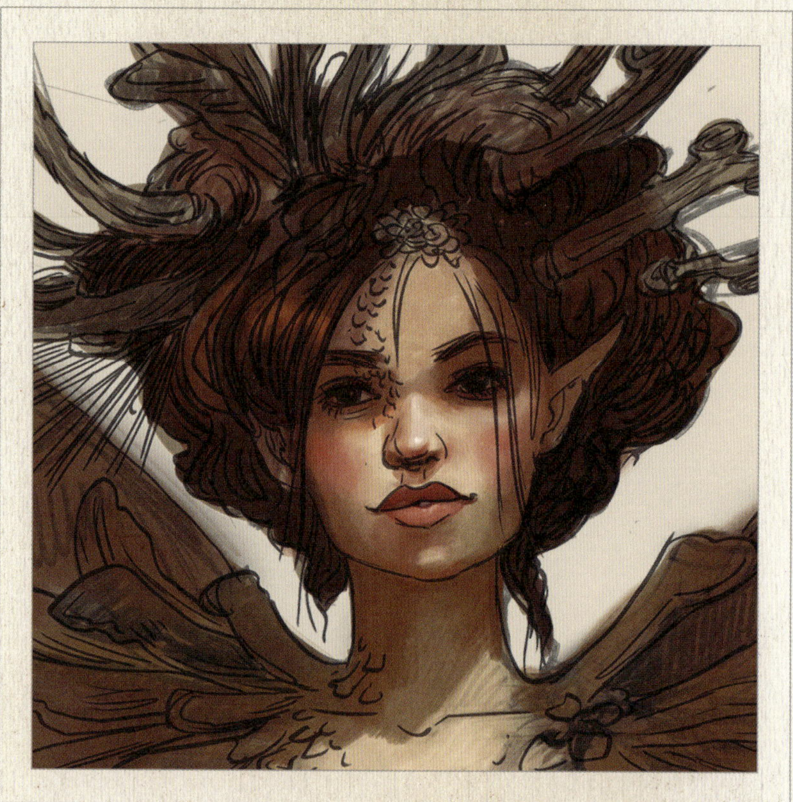

Add the details of the faery's face to convey her personality

RENDERING THE BODY

The next step is to start rendering and detailing the various parts of the body, including the pinecone elements. Take a moment to look back at your initial studies, as well as explore some photo references to get a good feel for the shapes, forms, and textures of pinecones. At this stage in the process, the character will really start to take shape. Work with the lights and darks to achieve the base form on the individual elements. Focus on the scales, but make sure you don't lose her overall shape to each individual pinecone scale. The design must still form a whole.

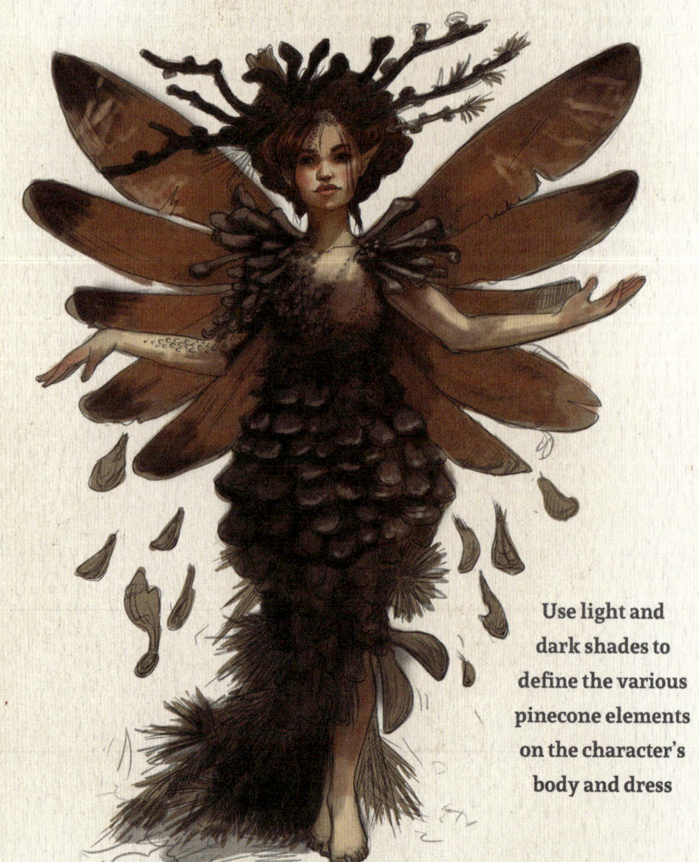

Use light and dark shades to define the various pinecone elements on the character's body and dress

LINE ART

Now you're well into the rendering stage, it's time to decide how important you want the line art to be. To see what the character looks like without the line art, simply toggle off the drawing layer. One approach would be to proceed with detailing the character without it. You can see how the lights and darks on the pinecone scales read fairly well without the line, and you could continue in this direction if you wanted a painterly final image. However, you've put a lot of time into the drawing and many of her characteristics could appear less interesting without the line.

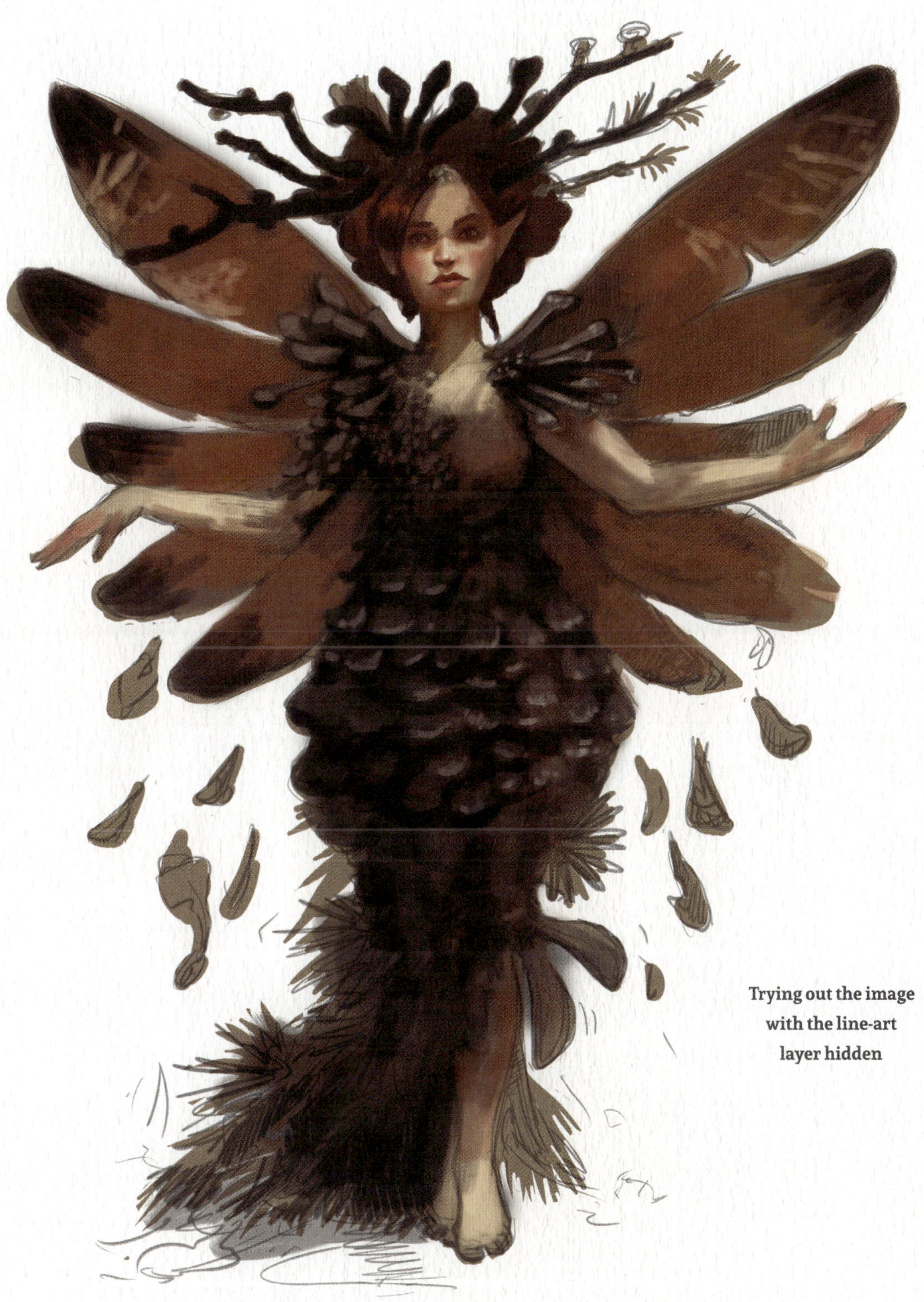

Trying out the image with the line-art layer hidden

COLOURING THE LINE ART

For this piece, we're going to keep the line-art layer included, but the darkness of it is currently overwhelming the colour palette. To fix this, select your sketch layer and use your digital painting software's hue or colour adjustment options to give the drawing a warmer grey tone. The character now feels warmer and still retains those nice details from the drawing – the best of both worlds. Next, look at the overall image and consider if there is anything you want to introduce or lose. The falling pinecone seeds, for example, may look a little messy at this stage, but in winter, seeds do get scattered by the wind or as animals pick, eat, and collect them. The falling seeds will be rendered in the next step.

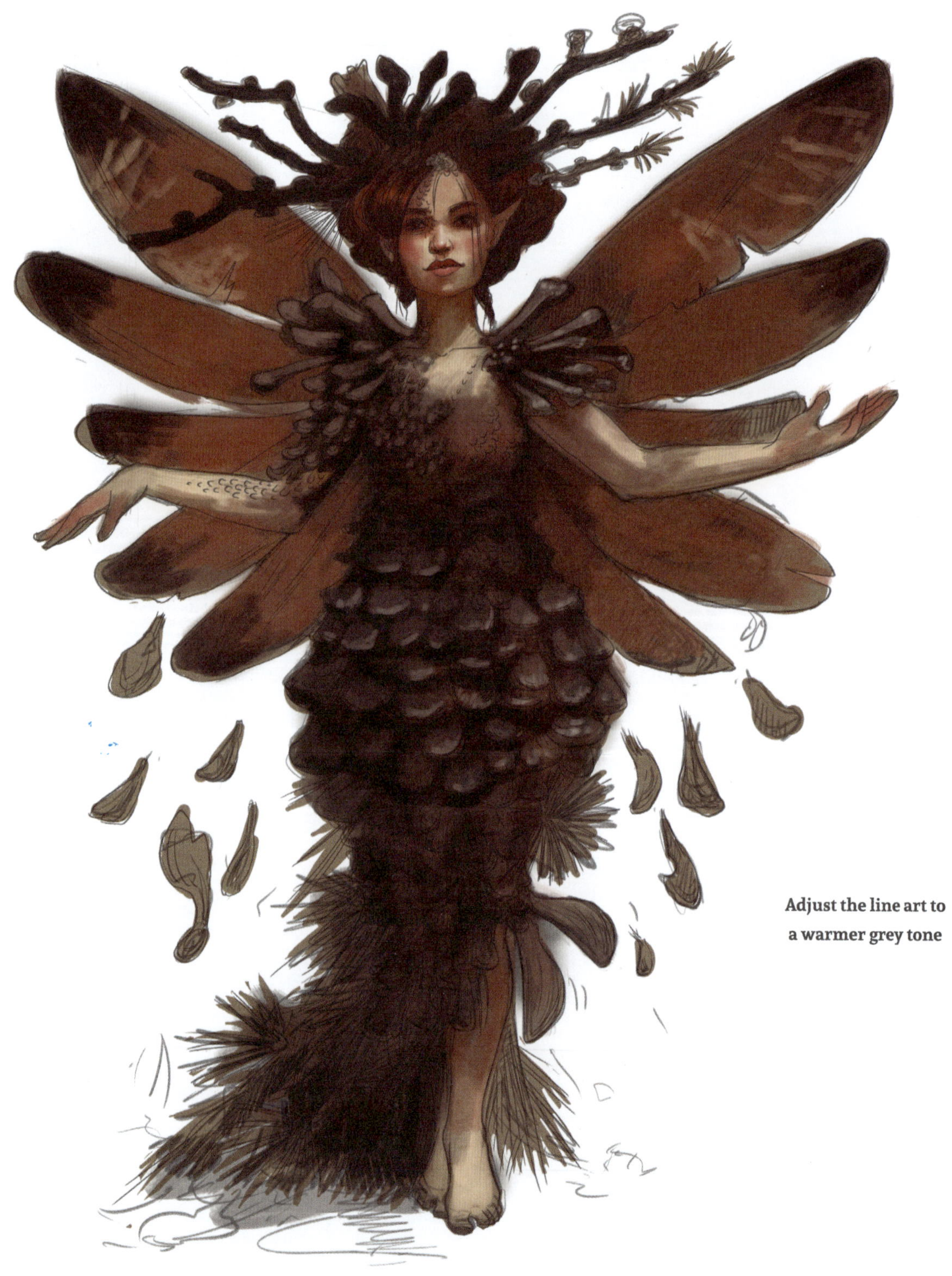

Adjust the line art to a warmer grey tone

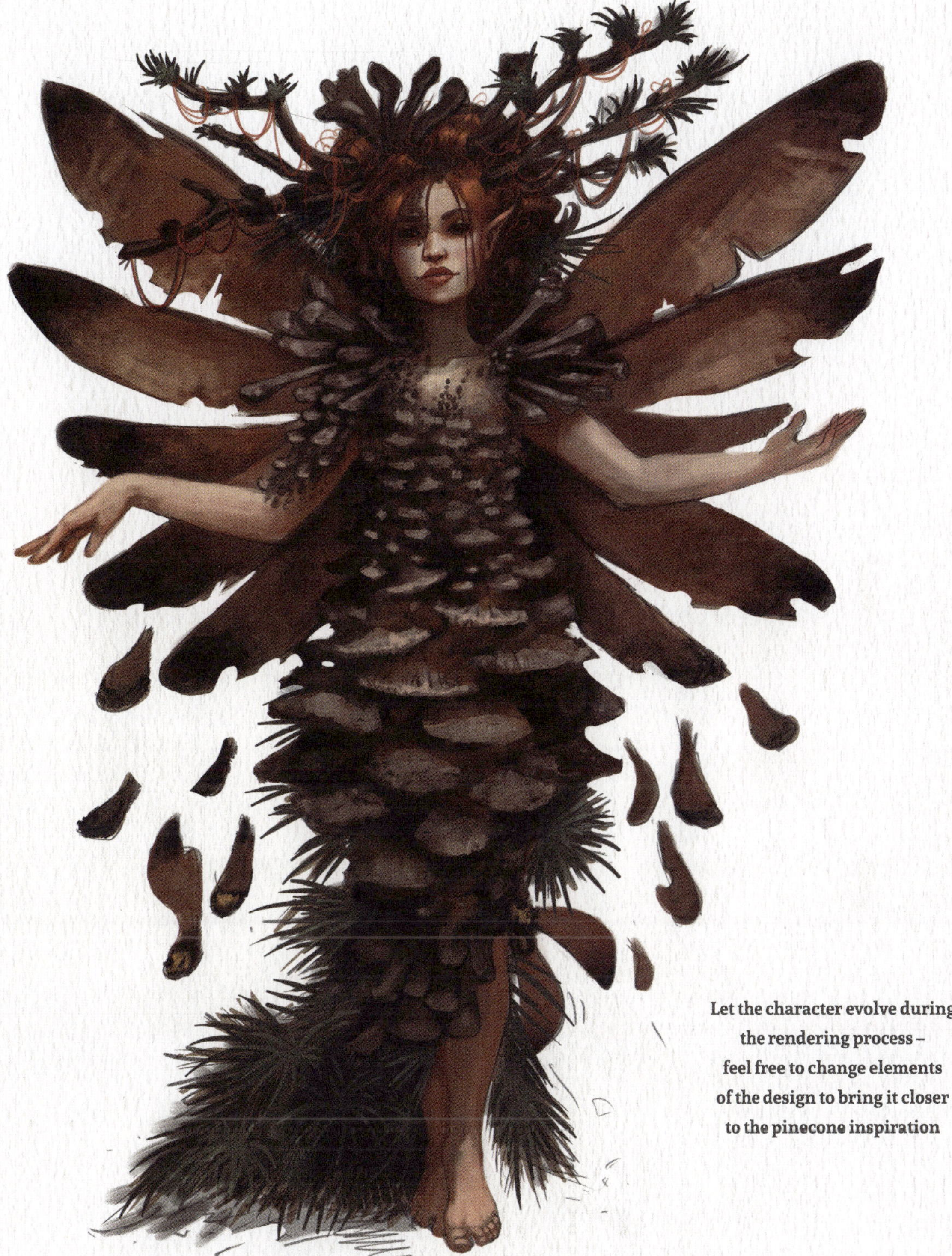

Let the character evolve during the rendering process – feel free to change elements of the design to bring it closer to the pinecone inspiration

RENDERING

This step is the most time-intensive part of the process. Start by merging your layers so it's all one layer, then begin rendering the character. As you render, you will be required to make a lot of design choices. Don't feel like you have to let your initial drawing dictate your rendering progress too much. Work organically and let the character grow and change as you render it out. Opt for bigger pinecone scales if you feel it's getting too busy with the smaller scales. Change parts of the wings to make clear they're made of pinecone seeds and not the classical dragonfly wing. Next, add more detail to her face and make her hair bigger. The hand on the right is too large, so make this smaller, then pull in some green tones to balance all of the browns. Green will suggest the colour of pines and evergreens, once again highlighting the winter theme.

FINAL DETAILS

Finalize the design by tightening up details and making any small adjustments needed. It can help to keep a mental checklist. Are the hands properly rendered? Is the face fully detailed? Did you incorporate enough pinecone elements? Is it easy to see what plant was the inspiration? Does she feel like a creature of winter? Is the rendering consistent across all parts of the character?

Paint in more woody scales on her arms and body, add some interest to the hair, and detail the face a little more. Let the piece rest for about a day, before returning to take a fresh look. There will usually be a few small things you notice that need adjusting after some time away. Once you're finished tweaking, your elegant pinecone faery is finished.

There will no doubt be numerous other directions in which you could have taken the design, as pinecones come in many different shapes and varieties. That's the fun thing about combining plants with human anatomy – there's always more to explore!

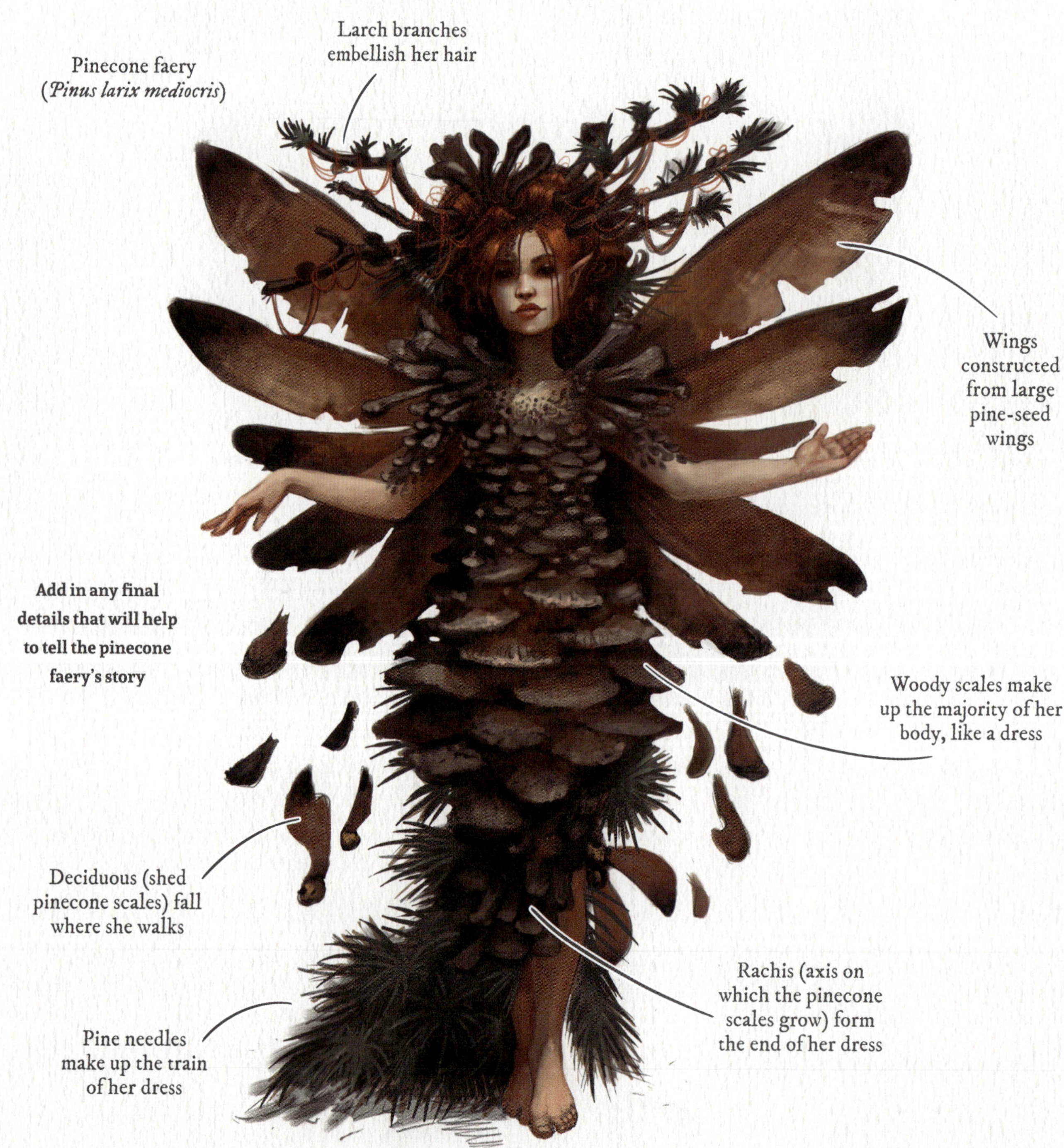

Add in any final details that will help to tell the pinecone faery's story

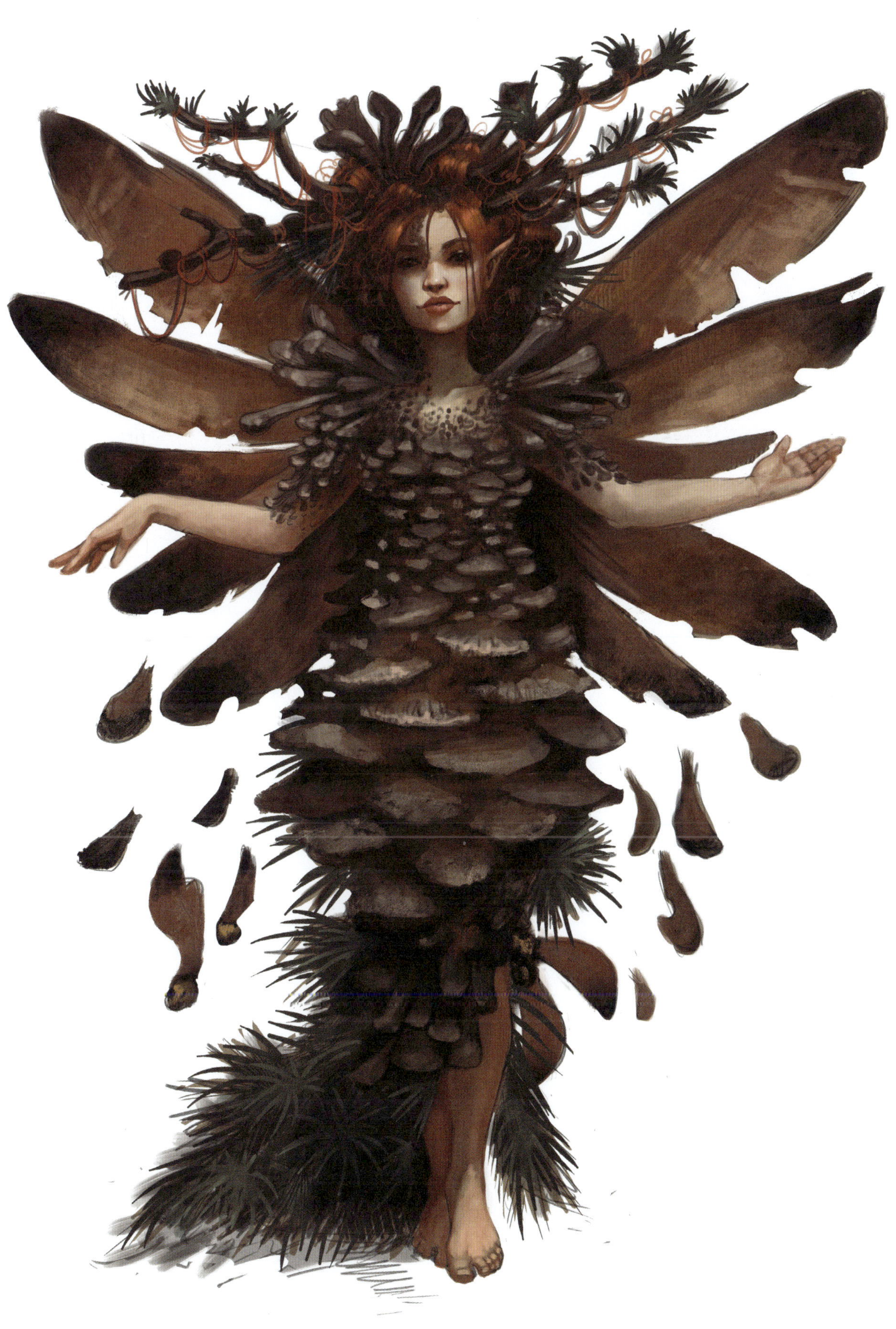

PINECONE FAERY

Final image © Kiri Leonard

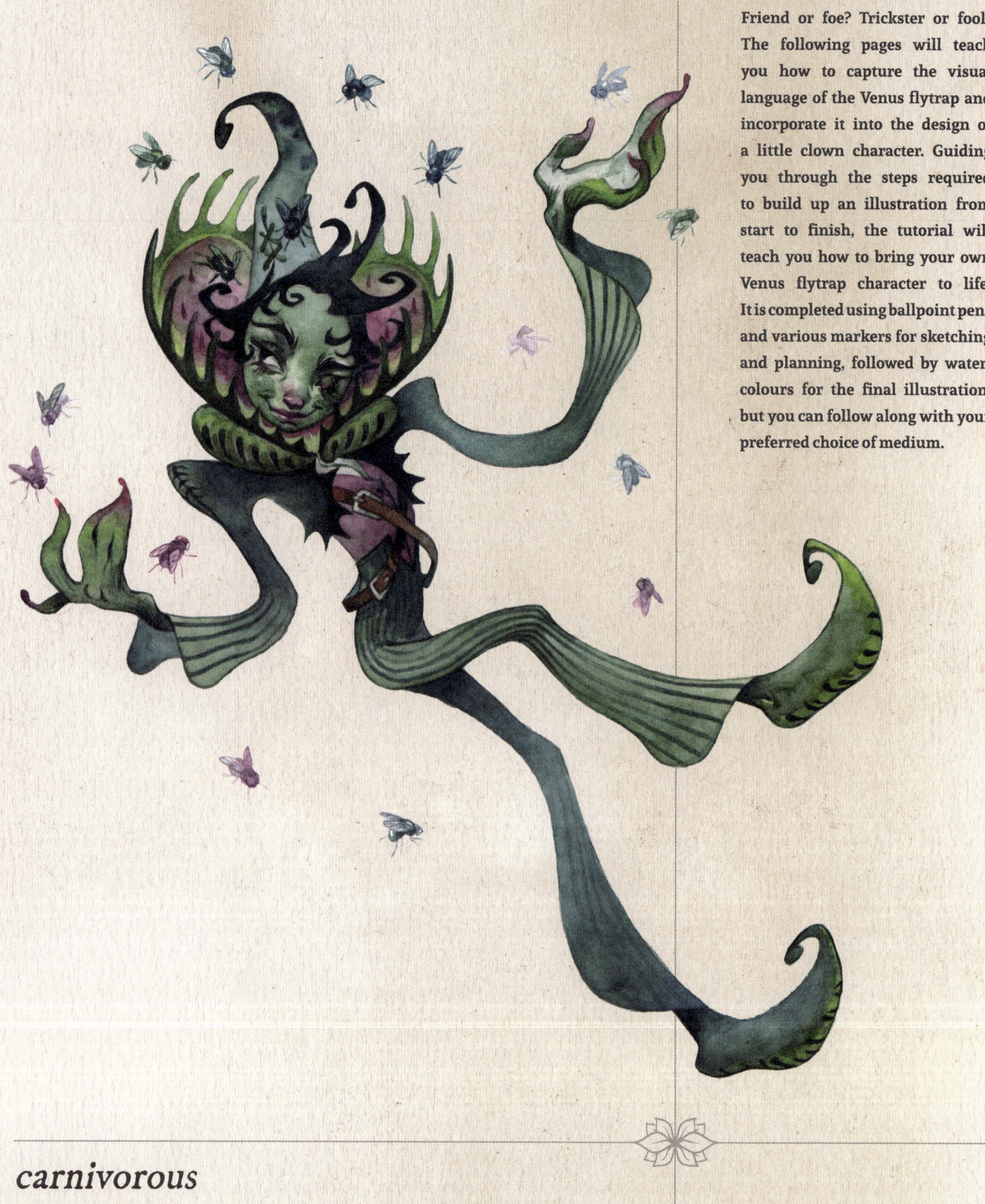

Friend or foe? Trickster or fool? The following pages will teach you how to capture the visual language of the Venus flytrap and incorporate it into the design of a little clown character. Guiding you through the steps required to build up an illustration from start to finish, the tutorial will teach you how to bring your own Venus flytrap character to life. It is completed using ballpoint pens and various markers for sketching and planning, followed by watercolours for the final illustration, but you can follow along with your preferred choice of medium.

carnivorous

VENUS FLYTRAP CLOWN

CHRIS HONG

START WITH RESEARCH

Begin by studying the Venus flytrap plant to find out what elements you might like to borrow for your character design. Gather reference images; look up photos from different angles and from various stages of its life cycle. Alongside the visuals, reading up on the etymology of the plant will provide inspiration for different design directions. The Venus flytrap is uniquely carnivorous, with its most iconic feature being its trapping mechanism. It can seem perfectly innocent as it waits patiently for an unassuming prey to land on its leaves and set off the trigger to be devoured. This trickery concept plays well with the clown or jester archetype, which provides a direction to follow for a character design. It can be helpful to assign an archetype like this early on to set some parameters and narrow the design process down to prevent it from becoming too nebulous and overwhelming.

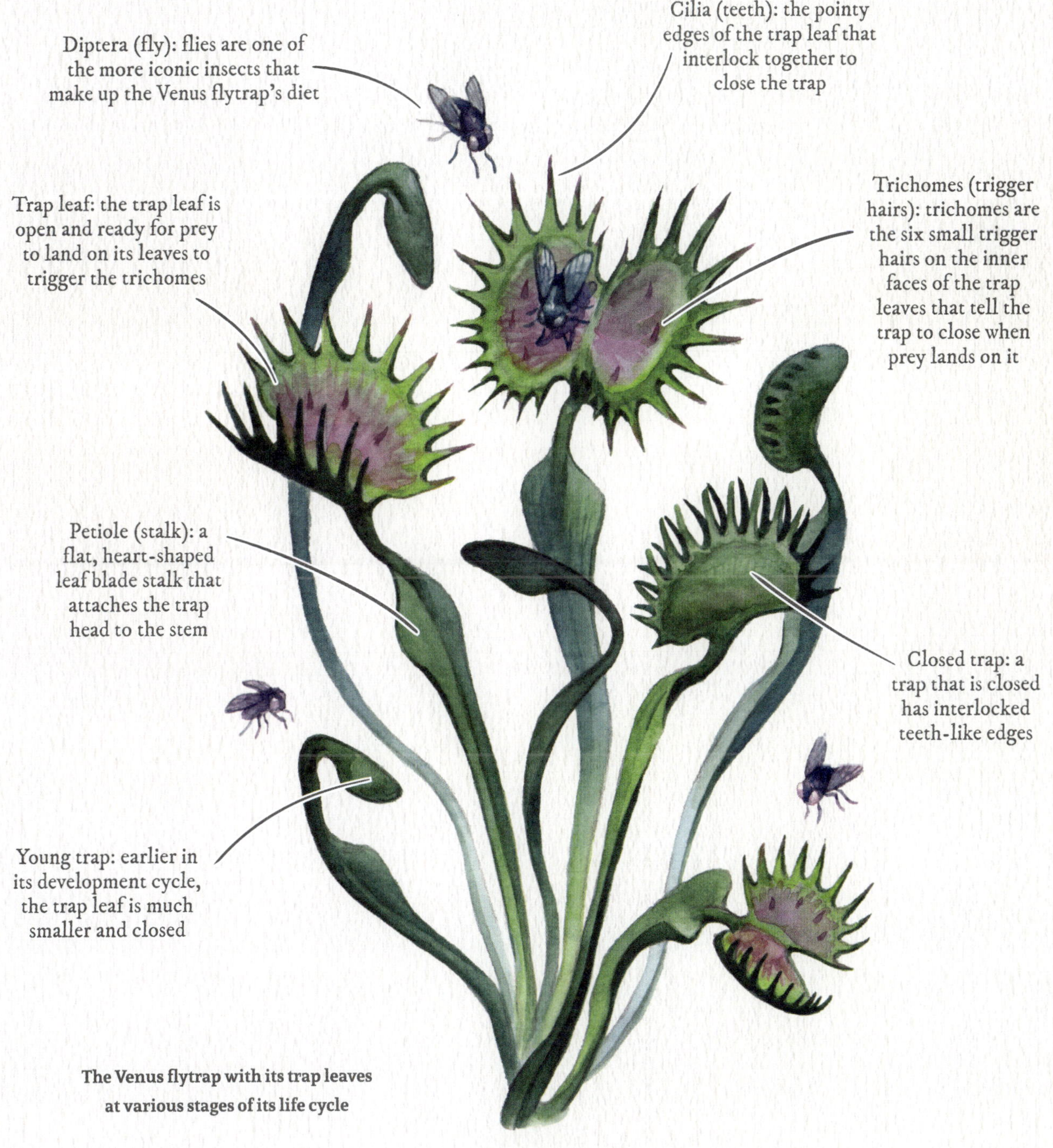

The Venus flytrap with its trap leaves at various stages of its life cycle

VISUAL LANGUAGE

Examine your reference images and intentionally copy what you see, making careful observations as you go. Visual language can be broken down into these key principles:

- Shape: what are the major shapes?
- Line: are the lines sharp with lots of joints? Or are they smooth and undisrupted?
- Proportion: how does one part of the image relate to another, and the whole?

As you study, make a note of these observations, such as the kidney bean-like shape of the head that feels so iconic and defining of the plant. Notice the certain curvature of the lines, like the S-shaped section that attaches the trap head to the petiole. Make a note of the general proportion and silhouette. Is it long and lean, or short and stubby? These are all traits that make up the Venus flytrap's visual language and can be incorporated into the character to embody the essence of the plant.

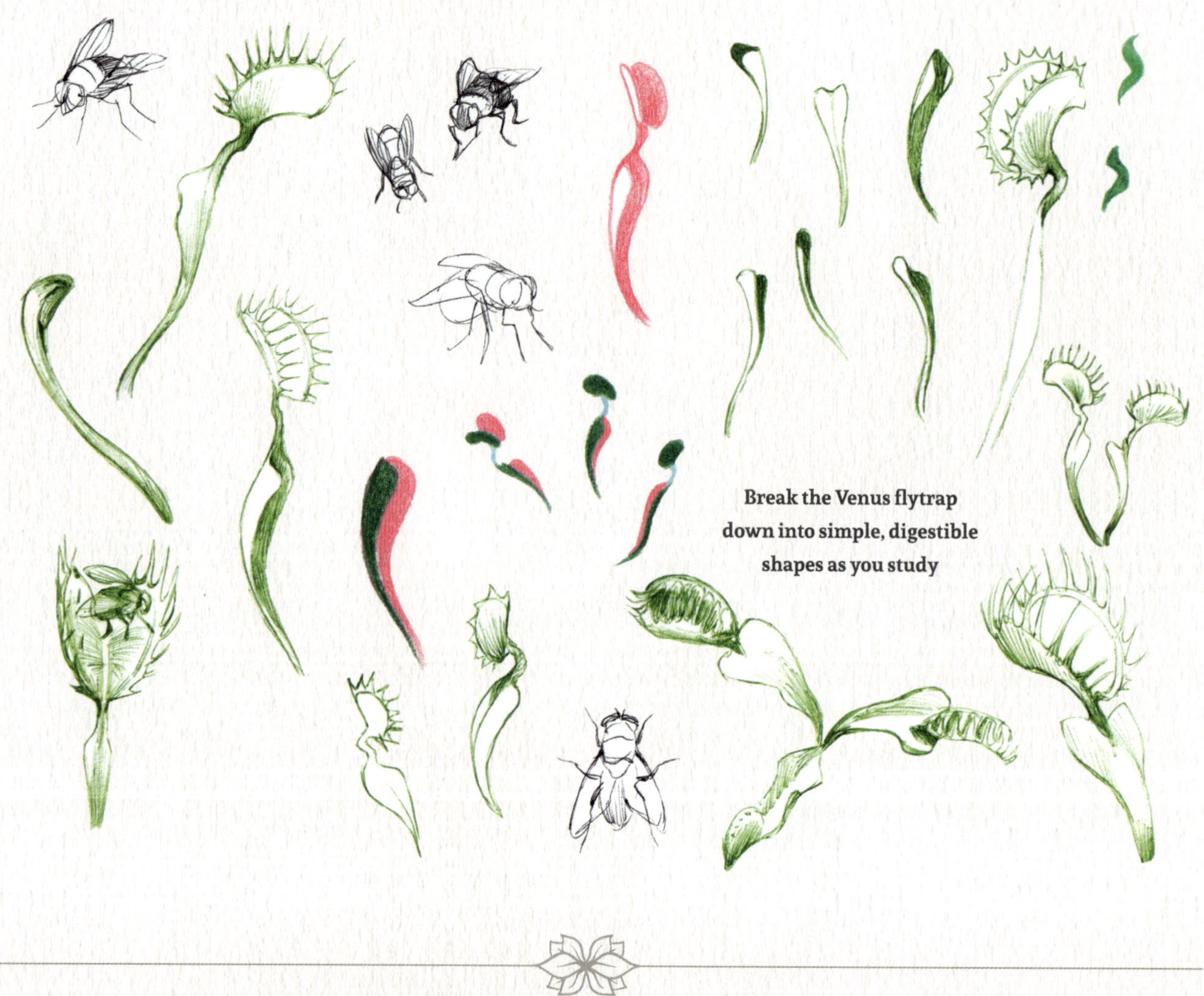

Break the Venus flytrap down into simple, digestible shapes as you study

EXPLORING THE TRAP CONCEPT

The trap head of the Venus flytrap is its main defining feature, so it should be the centrepiece of the character design. As this character will be a clown, try incorporating the trap into a clown-like collar or jester hat. Explore drawing the trap so it appears more open-faced, with the teeth pointing upward and framing the head. Or try sketching the trap leaf more closed over the head, with the character's face peeking through the teeth. Experiment with the shape of the teeth – are they long or short? Are they sharp or softer and rounded? The silhouette of the teeth should read clearly, no matter what the concept, so be mindful of this as you draw. Your goal is to create a collection of different ideas you can take further and flesh out.

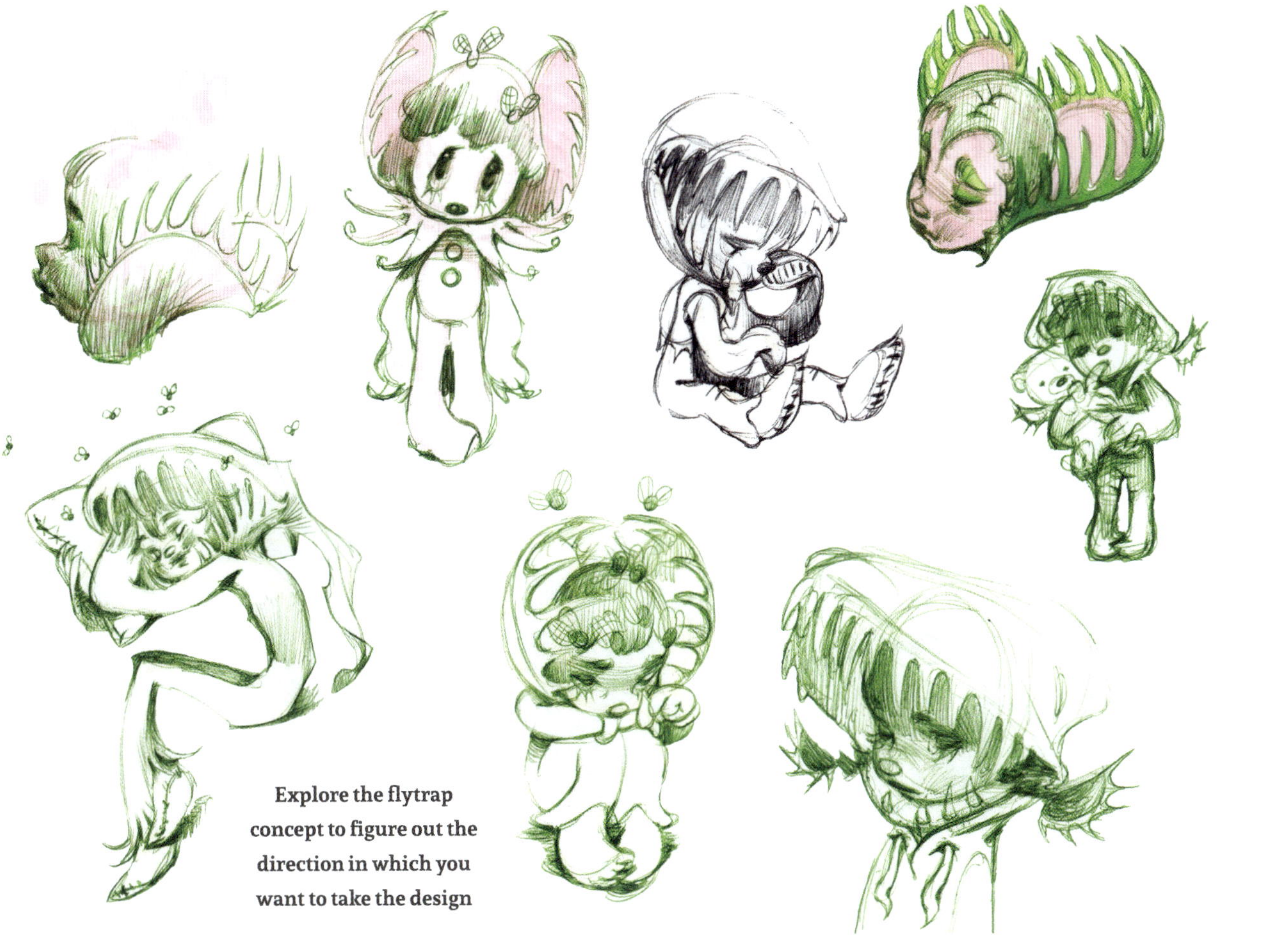

Explore the flytrap concept to figure out the direction in which you want to take the design

POSING

Once you have a concept you want to take further, draw your character in various different poses to explore their personality and develop the design. You might tend to think of the Venus flytrap as a villainous character due to its carnivorous nature and spiky teeth, so sketch the clown in poses that play on that idea. Drawing the character interacting with props can help to inspire ideas and bring out their personality. Sketch him with a whip as a ringmaster at a circus, which reveals a somewhat crafty and deceitful persona. You can also use the flies as props that interact with the character, imagining them as mindless fools being lured in by the clown's trickery. Focus on silhouette and readability, being mindful of making the trap aspect of the design easy to read. Posing the character in different angles will also help solidify the design and figure out any unresolved areas.

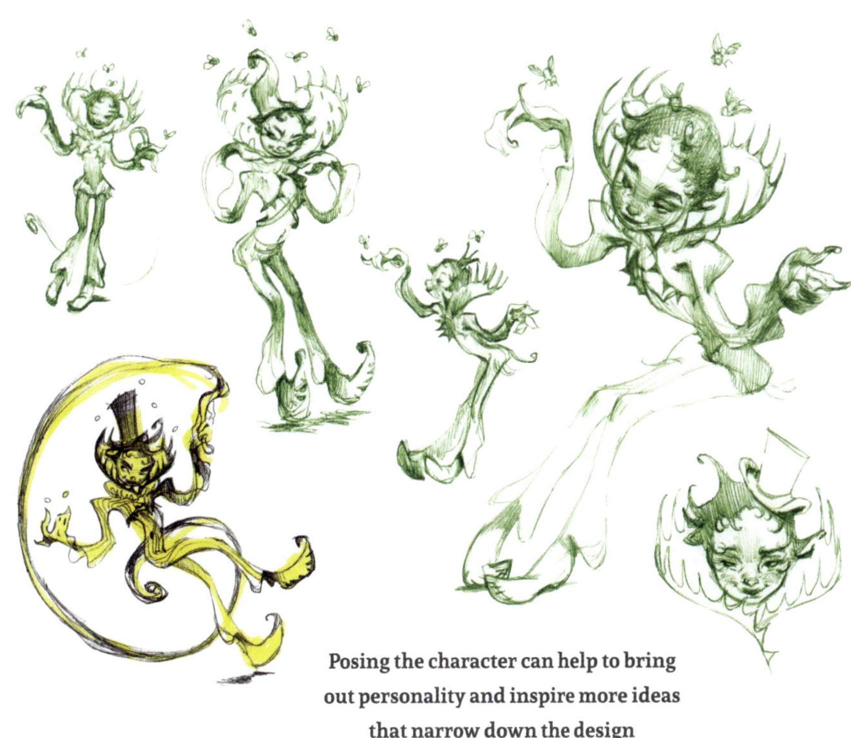

Posing the character can help to bring out personality and inspire more ideas that narrow down the design

TAKE YOUR TIME EXPLORING

Don't rush the exploration stage – wait for that 'aha!' feeling! It can take a lot of drawings and what might seem like bad ideas before you land on a direction you're happy with – one that also feels in line with your design sensibilities. If the ringmaster idea doesn't feel right, try some other circus options.

CHARACTER ANALYSIS

Moving away from the ringmaster design, this is the chosen clown concept sketch that will be developed into a final illustration. The following steps will take a closer look at how to break down the design into simple shapes to better understand how to draw it, as well as to see how the elements of the design have incorporated some of the visual language of the Venus flytrap. Every part of the design should be in support of the clown aesthetic and persona, as well as exuding the essence of the chosen plant.

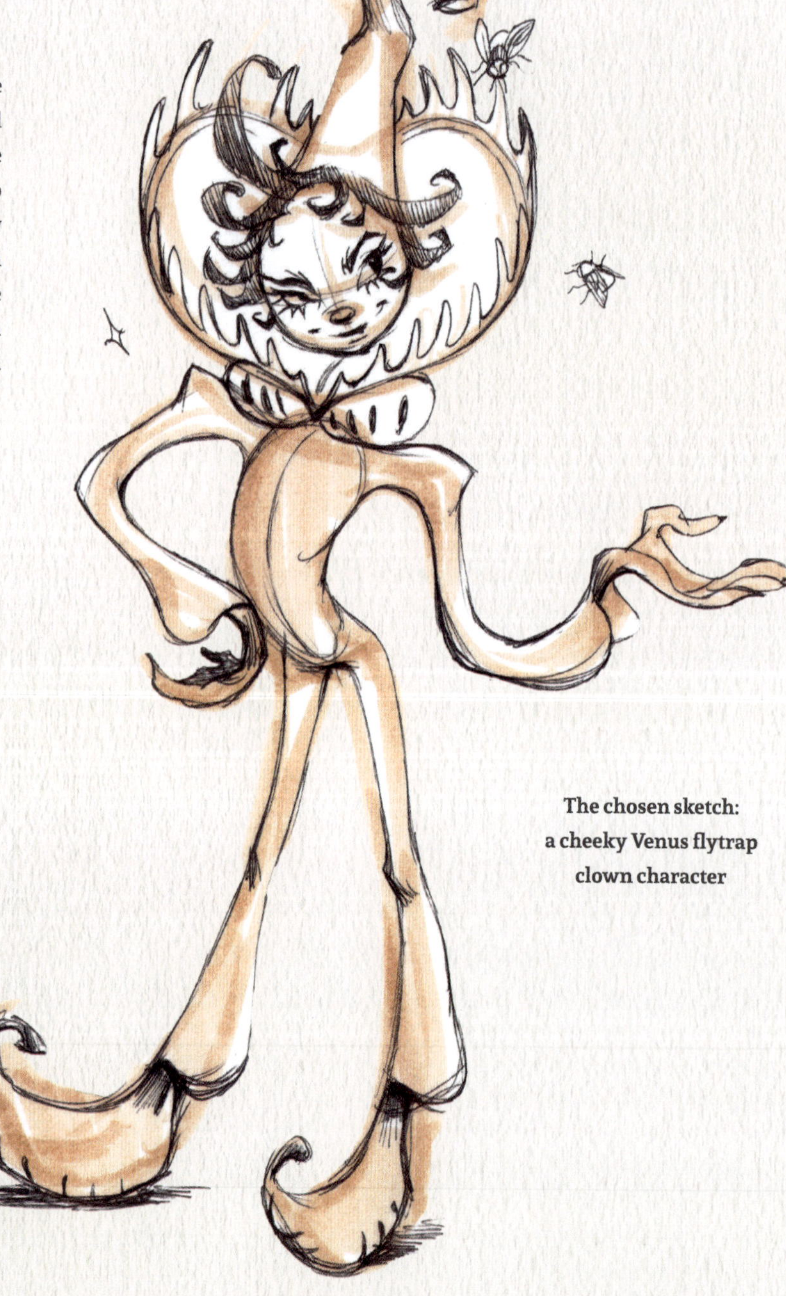

The chosen sketch: a cheeky Venus flytrap clown character

HEAD & TORSO

Start by drawing a circle to represent the head, then draw a heart shape around the circle to frame the head and represent the collar. For this crafty clown, the collar is ironically heart-shaped. Draw a long bean shape for the torso that is wider at the chest and narrower towards the hips. The silhouette of the head and collar combined with the torso should echo the silhouette of the plant – the head is the largest, then narrows at the neck, before widening at the chest, and then narrowing again down to the hips. This rhythm of thick to thin to thick shapes and flowing, curvy lines should be echoed throughout the character's design to mimic the plant.

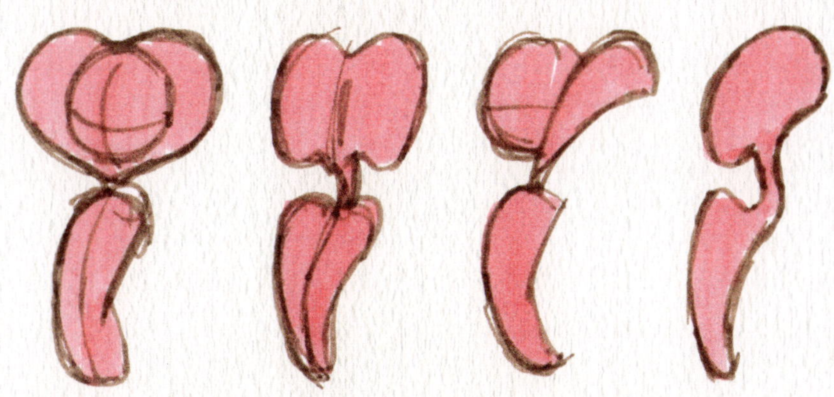

The silhouette of the head and torso should be reminiscent of the Venus flytrap's silhouette and shape language

SHOULDERS

The shoulders of the character are unique in how they're attached to the torso – they are very wide-set, as if the character were wearing shoulder pads. The shoulders come to a sharp point on the outer edges to contrast against the smooth, curved lines used in the design. To build the shoulders, draw a straight line at the top of the torso, extending well past where the shoulders would normally sit. Then draw a dip in the middle, following the natural shape of the collarbone, but exaggerated to be much wider. Notice the distinct upside-down U shape of the negative space of the armpits between the torso and the arms. Use that negative shape to guide you on where to place the arms and how wide to make the shoulders.

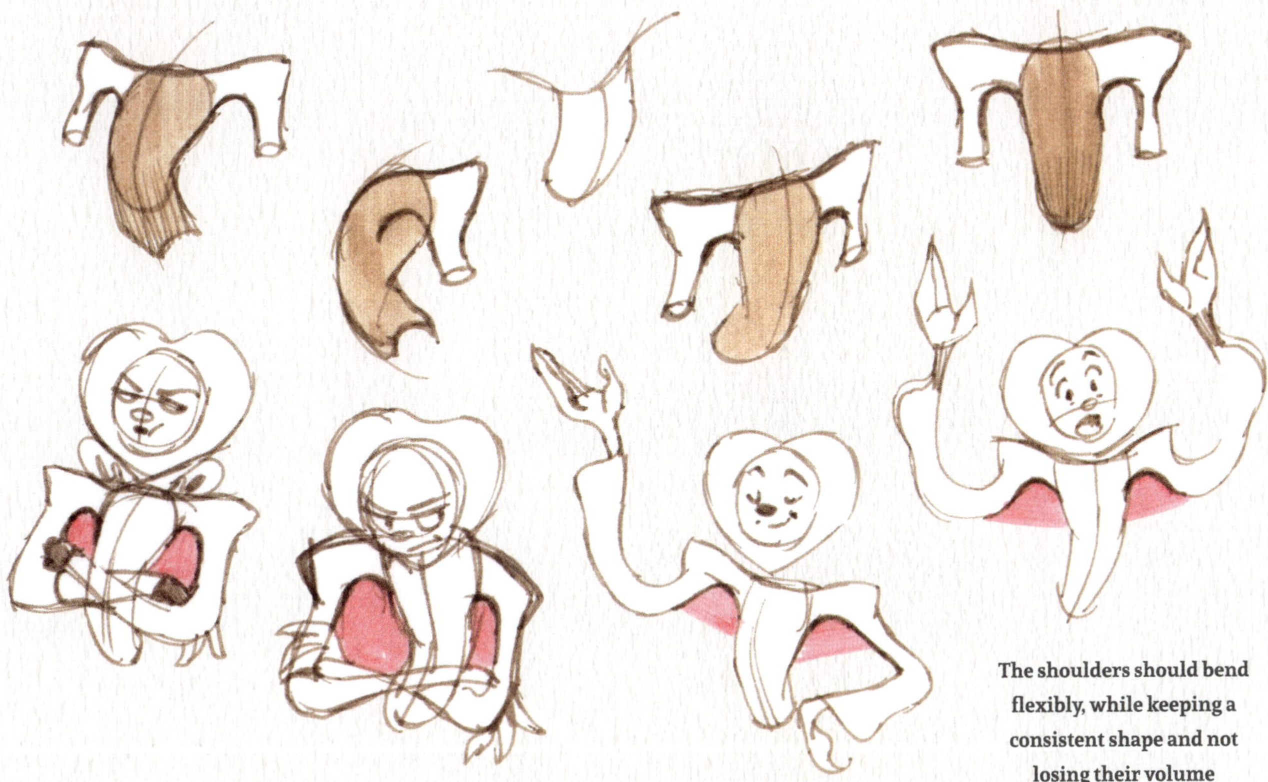

The shoulders should bend flexibly, while keeping a consistent shape and not losing their volume

ARMS

Each arm is inspired by the Venus flytrap plant. The long petiole stalk is the arm, the neck-like section at the base of the trap leaf attaching to the petiole acts as the wrist, and the trap head becomes the hand. The leaf blade of the petiole should widen towards the head to look as if the character is wearing bell-shaped sleeves. This widening also accentuates the narrow wrist and creates a more dynamic proportion with the hand. When drawing the arm, make sure there is no obvious bend or fold at the elbow as there would be on typical human arms. Instead, it should be more drawn-out and rounded to push the proportions and lengthen the arms to create an overall lanky appearance.

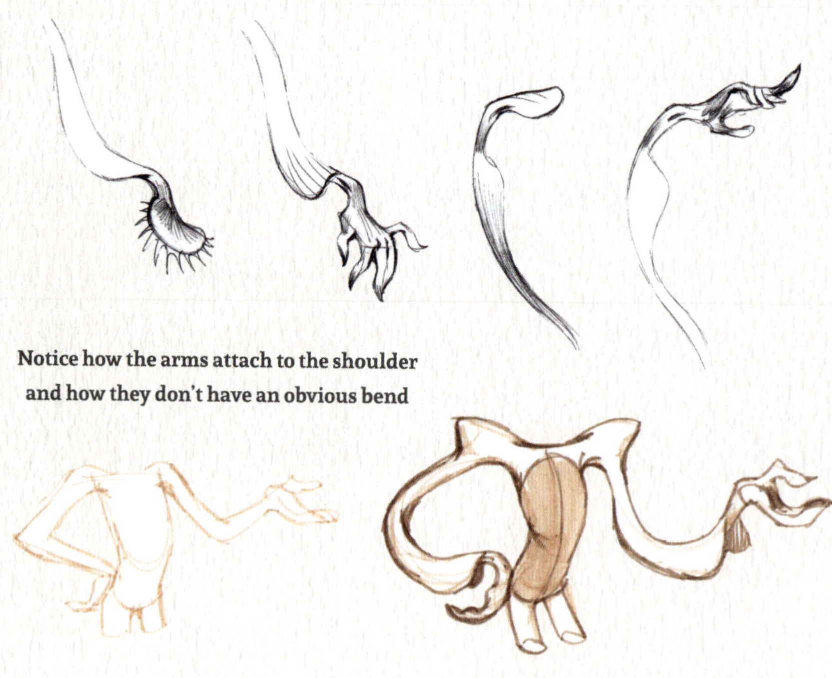

Notice how the arms attach to the shoulder and how they don't have an obvious bend

HANDS & FINGERS

As with the arms, the visual language of the plant can be imposed onto each finger to exaggerate the proportions. Start by blocking in the hand as you would with any other character design, then push the weight of each finger towards the fingertip to create a more bulbous end, as if each fingertip is the trap head of a single plant. Pushing the line of the fingers will make them look double-jointed, which adds to the fantastical quality. You can take this even further by adding the kidney bean-shaped curly detail at the end of the fingertips for extra flourish and playfulness.

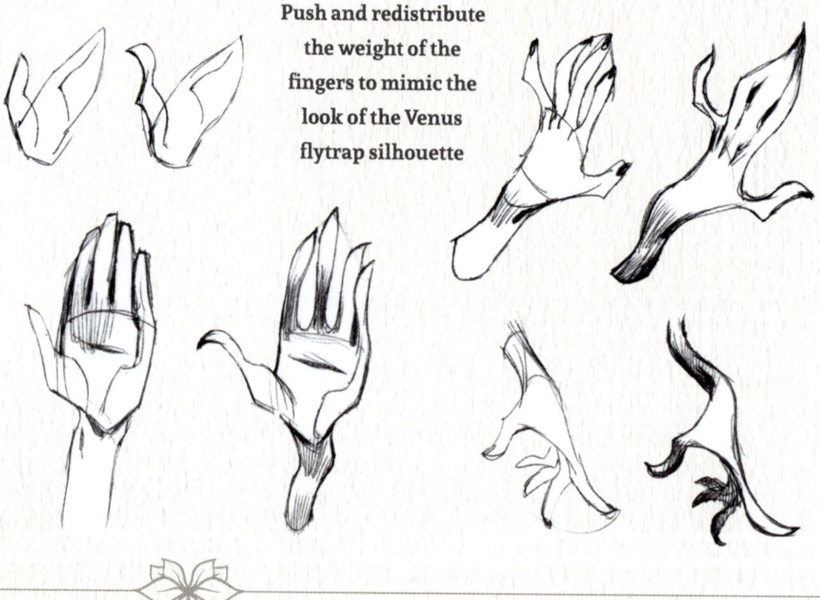

Push and redistribute the weight of the fingers to mimic the look of the Venus flytrap silhouette

FEET

Think of the foot as a closed trap, which resembles a foot in a sock due to its similar bean-like shape. Stylize the overlapping of the trap teeth. Instead of drawing the teeth individually overlapping one another, simplify the overlapping with small negative shapes that intersect the opening line of the leaf to resemble stitching down the middle seam of the sock. Since this character is a clown, exaggerate the size of the feet to cartoonishly large, adding curly tips at the toes to make it more playful and to add more plant-like details.

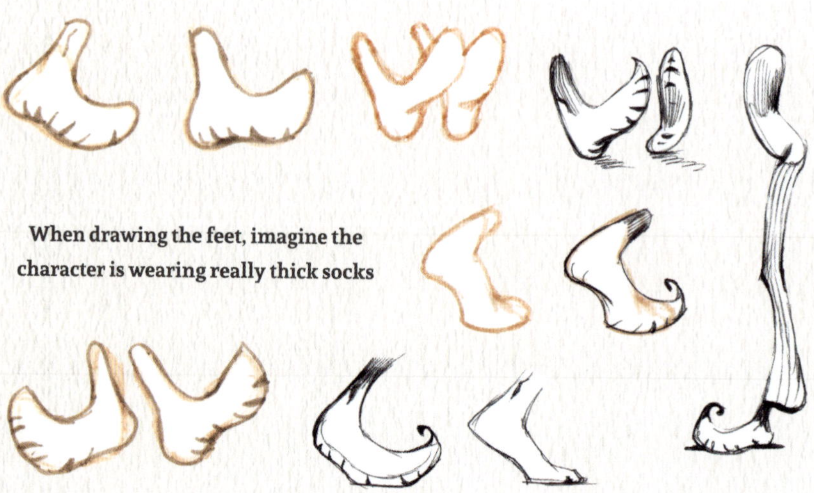

When drawing the feet, imagine the character is wearing really thick socks

FOLLOW YOUR DESIGN AESTHETIC

Staying true to your design aesthetic and intended direction or 'world' for the character will help you to make the them feel more like your own. For example, if you often draw big, clownish feet on your characters, it may feel natural to turn the closed traps into big clown feet. The stitching imagery on the feet feels doll-like and halloweeny, adding to the whimsical vibe. Drawing a secondary collar at the base of the heart-shaped trap of the character's head also adds to the quirky clown look.

LEGS

Legs can be approached in a similar way to the arms, except that the legs should have a defined knee joint to add a sense of structure. When drawing the leg, be mindful of the weight distribution; it should read like a triangle, with the bulk of the weight being on the feet at the base of the triangle. Stretch and elongate the proportions in relation to the rest of the body to make the legs look lanky, like the arms. The leg should narrow a little at the knee, then flare out dramatically towards the foot, as if the character is wearing flared trousers. This is to echo the proportions of the plant and to make the overall shapes of the leg, ankle, and foot more dynamic.

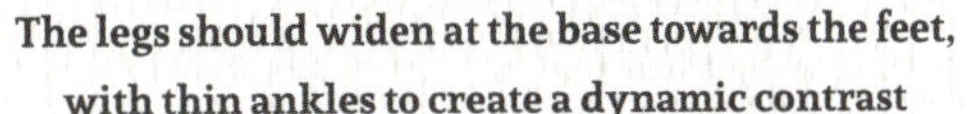

The legs should widen at the base towards the feet, with thin ankles to create a dynamic contrast

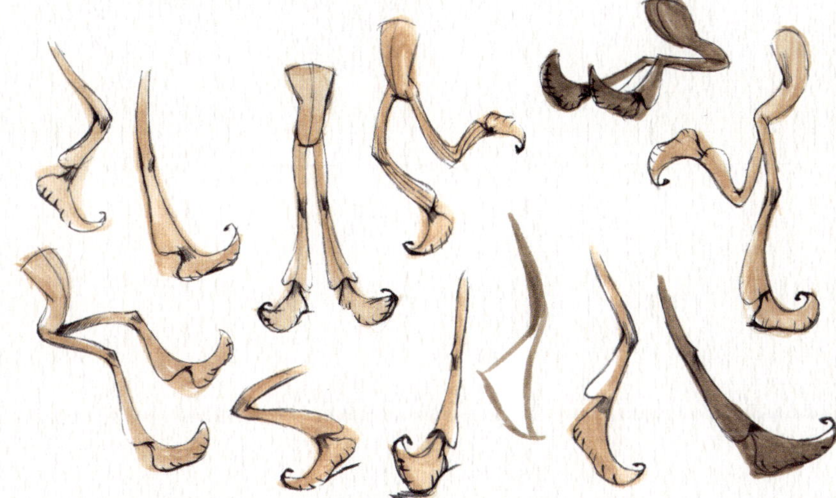

HAIR & EXPRESSIONS

The hair will be short, wild, and curly to give the clown a zany vibe. Start by drawing out three or four long C curves that branch out from the head. Next, add some bulk to each by drawing an even more exaggerated C curve to hug the first curve, almost like adding a belly. Draw smaller clumps to fill in between the main larger clumps, plus even smaller clumps to frame the face. The clumps should extend out in a curling fashion and reach haphazardly in different directions to make it look wild and unkempt. As with the fingers and feet, add a bulbous, bean-like end to each hair clump to mimic the bean-like trap heads in its earlier stage.

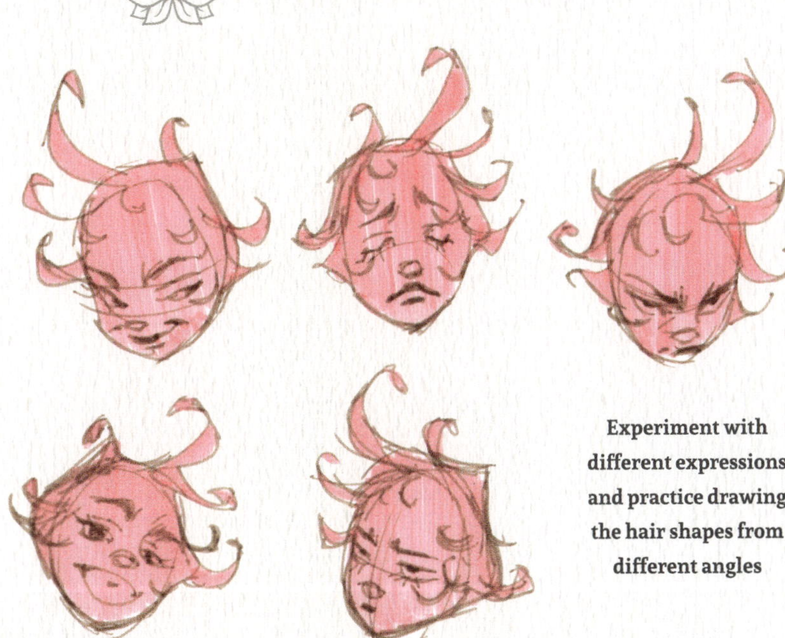

Experiment with different expressions and practice drawing the hair shapes from different angles

THE FINAL DRAWING

Now it's time to plan out the character illustration by deciding on the final pose. Start with a gesture drawing that showcases the character in the best light, then flesh it out as a larger drawing that you will use for the final illustration. This pose makes it look as if the crafty clown is luring in the flies, almost like the flies are circling around the clown as if in a trance.

By this stage you should have all of the design details figured out, so you're not designing as you're painting. Once you have a drawing you're happy with, use a graphite pencil to lightly draw it onto the watercolour paper. Going into the painting stage with a drawing you're happy with will set you up for success, so it's worth taking the time to get the drawing right.

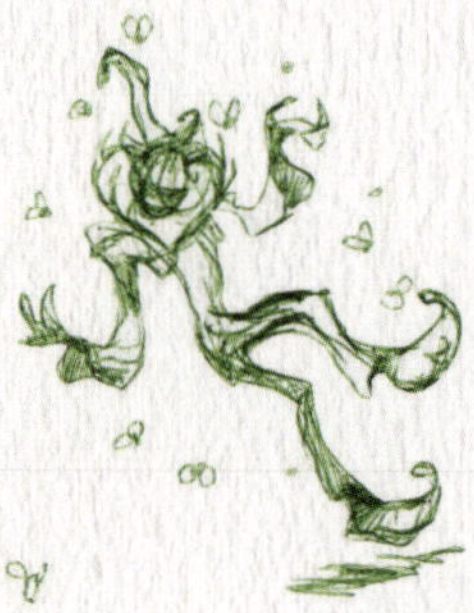

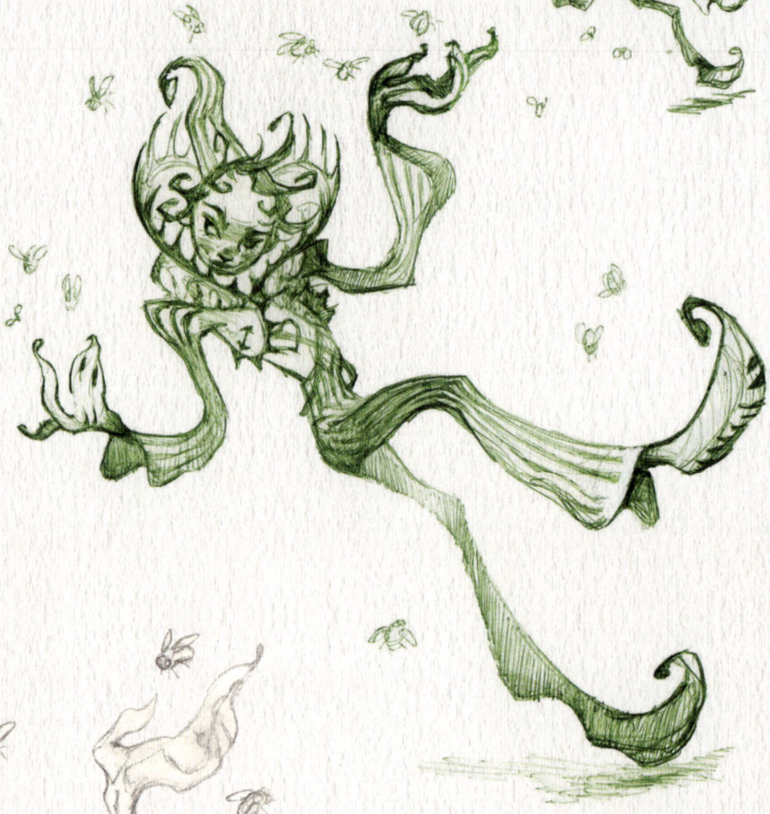

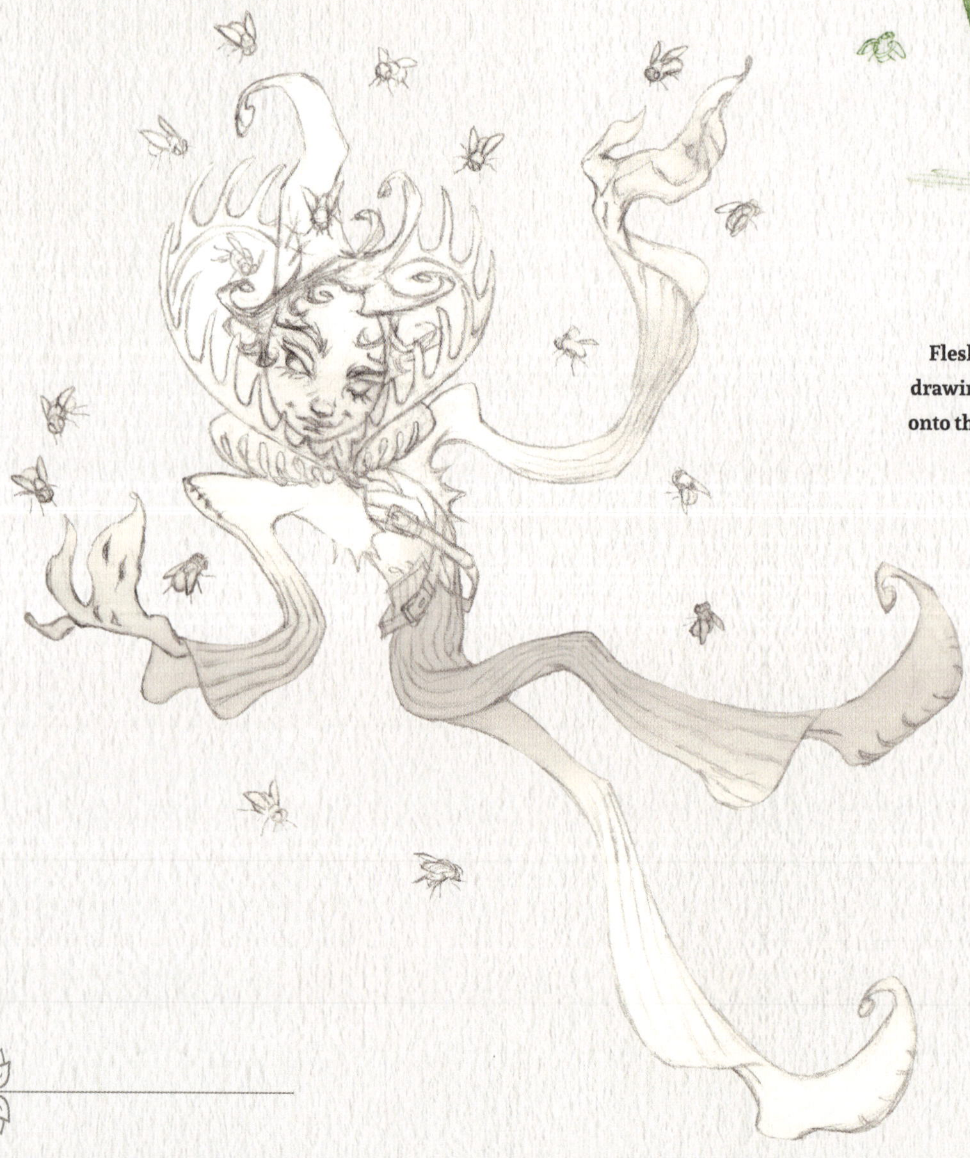

Flesh out the gesture drawing, then transfer it onto the painting surface

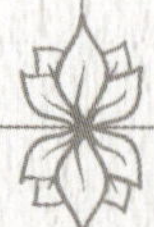

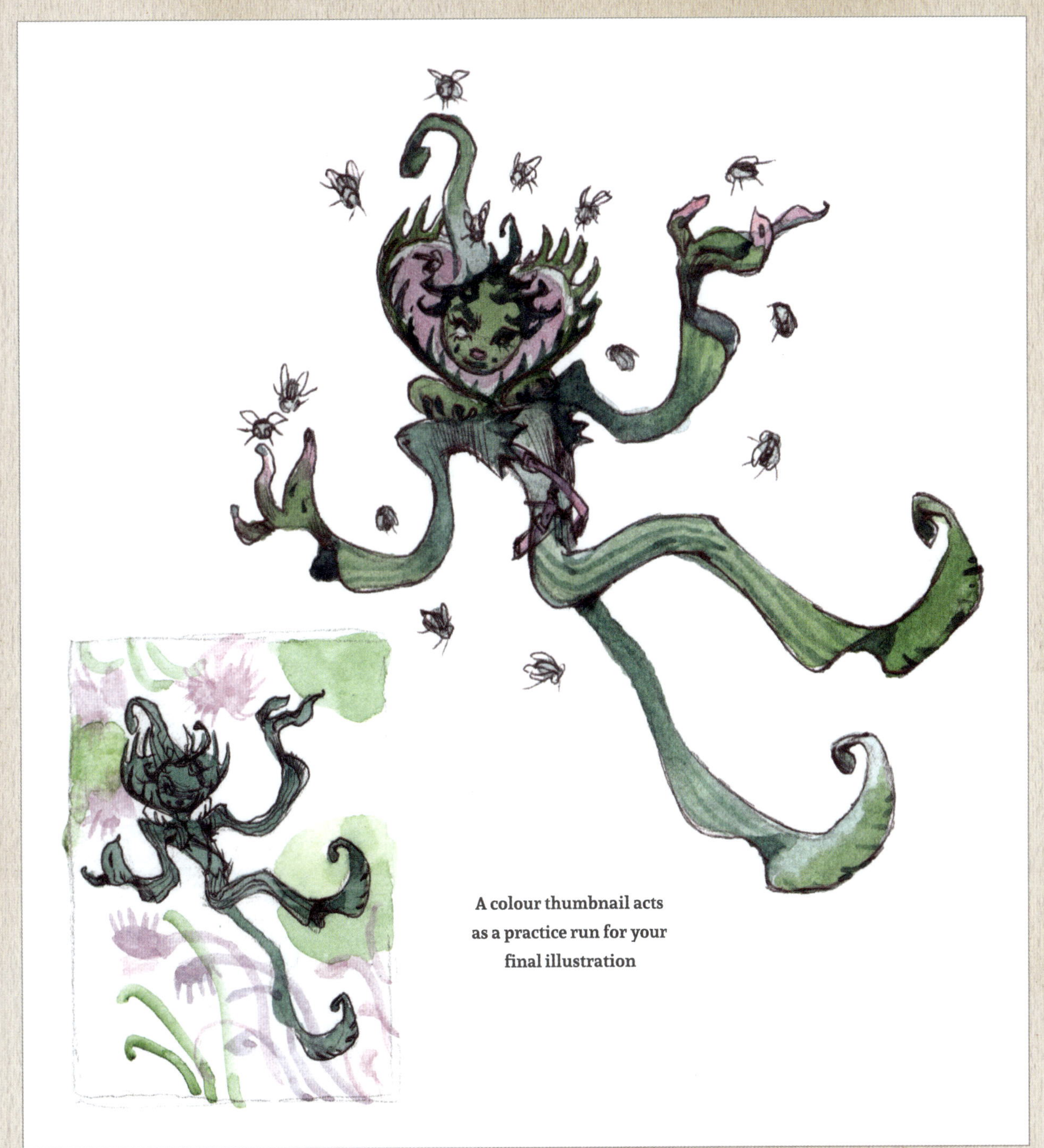

A colour thumbnail acts as a practice run for your final illustration

COLOUR THUMBNAIL

Before you start painting, it's extremely helpful to create a colour thumbnail to establish the lighting, colour palette, and overall style of the illustration to guide you through the painting process. Identify the key colours of the Venus flytrap and use these as the starting point. Choose a general colour temperature for the piece to select a colour direction; in this case, opting for a cooler palette. The thumbnail should also resolve where the light and dark values are situated in the image, with contrast in mind. This colour thumbnail uses a palette of mostly green, with a pop of cool pink around the head for contrast. Select a lighter tone for the face to stand out against the darker red for the inner trap. Instead of opting for a peachy colour for the skin, choose a light green to give the clown character an otherworldly, fantastical feel.

WASH OF COLOUR

Establish the colour direction right from the start by laying down a light, even wash of cool green all over the character. Since watercolour is a translucent medium, this cool green colour will show through all of the subsequent layers of colours, tying them together in a cohesive way. This is a quick and easy way to establish a colour palette, as it means less colour mixing on-the-fly. Once this underpainting layer dries, you can start to build up the base colours for each of the different elements.

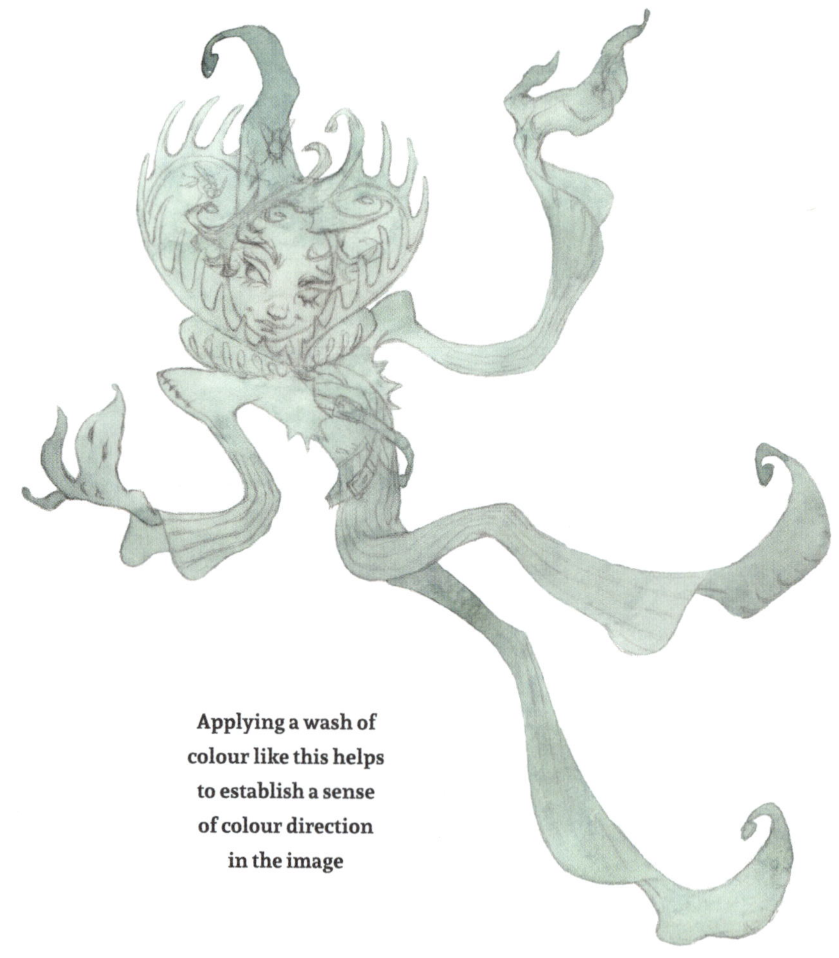

Applying a wash of colour like this helps to establish a sense of colour direction in the image

BASE COLOURS

Build up the main defining colours of each of the elements in the character. To add some variety to the greens, create a gradient from a darker, bluer green towards a lighter, warmer green near the hands and feet. This transition of colours will add interest and a sense of movement. Separate the front layer of the teeth on the main collar from the back layer of the teeth by assigning them with different greens. Next, paint the inner heart and vest pink to help break up the greens. Add some of the pink on the fingertips as well to echo the pinks of the plant. Keep each paint layer light and build up your saturation and value as you go to avoid going in too strong too soon.

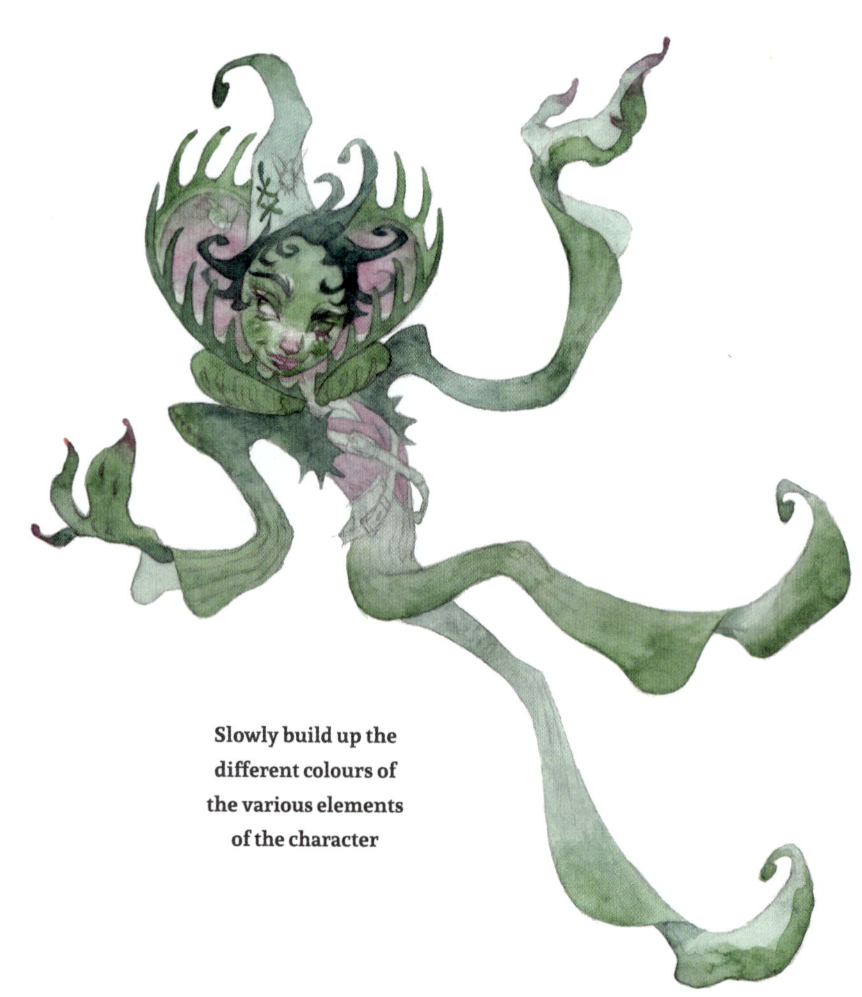

Slowly build up the different colours of the various elements of the character

SHADOWS & RENDERING

Establish the shadows by introducing darker values. Use the same cool green as a shadow colour when reaching for darker colours, as it will help to keep the colours cohesive and the guesswork out of mixing colours. Create a sense of separation in the sleeves by making the area behind the hands slightly darker and keeping the overlapping part in the front lighter. Focus your rendering effort on areas you want the viewer to pay the most attention to, such as the face. Creating an expression that reads clearly should be the top priority, followed by the collar design, then the hands and feet, and finally the rest of the image. For contrast, keep the shading on the sleeves and trouser legs as minimal and flat as possible. This will also help to mimic the look of the flat, leafy stalk of the plant.

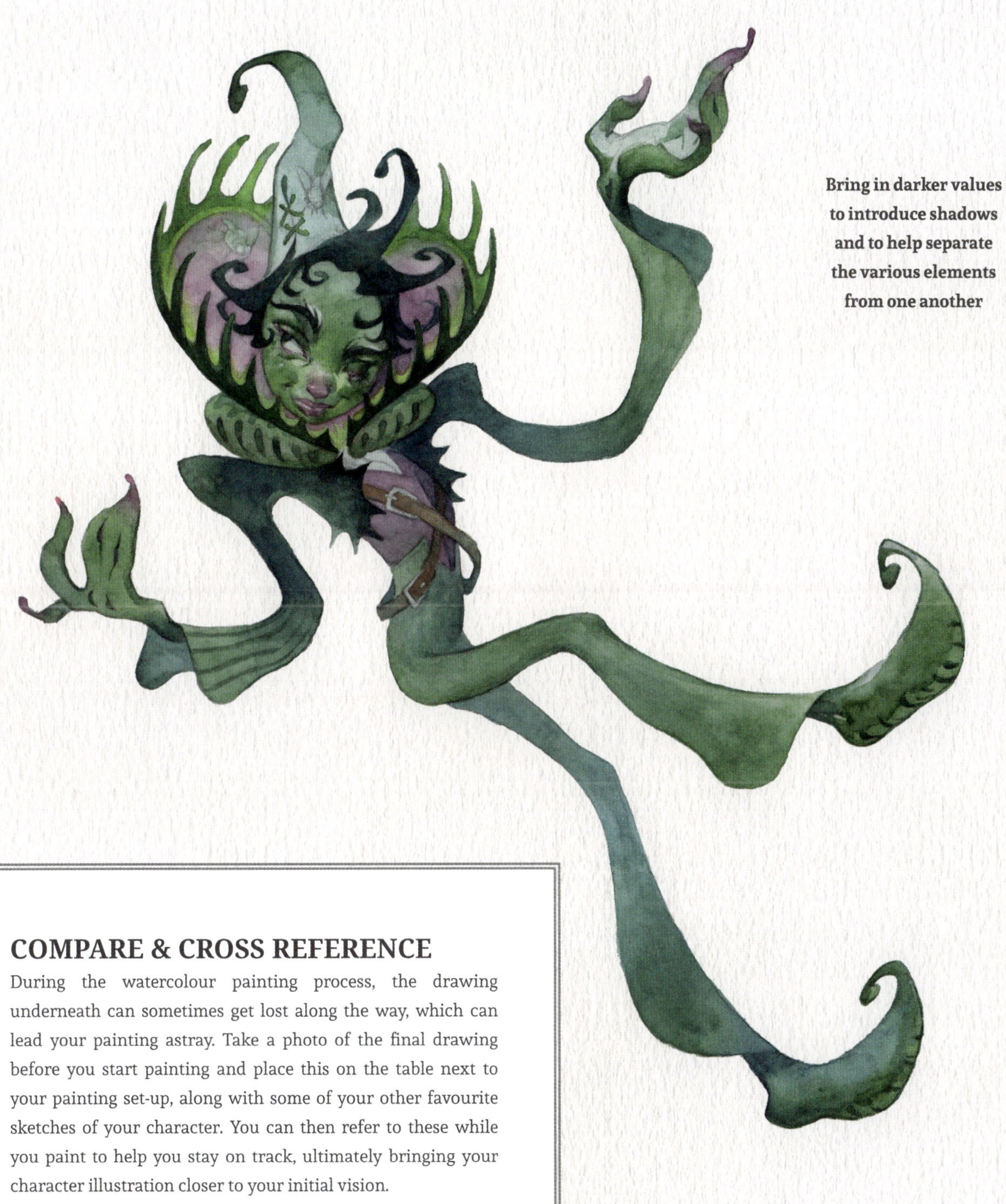

Bring in darker values to introduce shadows and to help separate the various elements from one another

COMPARE & CROSS REFERENCE

During the watercolour painting process, the drawing underneath can sometimes get lost along the way, which can lead your painting astray. Take a photo of the final drawing before you start painting and place this on the table next to your painting set-up, along with some of your other favourite sketches of your character. You can then refer to these while you paint to help you stay on track, ultimately bringing your character illustration closer to your initial vision.

TEXTURE

Once you've built up your painting, you can start to introduce details and textures to highlight certain aspects of the design and add more interest to the character. Paint some evenly spaced, vertical, pin-striped detailing along the sleeves and trouser legs. These lines hint at the circus aesthetic, while also helping to describe the form. Refer back to your initial drawings to see where you may want to introduce some additional textures to bring the essence of the drawing into the watercolour illustration. For example, you can mimic some of the shading lines from the initial drawings by lightly dry brushing lines in a few areas, such as the cheeks and along the hands. This helps to describe the form and brings slightly more emphasis to these areas. Take care not to overdo this, however, as you want to let the beautiful watercolour texture shine.

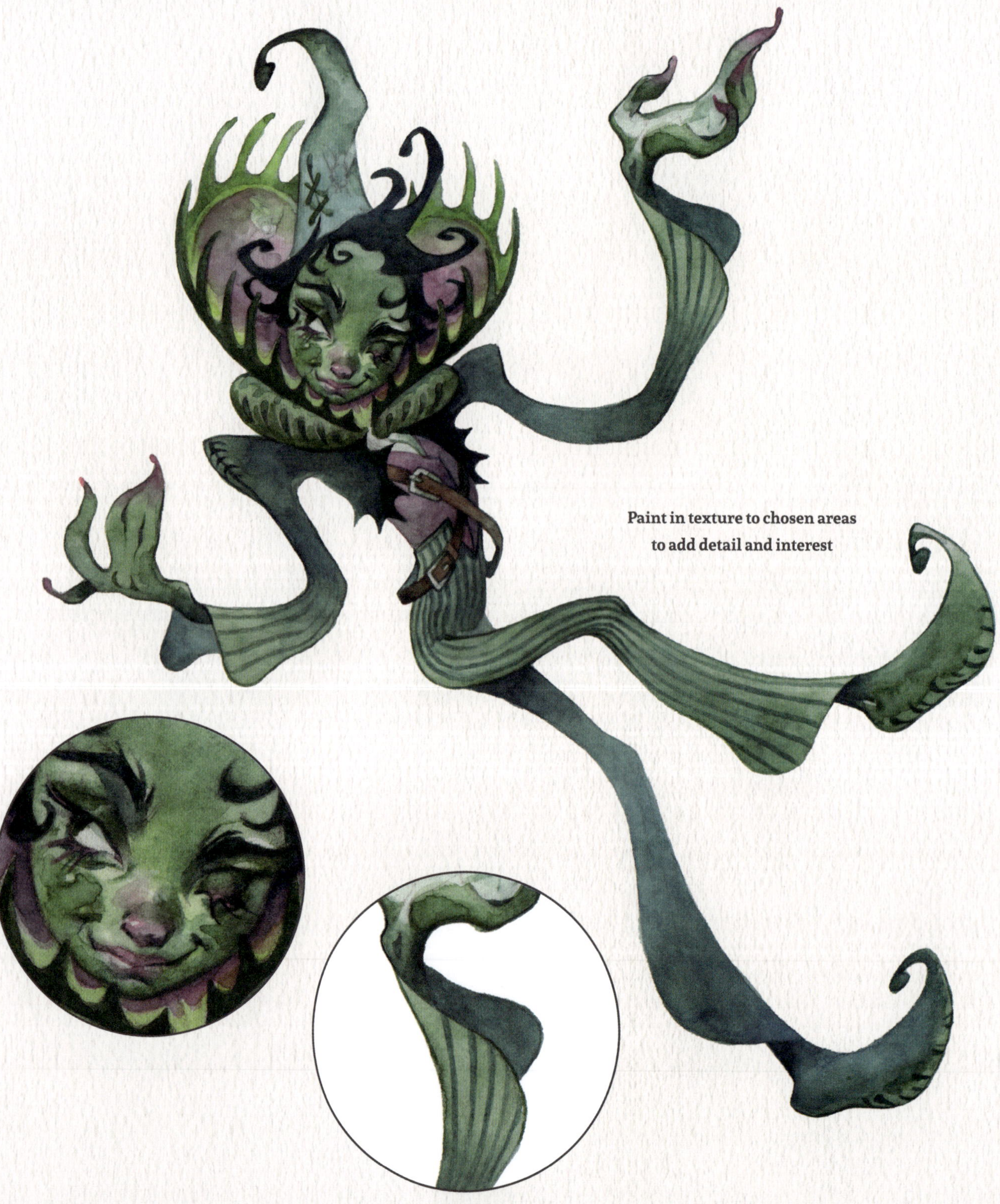

Paint in texture to chosen areas to add detail and interest

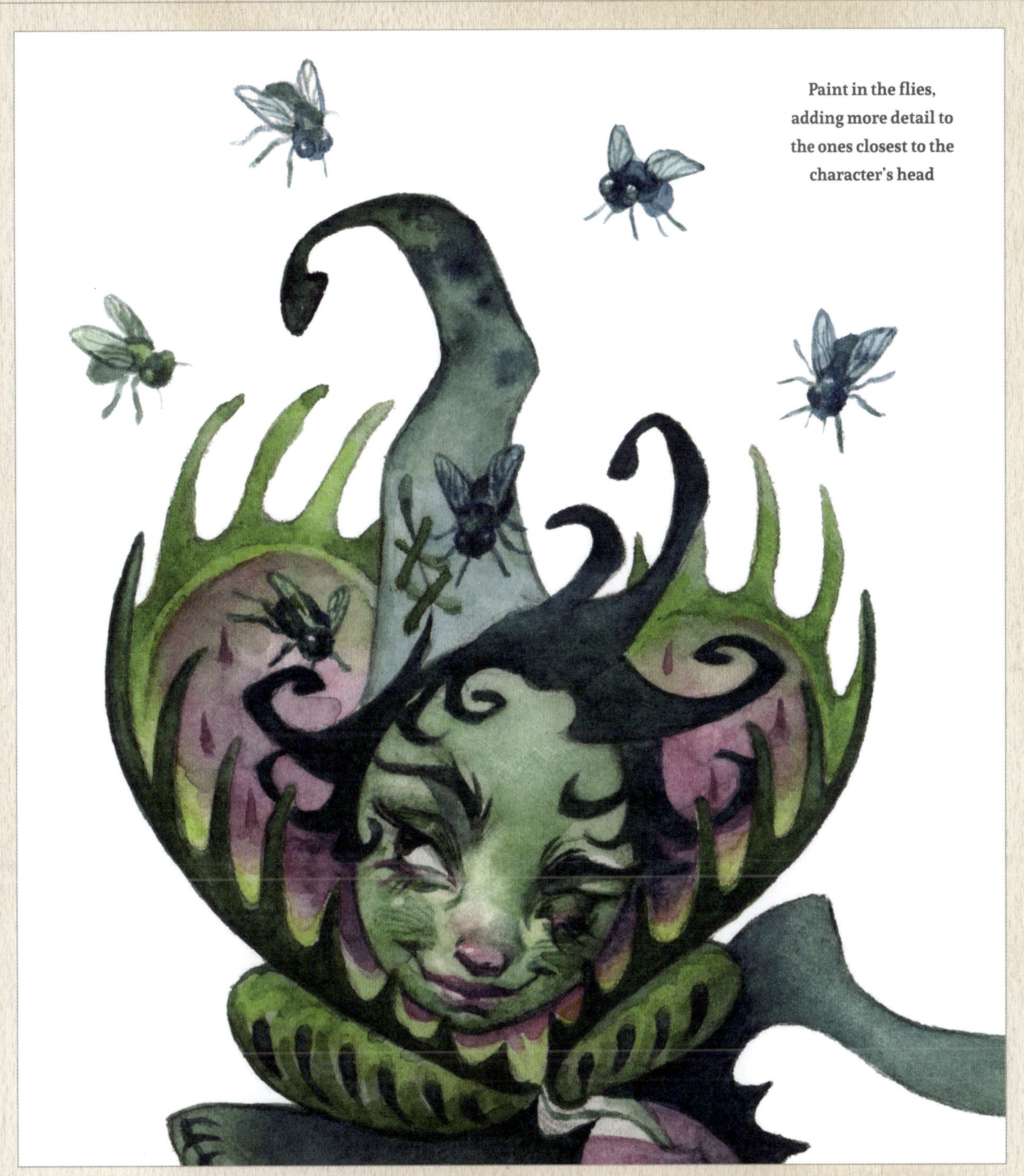

Paint in the flies, adding more detail to the ones closest to the character's head

PAINTING THE FLIES

The last remaining element is to paint in the flies. They will create a pleasing sense of movement throughout the composition and a sense of depth on the page. The key is to not treat them uniformly. Render the flies that are sitting on the character's head and closest to the head in greater detail and with a wider value range. Then for the flies scattered further away, simply fill them in with a light wash of colour and paint in minimal detail to keep them low in contrast. This will set them apart from the flies that are closer and more interactive with the character's head, creating an illusion of atmosphere and space within the page. Use the same colour palette that has been used throughout the illustration to ensure the flies appear cohesive with the character.

FINAL ILLUSTRATION

Once you feel the painting is nearly finished, you may find it helpful to take a step back and view the character from a distance. This will allow you to accurately evaluate it as a whole image, rather than focusing on smaller individual parts. When looking at the image as a whole, ask yourself: how does the focal point read? Do your eyes travel well through the image, or do they get stuck somewhere you don't want them to go? Does the character remind you of a Venus fly trap plant? Once you've satisfied these questions, carry out one last comb through your illustration; for example, to make sure there aren't any distracting white areas that haven't yet been painted. When you can't think of anything else to add or tweak, your character is finished.

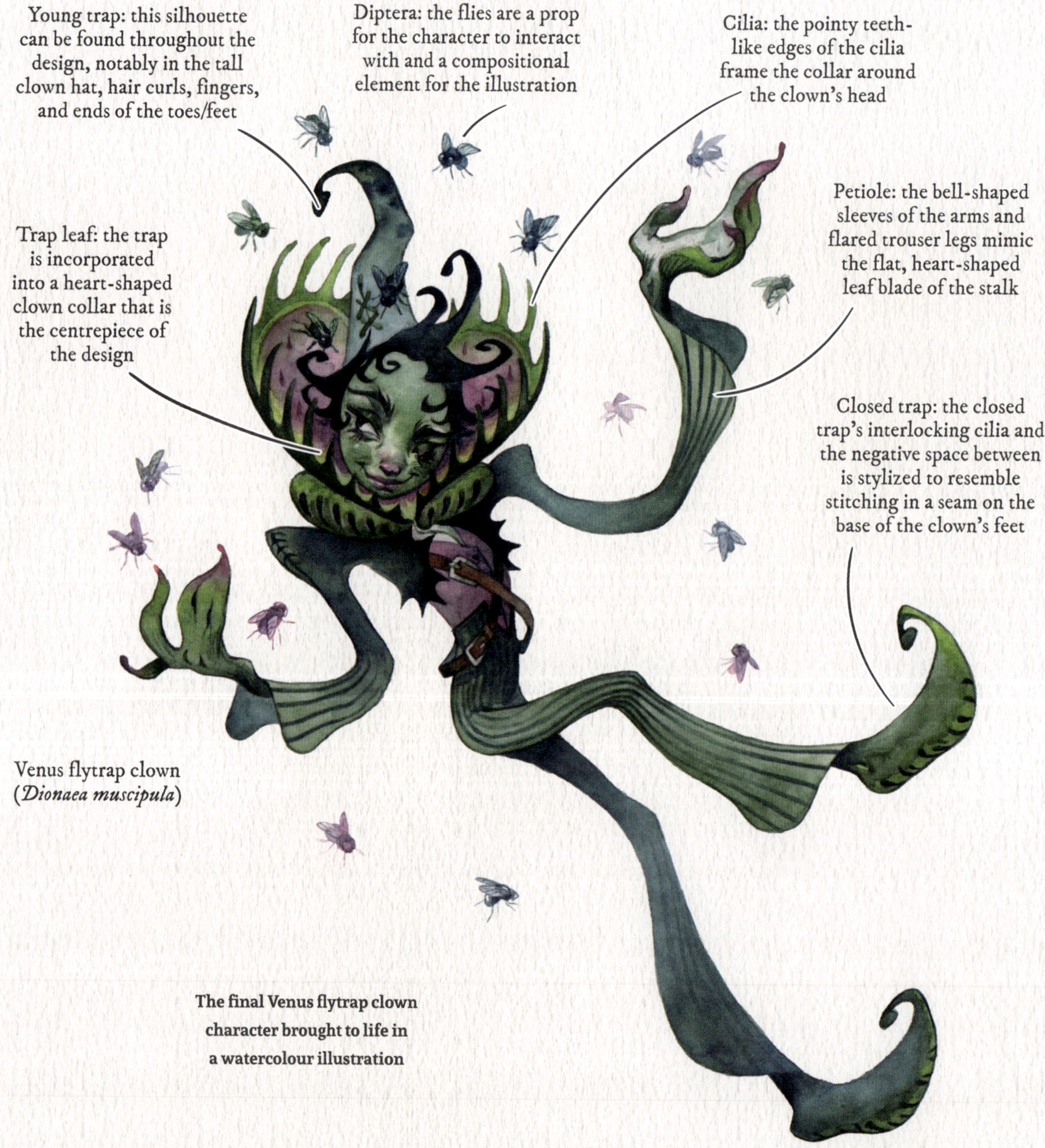

The final Venus flytrap clown character brought to life in a watercolour illustration

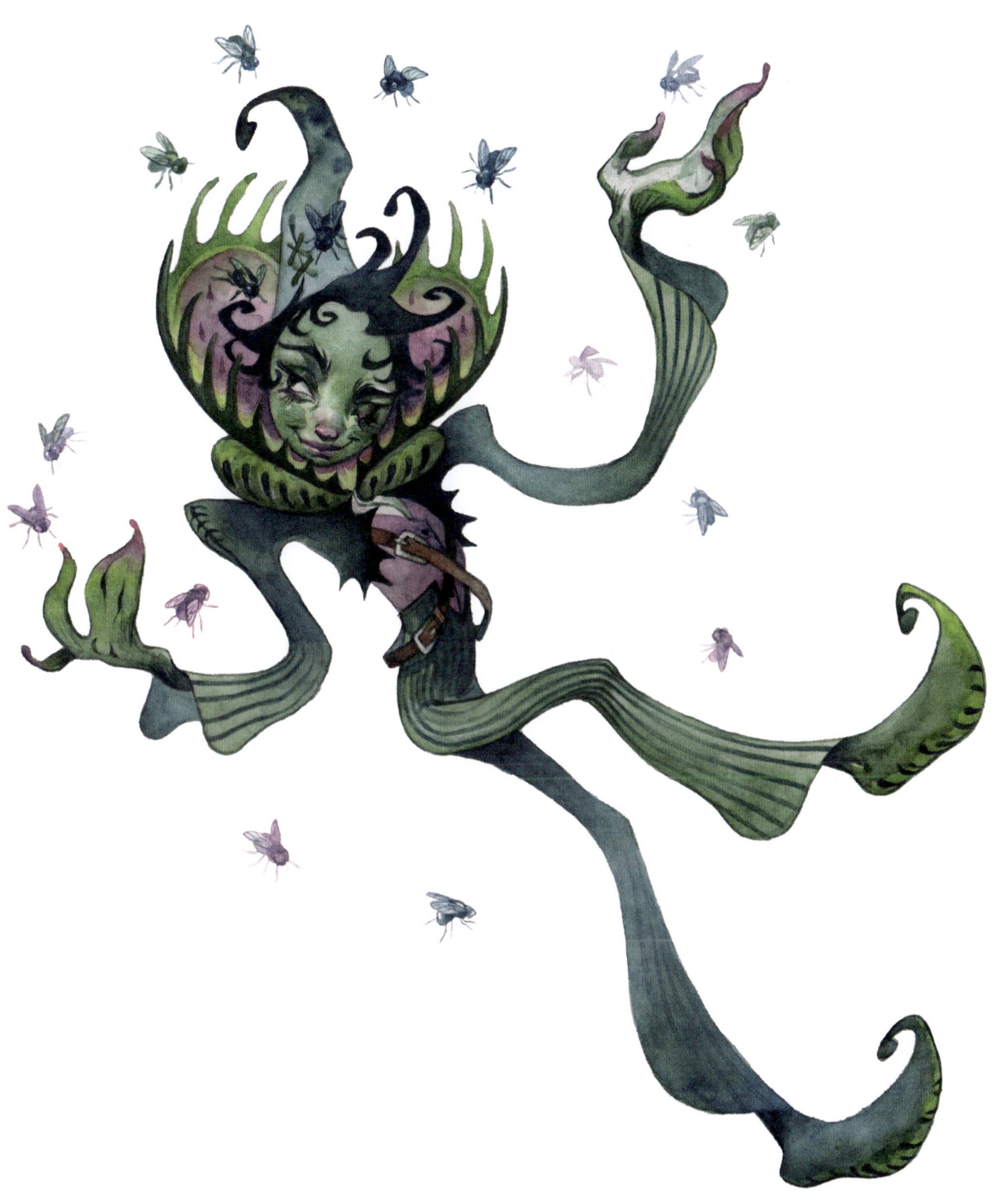

VENUS FLYTRAP CLOWN

Final image © Chris Hong

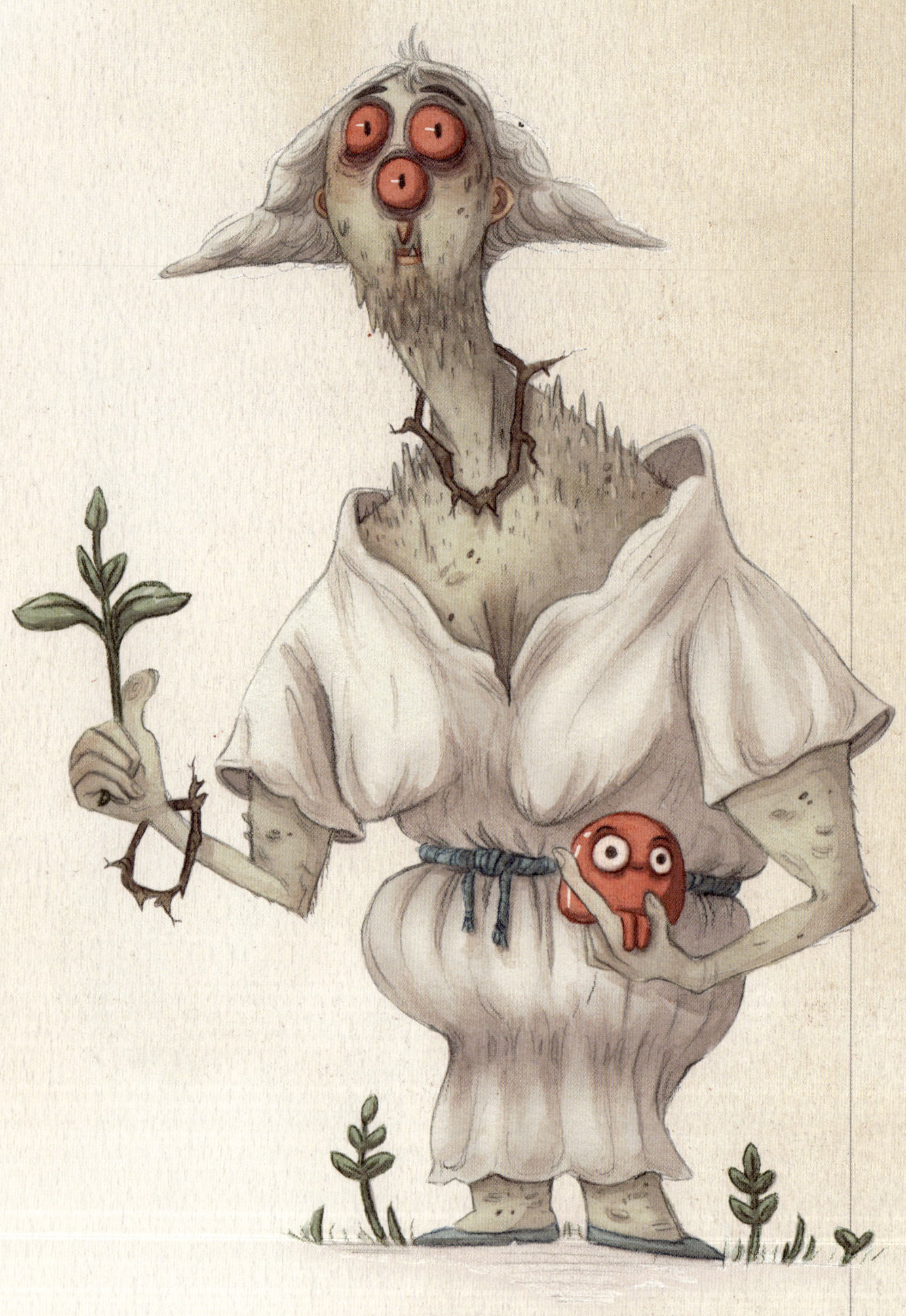

The following pages contain a step-by-step breakdown to creating your own character inspired by the wonderful world of fungi. For this design, you will be using the Devil's Tooth fungus (*Hydnellum Peckii*) in its youngest form as inspiration. The aim is to extract particular attributes of the mushroom to spark ideas and create a unique design with interesting shapes, colours, and personality. This tutorial will use watercolour combined with digital techniques to create a vivid character with traditional and botanical elements.

fungi

DEVIL'S TOOTH TROLL

CORAH LOUISE

START WITH RESEARCH

Begin by getting to know the chosen fungus. The Devil's Tooth, duly named for its grisly resemblance to a painful tooth, has many elements that can be used as reference material. Selecting a mushroom with unique and interesting qualities will ignite your imagination, and it's clear this fungus already has great shape, colour, and detail to draw from. Take note of the aspects of the mushroom that can be expanded upon or evolved into features of a character design, such as the stipe, cap, teeth, fine hairs, and red liquid droplets. This Devil's Tooth fungus is a very simple structure. Though its main feature is its striking studded cap of red spots, it's surprising what you can conjure up when you look closely at shape, texture, and detail.

Study the chosen mushroom, paying attention to the elements that intrigue you most

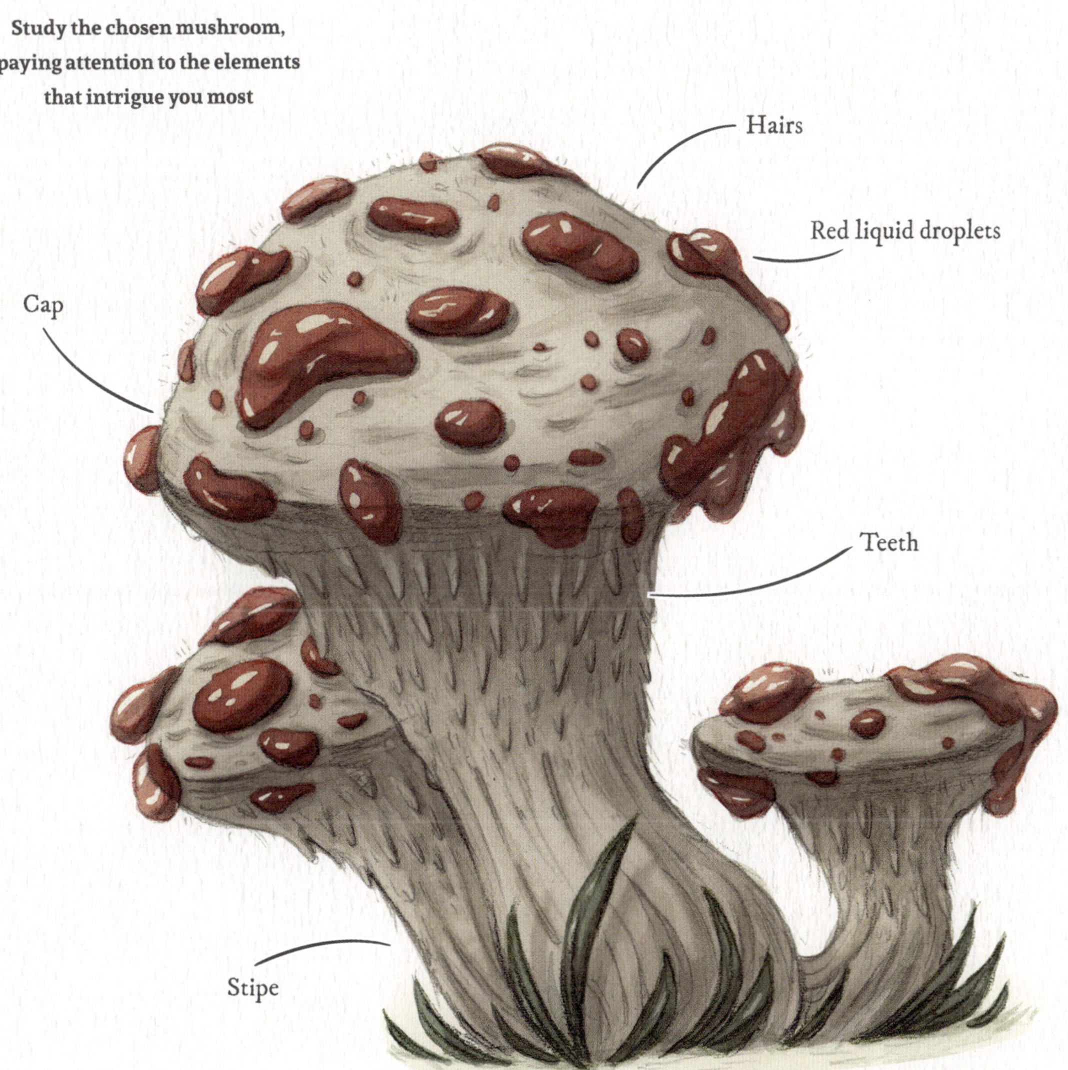

Devil's Tooth
(*Hydnellum Peckii*)

INITIAL SKETCHES

Before you start designing the character, take some time to become familiar with the various elements of the fungus. Sketch with a loose hand as you observe the basic shapes, colours, and textures. This could be the whole fungus, or you could zoom in and focus on particular spots to better understand how to draw them. The shape of the Devil's Tooth is stout and lumpy, with a wider cap. The oozing red droplets create a striking colour combination against the ivory shade of the stipe and cap, while the texture of the teeth beneath the cap is particularly unique and could bring more character and detail to a design.

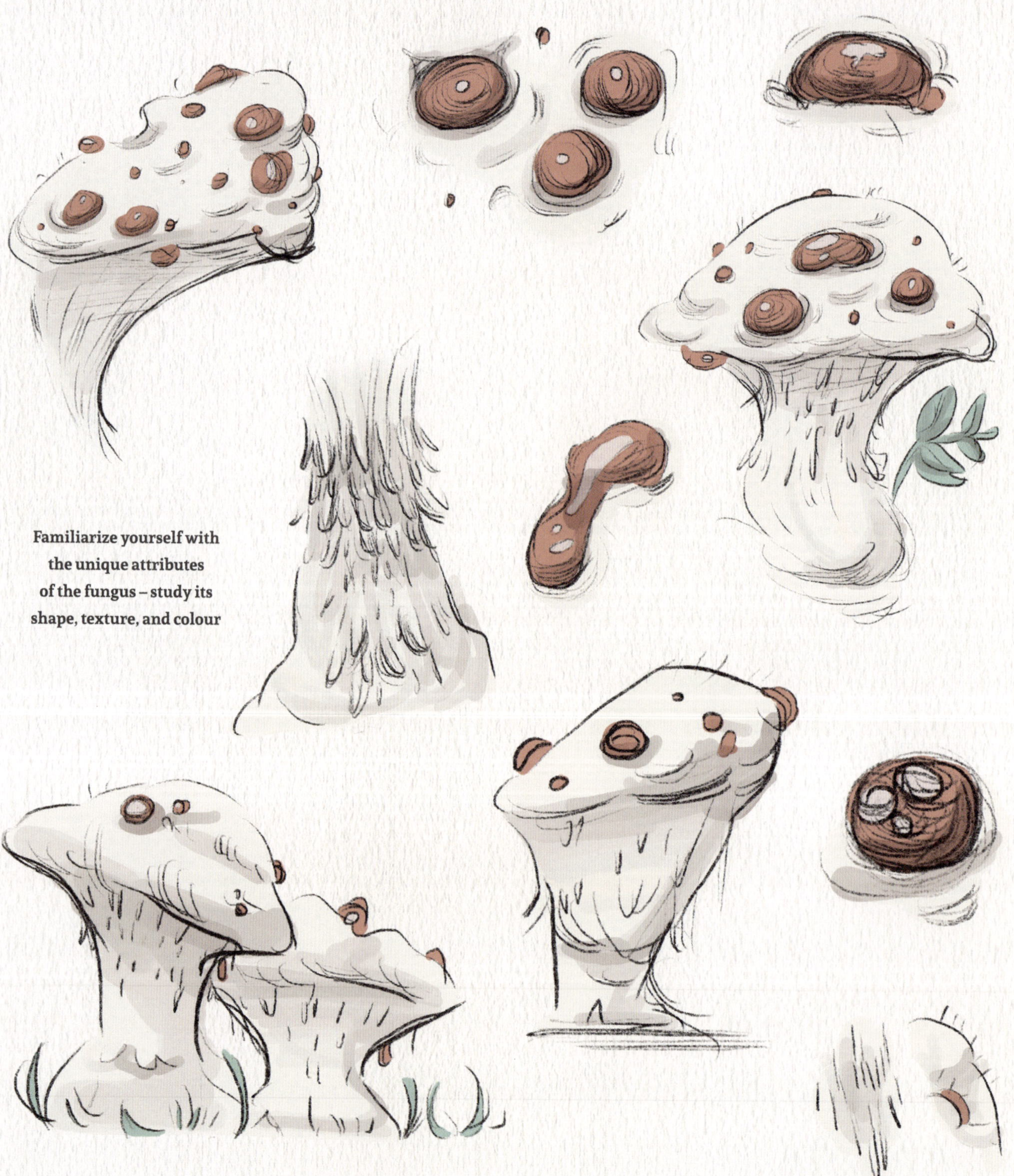

Familiarize yourself with the unique attributes of the fungus – study its shape, texture, and colour

THUMBNAILS

Now you have a better understanding of the mushroom and have practised sketching it, you can draw rough thumbnail designs for your character that focus on overview rather than detail. Use the initial sketches as inspiration to block in your shapes and simple monochrome colours to better visualise the silhouette. There are many attributes to be incorporated from the Devil's Tooth fungus. It flares out at the top, for example; this could be used for the overall shape of the body or for the head or hairstyle. It also has an uneven bulging stipe that could be mimicked and exaggerated within the curves of the character's body, plus striking droplets that could be referenced with large round eyes. Consider how the different elements could be used in a human or creature design, or if they already imitate those characteristics. For example, the teeth under the cap are similar to facial hair.

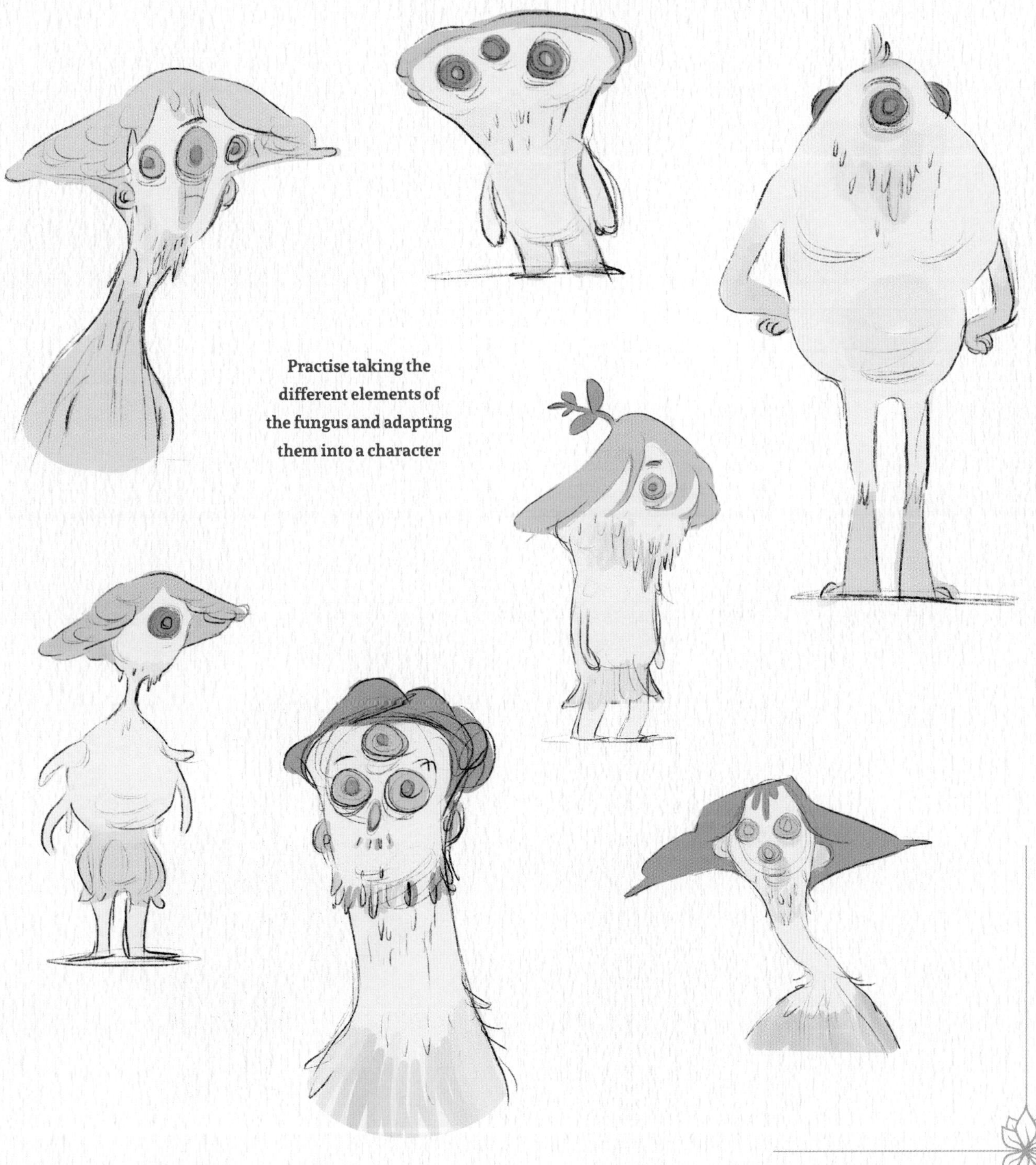

Practise taking the different elements of the fungus and adapting them into a character

FOUNDATION SHAPE

Once you've practised using the fungus for simple character designs, it's time to bring together all of the ideas that have been effective into one unique character. Look back over your thumbnails and observe the elements that have clarity and interest, and that you're happy with, and then see how you can develop them. Keep the sketch loose and use basic shapes to build an understandable base for the design. Think of it as a first foundation for your character that can be built on with detail later. This is great silhouette practice. Ask yourself, can you understand the pose and essence of the character from this simple map of it?

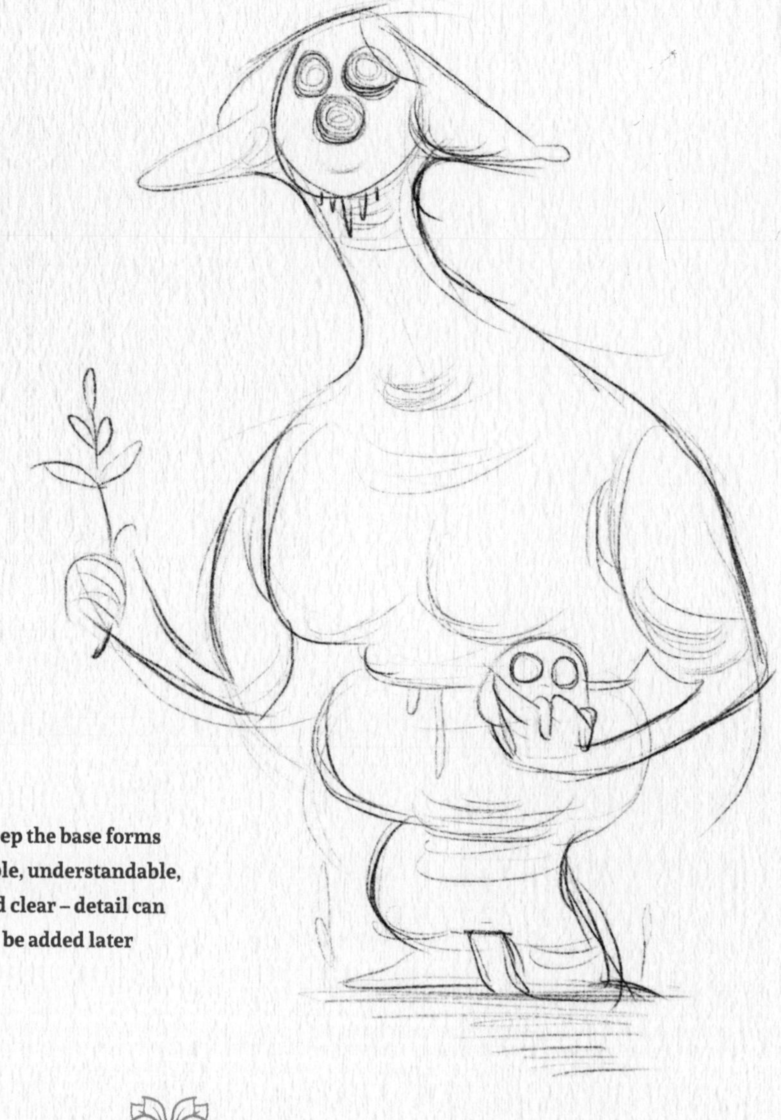

Keep the base forms simple, understandable, and clear – detail can be added later

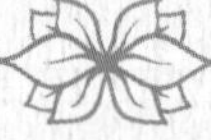

SILHOUETTING

Try testing the effectiveness of your thumbnails or foundation design by turning them into silhouettes. Block in the form of each sketch with one colour to remove all of its details, leaving you with just the basic shape. Are you able to read the pose clearly? Is it unique and engaging to look at? Can you see all of the different elements of the fungus you wanted to include? If you're unable to identify these in the silhouettes, try working with just the blocked-in colour to develop the design and create a silhouette that is clearer and more dynamic. Or why not start the design process by sketching a variety of strong silhouettes to practise your clarity and shape, before going on to develop detail afterwards.

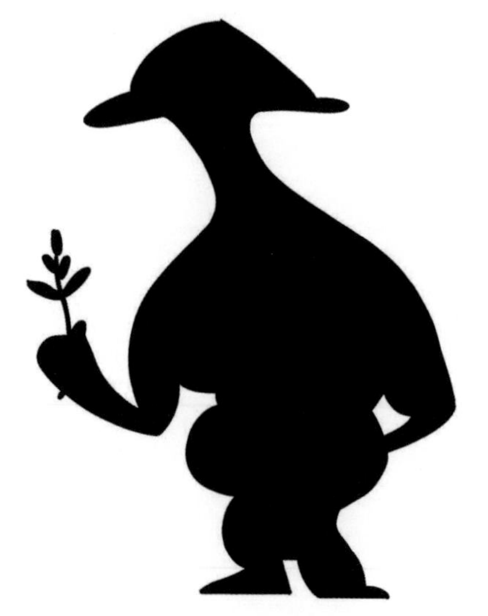

BUILDING CHARACTER

The next step is to add details that will develop the character and instil them with personality. Now you can incorporate the textures from your initial sketches, such as the teeth to mimic facial hair, the flow and bulging of the clothes to imitate the uneven, bulbous stipe, and fine hair and other textures that would be found on the fungus. Detail is important for creating a strong personality within your design; an animal friend, accessories, and props can provide a better understanding of who the character is. Plus linking them back to the original prompt – the fungus – helps to unite everything. The jewellery is crafted from nature, the pet is formed from the red droplets, the leaf prop indicates the natural world the character originates from, and the singular tooth is a tie to the fungus' name.

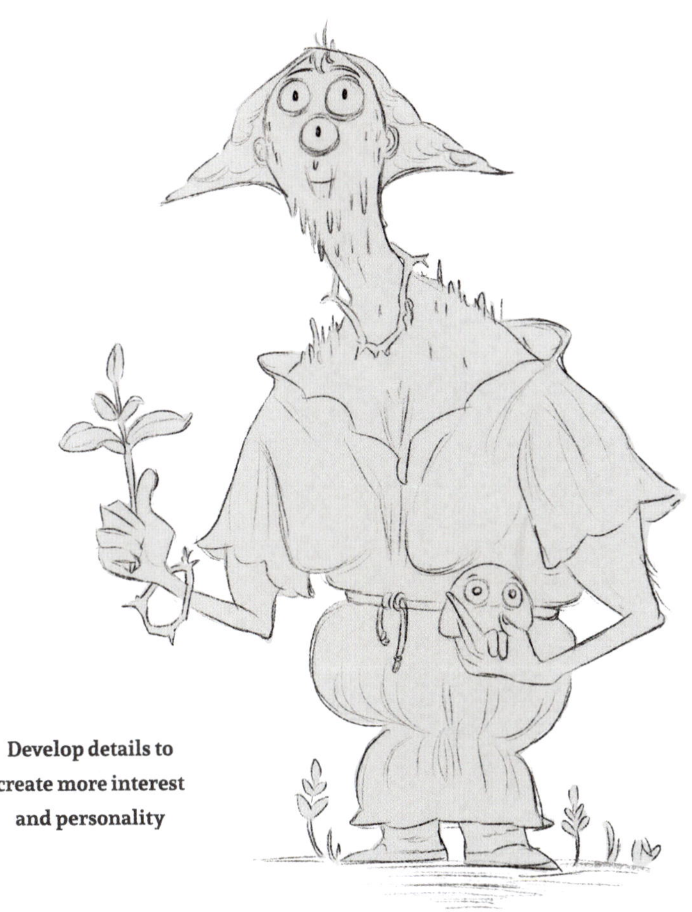

Develop details to create more interest and personality

FINAL SKETCH

Finish the final sketch by bringing the character to life with colour. Start by building a colour palette for your character, using the Devil's Tooth fungus as reference. The fungus is pale with strong red spots. Using the red spots for the eyes and animal friend creates interest and brings vibrancy to an otherwise fairly monochromatic palette. Keep the colours simple and natural, in harmony with the fungus world. You should also use them with purpose, choosing either to balance them out over the design or to draw attention to a certain attribute with colours or shades that stand out. Keeping the colours close to those of the reference material will create a stronger link to the chosen fungus.

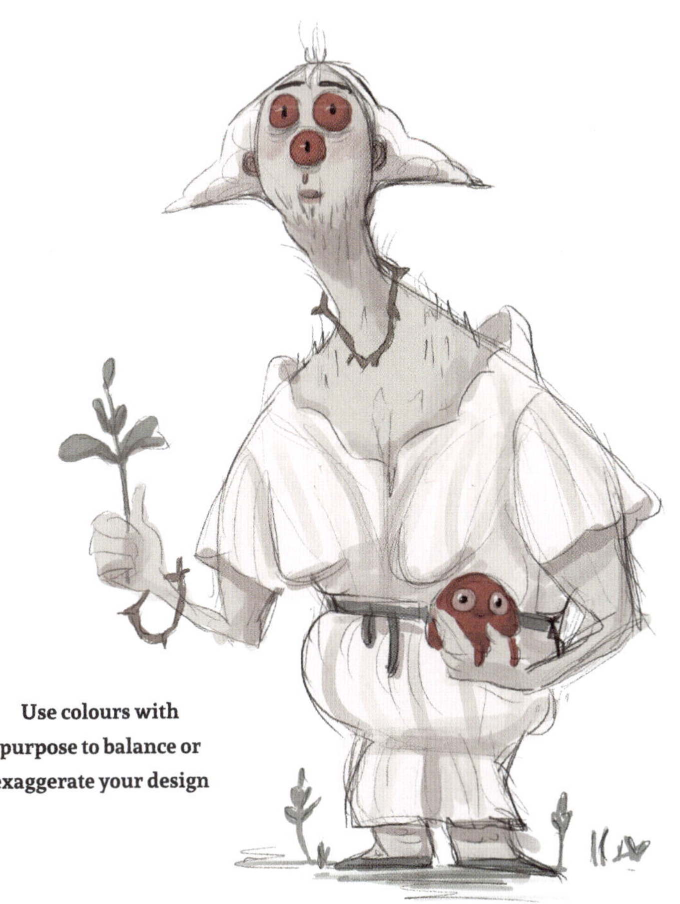

Use colours with purpose to balance or exaggerate your design

PENCIL SKETCH

Before you start painting the character, draw a detailed pencil sketch of the design onto watercolour paper. Here you can be more intentional with the texture and details, precisely planning out the design for the painting process. Keeping the lines light creates a textured look, which when paired with bolder lines, helps to differentiate between solid, smoother shapes and those with more textured edges. When drawing clothes or any fabric that drapes, keeping the lines loose will improve the flow of the garment and make it appear heavy and hanging. As you pencil in the lines and details, look back over your initial sketches and references to take inspiration from the elements you originally worked from.

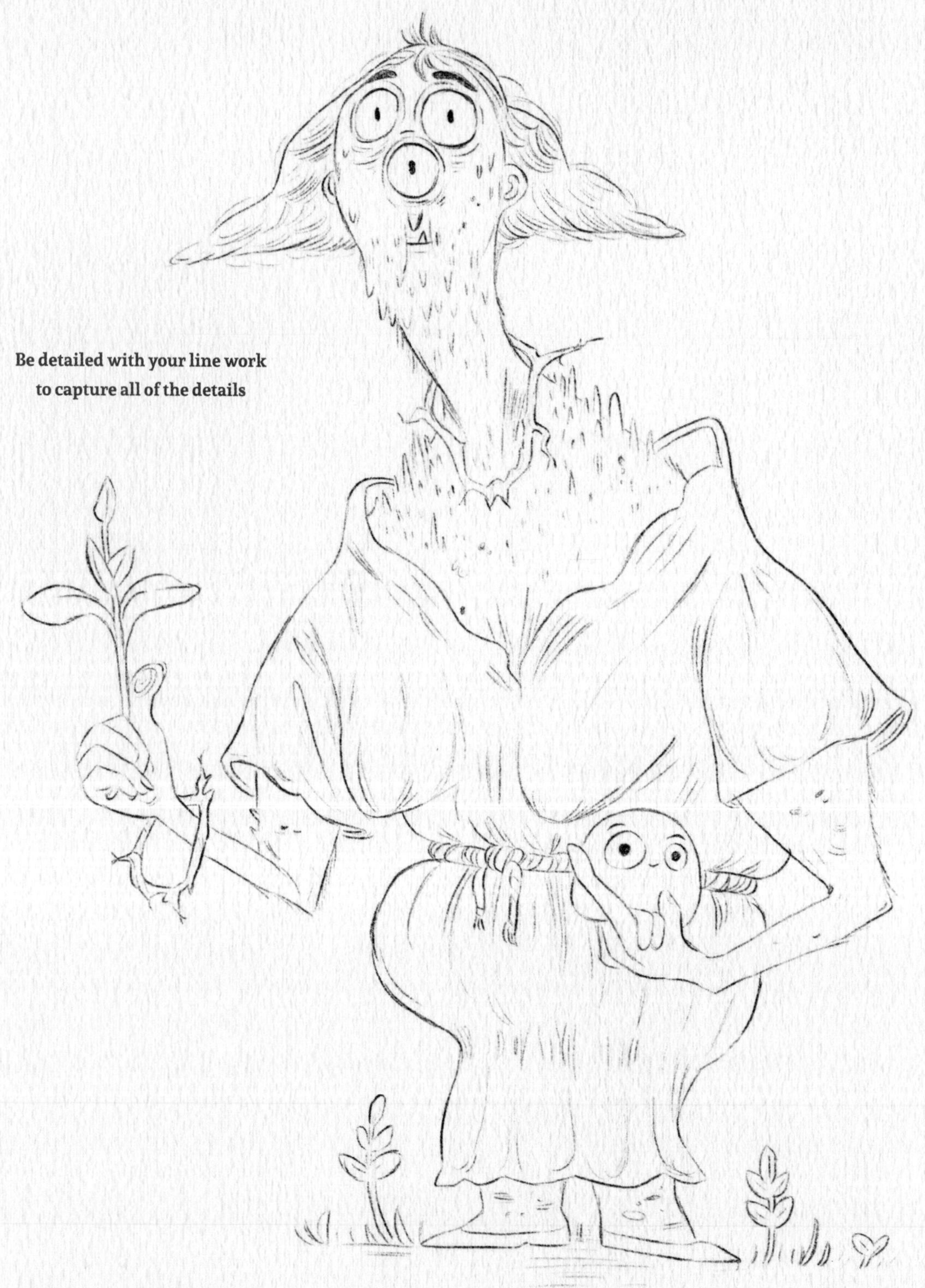

Be detailed with your line work to capture all of the details

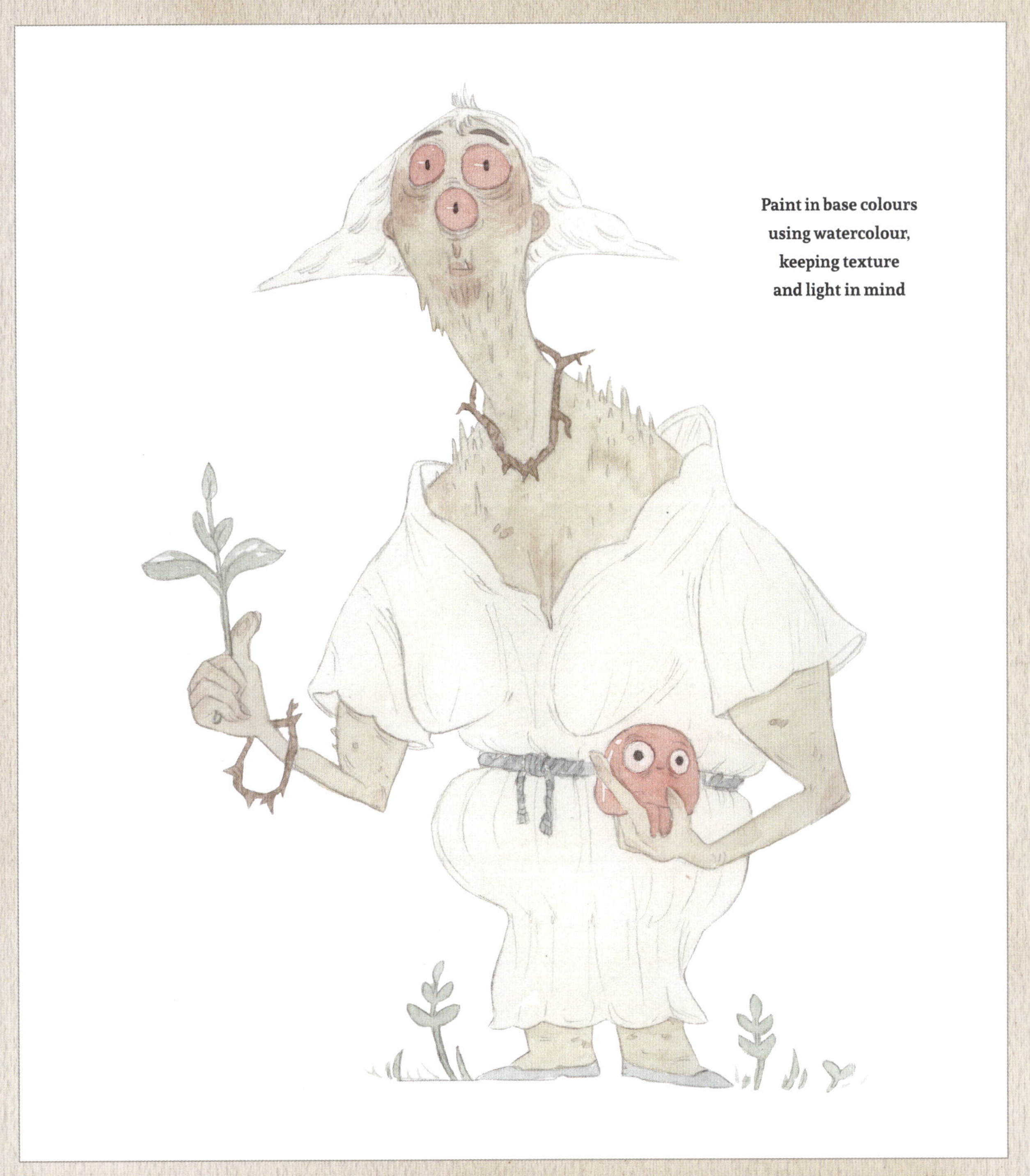

Paint in base colours using watercolour, keeping texture and light in mind

WATERCOLOUR BASE

Switching to watercolour, paint in the base colours you originally decided on in your sketched draft over the pencil sketch. Traditional materials such as watercolour can provide a natural and textured look that fits well with the natural theme of this fungi character. Use the brushstrokes to your advantage to create more interest. For example, you can layer the brushstrokes to create texture on the rope belt, lightly brush over opposing colours to create a nice blush on the face, or leave spaces unpainted to give the illusion of highlights, such as on the leaves, eyes, and blobby animal friend. Watercolour painting can produce accidental textures from the water placement and brushstrokes, imitating the uneven surfaces found in fungi and nature in general.

SKIN VARIATION

Introducing another colour, such as red or a deeper shade than the one you used for the skin tone, on certain facial and body features will make the skin look less flat and allow these features to stand out. This can be applied to areas including the nose, cheeks, ear, lips, and elbows. Skin is textured and different parts of the body will have lighter or darker colours and shades. Use this to your advantage to create interest throughout the design and to add to the character's persona.

WATERCOLOUR SHADING

Once you've applied the base colours, it's time to use shading to bring more depth to the design. Shading is a useful tool for emphasizing the textures you've taken from the fungus and incorporated into the drawing. Use your mushroom references to observe how the shadows and light acts on these differing textures and use this as inspiration. For example, this could be used in the character's clothing, skin, or hair. Rougher or looser application will add to the natural feel of it to link back to the original source.

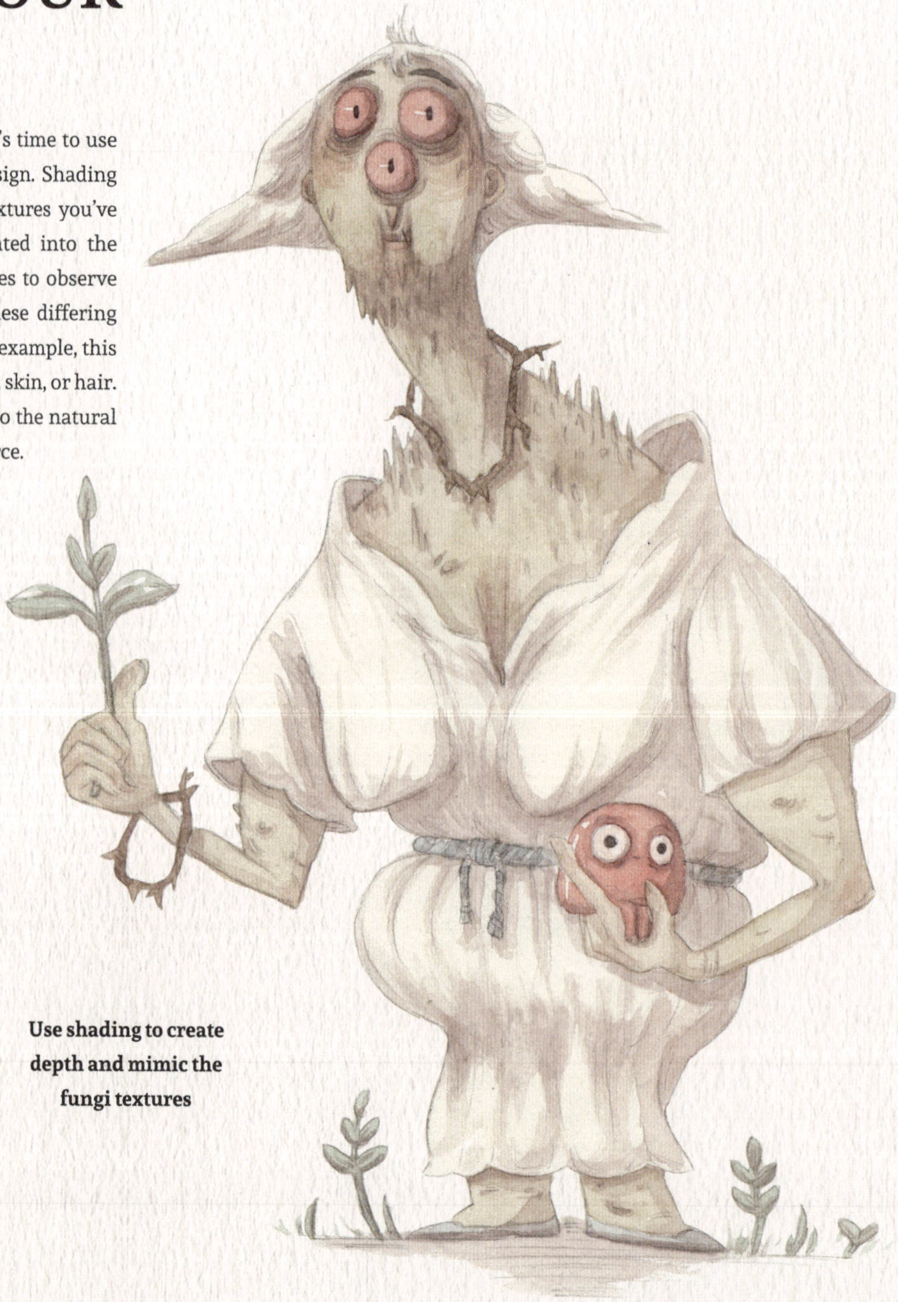

Use shading to create depth and mimic the fungi textures

PENCIL LINING

Now the shading and paintwork are complete, the next step is to unite the painting with an outline, using pencil for any final details and textures. Pencil is a good tool for creating finer details and enhancing subtle elements. It can be used to create wisps in the hair, around the fungi teeth on the skin to differentiate them from one another, or on the twiggy jewellery for the finer elements. The fine hairs observed on the Devil's Tooth fungus can also be added here on top of the skin. This not only adds another link back to the original fungi inspiration, but it also adds more texture to the piece.

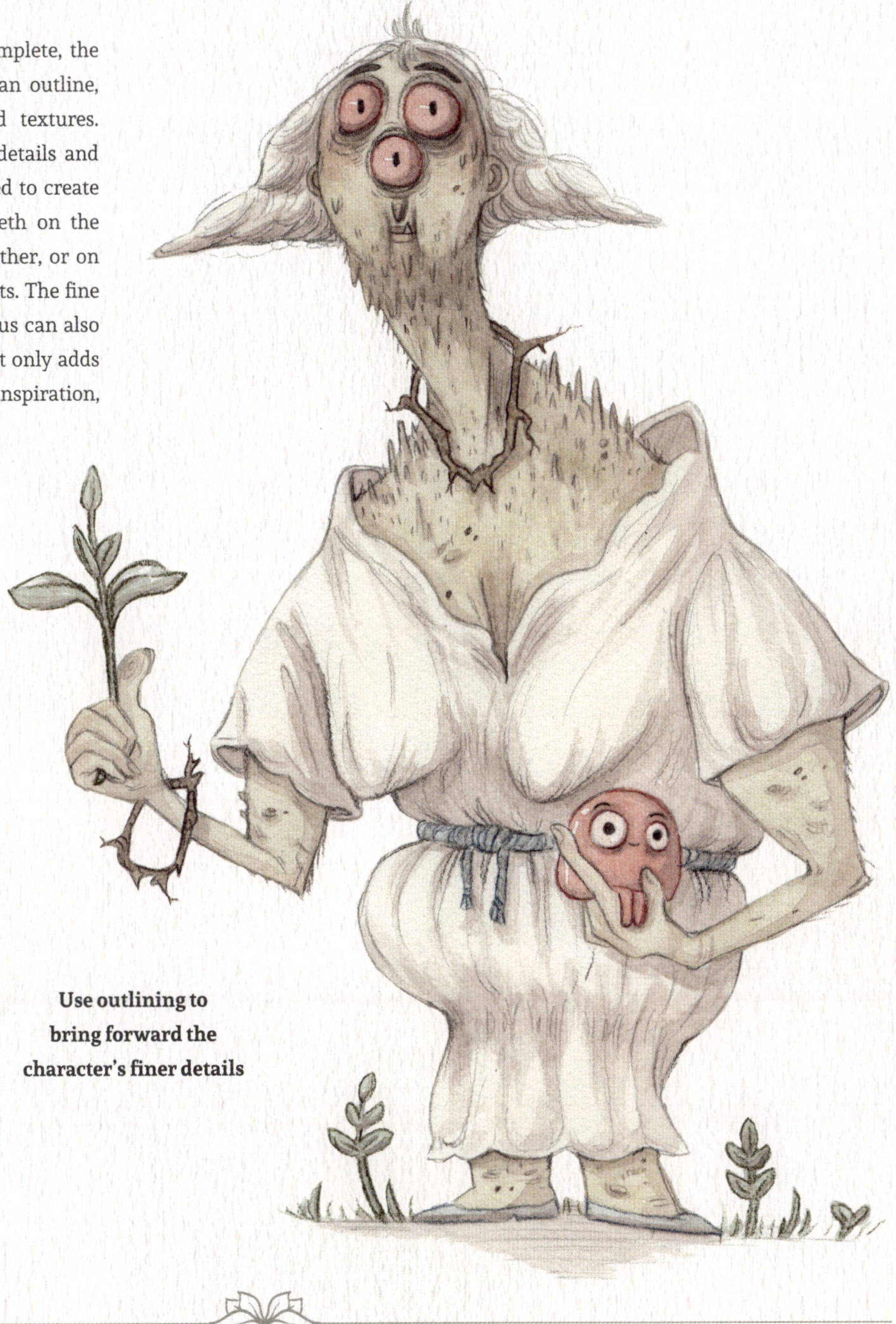

Use outlining to bring forward the character's finer details

DON'T LOSE THE FLOW

When painting and outlining your character design, try not to lose the flow of the original drawing. Sometimes outlining your character can make them look stiff, but staying close to the original draft, using loose lines, and holding on to strong shapes will instil the personality and quality you originally captured. While you should regularly stop and compare your draft to your outlined image to see if you've successfully captured these things, it's also important to allow yourself to develop new ideas throughout the painting process.

DIGITAL COLOURING

You can scan your watercolour illustration into your digital software of choice so that it can be edited digitally and developed into a final piece. Digital colouring will allow you greater control over the colours, depth, and vibrancy of the character. Use the digital tools on offer to adapt the base colours by layering onto your painted piece, bringing them closer to the Devil's Tooth colour palette. The reds can be made deeper and more striking, while the skin and clothing can be brought closer to that of a natural fungus in the wild. Here you can really make the colours pop and enhance the contrasts between the reds, blues, and greens throughout the design.

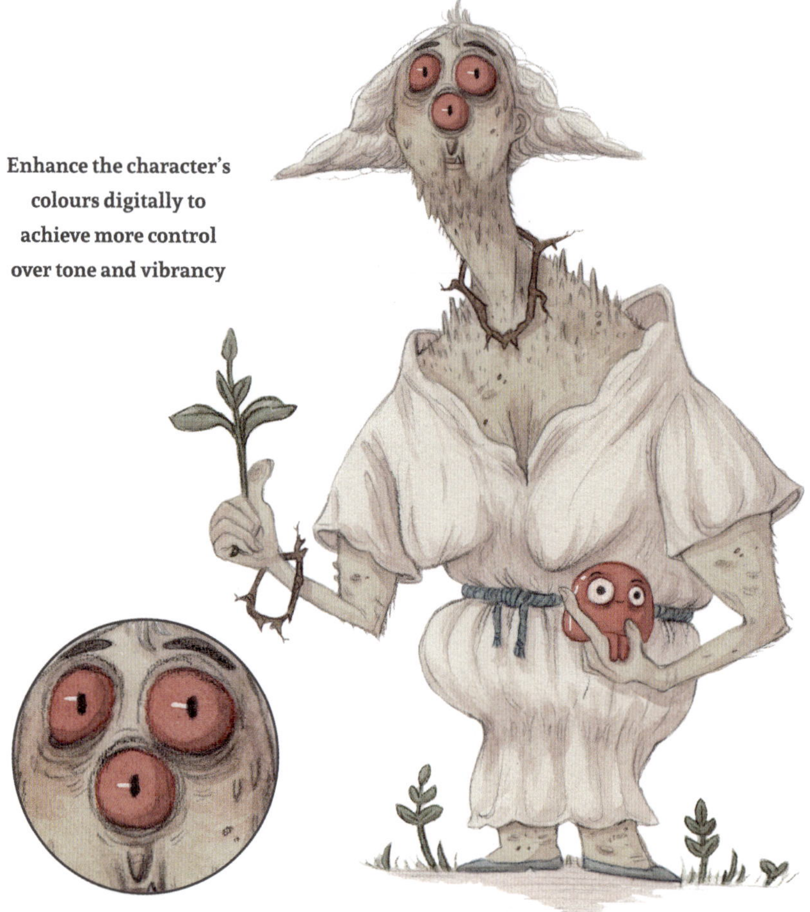

Enhance the character's colours digitally to achieve more control over tone and vibrancy

COLOUR DETAILS

Use digital colouring to manage and intensify the finer details; in particular, the stand-out colour of the design: red. The red liquid droplets of the Devil's Tooth are the most unique and eye-catching element of the fungus. The contrast of the crimson colour against the paleness of the stipe and cap plays a major part in the character design. Use digital tools, such as a hard or soft-edged brush on a suitable blending mode layer, to intensify the red in the eyes and pet. Balance this out with the blush throughout the body, using a feather brush on the cheeks, nose, lips, shoulders, chest, and elbows.

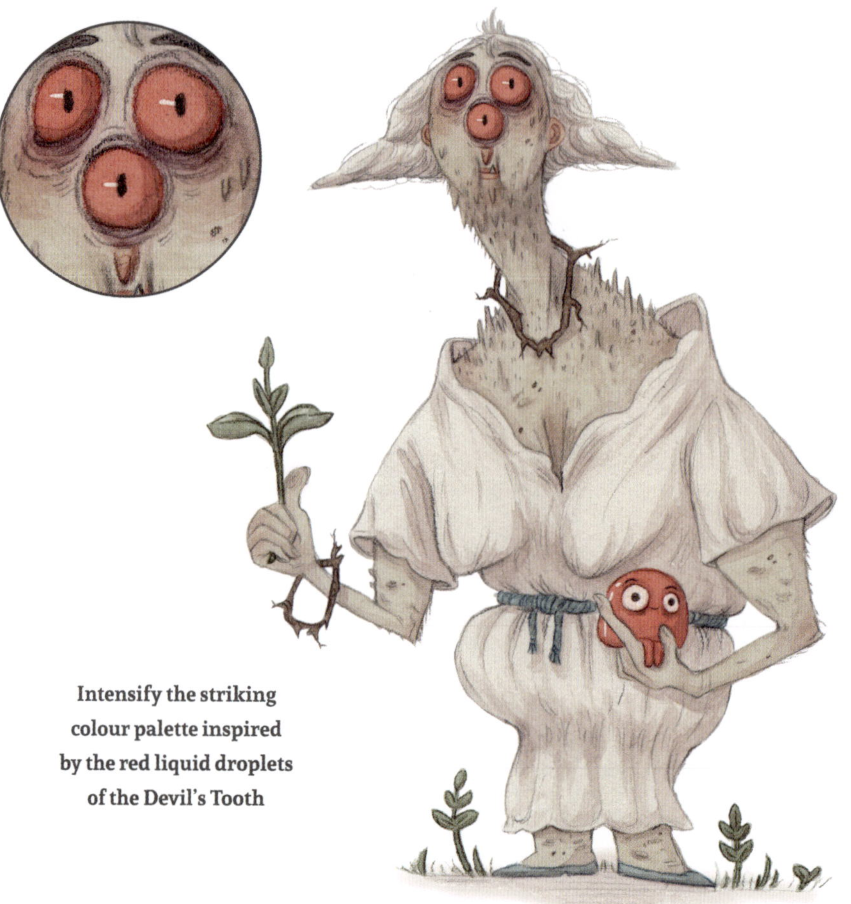

Intensify the striking colour palette inspired by the red liquid droplets of the Devil's Tooth

ENHANCE SHADING

Shade your character digitally to deepen the textured shadows you originally painted with watercolour. Using a feathered digital brush, etch out the shadows to make the textures pop, in particular enhancing the ripples in the clothing to imitate the same flow of the Devil's Tooth's stipe. Going around the individual teeth will help to brighten them, providing a stronger and clearer effect on the skin. Deepen the shadows where they will be darkest for more depth and dimension, such as in the sleeves and folds of the clothing. Next, paint in final touches and marks to the skin, such as the rough texture of a fungi cap.

Deepen the shadows using a digital brush to create depth and texture

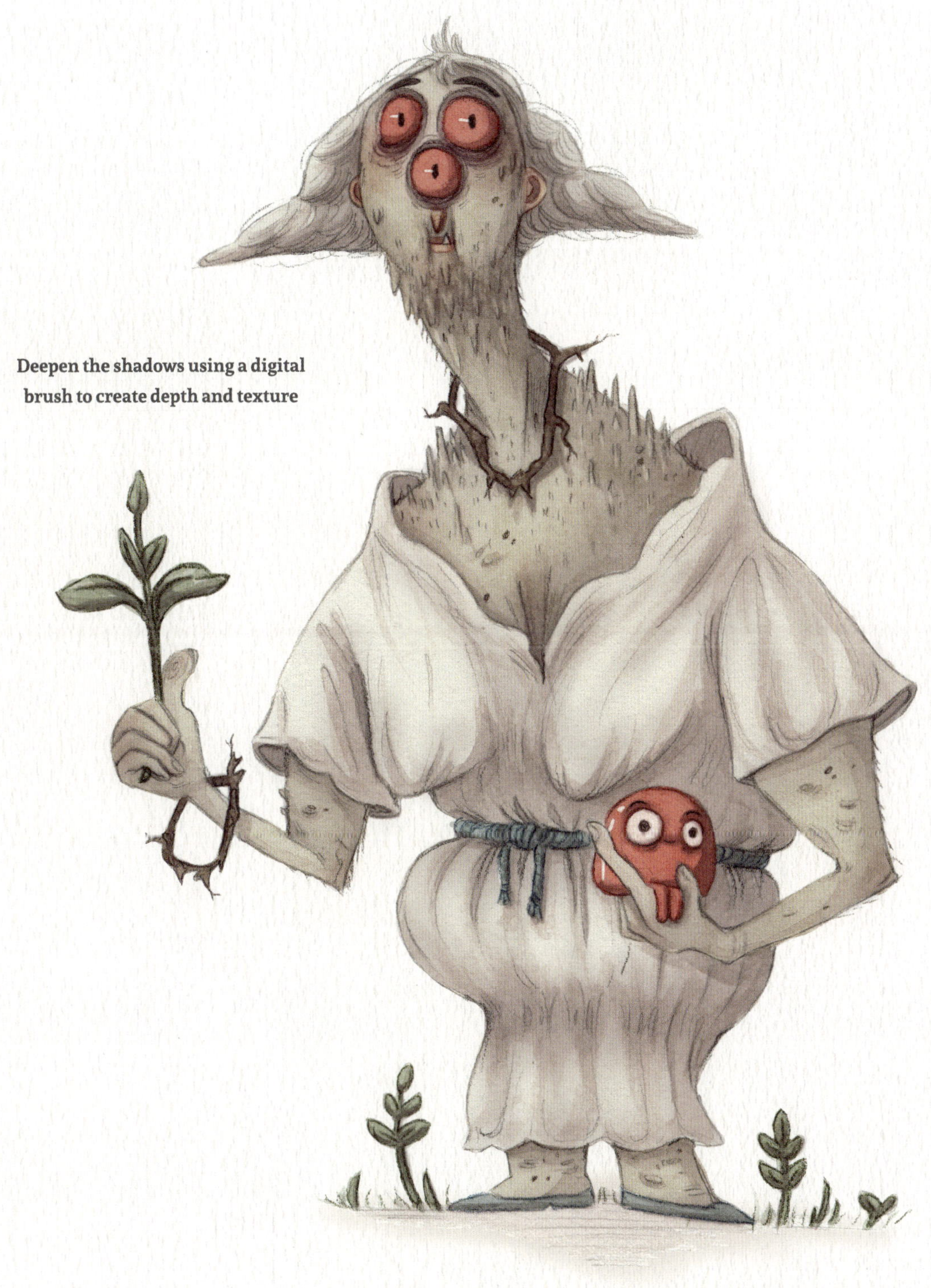

FINAL DETAILS

Here you can see how the Devil's Tooth fungus has influenced every step of the character design process as well as the final image. The red liquid droplets form the eyes and small pet friend, providing the design with an intense pop of colour. The teeth and texture of the fine hairs make the character look ancient and mythical, like a troll or sprite of the forest. The stipe and cap contribute to the base shapes of the character; a wide top and an uneven torso that's lumpy yet flowing.

Overall, the character design is full of personality and story due to the elements borrowed from the Devil's Tooth fungus. Inspiration from the natural world can help to broaden your imagination and develop your art, taking it to places it may not have gone otherwise. There are so many interesting and unique shapes, colours, and textures in the plant world that can provide inspiration. Why not pause and take notice of the fungi, flowers, and trees around you next time you're out in nature and see what elements you could use to create a character with.

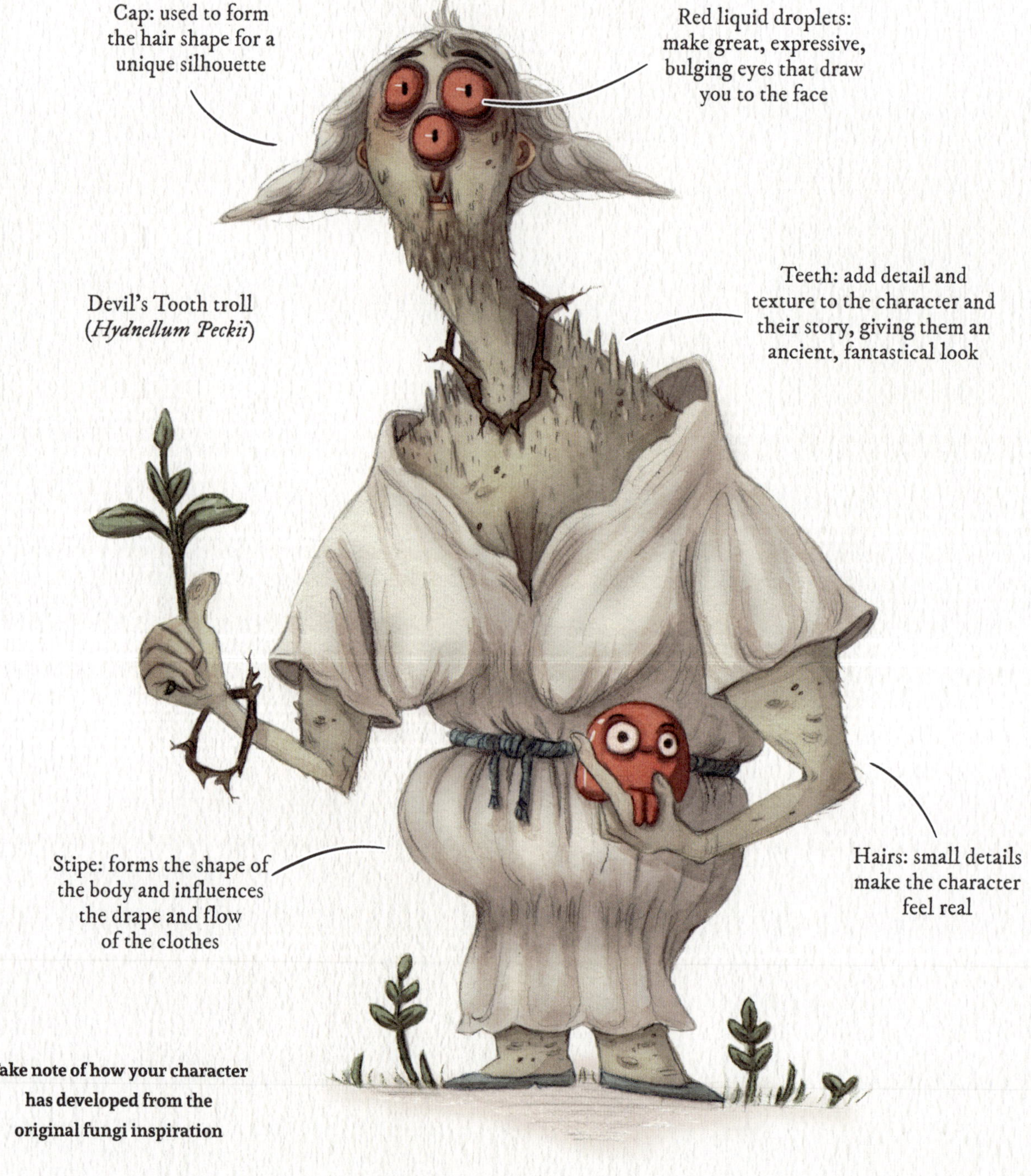

Take note of how your character has developed from the original fungi inspiration

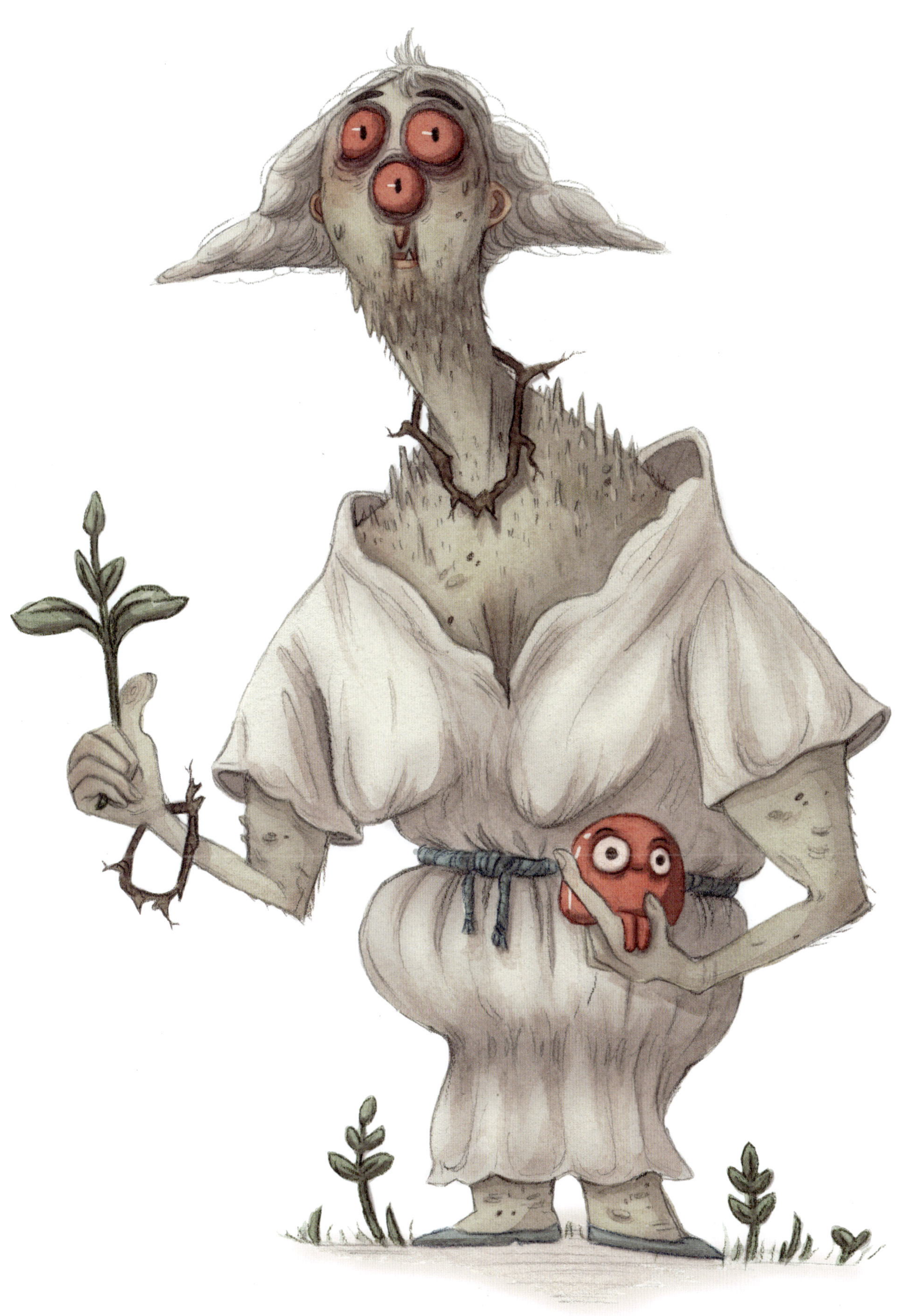

DEVIL'S TOOTH TROLL

Final image © Corah Louise

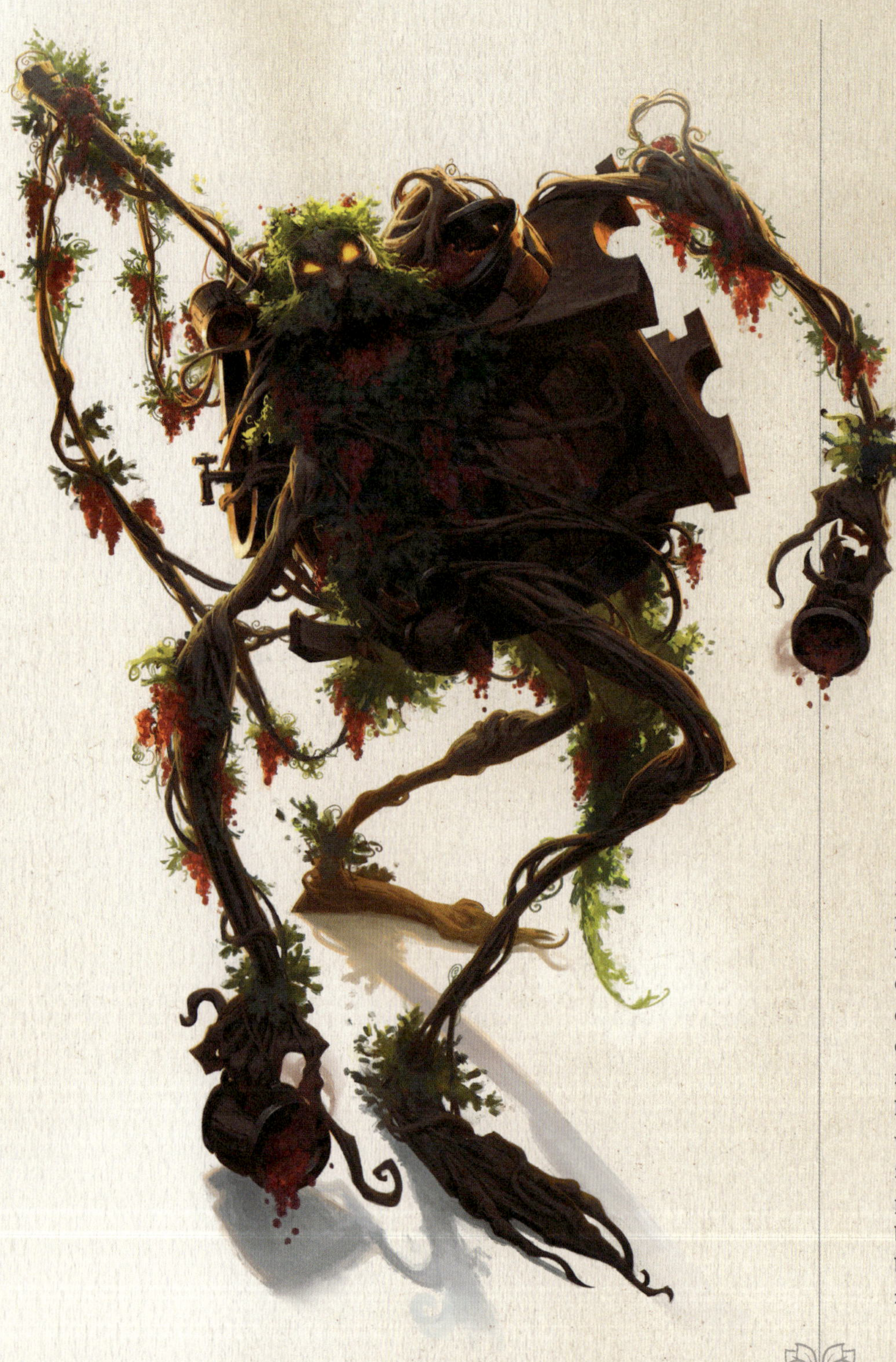

Home of the grapevine, vineyards possess an enchanting mix of nature's magic and manmade order. The grapevine golem character was sparked by the idea of the wilderness taking over and manifesting itself as a crazed, lumbering giant that haunts the vineyards. It also takes inspiration from vines, ivy, and climbing plants in general. This tutorial has been created using digital software, but you can follow along with the materials of your choosing.

vine

GRAPEVINE GOLEM

OGNJEN SPORIN

START WITH RESEARCH

Looking into different types of ivy plants, the grapevine stands out as an option with great storytelling potential. It would be apt to make the character drunk with wine; researching wine-making could lead to various ways to tie the character and his environment together. The creature could be a sort of golem that resides within a giant wine barrel in which the drink is perpetually fermenting. Another idea is that he could be carrying the big container, perhaps strapped to his back somehow, but the concept of the golem inside the barrel is much more innovative and fun.

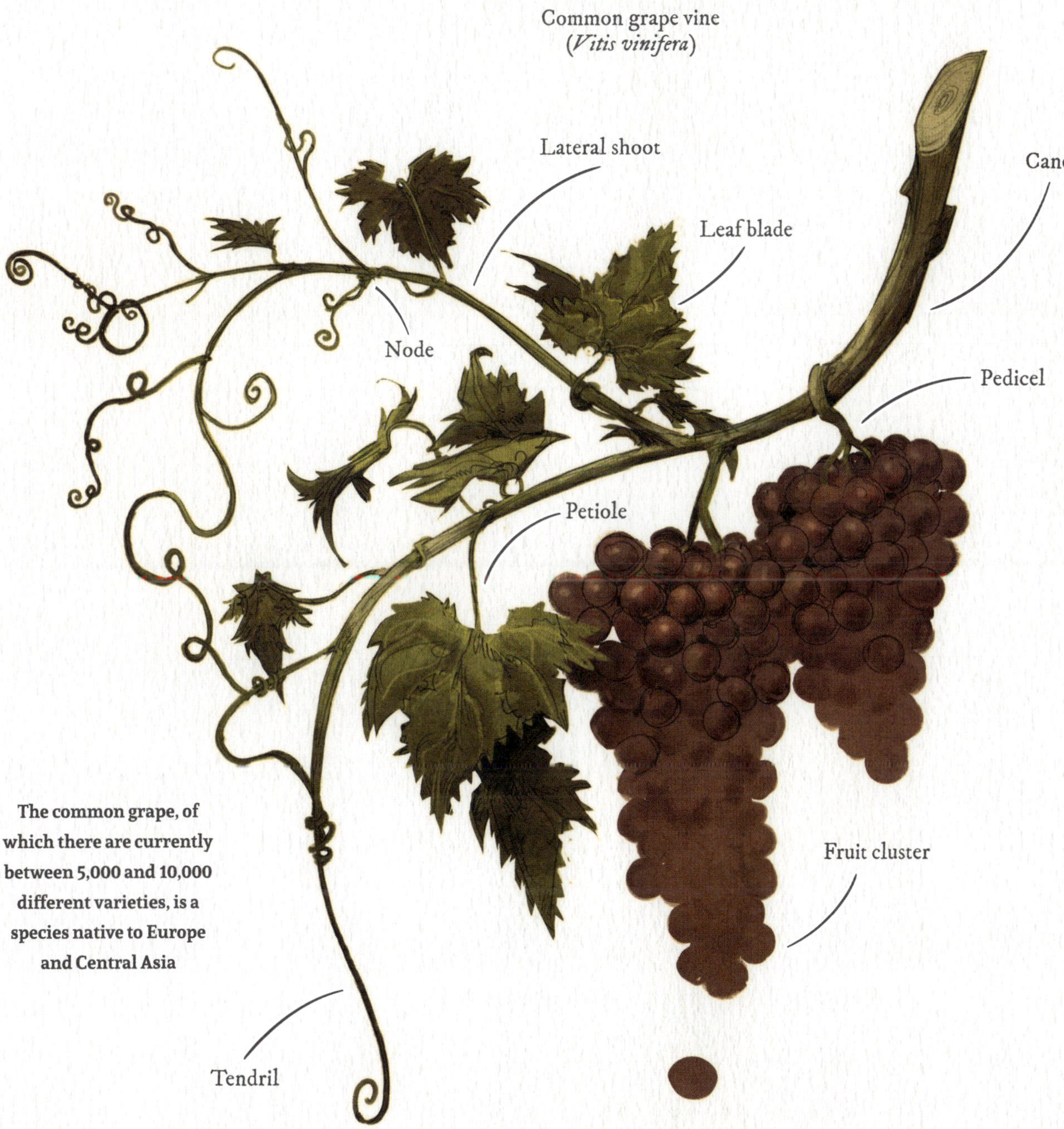

The common grape, of which there are currently between 5,000 and 10,000 different varieties, is a species native to Europe and Central Asia

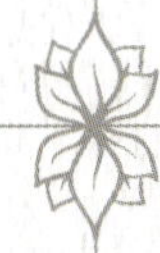

INITIAL SKETCHES

When beginning the sketching process, it's useful to have a reference board to hand, showing the broad idea you've come up with during your research. This idea will often dictate your overall shapes and proportions, which is the case here – a shape language of thin, spindly limbs and a round, broad torso seem already set out for the character.

It bears noting that each character or creature design you tackle will require a slightly different and distinct approach. In some cases, you might want to explore and brainstorm a few different ideas, but in others, you will have a much clearer idea of what you intend. Your sketching process might be iterative, with each sketch tackling only specific parts of the design while leaving others more or less the same, or you might use each sketch to build or expand on the same ideas you had in the previous one.

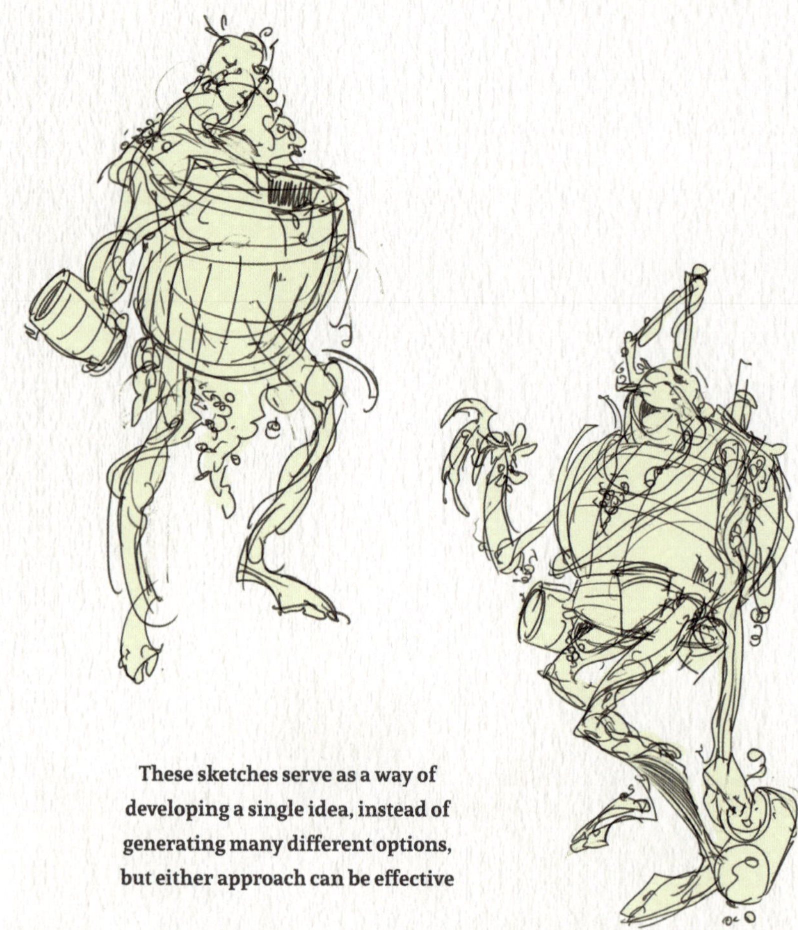

These sketches serve as a way of developing a single idea, instead of generating many different options, but either approach can be effective

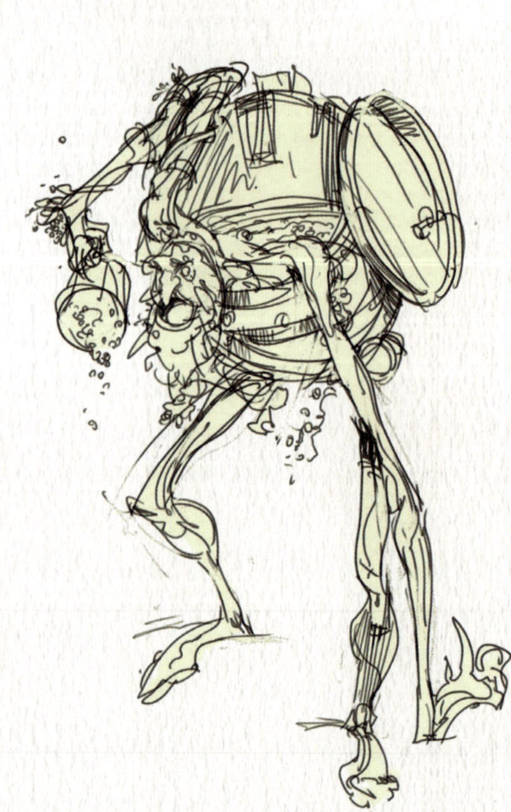

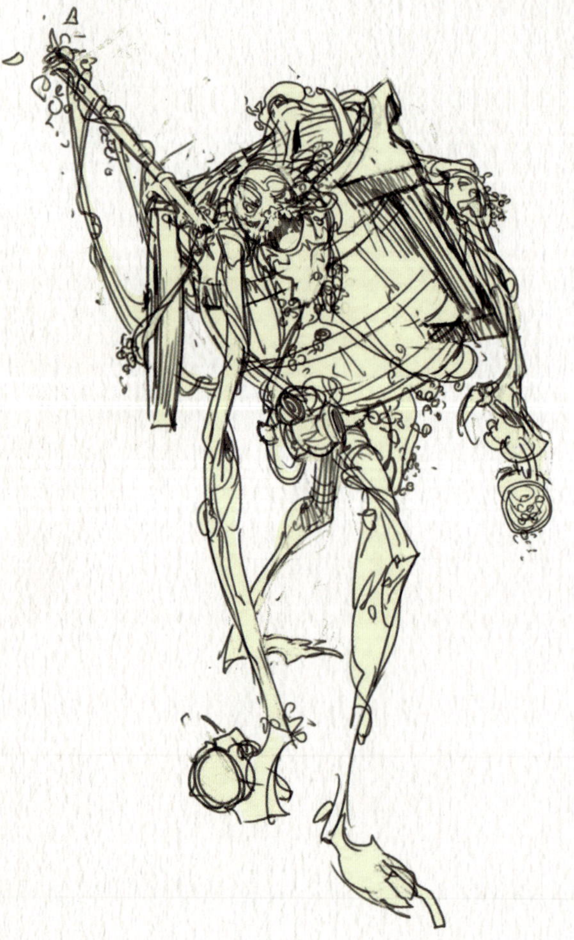

STARTING TO DRAW

If you struggle with transitioning from the sketch or thumbnail stage into building up a final drawing, try to consider the drawing as a separate entity from the thumbnail. Detach yourself from the sketch and don't hesitate to do away with anything and everything that doesn't work well as you refine it. A great, practical way to do this is to start a new drawing from scratch using the thumbnails only as reference, instead of working on top of the sketch.

Before starting the refined sketch, consciously analyse which aspects of the thumbnail work well. As you start drawing, keep those in mind, and try to not only maintain the good qualities but exaggerate them. Staying simple as you block in will allow you to make broad adjustments quickly. The sketch shown here is primarily focused on emphasizing the leaning, expressive posture and 'broad versus thin' shape language. It clearly shows the spindliness of the vines forming the character's limbs.

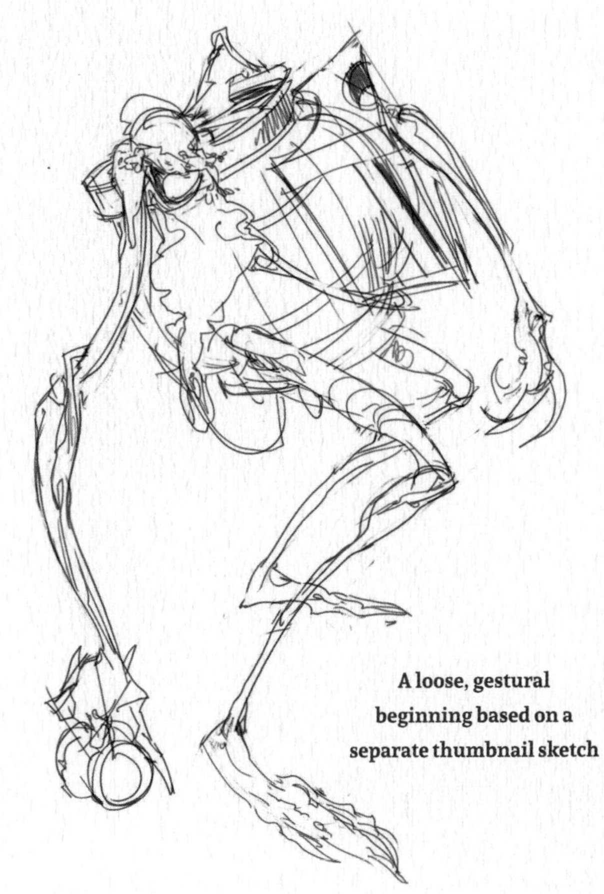

A loose, gestural beginning based on a separate thumbnail sketch

FINISHING THE SKETCH

At this point in the drawing, you can start zeroing in on smaller, more specific elements within the design. It's helpful to recognize the areas that are most difficult within the drawing, ask yourself why they pose a challenge, and focus more attention on them. For example, the barrel stand is a specific 'hard-surface' element that connects with the barrel in a tricky way; it needs to be constructed with precision to be believable. The face is another element that requires more care, in order to capture an intricate, manic, drunken expression. As you refine the drawing, you can also begin to add more details relating to the original plant, such as long, twisting canes for fingers and toes, clusters of grapes, and some leafy areas.

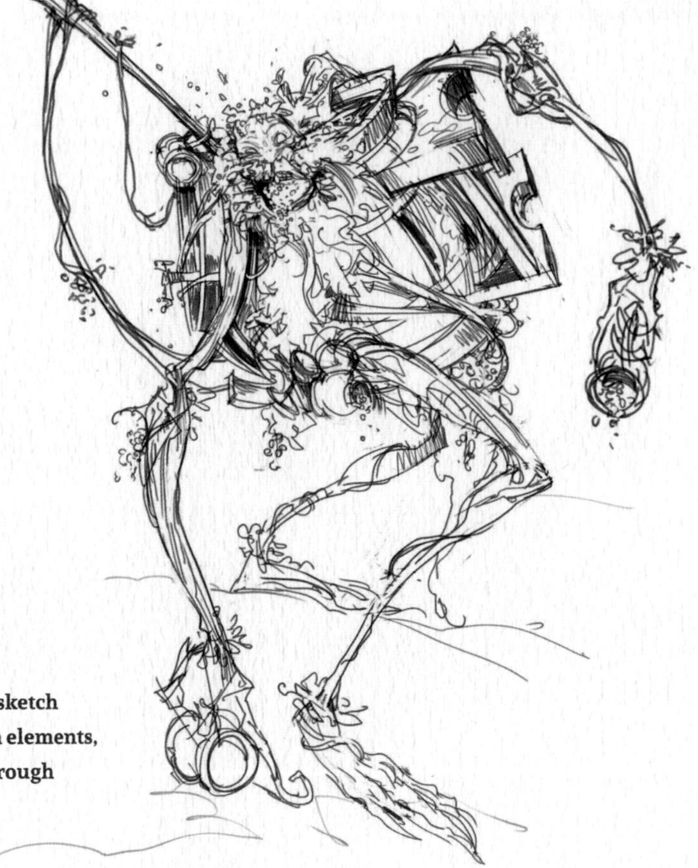

The finished line sketch contains all the design elements, albeit somewhat rough

CONCEPTUALIZING YOUR PROCESS

Each step of the illustrative process, including the drawing, is just a vehicle in service of advancing the image towards the final design. It can be a structured but fragmented process. Try to finish each step only as much as is necessary to move on to the next one. When deciding when to move on, the two factors that play the biggest role are prior experience and understanding of your comfort zone. For example, if creatures and organic objects are well within your comfort zone, you might opt to move on to the painting stage without having refined or detailed the drawing too much. However, if you are a beginner, it's wiser to take the step a bit further than you need, rather than not far enough. This is especially true for the drawing stage, which might be the single most critical piece in the illustration puzzle, upon which the whole painting is later built.

STARTING THE UNDERPAINTING

At this point, the sketch is taken as far as you need, so you can begin applying colour. Tint the lines a brownish colour and block in the silhouette with a flat hue. Start laying a very rough pass of umber values on top – not very careful or detailed at all, but just roughly indicating both local values and shadow/light shapes. Using semi-transparent strokes will help you to organically cover up the sketch.

This design will be lit by an ambient light source, without many strong or elaborate light and shadow patterns. Note how most of the leaves are grouped together to act as a beard and hair for the golem, but their specific shapes aren't indicated – only their overall shape and mass.

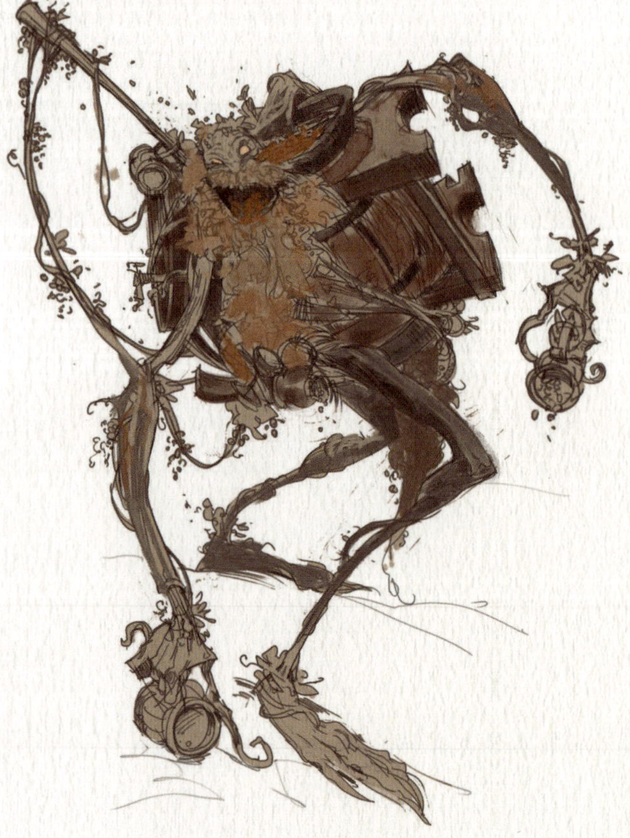

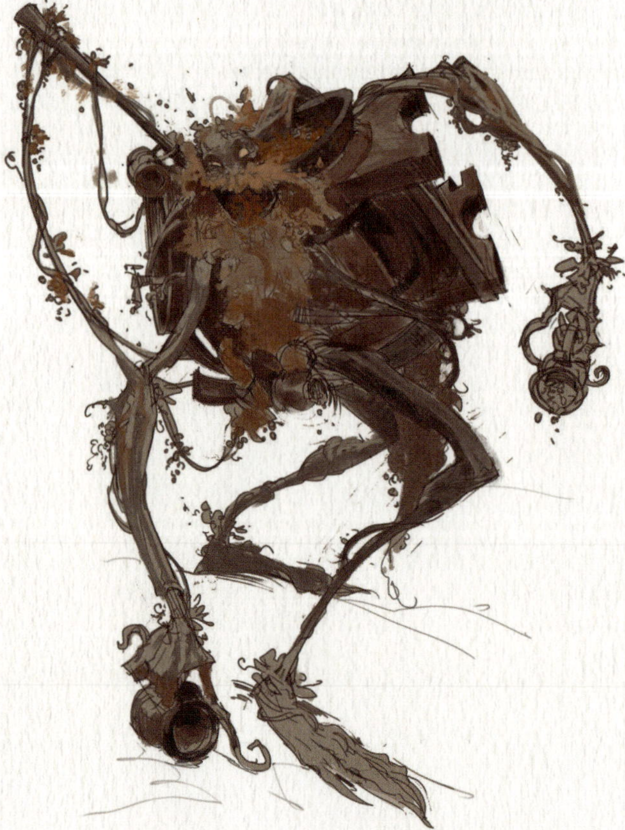

A rough colour foundation establishes the general light direction and value grouping

REFINING THE UNDERPAINTING

Continue to build upon the umber base, using more opaque strokes at this point. You can begin to add or change some smaller design elements, such as adding little vines or barrel boards, picking out the moustache as a separate volume, and adding more roundness and volume to the beard. Even though grapevines don't have big leafy canopies like this, you can take that artistic liberty with your design choice, counting on the fruit, overall structure, and wine barrel to clearly indicate the plant from which the creature is made.

In general, traditionally, an underpainting's use is twofold. It both establishes the light and value, and lays in a rich base colour that will shine through the strokes of thicker paint and create an additional layer of vibrancy. This is exactly the effect you are trying to achieve here, especially in the leafy areas. They will be greener and cooler later, so saturating the oranges in the underpainting will create colour accents that will punch through even in the final image. The brown areas of the vines will remain more or less the same.

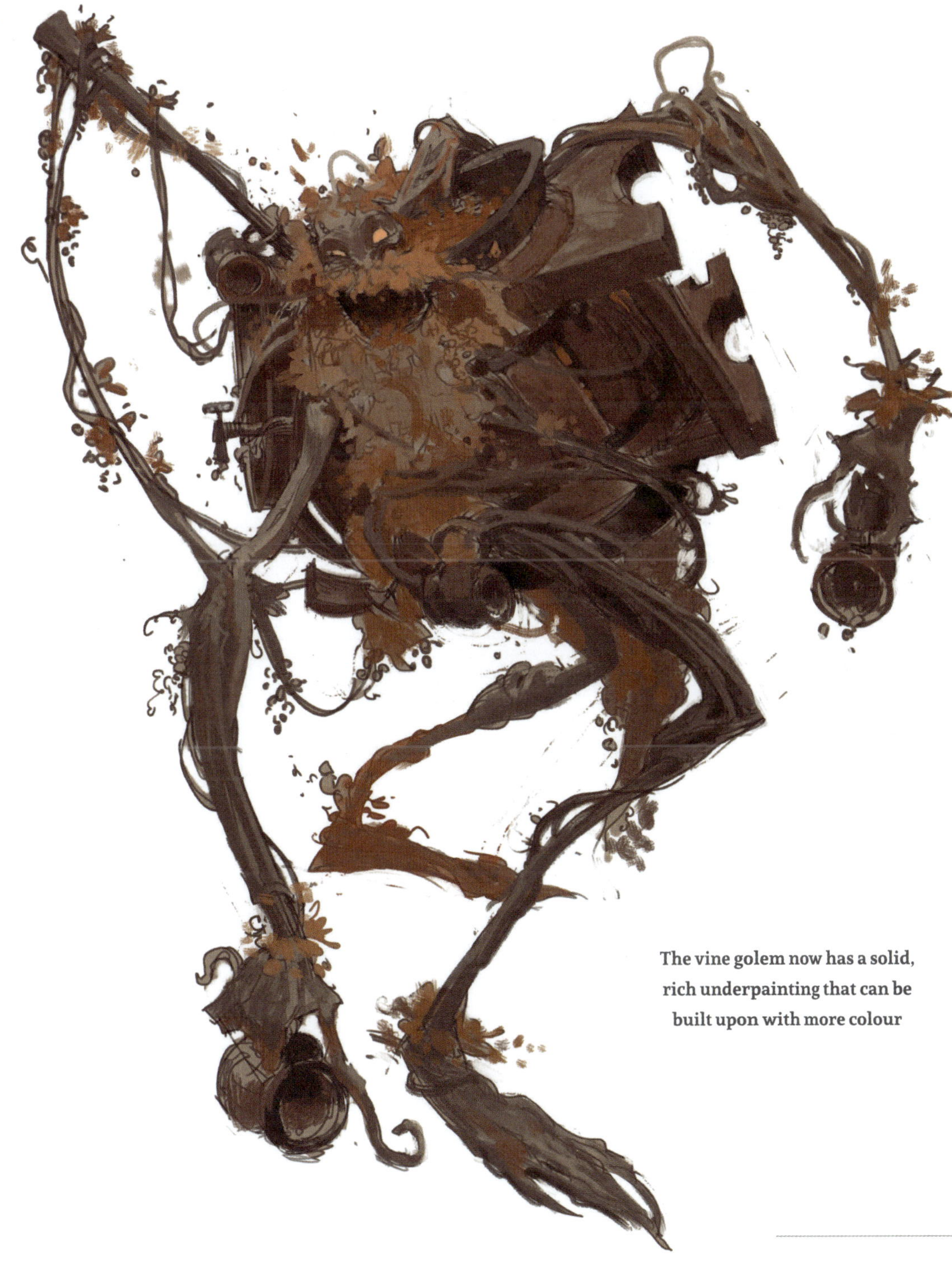

The vine golem now has a solid, rich underpainting that can be built upon with more colour

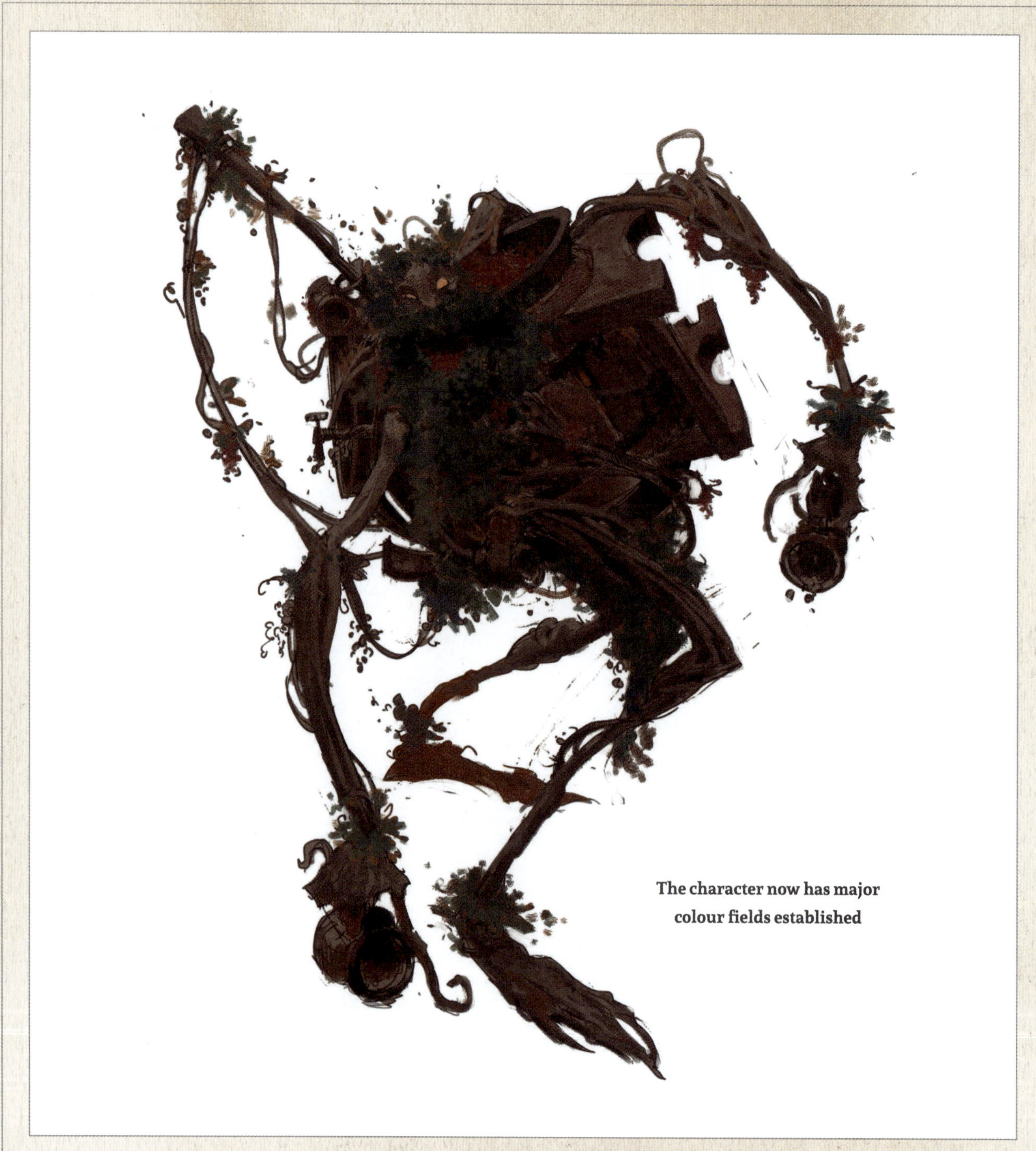

The character now has major colour fields established

ADDING INITIAL COLOURS

With the base tone in place, you can begin to build up the character's actual colours. Start laying in rough colours using thicker strokes and short, choppy movements, still using a large brush, trying to leave some underpainting colour showing through beneath. Red grapes create a complementary accent to the green of the leaves – purple or white grapes would not achieve the same 'pop'.

Don't bother with cleaning or tidying anything up yet – just focus on bringing the image towards its final colour and value range. It's helpful to focus on the most important task at hand at each step of your process, whatever those steps may be, so that your approach is more streamlined and linear. Most of the speed in painting comes from focus and decisiveness, rather than painting the actual strokes quickly.

FINAL ROUGH COLOURS

Continue building up the image, focusing on nearing the final value range and really emphasizing the value grouping of the silhouette. Since the character is lit with ambient lighting from slightly above, you should indicate this as simply as you can – make the planes that face upwards lighter, while darkening everything that faces downwards. The other big tool in creating form and depth is ambient occlusion, which is the soft, gradual darkening in and around the deeper nooks and crevices. Make sure to clearly model the roundness, lankiness, and twisting depth of the trunks and canes that make up the limbs.

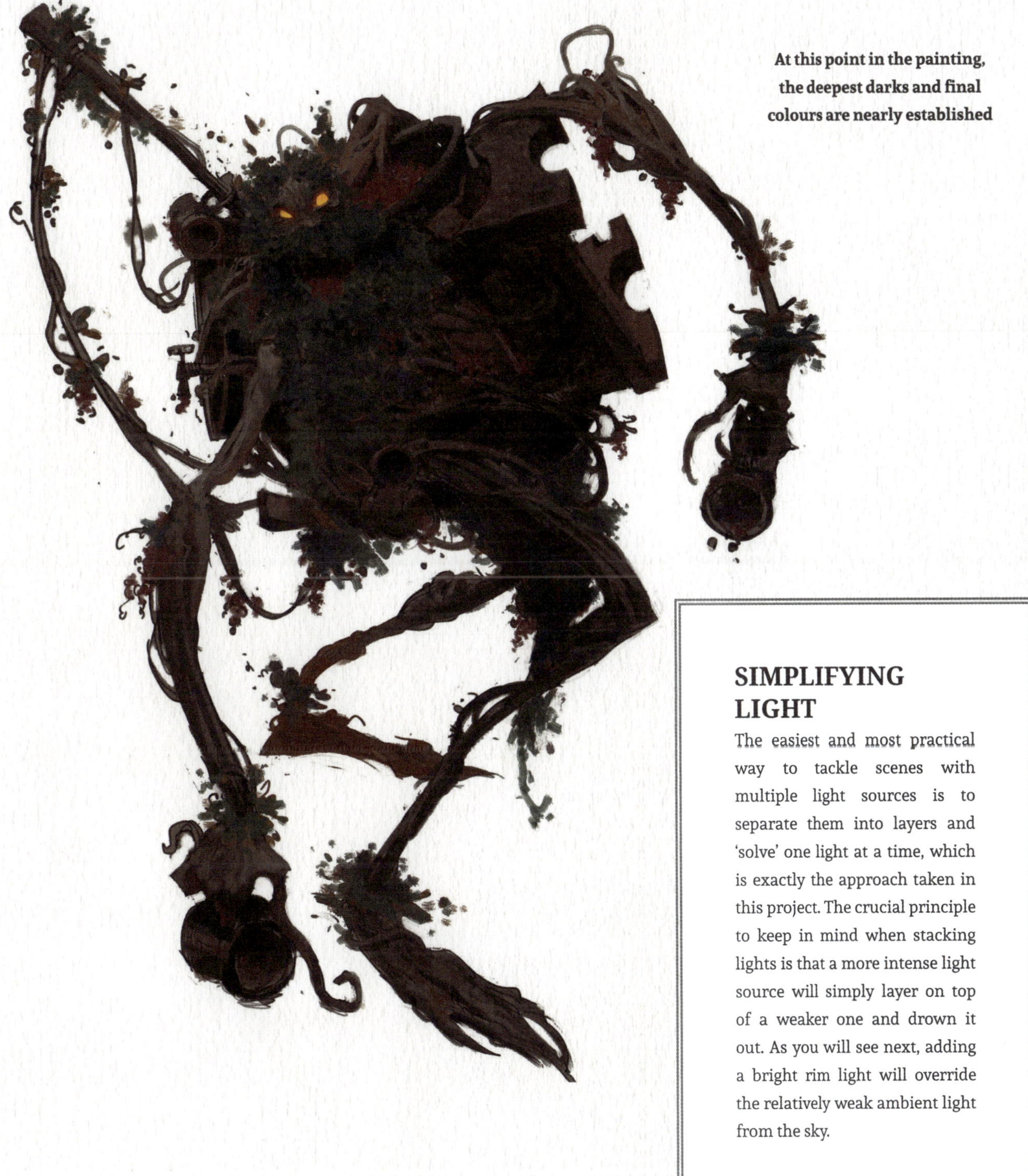

At this point in the painting, the deepest darks and final colours are nearly established

SIMPLIFYING LIGHT

The easiest and most practical way to tackle scenes with multiple light sources is to separate them into layers and 'solve' one light at a time, which is exactly the approach taken in this project. The crucial principle to keep in mind when stacking lights is that a more intense light source will simply layer on top of a weaker one and drown it out. As you will see next, adding a bright rim light will override the relatively weak ambient light from the sky.

ADDING RIM LIGHT

Once you're sufficiently satisfied with how far you have rendered the character in shadow, you can add the most intense light source, which will come from the back and silhouette the whole figure. If you find yourself overwhelmed when trying to light something, try to see the object as an abstract amalgamation of big, simplified planes. Imagine how those planes relate to the direction of the light source; the more perpendicular the angle between the light and the plane, the brighter the plane would be. As with most principles in art, the idea is simple but the execution is very difficult at first; practising with simple geometric forms is a great way to build up to lighting actual figures, faces, and creatures.

When it comes to rim lighting specifically, the worst mistake you can make when trying to add depth and dimension to an image is to use it as a simple outline. Notice here how the light comes into the silhouette, helping to describe overlapping forms and changing surfaces. The rim light on the golem's limbs emphasizes the long, spindly shapes inspired by the grapevine.

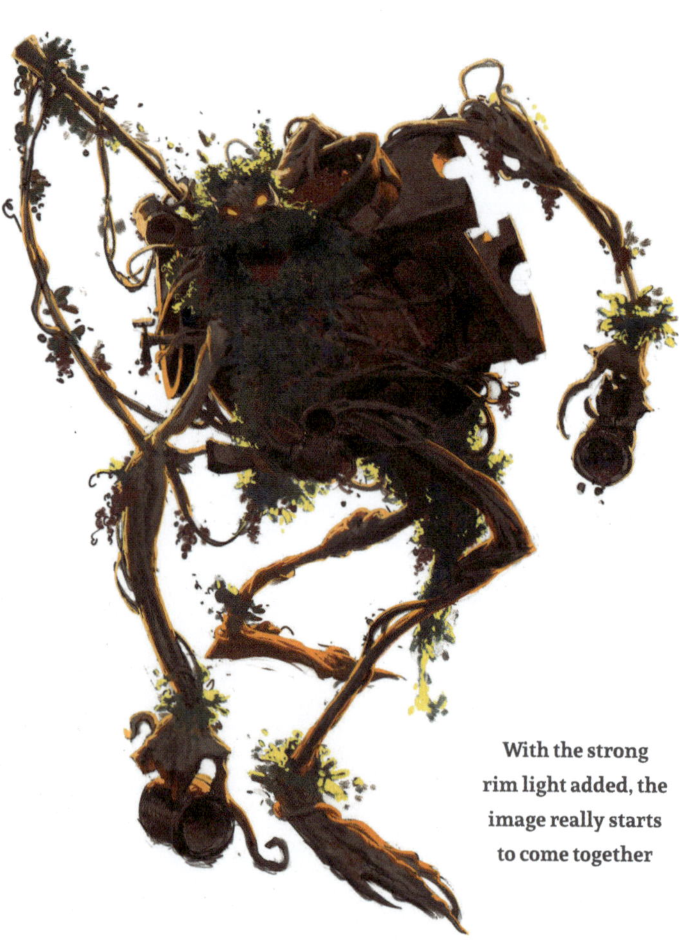

With the strong rim light added, the image really starts to come together

SUBSURFACE SCATTERING

Subsurface scattering is a light effect that occurs in materials that are slightly translucent, such as skin, leaves, fruit, milk, or wax. The light will hit the surface of the object and mostly bounce off it, but some light will come through the outer layer of the material, bounce around, and come out again. This visually causes a saturated, warm, glowing effect. This design presents many great opportunities to employ subsurface scattering and create some attractive colour accents.

Only after adding subsurface scattering do the red grapes really start to stand out. The strong pops of saturation attract the eye and emphasize the species of plant from which this giant is built. The punches of warm green help convey the leaf material more clearly.

At this stage, you can also add a drop-off in the rim light, so the head and upper torso are highlighted and the areas that are lower or closer to the viewer receive less or no light. Adding a cast shadow underneath the golem grounds the character in space.

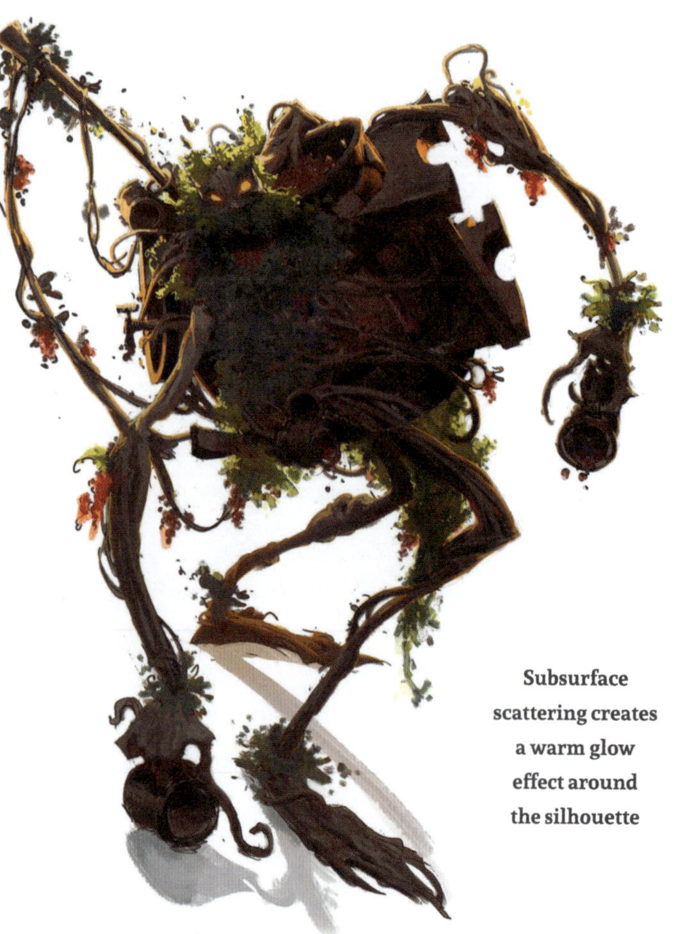

Subsurface scattering creates a warm glow effect around the silhouette

REFINING & CLARIFYING

With all the major elements now laid in, it's important to consider the overall clarity and readability of the character design. This is also a good time to ask a few trusted people for feedback, regardless of whether they are artists or not. Any comment you get, especially if it's the same comment from multiple people, needs to be considered very seriously. Try to separate yourself from the image in order to analyse it objectively. In this case, the feedback received is that the golem's head, especially the face, is hard to find.

This problem can be tackled by simplifying the hair shape, adding a nose, and trying to bring the head outside of the silhouette a little more. A cut-off branch for the nose achieves an iconic shape and a more immediately recognizable face. Extending and twisting some of the fingers and toes, to look more like grape cordons or canes, emphasizes the grapevine theme even further.

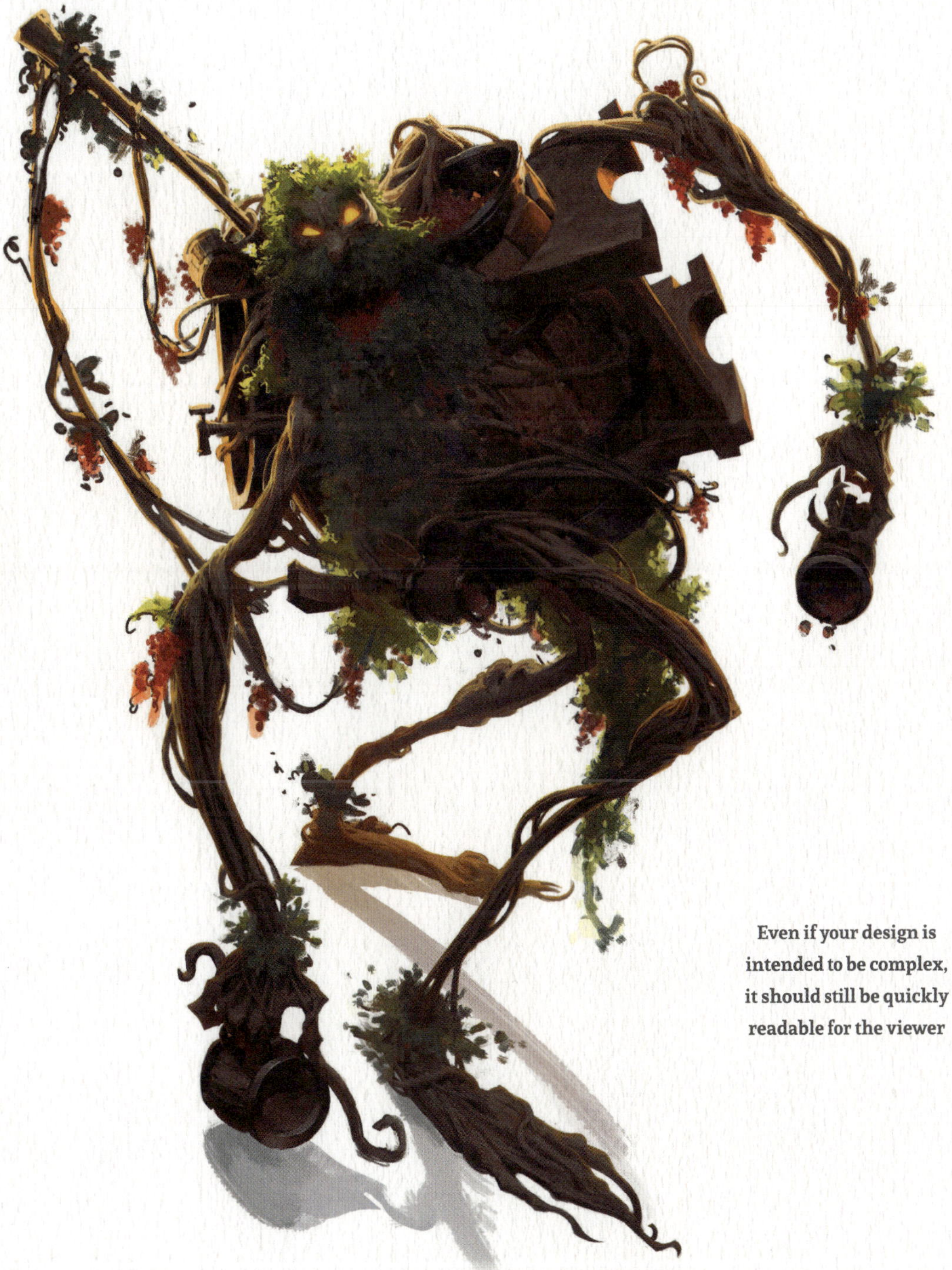

Even if your design is intended to be complex, it should still be quickly readable for the viewer

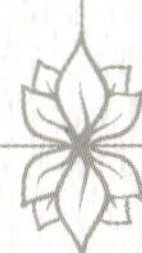

RENDERING & DETAILING

Most beginners tend to equate rendering with detailing, and to a certain degree, they are similar. However, a better way to think of it is asking yourself, 'As I render, how can I describe the form and materials in more detail, without undermining the qualities that the image already has?' Refining and detailing are a given at this point in the process, but maintaining (or even improving) the shapes, gestures, and expression is the difficult part – the goal to strive towards.

To ensure you don't mess up by over-detailing, it's helpful to constantly compare your progress to previous versions of the image. You can save these snapshots of your progress as JPEGs and place them on top of the file you're working on. Every so often, when you feel satisfied with rendering a chunk of the painting, open up a previous work-in-progress and use it as a guide to stay on track and check if you have truly improved on the issues you identified in them.

The design is becoming more polished now, including more small features of the plant's anatomy, such as thin tendrils, separate leaf shapes, and more grape clusters on the golem's beard.

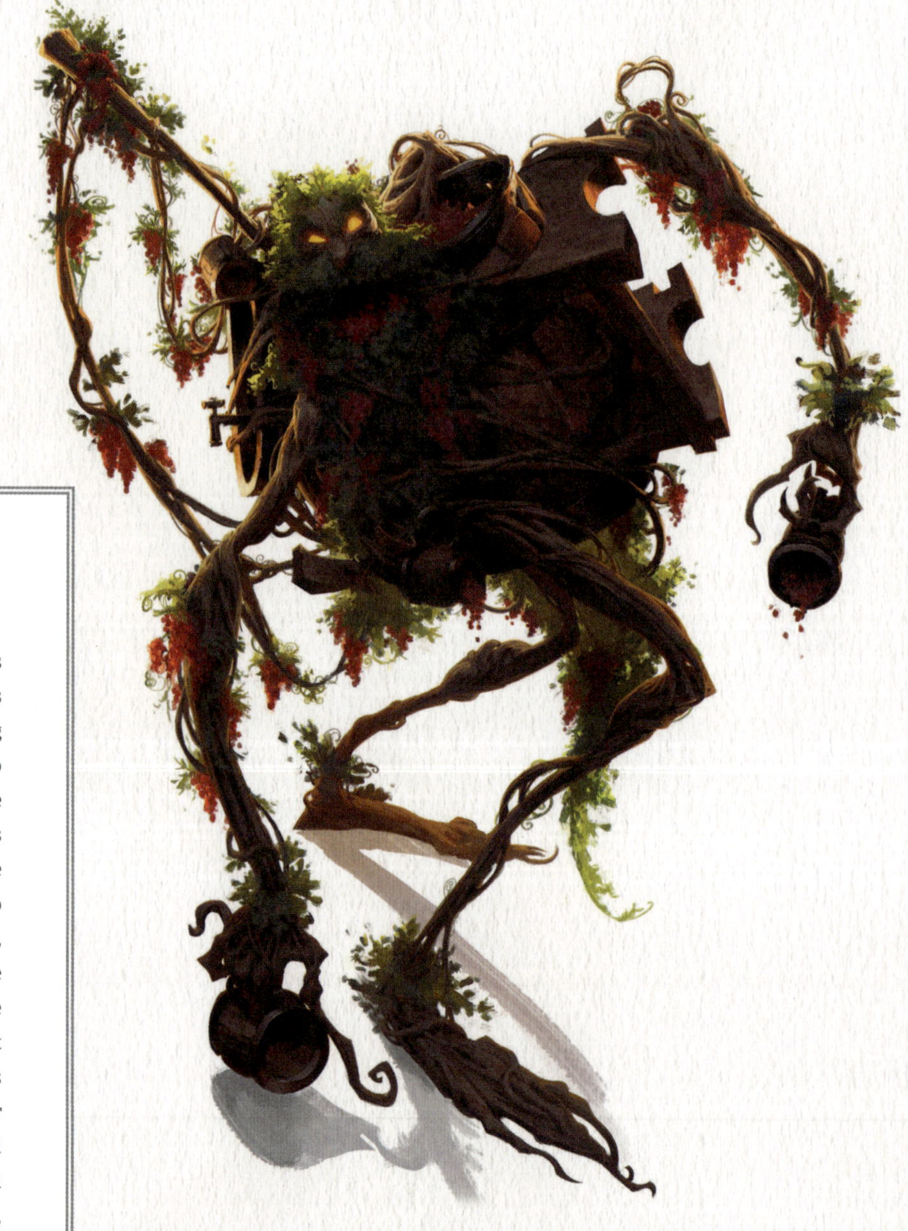

Rendering without overdoing detail is a skill that takes practice and frequent checks against previous versions

HAVE PATIENCE WITH RENDERING

Rendering can be very arduous and monotonous at times. As you move further into detailing the image, progress seems to slow down to a crawl, with the image changing visually less and less as you spend more and more time on it. It helps to listen to audiobooks or music, or to hang out with friends while performing these more mundane parts of the process. Just don't forget to keep taking small breaks to analyse your image! Another alleviating factor to keep in mind is that the more experience you have with polishing an image, the easier, more predictable, and more enjoyable it becomes.

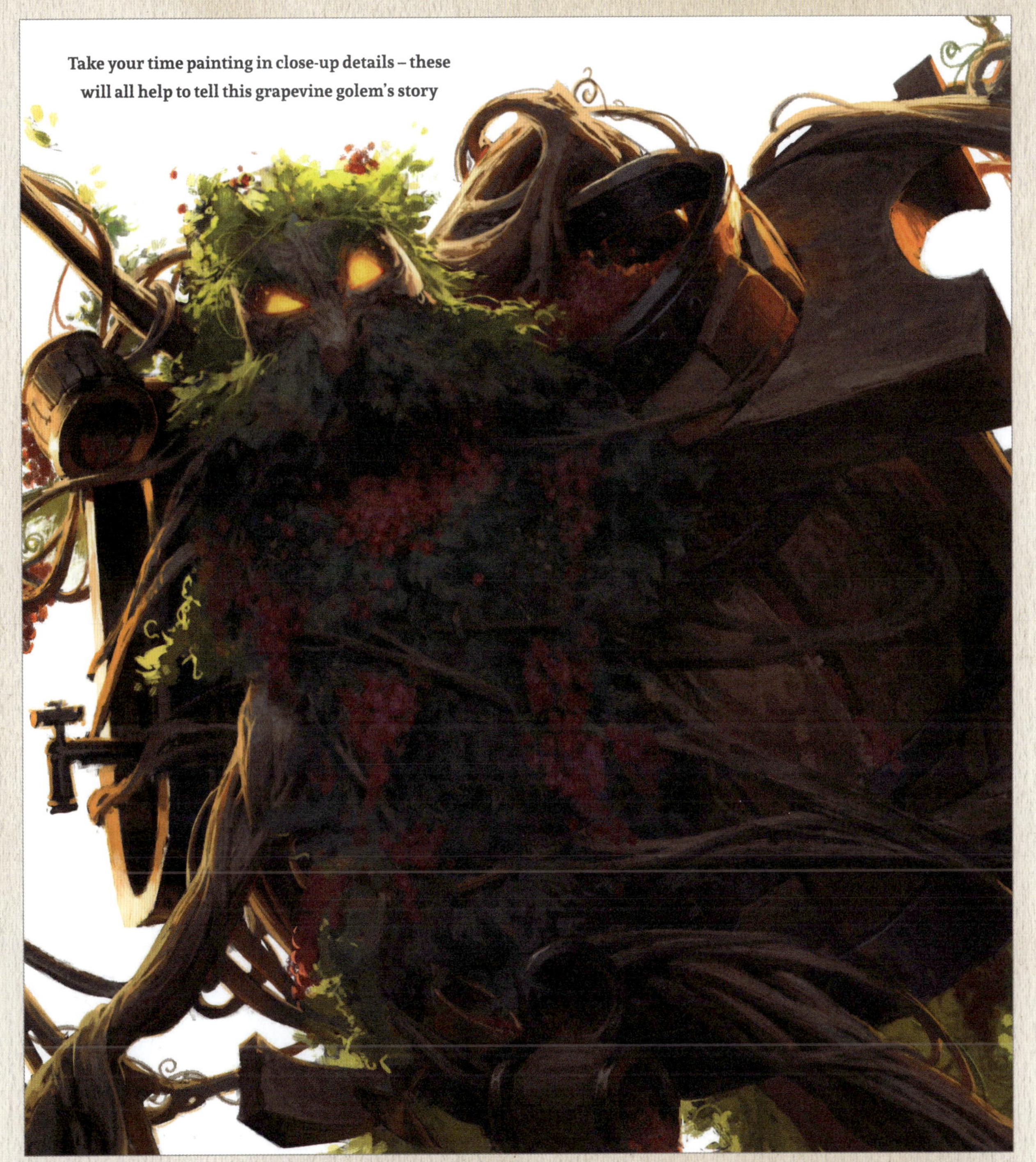

Take your time painting in close-up details – these will all help to tell this grapevine golem's story

CLOSE-UP DETAILS

By this point, the design doesn't really change, but only grows more detailed. In most cases, you will want to apply special care and attention to the areas with the largest amount of interest. When it comes to a humanoid character, the face, upper torso, and hands will tend to be the focal points of the design. Areas that are far away or strongly overlapped are good examples of places where you would want to apply less detail and contrast. Creating a good hierarchy of polish ensures that the image doesn't appear too stale or overworked – you will maintain a nice degree of freshness and brushiness in some areas, and a good amount of detail and crispness in others. Add final elements such as fermenting grapes and small grape shapes flying off outside the silhouette to capture the golem's drunken persona.

EVALUATING THE DETAILS

Final little tweaks and effects – such as liquefying, filters, glow, or particles – are added at the very last stage of the render. Enhance the atmospheric perspective on the leg to create some stronger depth; you can do this by fading it a little from the top, to simulate mist. See if there are any parts of the head and face that can be tweaked and improved by changing the shapes, adding more detailing, or introducing more rim light – this area needs to be readable from afar. Finalize the cast shadow by softening it in some areas and adding a little colour variation to it.

Here you can see how this giant golem derives inspiration from grapevines and vineyards. Twisted limbs burst out of the wooden barrel that forms the main mass of his lumbering silhouette. The smaller parts of the plant, such as leaves and fruit, are grouped into specific areas and features, while the big trunks and canes form the creature's frame. The clusters of green foliage and bunches of shining red grapes create a complementary pair that fits naturally with the warm browns of the golem's body.

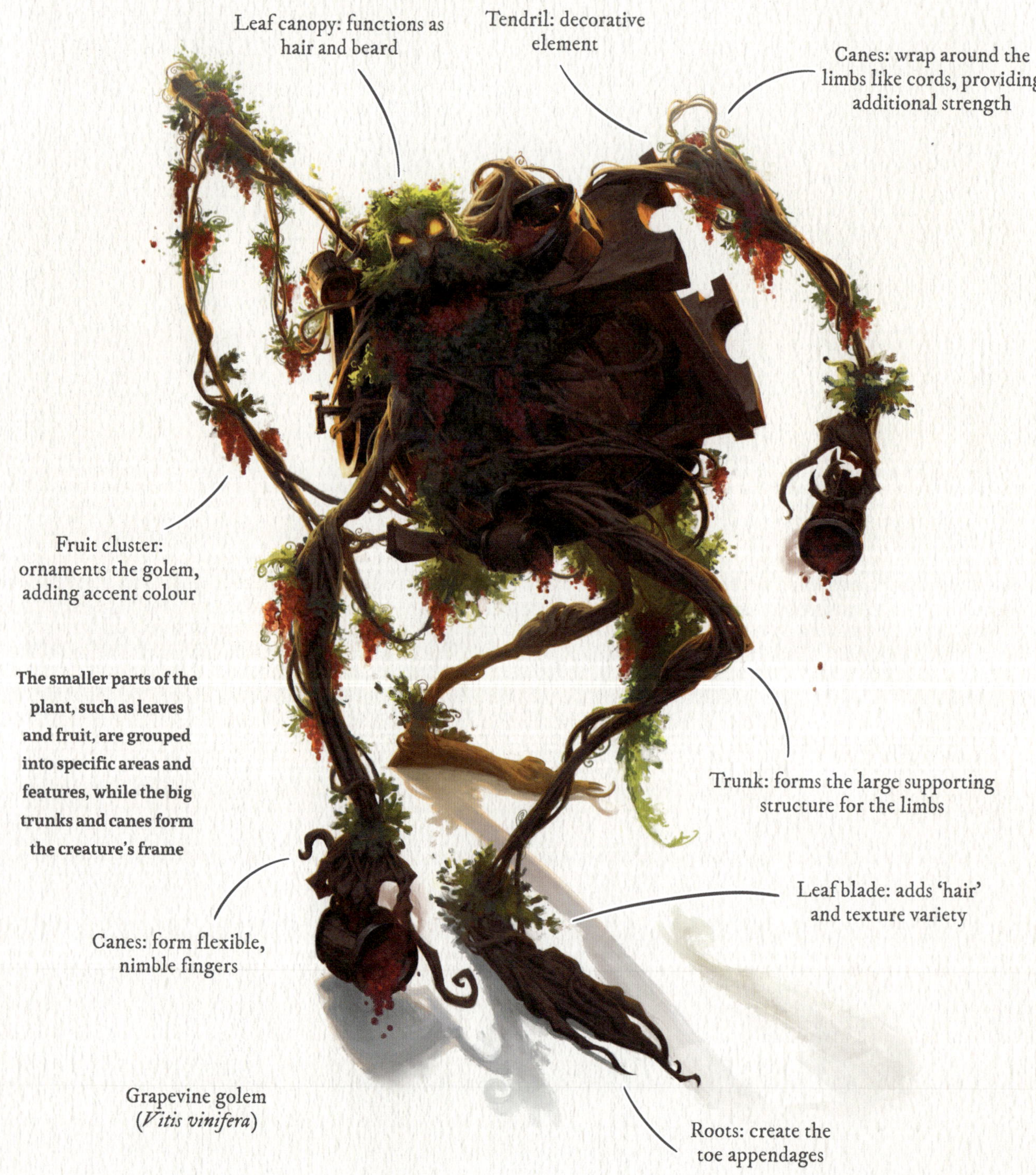

The smaller parts of the plant, such as leaves and fruit, are grouped into specific areas and features, while the big trunks and canes form the creature's frame

Grapevine golem (*Vitis vinifera*)

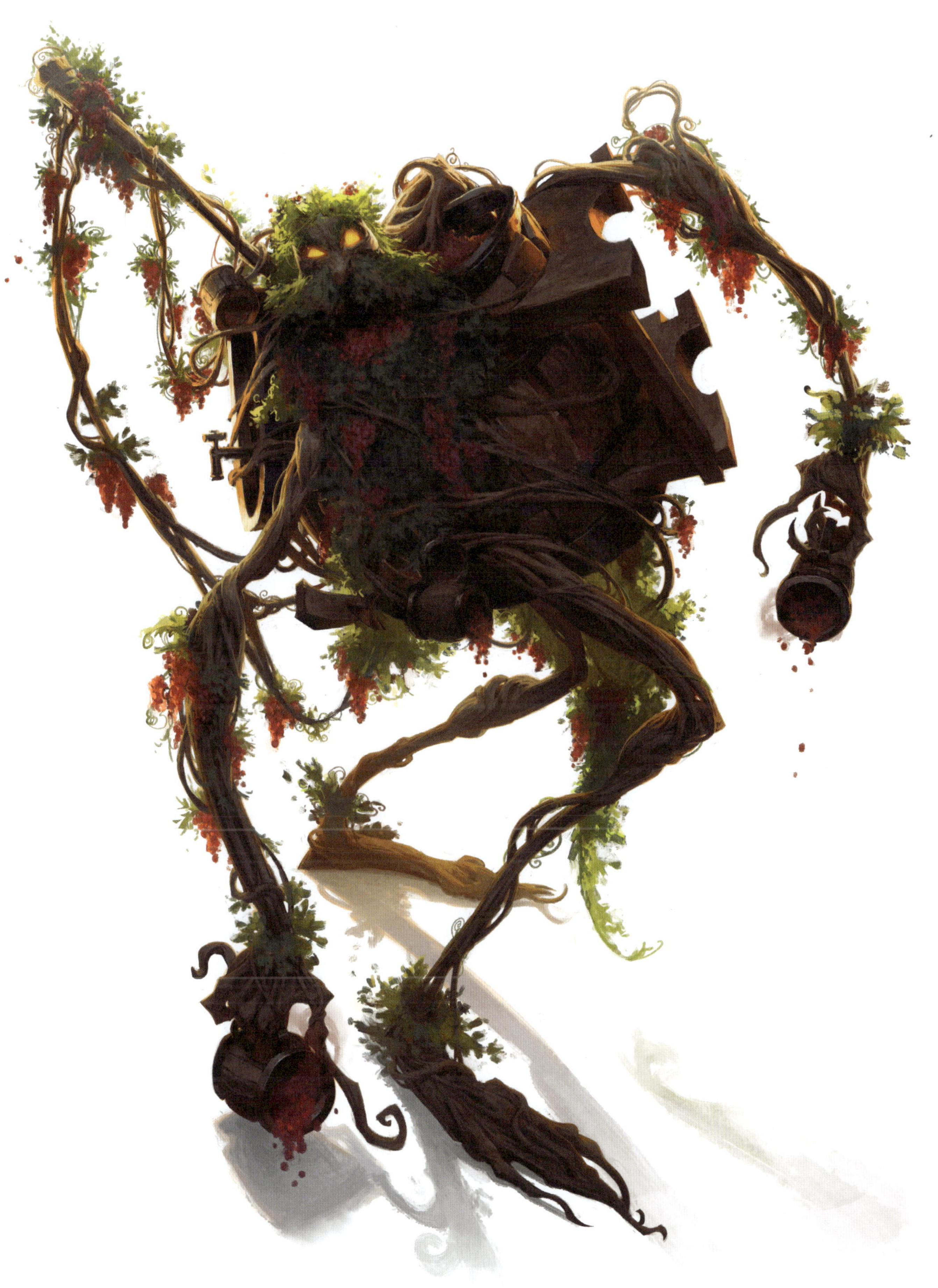

GRAPEVINE GOLEM

Final image © Ognjen Sporin

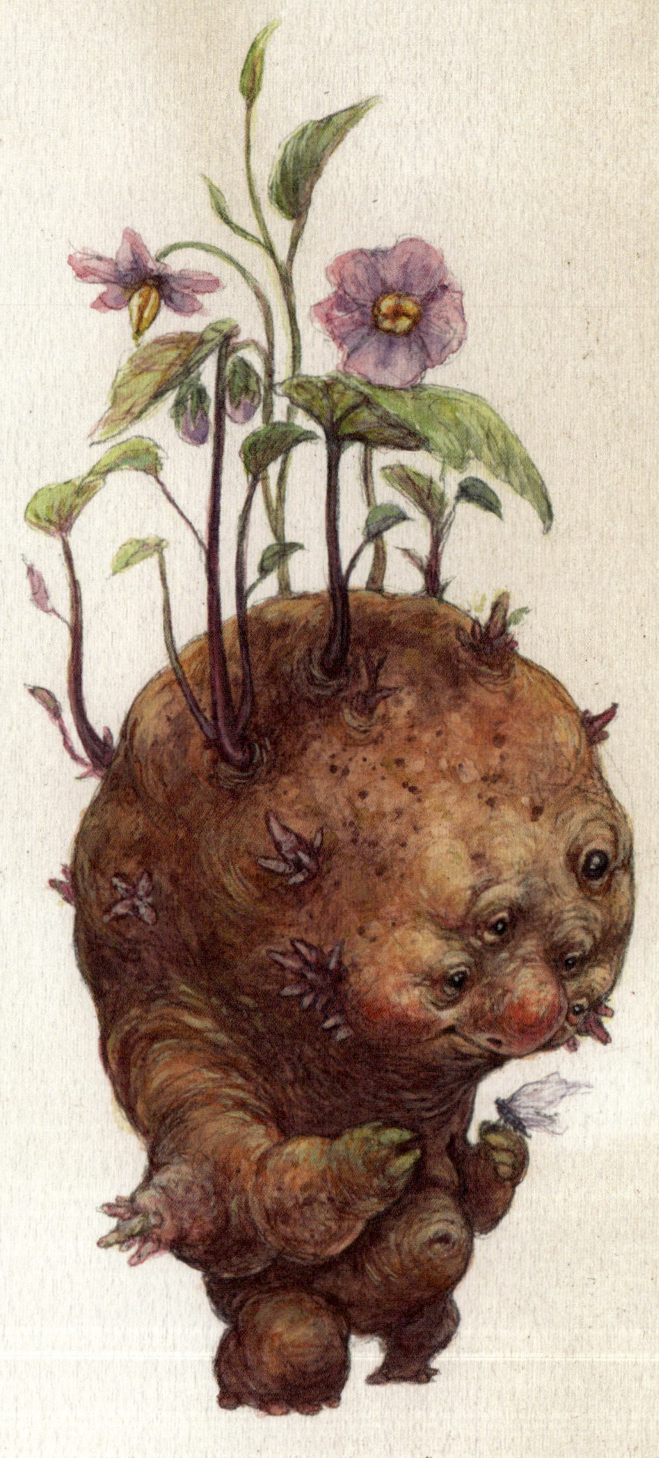

A member of the Solanaceae, or nightshade, family, the potato is a rustic root vegetable and dietary staple around the world. Many overlook its tuberous form as plain, ordinary, and mundane, but what if there was more than met the eye? What if this unassuming tuber were a peaceful creature, burrowed deep in the underground world of the vegetable patch?

Over the following pages, this tutorial will demonstrate how to turn the humble potato into a shy but adorable ground-dwelling creature called the potato pixie. The final character will be painted in watercolours, coloured pencils, and gouache, but you can follow along with the materials you have to hand. Anything in nature can be used as inspiration for an interesting character design – it's all about pausing, noticing, and letting the ideas come.

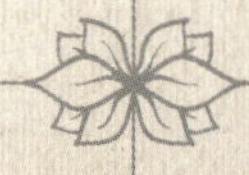

vegetable

POTATO PIXIE

IRIS COMPIET

RESEARCH & REFERENCE

Start by writing down as many different potatoes as you can think of. Research rare or forgotten potatoes, plus varieties you're not familiar with. Look for potatoes that have interesting characteristics you could work into a design. Even the standard potato has some quirky elements to work with. It has flowers, fruit, and leaves, plus lots of variation in shape, colour, and texture. It also goes through various stages as it ages. It's a common enough vegetable that you may well have it in your home to study first-hand, allowing you to watch as it grows wrinkly or starts to sprout over time. Finding reference images online is a great alternative as well. Collect lots of potato images, for example from a site like Pinterest, and create a reference board of inspiration.

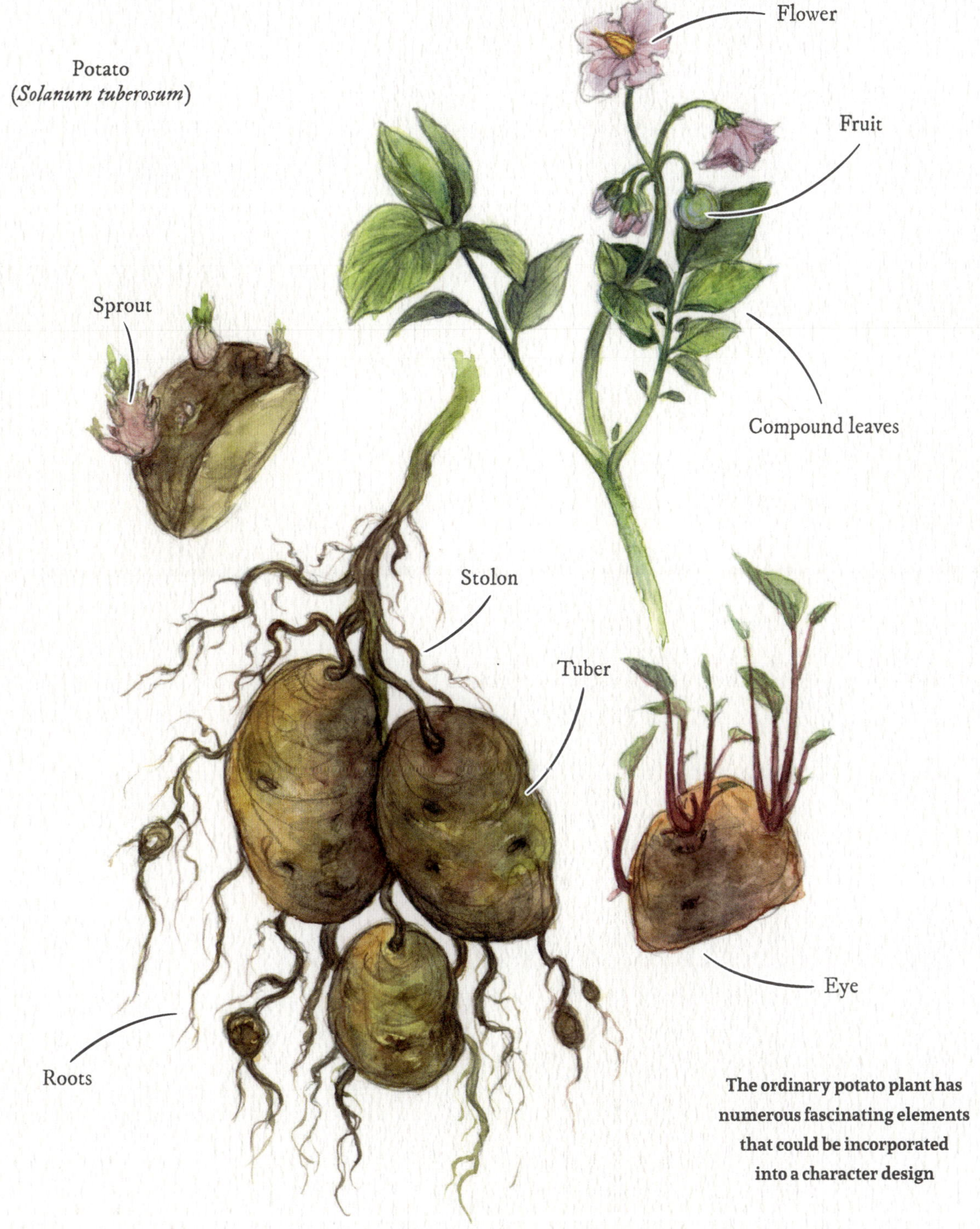

The ordinary potato plant has numerous fascinating elements that could be incorporated into a character design

SHAPES & SILHOUETTES

Begin by sketching rough shapes and silhouettes, rather than immediately jumping in and working on a concept for your character. Focus on creating interesting shapes, filling a page with rough sketches. Approaching the design in this way leaves a lot open to your imagination; you're not really thinking about the final design or what the character should look like. As you create these shapes, you should start to get a feel for the subject and the elements you want to incorporate and focus on. Slowly an idea will start to form and you will begin to get a sense of a story for the character.

The shapes where the top is heavier and bigger make for an interesting silhouette, whereas the elongated shapes feel goofy and silly. The pronounced hunch that seems to seamlessly morph into the character's head already hints at who the character could be: a kind, caring, and somewhat shy being.

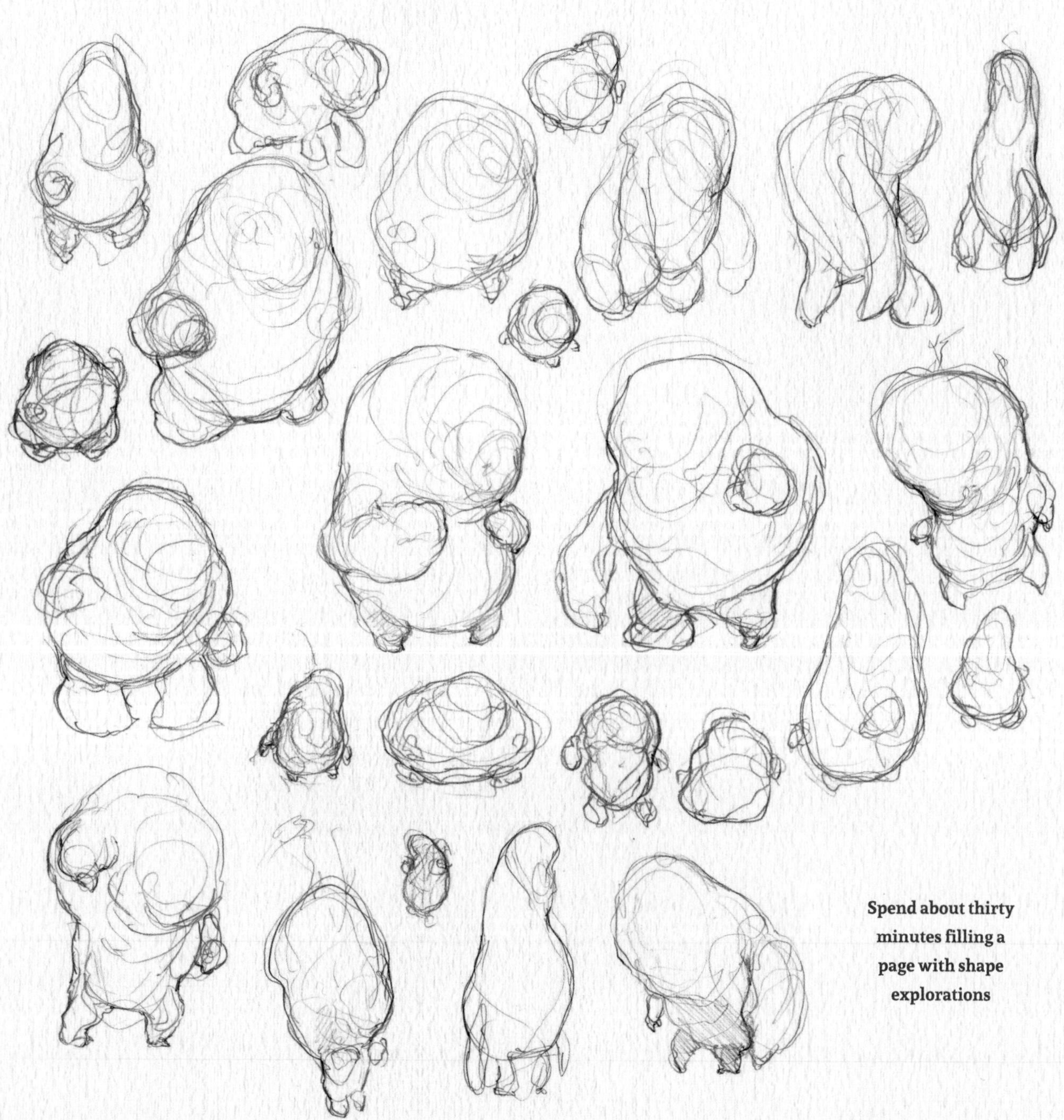

Spend about thirty minutes filling a page with shape explorations

FURTHER EXPLORATION

After sketching a reasonable amount of different shapes, choose the ones you like best and feel have the potential to be explored further. Which are the ones where the character feels top-heavy? Does it need to be even more bulbous? And what about its arms and legs? Those could be formed from sprouts, the little nubs turned into fingers and toes. Experiment with the proportions to see what happens if you give the base shape longer legs, shorter arms, or even multiple arms. The proportions you give your character conveys something about their story, so think about how you can communicate their personality.

Here the longer legs make it feel too big and take away from the sense of the character being shy. Keeping its limbs close to its head and stomach makes it feel more introverted, which is the personality you're trying to convey.

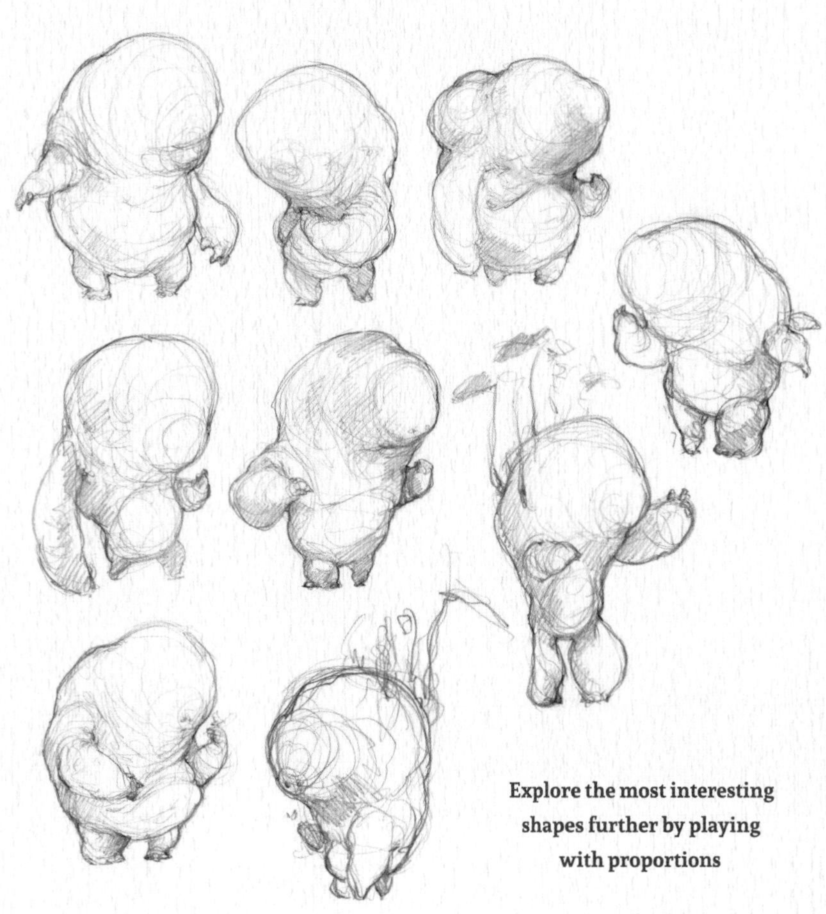

Explore the most interesting shapes further by playing with proportions

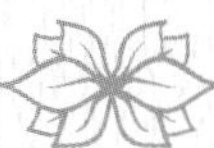

POSES

The focus up until now has been on the character's body shape, bulbous and slightly misshapen, much like potatoes can be. Besides playing with proportions and shape, you can also use pose to help tell your character's story. Sketch out various options to figure out which is the best pose to portray this character's caring nature, while also retaining enough of an interesting silhouette. What does it look like when this character is sitting down, running after something, or lying down? Maybe it's holding something small in its hand, like an insect. Not only does a pose like this help with the narrative, but it also provides a sense of scale. Feel free to make these pose sketches quite rough, as you're just trying to figure out what works; going into too much detail now would be distracting.

Find the best pose to convey your character's story

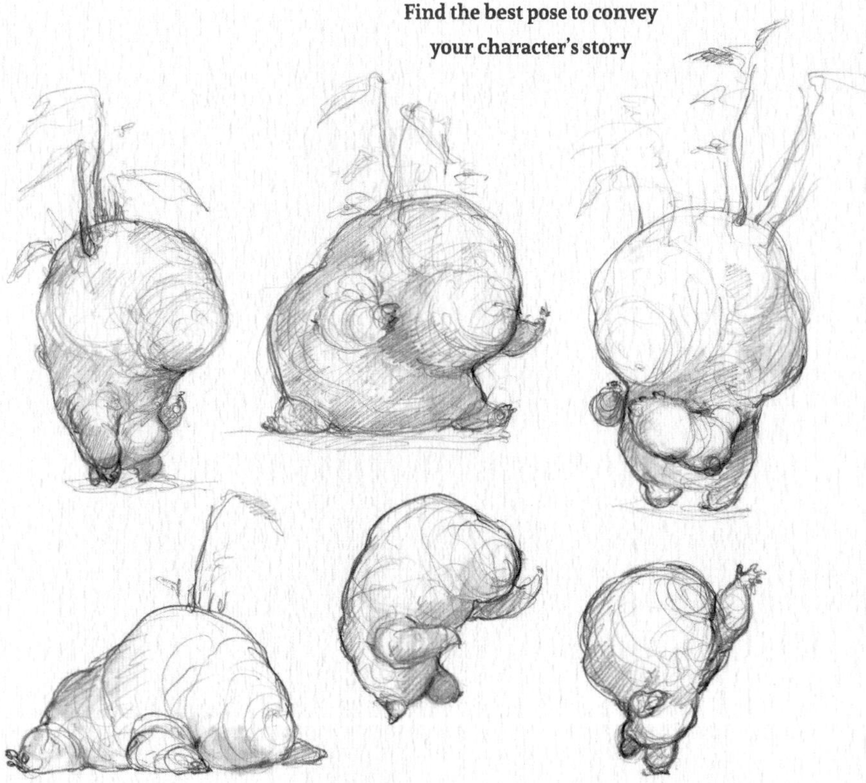

FINDING FACES

An important aspect of any design is the face, as it typically forms the main focal point of an illustration. As such, you should show it a suitable amount of attention and detail. Now you've chosen a shape and pose for your character, its story should be starting to form in your mind. The next step is to focus on giving it a little face to contrast against the misshapen, disproportioned body of the potato. Playing with these contrasting ideas could make for an interesting design. At first glance the viewer will see its bulbous, hulking shape, but as they take a closer look they'll notice its kind and gentle facial expression. Decide how humanlike you wish to make the face. Should it have a nose, and if so, what kind? How many eyes should it have? Does it need ears? And what about a mouth? Ask yourself such questions regarding the character and the way it looks throughout the design process.

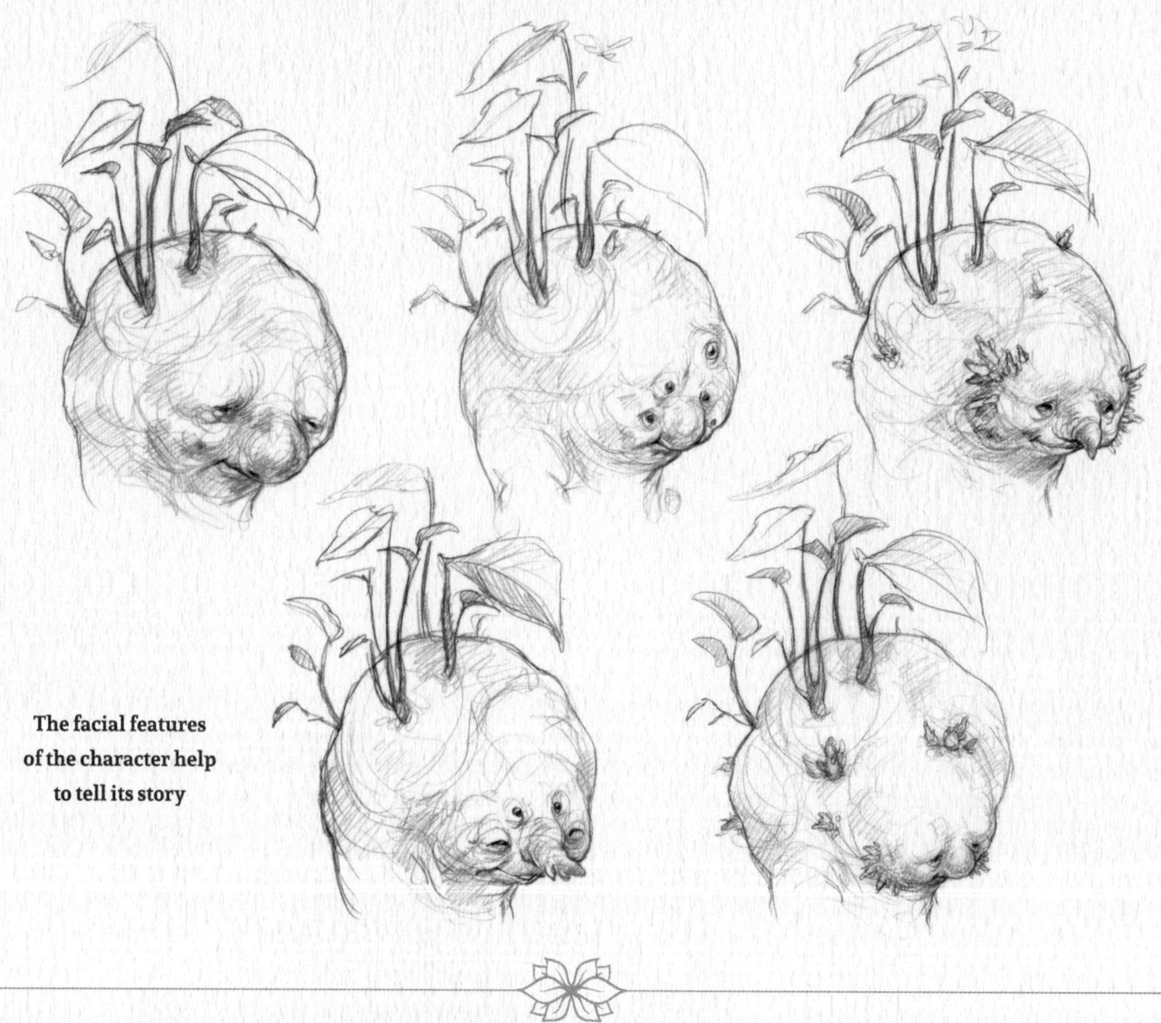

The facial features of the character help to tell its story

DON'T PLAN YOUR PIECE TO DEATH

You might be tempted to render everything, but it's important to leave room for adjustments in your design. Make sure your final sketch has enough detail to work with, so you know where the different elements need to go, but remember to leave room for experimentation too. Leaving your sketch very subtle, almost unfinished, provides you with the opportunity to respond to what's happening as you're working on your character. Not locking everything down leaves room for surprises and ideas that might change your design for the better as you're working. Keep the final sketch playful and it will bring life to your character.

ADDING INTERESTING DETAILS

Now you've figured out the body shape, pose, and facial features, it's time to put everything together. No sketch is wasted; take a look back over what you've drawn so far and see if there are any interesting elements that you might want to develop into the final design. For example, you could add little sprouts from one sketch to the chosen face. These add a little interest to the face and help to break up the shape. If you want to see how something will look before committing them to the sketch, simply trace those parts on translucent paper and lay it over your sketch to see if you like it. You can also move it around to see if it works better on another part of the drawing. Keep your final sketch fairly loose, only hinting at certain elements. This will allow you to change your mind if there are interesting developments during the colouring stage.

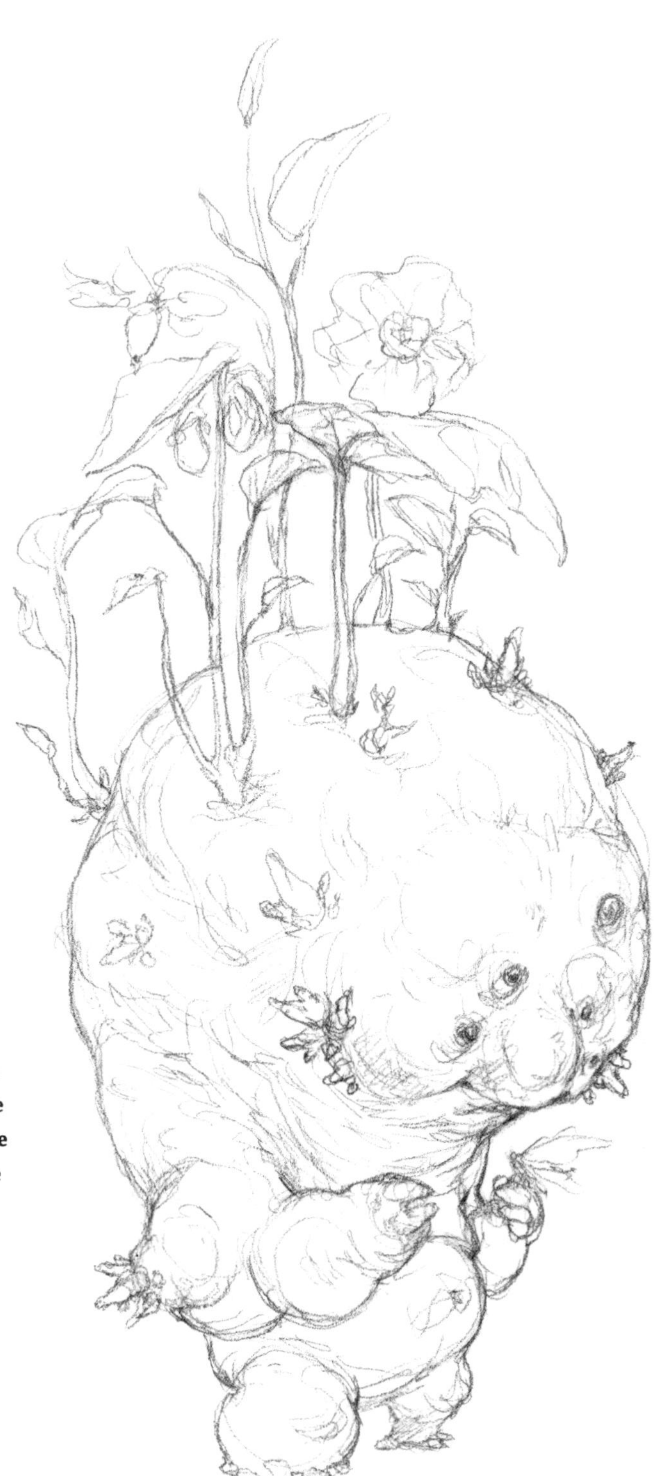

Keeping the final sketch loose will bring life to the final illustration, with the sketch remaining visible underneath the paint

COLOUR STUDIES

Before you start applying paint to the final sketch, first create some rough colour studies. These don't have to be elaborate; simply draw a few quick thumbnail sketches of your final character to add different colour schemes to. These studies will prove very useful in narrowing down what colour palette you want to work with. You won't have to worry about making these decisions while painting, as you've got the general direction for your colours already to hand. You will notice that the colour palette you choose for your character will have an effect on the way your character is perceived. Colour brings so much character and mood to an illustration; it can change the story dramatically. Choose the palette that best suits your character's story.

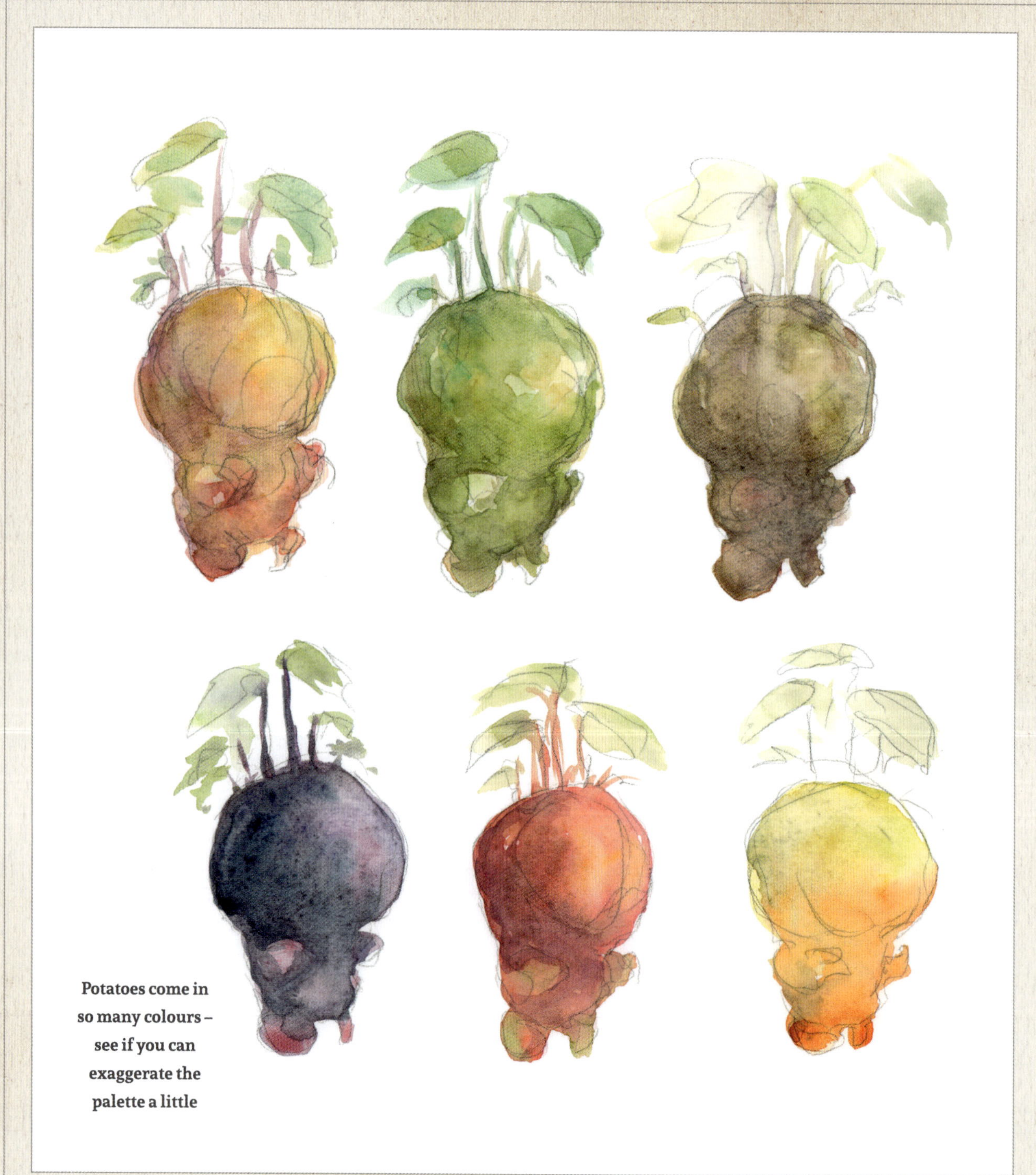

Potatoes come in so many colours – see if you can exaggerate the palette a little

SCAN ALL OF YOUR SKETCHES

Before you start painting on top of your sketches, make sure you scan them all. Scanning your images at a suitable dpi (minimum 300dpi for printing, if not higher) will ensure you have a file ready to print and work from afresh if you make a mistake during the colouring stage. Mistakes happen, especially when working traditionally; anything from using the wrong colour or overworking your final piece, to your cat thinking it's a good idea to sleep on your final artwork. Having a high-resolution file will allow you to easily print it out on watercolour paper using a printer that uses dye inks. Be sure to test if your printer uses dye inks and can handle thicker paper.

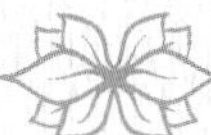

UNDERPAINTING

It's time to start adding colour to your sketch. When working with watercolours, you should work from light to dark. Before you start applying colour to your character, consider where the lightest areas will be and where the shadows are. It can help to paint a simple underpainting to help establish the areas where you want these lights and darks to sit, meaning you don't have to worry about this when you're painting the next layers. For the underpainting, use a mix of cadmium red and cobalt blue for the shadows. This will help you to build up the shape of the character without thinking about the colours just yet.

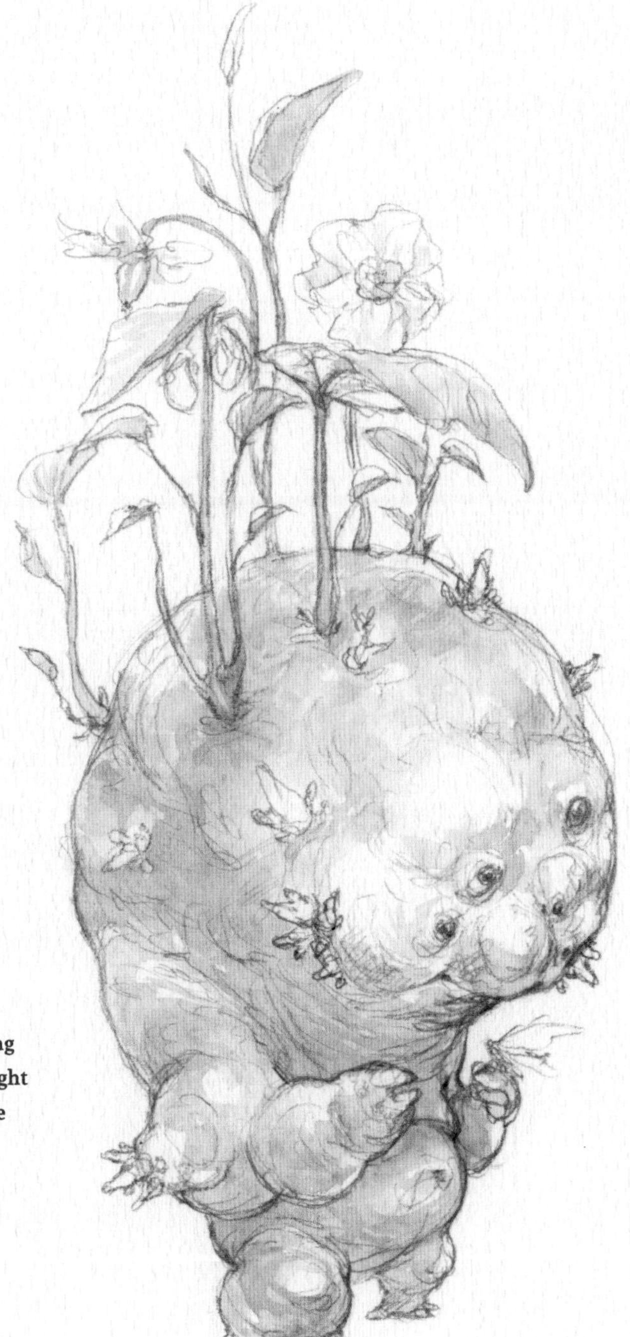

A simple underpainting establishes where the light and dark areas will be

GLAZING

The next step is to apply light washes, or glazes, of colour. The first wash is basically the undertone, the base colour, for this potato pixie. Use the first glaze to establish the area of focus by keeping the face the lightest. The underpainting is still showing and together with that first glaze of a warm tone, it already reveals much of the character's shape. Use the next layers to build up the tone and go darker with each wash, carefully building and defining the shape of your character. Keep each additional layer of colour very light and thin, using a lot of water, rather than opting for opaque colours immediately. This approach means there's always room for adjustments and changes, should you need to make any.

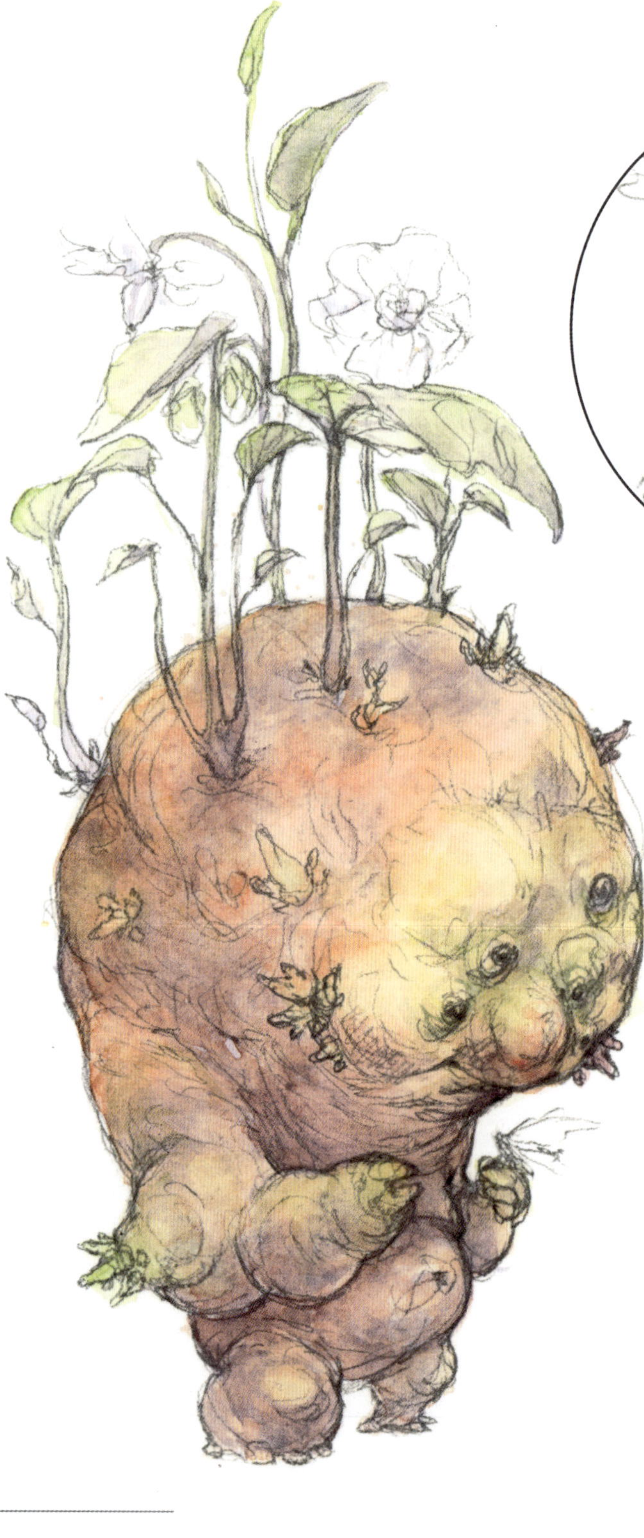

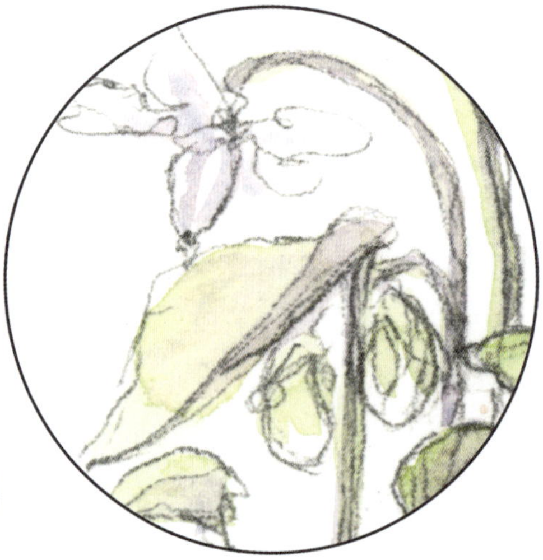

Build up light glazes of watercolour to define the shape of the character

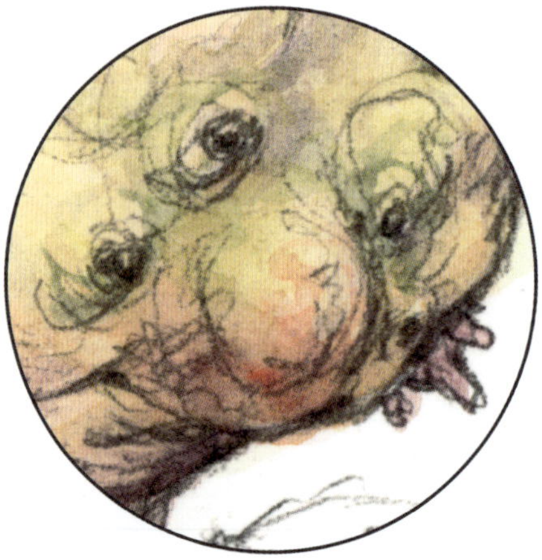

MORE LAYERS OF COLOUR & EFFECTS

Apply various painting techniques when laying down these first layers of watercolour. In the early stages, you may prefer to work wet on wet. This is when the area you're working on is quite wet, or damp, and when you add pigment to the surface, it bleeds into the pigments already on the paper. This can create wonderful natural-looking effects and textures. On larger areas, like the potato pixie's body, these textures can add a little interest without having to painstakingly paint on all of the textures by hand – just let the pigment and water do what it does best. Be sure to keep a hairdryer close by to speed up the drying process if you need to. Don't overdo the textures, though. Creating textures is a lot of fun, but you don't want to distract from the focal area: the face. Finding the right balance is key.

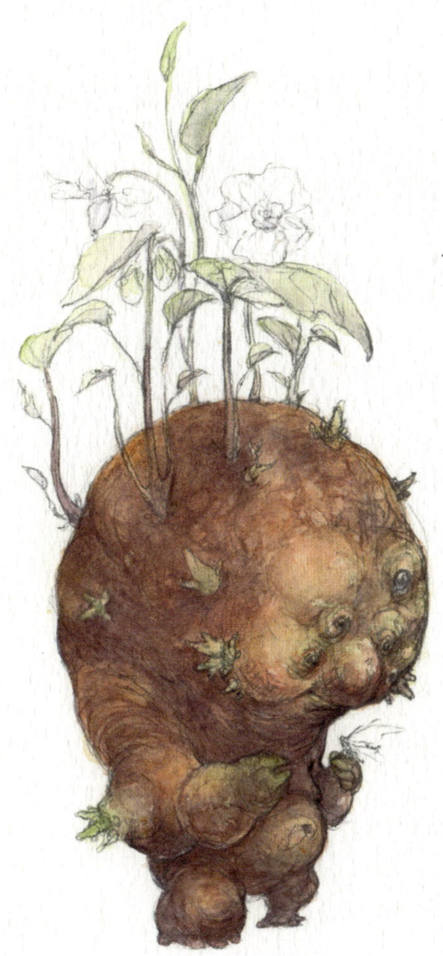

Adding wonderful natural textures by working wet on wet

DETAILING THE FOCAL AREAS

When applying the first couple of watercolour layers, your focus should be on establishing the shape, building the form by applying colour and tone. After working wet on wet for these first few layers, when you want to start adding more detail to render areas like the face, you will need the paper to be dry to prevent the colours from bleeding into one another. Rather than adding detail everywhere, focus on one area; in this case, the face. Plus, you can add detail to anything that leads the eye to that area, such as the hand holding the bug and the other hand pointing to it. Use a simple nail art brush to paint in these areas; they're cheap and are very small, which is perfect for this.

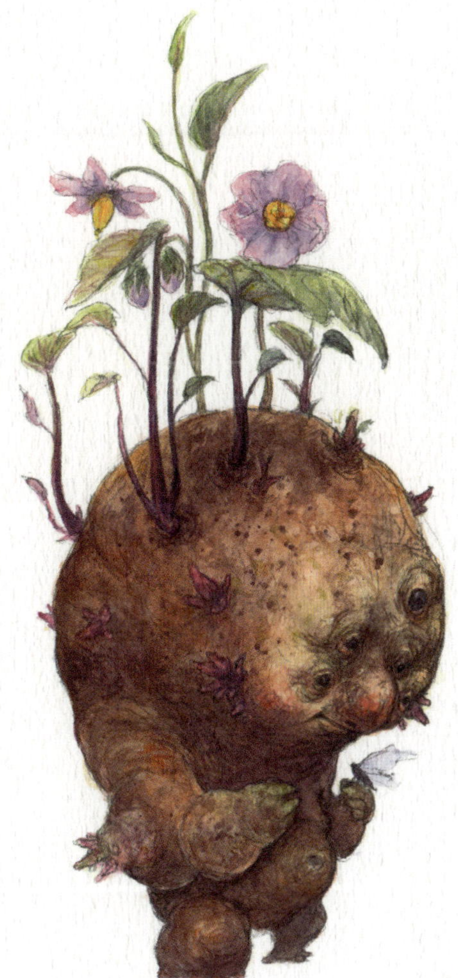

Paint in detail to the face, making sure the multiple eyes are clearly visible

COLOURED PENCILS

When you're starting to feel like the piece is nearly finished, go back in with coloured pencil lines. It's a nice effect when the sketch shows through the translucent layers of watercolour, but sometimes you can lose too much of the graphite when painting. To bring back the liveliness of the pencil lines, use a Prismacolor Col-Erase pencil – such as Tuscan Red, Brown, or Black, depending on the piece – to sketch on top of the painted character to enhance certain areas that need a little more added to the dark areas, without running the risk of picking up pigment with a wet brush. You wouldn't use a graphite pencil for this, as graphite is too shiny and doesn't look right on the surface. The coloured pencils, on the other hand, add a lovely texture.

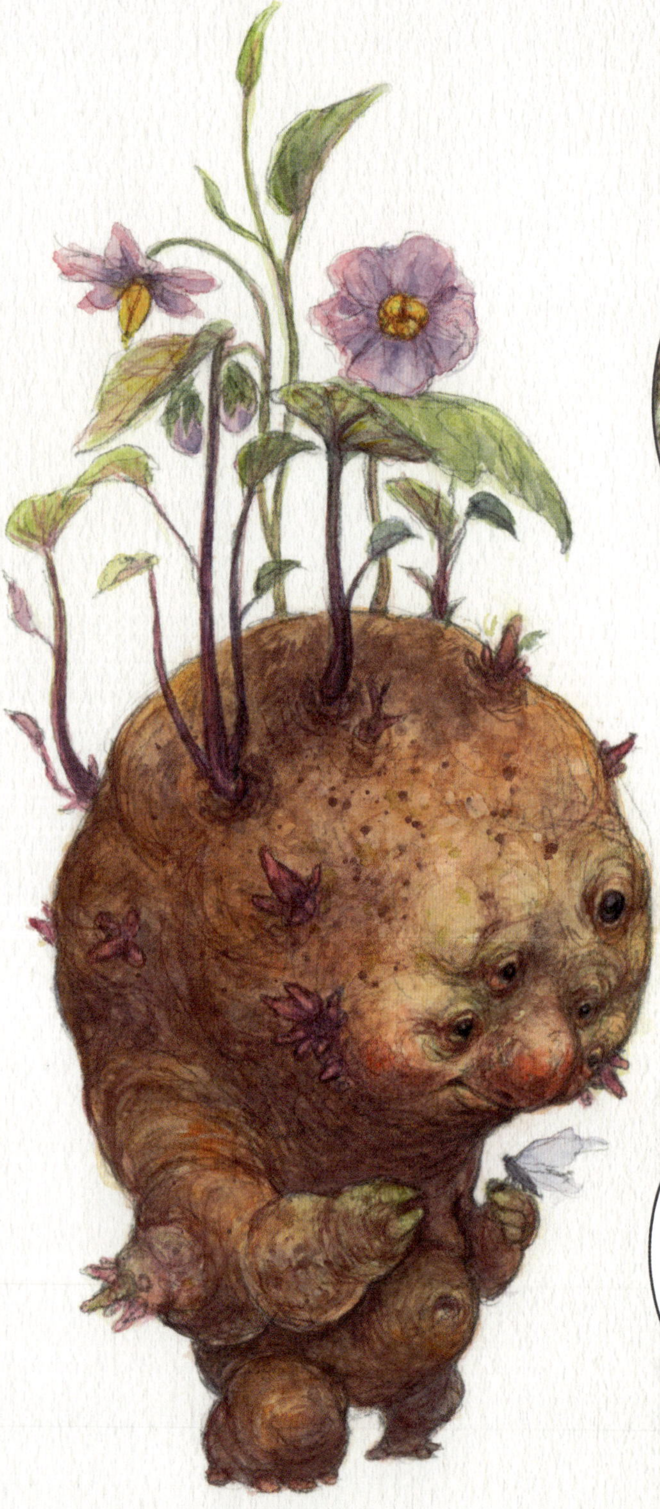

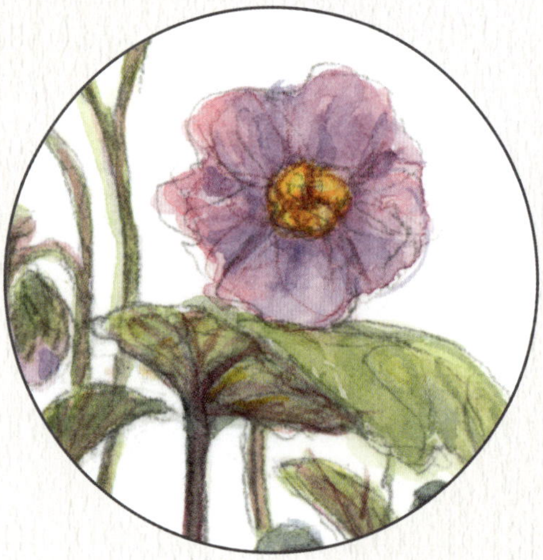

Use a coloured pencil to bring back some of the sketch lines that got lost under the watercolour

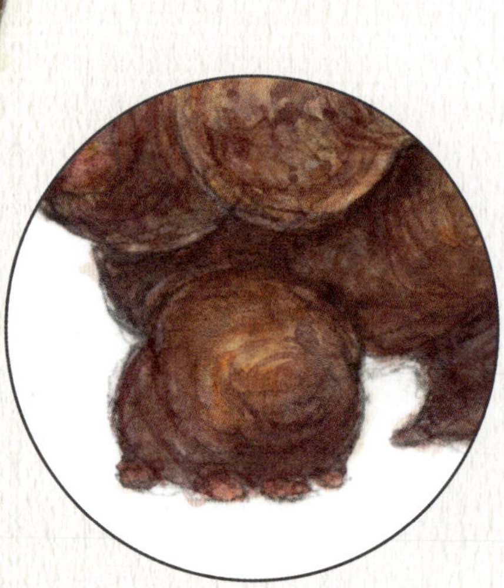

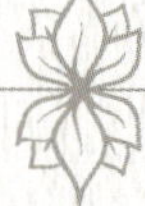

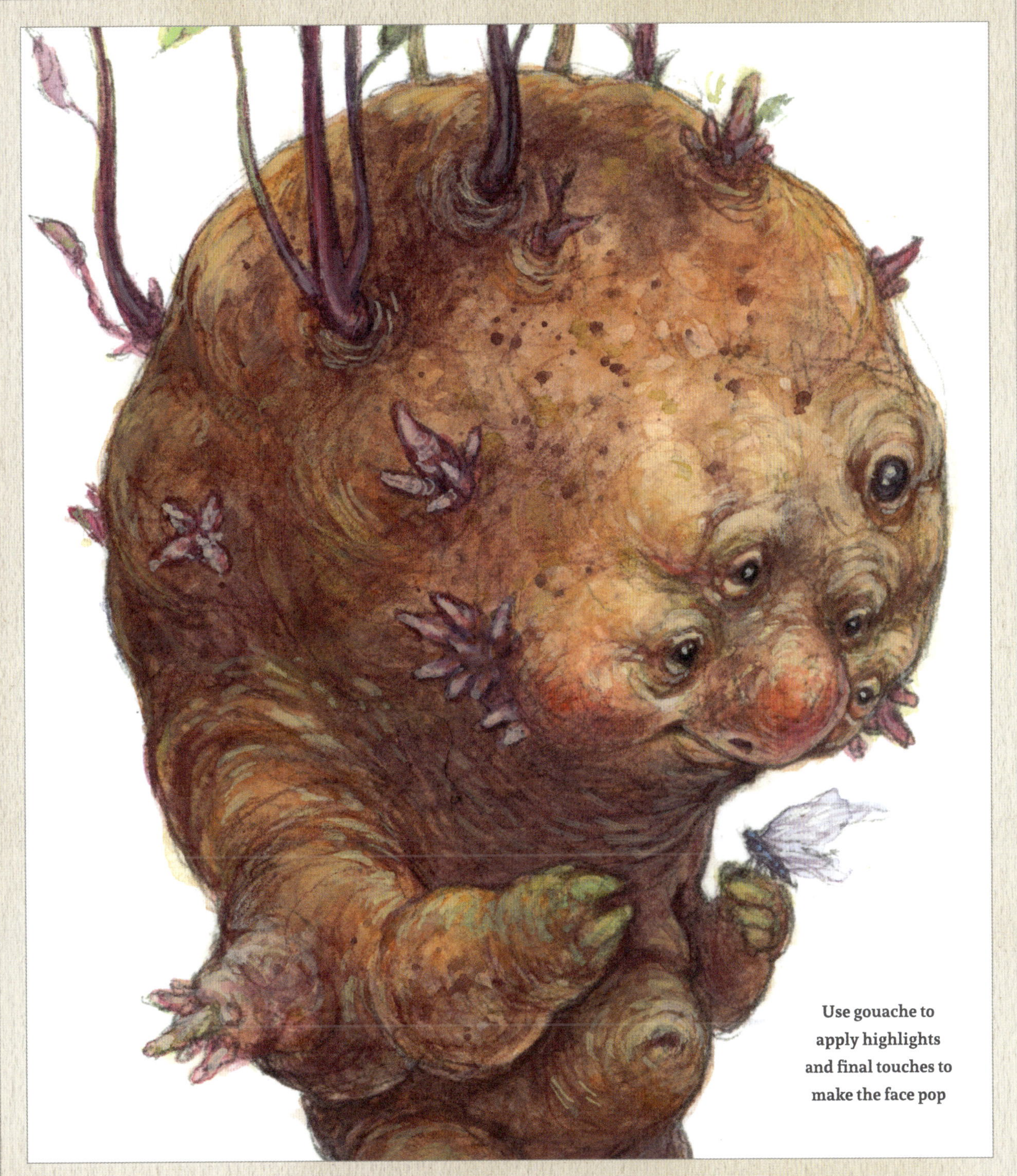

Use gouache to apply highlights and final touches to make the face pop

FINISHING TOUCHES WITH GOUACHE

After you've rendered some of the details with the coloured pencil, use gouache to add a few highlights throughout, but especially on the focal areas. You can also add highlights on elements such as the little sprouts, as these have become a little lost and need a bit more contrast to be visible. Avoid using pure white, as that would be too big of a contrast. Instead, try to mix a colour that is slightly lighter than your lightest colour on the character. You can then use this to highlight certain areas that need to stand out a little more; for example, around the eyes. Use regular gouache for this, rather than Acryla gouache, as this will allow you to change your mind. Acryla gouache won't go anywhere once it dries!

THE POTATO PIXIE

The potato pixie is a shy little character that spends most of its life burrowed deep beneath the soil, warm and safe, in a vegetable patch. In the darkness of the underground world, their bodies grow into weird, deformed shapes, giving them an outward appearance that at first glance can come across as monstrous. Yet these little pixies are the kind caretakers of everything that grows beneath the soil, keeping sickness at bay and tending to the roots and baby tubers. A peaceful creature with multiple eyes, it will dig itself as deep as possible at the first sight of danger. Mature potato pixies will travel above ground only when it's time to flower. When the first sprouts begin to form on their bodies, they know it's time for them to burrow upwards in search of light. Their flowers attract all kinds of insects that help them with their work, while their leaves provide them with shade against the sunlight.

Creating a character inspired by nature is both a challenge as well as a great adventure. Once you get started, the ideas will start to flow. How does a baby of this species look? Or maybe an elder? Character design isn't just about creating an attractive design, but rather about telling a story for the viewer to discover. You're not just creating a character; you're implying a world. That is the appeal of character design: to create something that 'could be'. Next time you're peeling a potato, you'll make sure it is indeed a potato and not a pixie...

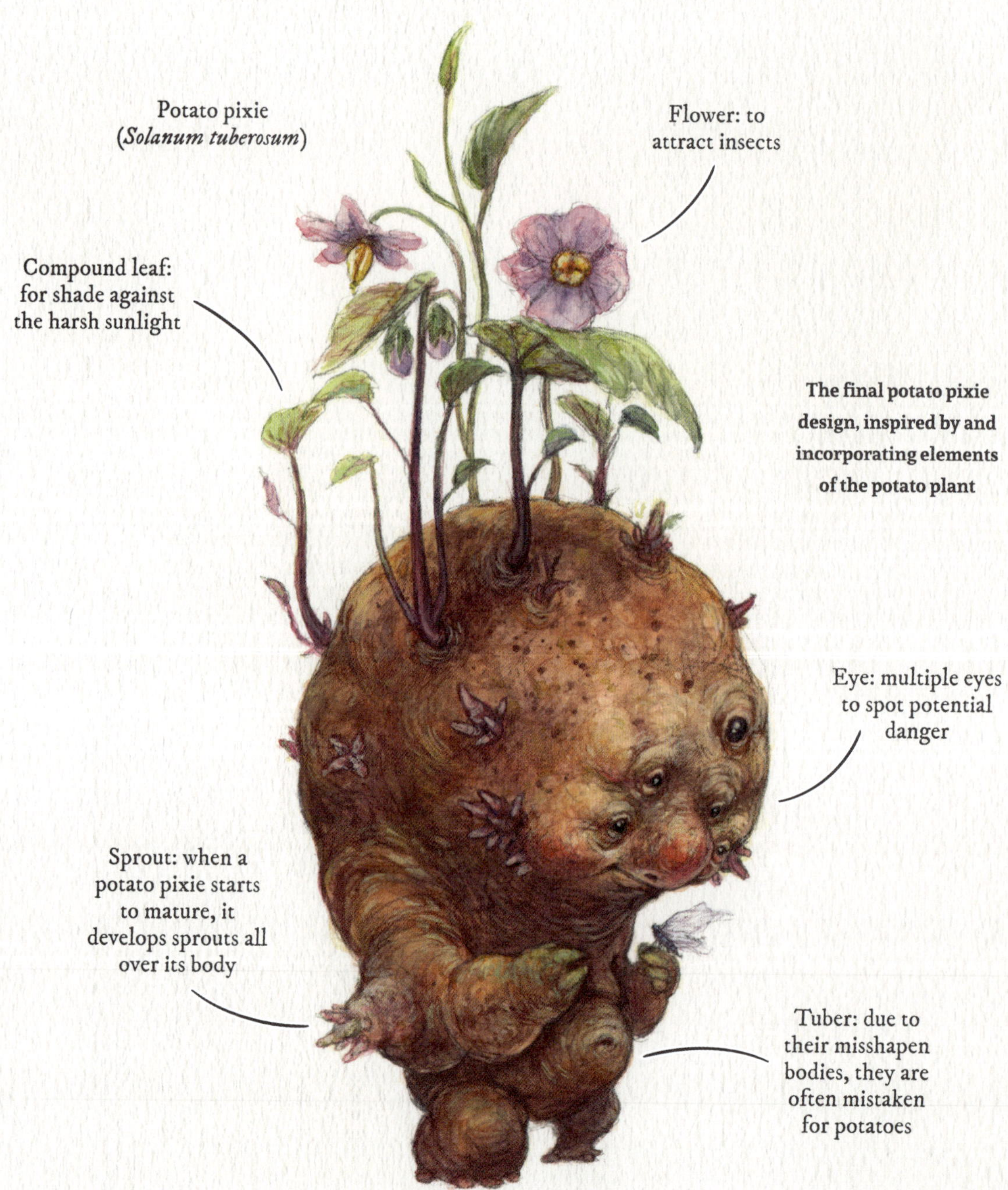

The final potato pixie design, inspired by and incorporating elements of the potato plant

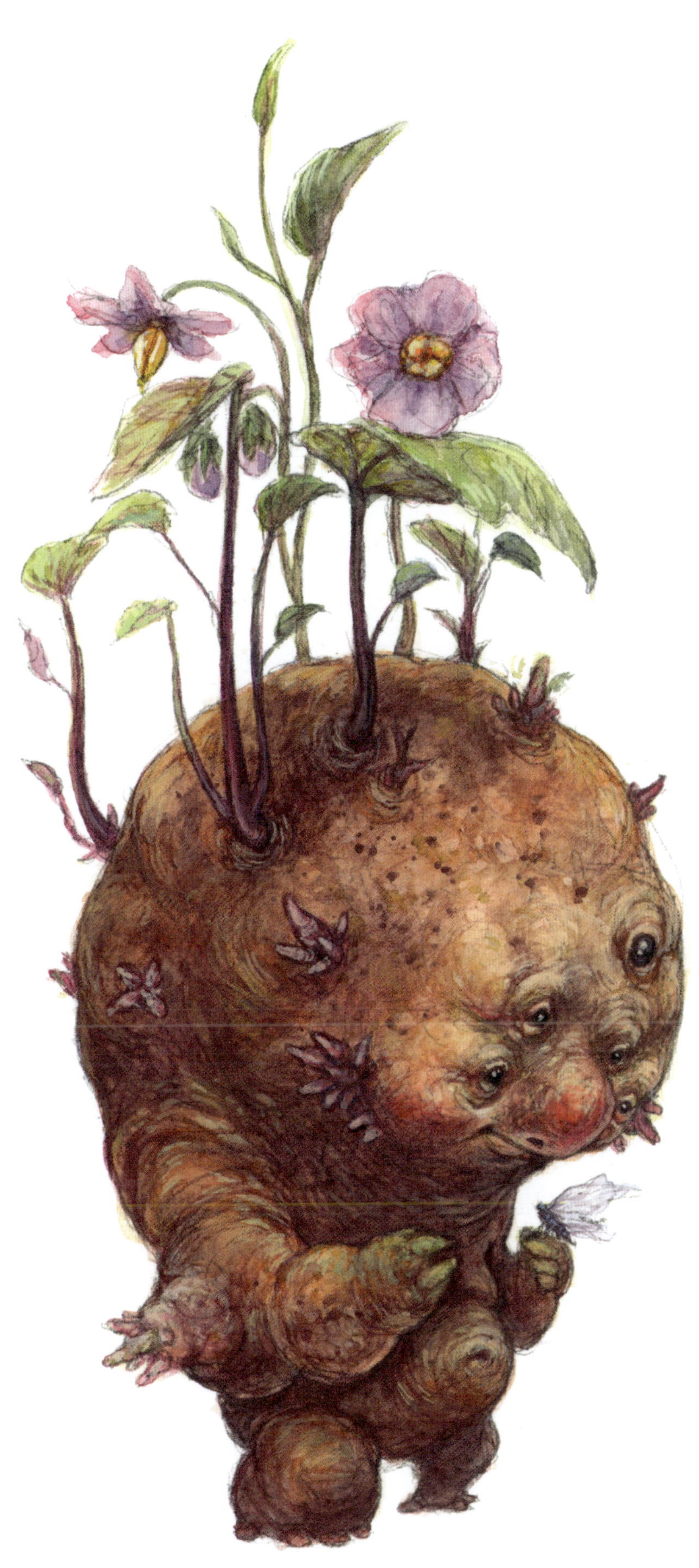

POTATO PIXIE

Final image © Iris Compiet

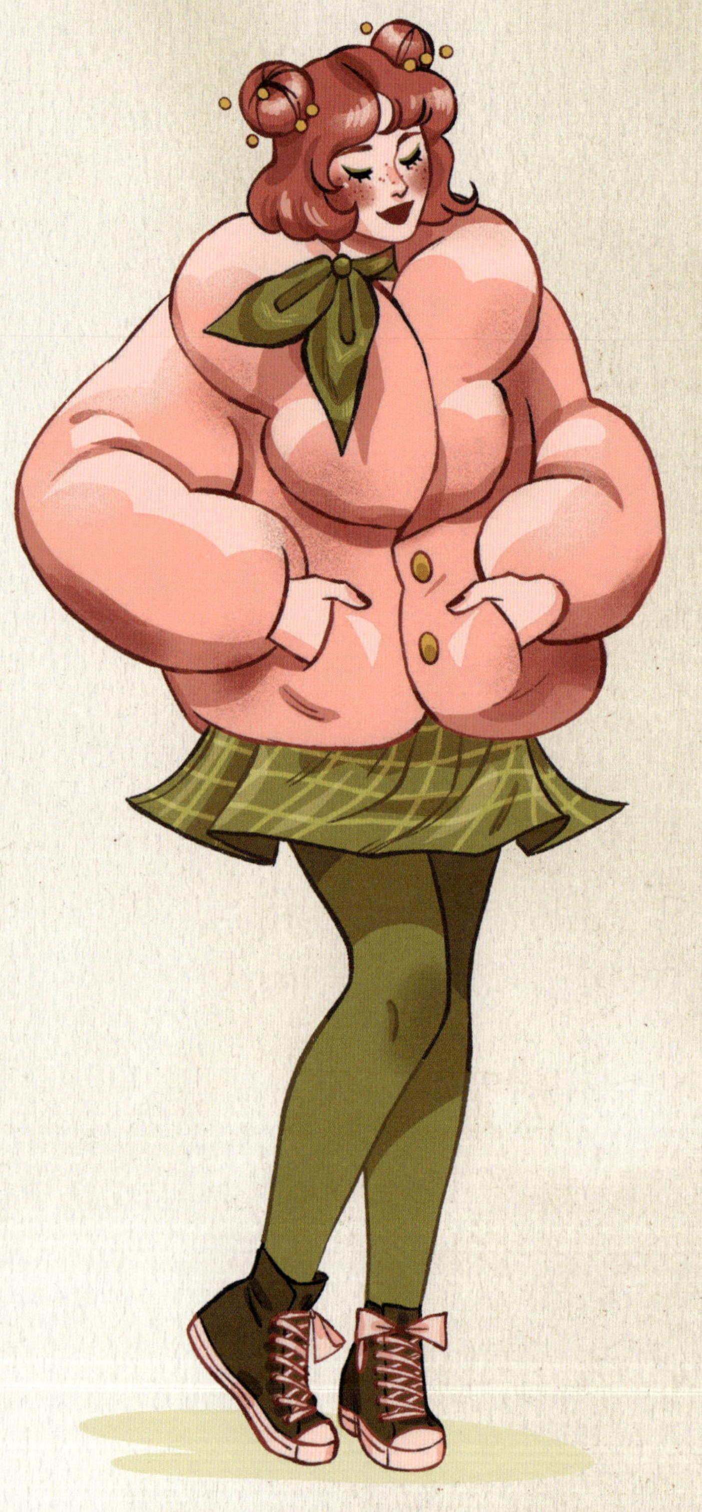

Nature is the greatest and most inexhaustible source of design inspiration that exists, displaying a wide variety of colours, shapes, patterns, and textures with the changing seasons. Always be on the lookout when collecting inspiration from nature, as even the smallest details can make a huge difference to your character.

This tutorial will teach you how to create a character based on *Prunus serrulata*, also known as the Japanese cherry tree. Its soft, soothing pink colours inspire poetic feelings of lightness, calm, and femininity. The iPad and Procreate will be used for this project. Digital tools are so useful for creating a character from scratch, as you are able to alter colours and shapes very quickly.

tree

CHERRY BLOSSOM GIRL

SIBYLLINE MEYNET

CHERRY BLOSSOM

The cherry tree is a majestic tree with many different varieties around the world, their flowers ranging from white to pink. When you think of a cherry tree, the impression of a floating pink cloud likely comes to mind, perhaps with touches of pink on the ground where the petals have fallen. In some countries, it's even an event to witness cherry trees in bloom. Choosing between white and pink flowers is difficult, but the pink blossoms of *Prunus serrulata* will allow this character to stand out.

This kind of cherry tree, *Prunus serrulata*, is mostly found in Japan, China, and Korea

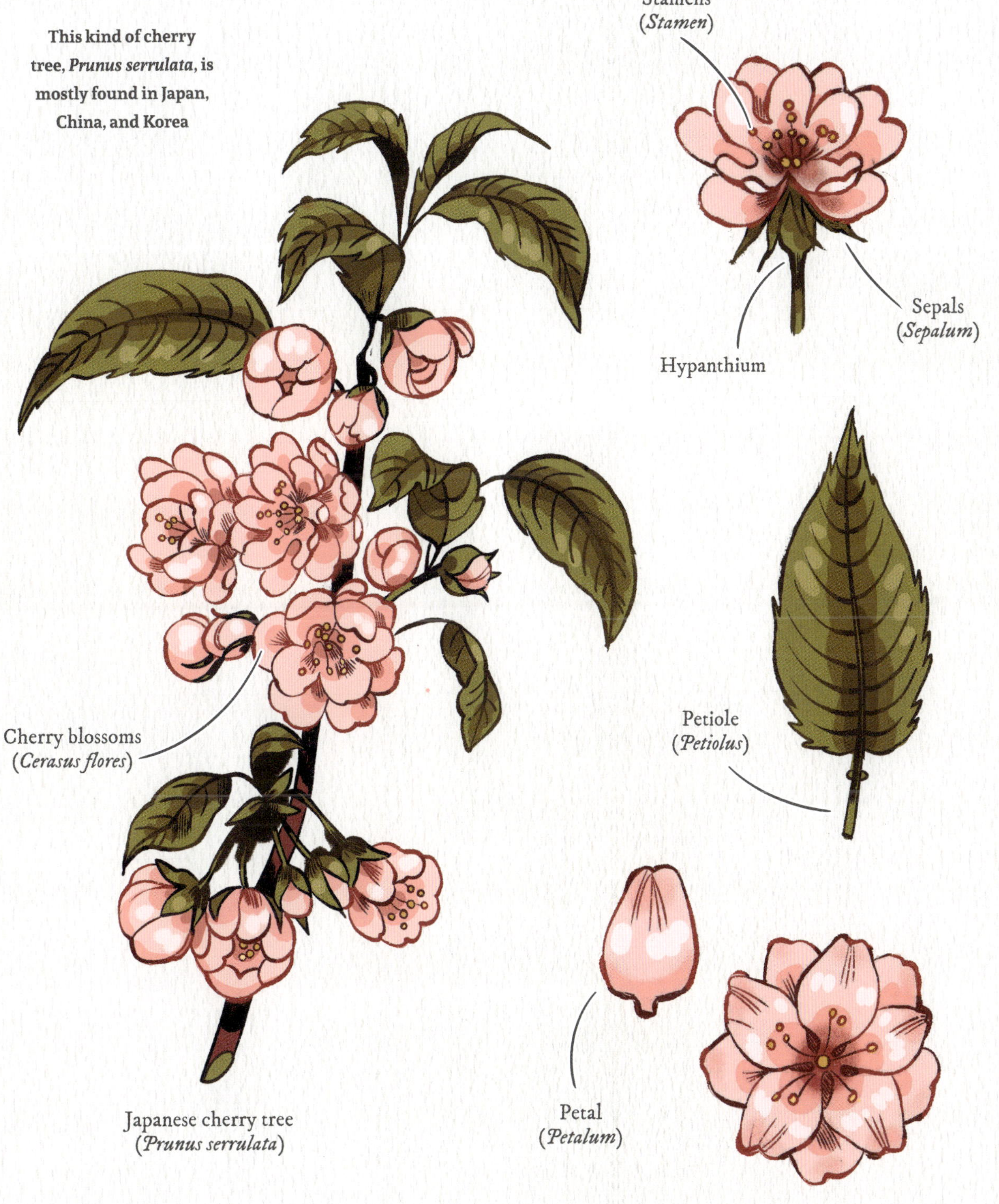

INITIAL SKETCHES

Start by considering what attitude the character will have. As mentioned in the previous step, the cherry tree inspires feelings of lightness, poetry, and calm. It would work well if the character is also calm, perhaps waiting or daydreaming. Begin looking for character shapes by studying and drawing the shape of the cherry blossom and branch. For example, the flowers are round, the leaves are teardrop-shaped, and the branches are long and thin. All three elements are interesting, but your focus can be narrowed down to two elements for this initial brainstorming stage. While the leaf is very compelling, the flower is already round, so you don't really need to explore two similar ideas. Instead, try exploring two opposite takes on the character: one round and flower-shaped, the other thin and twig-shaped.

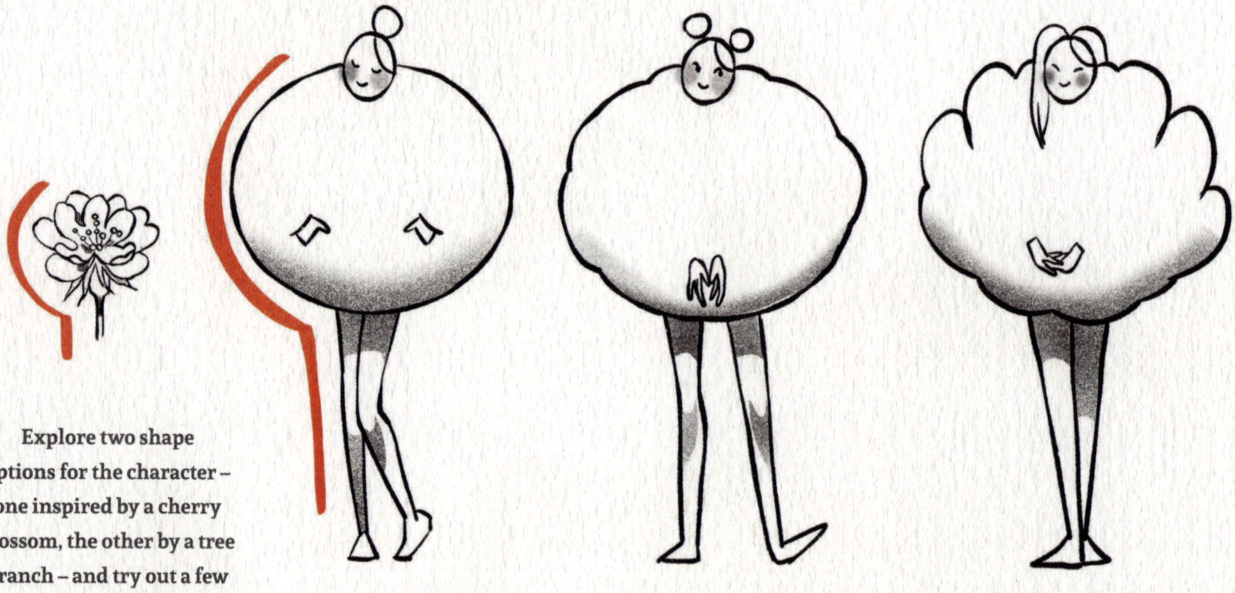

Explore two shape options for the character – one inspired by a cherry blossom, the other by a tree branch – and try out a few poses to see how she occupies the space around her

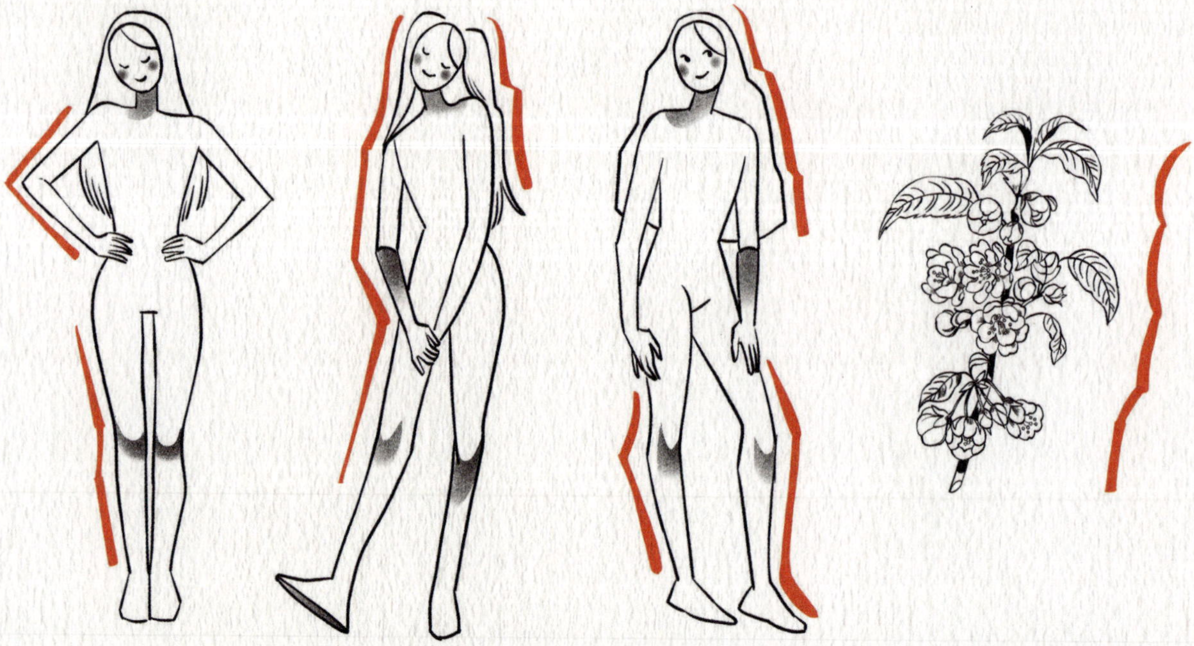

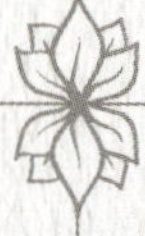

SHAPE OPTIONS

Dig a little deeper into the two shape options. Which do you think is most similar to the cherry blossom? You can work this out by drawing a silhouette for each shape and refining it. For the round version, draw the whole body first, then add her puffy clothes afterwards – this will ensure her body is anatomically correct underneath. If you're struggling to get your characters' proportions and posture correct, try taking a photo of yourself to use as a reference. This is a very practical, useful way to understand how the body works and how the arms, legs, and feet give the character a lively and expressive attitude.

Here the flower keeps its initial round blossom shape, which could inspire a big fluffy jacket. Likewise, the branch maintains its thin shape, which can be dressed with flowers later.

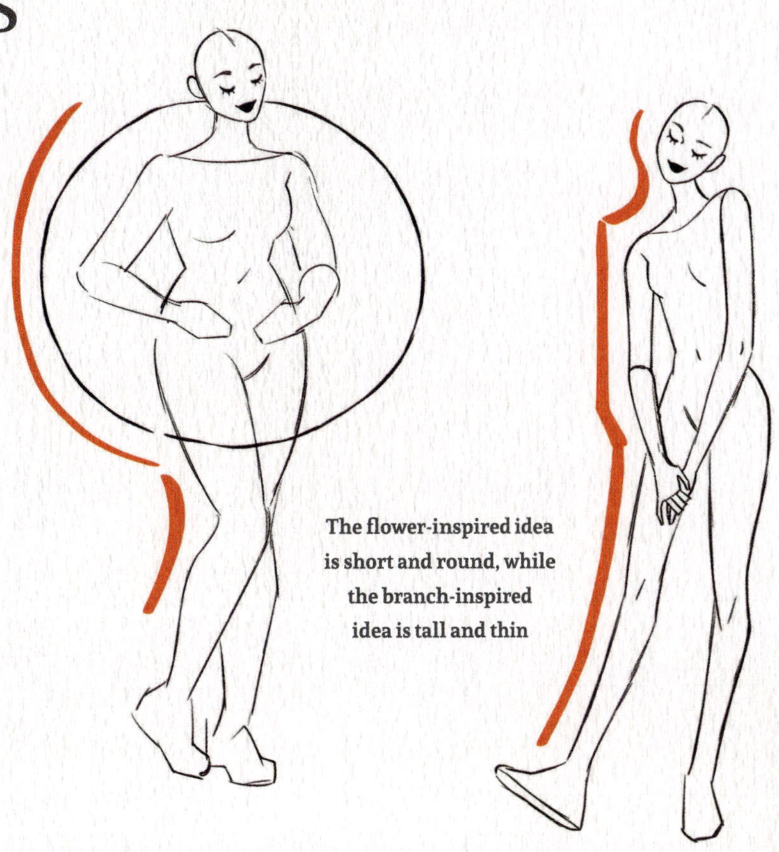

The flower-inspired idea is short and round, while the branch-inspired idea is tall and thin

HAIRSTYLE IDEAS

Shapes are important not only for the morphology of your character, but also for accessories, hairstyles, and anything else the character will wear. Here are several examples of potential hairstyles for the blossom character (round) as well as for the branch character (long). The round hair is shorter and full of volume, while the long hair is straight and angular.

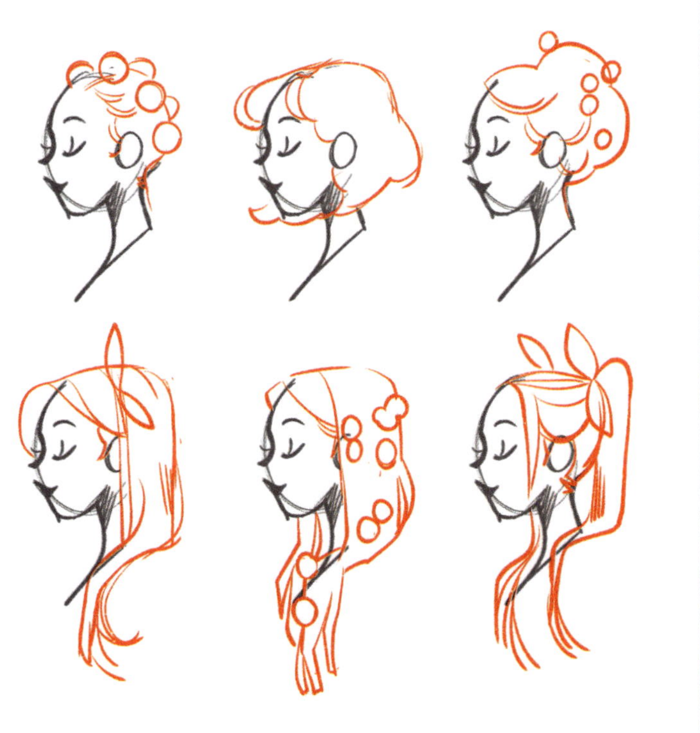

THE PERFECT SHAPE

Finding the perfect shape for the figure is now the priority. You can begin to see that the round character is more recognizable as cherry-blossom-themed, while the branch's slender silhouette doesn't have such a strong impact. It's still worth taking the time to explore the branch character in order to decide on which design to keep. Experimenting with different concepts is the main focus of character design. The more unique ideas you find, the more interesting elements you will have stored up for your final design.

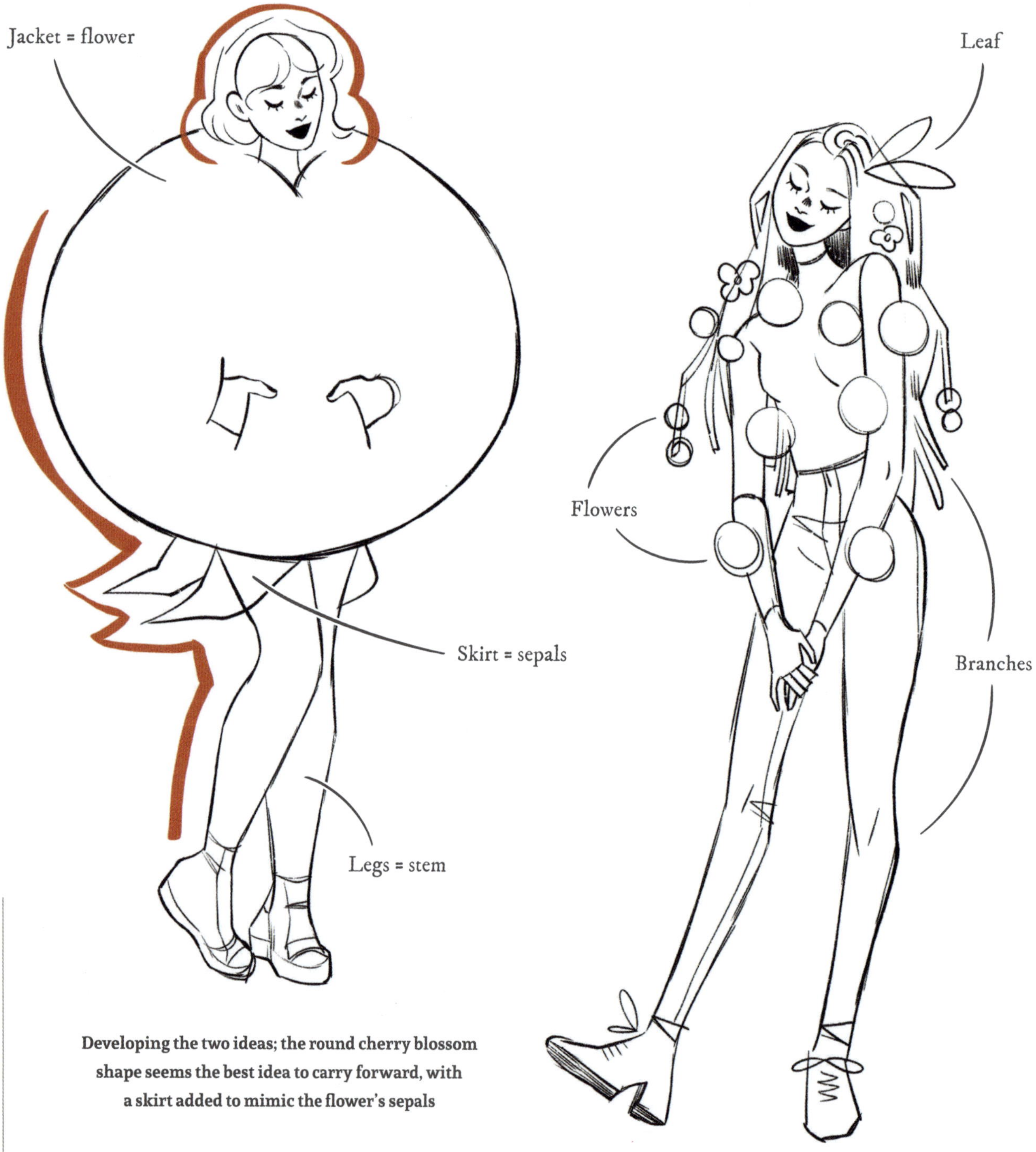

Jacket = flower

Skirt = sepals

Legs = stem

Leaf

Flowers

Branches

Developing the two ideas; the round cherry blossom shape seems the best idea to carry forward, with a skirt added to mimic the flower's sepals

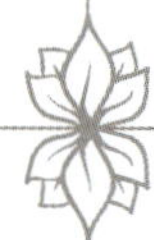

STYLING YOUR CHARACTER

Clothes, accessories, and hairstyles can help make your character more recognizable. Try drawing two or three different silhouettes based on the flower's shapes combined with current or past fashion styles. This is the part where you can really get creative and have fun! The ideal cherry blossom character would have a flowing yet also fluffy look – a reassuring shape that resembles a cloud – but this will also be a modern girl dressed in 'real' clothes. This means the design must move away from the somewhat vague, fantastical circle shape.

It makes sense that the character is wearing a large puffy jacket with tight trousers or a fitted dress, creating the impression of a round flower and stem beneath. The jacket could be a bomber jacket, puffer jacket, or a fluffy coat. She will also have a round hairstyle to echo the flower's buds, petals, and stamens.

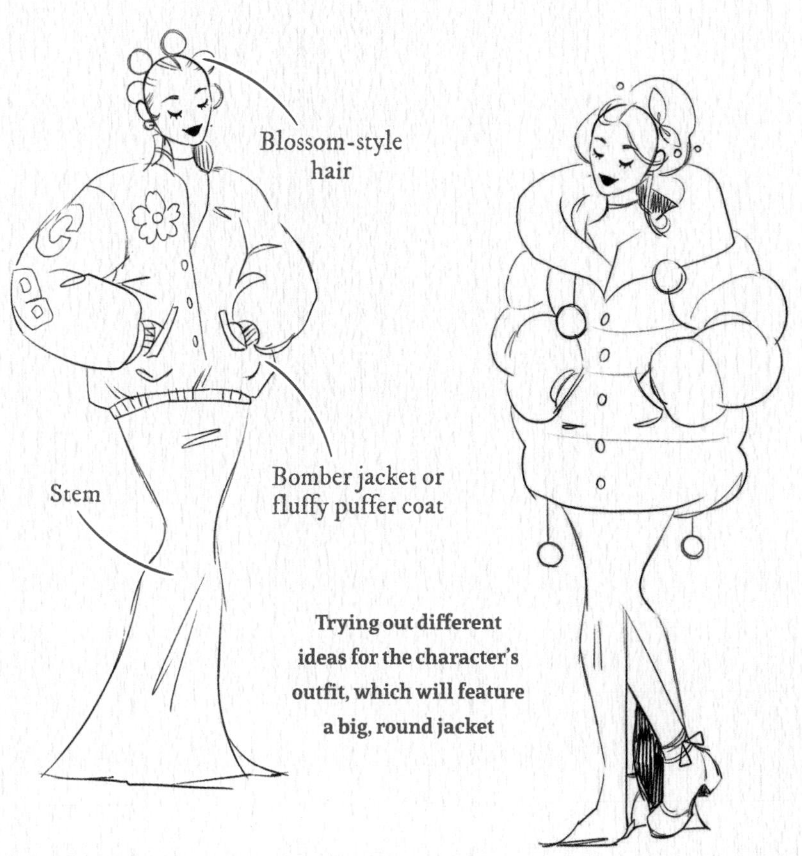

Trying out different ideas for the character's outfit, which will feature a big, round jacket

THE FINAL SKETCH

The strongest idea is the big, fluffy coat paired with a skirt that recreates the shape of the flower's sepals. The character will have two side buns that recall the flower's buds. All this will help to ingrain the theme even more strongly into the design – no detail is left to chance. You can now finalize your sketch, adjust the shapes, refine the features, and add details that will make your design unique. Once you're happy with the character's outfit and overall look, try sketching a few poses that give her life for a short moment. See if her silhouette still works well with the theme, even when she moves!

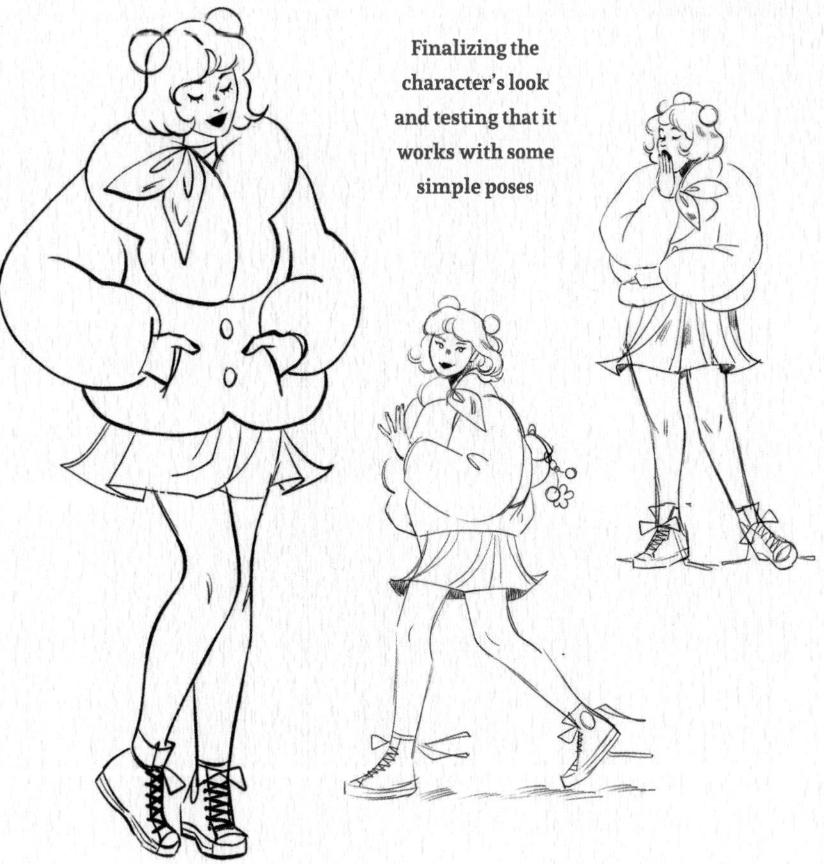

Finalizing the character's look and testing that it works with some simple poses

LINE ART

For the line art, use the Dry Ink brush from Procreate's Ink brush menu. Line art often lacks the charm of the initial sketch's somewhat messy lines, so using a slightly rough brush helps to keep a bit of that original spirit. The inking stage is typically when you will begin to visualize the design's proportions more clearly; once the drawing is finished, you can change any details that seem incorrect. Flipping the canvas allows you to check if your character is standing straight, if their face is symmetrical, and if their attitude seems natural. Once the canvas is flipped, you can modify your line art to fix any minor defects, and then flip it back again when you're finished.

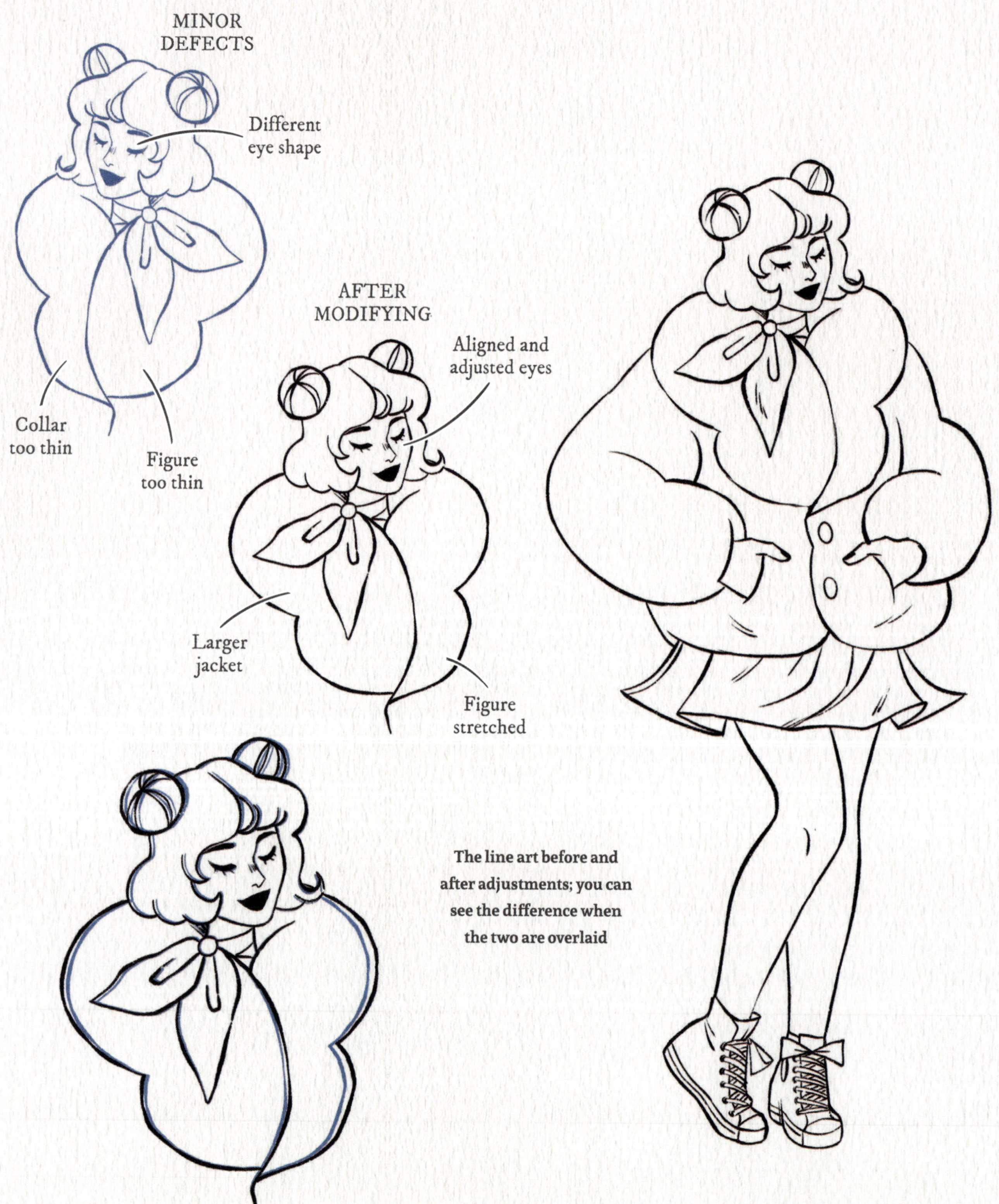

The line art before and after adjustments; you can see the difference when the two are overlaid

COLOUR BASE

Colour provides a character with personality and atmosphere. The colours of a cherry tree are quite limited, but that will work to your advantage here – a limited colour palette can make a character design even more recognizable and impactful. For this character, use a variety of pinks (for the flowers), a very dark fuchsia (for the trunk/branches), and green (for the leaves). These colours will create contrast and are pleasing to the eye, but can be reworked slightly to make the colour palette your own.

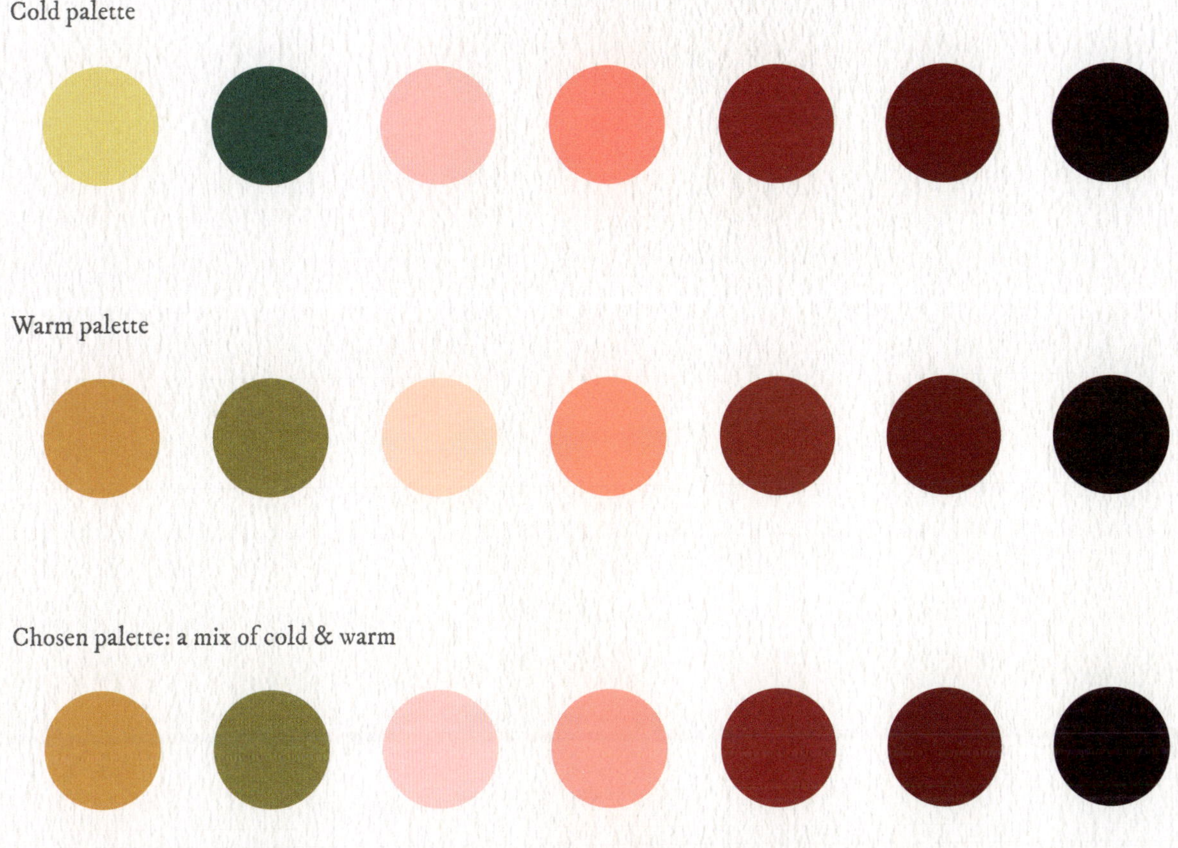

There are many different types of cherry trees that you could reference here; for example, the white flowers of the sour cherry (*Prunus cerasus*) could make for an interesting palette too

WARM OR COLD?

When picking colours straight from the cherry-tree reference, they will need to be reworked a little to find the ideal colour temperature for your character. Here you can see the difference between cold and warm hues of the same colours. It's fun to build your own palette from a mix of warm and cold tones – it's the best way to create an appealing contrast and find a unique colour scheme that you're comfortable working with.

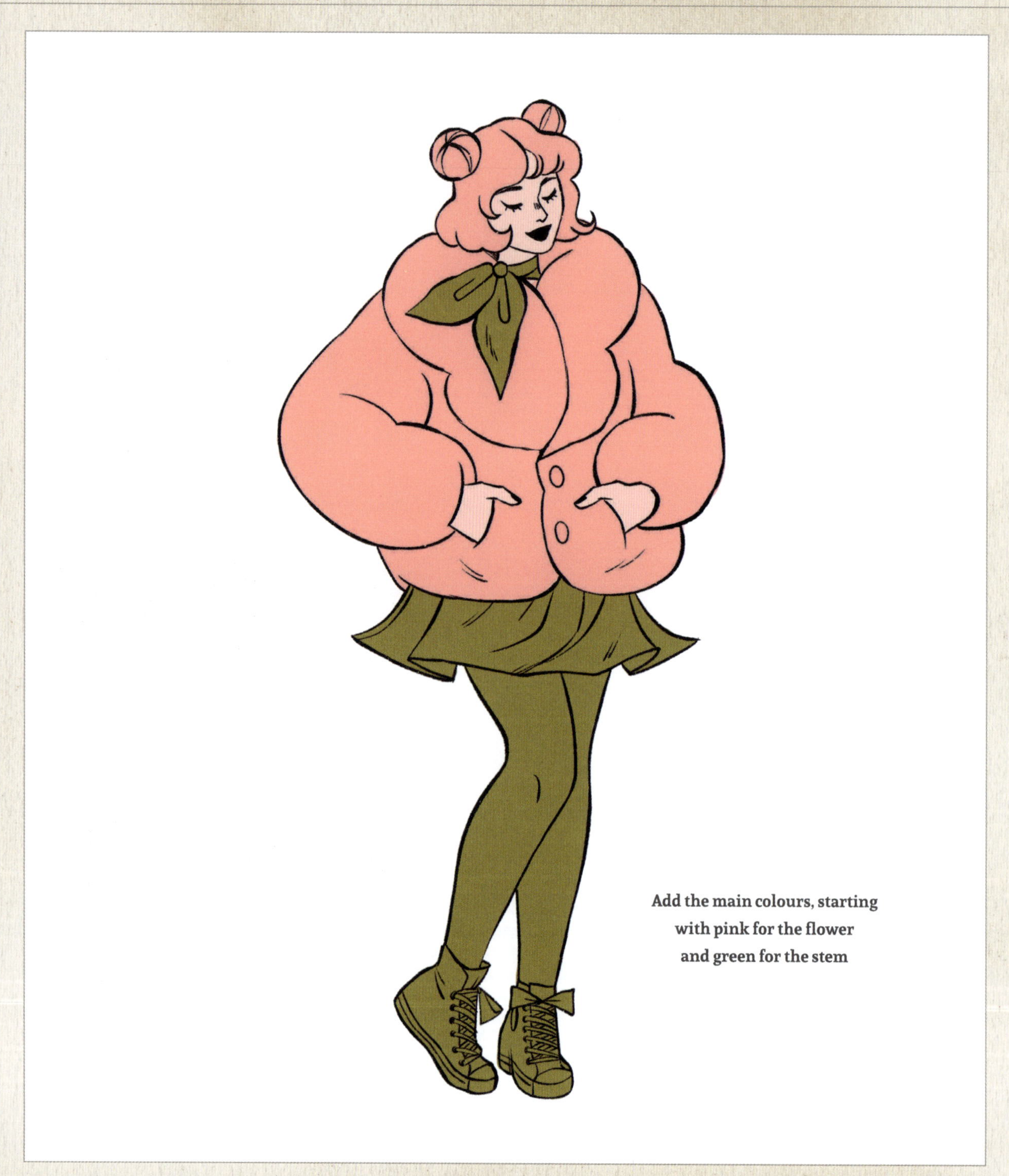

Add the main colours, starting with pink for the flower and green for the stem

ADDING COLOURS

Add the colours to your character, using a new layer underneath your line art. This stage is when you can experiment with the colours, try different combinations, see what is most harmonious, and explore what makes the most sense for a flower character. To create the effect of a cherry blossom on its branch, paint as much pink as possible at the top of the character, using a variety of different pinks for her clothes and hair. Staying within pink tones will keep the palette coherent. Next, use the greens for her scarf and legs, which mimic the plant's leaves and stem.

ADDING SHADOWS

The light source will come from above the character's head, so the shadows must follow that direction. As the character is a dreamer, the light (and therefore the shadows) should be soft and soothing. To create the shadow colours, take your existing colours and darken them slightly, either keeping the same temperature or making them a little warmer.

If you want to create soft, warm shadows, don't mix your initial colour with black – this will only desaturate the colour and make your palette neutral and flat. To give warmth and life to your artwork, always shade with a mix of colours. If you can't find the perfect colour for your shadows, create a new layer, set it to Multiply mode, lower its opacity, and use that for painting a shadow colour. This is an easy way to create shadows that are harmonious and consistent with the rest of the image.

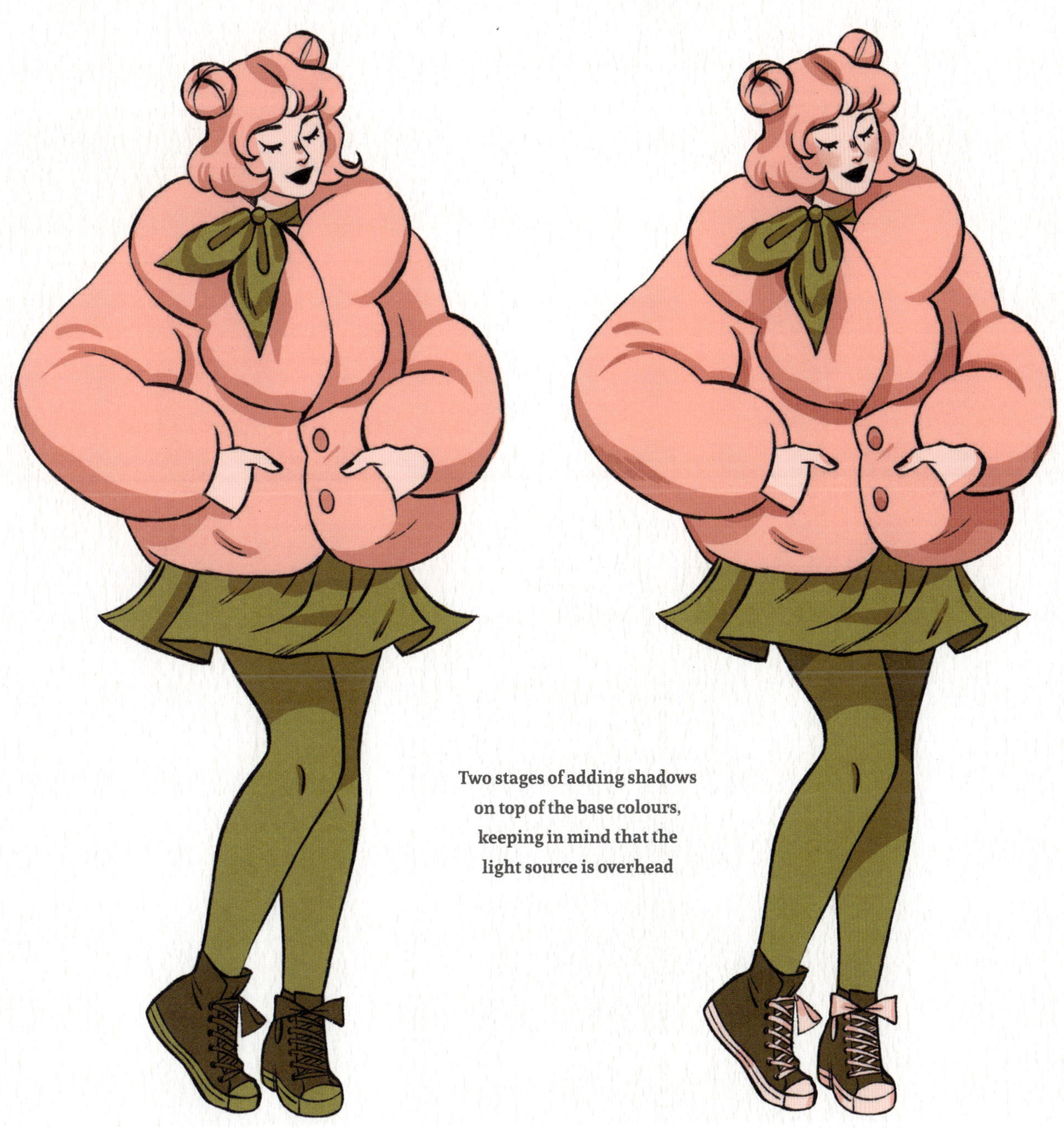

Two stages of adding shadows on top of the base colours, keeping in mind that the light source is overhead

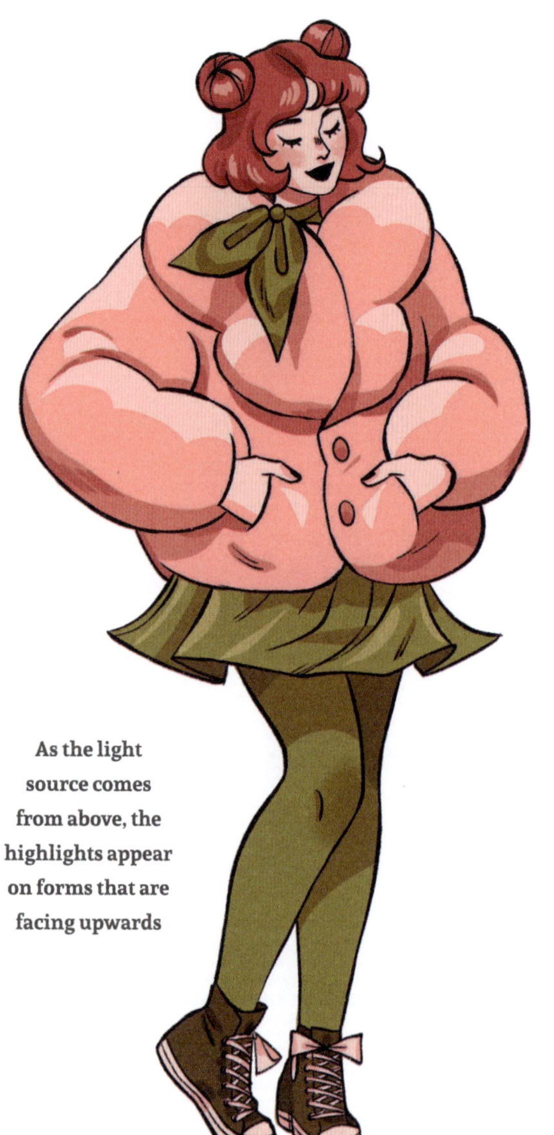

As the light source comes from above, the highlights appear on forms that are facing upwards

ADDING HIGHLIGHTS

Highlights will make certain elements of the character pop, as well as indicating where the light source comes from (the shadows help with this too). To quickly add highlights to your character using Procreate, create a layer set to Overlay mode, paint on it with a light colour, and modify the layer's opacity to your liking. White is an effective colour for Overlay mode if you can't decide on a colour. Add a few touches of light according to the light source's direction. At this stage, adjusting the character's hair to a darker pink helps to frame her face and show her hair's shading more clearly.

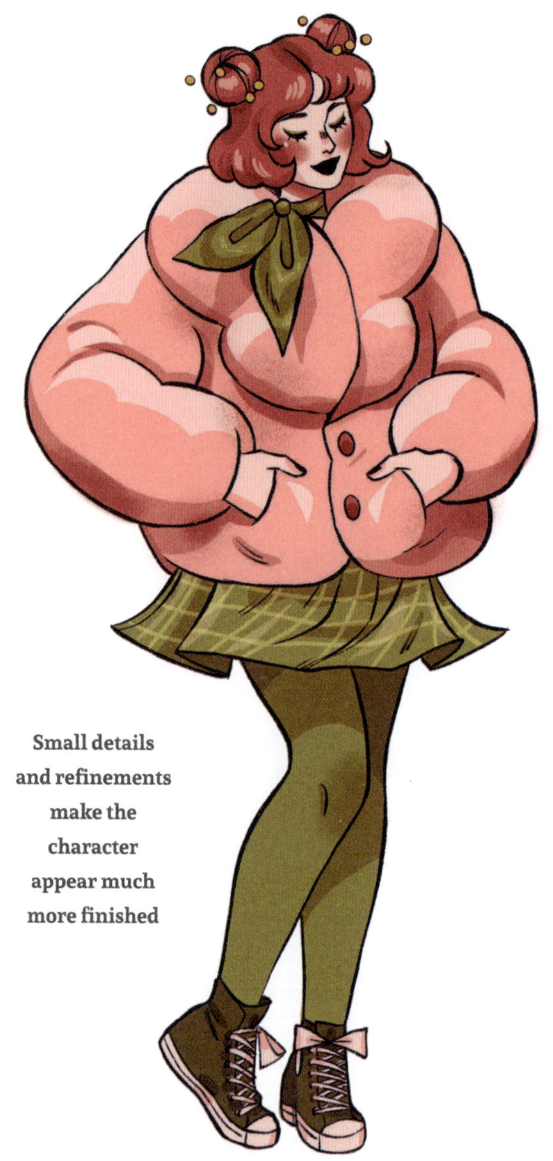

Small details and refinements make the character appear much more finished

BUILDING UP DETAIL

Once the character is almost complete, the next step is to add the last little details that will give the design a more finished look. Though small, these refinements can really make a difference. Which elements of the cherry tree could be added to make the design even more impactful? The flower's stamens, which are usually yellow or pink, are a fun detail to add. They take the form of yellow dots in the character's hair, making her appear more dreamy and thoughtful as they appear to float around her head. The yellow also creates an interesting contrast with her dark pink hair. Adding pink cheeks and green make-up completes her floral-inspired look.

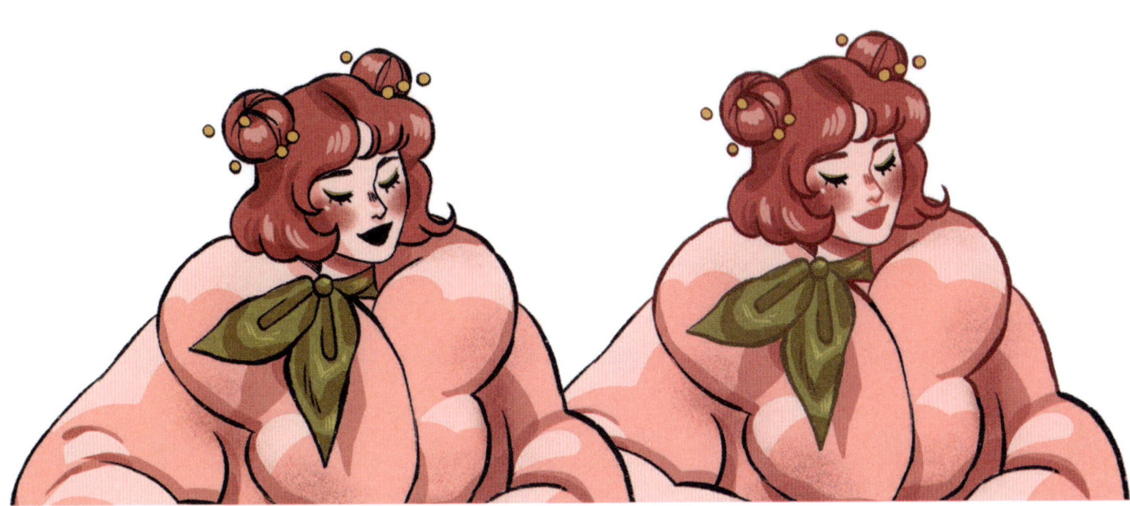

COLOURING THE OUTLINES

One approach to making your illustrations look even more refined is to colour the line art. To do this, create a new layer on top of the line art and change it to Lighten mode. Then colour the black lines with your choice of colours using the Studio Brush from Procreate's Inking set. Using a slightly darker colour than the ones used to fill the character will give your illustration a softer look.

CLOSE-UP DETAILS

The character is now almost finished. Take some time to look over the whole image, especially the fine details, to check that the design is well balanced. The little details can be as important as the overall silhouette, but knowing when to limit yourself is key – especially with a theme such as this, which offers many compelling elements to potentially include. It's tempting to include as many fun details as you can think of, but when you do that, you will often overdo it. Keep in mind the saying 'less is more' and limit yourself to the ideas that have the most impact on your character. In this case, all it takes to polish the design is colouring the line art and painting in details such as coat buttons, extra freckles, and subtle hair textures.

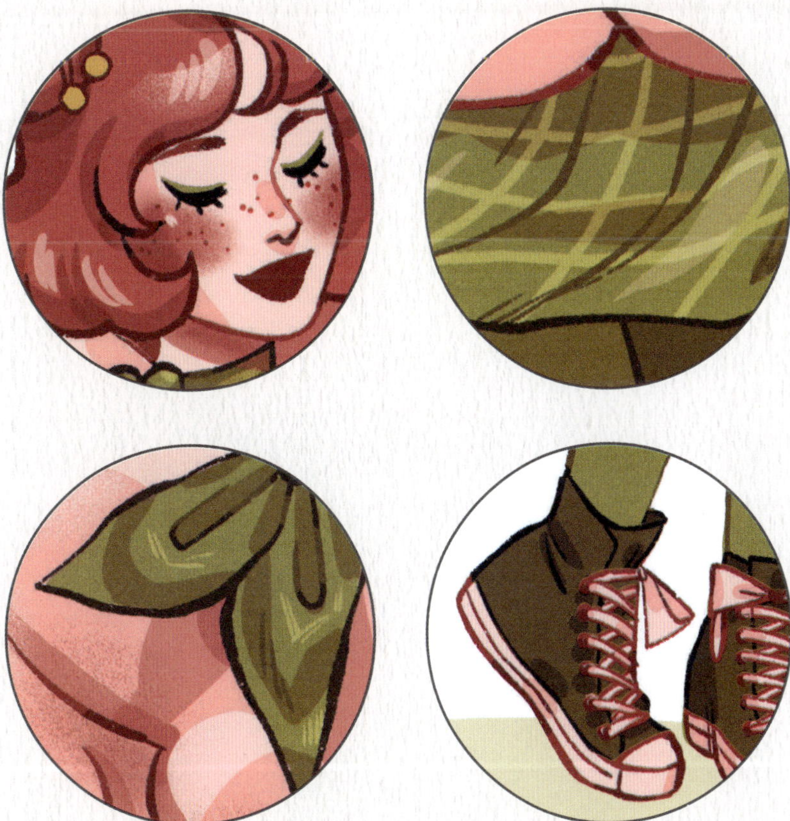

Check over the small details and make final refinements, but don't overdo them

THE FINISHED DESIGN

Character design is fun and without a doubt a great exercise to practise every aspect of storytelling. Bringing characters to life can offer boundless opportunities to explore, push out of your comfort zone, and tell stories through memorable silhouettes, interesting shapes, and loveable personalities. This particular cherry blossom girl is round and sweet; she likes to daydream and loves spring, but keeps her fluffy coat on because of the wind. She likes fashion and pastel colours, but her priority is to stay warm and comfortable. Haiku poems are written about how whimsical and beautiful she is, but she's humble and would sometimes prefer to hide away. Her presence is comforting and calming. Now, how else could you interpret a cherry blossom character?

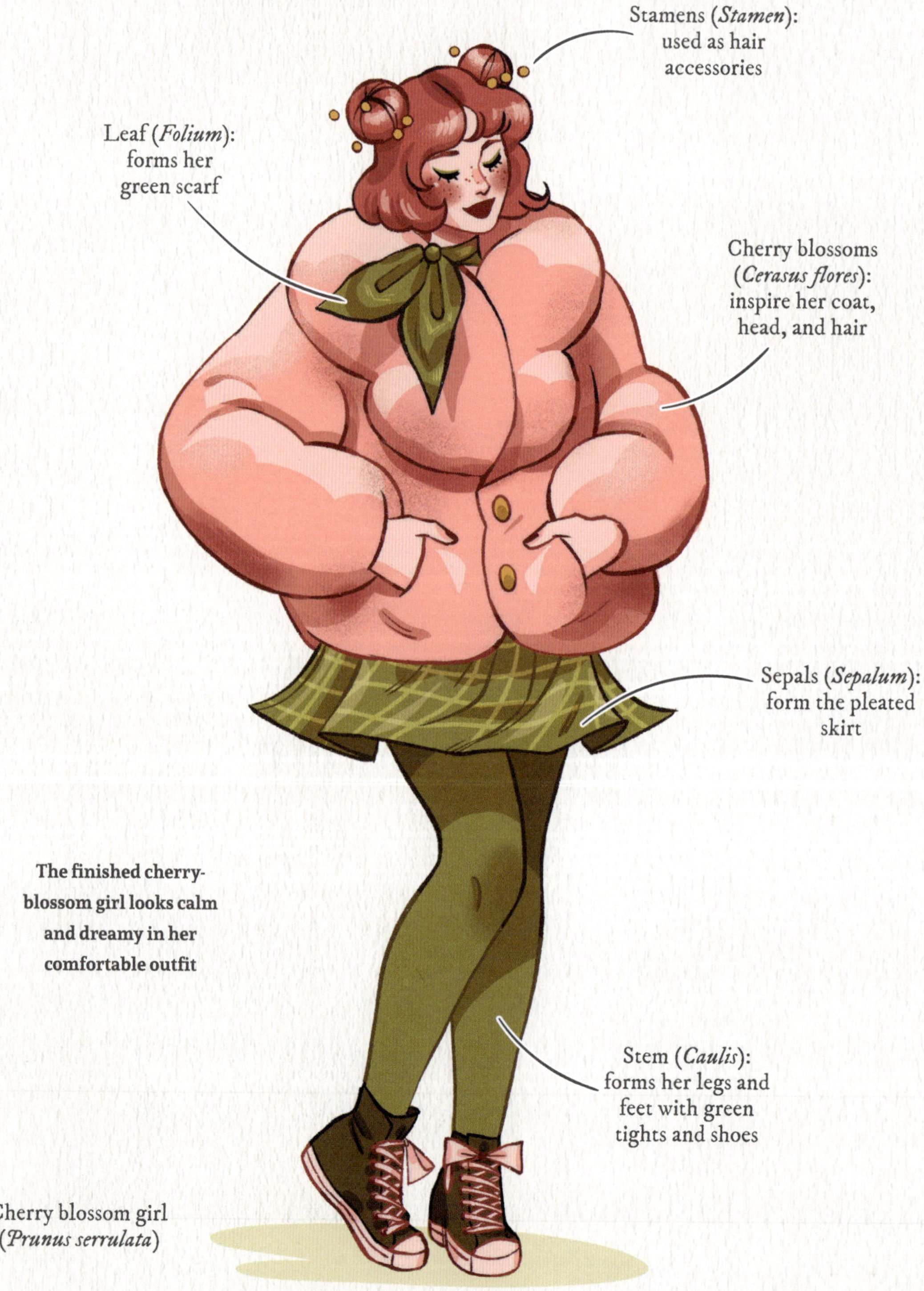

The finished cherry-blossom girl looks calm and dreamy in her comfortable outfit

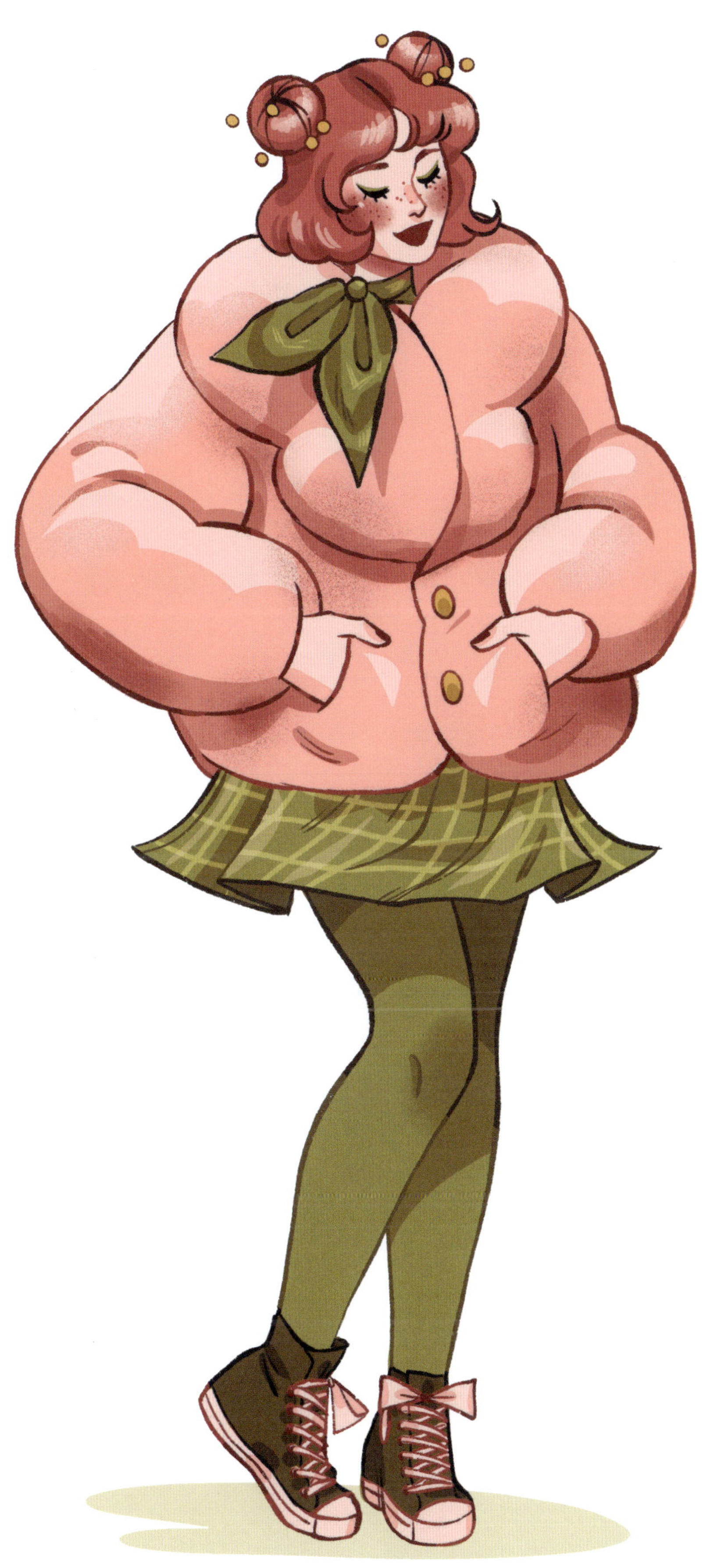

CHERRY BLOSSOM GIRL

Final image © Sibylline Meynet

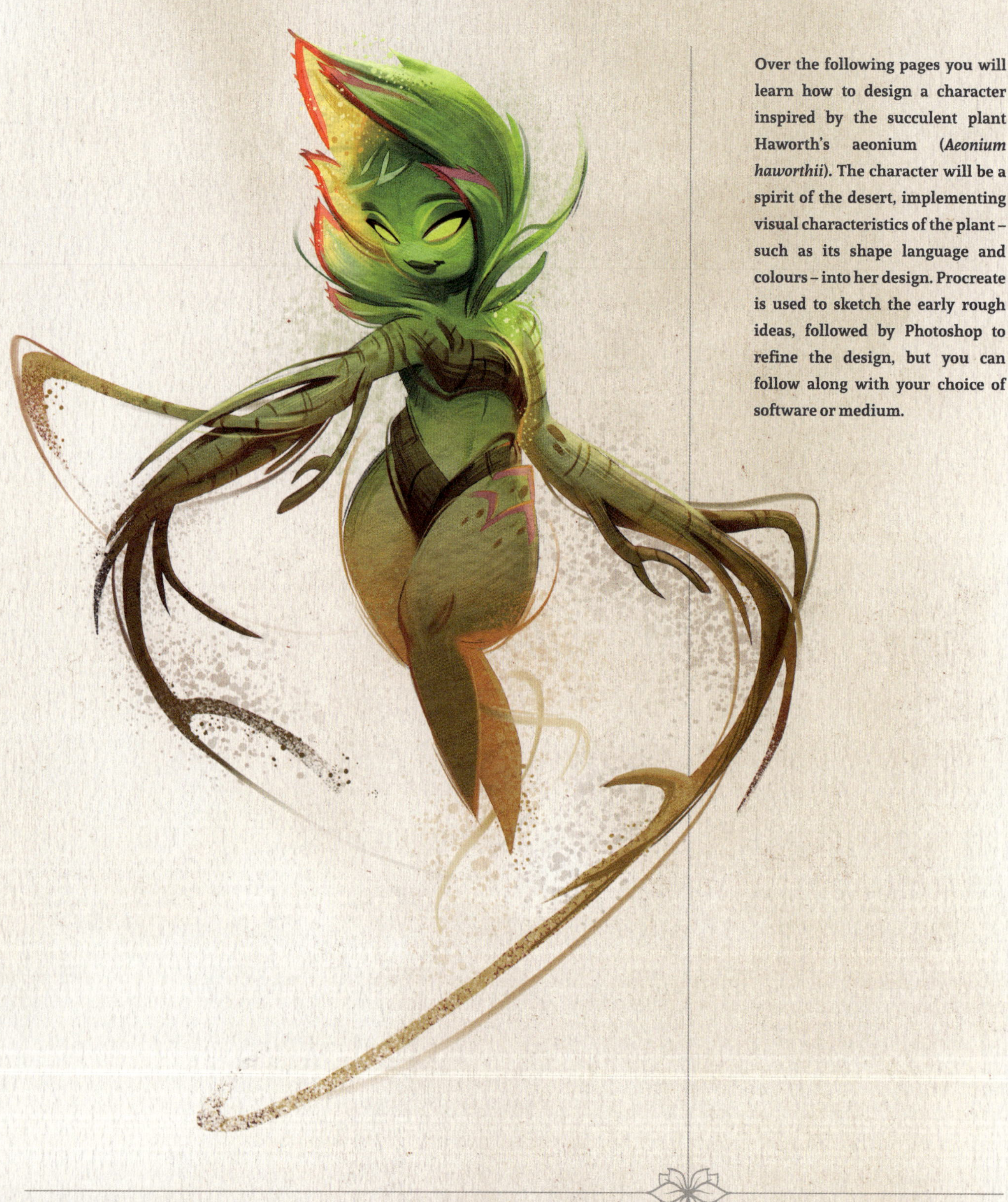

Over the following pages you will learn how to design a character inspired by the succulent plant Haworth's aeonium (*Aeonium haworthii*). The character will be a spirit of the desert, implementing visual characteristics of the plant – such as its shape language and colours – into her design. Procreate is used to sketch the early rough ideas, followed by Photoshop to refine the design, but you can follow along with your choice of software or medium.

succulent

DESERT SPIRIT

ESTER CONCEICAO

START WITH RESEARCH

During the research stage, it's important to carefully study and form an understanding of the plant's shape and main characteristics. Focus on simplifying the shapes of each section of the plant and start analysing these characteristics from top to bottom. As you're not using colours just yet, keep in mind how the colours might translate into values, as this will help to figure out the design later.

The aeonium plant has green leaves that are triangular or droplet-shaped, edged with small 'eyelashes' (cilia). These leaves come in a variety of thicknesses. The colours have some hue and value variations of green and pink or red. The plant also has woody stems with a lighter tone, and the roots can vary between thick strands and thin hair-like strings.

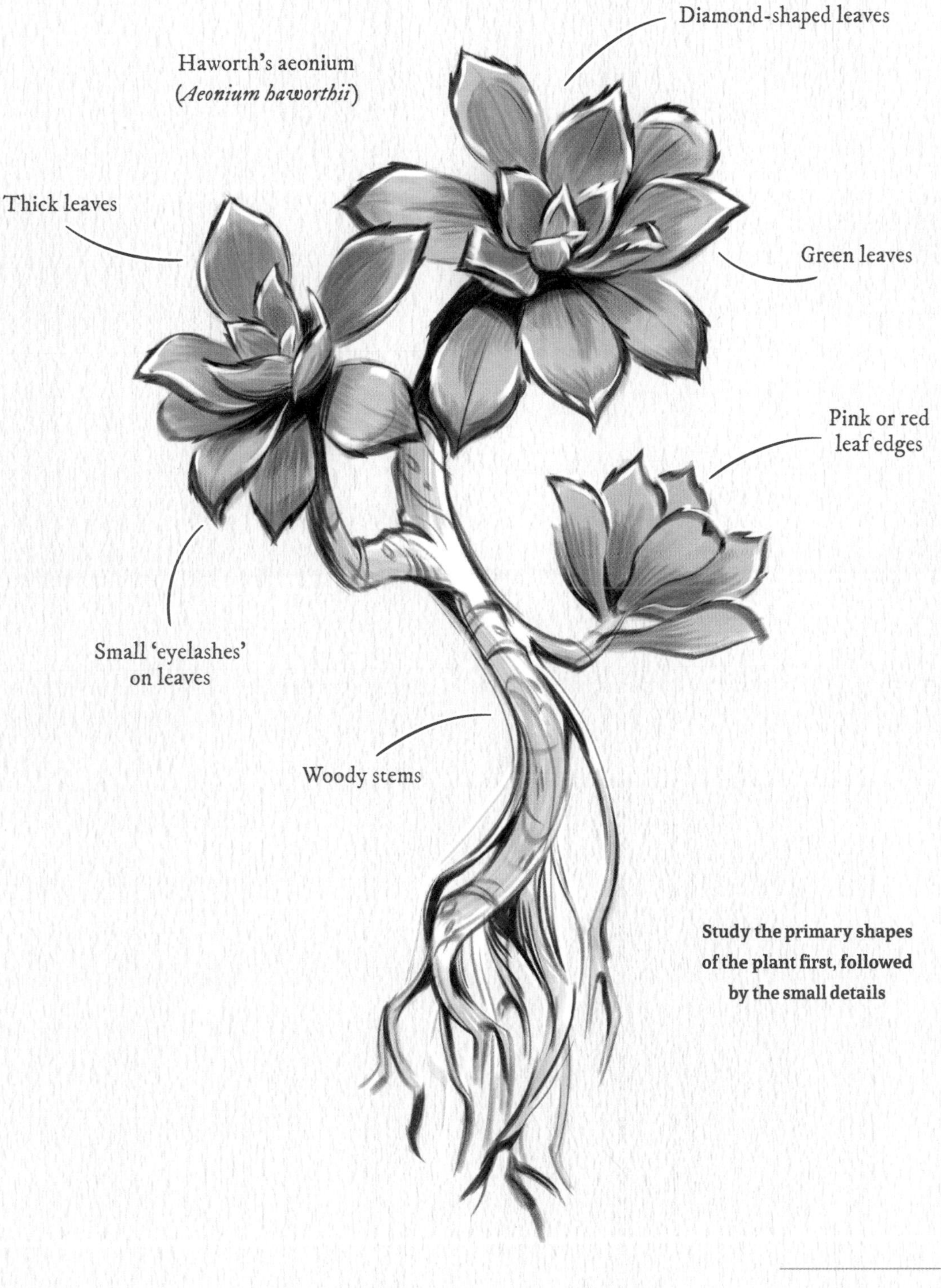

Diamond-shaped leaves

Haworth's aeonium (*Aeonium haworthii*)

Thick leaves

Green leaves

Pink or red leaf edges

Small 'eyelashes' on leaves

Woody stems

Study the primary shapes of the plant first, followed by the small details

INITIAL SKETCHES

The objective is now to experiment with different variations of shapes without worrying too much about adding fine details. Try to incorporate elements of the aeonium plant as parts of her body to communicate the idea of her being a desert spirit. You can also think about where the plant comes from and how the people from that desert region dress. This can inspire ideas like shaping the leaves into a hood or trousers.

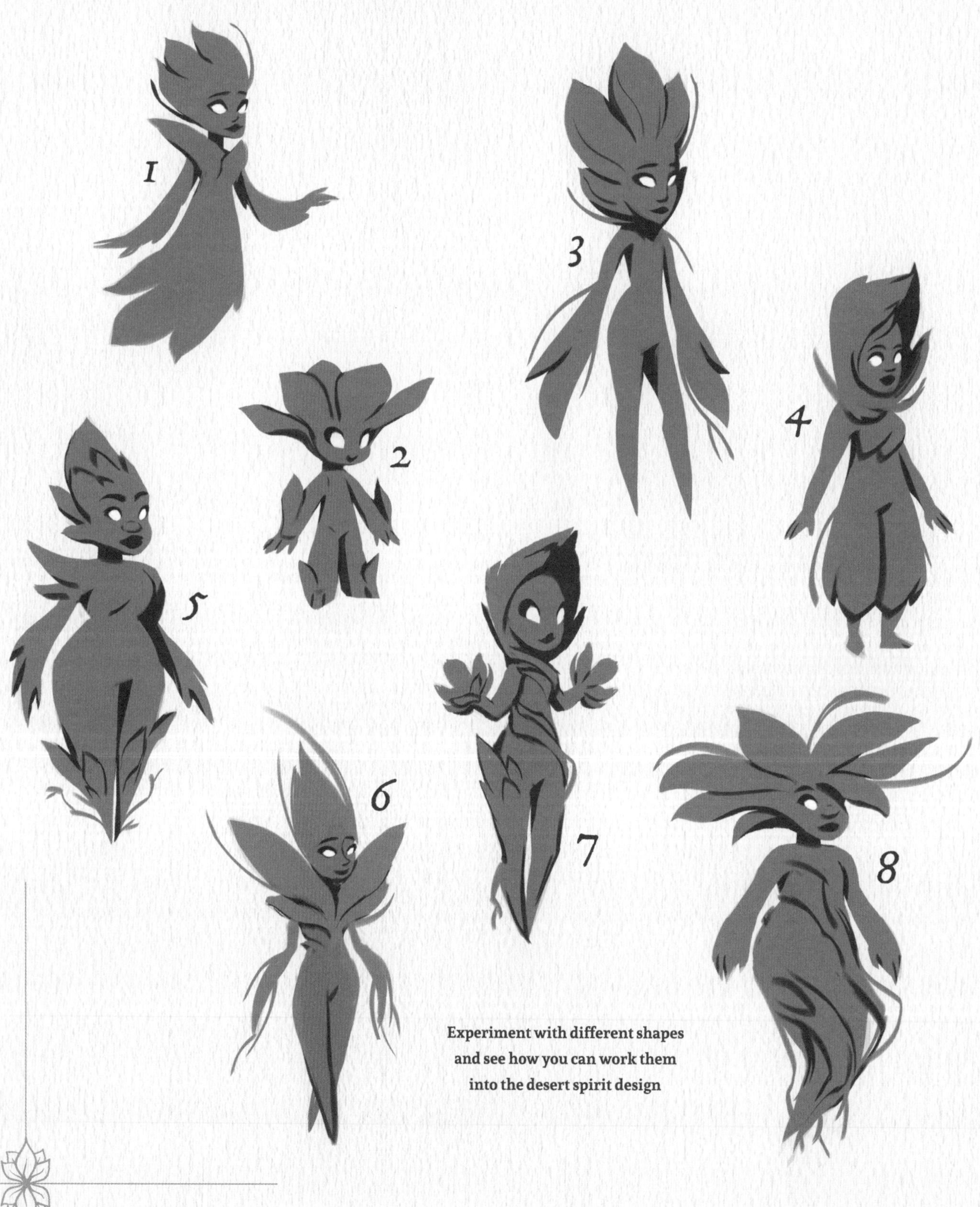

Experiment with different shapes and see how you can work them into the desert spirit design

REFINING THE DESIGN IDEA

Once you're confident with your initial sketch thumbnails, start combining the elements that have the strongest silhouettes and best match your character's description. For example, the arms of thumbnail 6 fit well with the main body of thumbnail 7. When you've finished mixing and matching the parts, make sure the combined elements look as solid as possible before moving on to the next step. Refer back to the original look of the Haworth's aeonium to help with this. Add the hood of leaves around her head, roots that wrap around her body and morph into her lower arms, and the leaves on her shoulders and legs.

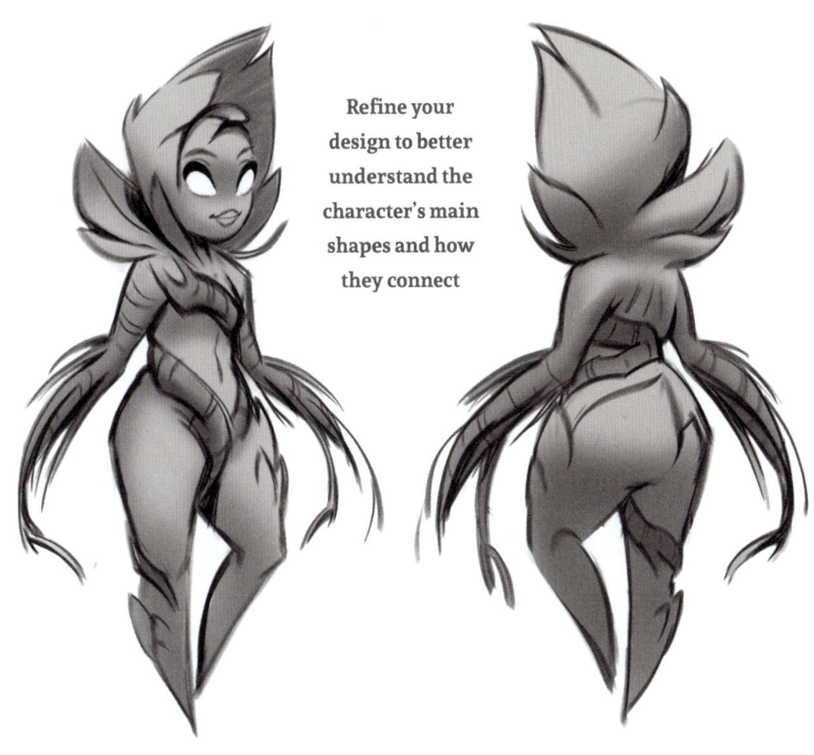

Refine your design to better understand the character's main shapes and how they connect

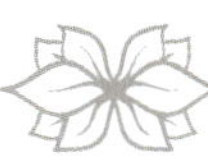

COLOUR IDEAS

The aeonium plant has a variety of shades of green and yellow in its base, and pink and red on the edges of its leaves. These shades vary in saturation and value, so try exploring a few different options. As this character is a desert spirit, option D works well, as the yellows and pale greens sell the idea that she lives in a dry environment. Note how the more saturated greens are located around her head, reflecting how the aeonium retains water in its leaves.

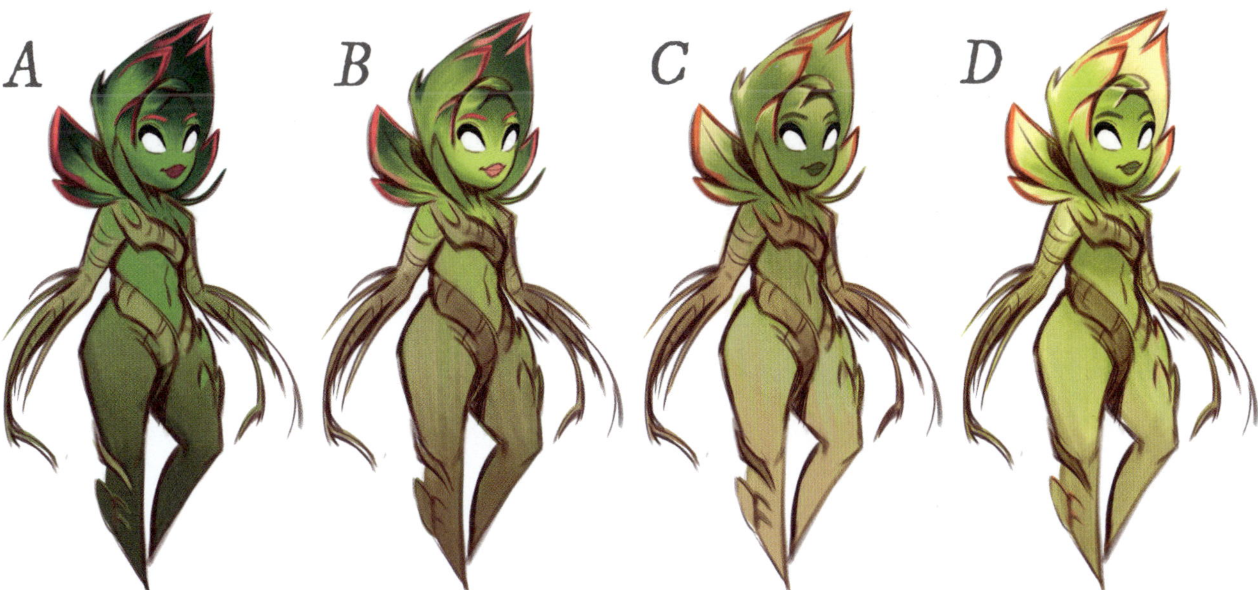

Experiment with different colour options to find the best fit for the character

REVISE BEFORE REFINING

Don't be afraid to make adjustments at this point, before you move further into the final stages of the design. You need to have clarified all of the core elements of the design before you can begin refining it or drawing poses. Ask a fellow artist, friend, or family member for their opinion, as it will help you to determine if the character's anatomy, silhouette, and design are visually appealing!

CLEANING UP THE DESIGN

You can now start to clean up the design by removing the rough line work and adding local colours. This helps to give more clarity to the character's shapes and harmonizes the colours with her design. For now, there's no need to add heavy shading – just use the different hues and values to simply sculpt the large, medium, and small forms. When painting digitally, it's useful to keep some colour swatches nearby to avoid picking the wrong colours and mixing them up. Once those base colours are added, you can add a soft layer of shadow to make her shape pop a little more, plus some line art to separate any elements that overlap, such as her arm and torso. You can also begin to add the tiny eyelash details to the leaves.

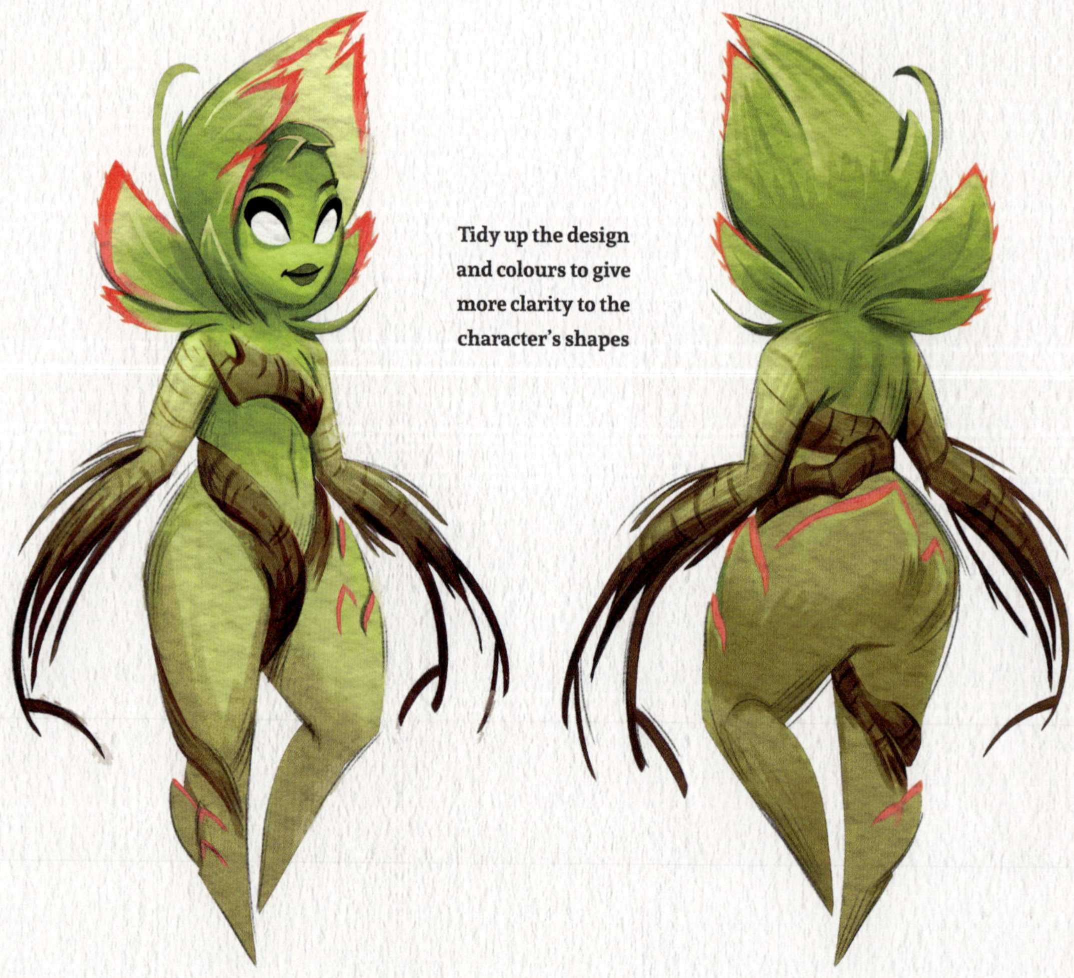

Tidy up the design and colours to give more clarity to the character's shapes

POSE EXPLORATIONS

Now that you have a solid foundation of the character's design and an understanding of her three-dimensionality, you can start sketching quick ideas for poses and expressions. At this stage, there's no need to add all the small details – your goal is to figure out a silhouette that transmits the essence of the character's spirit and personality.

She would move around the desert almost as if she's dancing, to reinforce the idea of her being a magical being. Don't be afraid to exaggerate how she moves her arms, legs, and torso, and experiment with how her arms and roots stretch as she moves around.

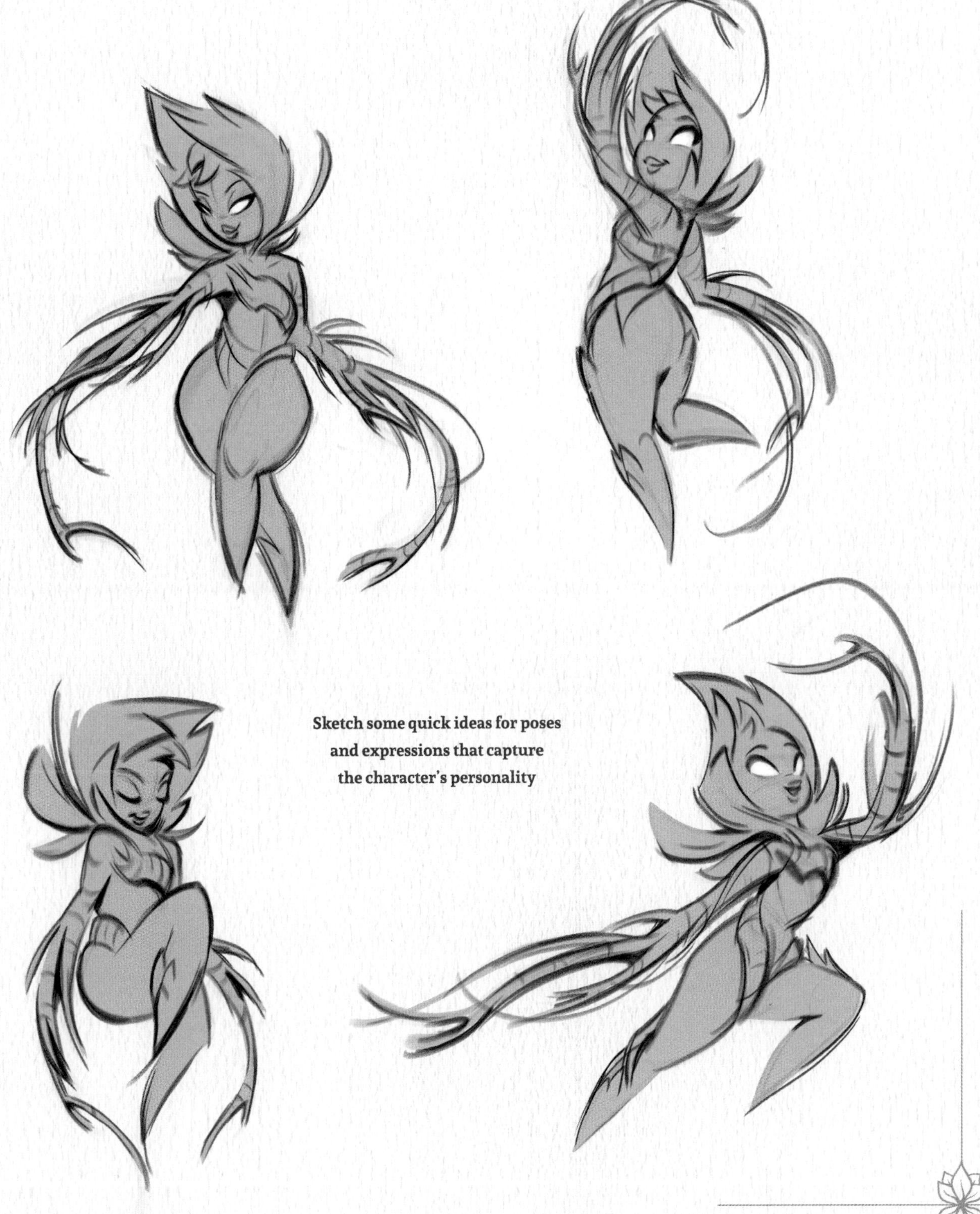

Sketch some quick ideas for poses and expressions that capture the character's personality

REFINING THE POSE

The first pose is the best option for offering a clear view of the character while also showing her in motion. Since her arm roots can grow and stretch in length when dancing or moving, you need to elongate them and add a few more thin strands to make them appear even more dynamic. Drawing all of these details can quickly become tricky – avoid drawing roots randomly without first considering which direction they're travelling in. It can be useful to simplify the root shapes into cylinders and draw grid lines that wrap around them, helping to visualize their form and direction. Once this is done, start cleaning up the sketch and construction lines so that the drawing looks clearer and more polished.

Exaggerate the roots and simplify them into gridded cylinders

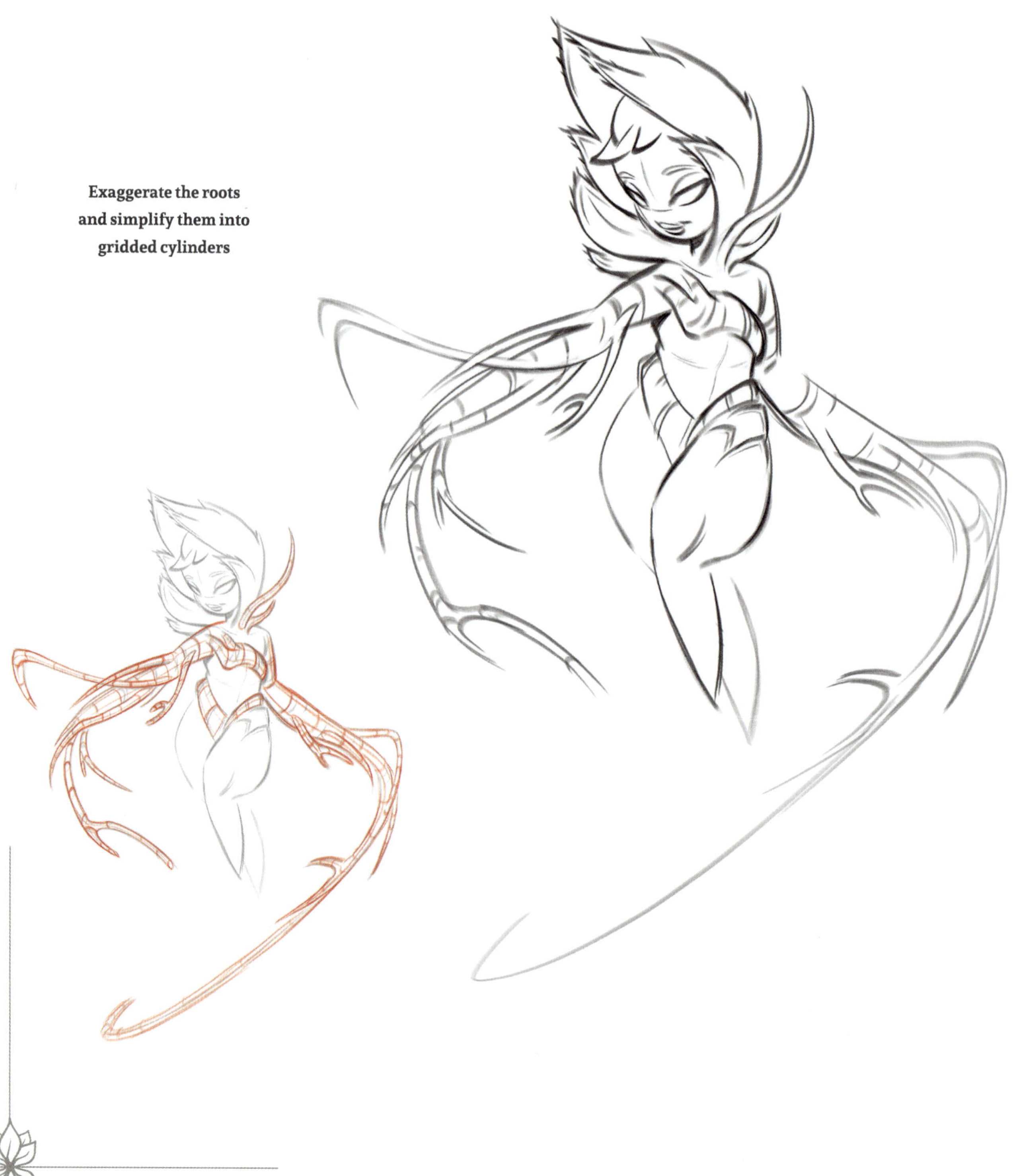

PLANNING THE COMPOSITION

Before you move into colours, it's important to plan out the composition of the painting: determining the use of values, the light source, shadows, and focal point. The goal is to make the character's face and eyes the centre of attention and to use the flow and rhythm of her arms to lead the viewer's eye through the image. To achieve that, start by painting the local value, then create a Multiply layer on top to add an overall shadow. Make sure to keep her eyes bright for more contrast. To add mood, use a Linear Dodge layer to add a rim light behind her on the right.

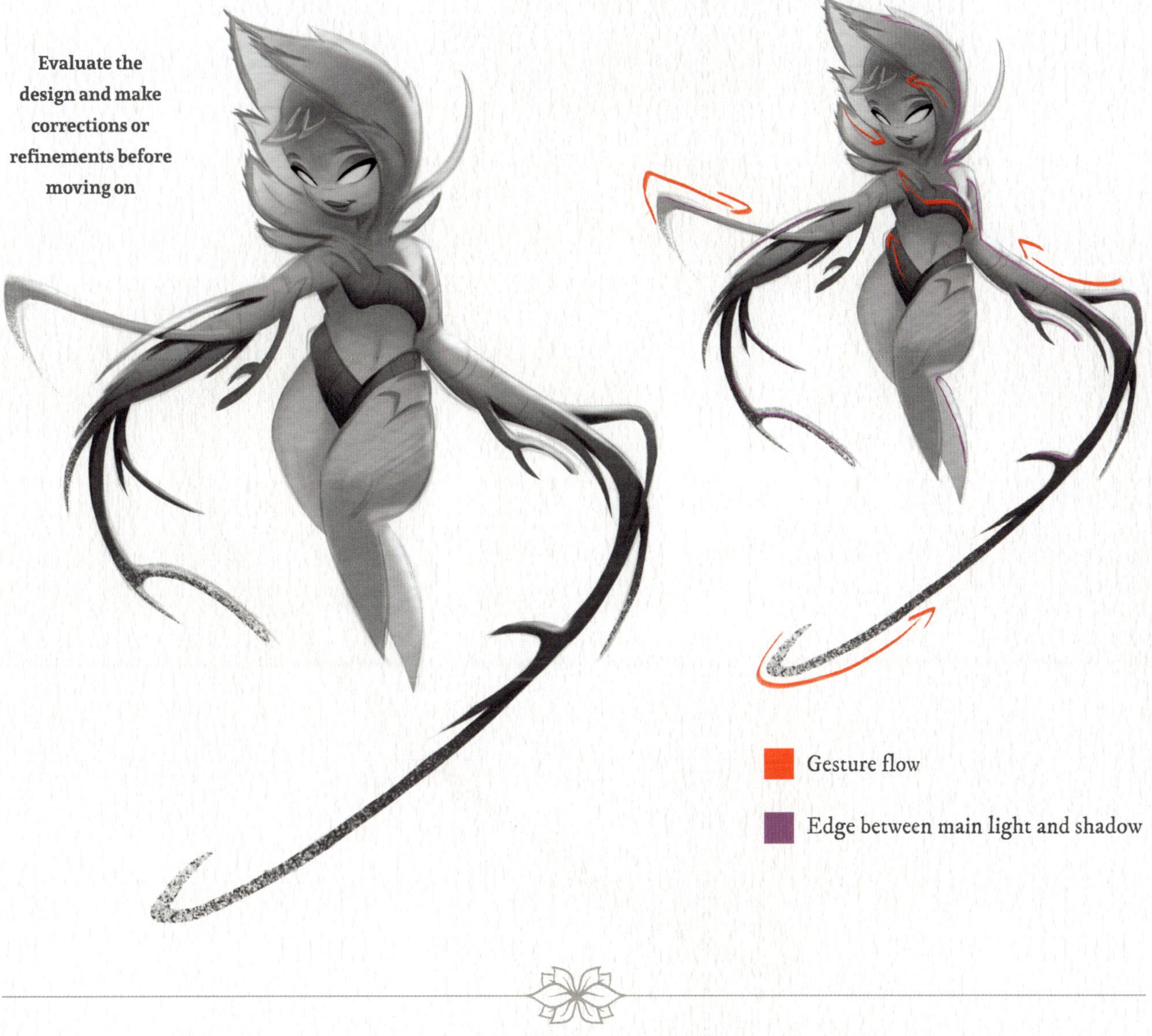

Evaluate the design and make corrections or refinements before moving on

SQUINT YOUR EYES

As you progress with the painting, you might find yourself zooming in too close to the canvas, which can lead you to lose track of the main goal of the composition. Squinting your eyes and/or looking at the character from a distance will enable you to keep the shape of the rim light simple and see how it impacts the whole design, whereas zooming in for too long can tempt you to focus on the small bumpy shapes of her arms too much.

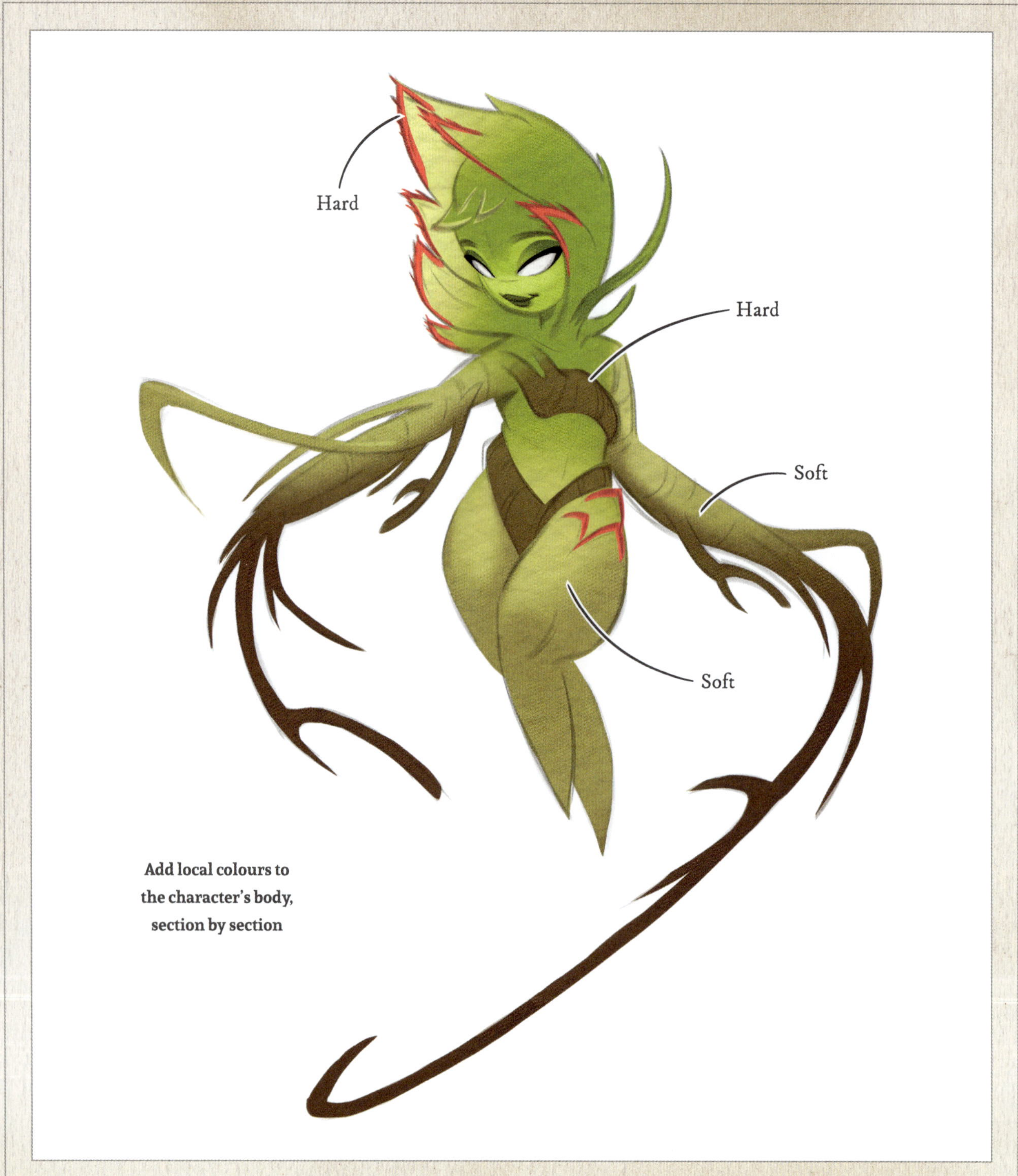

Add local colours to the character's body, section by section

LOCAL COLOUR

Once you're confident with the composition and greyscale values, you can start adding local colour. Lower the opacity of the line-art layer so you can use it as a guide to divide each section of the character's body. Start by using a soft brush to add colour to the body parts where there are soft colour transitions, such as the legs, which are dark yellow at the bottom and light yellow at the top. You can then use the Lasso tool for areas that don't have a soft transition, such as the roots wrapped around her torso and hips, the red leaf tips on her hood and legs, and some of the facial features (the eyes, eyelashes, and lips).

ADDING FORM

So far, you have given the character life little by little, but now you can really work on sculpting the design's volume. On a new layer, add the occlusion shadow on her neck and in between the roots on her arms. These are the areas where the light cannot reach, so keep in mind the direction of the main light source to help you determine where to add occlusion. Use slightly darker versions of the local colours of her head and torso roots to create more dimension in those areas. Do the same to the pink tips of her leaves, so they don't look too flat, by adding a slightly darker tone to some of the edges.

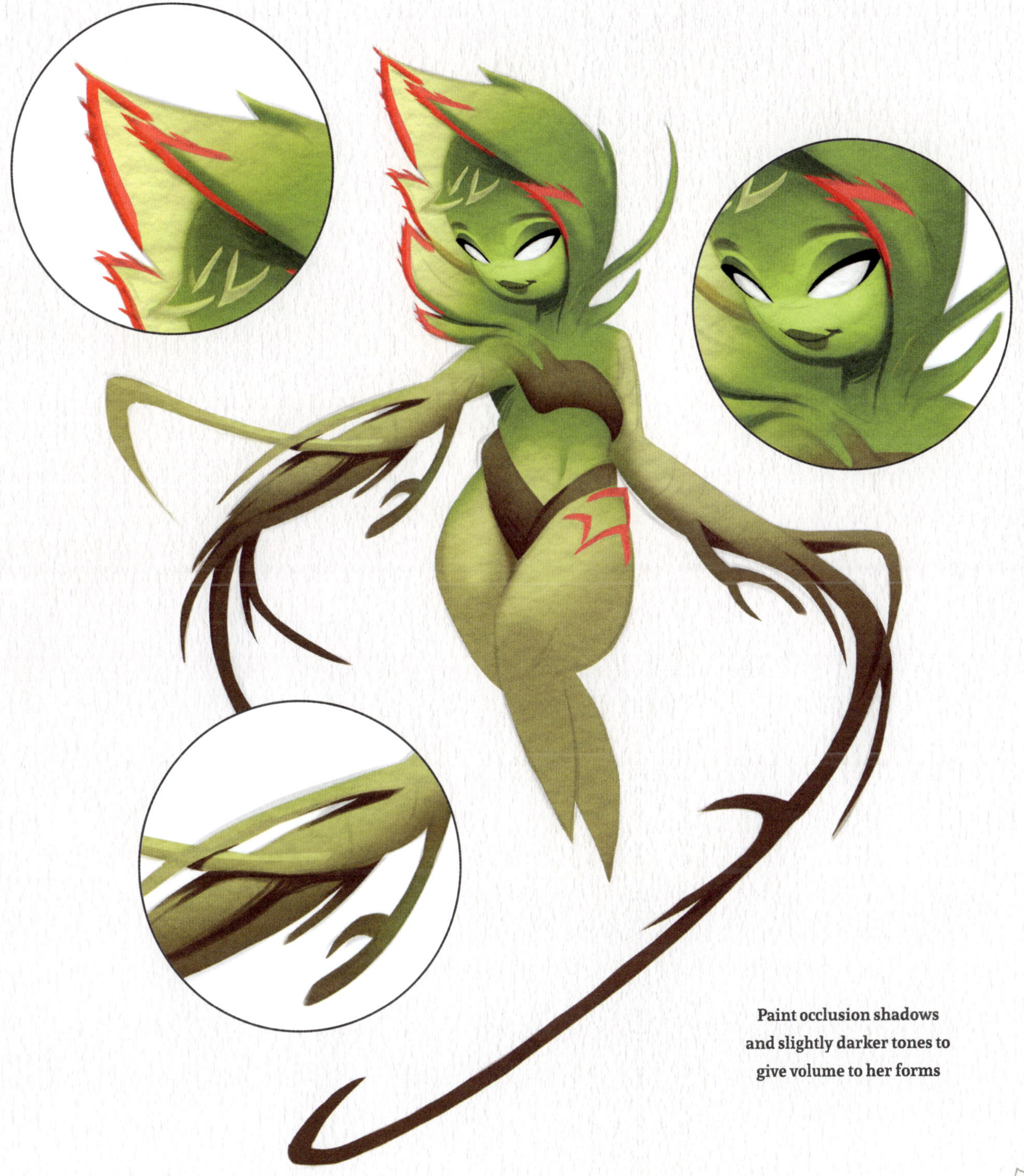

Paint occlusion shadows and slightly darker tones to give volume to her forms

ADDING TEXTURE

There are some soft edges that need more texture, which will give the character's pose a sense of movement and life. Add some hatching lines that follow the form of that specific body part – this will help to reinforce its direction and perspective. Sketch more hatching into the colour gradients, such as on her legs, upper arms, and torso roots.

Create a Multiply layer on top and draw the woody texture of the stems, and add a few small dots to some areas of her arms and leg leaves. Finally, use a textured brush on a layer mask to slightly fade some of the tips of the roots, as if they are blurred in motion.

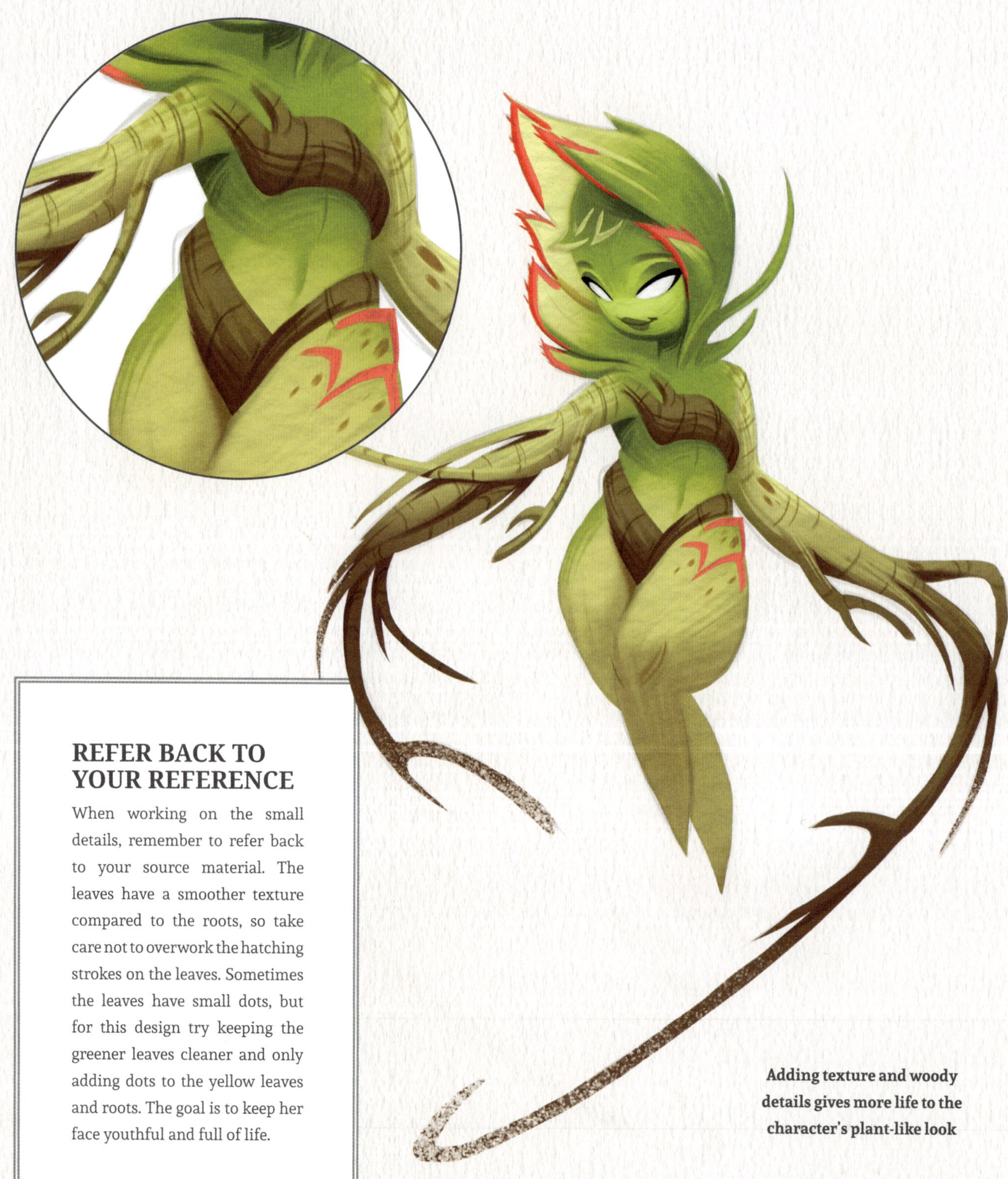

Adding texture and woody details gives more life to the character's plant-like look

REFER BACK TO YOUR REFERENCE

When working on the small details, remember to refer back to your source material. The leaves have a smoother texture compared to the roots, so take care not to overwork the hatching strokes on the leaves. Sometimes the leaves have small dots, but for this design try keeping the greener leaves cleaner and only adding dots to the yellow leaves and roots. The goal is to keep her face youthful and full of life.

DESERT SHADOWS

Now that the character has enough volume, you need to make her feel as if she's in a desert environment. Even without a full background, this can be achieved subtly with the use of shadows. Add a layer of very light, pale blue over the character and set it to Multiply to give the design a cooler tint. This will give the viewer the idea that it's daytime, with the blue of the sky reflecting in the shadow. Create a Darken layer and paint a darker, warmer gradient over the character's lower body; this will bring balance to the cooler colours above, as well as bringing more focus to the upper body.

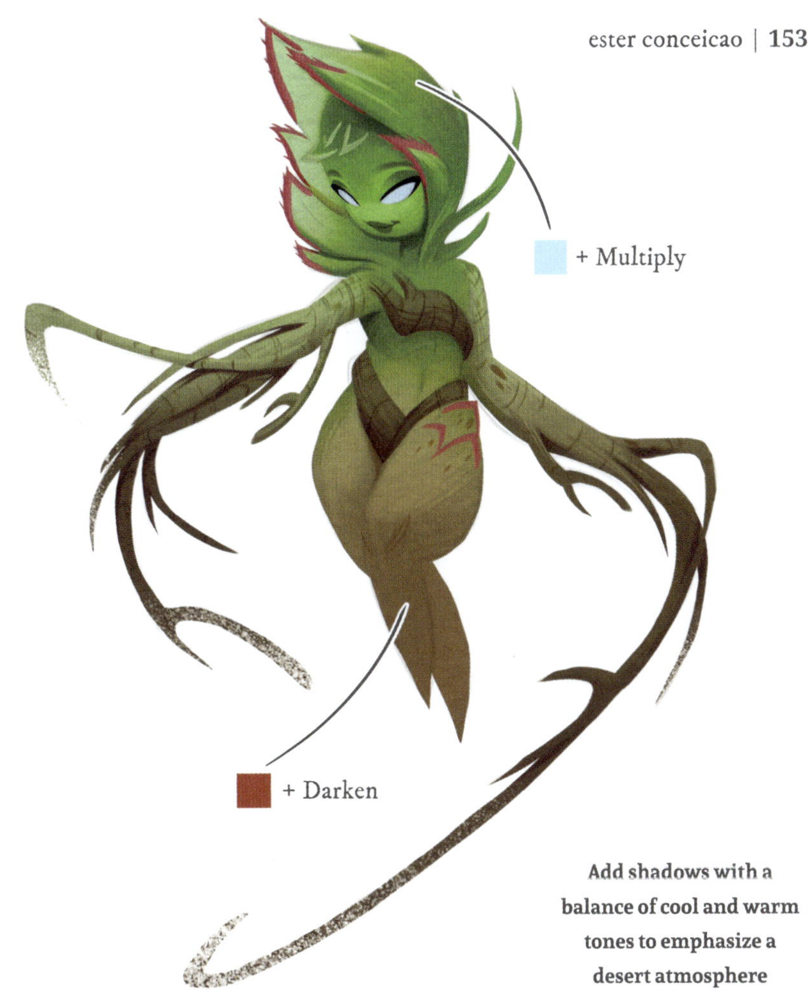

Add shadows with a balance of cool and warm tones to emphasize a desert atmosphere

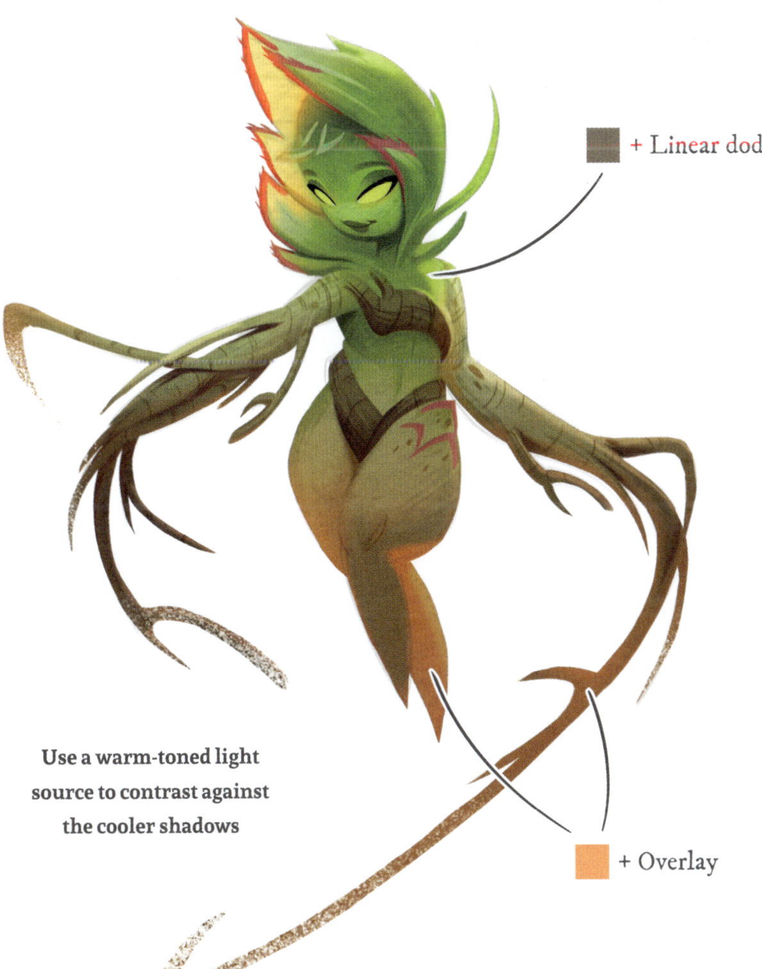

Use a warm-toned light source to contrast against the cooler shadows

MAIN LIGHTING

Now it's time to add the main light source. Add a new layer set to Linear Dodge and begin painting some warm colour onto it. The sunlight would pass through the leaves of the character's hood, so paint that area with more saturation. Light also tends to bounce in different directions when it hits a surface, so use an Overlay layer to add a warm glow bouncing up from the desert sand. This adds depth to her pose, bringing one leg forward and pushing one arm back. You can also add some colour to her eyes to give them more life and contrast.

FINAL TOUCHES

The character is now very close to completion and all the characteristics of the aeonium plant have come to life. As a finishing touch, you can add more texture to the painting to give it a slightly more traditional look by removing the line-art layer and creating a new one, with sketchier pencil lines around her form. Draw parallel hatching lines and focus on adding them in the darker areas, with only a few in lighter areas.

It's important to focus on adding details in the right areas. Be careful not to overdo it. Paint some extra thin, flowing strokes around her roots to create more variety in thickness, and add more of these thin lines around her legs, torso roots, and hood. Finally, use a textured brush to paint various tiny dots where the tips of the roots fade, and in the areas between the background and the main light source, as if particles of dust and sand are catching the light. These small touches enhance the succulent desert spirit's final look and add variety to the details.

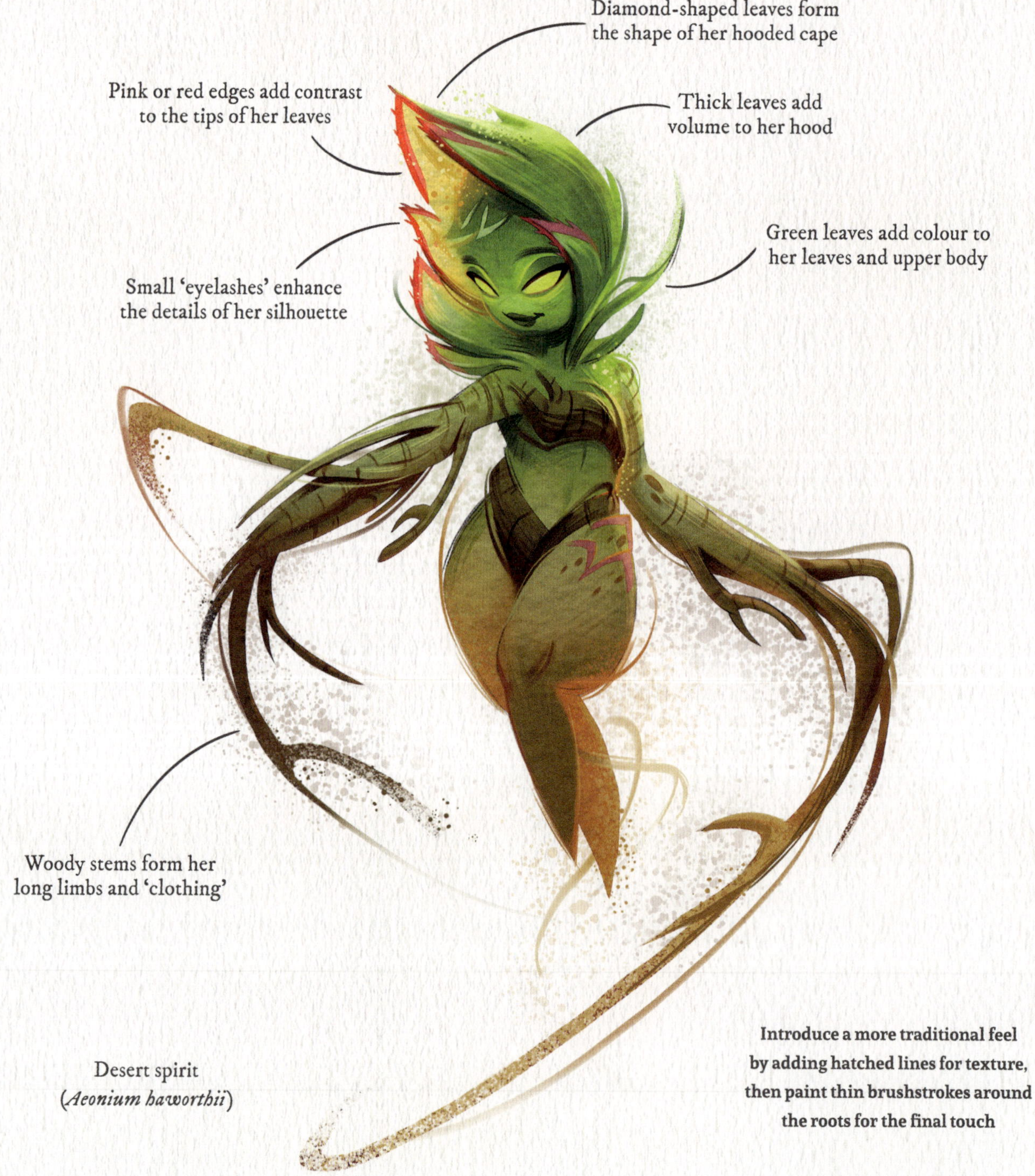

Desert spirit
(*Aeonium haworthii*)

Introduce a more traditional feel by adding hatched lines for texture, then paint thin brushstrokes around the roots for the final touch

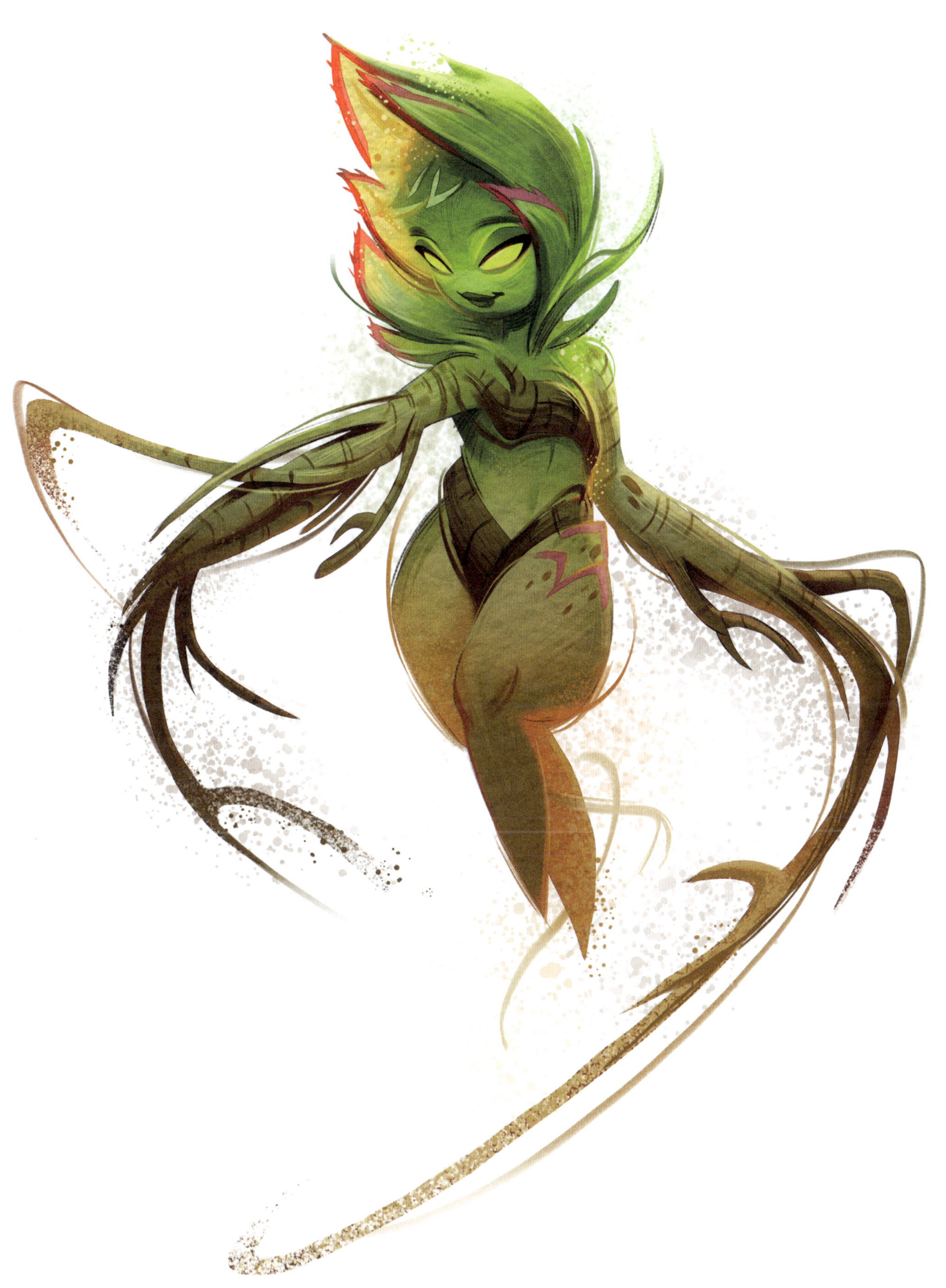

DESERT SPIRIT

Final image © Ester Conceicao

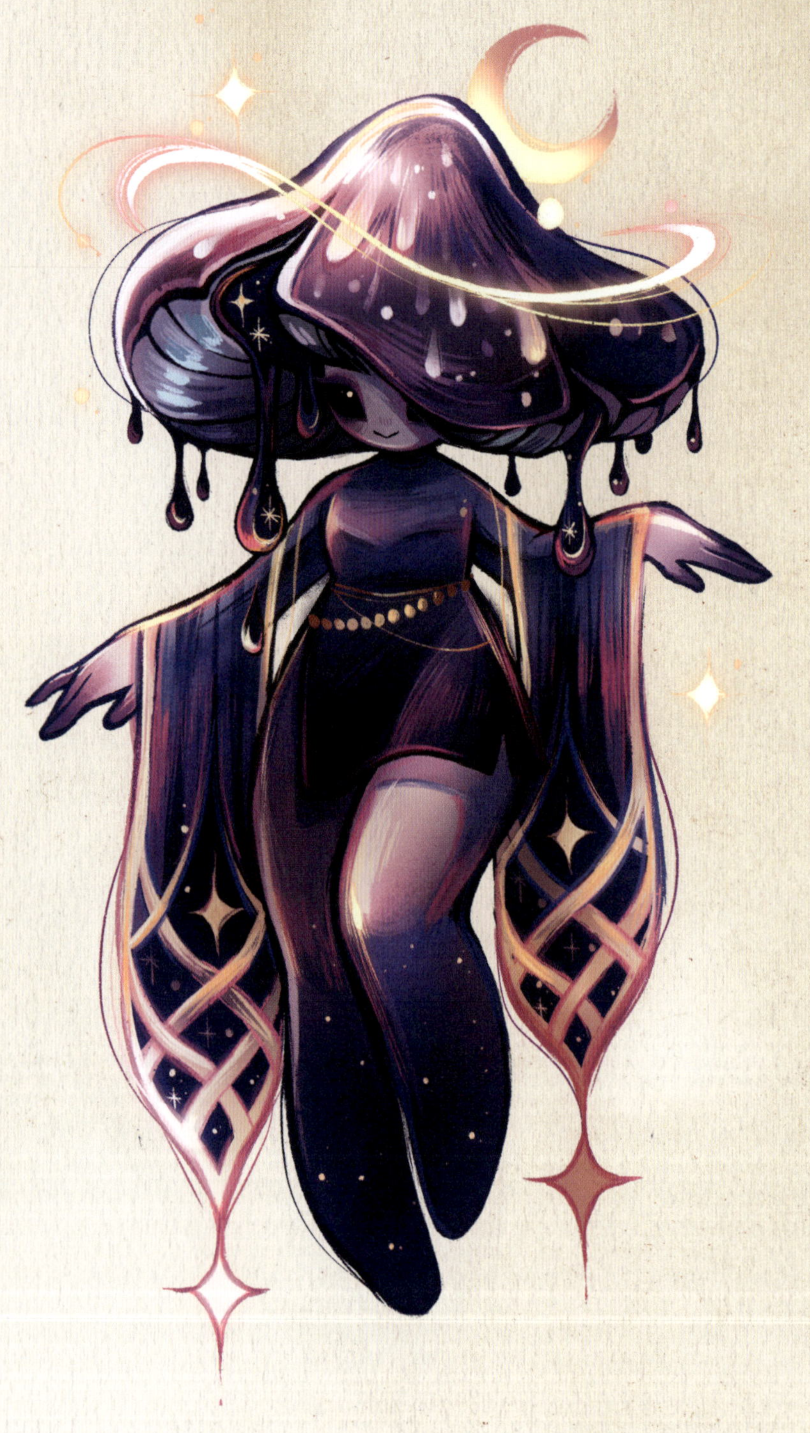

Not quite flora or fauna, the fungi kingdom is something wholly in-between, offering an endless source of inspiration with its abundance of weird and colourful species. The Cortinarius iodes, also known as the spotted cort or viscid violet cort, is widespread and undeniably striking. It has a slimy purple cap with white spots, reminiscent of a lilac starry sky. This is perfect for anthropomorphizing into a celestial being, transforming it into the magic mushroom it was always meant to be! This character will be created using Procreate on the iPad Pro.

fungi

CELESTIAL MUSHROOM GIRL

FEEFAL

START WITH RESEARCH

Begin by researching the chosen fungi and familiarising yourself with its traits. *Cortinarius iodes* is a relatively common fungi in the *Cortinariaceae* family, which is suspected to be the largest genus of agarics, containing over 2,000 species! They are woodland mushrooms, with cinnamon-brown spores and a cobweb veil. This colourful mushroom likes to grow on the forest floor, primarily around dead wood. (It has a preference for oak trees.) They have a slimy cap, best seen after a gentle downpour of rain. Other than its enticing violet colour, it's relatively plain and lacks any strong characteristics, allowing you plenty of freedom to form your own narrative for the character.

Cortinarius iodes
(Spotted cort or viscid violet cort)

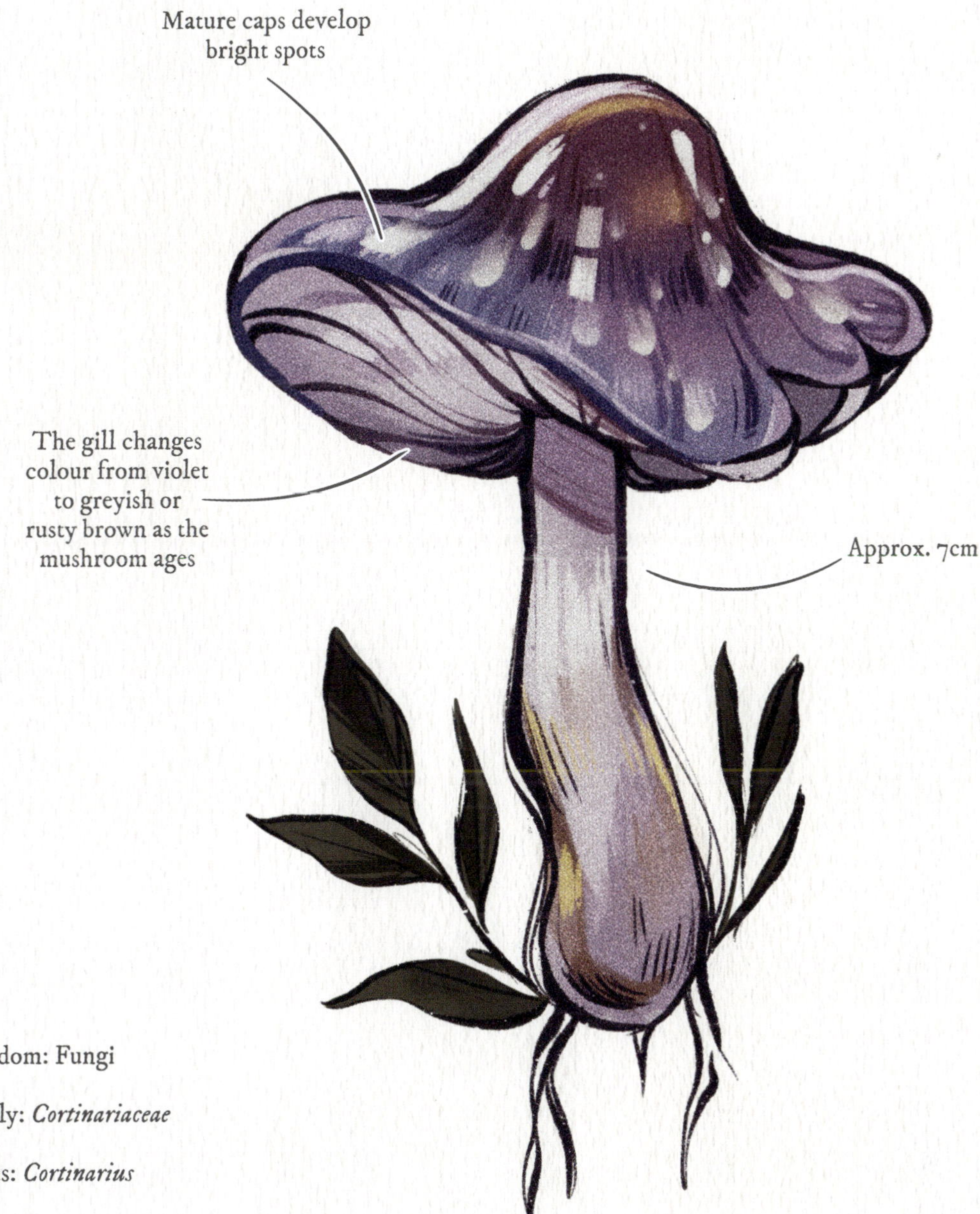

Kingdom: Fungi

Family: *Cortinariaceae*

Genus: *Cortinarius*

Species: *Cortinarius iodes*

INCORPORATING THE MUSHROOM

Before starting the design process, take a moment to consider how you can incorporate the fungus' shape into a human-like character design. The most common way is to use the mushroom cap as a hat, transforming it into some kind of gorgeous headwear. Another approach would be to craft the mushroom so it's growing out of the character's body, maybe even replacing certain body parts. It all comes down to how strange or fantastical you want the design to be, and where on the human-mushroom spectrum you want your character to land. The more you lean into the fungi aspect, the weirder and more hybrid it will seem. If you want to preserve something of the character's humanity, however, you may prefer to integrate the mushroom aspect into the character's clothing design instead.

Take note of the traits your fungus possesses. Incorporating these characteristics into the design is a wonderful way to further the lore of your character. If the mushroom is poisonous, you could give the character a sinister edge to visually portray danger. Researching your fungi is important because it helps you to explore new concepts that may not have otherwise come to mind.

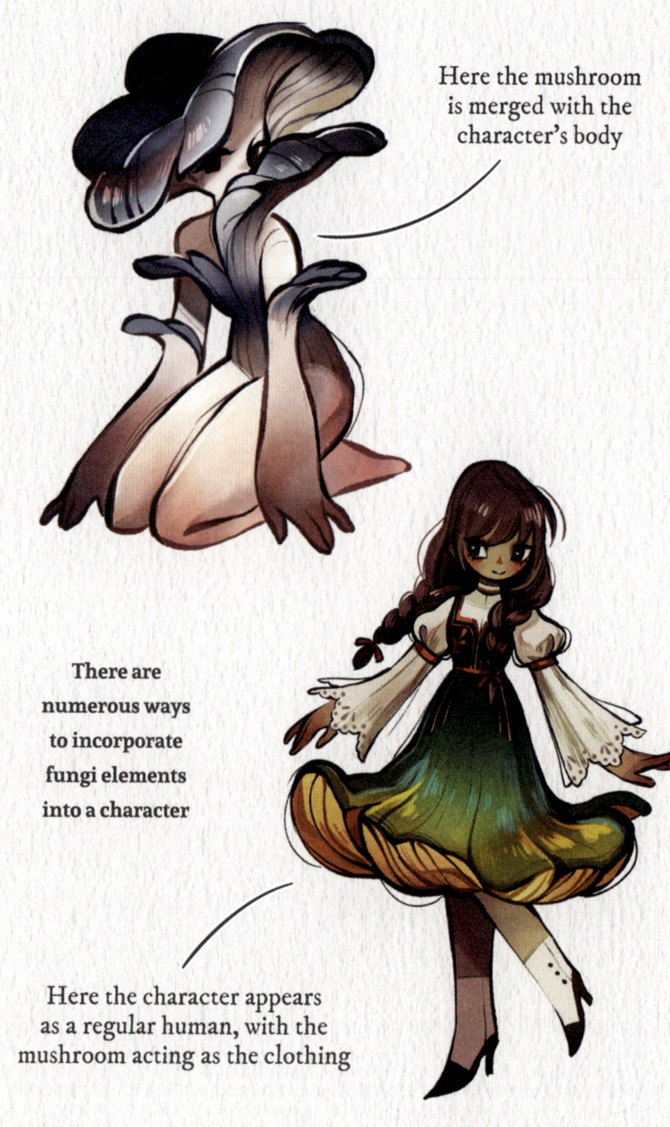

Here the mushroom is merged with the character's body

There are numerous ways to incorporate fungi elements into a character

Here the character appears as a regular human, with the mushroom acting as the clothing

FUNGI INSPIRATION

Mushrooms aren't plants and don't depend on the sun to live. In fact, they thrive in complete darkness. Instead, they gather nutrients by breaking down organic material, or put more morbidly, they live as a parasite on living plants. They're like these eldritch entities that embody the line between life and death, turning decay into new life. Some mycelium have crazy abilities, such as lethal toxicity or even mind control, which could be excellent sources of inspiration. It's interesting to think about how these characteristics would translate if given sentient form.

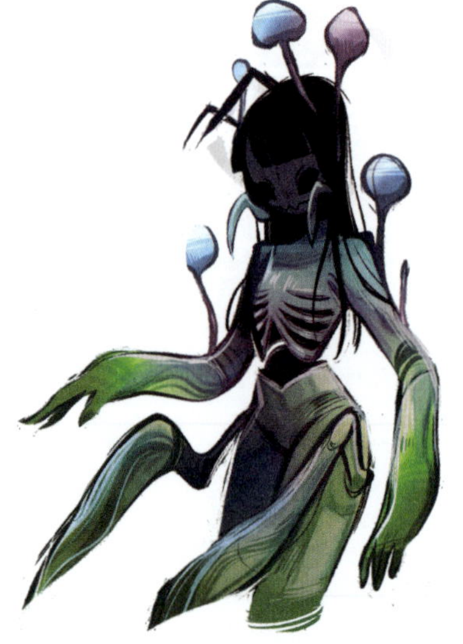

A character based on the Ophiocordyceps, also known as the zombie-ant fungus, a parasitic fungi that attacks ants and hijacks their brains and bodies. The character itself is based on a hollowed-out ant, with the fungus acting as the puppet master

SKETCHING

On observing the mushroom, you can see that it's round and colourful, with a mystical edge. Keeping these keywords in mind, start to loosely sketch out ideas for the character, prioritizing round, flowing shapes. As the mushroom cap vaguely resembles a night sky, you could choose to exaggerate this in your design by incorporating a space theme. By making the limbs thick and billowing them out towards their extremities, the anatomy appears more organic and veers away from a typically human shape. Embrace the opportunity to break away from the limitations of realistic human anatomy and feel free to exaggerate shapes.

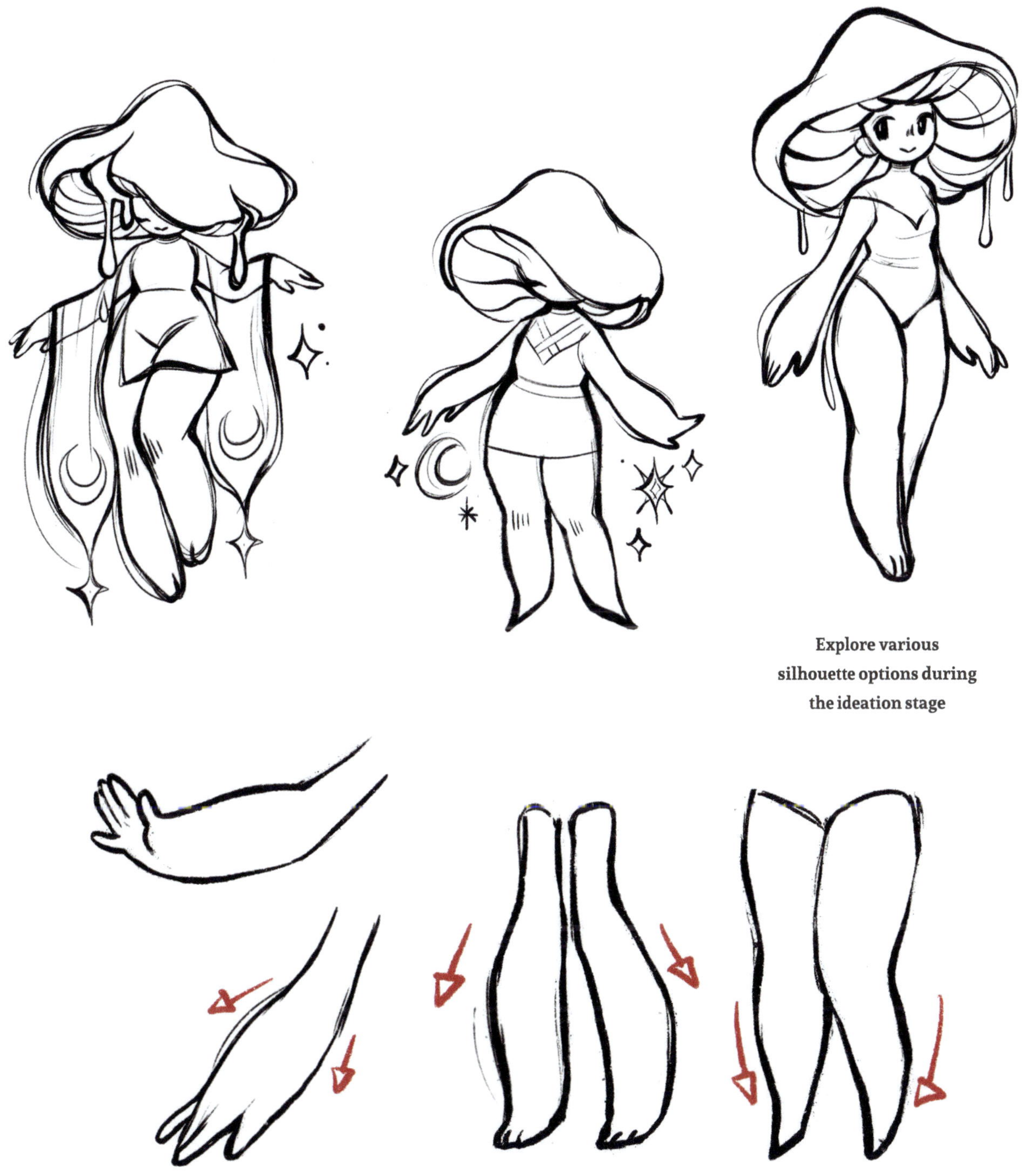

Explore various silhouette options during the ideation stage

LINE ART

Once you have a sketch you're satisfied with, it's time to start drawing the line art. Using a brush with texture to draw line art can lend a sketchy feel to the final result, which can be helpful if you struggle with drawing neat lines. A rougher brush is more forgiving, as small imperfections won't be as noticeable. To create this final outline, lower the opacity of your original sketch and draw on top of it on a new layer. Try to vary the thickness in your line art, making it thicker towards creases and bends, and thinner on longer forms, such as the arms and legs. Adding weight to your lines adds life and can be used to draw attention to detail or indicate shadow.

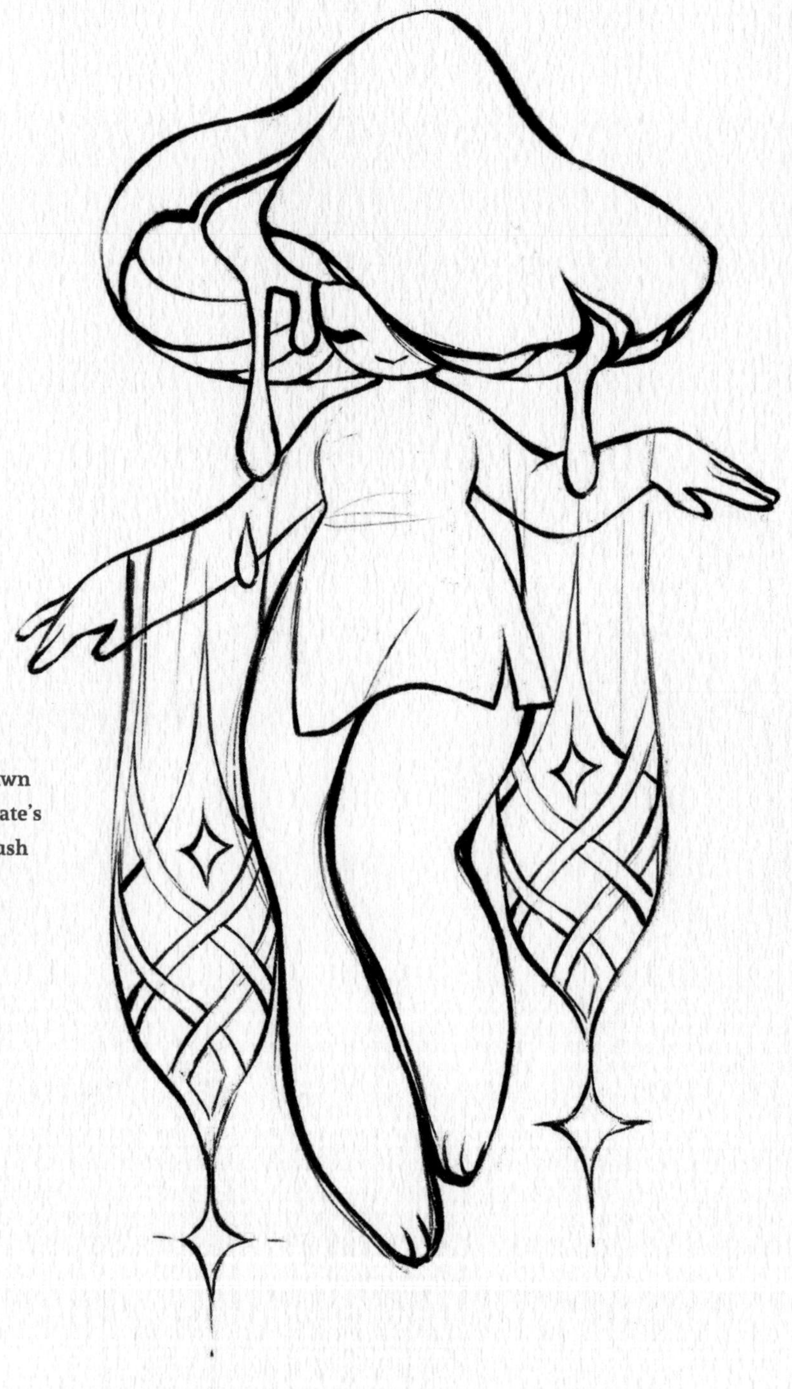

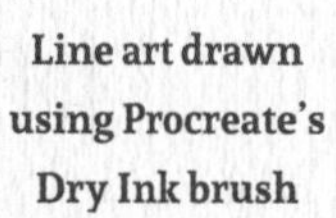

Line art drawn using Procreate's Dry Ink brush

DIRECTION & NARRATIVE

When creating a character inspired by nature, consider the direction you want to take. Fantastical and whimsical, or earthy and rooted in your source material? Adding a little fantasy into the mix is a terrific way to make the design appear more exciting, but if you stray too far from the source material, it's easy for the original narrative to get lost. A good character design isn't necessarily defined by its complexity, but its ability to tell a story.

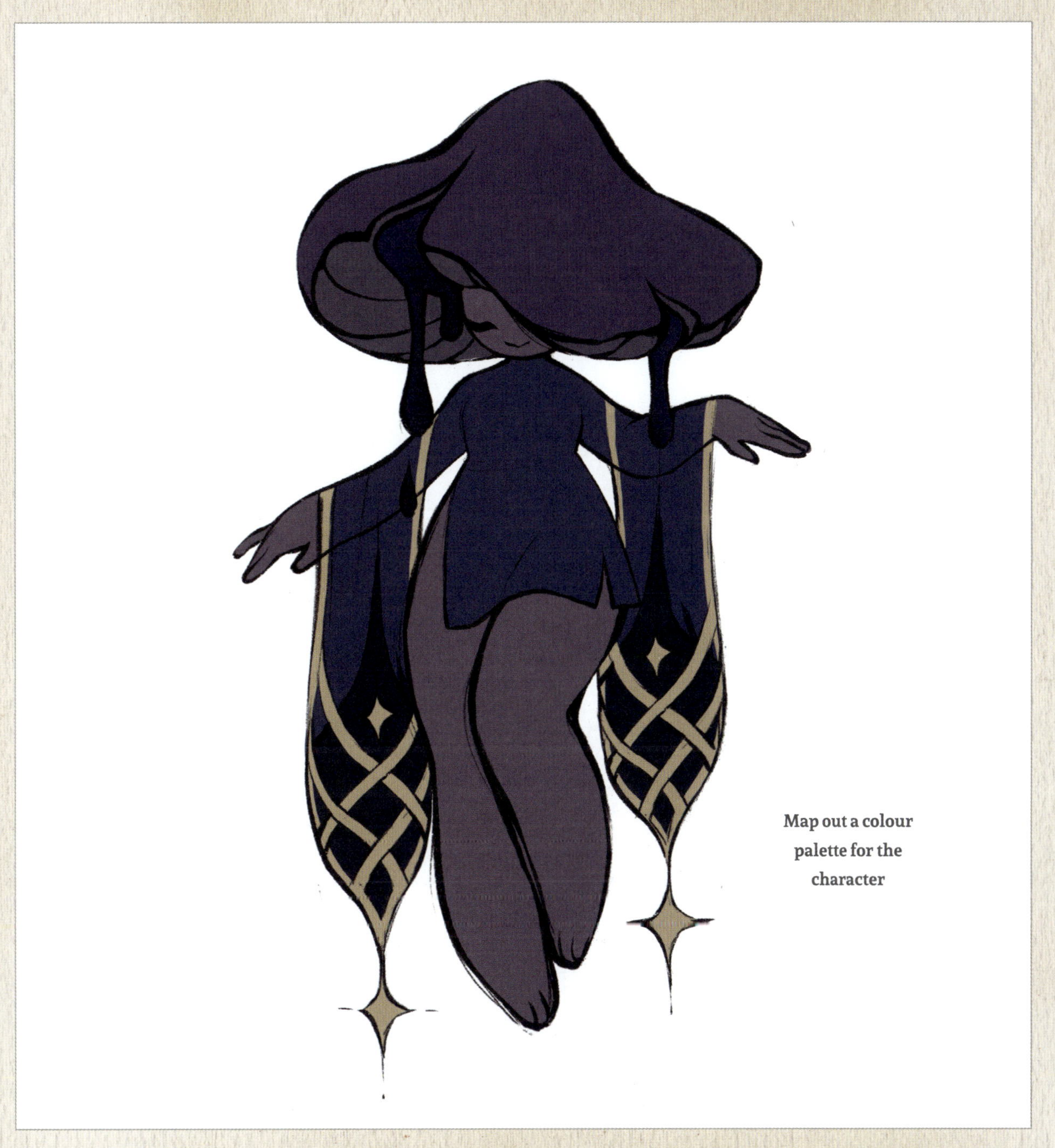

Map out a colour palette for the character

CHOOSING A PALETTE

One of the many benefits of using fungi as a reference material is that you already have your colour palette chosen for you. As this is a purple fungus with white spots, these will be the colours you will be working with. This is quite a limited palette, but you can introduce both warm and cool hues of purple/blue in order to include the full spectrum.

To find your colour palette, try assigning your mushroom different parts of the human body. Mushrooms often have a cap that's different from the colour of the stem and gills. The stem acts as the body of the mushroom, so you may like to use this as the character's skin tone. The cap of this mushroom is a slightly darker purple than the body, so you could use this colour for the clothes and headpiece. The colour of the gills can be used for her hair, and the spots could be the colour of her freckles.

ADDING BASE SHADOW

The next step is to paint in the base shadows. First decide on the direction of your light source, so you know where the light is coming from. For example, if sunlight is shining from the right, the shadows should sit on the left. You also need to locate cast shadows, as this is where you will add more pronounced dark shades. For example, the mushroom cap will cast a dramatic shadow across the face, just like a large hat would.

One thing to note is that fungi have a different texture to human skin, so begin to add a rough texture to the legs and cap. These textures play a role in how your character exists in day-to-day life, as well as how light interacts with their physique. Keeping this in mind will enhance the authenticity of your design.

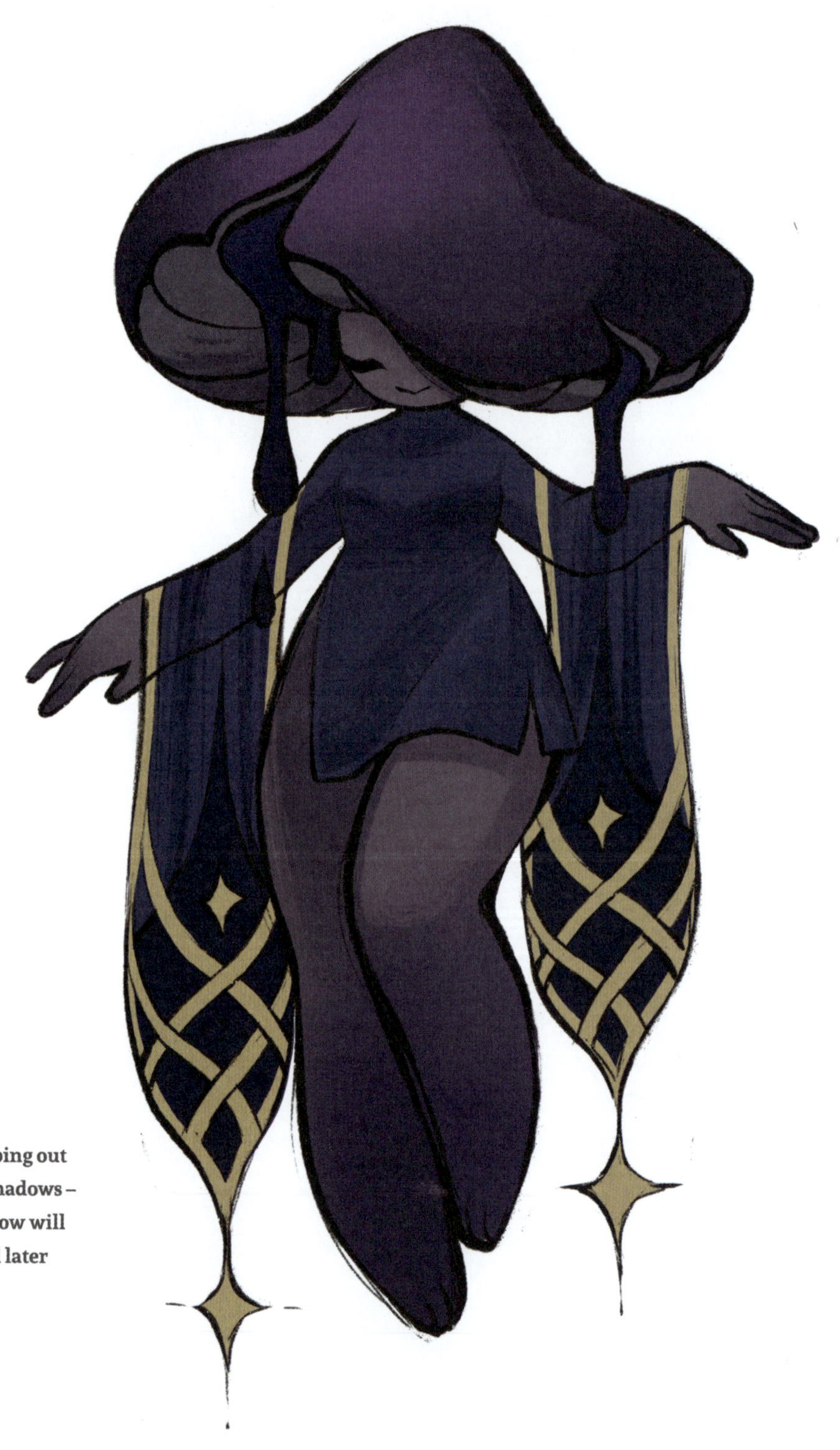

Start mapping out your base shadows – more shadow will be added later

ACCENT COLOURS & TERMINATOR LINES

Once you've painted in the base shadows, you can further accentuate the shapes by marking them with a darker edge. These harsh lines are referred to as terminator lines; they act as transition zones between the areas of light and shadow. The darker part of the shadow will begin directly after the terminator line ends. They're commonly taught in figure drawing and are very useful when conveying form. Adding a darker band to the highlight edge clearly separates lighting and conveys a better sense of form and solidity. If your mushroom is surrounded by greenery or another background element, you can draw the terminator line in this colour to tie it all together.

Paint in blue and pink terminator lines to further accentuate the forms

ADDING GRADIENTS

The fungi kingdom possesses a variety of colour gradients, since many species start to brown or become less vibrant with age. Others have a more saturated hue at the peak of their caps, which desaturates towards their brim. Incorporating gradient colours is a great tool for adding more variety and interest to your palette. You can use gradients to accentuate the focal points in your image, as the viewer's eye will naturally be drawn to the brightest part of the gradient.

To add a darker gradient colour, add a Clipping Mask layer on top of the layer where you want to add the gradient. Set this clipped layer to Multiply, and paint on a light colour using a soft airbrush. The Multiply setting combines the colours on the layer with the layers beneath it, resulting in an attractive flush of colour.

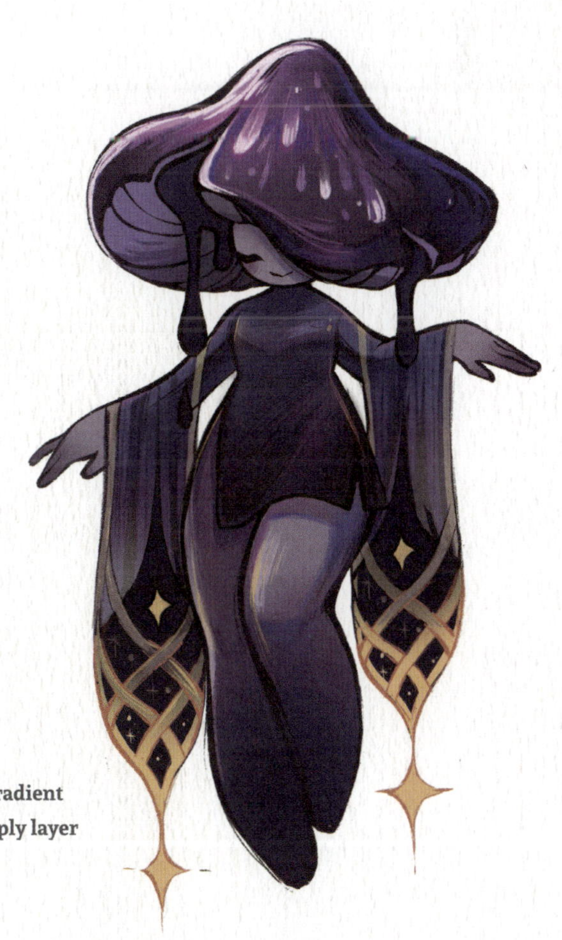

Paint in a darker gradient colour using a Multiply layer

HIGHLIGHTS

To add highlights, start by roughly sketching on a lighter version of your base colour. Paint it on the natural peaks of the forms, such as the top of her hands, her thigh, and the mushroom cap. Since this particular fungi has a slimy cap, paint a stark white highlight onto the cap to really increase the gloss factor. Try to be frugal with your usage of white highlight; reserve it for places where the light is directly reflected.

Light is also important for setting the environment. If your character is located on a forest floor, as most fungi are, light that's been scattered due to the tree canopy above would be a good indicator of the surroundings. However, as this is a space mushroom, feel free to ignore this advice and opt for what you think looks more fantastical instead. Paint rim lighting on various edges of the body. This is light placed on the contour of the subject that adds a dramatic effect and breaks up the monotony of the line art.

Paint a bright highlight onto the fungi cap to convey it's glossy, slimy texture

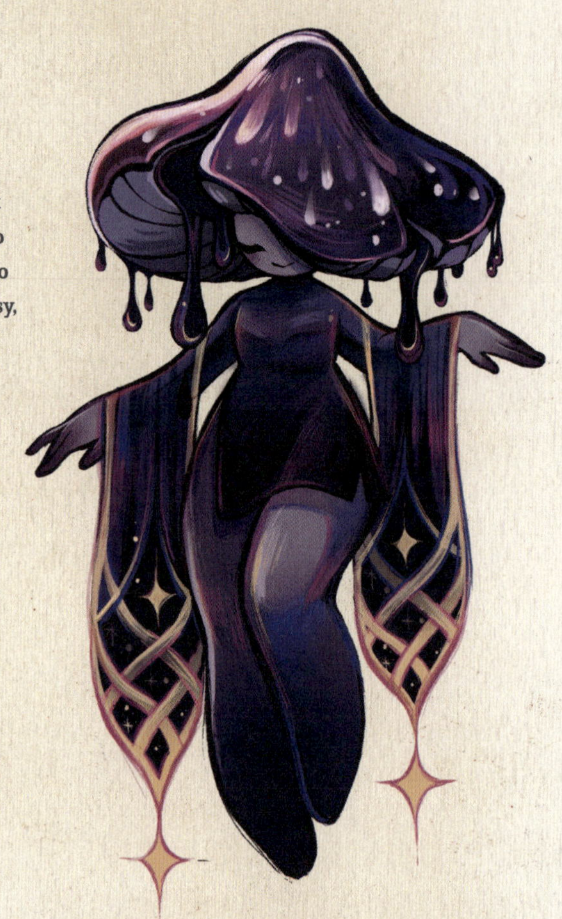

CLOSE UP

When you feel like the character is nearly finished, take a closer look and analyse whether anything feels off. This could be an anatomical error, such as one arm being longer than the other, or a discontinuity error. Procreate lets you flip your canvas, which can give you a new perspective and help you to spot imperfections. In this case, the expression doesn't quite fit the vibe of the character. Sometimes it can take a while for a creature to really make sense, so you may find that you don't finish painting the face until you have a firm grasp on the rest of the design. Fungi are quite otherworldly, almost alien-like, so paint in a big alien eye to continue the character's eery space theme. (Her second eye is hidden by the mushroom cap.) Keep referring back to your fungi reference to see how it can inspire each element of the character's design.

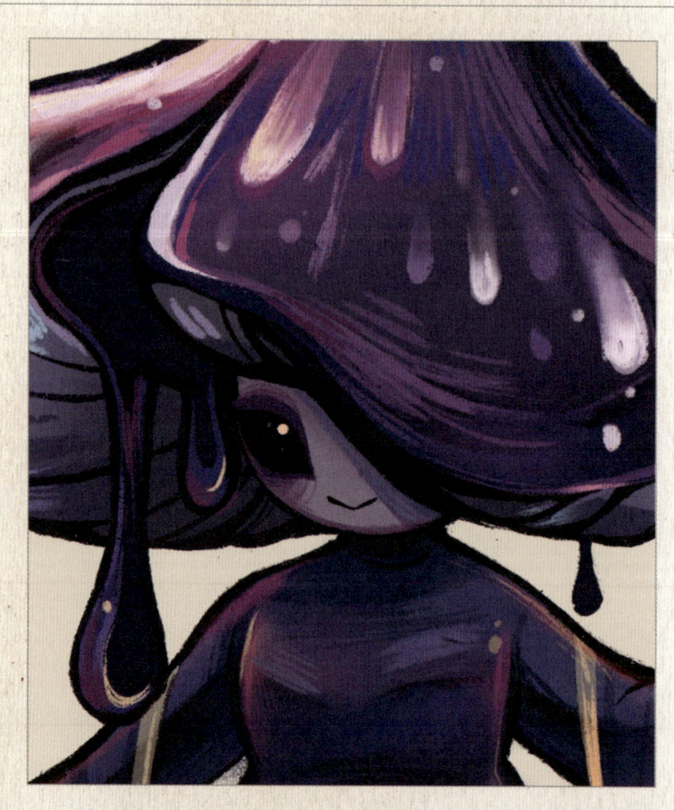

Paint in a big alien-like eye to convey the fungi's otherworldly nature

ACCESSORIES

Another way to tell your character's story and capture who they are is through the accessories they carry. These will lend an insight into their personality and how they choose to portray themselves. A character who wears a lot of fancy jewellery might value aesthetic over practicality, whereas a character that carries around a blade could signify a combative or survivalist nature. When adding accessories, consider what your character would gravitate towards, plus what they would have access to in their natural habitat. What are the local plants that surround their environment?

As this character is more themed around space than earth, you may want to include a few small accessories that make her appear more cosmic and celestial. Paint in a shimmering chain belt and starry sparkles in a yellow accent colour throughout various parts of the design. These add a magical and whimsical feel, which fit the space theme perfectly.

Add some celestial accessories and sparkle to convey her cosmic theme

COMPANION

Introducing a pet or companion can elevate your character's story. Even in real life, pets tend to reflect the nature of their owner, and this can be exaggerated even further when creating a character. Slimy and a bit strange, mushrooms and frogs are soul companions.

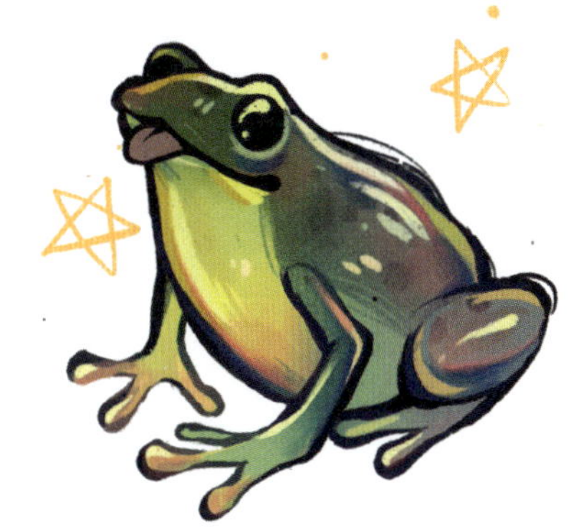

FINAL SHADOWS

If you get confused going back and forth between numerous layers, you can flatten them into one at this point. The next step is to use the Multiply tool to add extra vibrancy and darkness to your character by painting in some more gradients to the whole image, increasing contrast and vibrancy. This is a quick way to add some exciting hue variation in your piece. Using a soft airbrush, paint broad strokes of blue and pink. Avoid colours like grey and black, as these will muddy out your other colours.

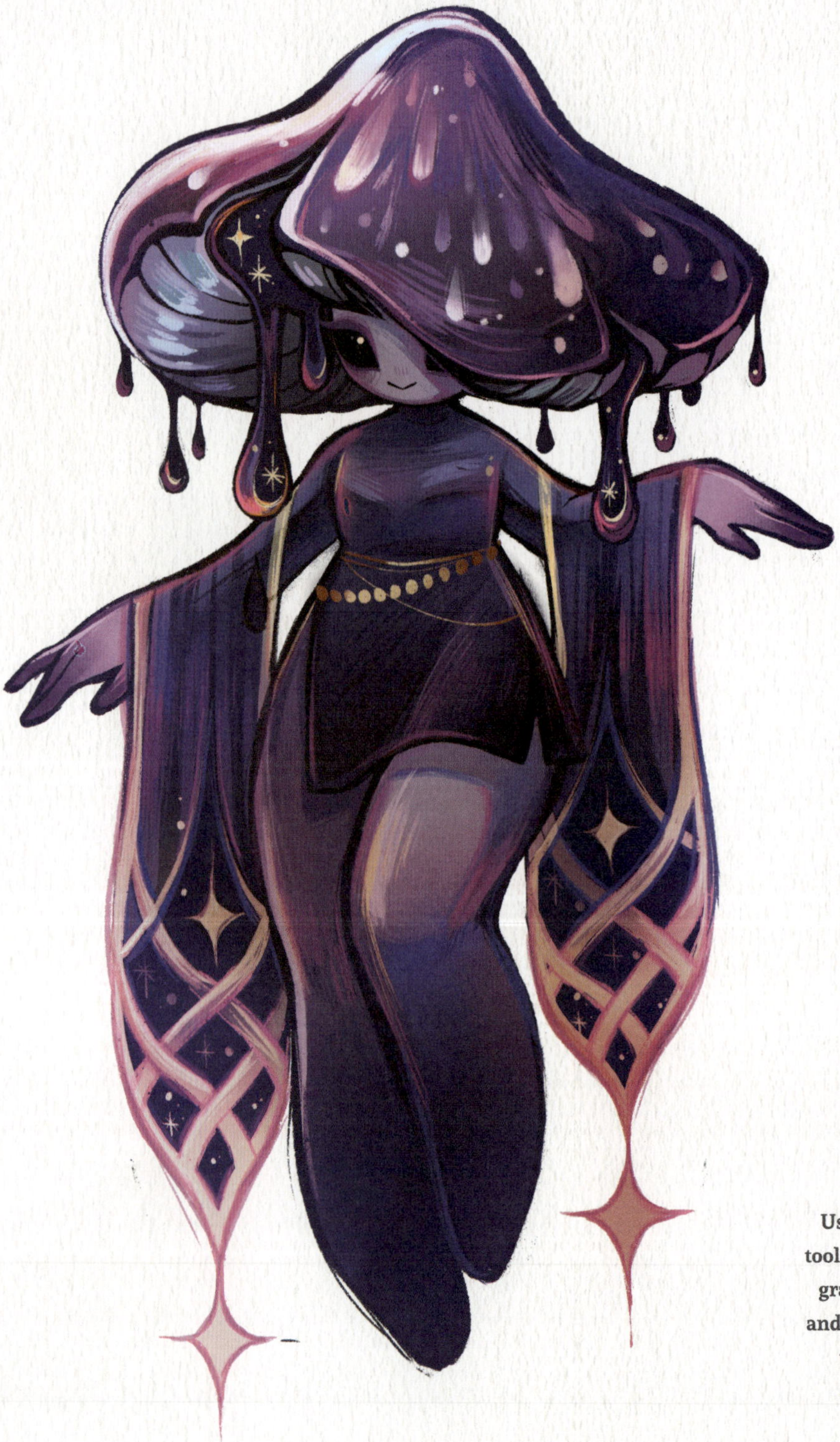

Use the Multiply tool to paint in more gradients in pink and blue to increase the vibrancy and contrast

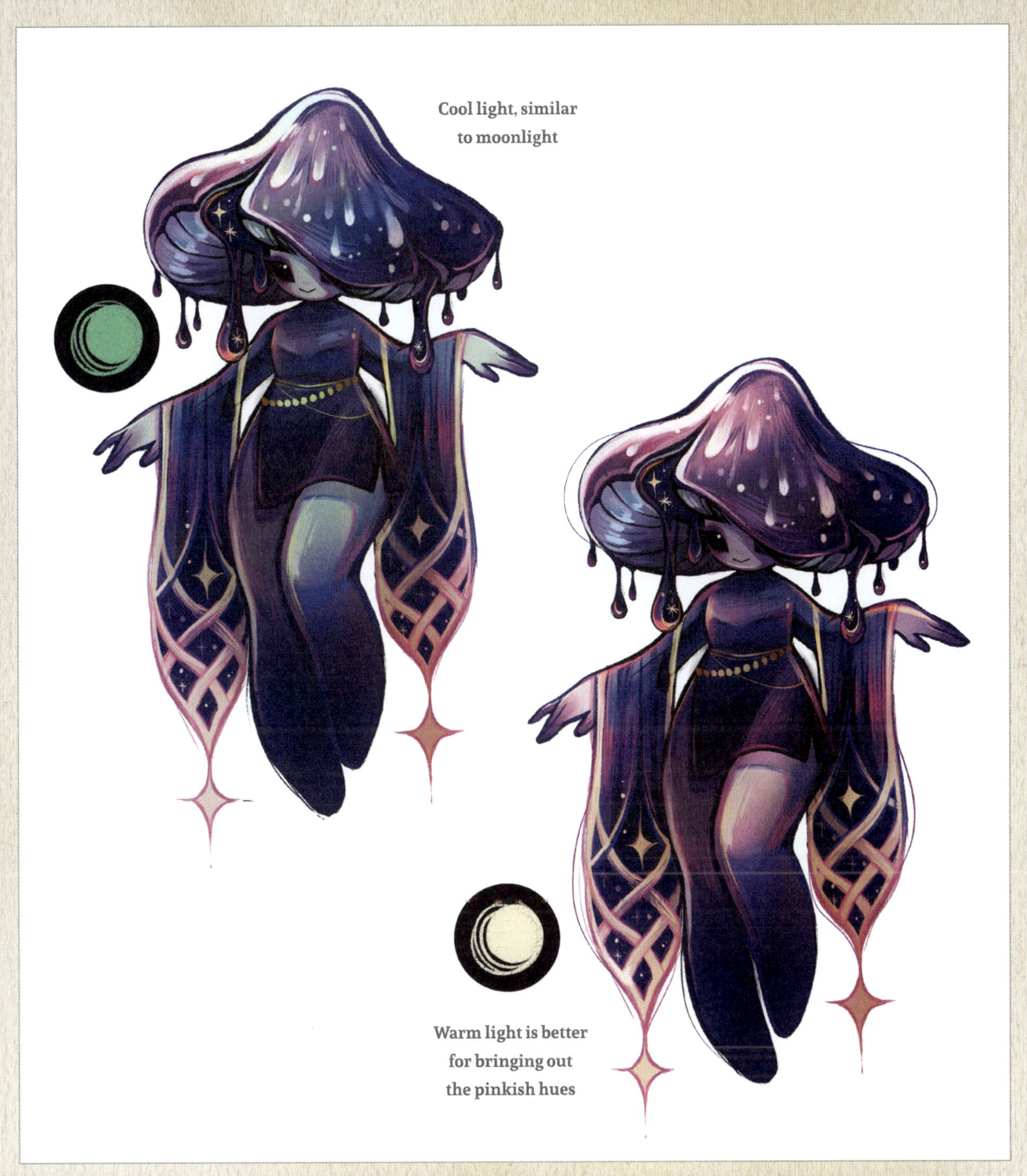

FINAL HIGHLIGHTS

Increase the light by creating a layer mask with the Overlay blending mode. Overlay works like a combination of the Multiply and Screen modes, both lightening and darkening images by shifting the midtones. Dark blend colours shift the midtones to darker colours, whereas light tones shift the midtones to brighter colours. This layer mask is useful when adding quick highlights, as it doesn't brighten your line art. Painting on the Overlay layer with a pale yellow will create a nice warm light, while painting with a cooler tone will result in lighting that's more reminiscent of moonlight. As you want the character to be engulfed in a warm light to bring out the pinkish hues, opt for the warmer option.

FINAL DETAILS

The final step is to add more celestial elements. Paint in a crescent moon, some stars, and extra sparkle using the Dry Ink brush. Introducing simple background elements like this will elevate your character from a standalone design to a final piece. Finish by selecting Adjustments and increasing the Bloom function to about 40%, which will produce a magical glowing effect that captures that otherworldly atmosphere of the Cortinarius iodes. It's okay to prioritize the theme and energy of your subject rather than accuracy and faithfulness to the source material. The fungi kingdom is equally beautiful and bizarre, and there's so much inspiration to be taken from it, however loyal or creative you decide to be.

Reflecting back on the design process, it was important that the character had a similar look and shape to the Cortinarius iodes, so elements such as roundness, colour, and texture were carried over into her design. The mushroom's striking cap, which looks like a piece of space contained within a fungus, inspired the celestial theme. These white spots were enhanced to appear even more star-like, and extra cosmic elements were added throughout the design to enhance the idea.

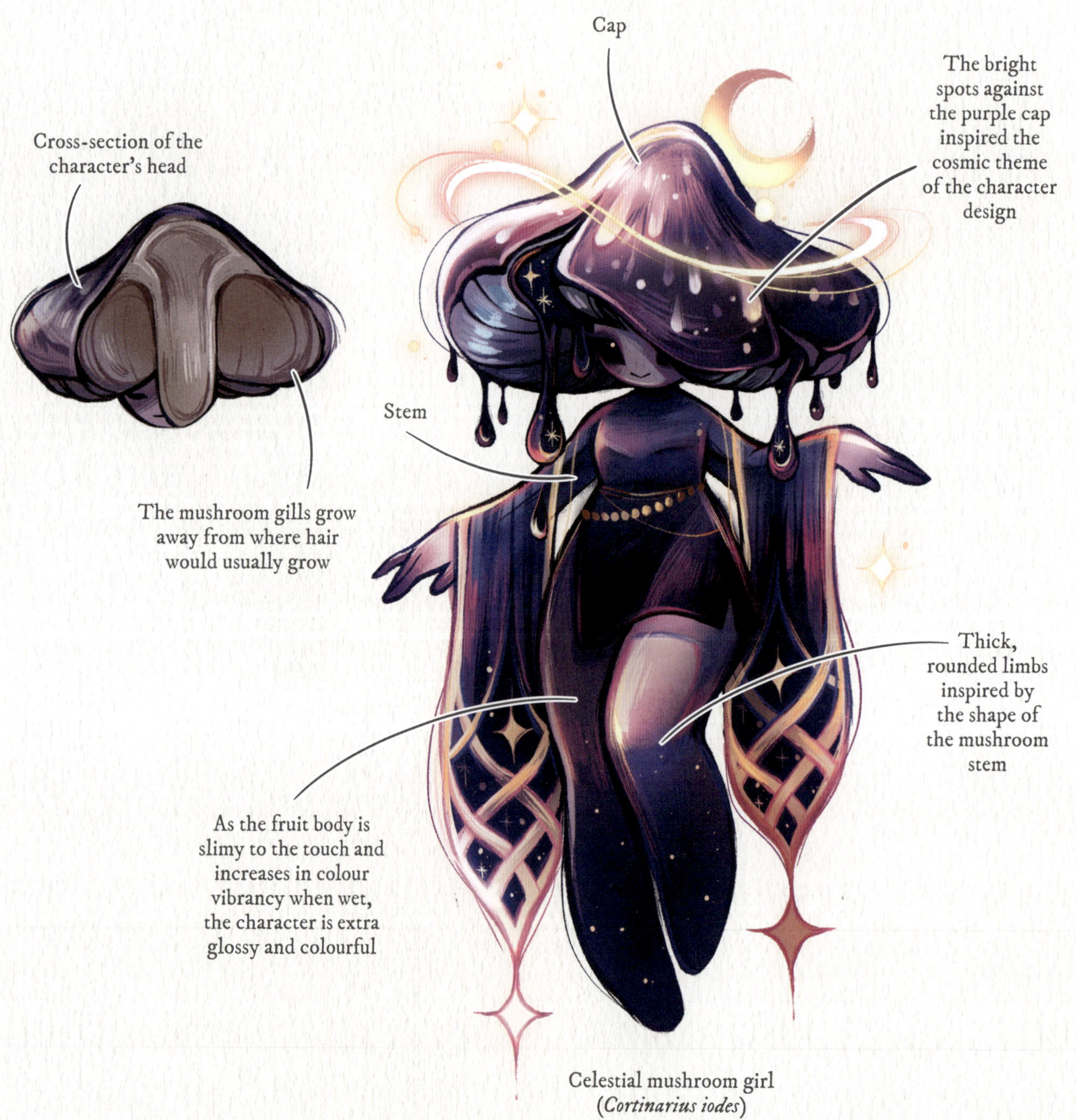

Celestial mushroom girl (*Cortinarius iodes*)

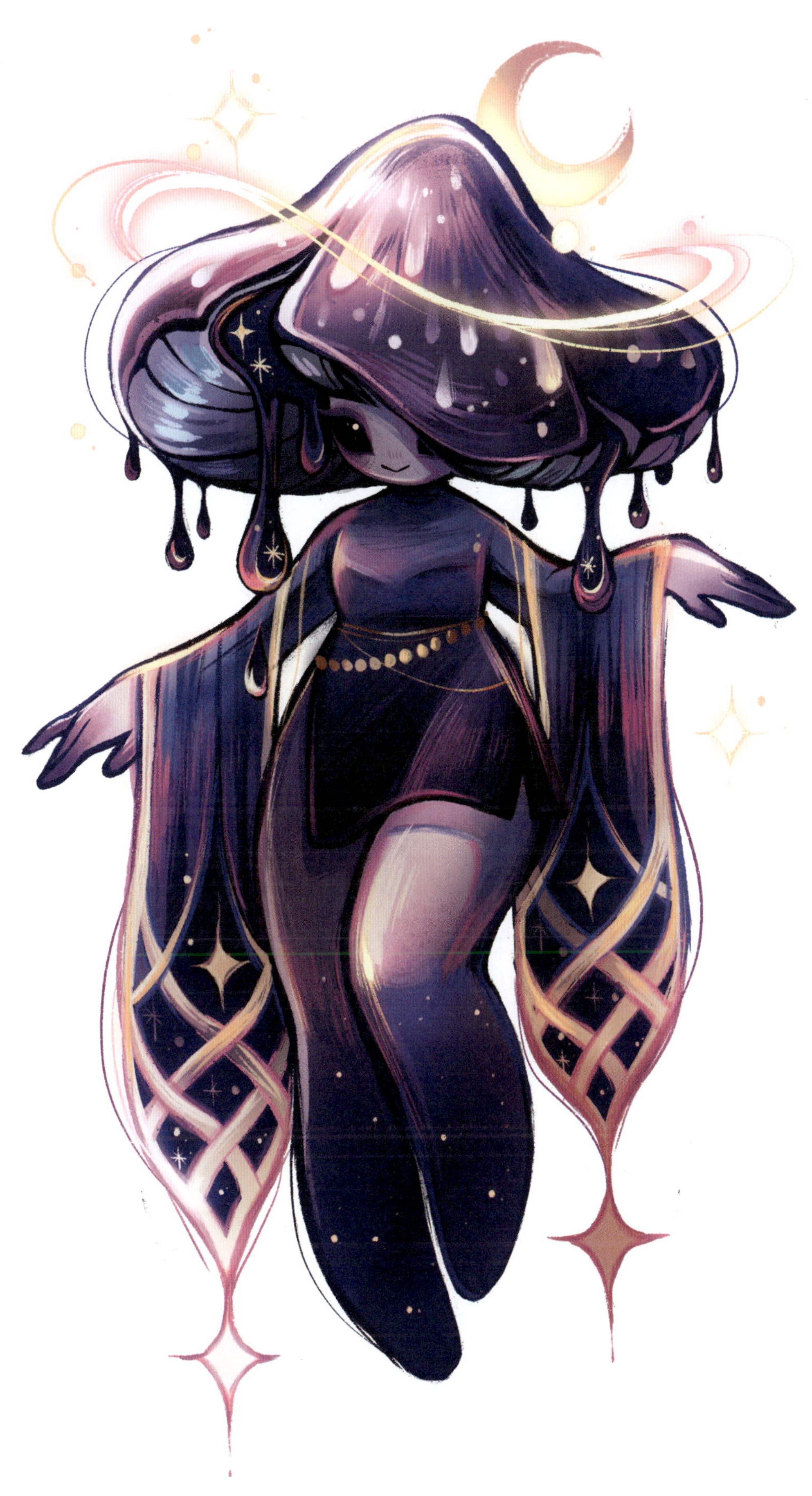

CELESTIAL MUSHROOM GIRL

Final image © Feefal

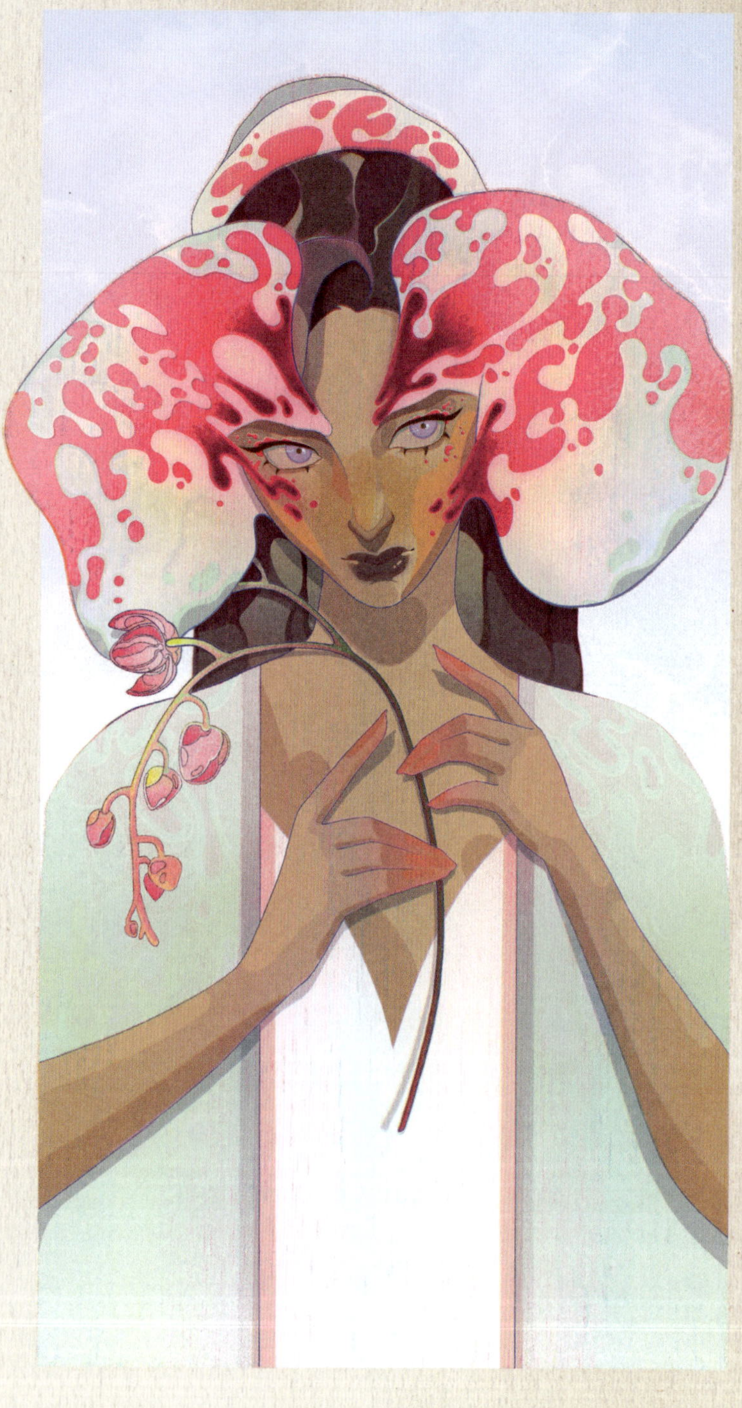

This tutorial will demonstrate how to create an ethereal enchantress character inspired by the exotic and universally beloved orchid flower. It will cover subjects such as seeking out inspiration from multiple sources, how research can help inform creative decisions, how to balance direct sources with aesthetic choices, and how to use colour fearlessly and purposefully. Using the Procreate app on the iPad is recommended, but you can follow along with any software of your choice.

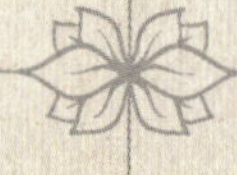

tropical

ORCHID ENCHANTRESS

LARA GEORGIA CARSON

ONLINE RESEARCH

A simple internet search shows that orchids are one of the oldest known flowering plants to span the globe. Interestingly, their significance across many cultures is the same, recognized worldwide as a symbol of beauty, power, luxury, fertility, and feminine grace. In Victorian Europe, there was even a condition known as 'Orchidelirium'; those who suffered this 'affliction' were obsessed with collecting rare and beautiful orchid specimens. That covetous behaviour will inspire this orchid character, who could perhaps be guarding a younger flower. When creating this design, you need to keep in mind this mesmerizing, almost hypnotic allure that orchids have had throughout history.

From this initial research, you can extrapolate that the character will be female, exuding beauty and grace, and perhaps giving off an air of bewitchment, royalty, and confidence. There are thousands of species of orchid, so narrowing references down is tricky. There are some really interesting, alien-looking orchids out there, but you want to choose a type that will be easily recognizable; the orchid inspiration needs to be obvious enough for viewers of the final design. The genus *Phalaenopsis*, also known as moth orchids, would be perfect for this.

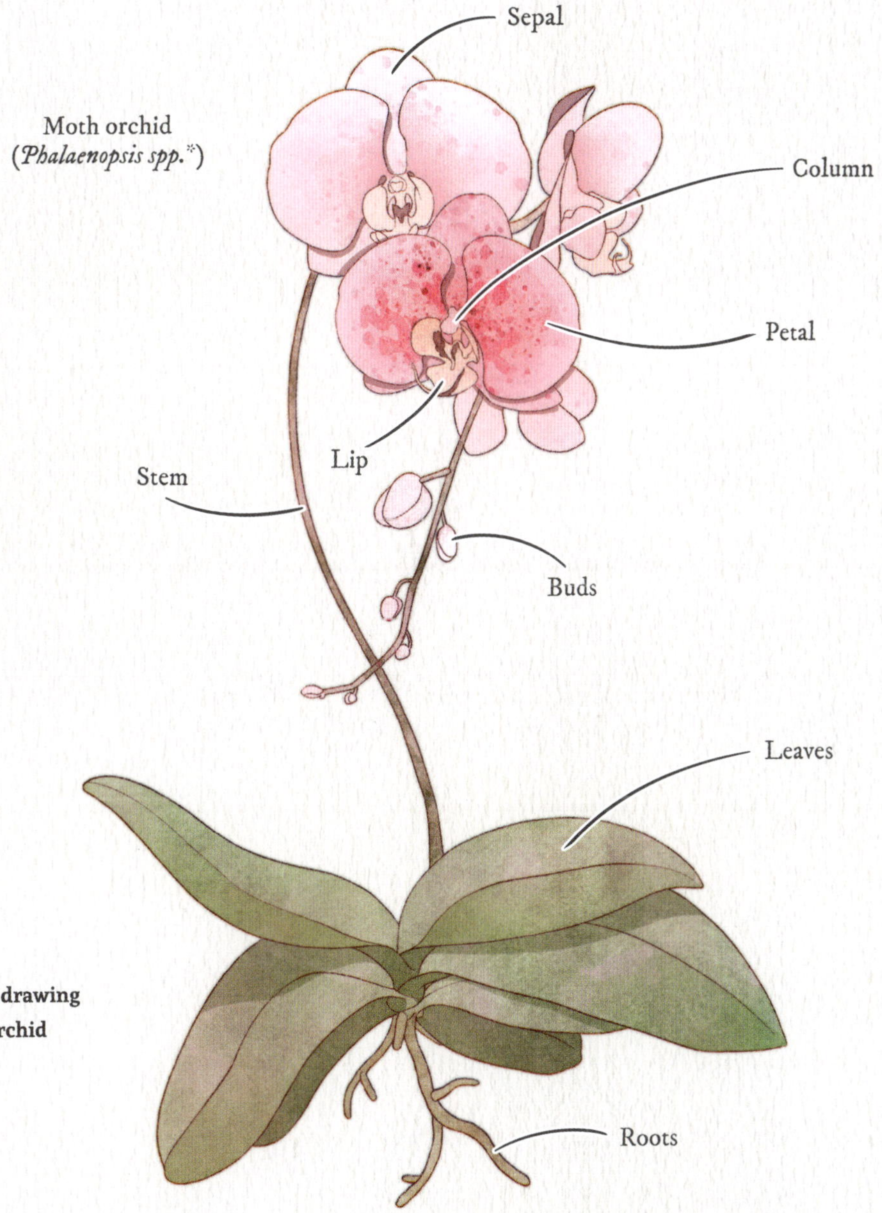

Sepal
Moth orchid
(*Phalaenopsis spp.**)
Column
Petal
Lip
Stem
Buds
Leaves
Roots

An anatomical drawing of a moth orchid

*'spp.' stands for *'species plurimae'*, meaning there are multiple species of the genus (*Phalaenopsis*) and this is just a generic example of a moth orchid

OFFLINE RESEARCH

After choosing your orchid and researching its biology and cultural significance, you may find yourself stuck. It's easy to feel overwhelmed by the options and imagery that you have access to online. A great solution is to go out and try to find your inspiration in real life. Orchids are a popular house plant, so visiting a local plant shop or botanical garden, taking along a sketchbook or just a camera, will help you to get inspired much more directly and take the exact reference photos you need. You can use these studies to get a feel for what draws you in; for example, in person, the pattern and colour of this white and pink orchid variety is captivating. It will definitely be a strong focal point to translate into the character.

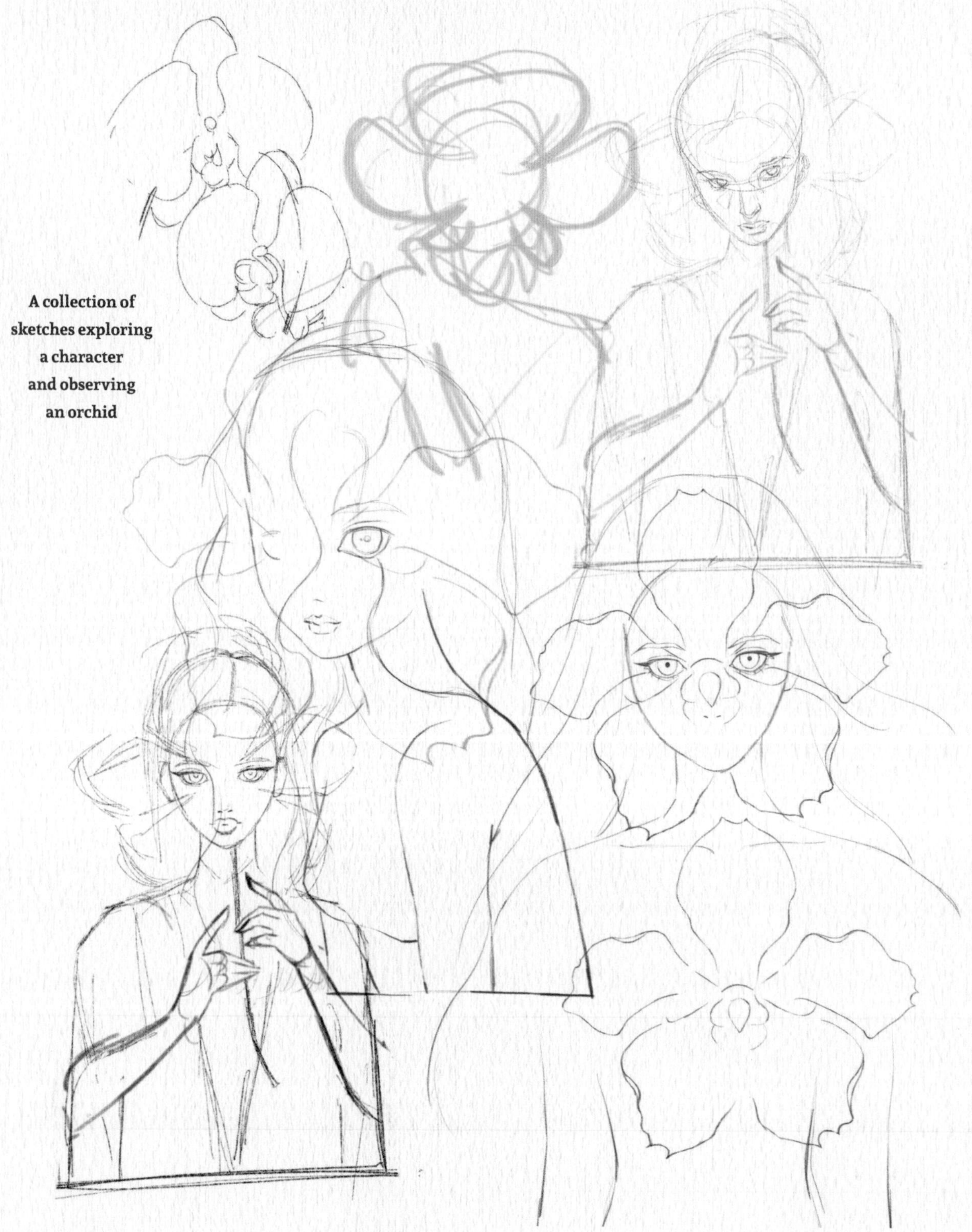

A collection of sketches exploring a character and observing an orchid

INITIAL SKETCH

At this point you have enough research and reference material to begin sketching a character. The orchid only has a handful of petals; its simplicity is deceptively challenging, as there are fewer shapes to work with than a many-petalled daisy or chrysanthemum. You will have to be very specific about the shapes used.

The character's face will be the focal point of this design, integrated with the very distinctive shapes of the orchid's petals. The shape of the column is reminiscent of a nose or lips, which can be used to your advantage when making sense of merging plant and humanoid. In these sketches, you can experiment with the angles of the face and how best to display them. Keep your drawings simple and loose for now.

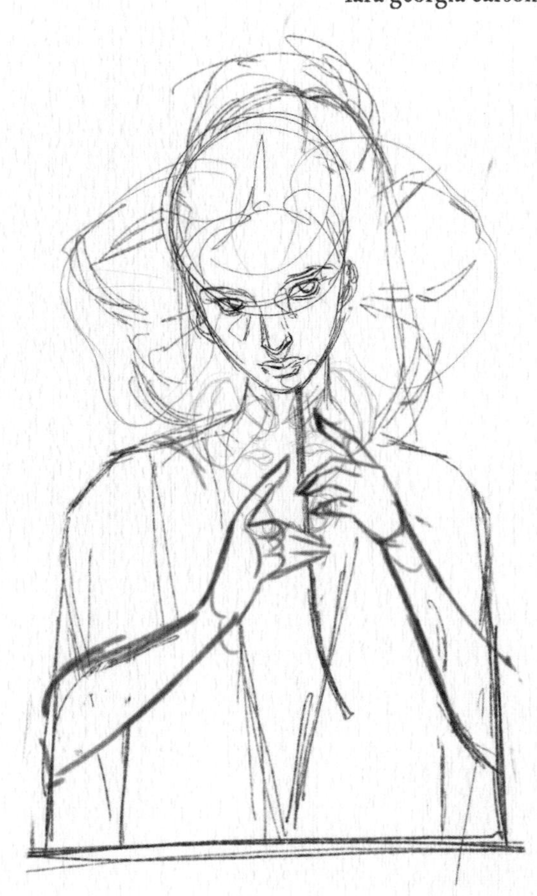

A very rough character sketch to get the basic forms down

FOUNDATIONS

You can easily build upon your favourite sketch by lowering its opacity and creating a new layer on top, then making a new sketch using the rougher one as a guide. Refining the sketch can take several passes, and it's here where you can experiment with expressions, line weight, and brush options. The character needs to look confident yet mysterious, just like real orchids; they are very proud-looking flowers, but still an enigma, with several species that we know little about. Looking at yourself in a mirror while pulling faces can be a great help for inventing an expression or capturing a tricky emotion.

Block in a light grey below the line art to check the character's silhouette as you go along. This can really help to provide a different perspective on things, highlighting any weird tangents or cutouts that aren't working. It's easy to move things around at this point, as there is no detail or colour, so be liberal with your adjustments! Instead of designing the stem so it runs straight up into the face, you can refer to your research findings for a more interesting solution. The Victorians hoarded these exotic flowers, so the character could be holding a stem of buds close, maybe as a lure or perhaps protectively.

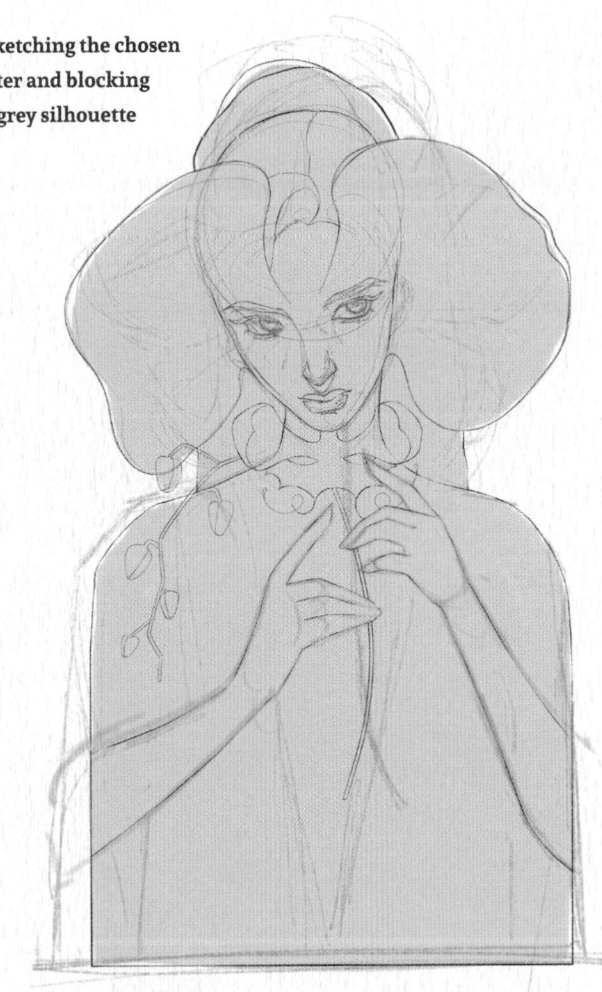

Roughly sketching the chosen character and blocking out a grey silhouette

FLIPPING THE CANVAS

Flipping your canvas at this stage is highly beneficial, providing you with a fresh perspective and getting any distressing surprises out of the way early on. You can achieve this digitally by flipping your canvas or layer horizontally. If you're using traditional media, you can achieve the same effect by taking a photo of your sketch and flipping it with your phone's photo-editing options. You could also hold your drawing up to a mirror, or even flip your paper over and hold it up to a bright light or window.

FINAL SKETCH

At this point, you should feel confident in your sketch and ready to clean it up. Once again, lower the opacity of the rougher sketch to aid visibility of what's important; you can go over the cleaner sketch one last time, but try to use as few strokes as possible to achieve a smooth, tidy finish. It doesn't have to be absolutely perfect – that's for the next stage – but having a clean sketch will prevent you from getting distracted by messy contour lines later.

It becomes apparent that the neck collar/column area isn't reading clearly and doesn't make much of an impact on the story of the character. Redrawing the stem and buds creates better flow, a more appealing balance of detail, and a more interesting character moment.

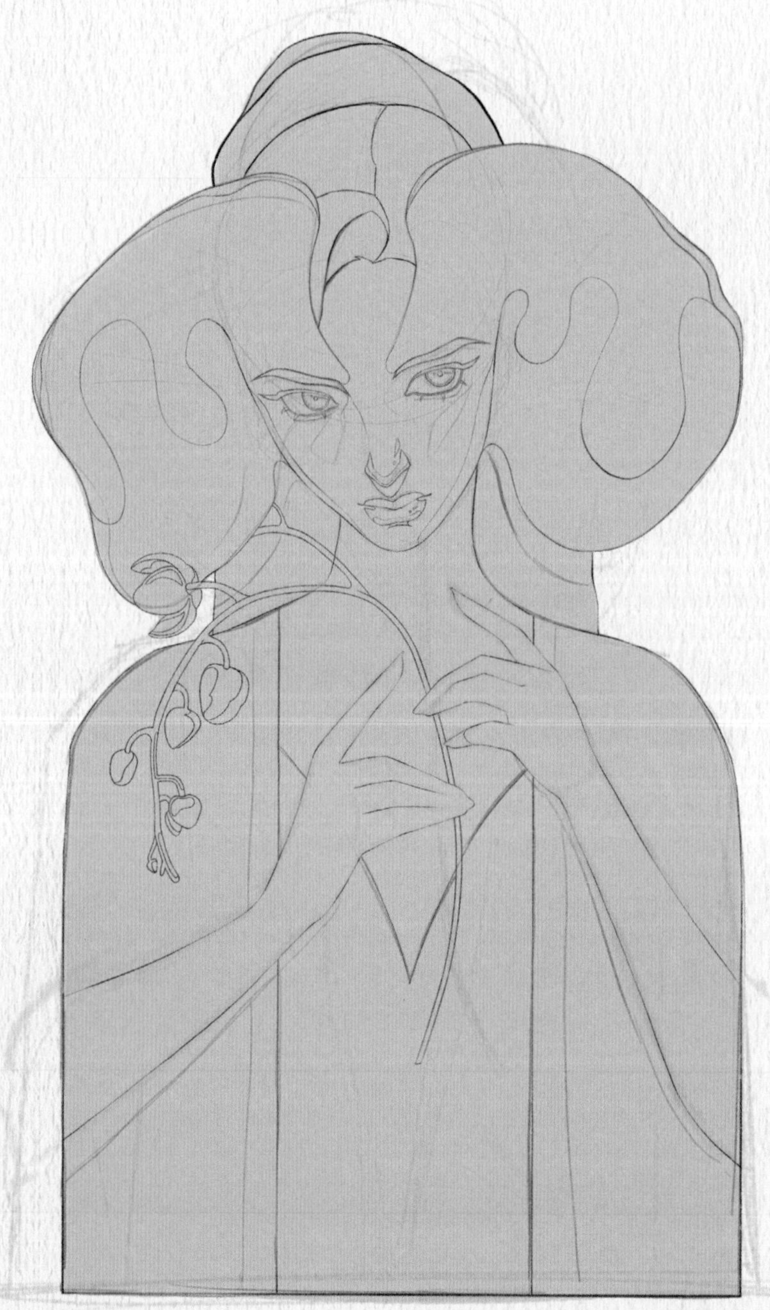

A clean sketch without rough sketch lines; the final checkpoint for making any major changes

LINE ART

Once you have your cleaned-up final sketch, you're ready for the next stage of the lining process. Choose a brush that imitates a sharp pencil or ink pen, with a little texture, set it to a very small size, create a new layer, and trace over your sketch to create smooth line art of the whole character. Don't worry about marking out patterns or shapes that can be created with colour later on. Instead, focus on the major outlines and facial features. Perfectionist tendencies often surface at this stage and can sometimes hinder your progress. Taking a break for a snack or a stretch and then coming back with fresh eyes can help alleviate common frustrations when drawing line art. When the clean line art is complete, tidy up the grey silhouette and replace it with a pink fill; you can use digital wet-media brushes to give the fill the marbled texture of a watercolour wash.

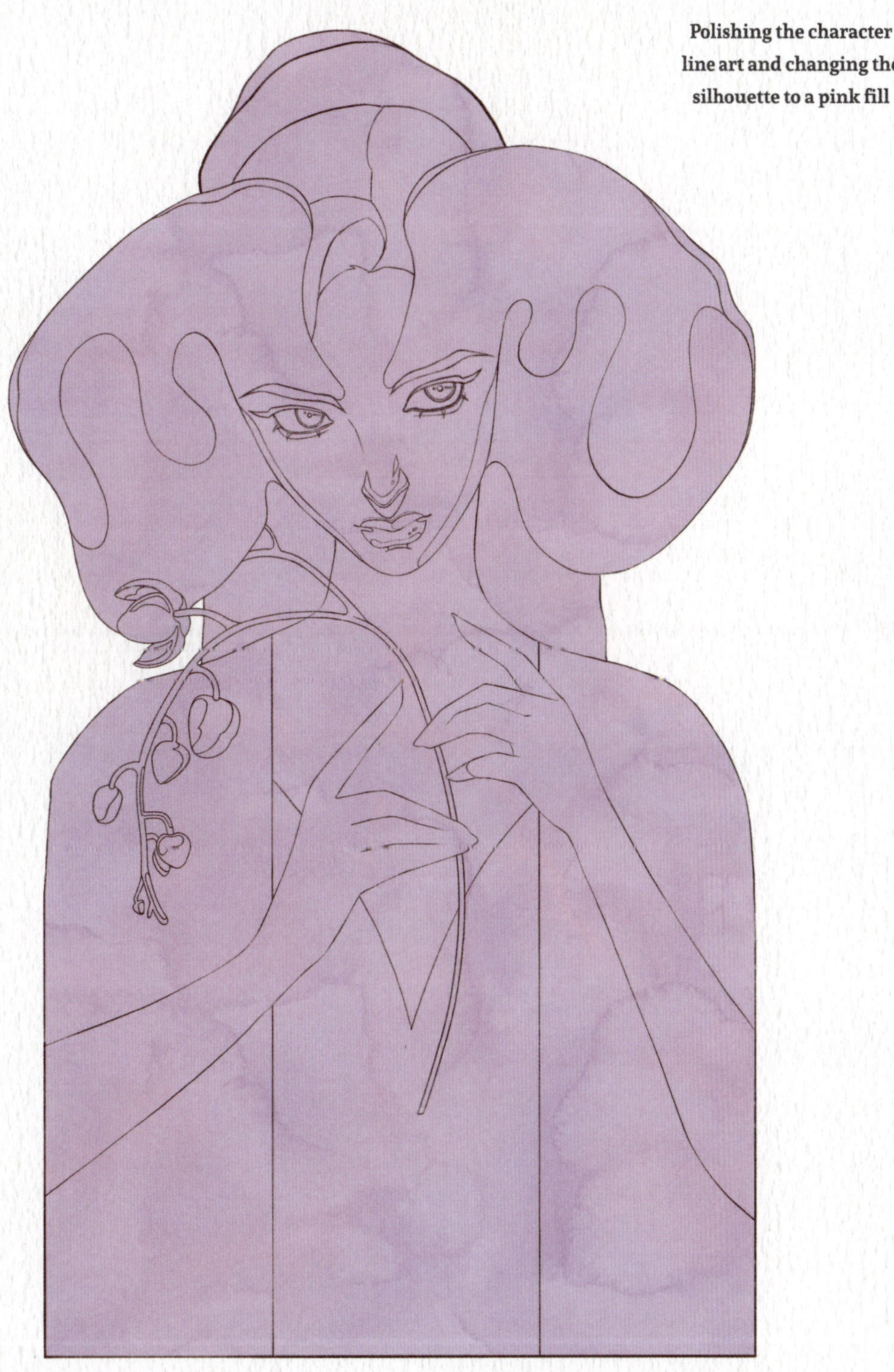

Polishing the character line art and changing the silhouette to a pink fill

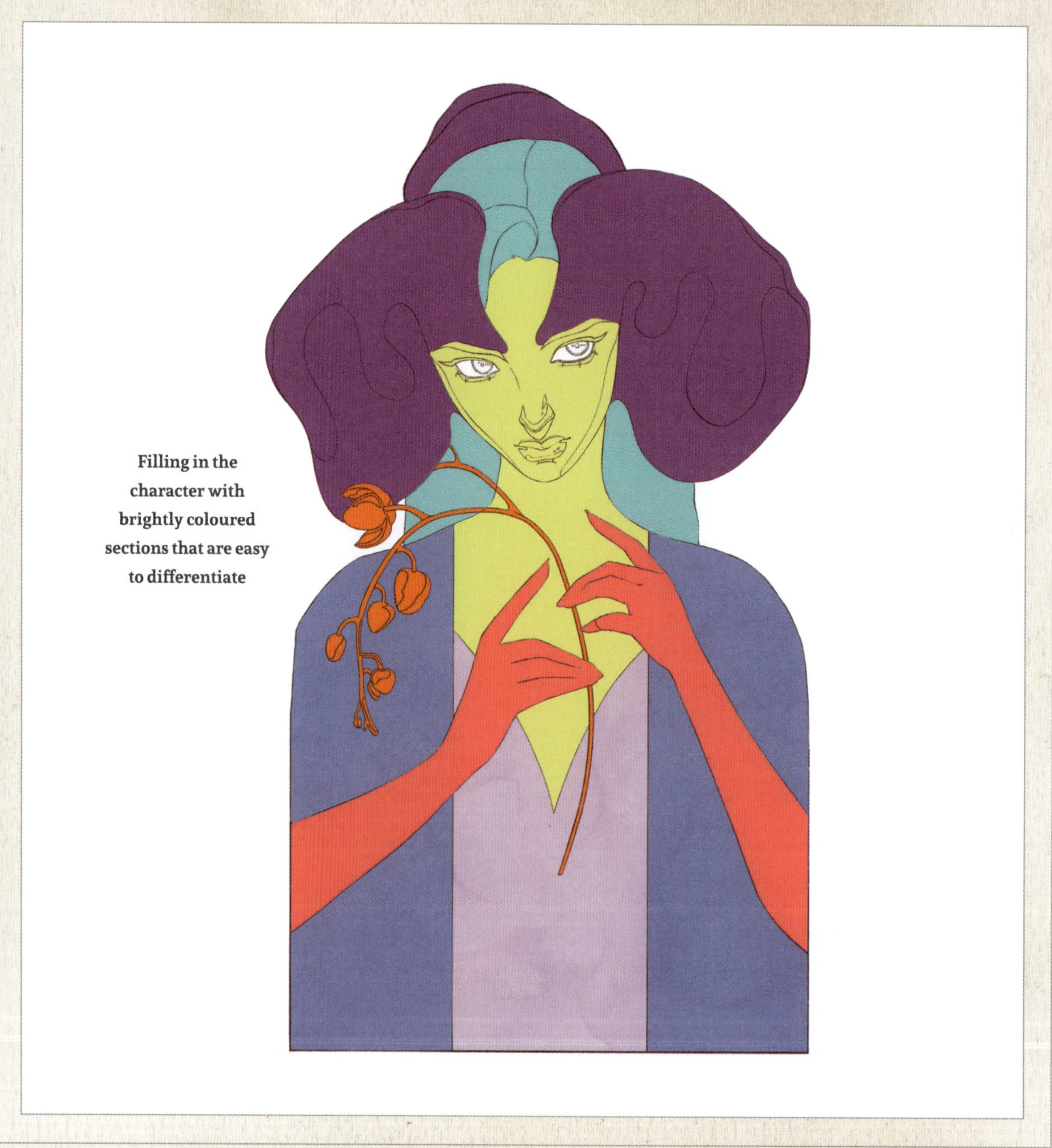

Filling in the character with brightly coloured sections that are easy to differentiate

COLOUR BASE

When you start introducing colour, it can be tempting to go wild. You want to get straight to the fun part and go all in on rendering your favourite feature – usually the character's face! However, it's important to continue building the base and setting your image up for an easier rendering process later on. This step is fairly simple, but totally essential across many art pieces. By blocking out elements first, you can clearly determine what lies on top of what and think about your piece in a more three-dimensional space.

Create separate layers for each important part: the face/neck, petals, hair, arms/hands, shirt, cape, and budding flower stem. If you're working digitally, the colours used here don't matter at all; you can use very bright colours to help delineate areas clearly from each other. Check the petal shapes thoroughly here, and adjust them if necessary, since any flaws in their shape will be highlighted by this blocking technique. They need to capture the distinctive shape of the moth orchid.

ADDING COLOUR

Now you've arrived at the most fun, experimental stage of the process: exploring colour combinations. Since you've already gone through the trouble of blocking out sections, you can now either apply Alpha Lock to each layer or create clipping layers attached to them. Either method will allow you to paint each shape without worrying about staying within the lines, as the transparent areas around them will be locked.

Look back on your collection of reference images to see what colours to use. Since this will be quite an obvious orchid design, using as much white as possible will create a classic, recognizable orchid palette with connotations of elegance. It will also form a great backdrop for some more vibrant patterns of colour that you can introduce to the petals. However, although the overall colour appears 'white', you will find many soft-pink veins and tints if you look more closely. Other moth orchids mostly seem to be pastel hues, which is something else you can try to tie in.

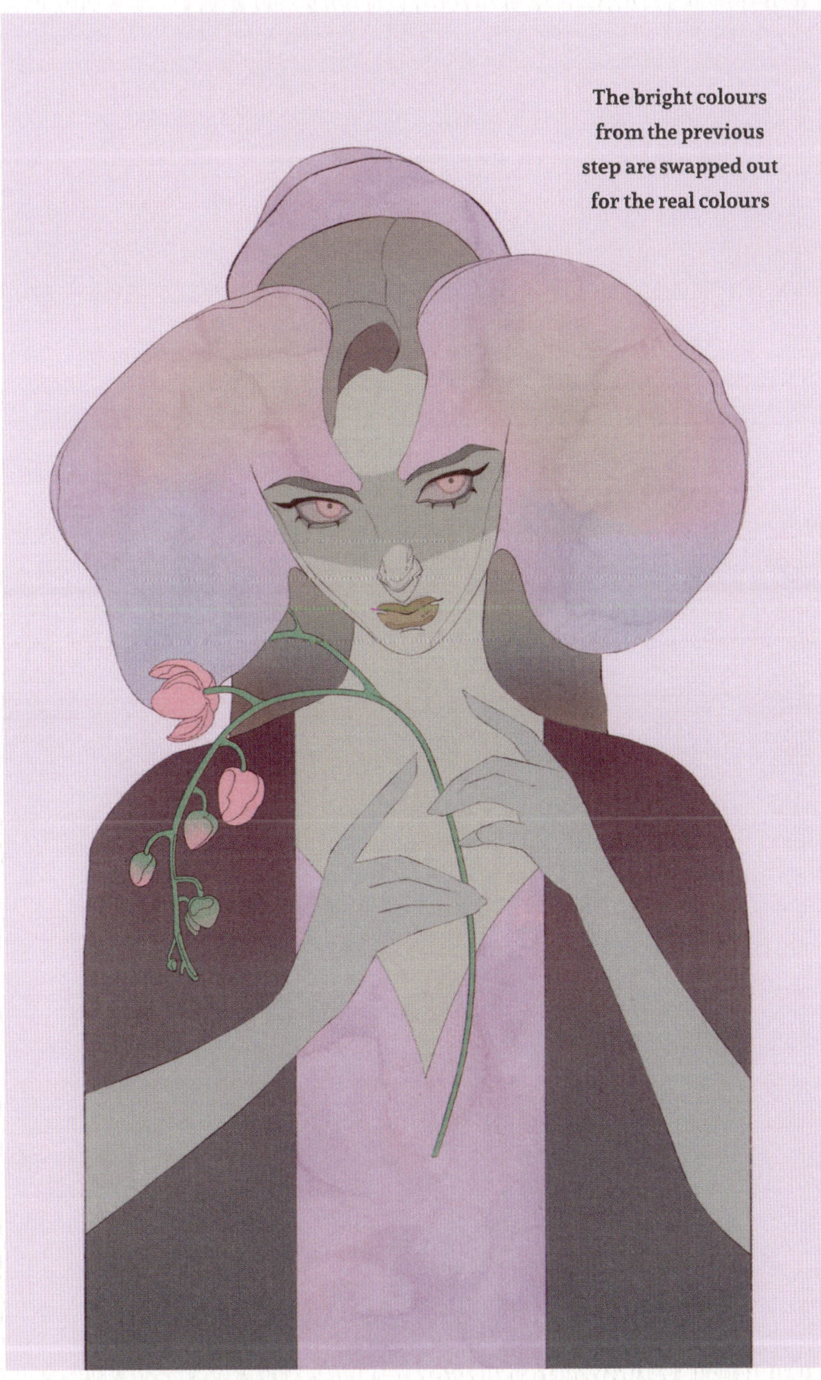

The bright colours from the previous step are swapped out for the real colours

PAINTING WITH WHITE

White gets a bad reputation as being boring or blank, but it can be very versatile with a little colour theory applied. At the most basic, white reflects colour and is very affected by lights and shadows. This means you can tint white to essentially be any colour you like; as long as its value is the lightest thing in comparison to the surrounding elements, it should 'read' as white! Don't feel limited to using pure white or grey; try using colours with light, bright values instead to add more life and interest.

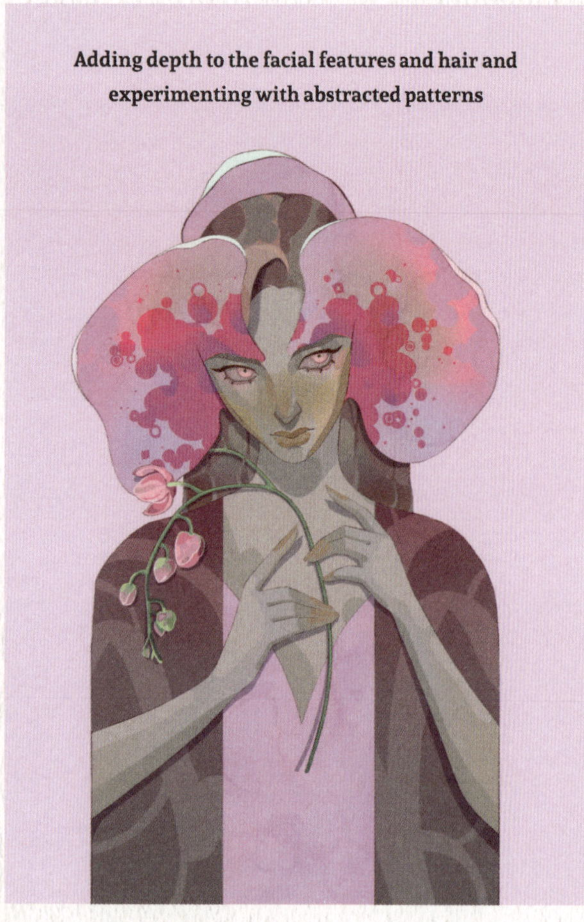

Adding depth to the facial features and hair and experimenting with abstracted patterns

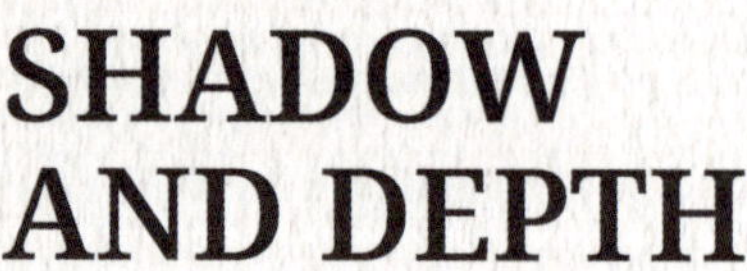

SHADOW AND DEPTH

Continue exploring colours by adding shadows and depth between the separated elements. The planes of the face and hands can be sculpted out by adding shadows and contrast. Experiment with a kind of abstract rendering, pushing and pulling shapes into the forms; for example, giving the hair long, segmented shapes to convey what it is without detailing each strand of hair. Start thinking about the pattern of the petals – keeping the petal headdress on its own layer will allow you to make several iterations. The specific orchid shown on page 171 has bold splashes of bright magenta, likely as a way for the flower to attract pollinators. Those vivid colours make it stand out from the pale pastel varieties, so try to mimic those qualities in this design to make the character especially captivating.

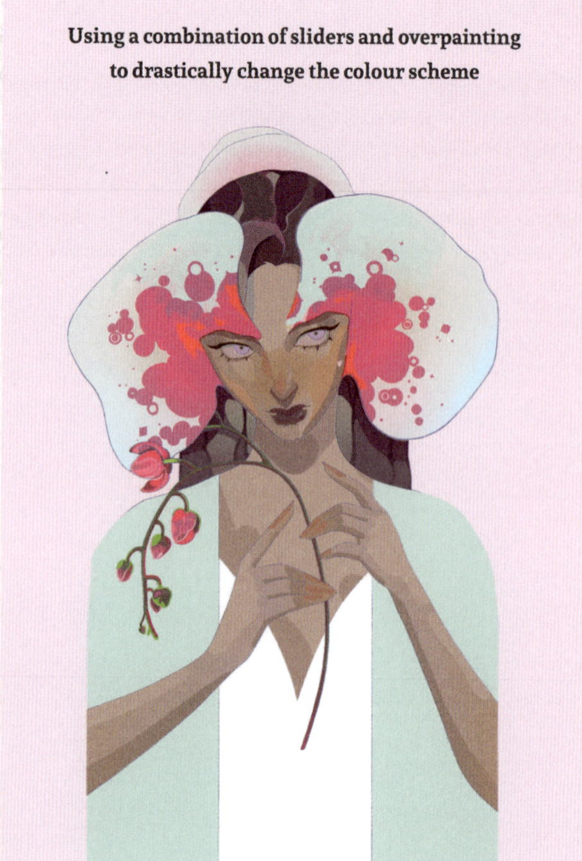

Using a combination of sliders and overpainting to drastically change the colour scheme

COLOUR ADJUSTMENTS

The colour scheme needs some higher contrast to make those tropical colours pop – it's a little too soft and subtle, so the character looks washed out, almost dead. She needs more of that powerful punch that came through in the research stage, with a vibrant boldness that draws in the viewer (or maybe a bee!).

The prep work you did in the Colour Base step (page 176) allows you to use the adjustment sliders on each individual segment to push it towards your preferred colour scheme. Try using a mixture of the Curves tool and the Hue, Saturation, Brightness sliders to test out new combinations, aiming for a warmer palette with higher contrast. Merging excess layers (but keeping sections separate) can help you to make faster colour changes, but comes with the risk of losing a layer that you might need separately later. It's a good idea to save a spare version of your file before you start merging them, just in case.

SMALLER DETAILS

The image is progressing quickly towards completion, but there are still opportunities to think critically and make changes. For example, the initial pattern on the petals felt too whimsical and not as mysteriously alluring as the original intended plan. A punchy, more organic form suits the character better. In this revised version, the viewer is drawn into the centre of the flower, and it feels more functional this way. You can also remove some of the initial line work or replace it with coloured lines to help the design blend together more cohesively. Line art doesn't need to stay black – simply changing its colour to something complementary to the piece can make a huge difference. At this stage you can also add smaller details such as the highlights in the eyes and additional patterns on the petals and clothing.

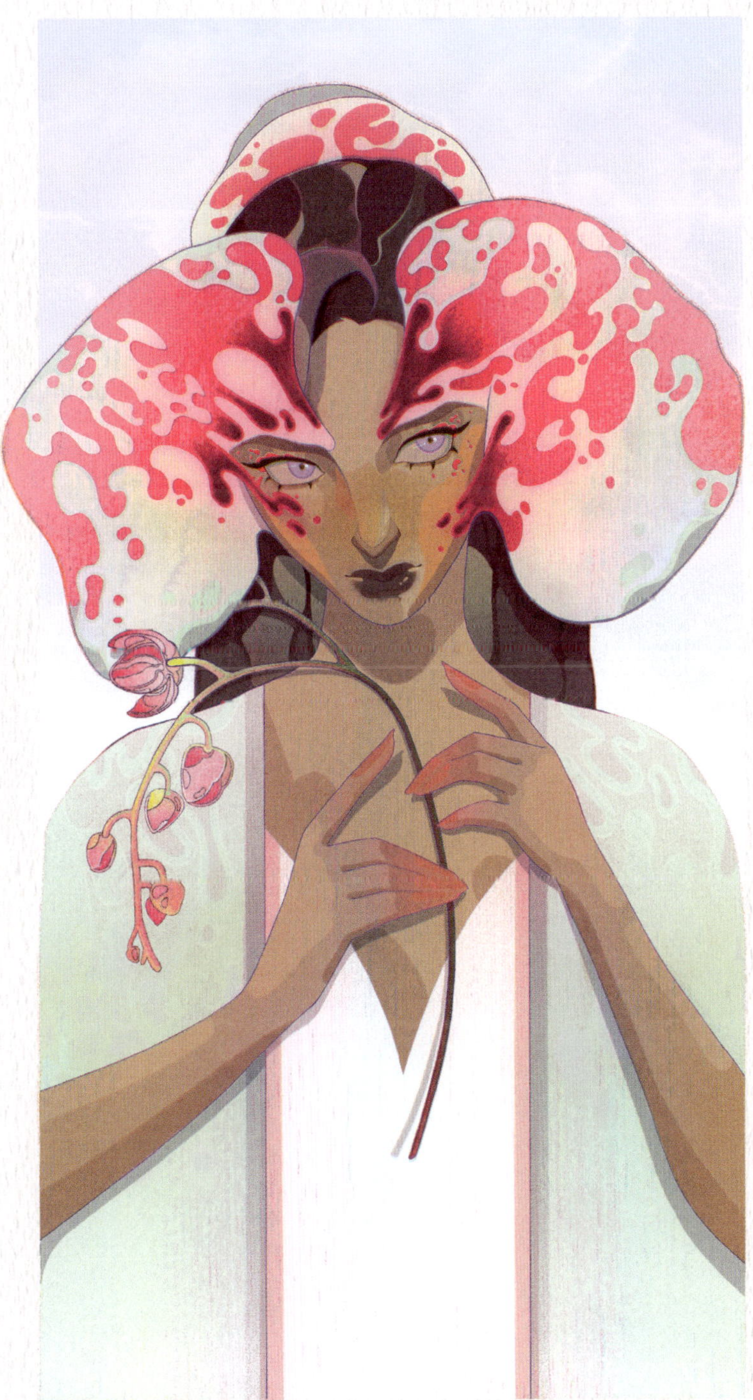

Adjusting the character's petals and adding smaller details

ADDING TEXTURE

Texture will be the 'cherry on top' of this design. This is the last major stage of the process and can involve throwing a lot of things at the image to find what works best. Digital images can sometimes appear very flat, or too perfectly smooth and clean, and a great way to counter that is to create a texture. This can be done using various sources and will really add something special to your artwork.

Orchid petals, upon very close inspection, have a very delicate veining and translucency. The easiest way to imitate this effect is with watercolour brushes on a new layer. Test different layer blending modes and levels of opacity until you achieve that petal blush texture; lay brushstrokes down and then creatively erase them to achieve more varied effects. Add another layer and use more canvas-like brushes to create a more traditional look. Finally, add a layer of grain or 'noise', which is extremely effective at reducing the 'flat' feeling of a digital image. You can apply these textures with quite a heavy hand at first, then lessen them before proceeding to the final detailing.

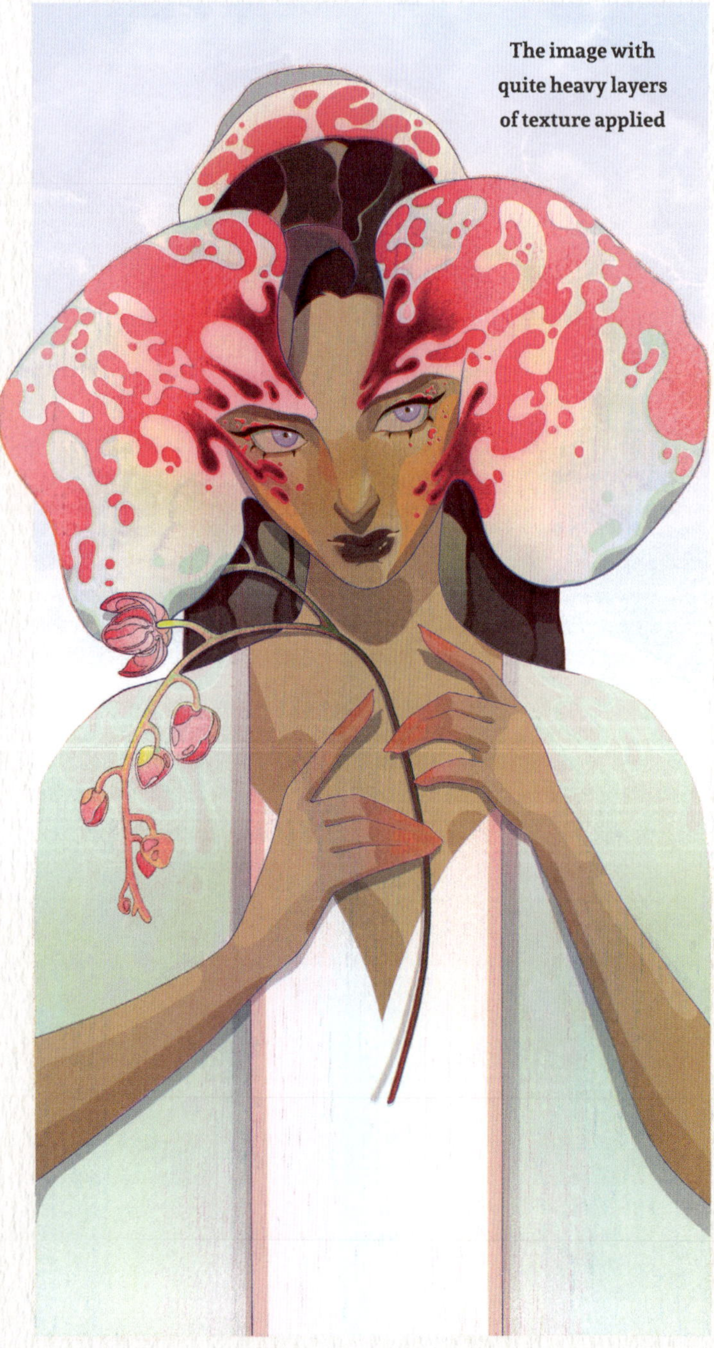

The image with quite heavy layers of texture applied

SOURCING TEXTURES

You can also overlay imported images, such as paper textures or watercolour splashes. There are many free and paid-for resources available online. Even better, you can create your own: try scanning paper textures and watercolour splashes, or taking pictures of fabric, carpet, and cardboard. Experimenting with image textures, layer modes, and masks in combination can be very rewarding and an easy way to add a little 'oomph' to your piece. The possibilities are endless!

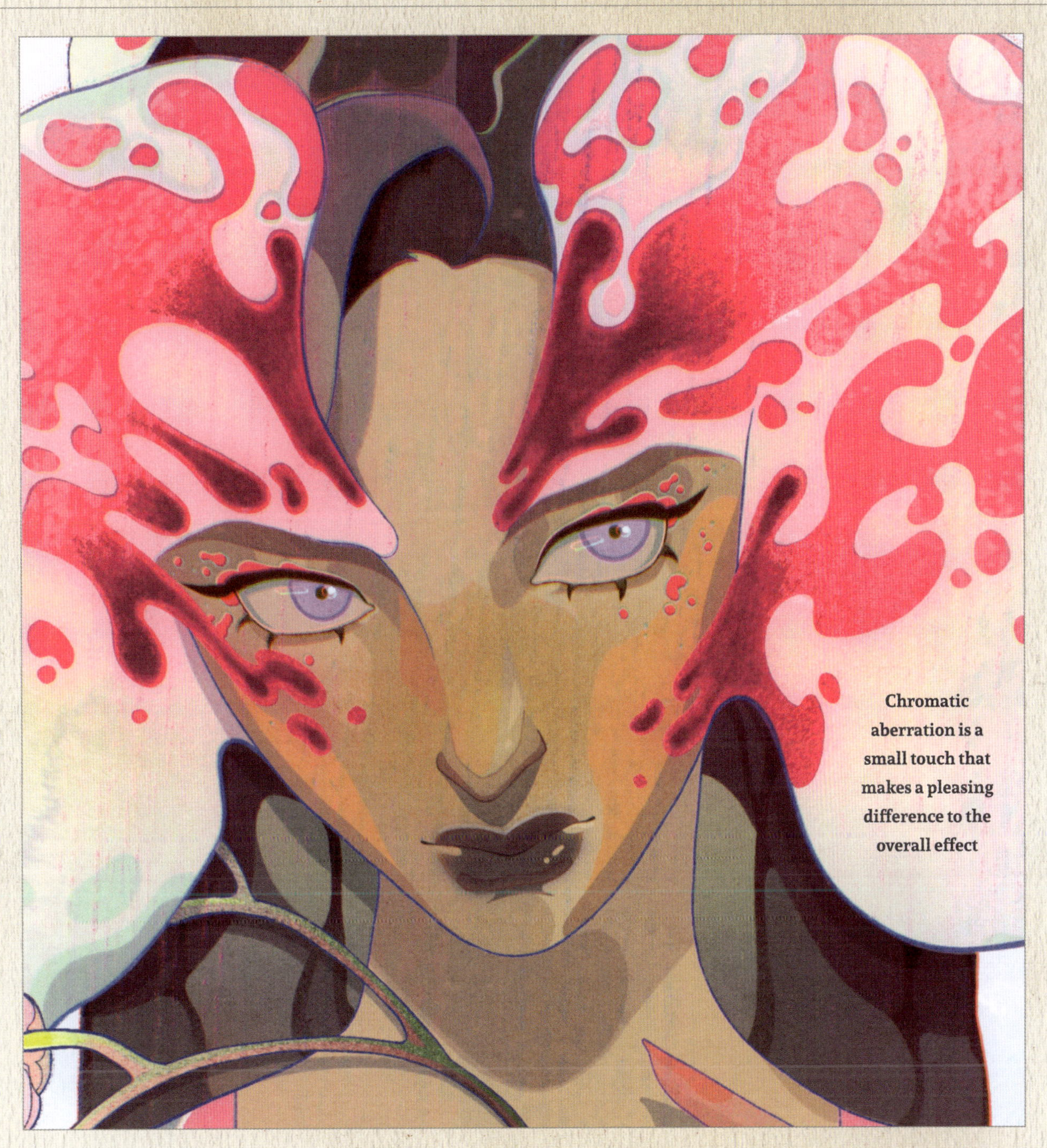

Chromatic aberration is a small touch that makes a pleasing difference to the overall effect

FINISHING TOUCHES

The absolute last possible details are added at this stage. For example, the petal pattern can be given a little extra attention to make sure it really mimics the rich splashes of the reference. See if there are any other areas where you can add a little more dimension and contrast.

Once you're happy with everything, save a spare copy of the image and merge all the layers together. On this flattened copy, you can add a little chromatic aberration; this effect creates coloured edges as the image's colour channels separate. This psychedelic, entrancing look will help push the narrative that this orchid enchantress toes the line between alluring and sinister, leaning on the idea of these flowers seeming to induce a mania in people. Check if any overall colour and texture adjustments are needed after this, then finally zoom in close to inspect the image thoroughly for any leftover lines or blobs that shouldn't be there.

THE FINAL DESIGN

The patterns on the character's robe, coupled with the textures and effects added in the meantime, have become a little too distracting. Removing them in favour of a simpler, almost bridal look works better, and feels more fitting, since orchids are often found in wedding bouquets. You want to focus on what makes the piece and narrative pop, and for this design, that's the petals. It's never too late to make changes and cut elements that don't bring something new or specific to the character.

The final design has that mysteriously alluring and quietly powerful quality that was aimed for from the start. Here you can see how the references, inspiration, research, and planning all come to fruition. The bright patterns on the enchantress's petal headdress seem to dance, entrancing those who are fortunate (or perhaps unfortunate) enough to gaze upon it. This character embodies 'Orchidelirium', perhaps intentionally inducing it in anyone foolish enough to try to steal her closely guarded buds.

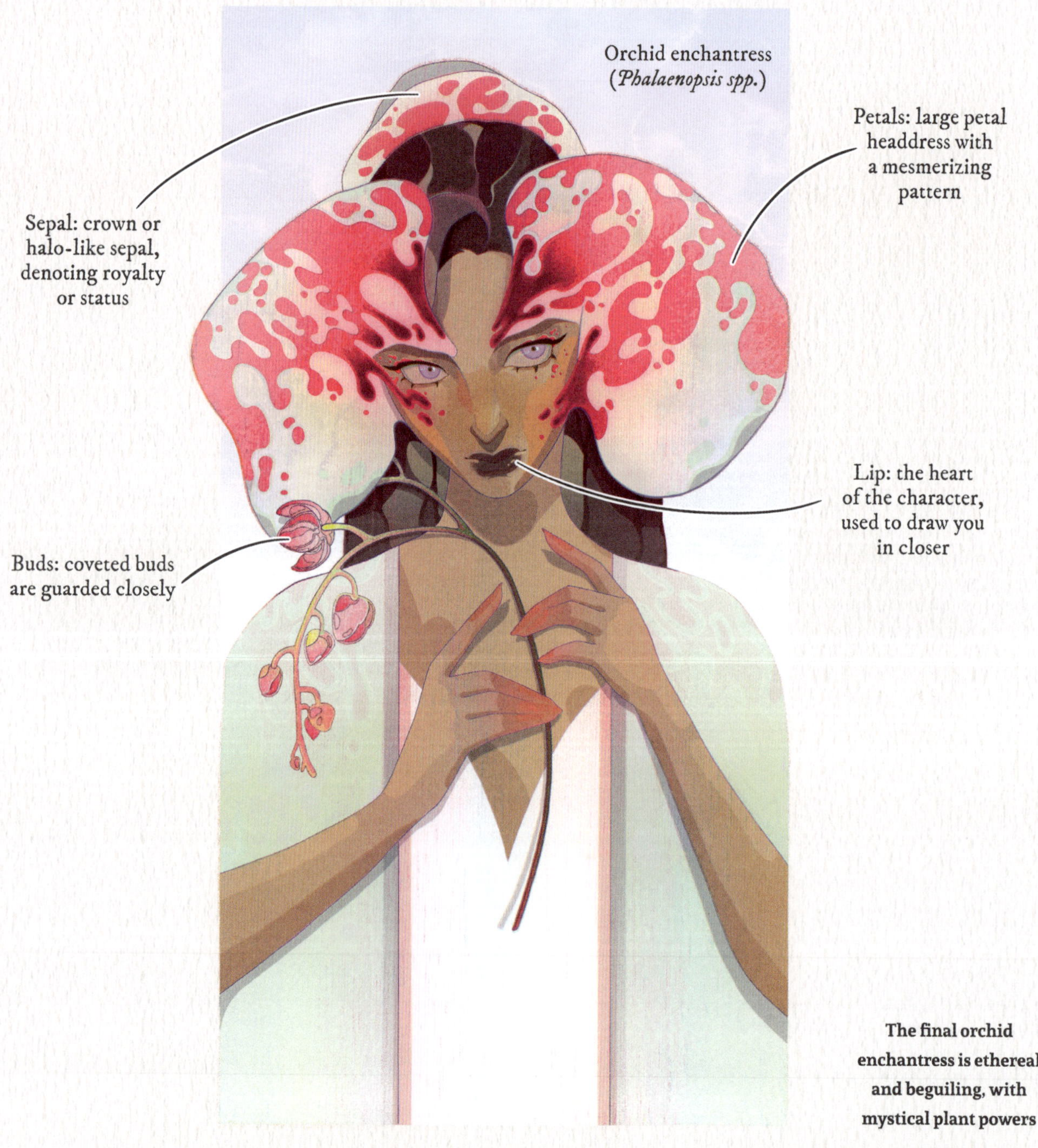

The final orchid enchantress is ethereal and beguiling, with mystical plant powers

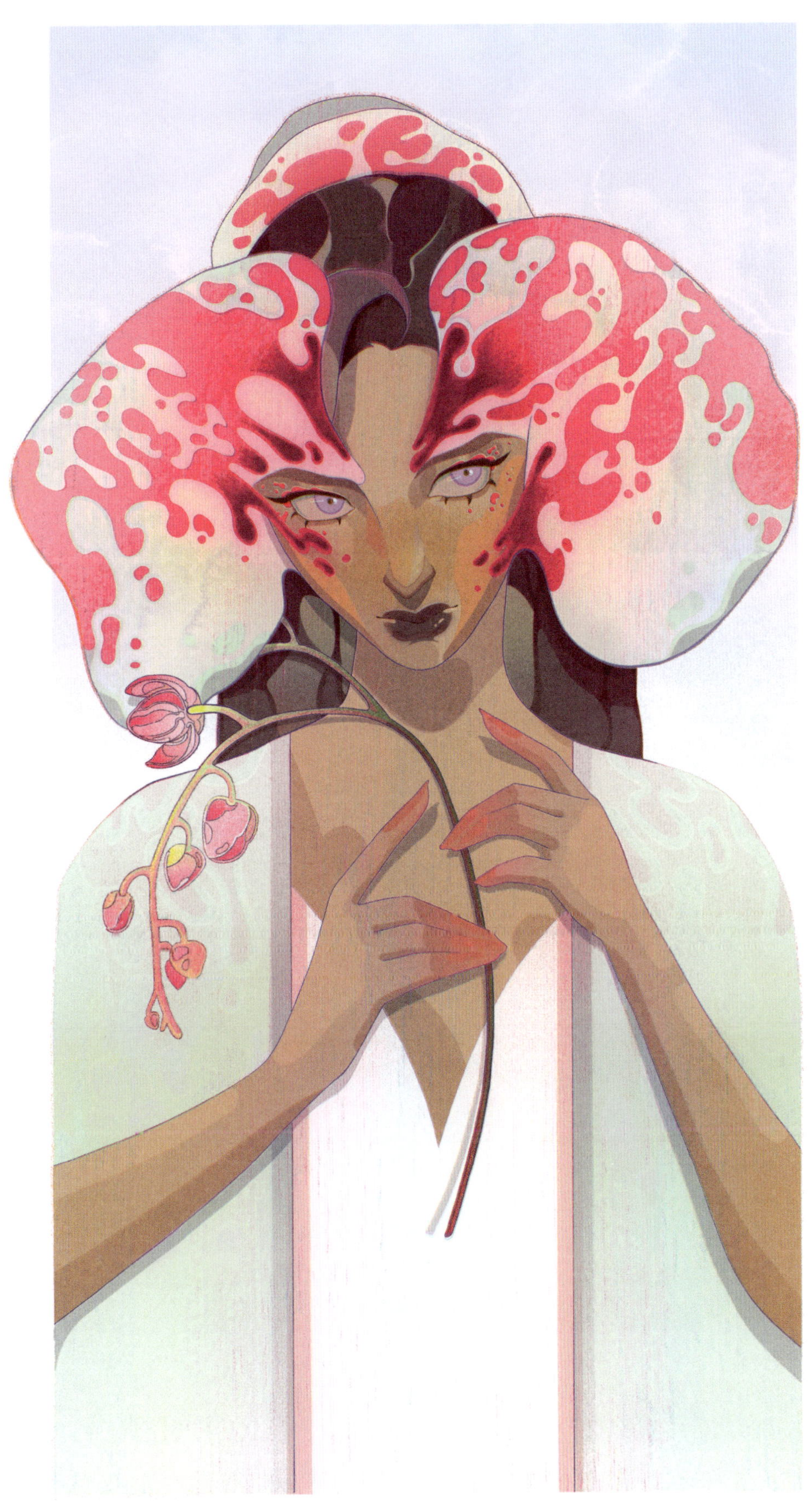

ORCHID ENCHANTRESS

Final image © Lara Georgia Carson

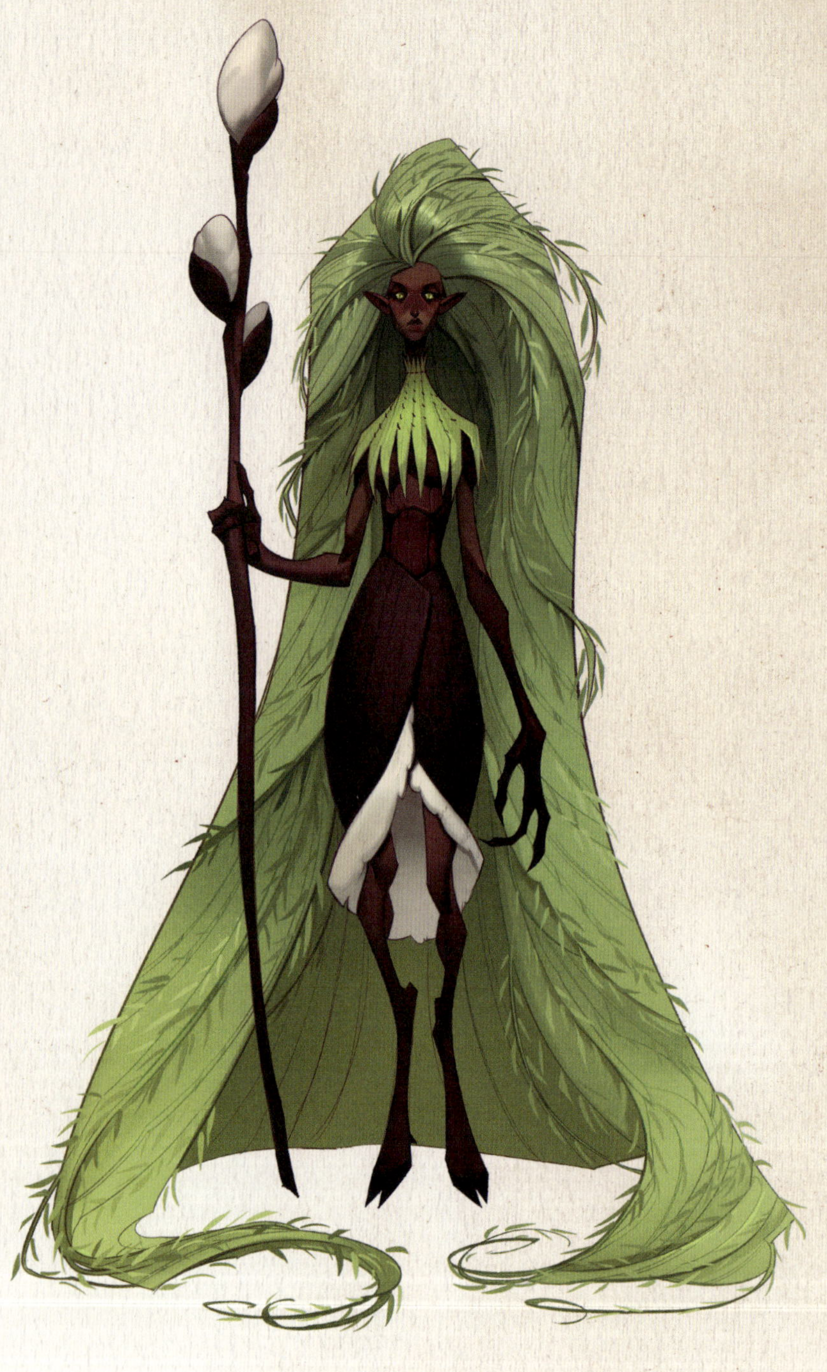

Sometimes you might find it hard to come up with ideas for a character, but inspiration can easily be found in the natural world just outside your door if you know where to look! This tutorial will walk you through the process of designing a character inspired by a weeping willow tree, providing helpful advice and tips that can be used in your workflow. The character will be created in Procreate on the iPad, however you can use whatever media and tools you're comfortable with.

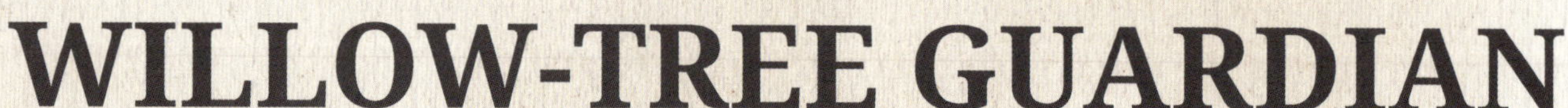

tree

WILLOW-TREE GUARDIAN

ROMA GEWSKA

Final image © Roma Gewska

START WITH RESEARCH

Start the design process by familiarizing yourself with your tree of choice, in this case a willow tree. Pick a few key elements that you would like to incorporate into your design and study them closely, considering how you could translate them into a humanlike character. Willow tree bark has a rough texture that has the potential to be an interesting detail; perhaps an armour? Willows are also well known for their catkins. In Slavic cultures they have a sacred meaning, taking root in pagan rituals and merging with Christian beliefs over time. It would be interesting to somehow include such symbolic details in the design. Finally, arguably the most iconic feature of the willow tree is its long leafy branches.

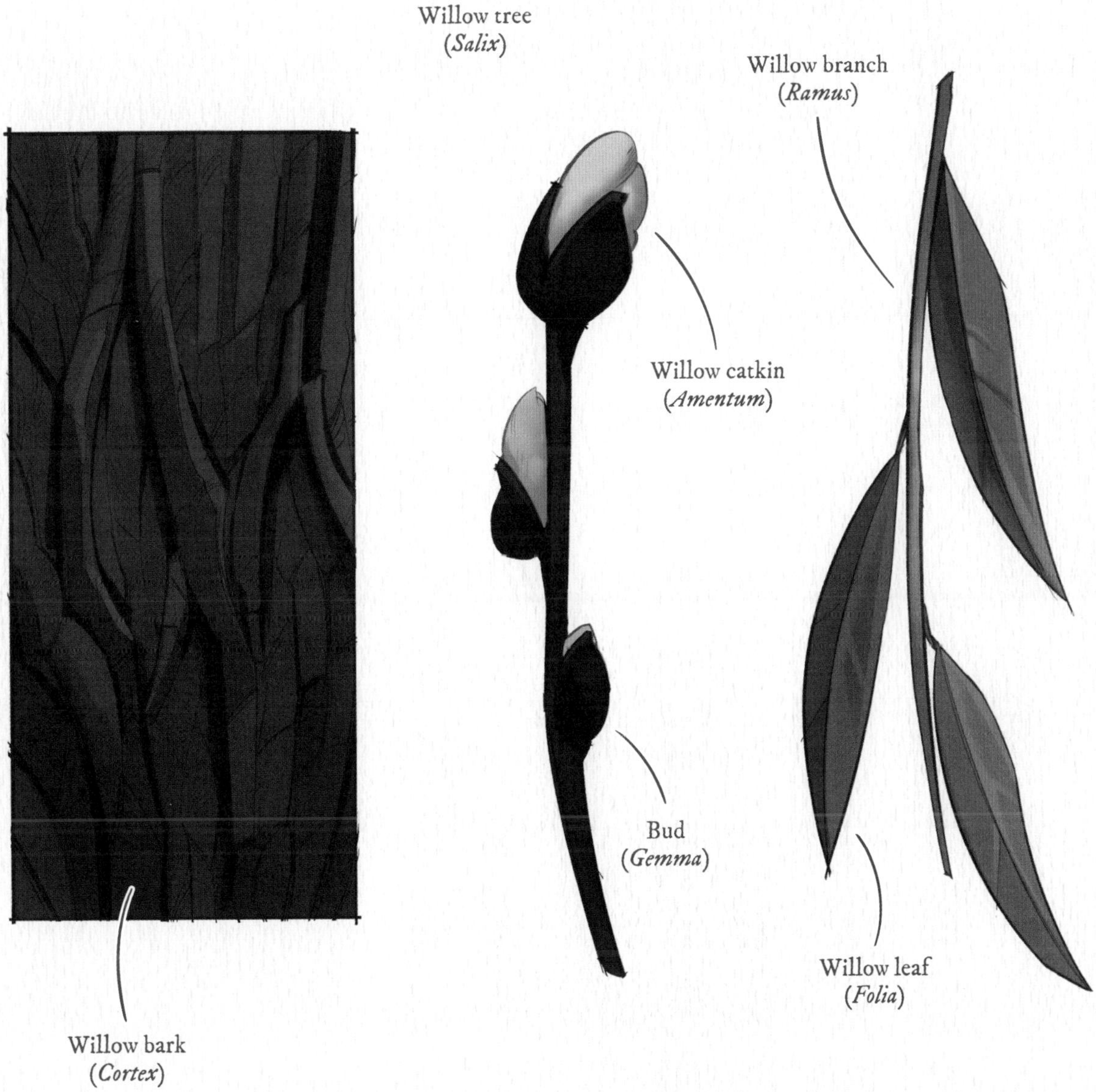

Willow tree
(*Salix*)

Willow branch
(*Ramus*)

Willow catkin
(*Amentum*)

Bud
(*Gemma*)

Willow leaf
(*Folia*)

Willow bark
(*Cortex*)

Sketching the main features of the willow tree to familiarize yourself with the plant

INITIAL SKETCHES

Think about the essence of a weeping willow tree. Not only is it a very iconic tree, but it has lots of parts that will translate well into a character design. For example, its foliage hangs in a manner not too dissimilar to human hair, while its twisted trunk could be mistaken for a hunched-over figure. It also possesses a slightly mysterious vibe, like it's hiding something behind all of its leaves and branches.

An ancient creature, an old guardian of the forest, a powerful being that existed long before the oldest tree in the forest was even a sprout; this is the kind of a creature that comes to mind when thinking of a willow tree. Draw a series of sketch explorations for how this guardian character might look.

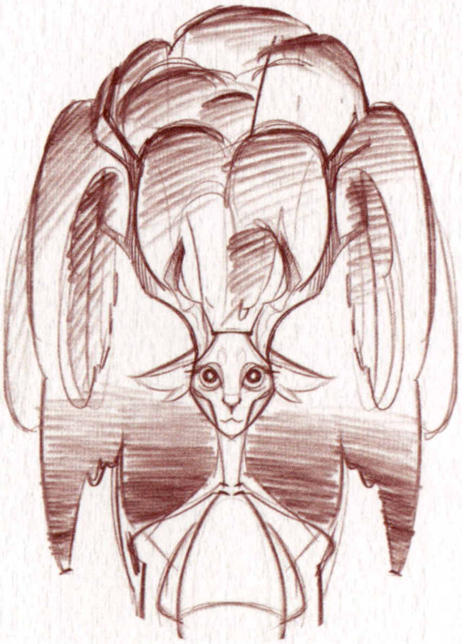

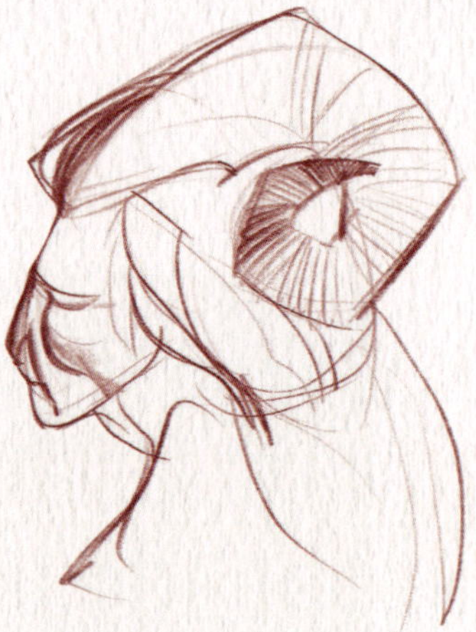

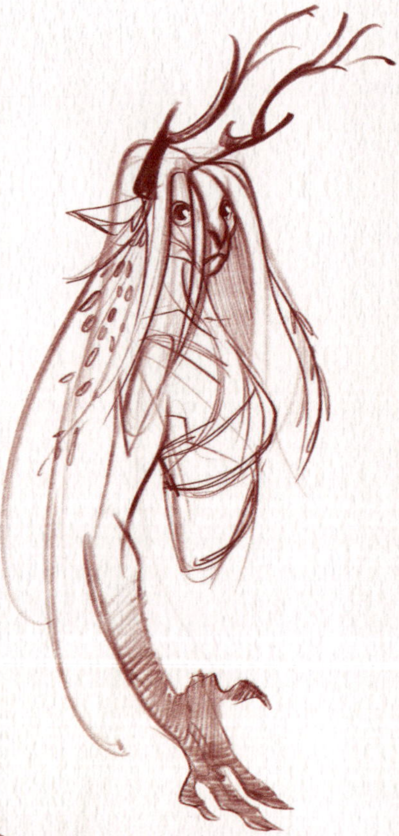

Exploring potential designs with quick rough sketches

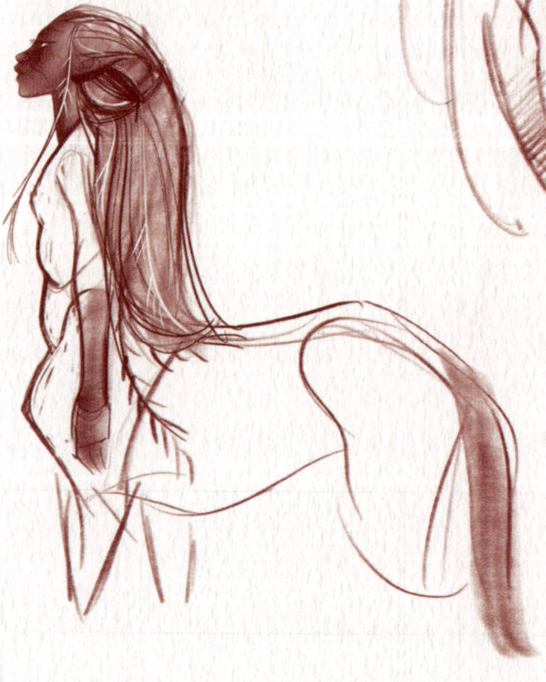

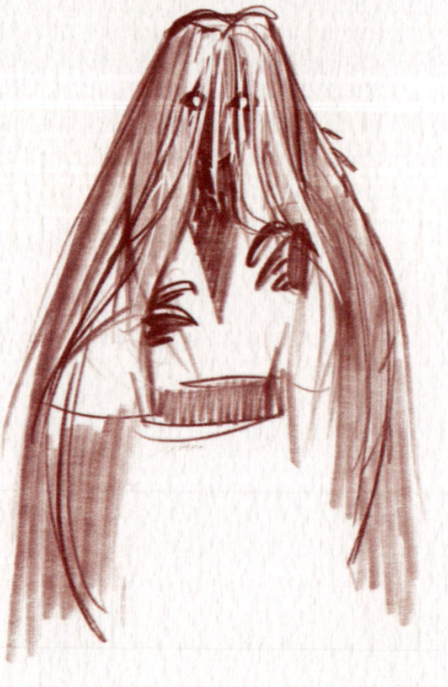

THUMBNAILS

Once you have a general idea for the character, move on to the thumbnailing stage. When sketching thumbnails, keep each one simple, drawing general forms and tones. Try to make each sketch as different from the previous one as you can, as this will give you more options to choose from. Think of a feature that will remind the viewer of a willow tree when they look at your design, such as the foliage – it's long and lush, resembling human hair – then try different ways to incorporate this into your design.

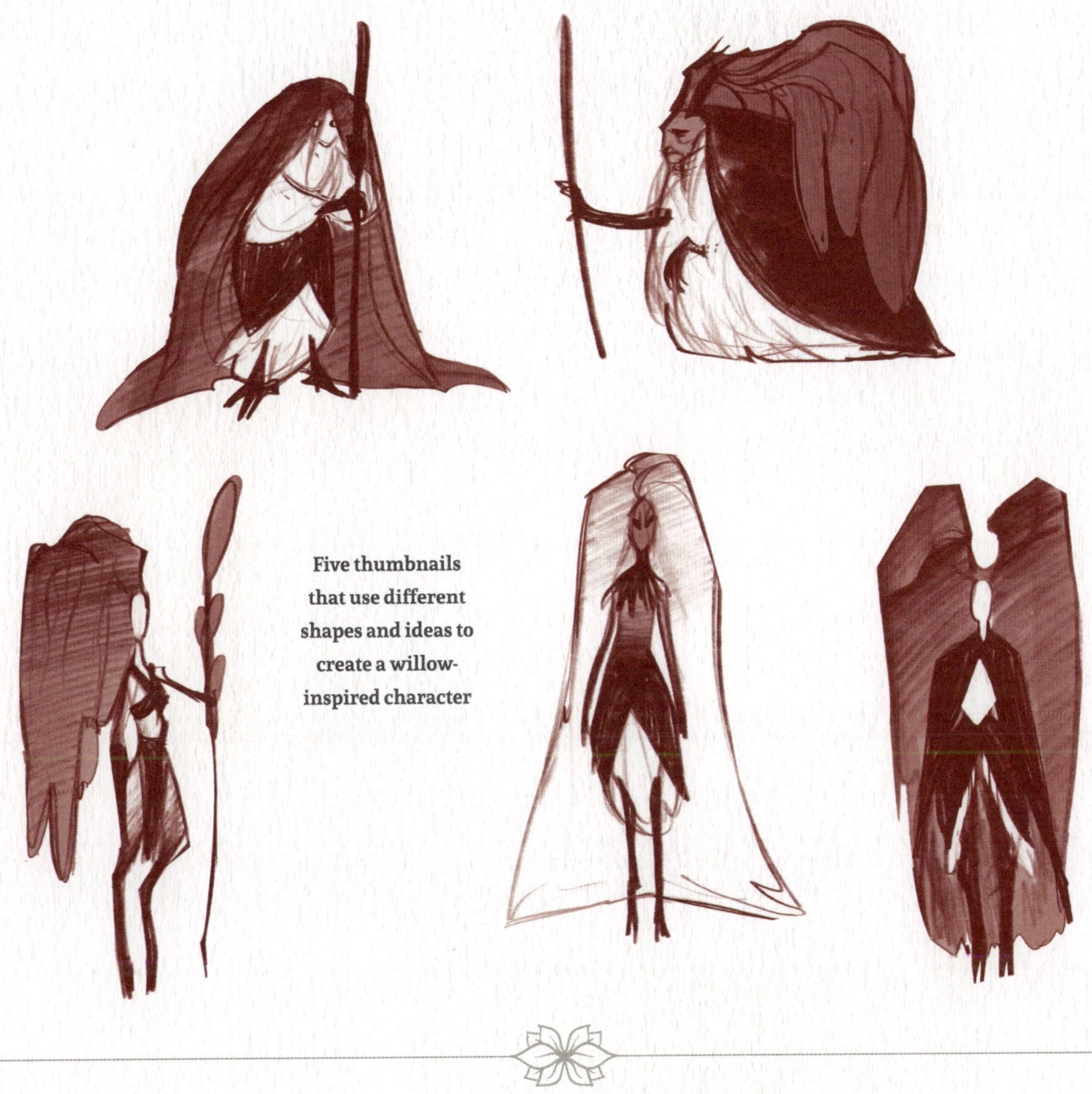

Five thumbnails that use different shapes and ideas to create a willow-inspired character

SHAPE LANGUAGE

Pay attention to shape language when sketching your character. There are three basic shapes: square, triangle, and circle. Square is a very firm and static shape, typically used for characters that are strong, stubborn, and stoic. Triangles are angular, dynamic, and have multiple purposes. They're often used to design quick, agile protagonists, or mysterious villains in capes. Circles are used for designing cute or friendly characters due to the soft, round nature of the shape. Experiment and combine different shapes and forms during the thumbnailing stage to create different results.

FOUNDATIONS

Once you're happy that you've explored a suitable number of thumbnails, choose the strongest and proceed on to sketching a foundation. Start with simple shapes for the character's torso, head, limbs, and any additional elements that are necessary in your design. Focus on the anatomy rather than adding any details just yet. Introducing detail at this stage would only be distracting and could risk causing disproportionate or jumbled anatomy. Don't be afraid to alter elements from your thumbnails. For example, though the chosen thumbnail didn't have a staff, it would make for a more imposing silhouette if the forest guardian held a sacred staff hewn from a branch of willow catkins. Sketch a general outline of where it should go.

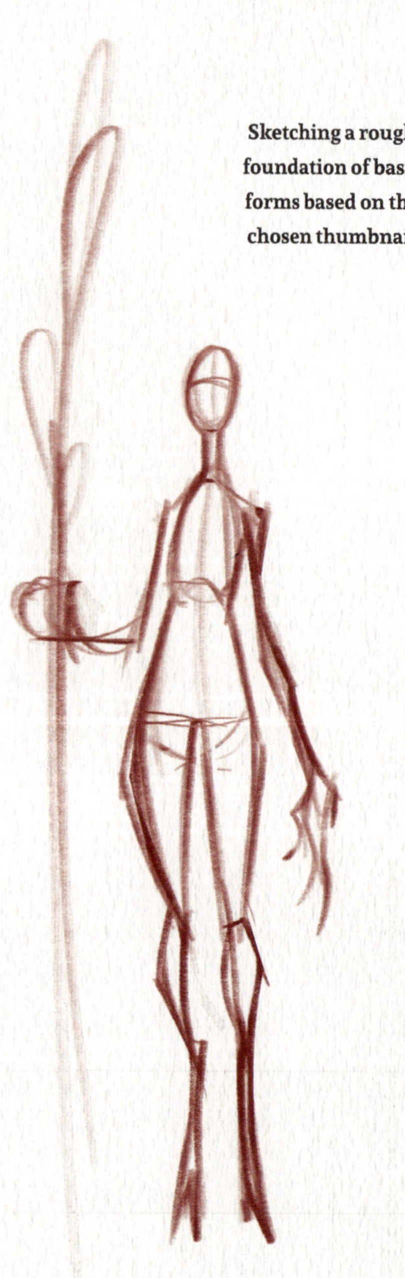

Sketching a rough foundation of basic forms based on the chosen thumbnail

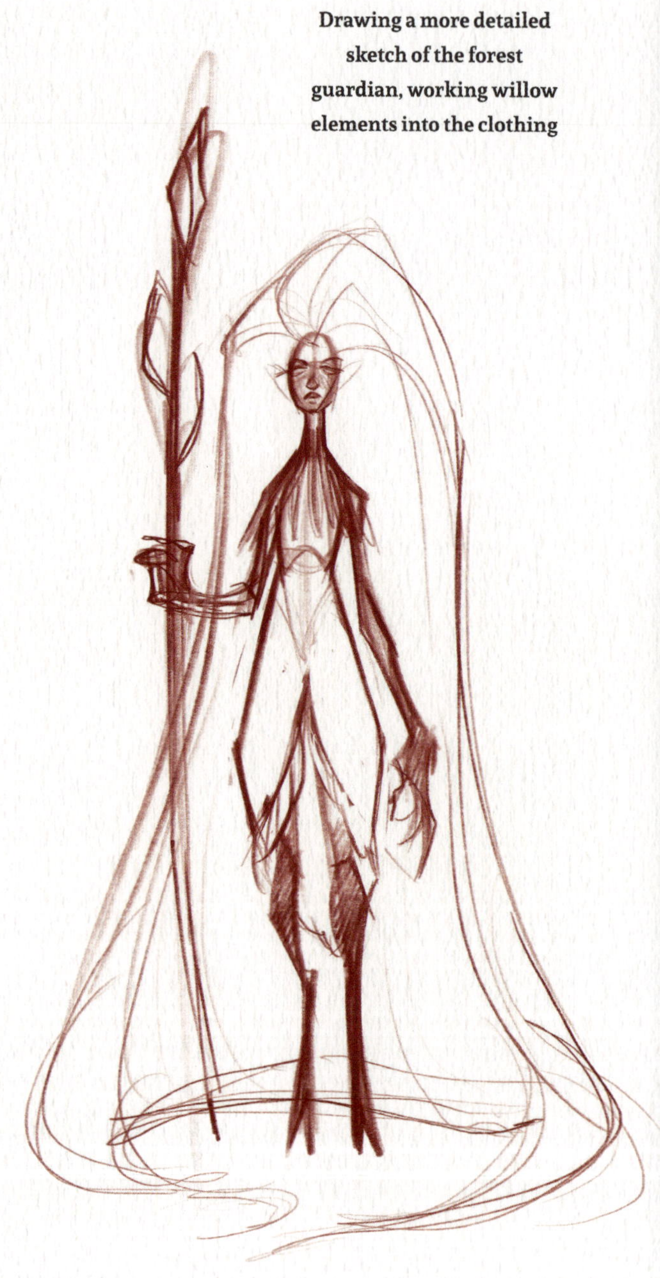

Drawing a more detailed sketch of the forest guardian, working willow elements into the clothing

BUILDING UP

Begin to build up the design and add in detail, such as outlining the face and clothing elements. Sketch her iconic willow-branch hair to give the silhouette a soft triangular shape. This will help to guide viewers' attention into what's going on inside of the design. The guardian's frame is long and slender, like a tree, and drawing a long neck piece fashioned from slim willow leaves will accent it even more, as well as making the design more believable. Next, draw her skirt piece based around willow buds; their shape is perfect for sculpting into clothing and armour.

FINAL SKETCH

Continue to detail your sketch. During this stage, focus on solving any problems that might make the next steps harder. In this case, the most unresolved area from the previous step is the torso – it's empty and boring. Draw in armour crafted from tree bark on her upper body, coupled with a willow bud skirt. This adds more noise to the overall design, but makes it more interesting and thought out. Keep in mind that the character's face is the most important part of the design, as it's the first thing the viewer will look at. Sketch in more detail on the character's face and fix any anatomy problems present in the previous sketch.

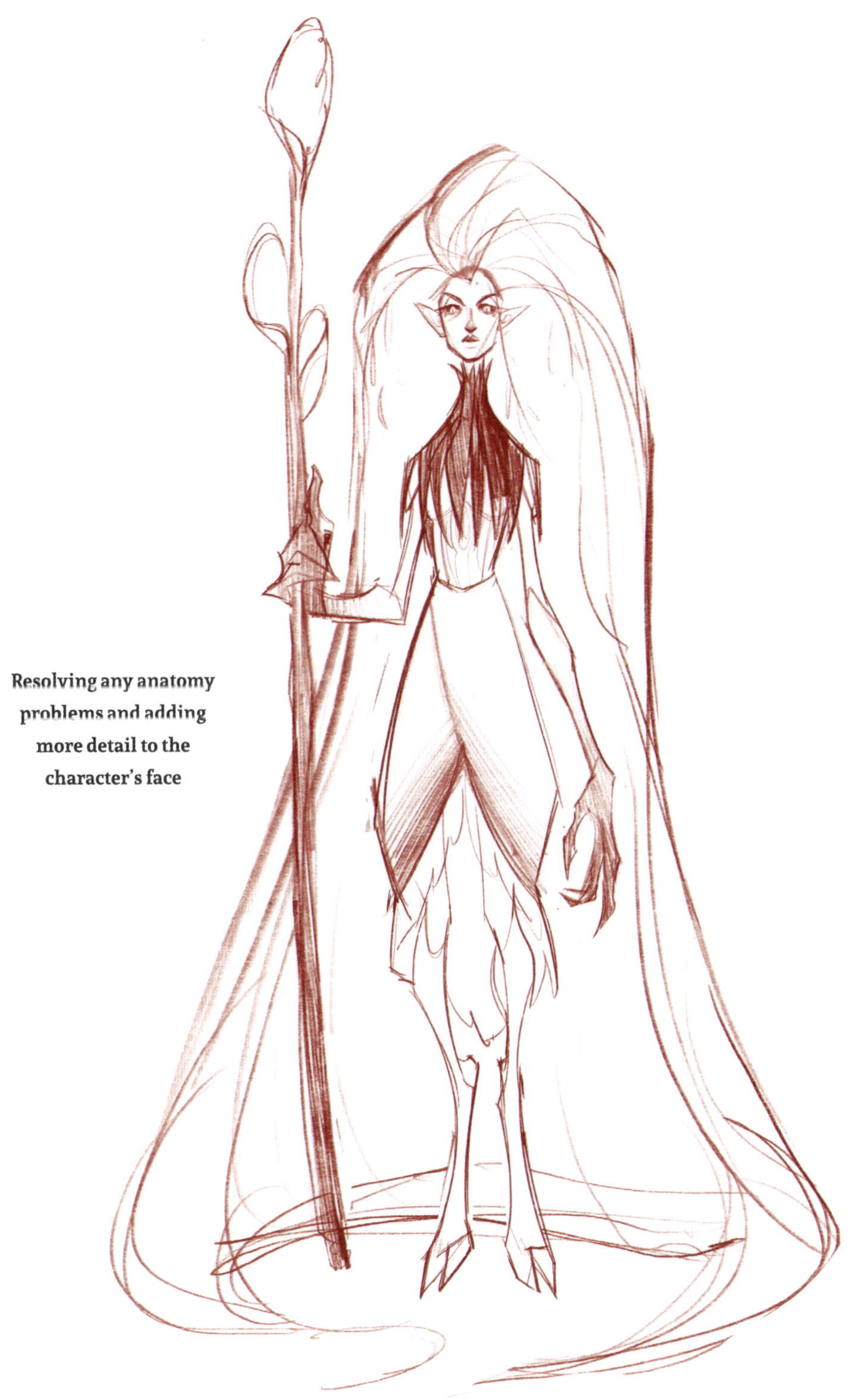

Resolving any anatomy problems and adding more detail to the character's face

LINE ART

After the sketch is complete, move on to the line-art stage. Aim to make your lines as confident as possible by trying to draw smooth lines in one swift motion, rather than lots of smaller, stop-start, broken lines. This will take a lot of practice and do-overs. Your lines don't have to be perfect; a little messiness can add personality. Once the main outlines are finished, add textures in places where you feel they're needed. For example, this guardian wears wooden armour covering her upper torso, so adding a tree bark texture will show this.

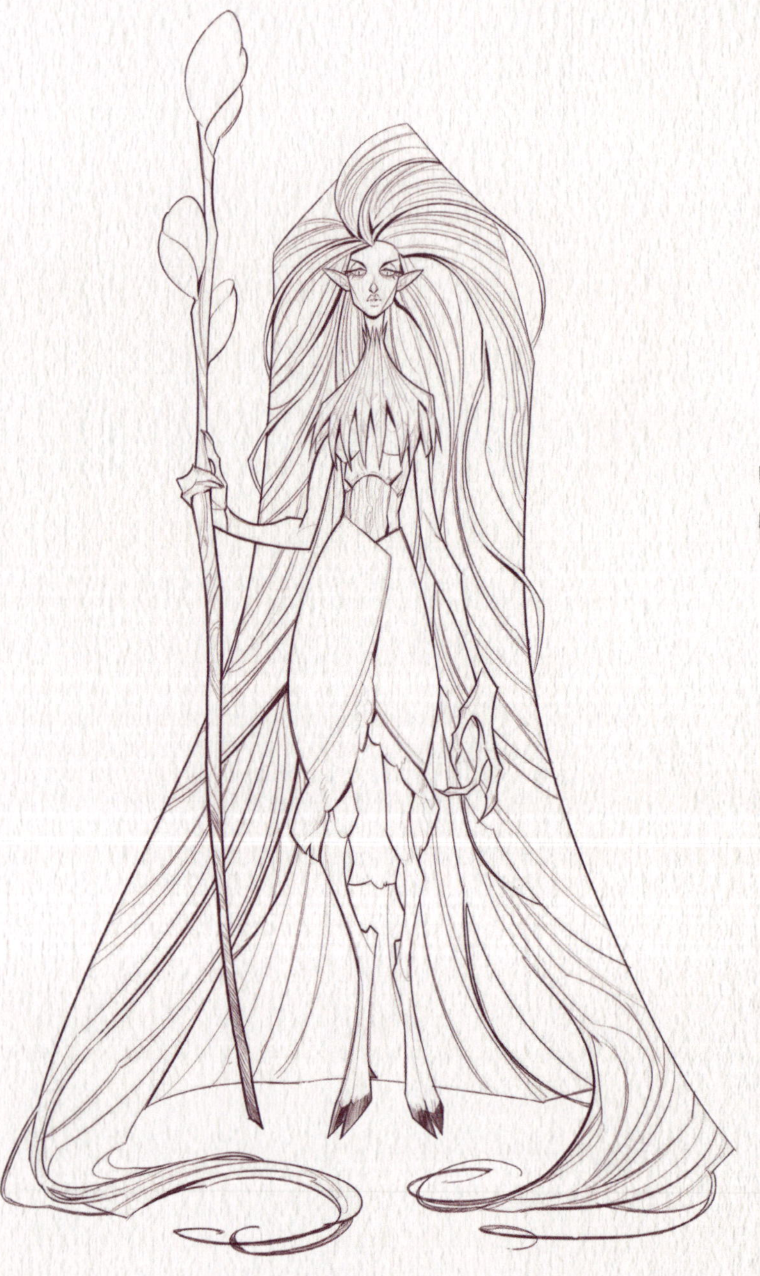

Drawing the line art with smooth lines, then adding texture to the wooden armour

LINE ART & COLOURS

Many artists play it safe and choose only one colour for their line art; however, you have the freedom to use different colours. The colour of your line art influences the way the other colours look. It can also be used to accent various elements without necessarily getting rid of others. Experiment with changing the colours of your lines depending on what they outline. For example, you could make the outlines of the character's hair a light green colour to prevent them from being too dark and distracting.

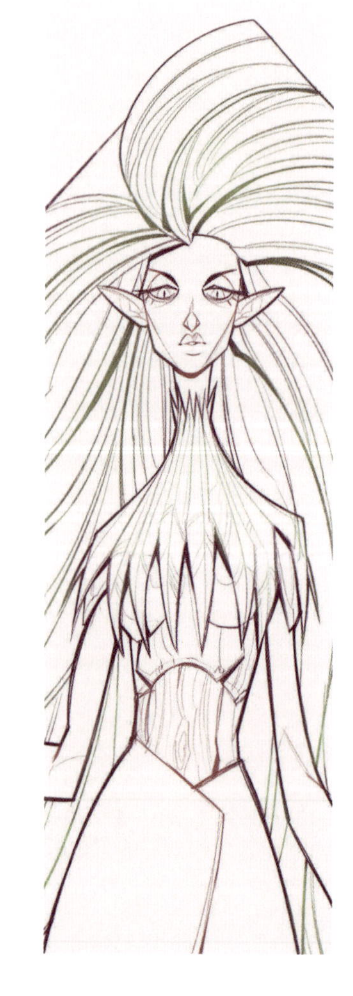

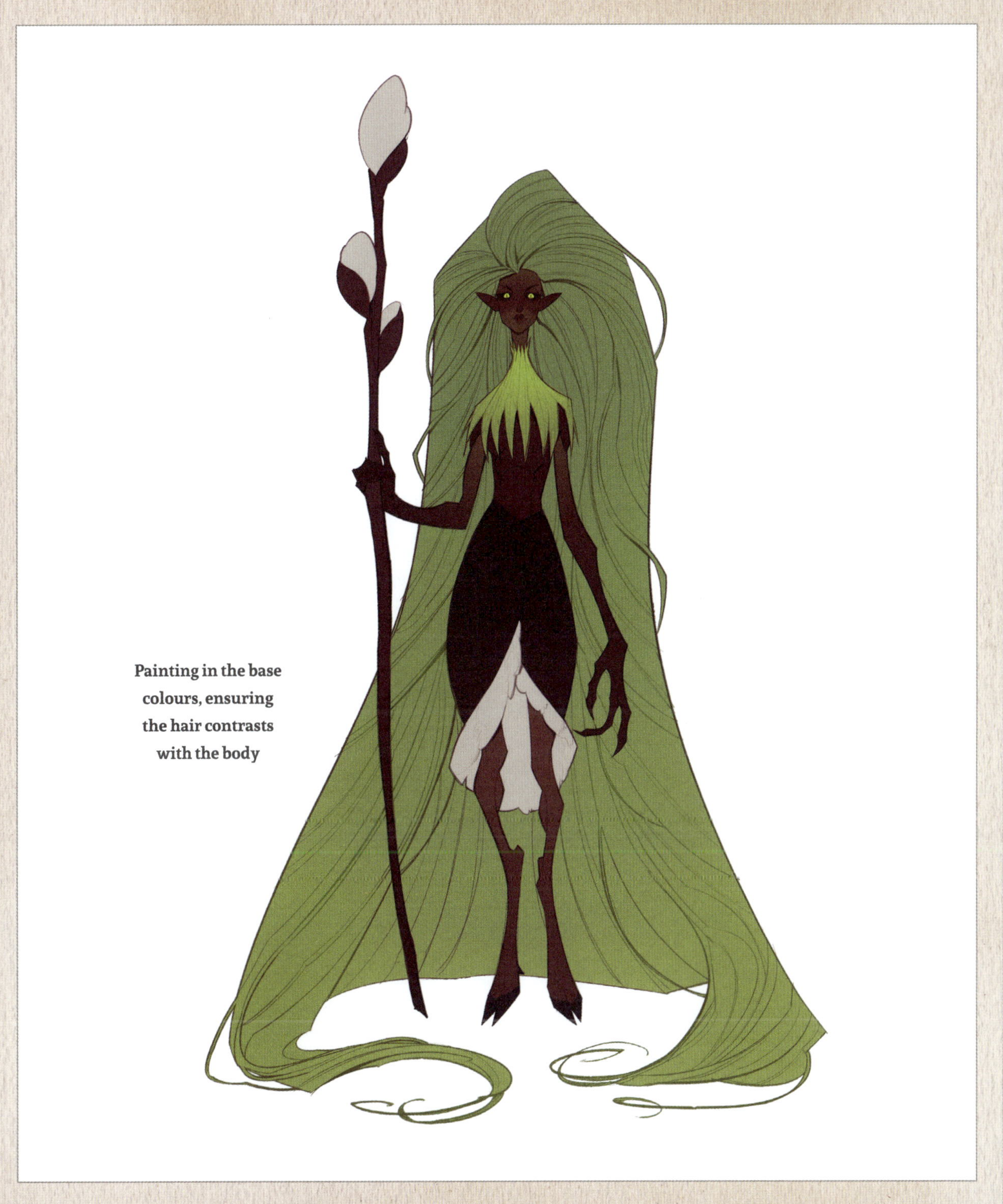

Painting in the base colours, ensuring the hair contrasts with the body

COLOUR BASE

Now the line art is finished, you can start to select the colours. This stage can be a little tricky, because you need to keep in mind not only the hue, but also the tone of the colour you chose. With a willow tree, there are three main colours to experiment with: brown, green, and grey. The character's body should contrast with her hair, so choose a dark, warm shade of brown for her torso and a light, cool shade of green for her hair. Her leaf necklace is a great accent piece, so colour it with an even lighter green.

ADDING AMBIENT OCCLUSION

The easiest way to add volume to your drawing is to add ambient occlusion. This is a type of soft shadow that occurs when indirect or overcast lighting is cast on an object. Choose a dark colour and use it to paint soft shadows in places where one object is overlaid by another. For example, the neck under the head, the drop shadow under the hand holding the staff, legs that are covered by the skirt, and so on. You can also use it on the face in places like the eyes, eyelids, nostrils, and upper lip. Be careful with it, however, as too dark a colour risks covering over the detail. It's better to return and add more occlusion in the later stages than to apply too much of it at this stage.

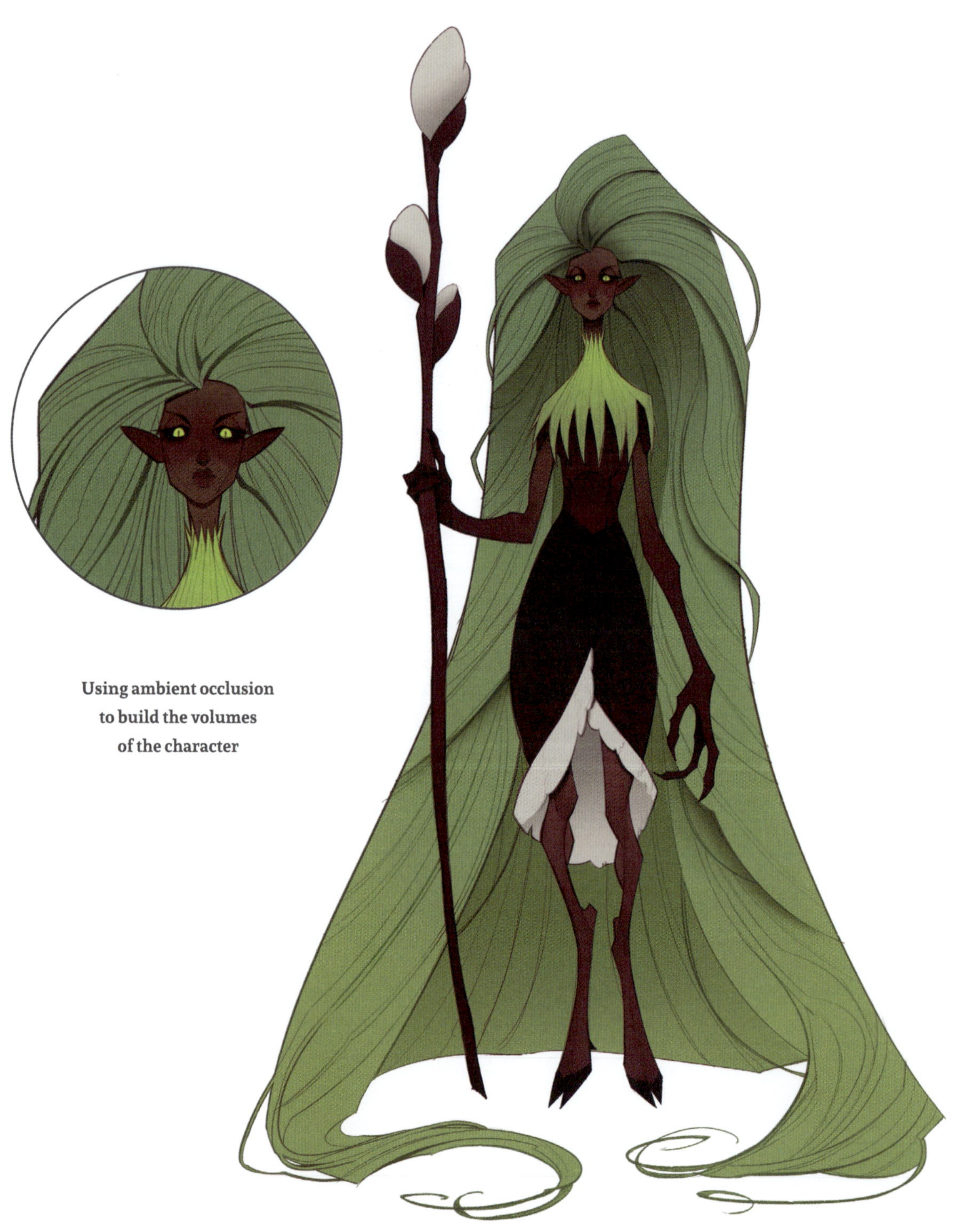

Using ambient occlusion to build the volumes of the character

ADDING SHADOW

When painting shadows on your character, think about the shape you're drawing. Organic objects typically have a softer shape, so try to keep your shadows on the softer side. Keep the various textures of your design in mind during this stage as well. The easiest way to show texture is to vary the contrasts of the shadows and lights. The more matte the material is, the less contrast the lighting has. Wood and catkins are the most matte out of all materials this design has, so they require the softest contrasts. Her hair and branches will need the most contrast, so you can make the shadows a little sharper on these areas.

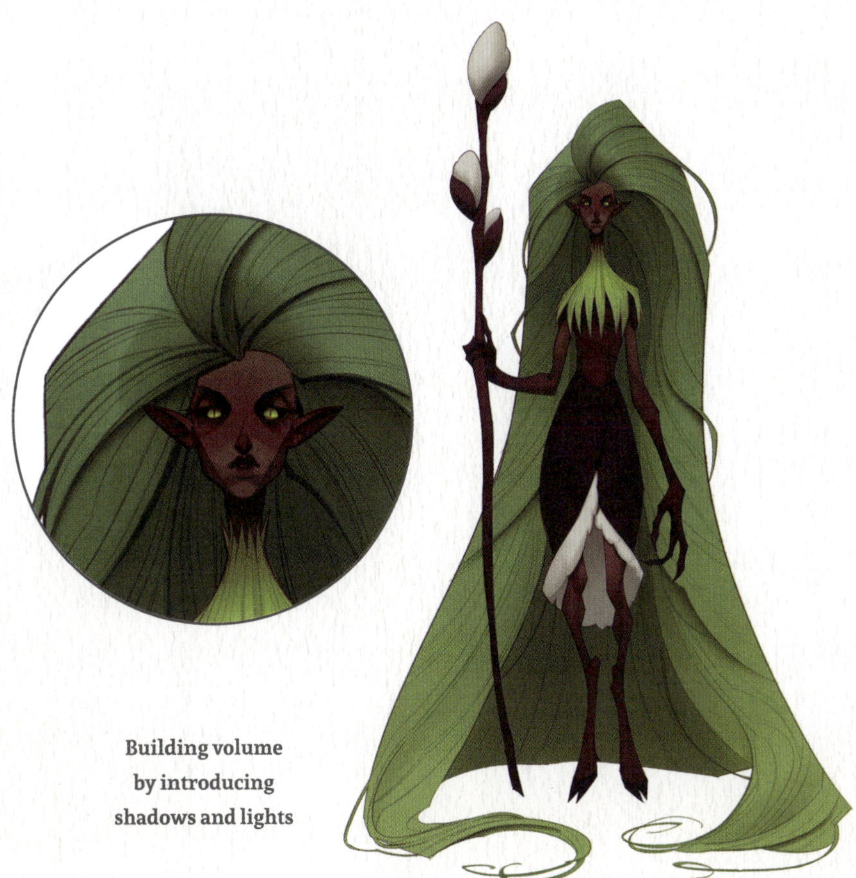

Building volume by introducing shadows and lights

HIGHLIGHTS

When adding highlights to your character, it's also important to consider the textures. Highlighting adds dimension and depth, making the forms more visually interesting. Objects will gradually become darker towards the bottom if they're under direct overhead lighting, such as sunlight. By keeping your lightest colours at the top of the design, you can create a more realistic effect. This will make your character more engaging to the viewer, as it will appear more natural and pleasing to the eye.

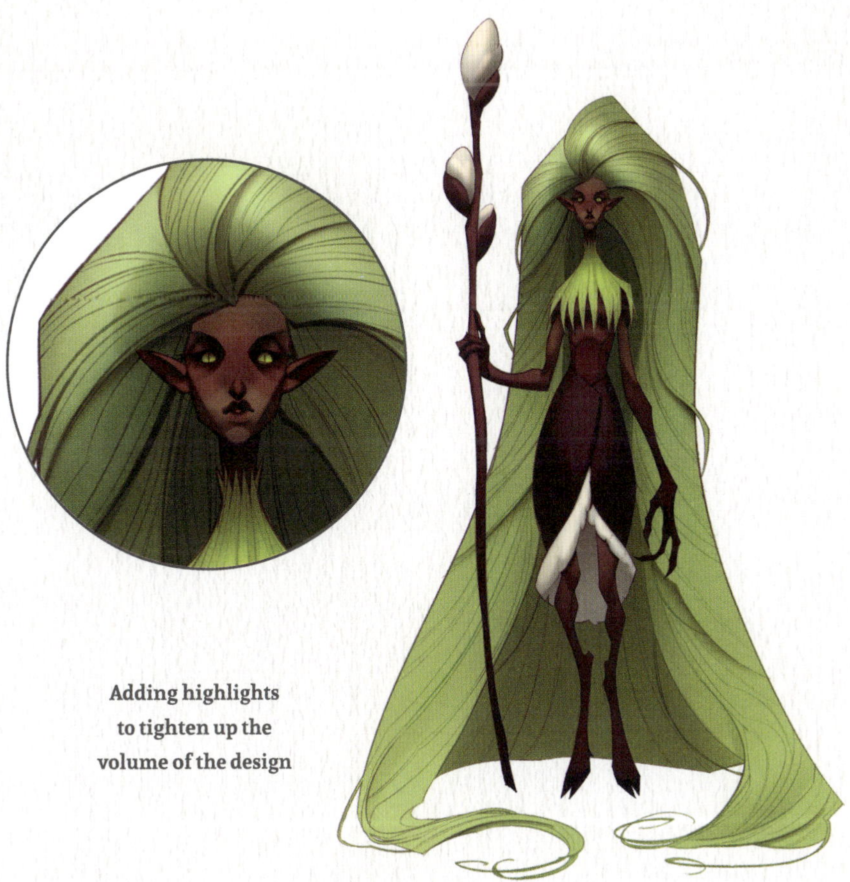

Adding highlights to tighten up the volume of the design

POLISHING

Once you're happy with the lighting, it's time to go over your design once more, polishing and tightening it up. Fix crooked shadows, add occlusion where and if needed, and paint in highlights to the character's eyes, hair, and nose. Take a short break before and after starting this stage. Pausing in this way will allow you to return to the design with fresh eyes, enabling you to spot any mistakes. It will also give you time to think of any additional willow-tree elements you might like to add to the character.

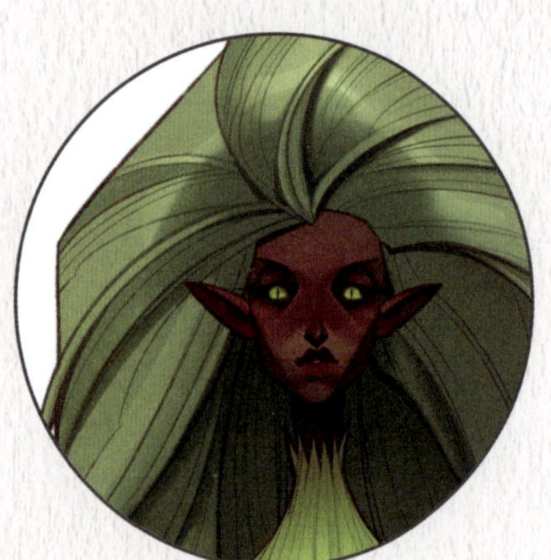

A polished version of the character, with added lighting

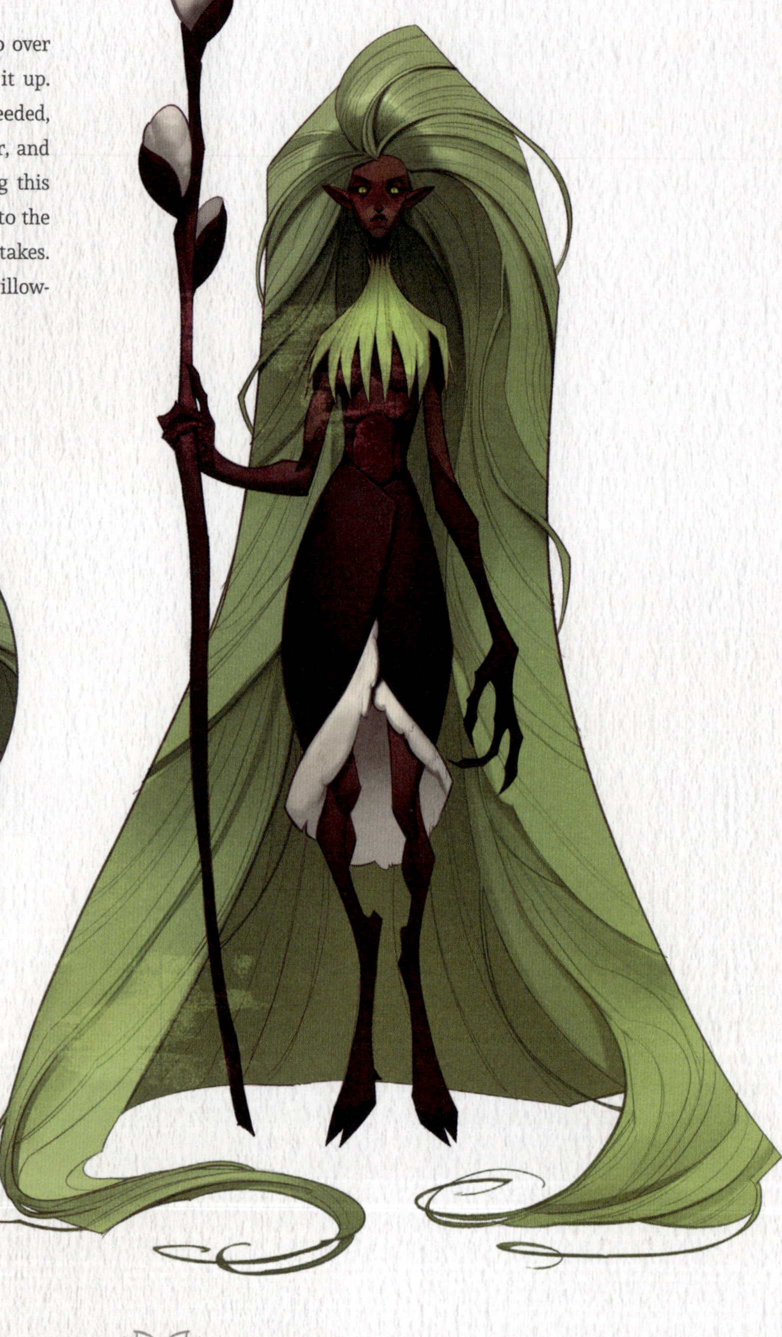

TAKE A BREAK

It can be very helpful to step away and take a break from your work from time to time. When constantly working on one character, your eyes gets so used to it that they may fail to notice crucial details, including glaring mistakes. Try not to look at or think about your drawing while on the break. This will allow you to return to it with renewed energy and the ability to notice if there are elements that need fixing or improving.

ADDING DETAILS

While the shape of the hair is strong, it looks like sleek green human hair rather than vines and leaves. Paint in vines of willow leaves to allude to the willow tree this character is inspired by. The next element that seems a little plain is her necklace. Adding small stitches to hold the leaves together will make its design more interesting and realistic. Finally, the skirt is also a little plain and requires some kind of a pattern. Simple vertical lines successfully accent the character's slender build and work well with the other vertical guidelines, including the leaves, bark texture, and vines.

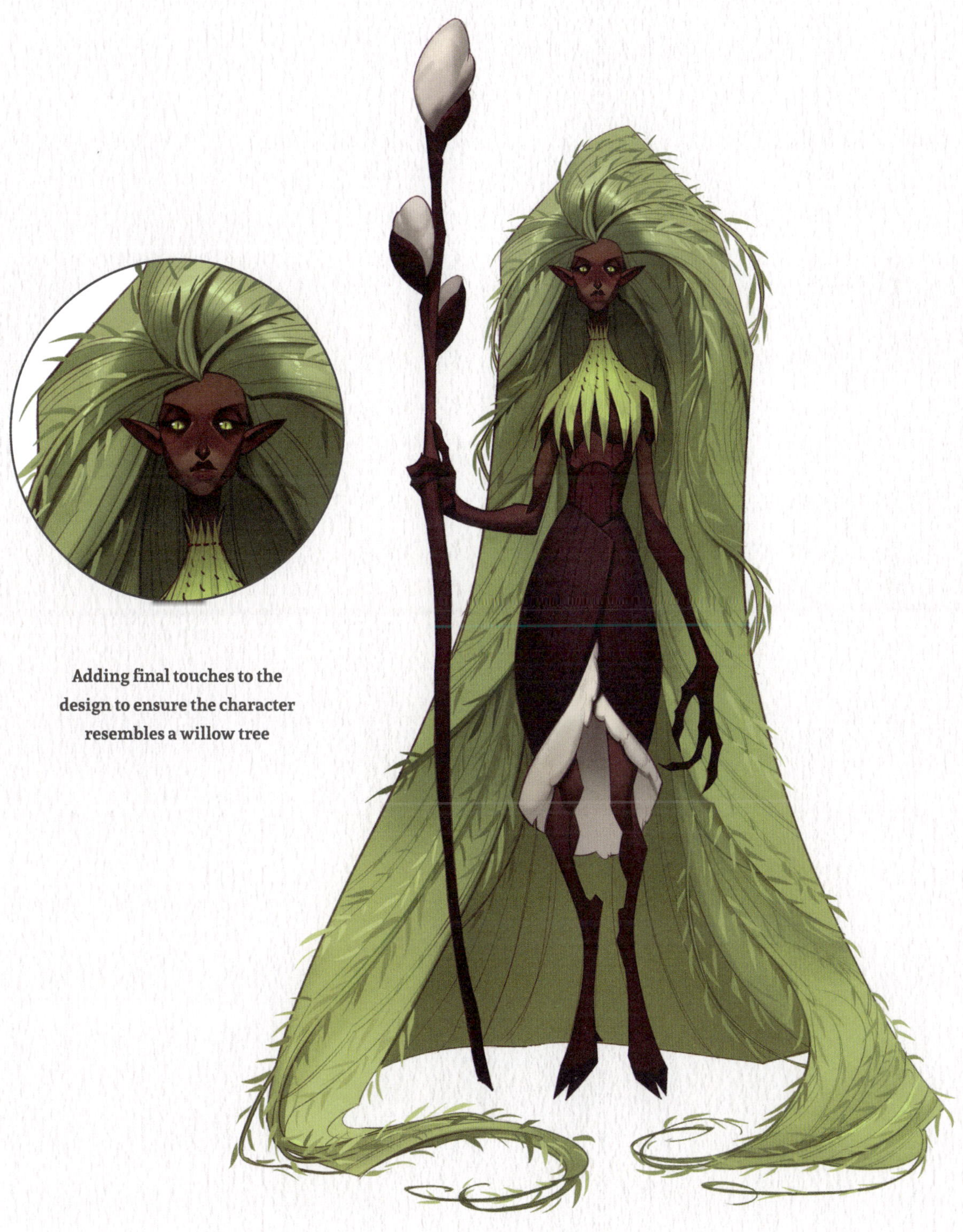

Adding final touches to the design to ensure the character resembles a willow tree

FINAL DETAILS

Once the final details are added, you can reflect on the final willow-tree guardian design. The character's hair is formed from branches, vines, and leaves, hanging long like the leafy vines of a stately weeping willow. Her necklace is also crafted from leaves, adding an elegant accessory to her outfit. The fluffy catkins on her staff are decorative, while the catkin lining on her skirt provides a practical warmth. Her protective torso armour is crafted from willow bark and her wooden branch limbs and willowy tree-like figure all allude to her willow-tree origin.

By following the process outlined in this tutorial, you can create a captivating design that honours the beauty of this beloved tree. Taking inspiration from plants and trees found in nature and incorporating them into your work is a great way to expand your visual library and enrich your portfolio with truly unique characters.

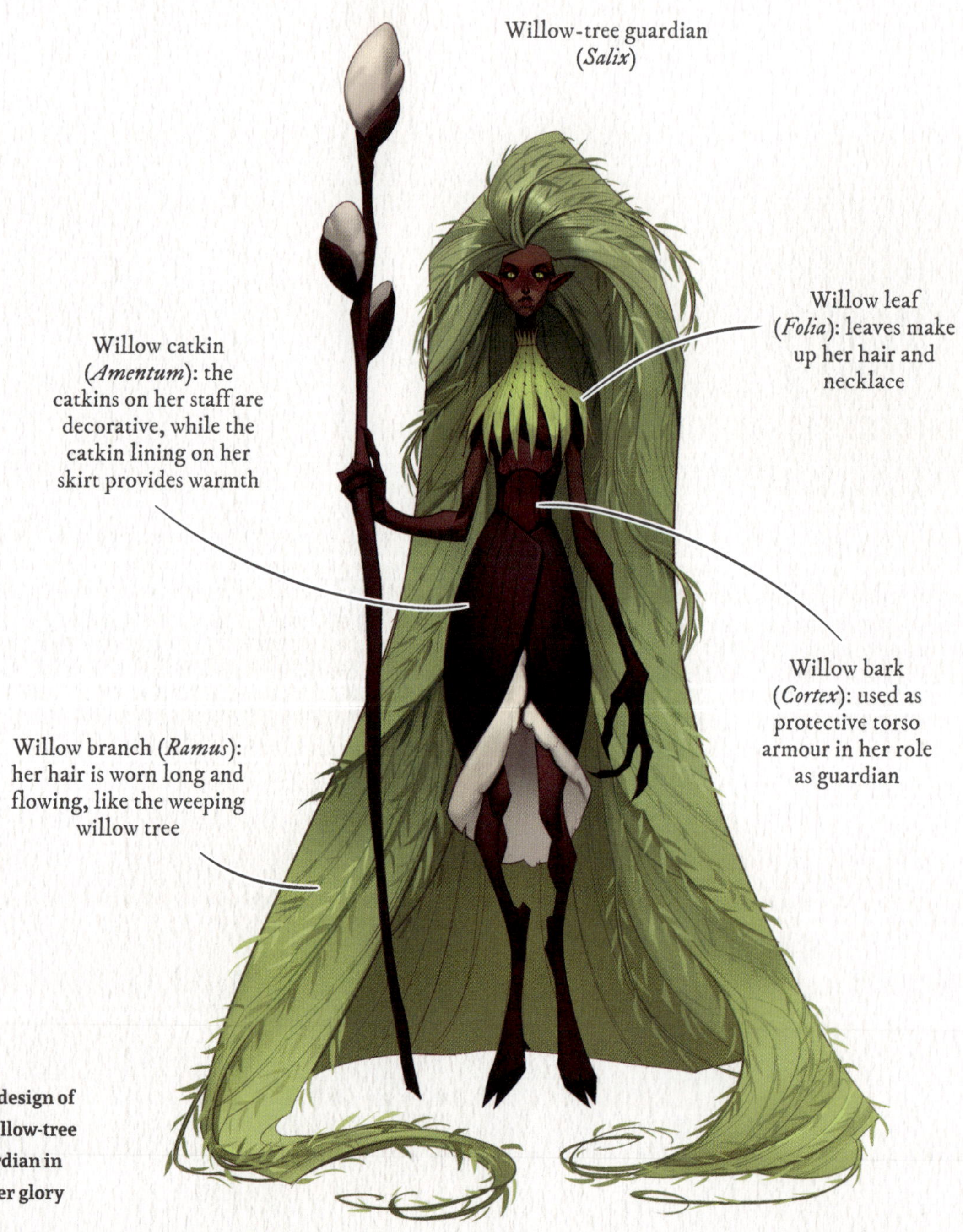

Final design of the willow-tree guardian in all her glory

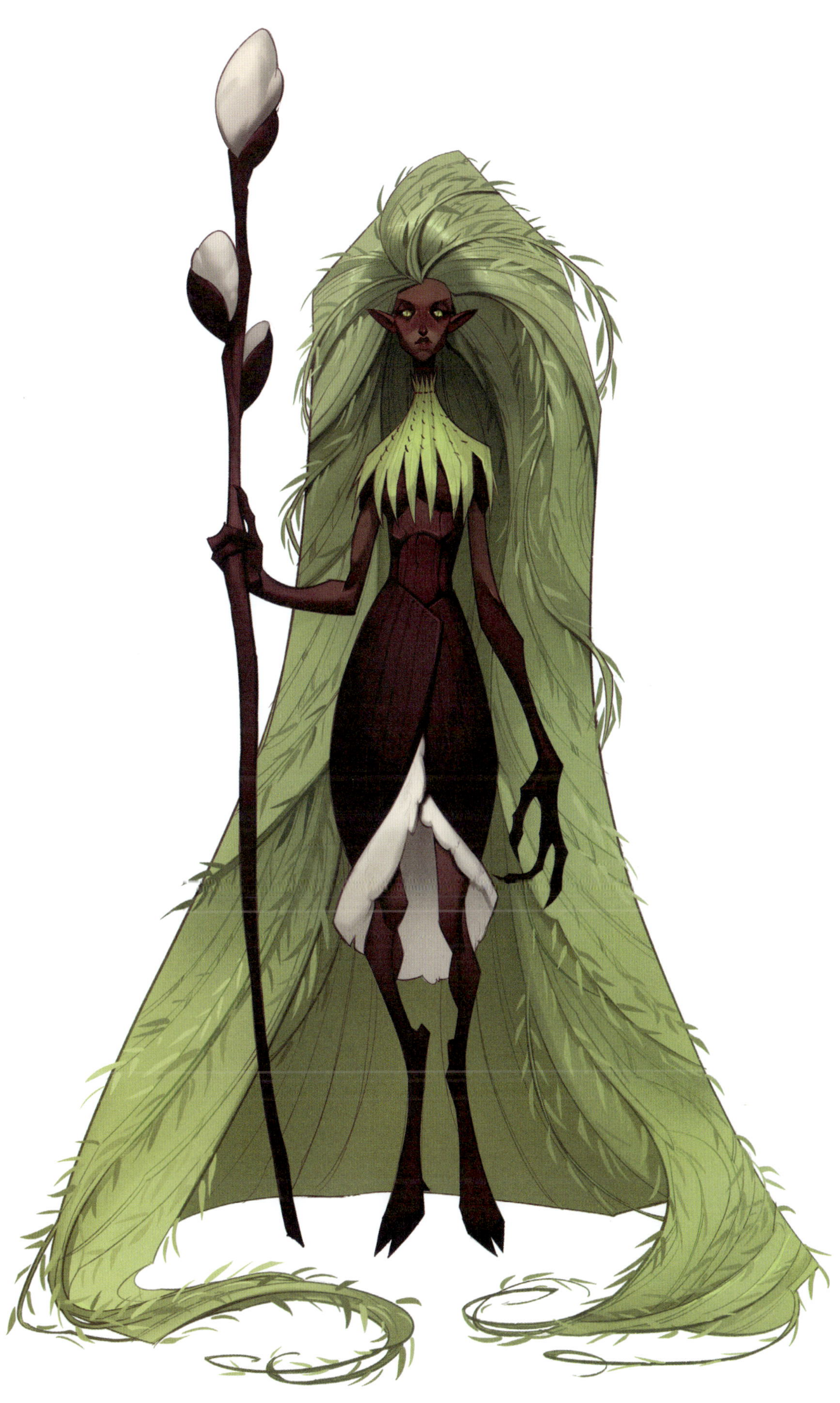

WILLOW-TREE GUARDIAN

Final image © Roma Gewska

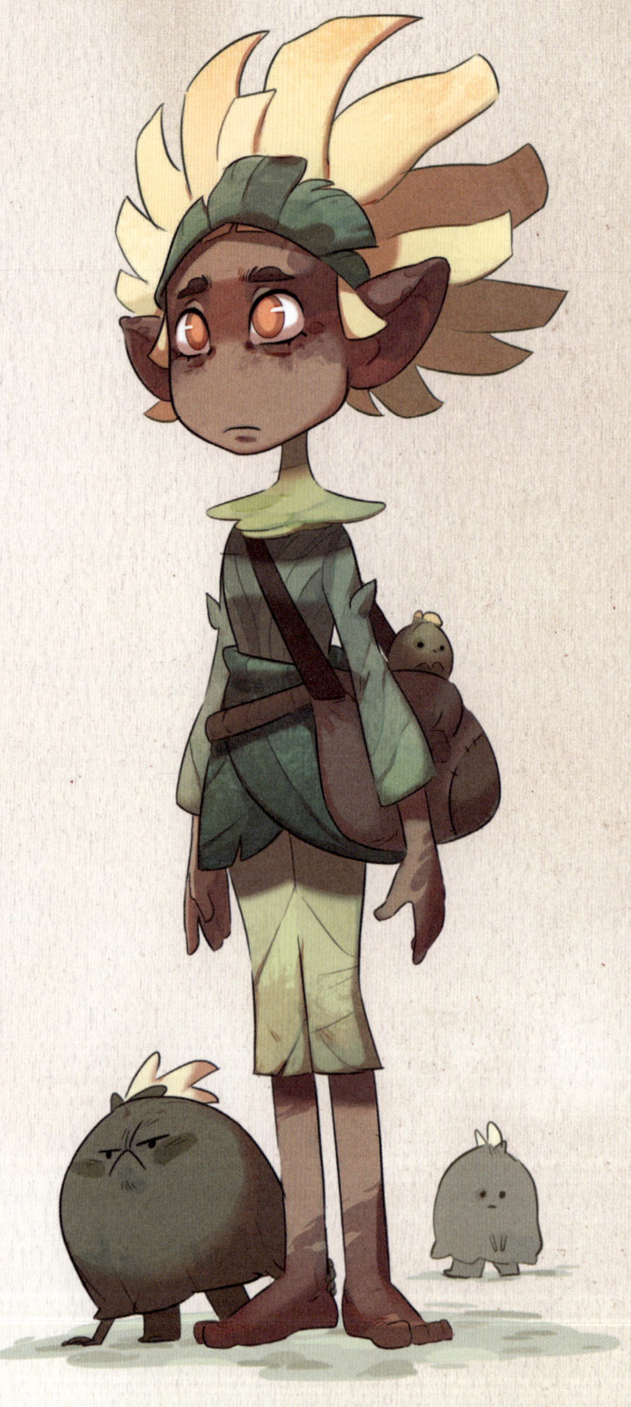

The common dandelion may not seem to have much use, other than for making wishes while you blow its seeds into the air, but in fact it has great strength in the wild, as well as many nutritional qualities. Its name comes from the French *dent de lion*, meaning 'lion's tooth', referring to the shape of the leaves. Perhaps the humble dandelion is hiding a heroic secret? In this tutorial, you will learn how to turn this herb into a character that tells a story and is ready to be used in an animation. The first sketches are created in Procreate, while the following steps use Photoshop.

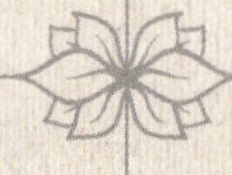

herb

DANDELION HERO

DAVID NAVARRO

START WITH RESEARCH

To begin, take your time looking for information about the dandelion. You can find a host of useful facts online, as well as reference photographs, art, and even videos to help you understand how the plant moves and changes. The research step is very important to ensure the basics of the character design work well, and it ends up as something original and eye-catching. It is interesting that the dandelion is often considered a weed that grows everywhere and doesn't have much value. This provides an idea of the type of character you could create.

Dandelion
(*Taraxacum officinale*)

Family: *Asteraceae*

Genus: *Taraxacum*

Native: Eurasia and North America

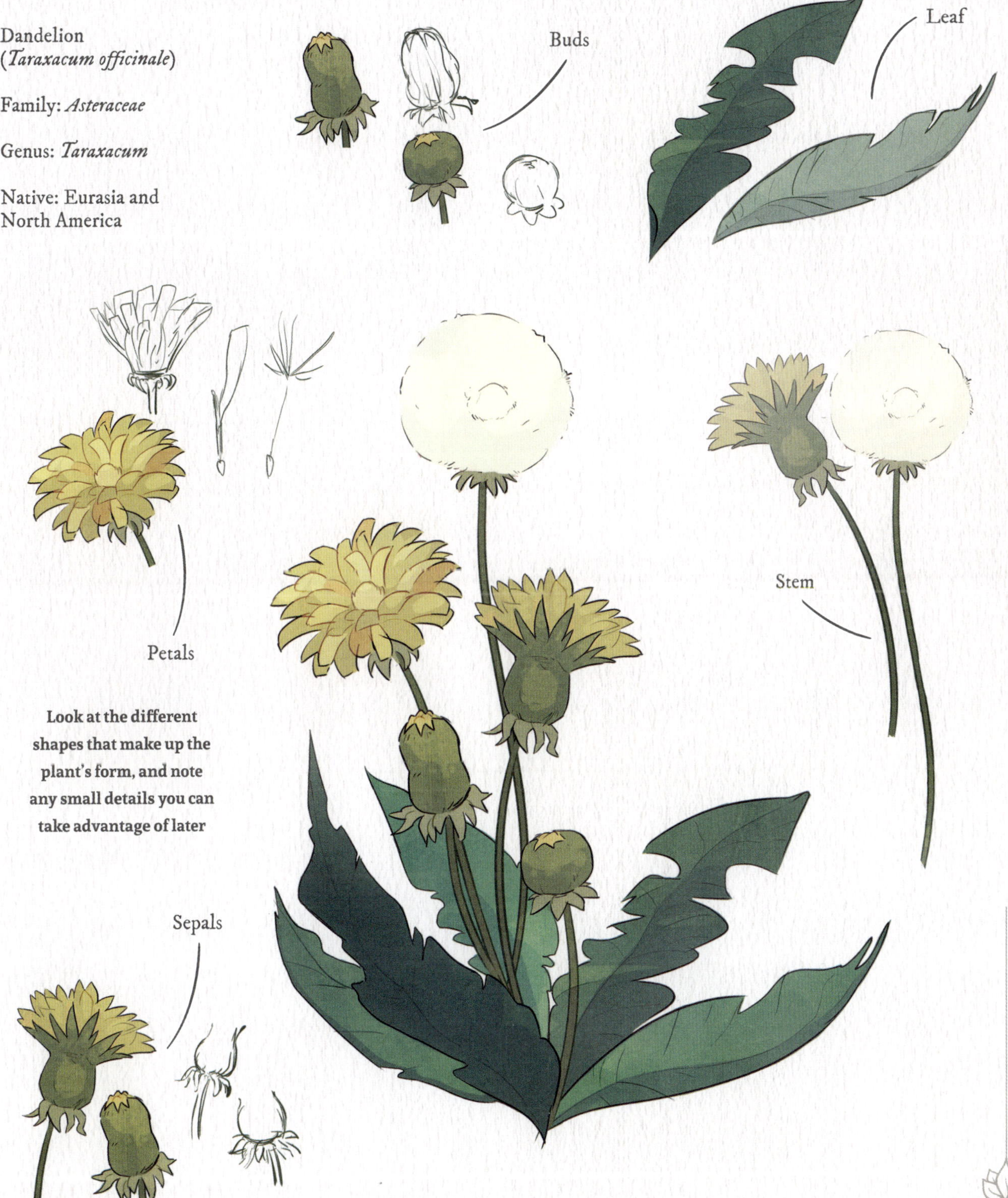

Look at the different shapes that make up the plant's form, and note any small details you can take advantage of later

UNDERSTAND THE REFERENCES

Study the references carefully. See how the dandelion grows, what kind of textures it has, the colours and proportions. All of these elements will provide valuable information. In this case, the way the flower grows seems clear and symbolic. The bulb grows little by little, with the changes clear to see thanks to the way it opens and sprouts yellow petals. At the end of its life cycle it turns completely white and thin, almost like an elderly human. This is a wild plant that symbolizes survival and prosperity; a weed that can grow almost anywhere. Perhaps this is a character that is not well off, but has a certain strength. Research tells you that the dandelion usually doesn't grow alone, and that the size and colour of the petals are a symbol of its age.

Experimenting with the dandelion growing from young to old as a character

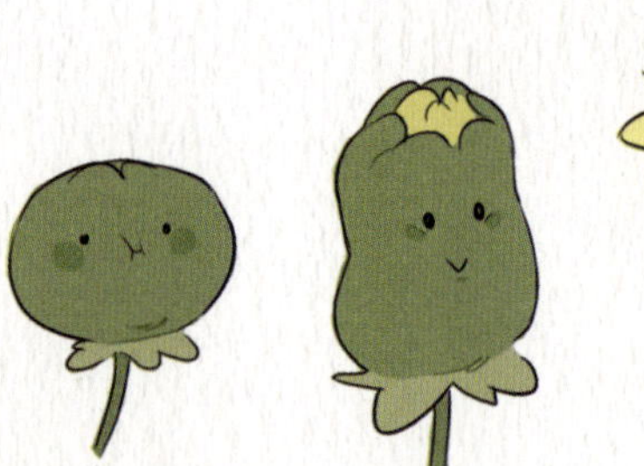
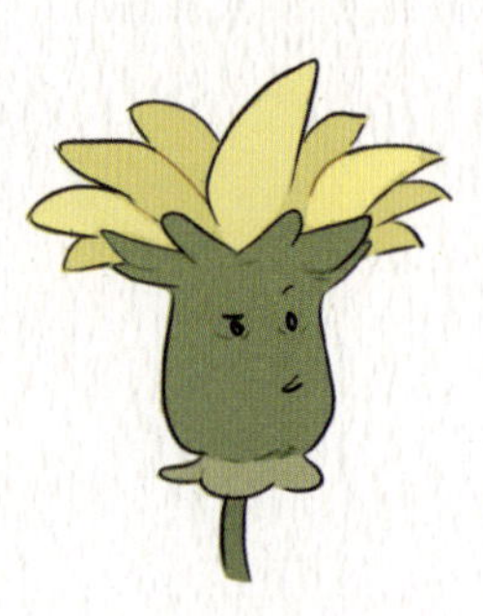
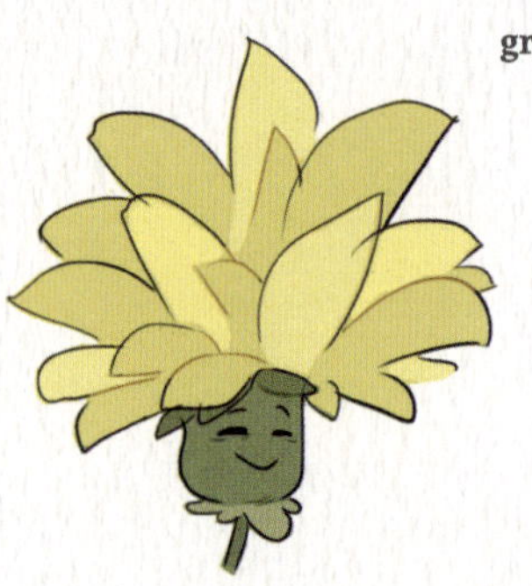
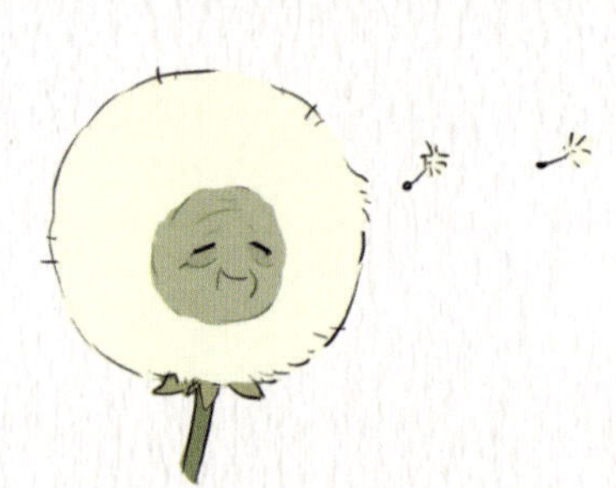

LOOSE SKETCHES

Now it's time to start drawing. This can be the best part of the process if you allow yourself to explore freely. Keep in mind the information you have gathered up to this point, then draw whatever comes into your mind. Any sketch can help – whether it's just a face or a full-body silhouette. Use these initial drawings to think about the story of your character. If you don't have an exact description to follow, sketching and trying different approaches and styles can help build your character. Ask yourself: Who are they? How are they? Where do they live? Your idea might remind you of a person you know, or a fictional character, and you can either move towards or away from these ideas. Don't limit yourself. Explore a large range of characters and approaches – you can decide which to move forward with later.

Explore lots of ideas at this stage – have fun!

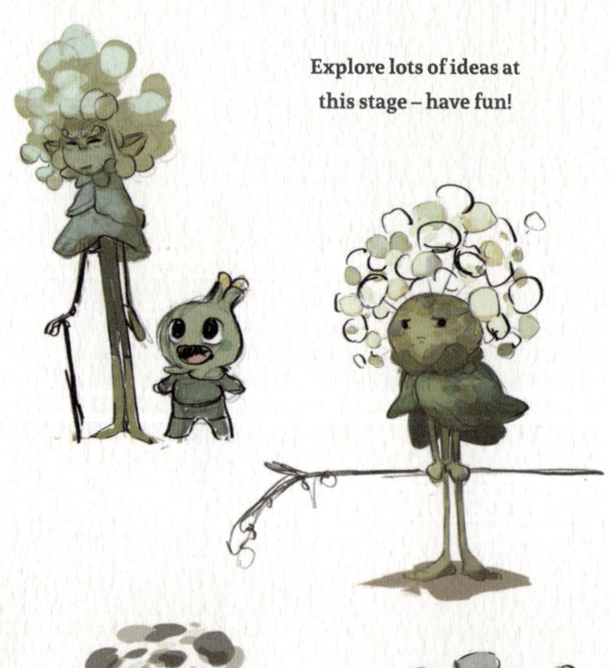

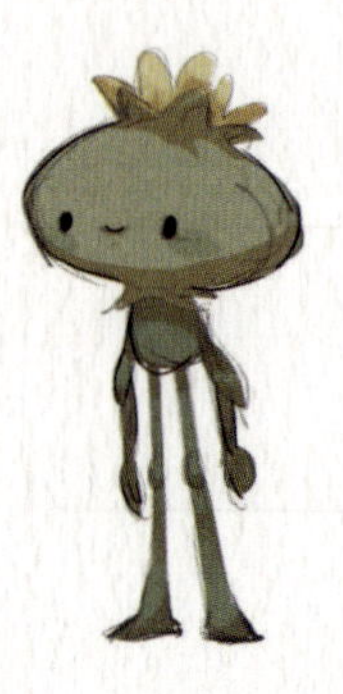
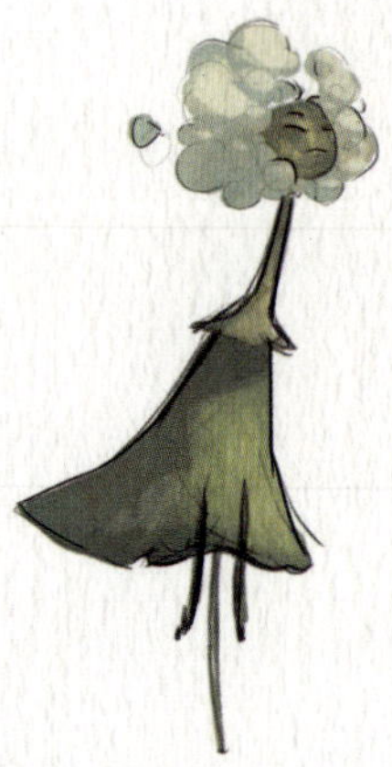
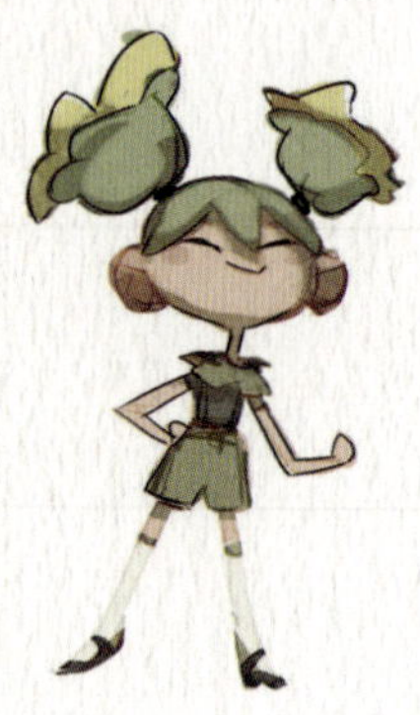
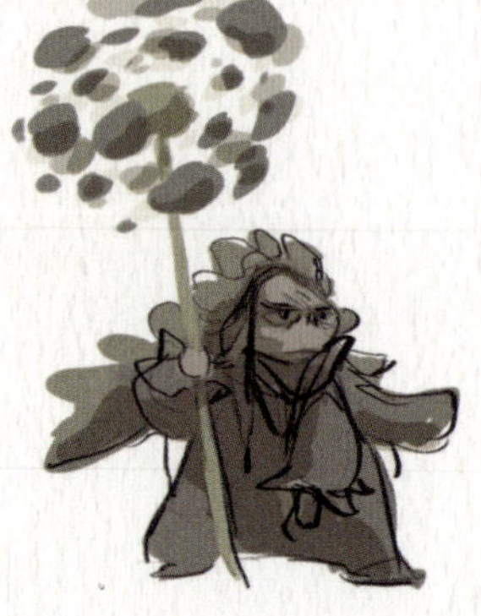
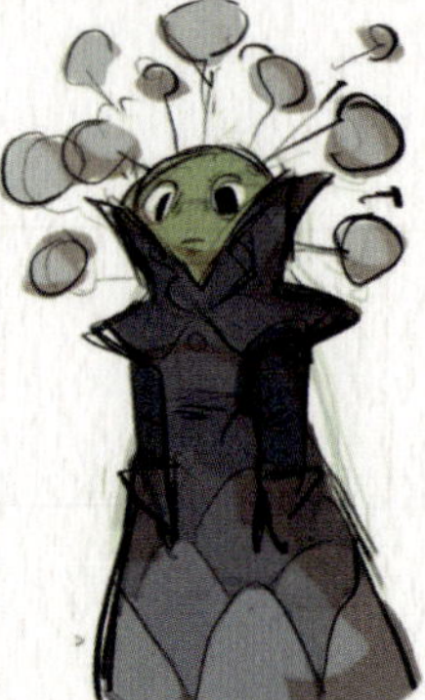

KEEP EXPLORING

You can now start to make choices. Look at the exploratory sketches from the previous step and decide what type of character appeals to you. For example, do you want them to be more plant or more human-like? It's not about the colours or clothes yet, just the kind of character it will be. Perhaps a goblin-type look could work with the dandelion aesthetic. Create some more sketches based on this idea – again keeping them quite free, with different proportions, clothes, and styles. This will enable you to see stories emerging, and that's the key point – the viewer needs to see a narrative in the character's design.

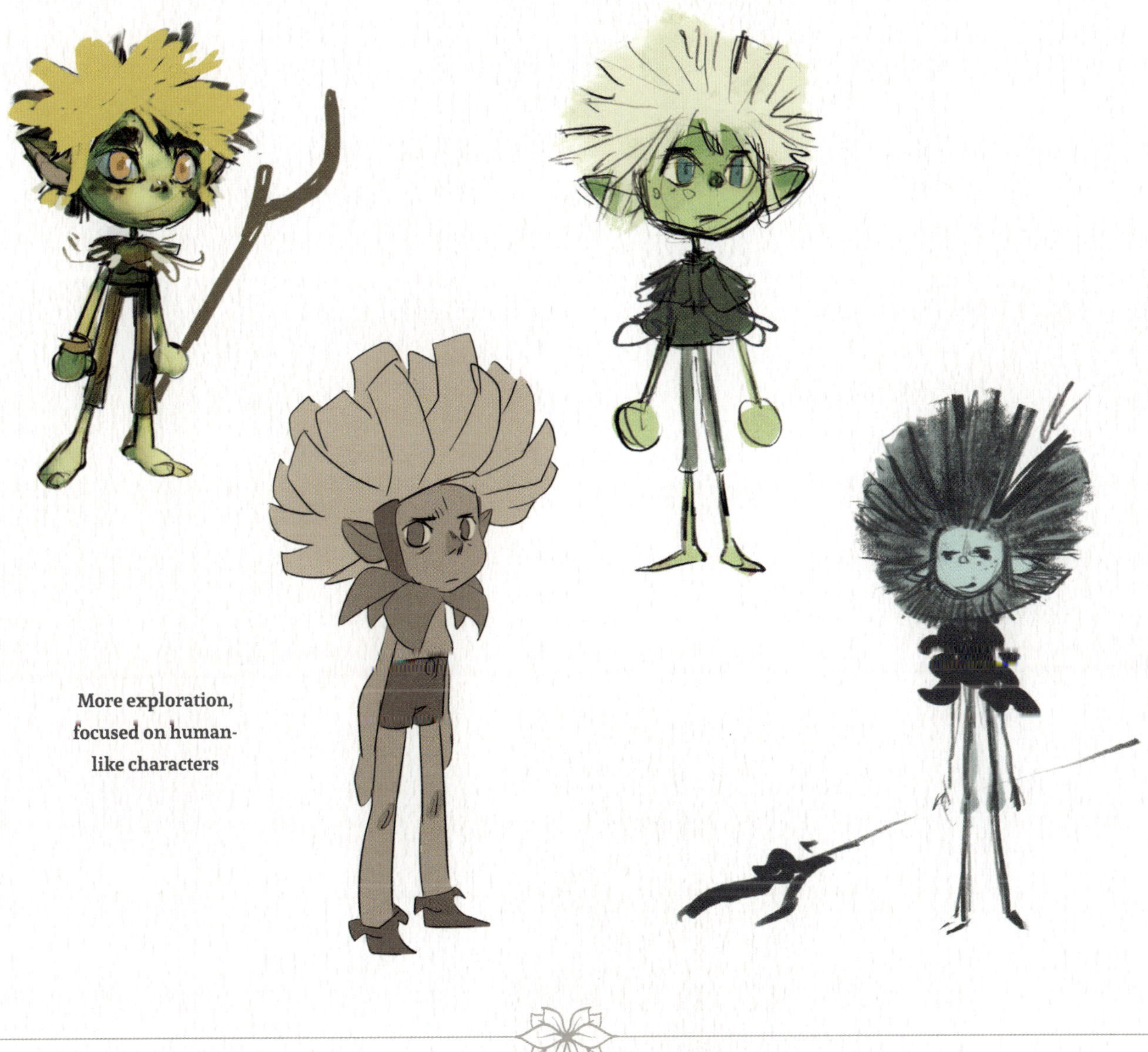

More exploration, focused on human-like characters

QUICK COLOUR SKETCH

Sometimes it's a good idea to add some colour to your sketches during these exploration stages. This depends on your personal process, but it can give you a glimpse into how your character might look in the final design, and help you to make some early decisions.

MAKING DECISIONS

The overall feeling of the character is now starting to come through, thanks to all of the decisions made so far. This step is for pulling it all together and doing the final explorations. It's a good idea to experiment with proportions, as well as costume and props. All of the clothes the character wears and the items they carry should tell the viewer something useful about them. Be careful not to stray too far from the main narrative. Always ask questions: Is this still a dandelion? Does it tell the story you need or want to tell? It's an important part of the creative process to trial and change things, but be careful not to lose your vision through iteration. Also, try to keep the design clean. Details are great, but too many could make the image hard to understand. Some parts (such as the face) should remain free of clutter, so the viewer can see the expression and empathize with the character. This variation between busy and calm areas will also build good contrast and rhythm – probably the most important thing to create character appeal.

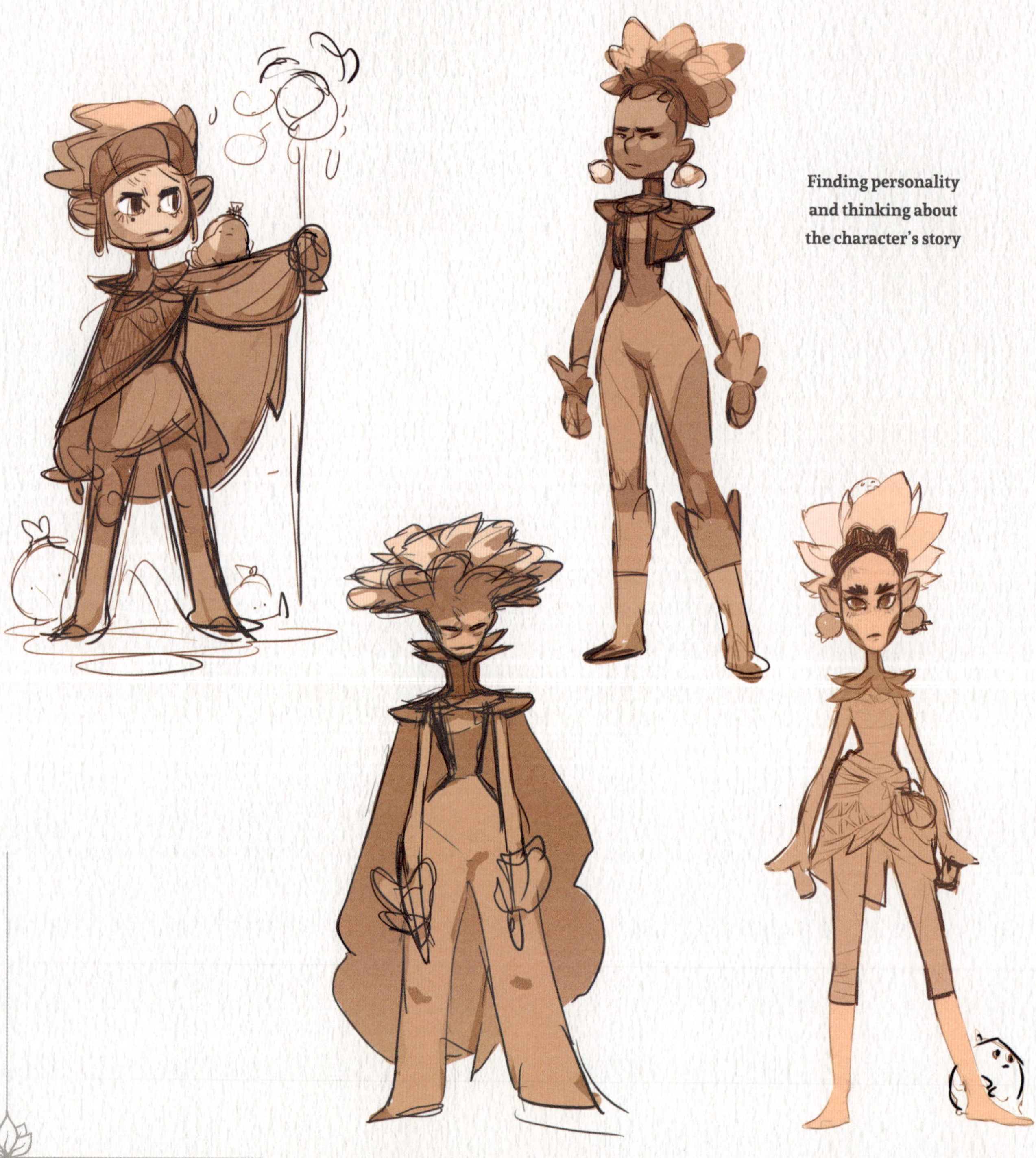

Finding personality and thinking about the character's story

THE LAST SKETCHES

As a last step before moving on to line art and colour, create some final sketches to work from. Decide the proportions of your character and assemble all the choices made so far. This step will provide the base of the character, with just a few details left to explore. Take this time to make final decisions on the costume, face, hair ... all the things that make up the final look. These sketches show the character at different ages, but only one of these will be taken forward to the final design.

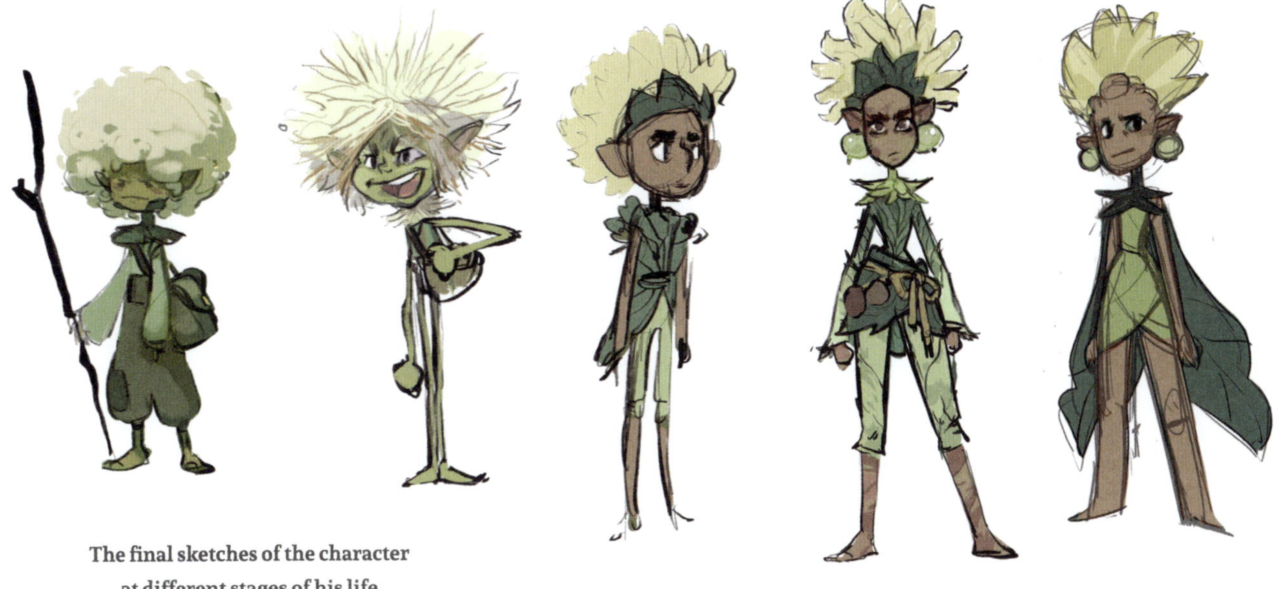

The final sketches of the character at different stages of his life

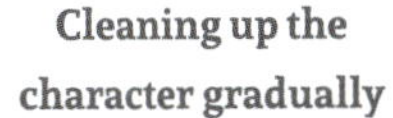

LINE ART

Choose a design to move forward with. You may still feel unsure about your decisions, but moving forward is important. This is your character, with all its hits and misses. Another artist might make different choices and that's okay – this character is yours. Clean it up by inking the lines and defining everything clearly. The drawing of the line art can be repeated two or three times, if required, as you work out the details and refine it. Pay extra attention to the details, thinking about every part of your character and ensuring everything matches with the story you're trying to tell.

Cleaning up the character gradually

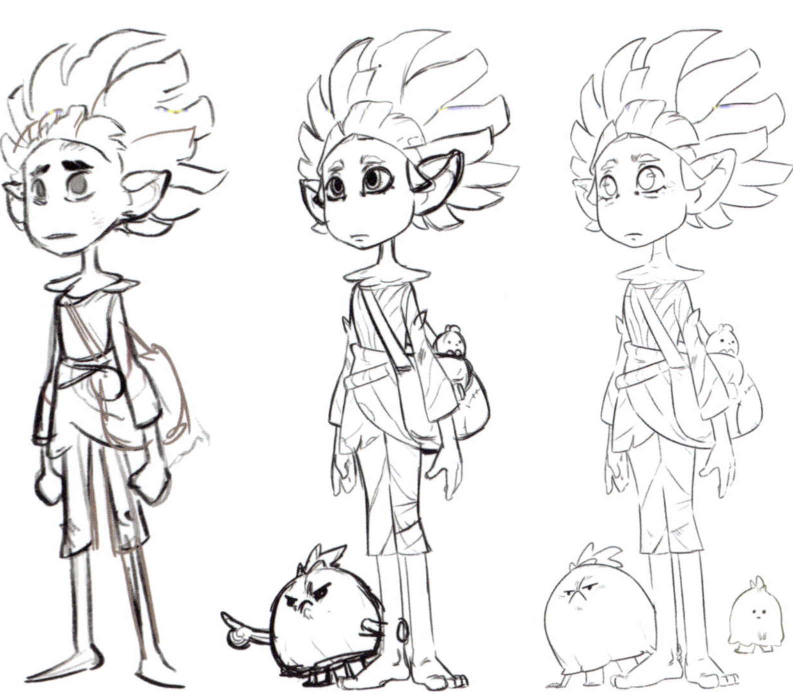

COLOUR BASE

You may have a clear vision of the colours you want to use, but even in these situations it's a good idea to create two or three tests to choose the final palette. Try to keep the original colours of the source inspiration pretty clear, in this case the dandelion, as this will make it more recognizable. With this in mind, there's a large variety of greens and yellows to work with. Use this step to add the local colours to the character – these are flat colours that define an area or thing, unaffected by any kind of light or shadow. These flat colours are impossible to see in the real world, but provide a solid base to work from in character design.

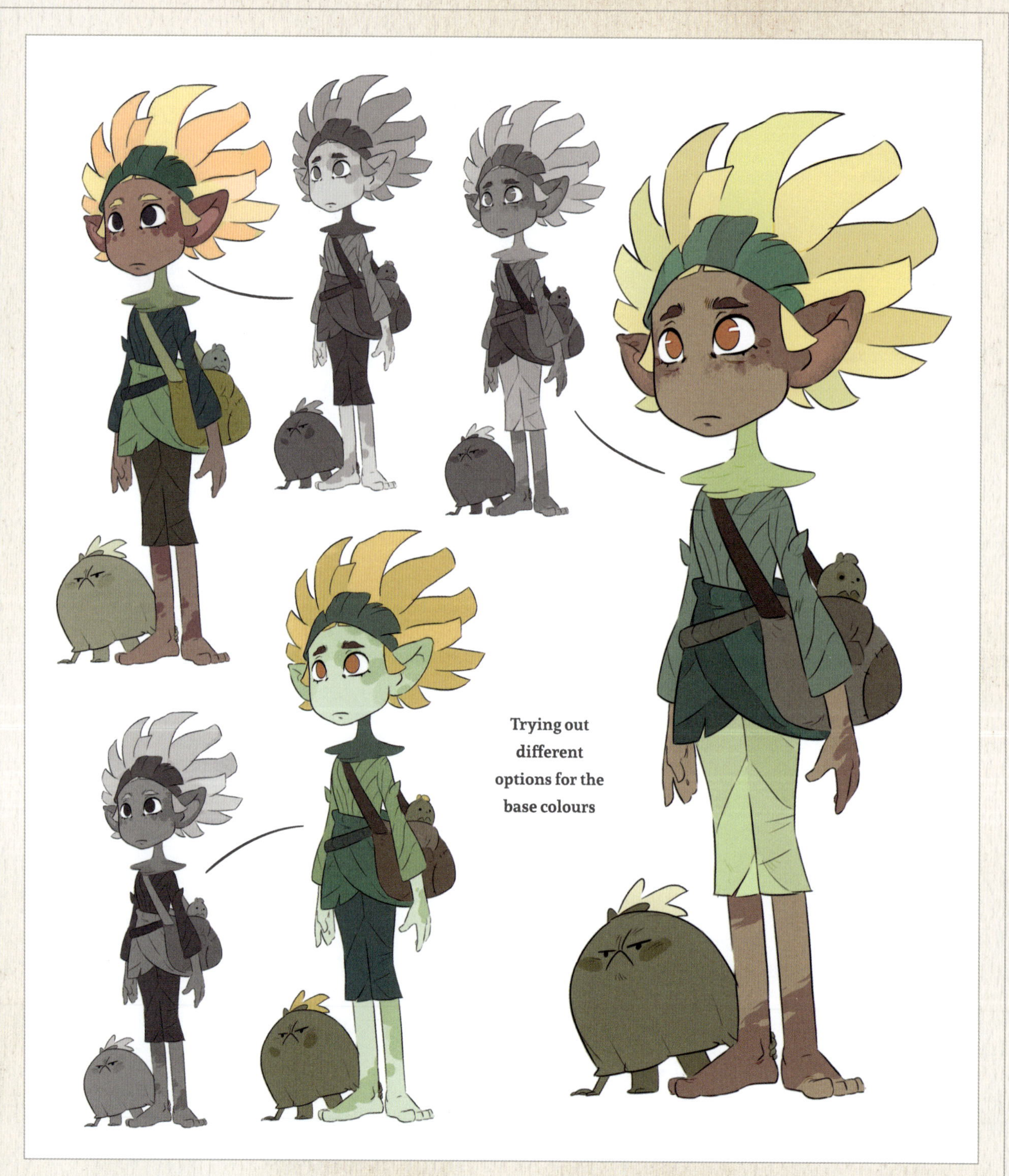

Trying out different options for the base colours

CHECK YOUR VALUES

Always check your values (the balance of dark and light areas) on colour tests – they are so important and you need to work on them right from the start. Add a layer on top of everything, fill it with black, and set its blending mode to Colour. You can then easily activate this layer to see the image in greyscale and then turn it off to keep working. A quick trick for achieving good values is to use the 'chess pattern'. This means that every part of your character with a darker value needs to sit next to a lighter one.

ADDING TEXTURE

Adding textures will give your character variety and make them more believable. Try to avoid flat colours unless that's part of your style. Think about the materials and textures in the image, and also about your character's narrative. Maybe this is a character that's always dirty after going on adventures? Remember that the dandelion is often considered a weed, so making the character look a bit dirty and downtrodden will convey this idea.

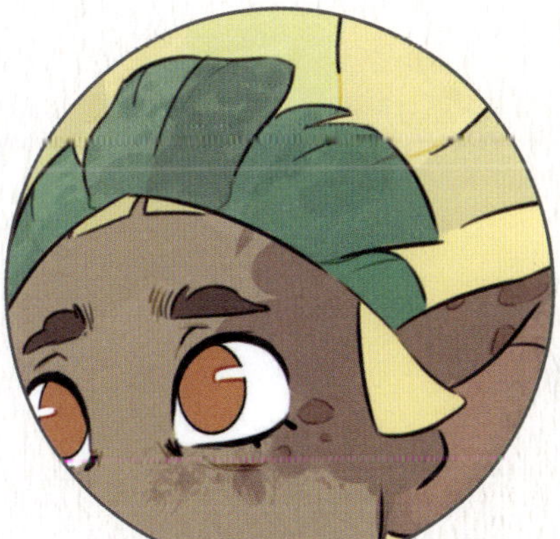

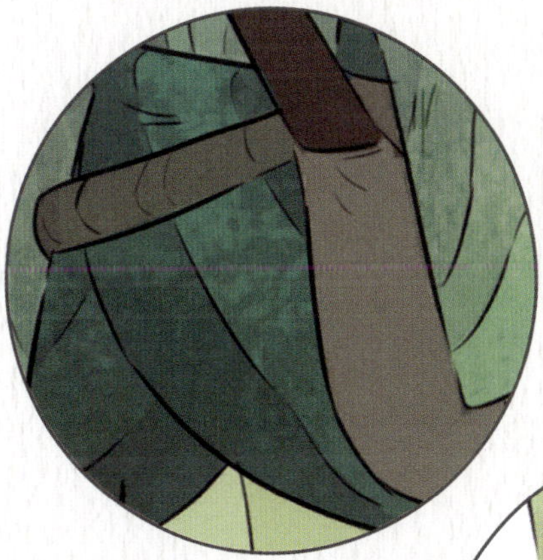

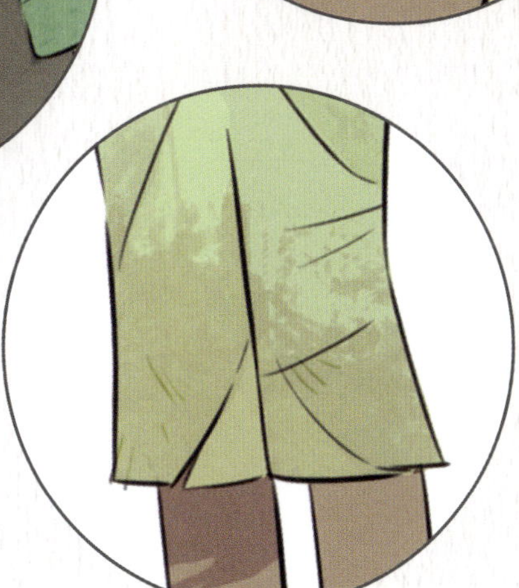

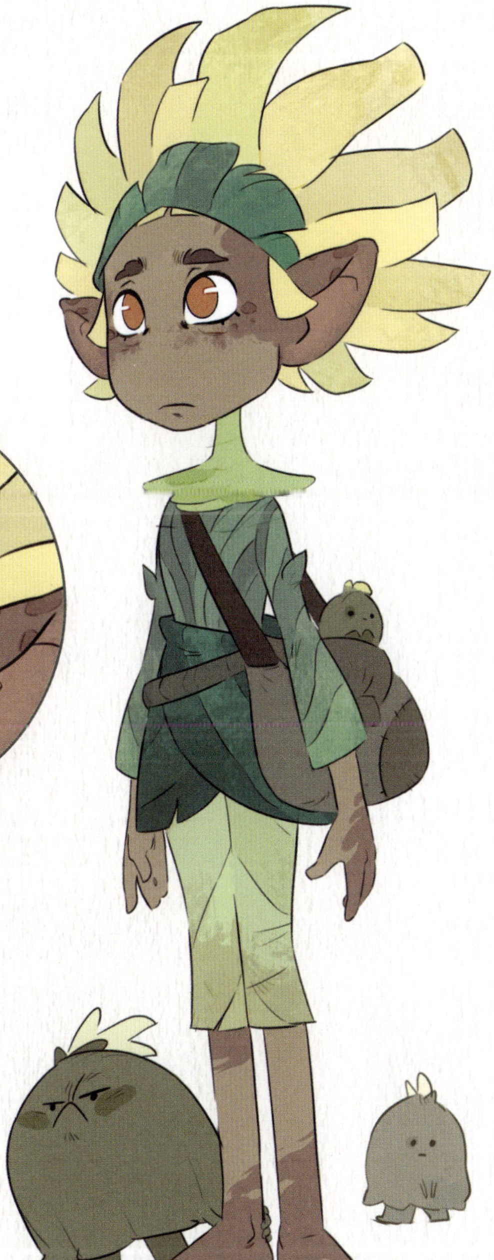

Adding textures to give some life and realism to the character, avoiding perfection

ADDING SHADOW

Finish the character by rendering him a little and painting in shadow and light. To create the correct shadows, you first need to understand the volumes. Try to see the character in 3D, consider which parts sit above others, and what would cause shadows if light comes from above (for example). This is a step that should be taken slowly to ensure it's done well. Try out different colour atmospheres – if your character image doesn't have a background, you can be experimental with this and see which palettes work best.

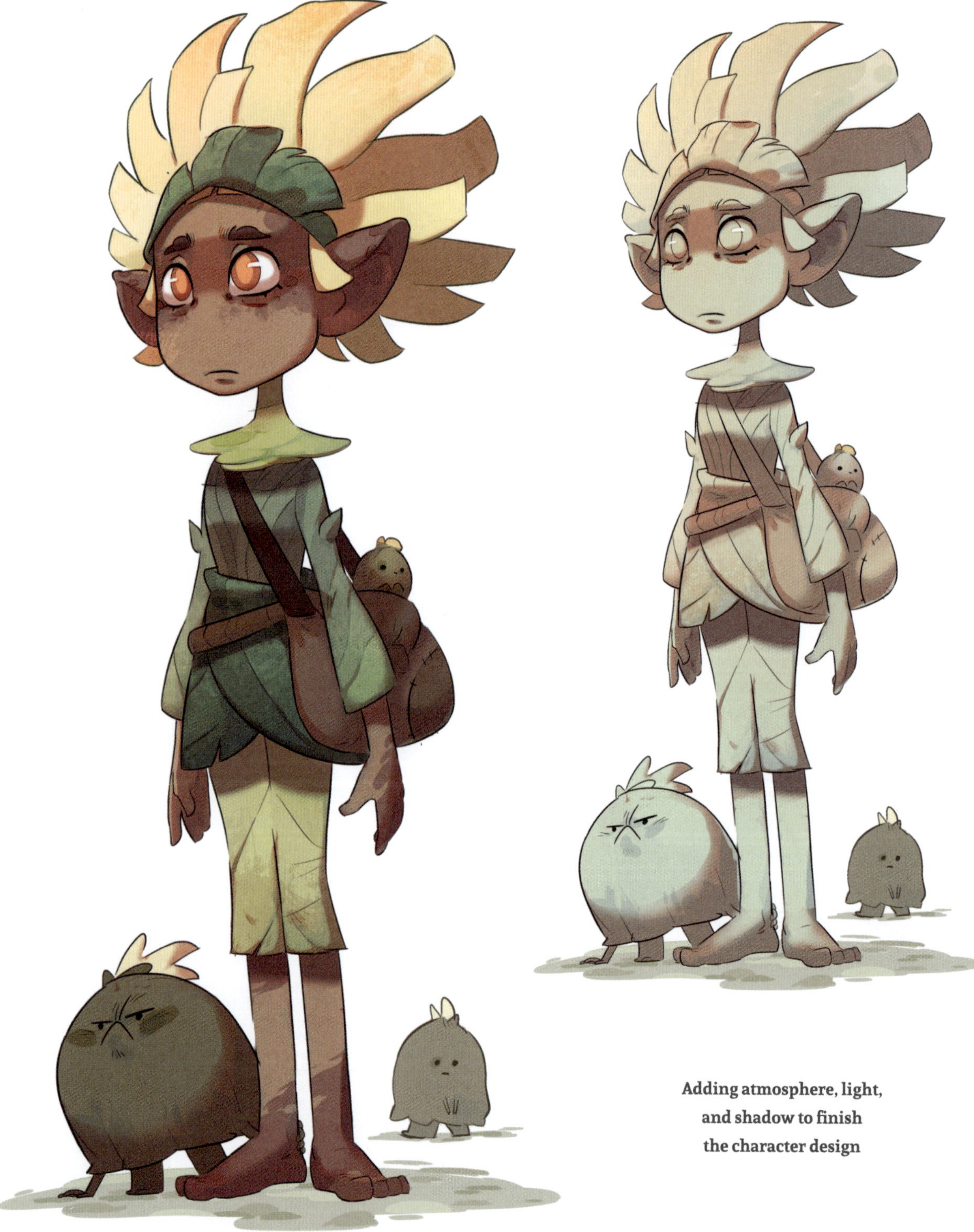

Adding atmosphere, light, and shadow to finish the character design

TURNAROUND SKETCHES

In order to prepare your character for use in animation, you will need to create turnarounds. This can be a challenging exercise, but it will give you (and others) more knowledge of your character. Seeing it from every angle will provide invaluable information about its volumes and lengths, and provide a profile and back view. This might almost feel like starting again, as you will need to make decisions about how it looks from every angle. Perhaps the character has something on their back? How do their clothes look from the side? Give this step some time, starting from rough sketches based on the big volumes and understanding how the body is posed. Return to your original references – they will help when drawing petals, leaves, and more from different viewpoints.

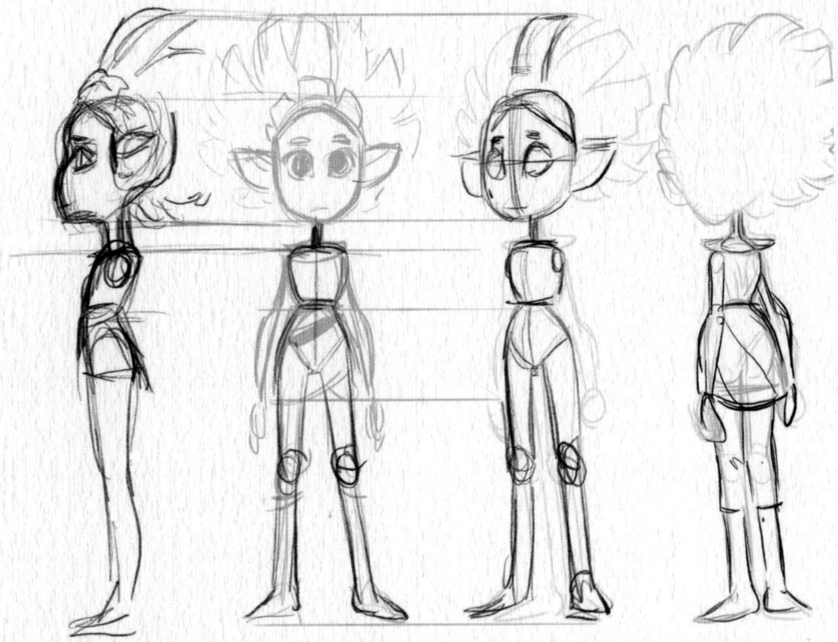

Sketching the different angles, always keeping the proportions true to the original design

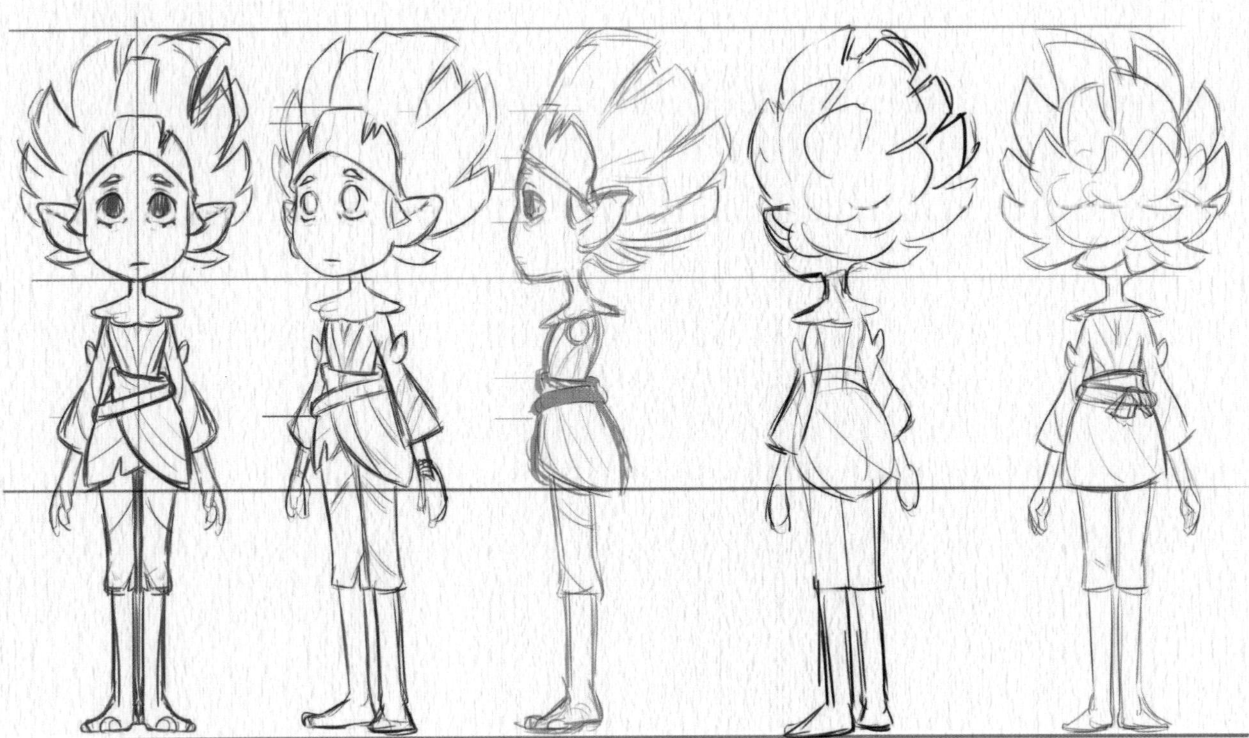

FINAL TURNAROUNDS

Clean up the turnarounds and add the local colours. Again, this can be a challenge, but it's important for the shape and base colour to be correct from all angles. This is a common exercise in the industry of animation and video games. As a character designer, you will need to pass all the information to other artists or teams, and explain your character clearly. A 3D modeller or animator can then take your character and know exactly how its body works and moves. Be sure that all the things you designed with intention don't get lost in this step.

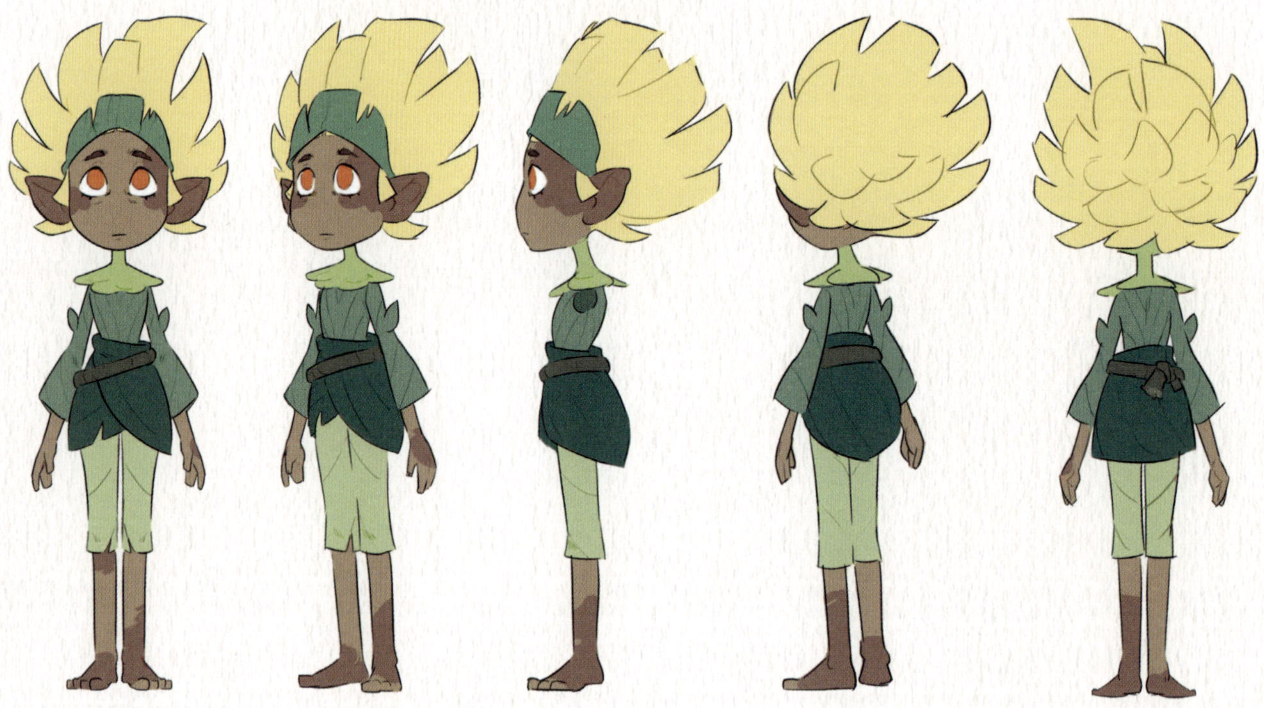

The final turnarounds, ready for animators and modellers to use

DON'T SKIP THE HARD PART

There will always be parts of the design process you enjoy and some you really dislike. This is the same for every artist. But those less-pleasing parts should never be skipped. Often the reason you dislike them is because you've not practised them enough, meaning you're the least confident or competent at them. There is nothing wrong with this. With practice you will get better! Don't put too much pressure on yourself and remember that nobody does everything perfectly.

EXPRESSIONS

This step can be one of the most exciting parts of the process. You've created a character from scratch, you know the volumes and the way they move, and now you can bring the being to life. Through different expressions, the character can show emotions, interact with the world around them, and express every feeling. Every character has a unique 'voice' – the way it moves and expresses itself. Choose the character's dominant expressions carefully to portray them in the right way. Are they shy? Are they brave? Also, think about the character's backstory and the target audience. A character won't move the same way on a children's television show as they do in a feature film for adults. Consider also how to use their physical characteristics – in this case, perhaps the petals on the head, which provide a recognizable silhouette, could also provide a first look into the character's feelings? For example, they could be tall and pointed to show surprise or anger, and loose and wilting to represent sadness.

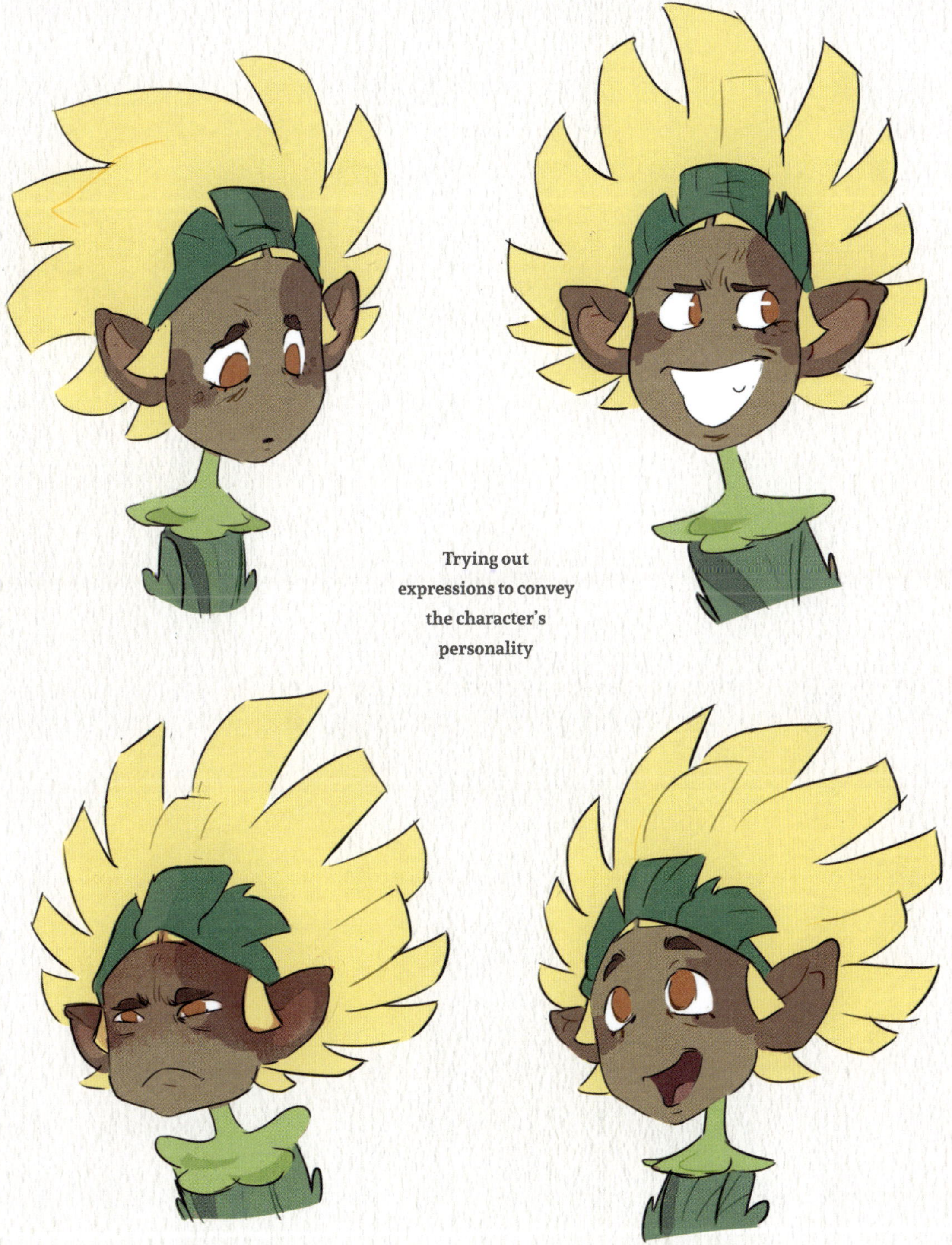

Trying out expressions to convey the character's personality

LOOKING BACK

Look back and dissect the dandelion to see where you used each part of the original reference. Starting with a common dandelion, you separated all the parts that could be used and worked on the character's story through exploratory sketches. Some parts from the original plant were inspiration for clothing and accessories, while others were incorporated into the silhouette. All of this provided an overarching feeling about the personality of the character.

For the final image, present your character in the best possible way – a striking pose, well rendered, showing off the volumes, colours, and textures. Create an expression to show how the character interacts with the world around them, and to give a first taste of their personality. This is a being that is seen as wild and not particularly special, but must face big challenges and survive hard times. The textures and dirt suggest the character isn't wealthy, living with just the basics and taking care of their tribe; a hero among the weeds.

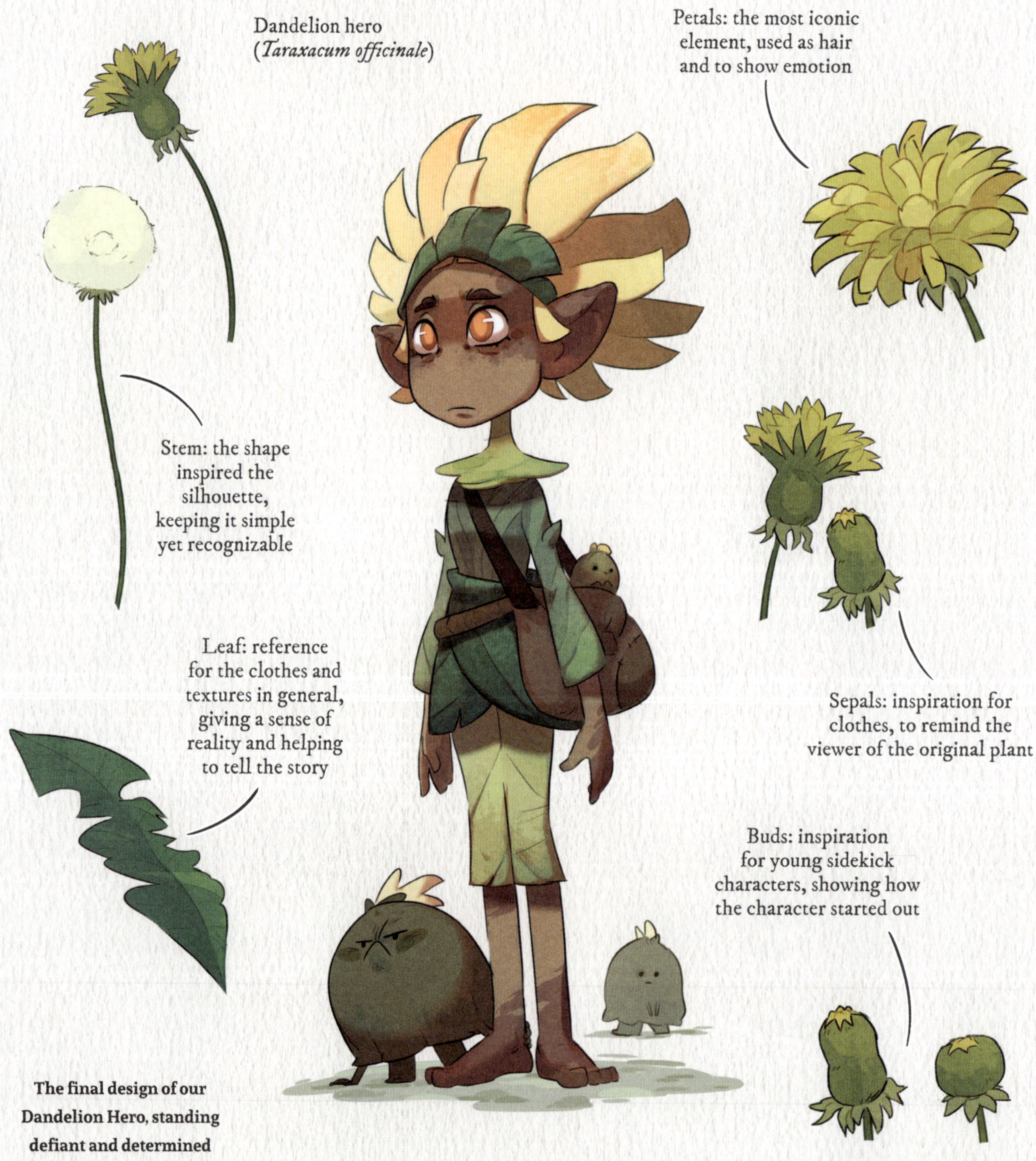

The final design of our Dandelion Hero, standing defiant and determined

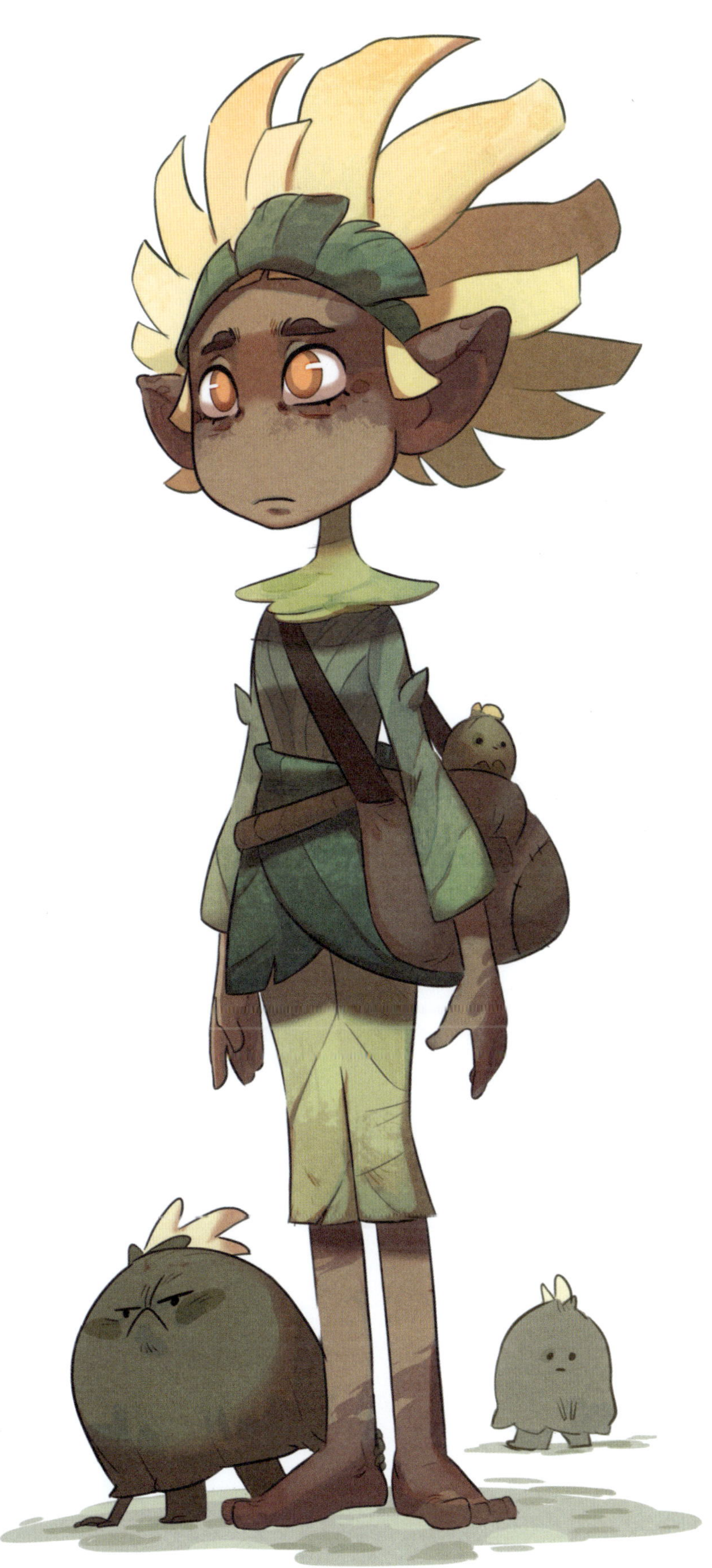

DANDELION HERO

Final image © David Navarro

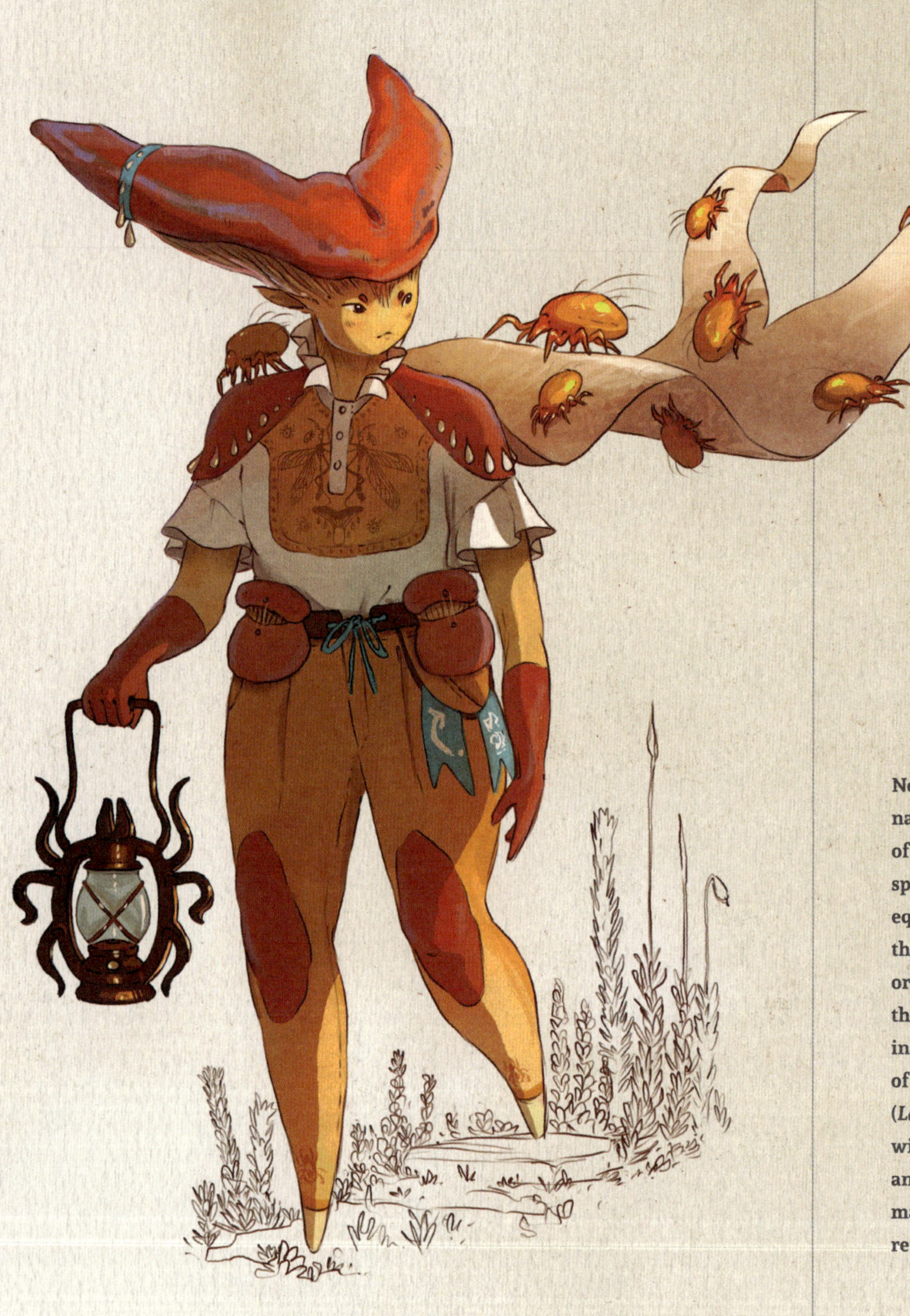

No organism exists in isolation; nature is a highly complex web of interrelationships between species and these interactions are equally as inspiring for design as the physical forms of individual organisms. This tutorial will detail the process of designing a character inspired by the form and ecology of the weeping milk cap fungus (*Lactifluus volemus*). The character will be created using the iPad Pro and Procreate, along with the macOS app VizRef for organizing reference images in one place.

fungi

WALKING MILK CAP FAERY

DOMINIQUE VASSIE

START WITH RESEARCH

For nature-themed projects like this one, try opening a big natural history guidebook for inspiration. In this case, *Mushrooms and Other Fungi of Great Britain and Europe* by Roger Phillips is a good starting point for finding visually interesting fungi. Natural history books are a really useful way to explore potential inspiration without being biased towards the famous organisms you already know.

The weeping milk cap's velvety texture and beautiful colours make it a strong candidate for a character design. As well as an unusual appearance, it has a remarkable relationship with insects, mites, and plants. Designing a character that incorporates both the appearance and ecology of the weeping milk cap will be a fun challenge and an opportunity to create something truly unique.

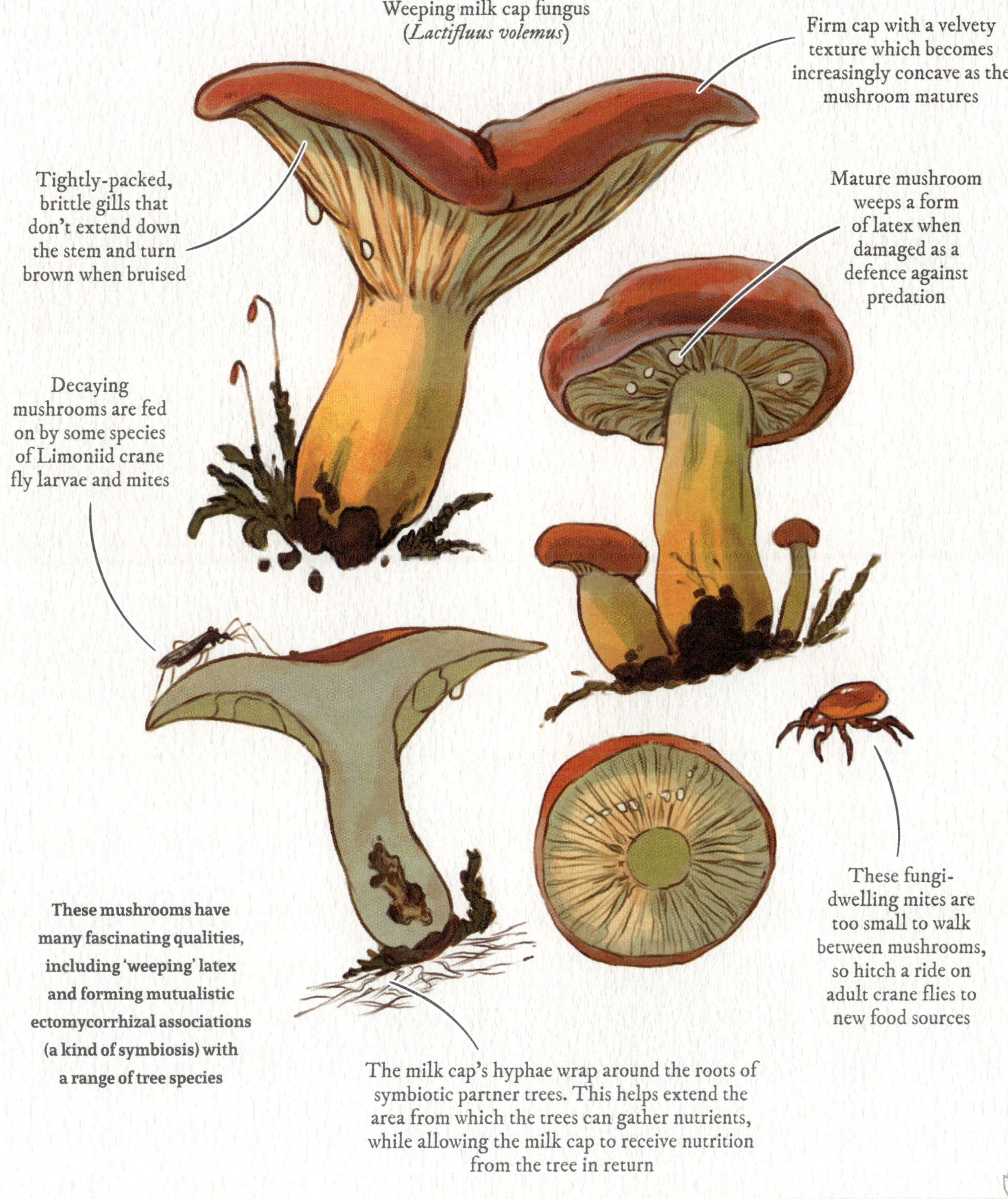

These mushrooms have many fascinating qualities, including 'weeping' latex and forming mutualistic ectomycorrhizal associations (a kind of symbiosis) with a range of tree species

INITIAL SKETCHES

Start by creating a series of small sketches to explore the shapes of potential characters, using the milk cap's shape and ecology as inspiration. To challenge yourself, try to avoid a very classical mushroom shape for the character; instead, draw more inspiration from the concave-shaped mature mushroom and mix in the associated organisms. The weeping milk cap is quite a sturdy-looking mushroom, so giving the character a more stable stance and base would reflect this. You can even try using the shapes in different orientations, such as an upside-down mushroom with its hyphae in the air instead of at ground level.

Tiny thumbnail character drawings exploring overall shapes

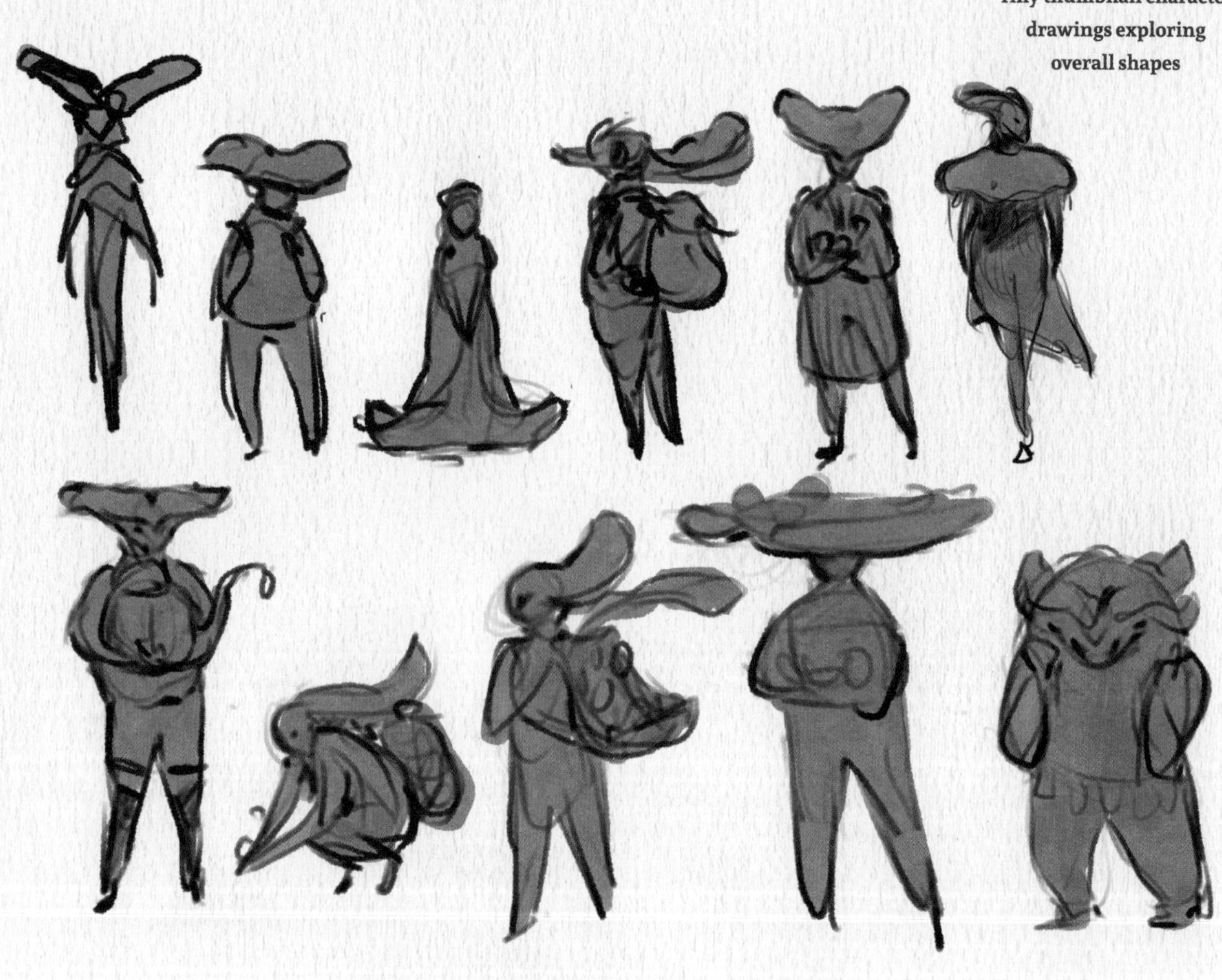

RESEARCH WITH CARE

For this tutorial, you are looking at a specific species of fungus. Search engines can throw out images of all sorts of organisms that are not correct, even for very familiar animals. It's better to start your research by reading a little about the organism on a trusted natural history website, or even just on Wikipedia, so that you know what you're looking for. For fungi, plants, and invertebrates, it's really useful to also search by scientific name, as organisms often have multiple common names or ones that are used for multiple unrelated species.

REFINED SKETCHES

Choose the elements from your thumbnails that you like best and develop them while thinking about the character you want to portray. At this stage, the most intriguing ideas are the concave heads inspired by the mature milk caps and the masks inspired by crane flies. The concept of the fungi-dwelling mites hitchhiking on the crane flies (an interaction known in biology as 'phoresis') is so fun and could be great inspiration for the character's role.

All these elements lead to the idea of a milk-cap-inspired faery who works as a bus for mites, transporting them where they wish to go in the forest as their little legs don't carry them far. The faery character would need to look ready for walking and have a place to comfortably carry their mite passengers. You could also draw inspiration from the milk cap's interaction with plants if you read up about ectomycorrhiza.

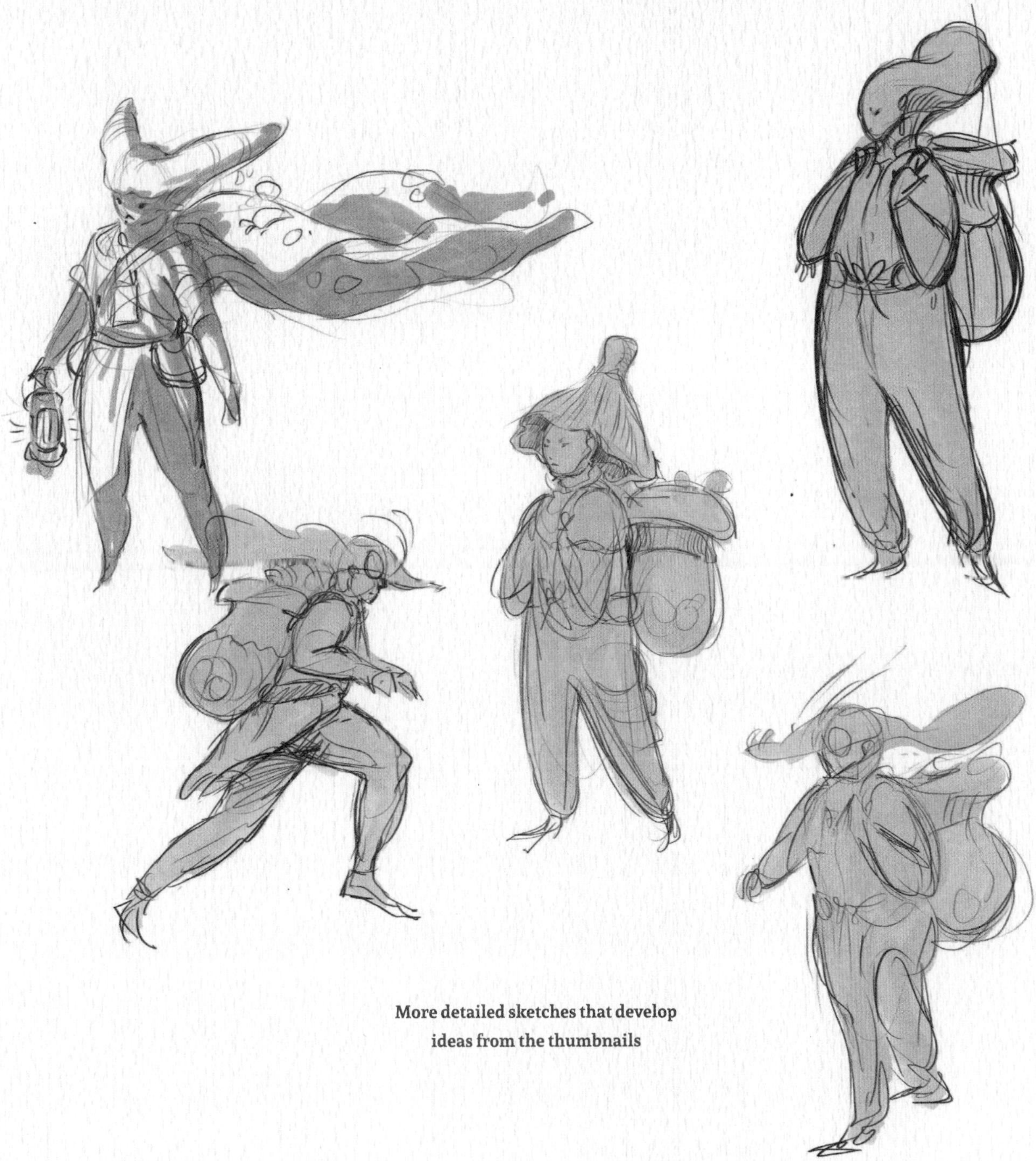

More detailed sketches that develop ideas from the thumbnails

POSE AND FOUNDATIONS

Having chosen an approximate design path, you can now think about how the pose of your character might help communicate their personality or story. For this character, it would make sense to draw them walking, sitting along the path having a rest, or interacting with a mite customer in some way. A basket for the mites might not be the best mode of transport; instead, they could cling to a floaty, magical piece of fabric, like a cape or cloak. Mites prefer to grip the outside of things, so they would be more comfortable travelling this way, and it also gives a more magical, fairy-tale feel to the character.

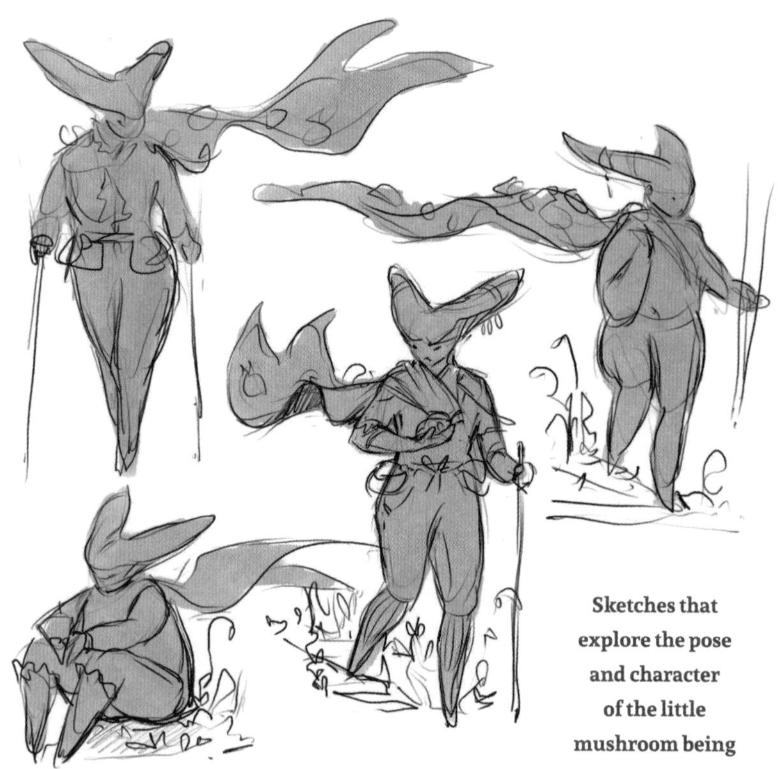

Sketches that explore the pose and character of the little mushroom being

BUILDING UP

The walking pose is ideal for showing off the character's design, as well as putting them in context a little. You can now begin refining the anatomy and thinking about the shapes of the clothing and other details. The character will be about mushroom-sized, with clothing that looks like it's made from the milk cap mushroom. Ruffled fabrics create an ethereal feeling and resemble the mushroom's gills; white decorations on the body and clothes draw inspiration from the 'weeping' latex. There are so many opportunities to include nods to the ecology of the milk cap: for example, the lantern is shaped like a fungus mite, and the clothing has plenty of space to include patterns based on the crane flies and hyphae.

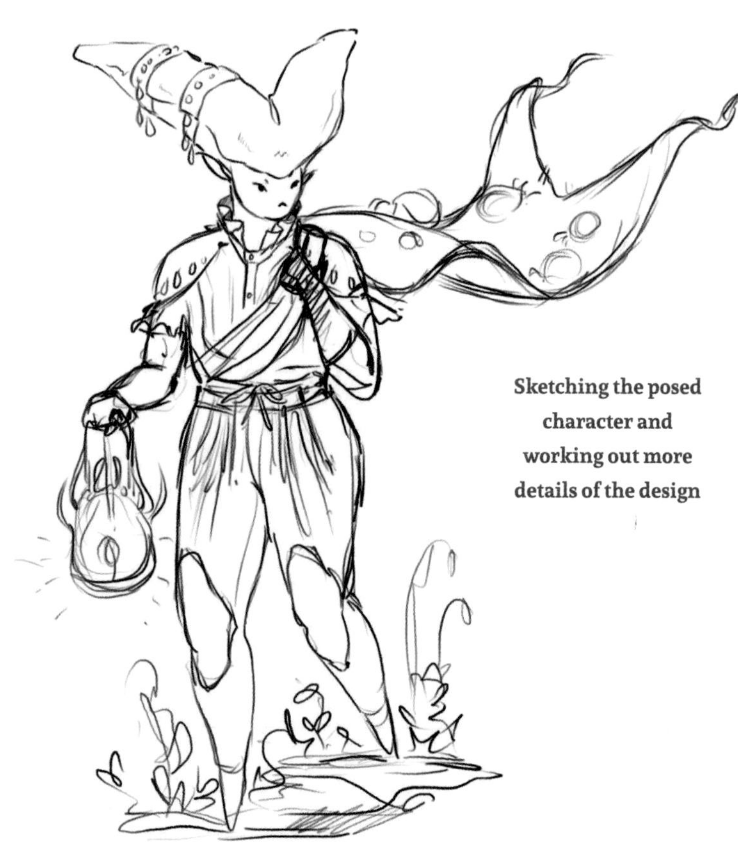

Sketching the posed character and working out more details of the design

FINAL SKETCH

Your final sketch doesn't have to be neat, but make sure to work out the locations and shapes of all your character's details. This will make tidying the sketch into line art much easier. Here the character's head has been adjusted into a more swept-back shape that worked well in an earlier sketch, and flags have been added to the faery's hip to show the direction of travel. For most paintings, it can be very helpful to apply a rough pass of colours at this stage, just to check if any shapes are not setting well and to get a sense of how the whole image will work.

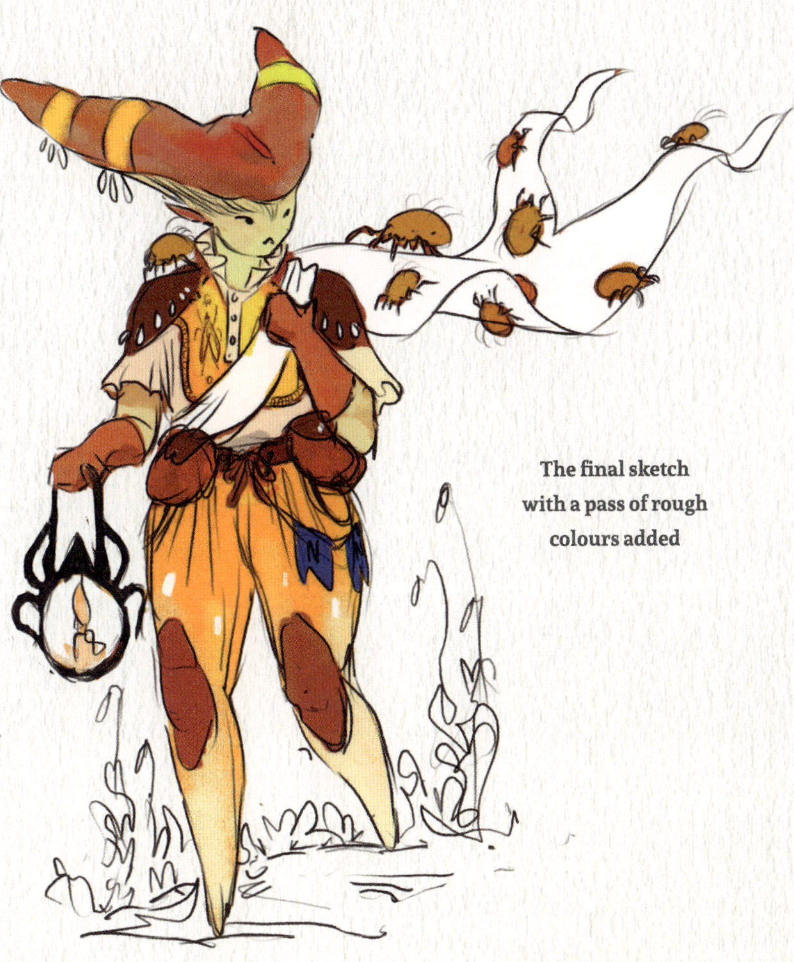

The final sketch with a pass of rough colours added

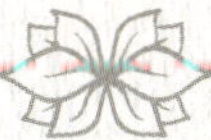

DON'T BE AFRAID TO USE REFERENCES

When starting out, it's easy to assume that professional artists are magically able to draw everything from their minds, but this really isn't the case. Whatever your skill level, you will find yourself reaching for a helpful image search. For example, the initial sketches of the character's frilly sleeves were drawn from the imagination and just didn't look right. Compiling plenty of reference photos of frilly sleeves was essential in finally understanding what they should look like. It's always best to learn from the real thing!

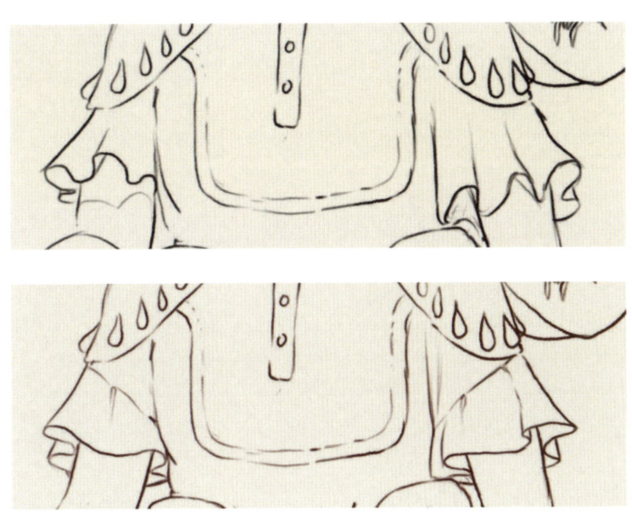

FIND INSPIRATION IN UNUSUAL PLACES

Every little object within a character design can be experimented with and carefully designed. The character's lantern is inspired by mites, an animal that is usually ignored or dismissed as ugly and horrible. The challenge is to turn this misunderstood critter into an elegant lamp. Using your reference images for inspiration, play with the shape of the mite, trying out both complex and simple shapes. Their smooth round bodies contrast nicely with their eight spiky legs!

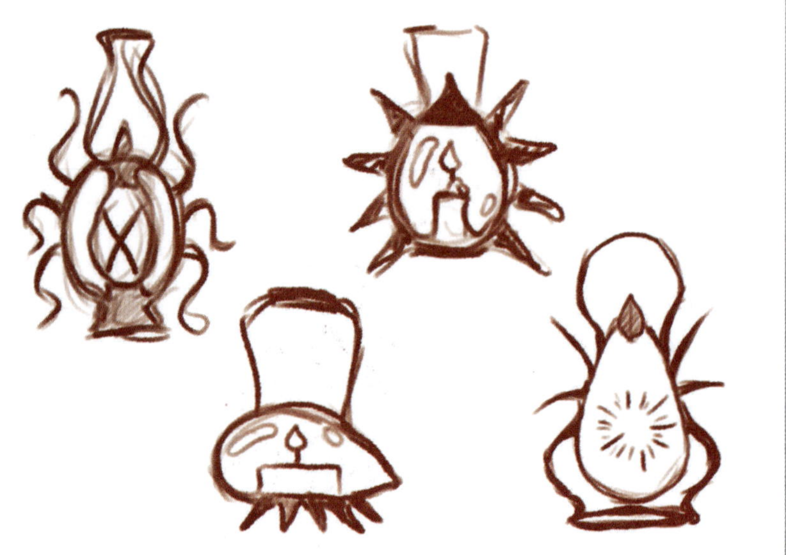

LINE ART

Next it's time for the line art. Reduce the opacity of the sketch layer and work directly on top in a new layer, using a pencil-like brush to create lines with varied opacity and strength. During this step, use visual references to help you refine the details of the design. Image-search niche subjects and small details if needed to help your drawing; for example, you may need more photos of fungus-dwelling mites, flowy clothing, lanterns, mosses, and flags to help finish the line art with confidence. Vary the thickness and heaviness of your lines to create stronger focus on certain areas and hint at areas of shadow. If you prefer, you can go straight from sketch to colour and paint in these details instead.

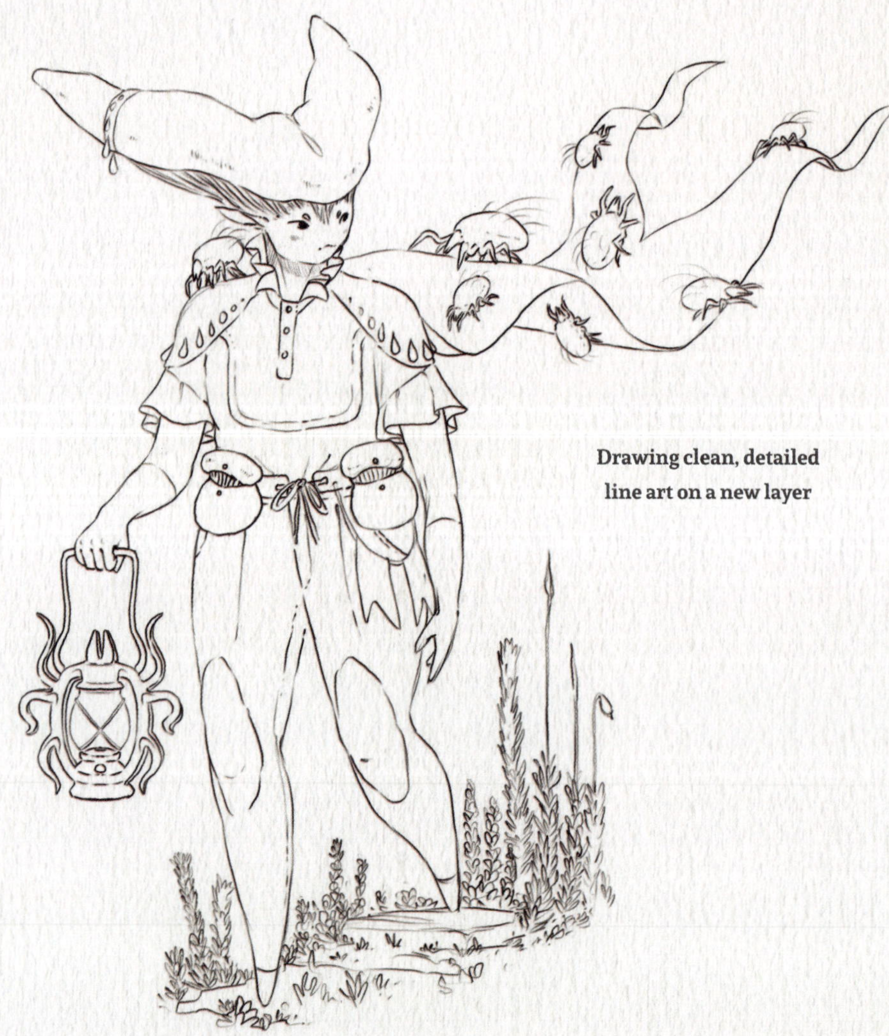

Drawing clean, detailed line art on a new layer

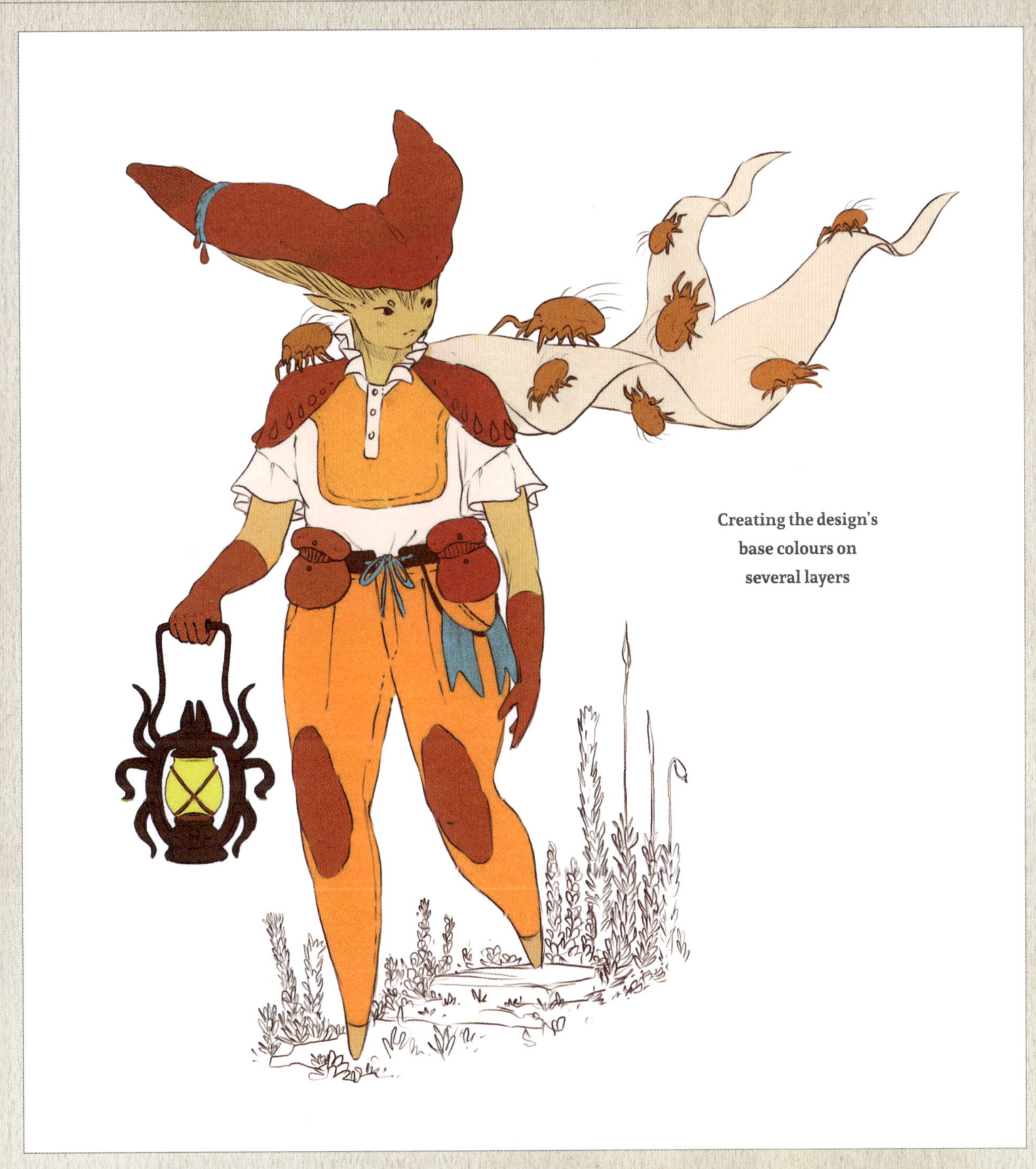

Creating the design's base colours on several layers

BASE COLOURS

To create the colour base, you can fill the whole silhouette with one colour using selection, colour fill, and brush options. A freehand selection lasso is helpful for blocking out large areas, ensuring you don't miss out any tiny sections in the centre that need to be fully opaque. Next, create new layers for different blocks of colour on the body and set each to be a Clipping Mask layer on top of the base colour layer. You don't have to colour every single thing on a separate layer – just make the various elements separate enough that you can recolour them easily by setting the layer to Alpha Lock when playing with potential designs. At this stage, you can also experiment with changing the colour of the line art if you find the black looks too harsh against the chosen colours. You can do this by colouring in another Clipping Mask above the line art layer.

BUILDING UP COLOUR

You can now begin painting properly over the colour base, using a brush with a tiny amount of Hue Jitter in its settings to add colour variety to your brushstrokes. Have plenty of photos to hand for reference as you work. Draw inspiration from the textures of the milk cap and its yellow, orange, cream, and ochre colour scheme. Add a pop of blue here and there for colour contrast. The shoulder pads, knee pads, and gloves all need to look like they're made from a kind of mushroom leather (like amadou fabric), so bring the colours of the mushroom's cap into those areas. The billowing fabric to which the mites are clinging will have a rougher texture, resembling the milk cap's hyphae in soil, so use painterly brushes and scruffier strokes to suggest that.

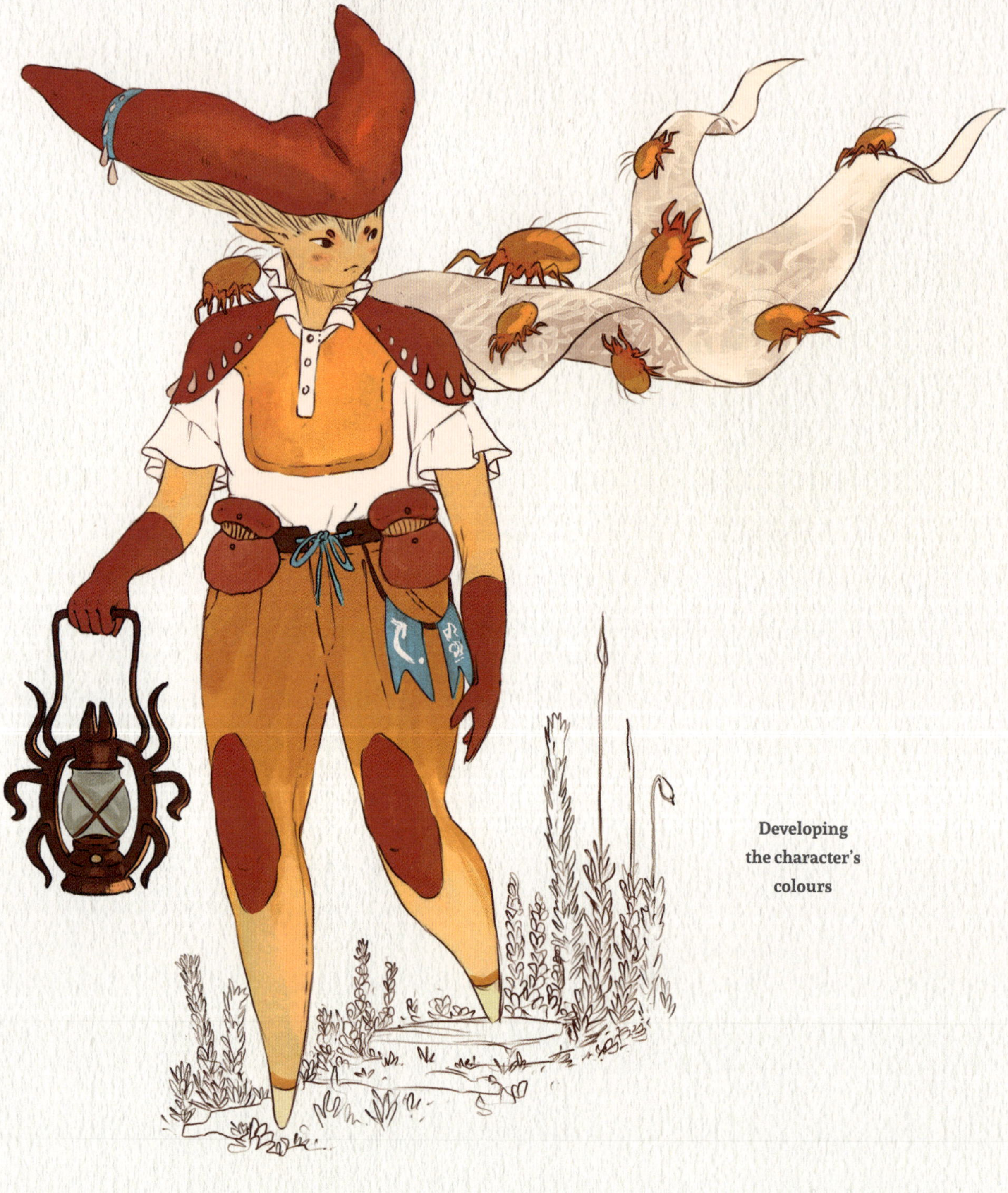

Developing the character's colours

MINOR SHADOWS

For the shadows, create a new layer on top of all of the colour layers and set it to Multiply mode. You can make this layer a Clipping Mask attached to the colour base for ease. Select a low-saturation colour, such as a neutral mid-brown or blue, depending on the desired effect. Start adding small, dark shadows to areas where planes meet and block out the ambient light (an effect known as ambient occlusion). For this illustration, those would be places such as fabric creases, under the character's jaw and cap, and where the mites' bellies touch the cloth.

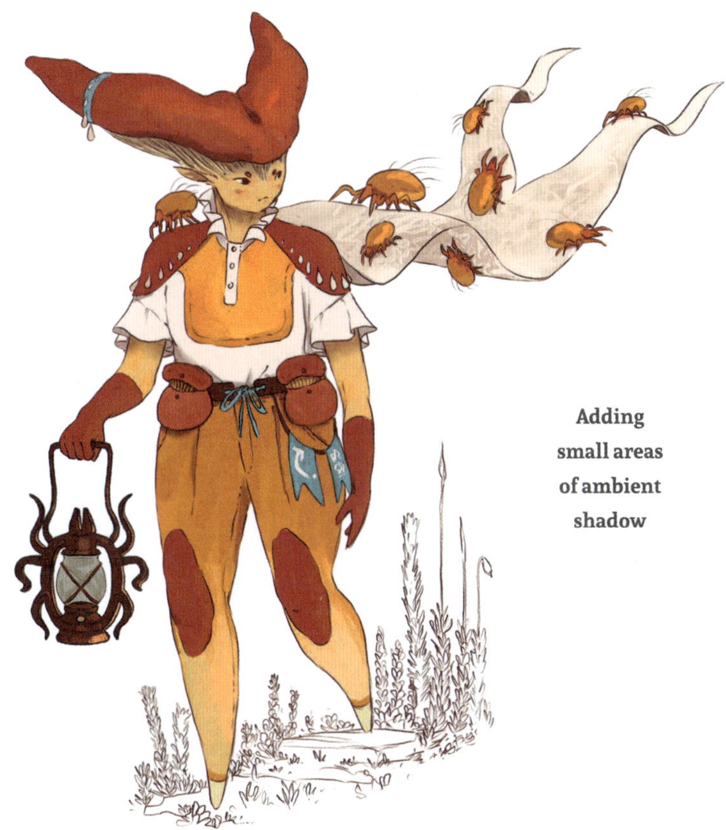

Adding small areas of ambient shadow

MAJOR SHADOWS

Before adding the main shadows, you must first choose a light direction. For shading any image, having a concrete idea in your head of where the light source is placed is very important. In this case, to make the character look adventurous, they will be lit somewhat dramatically from the rear left, as if walking away from a sunset or sunrise. Use a soft-edged brush for the shadows on the hyphae cloth to give it an ethereal floatiness, and a hard-edged brush to paint harsher shadows on the character's body. Once blocked out, Alpha Lock the shading layer and try using a large brush to play with subtly different hues within the shadows. Start with a warm, neutral brown and add in slightly cooler neutrals here and there for some variation.

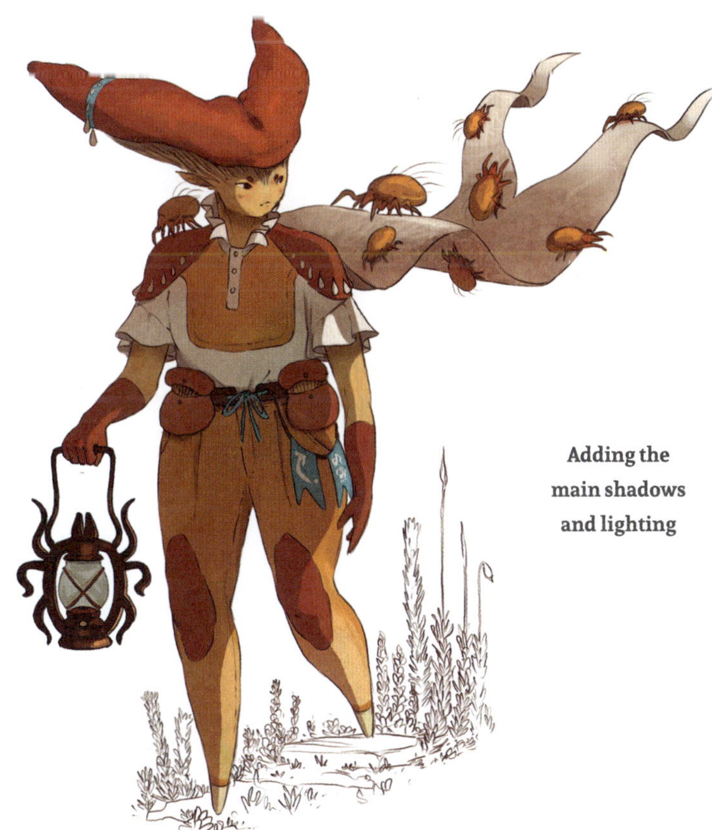

Adding the main shadows and lighting

HIGHLIGHTS

The velvety texture of the weeping milk cap's cap is a great feature to include in the design. From your reference photos, you can see that the velvety texture is achieved through soft areas of lighter colour in places where the form changes direction away from the viewer. Try to emulate this in the character painting, adding this soft, subtle texture to the cap, gloves, shoulder pads, and knee pads. At this stage you can also add some golden glow to the lighting. Make a new Clipping Mask for the character, which sits above the shadow layers, set it to Overlay mode, and use a large, soft airbrush to add just a hint of gold around the character's face and shoulders. Adjust the opacity of this layer until it's just right.

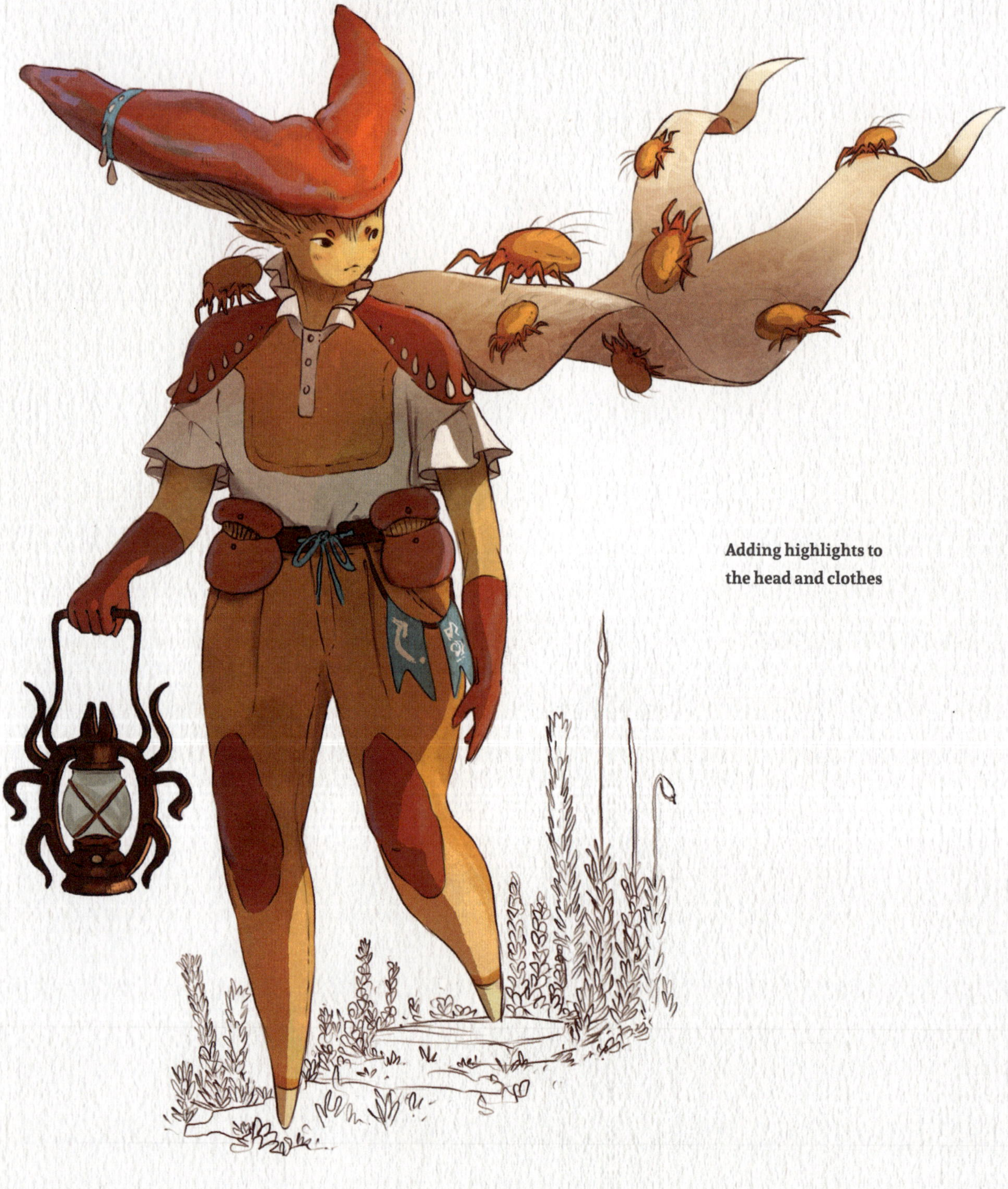

Adding highlights to the head and clothes

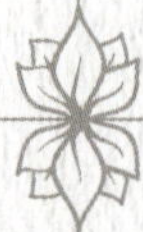

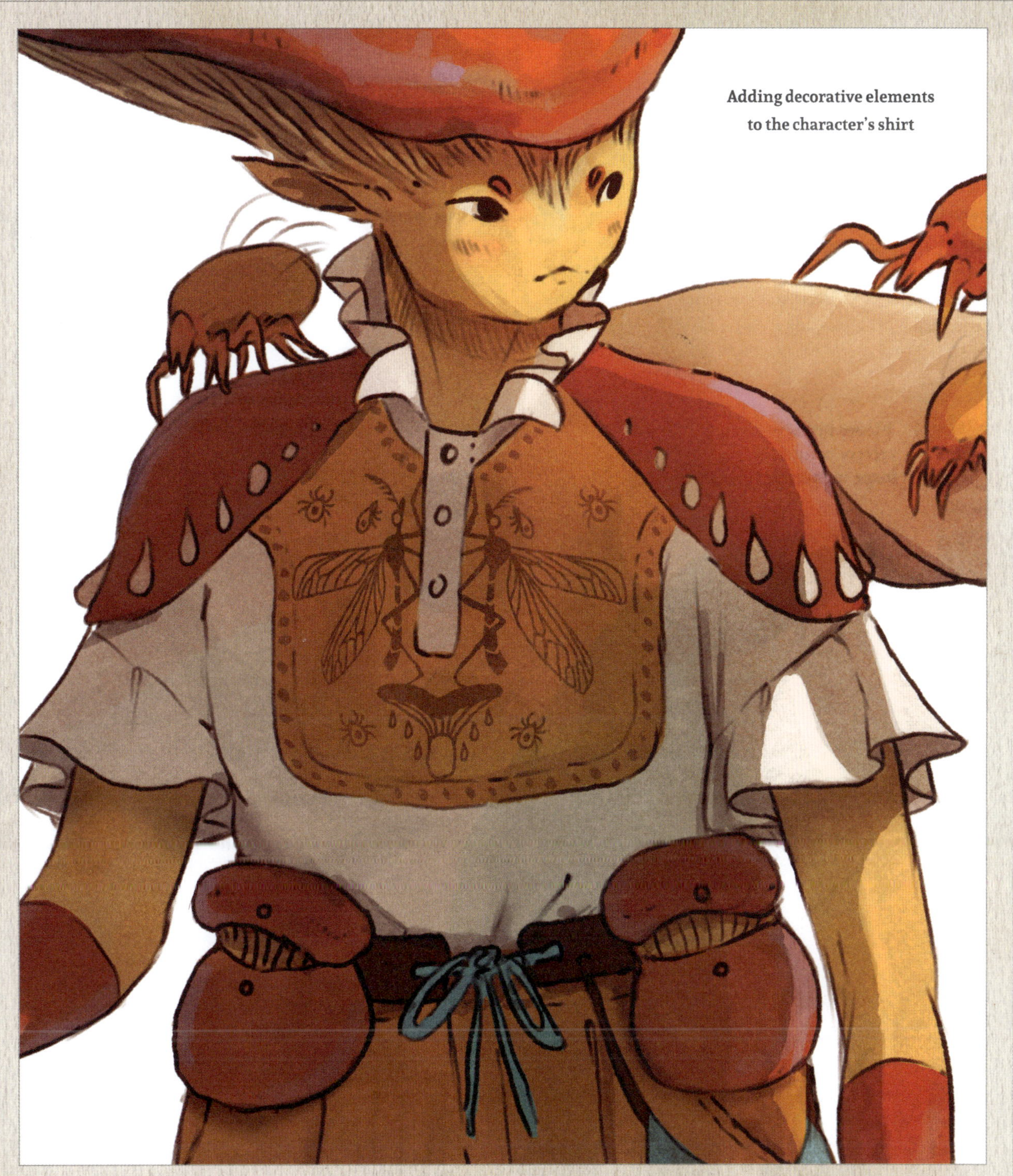

Adding decorative elements to the character's shirt

CLOSE-UP DETAILS

You can include more nods to the weeping milk cap's ecology and associated organisms through small patterns and details. For example, the faery's clothing could feature an embroidered pattern of crane flies (the real-life mite-taxis) with mites around them and a weeping milk cap in the centre. Insects and invertebrates are fascinating creatures, but aren't usually depicted in beautiful and elegant ways! Also, a friendly faery that helps little mites around the forest shouldn't look too intimidating. Try playing with their facial expression to give your milk cap faery the personality you want to portray.

FINAL DETAILS

The last step is to make a new layer on top of everything else and use a painterly brush and the Eyedropper tool to fix any remaining details that you feel aren't quite right. This can include painting over the line art in places. The latex-inspired decorations should sparkle like the fluid that oozes from the weeping milk cap, so add bright white highlight spots to capture that wet glisten. Similarly, reference images of the fungus-dwelling mites show that their bodies catch the light in places, so add warm yellow highlights there. To make the brass lantern look shinier, add some high-contrast highlights to make the metal and glass stand out a little more.

You can now leave this finished faery to wander off among the mosses, gently delivering mites between mushrooms, or you can continue adjusting details and exploring other angles to really iron out all the elements of the design. You could even start the process again from the beginning, still using this single fungus as inspiration, and see whether you meet a different character or creature along the way!

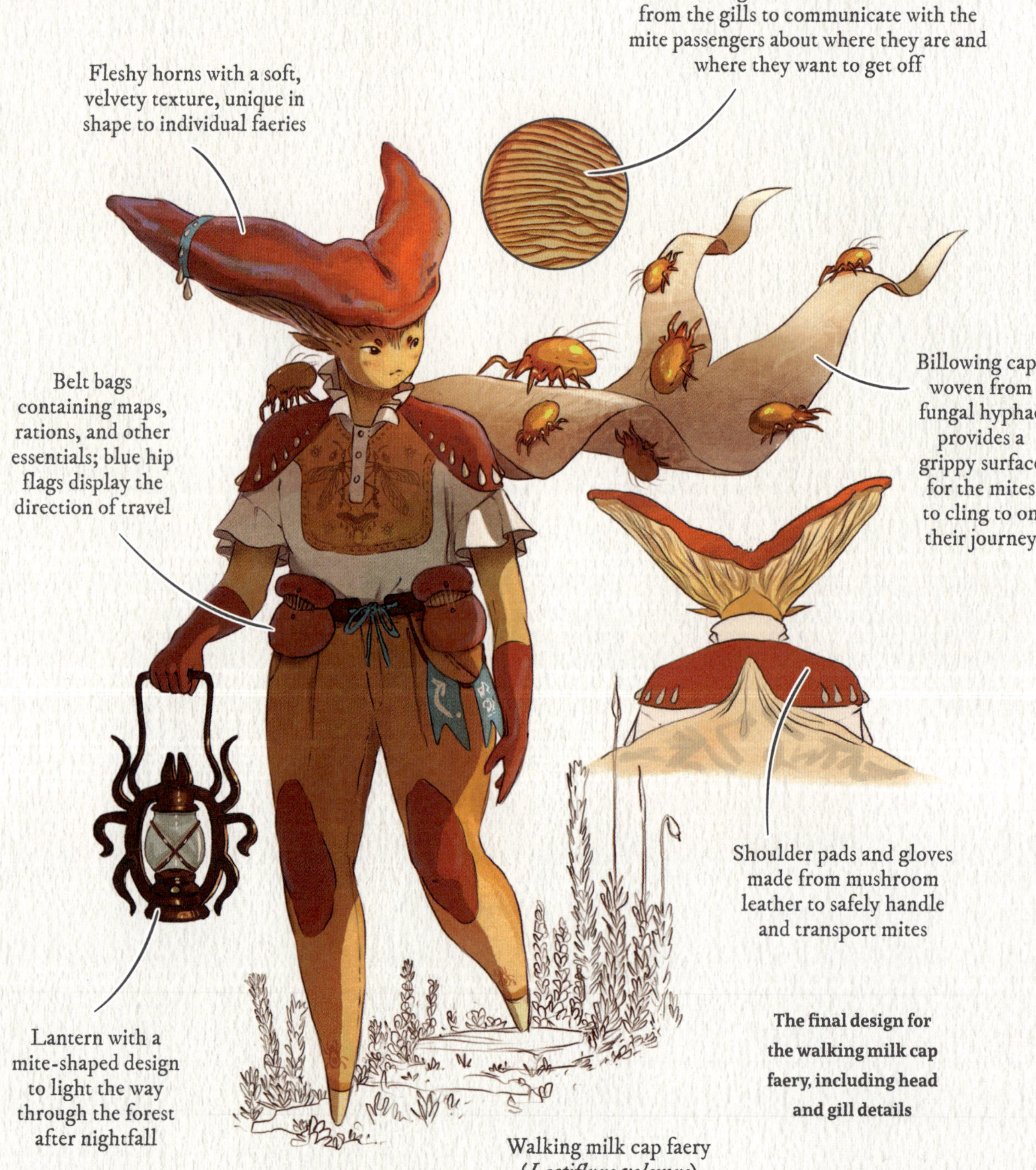

The final design for the walking milk cap faery, including head and gill details

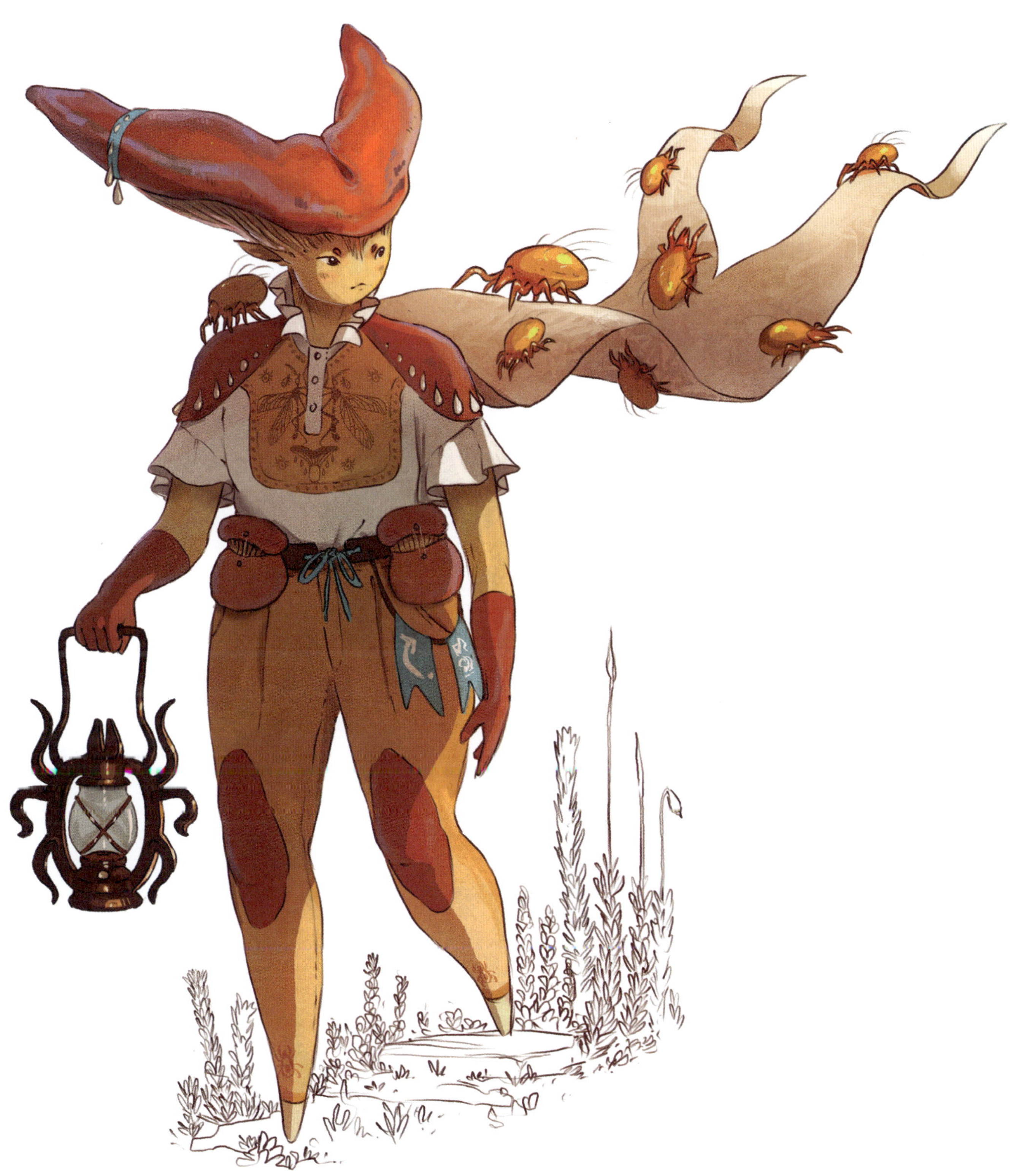

WALKING MILK CAP FAERY

Final image © Dominique Vassie

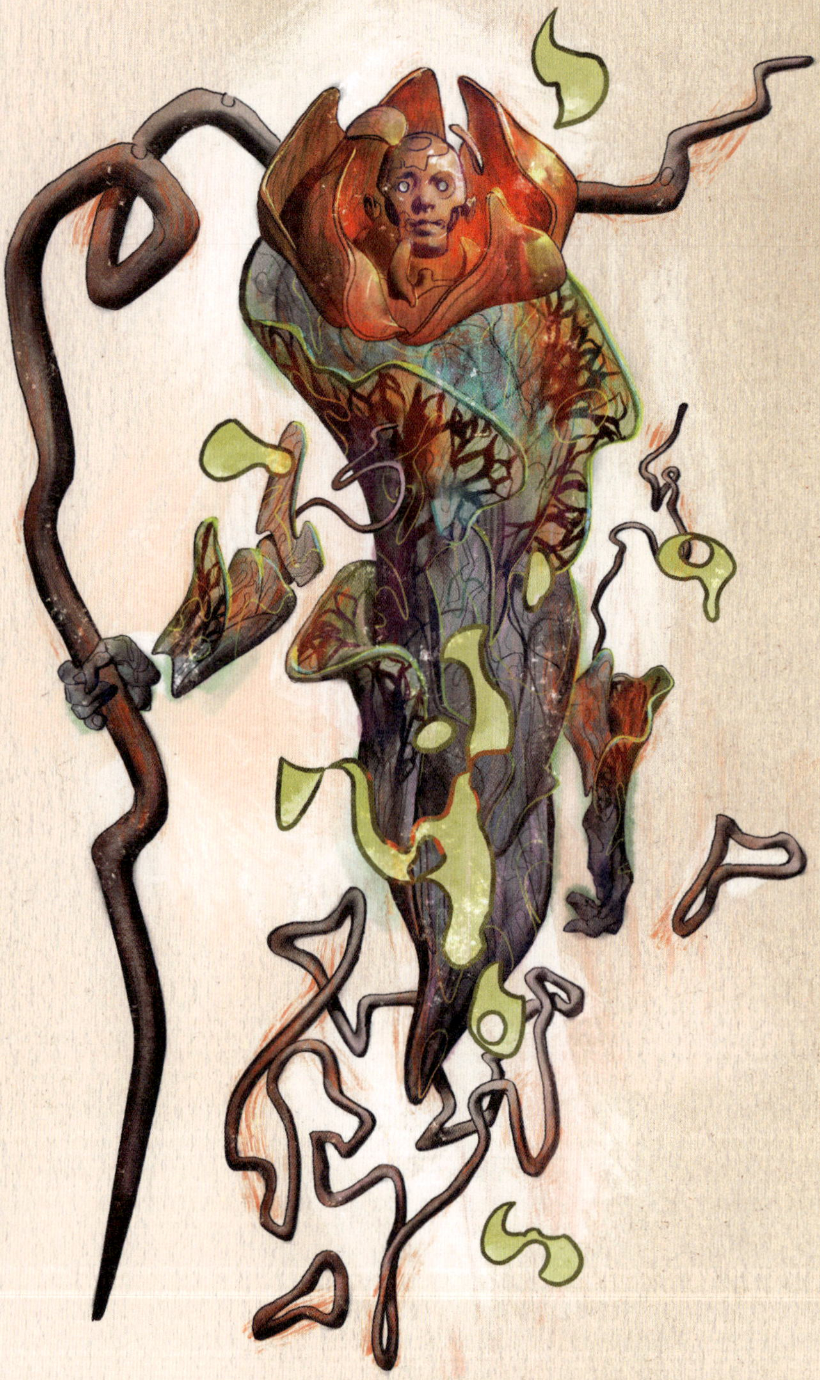

Sarracenia purpurea, also known as the purple pitcher plant, is a carnivorous wetland species. Its red colouring and marbling are a distinctive feature that can be used as inspiration for a character in this tutorial. The pitcher plant's flowers look very different from the rest of the plant – another strong focal element to capture in the anthropomorphized design. This tutorial will be completed using Procreate, but you can follow along with any digital software.

wetland

PURPLE PITCHER SPIRIT

ELIZA IVANOVA

START WITH RESEARCH

Gathering multiple reference photos of the pitcher plant, and also of the flowers, at different angles is crucial in figuring out the plant's most distinguishable features. Unlike other carnivorous plants, the pitchers grow in a bunch from the roots, which creates interesting abstract shapes due to the frill-like leaves. The flower bulb, on the other hand, towers over the pitchers and has a beautiful red sheen. The pitcher plant has an alien look, particularly the shiny skin and fractal-like textures that the veins create. The fact that the plant is also carnivorous adds to the otherworldly feeling that will inspire this character.

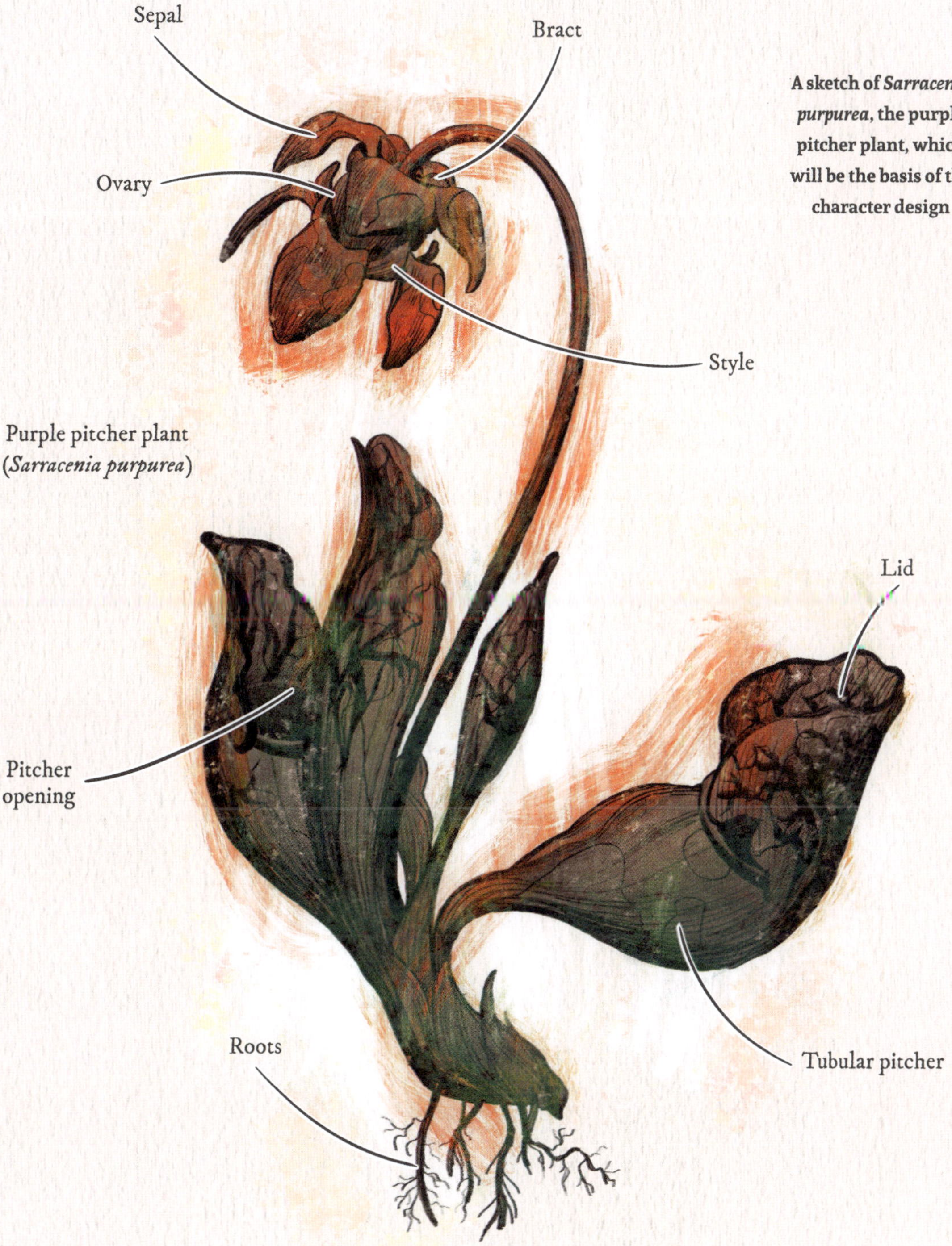

Sepal

Bract

Ovary

Style

Purple pitcher plant
(*Sarracenia purpurea*)

Lid

Pitcher
opening

Roots

Tubular pitcher

A sketch of *Sarracenia purpurea*, the purple pitcher plant, which will be the basis of the character design

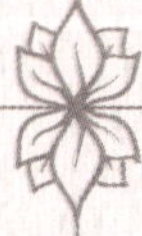

INITIAL SKETCHES

Begin exploring ideas for the character by sketching loose thumbnails based on different blooming *Sarracenia purpurea* plants. Try to capture a general flow that is functional and abstract at the same time, going through a few iterations until you find something that has a clear silhouette and statuesque demeanour. This character will appear strong, wise, and tranquil, but also somewhat abstract and alien. Creating a clear silhouette will be crucial in conveying that this abstract figure can also exist as a functioning being in its own world.

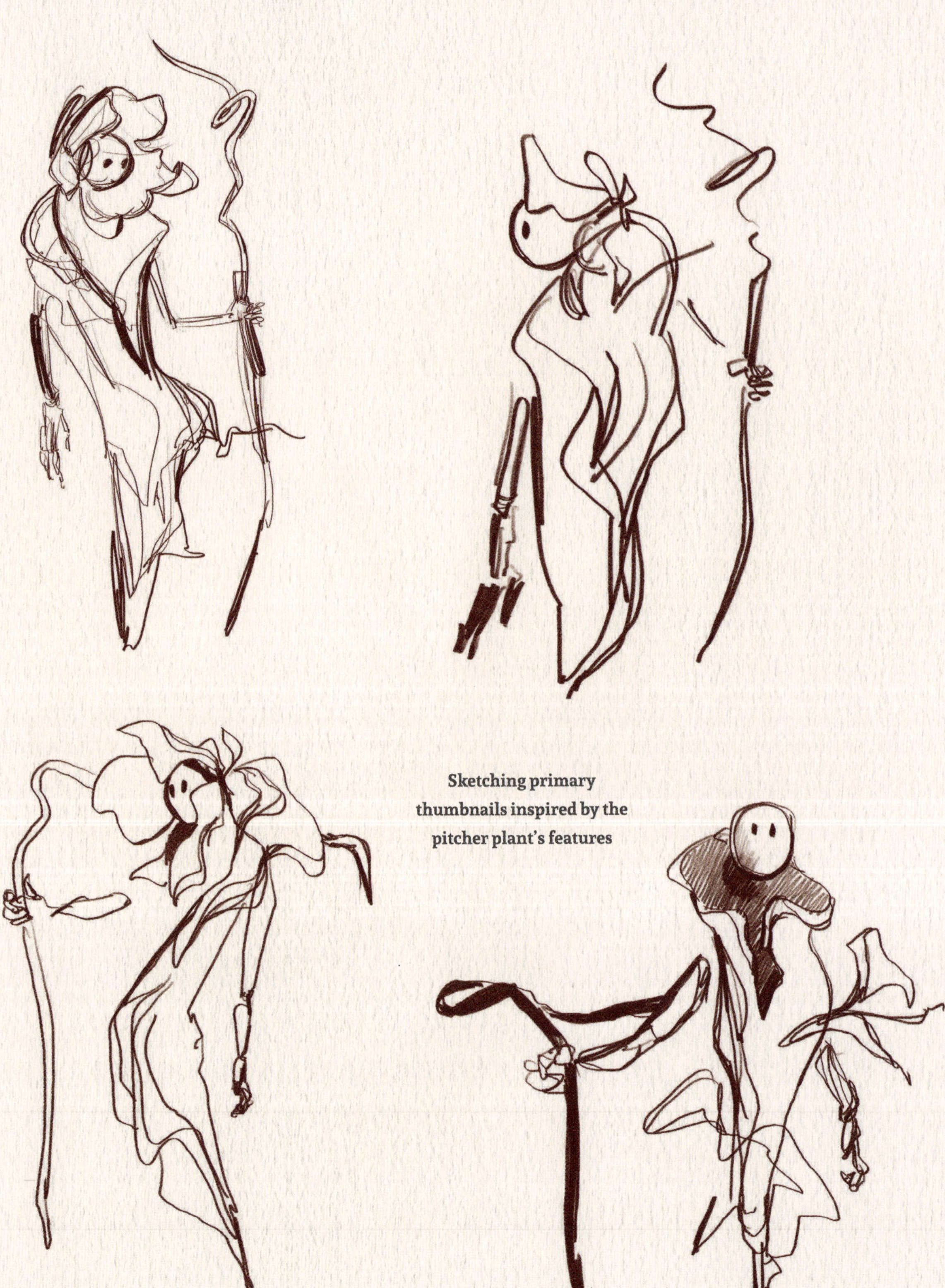

Sketching primary thumbnails inspired by the pitcher plant's features

FIRST ROUGH DRAFT

Based on the chosen thumbnail, draw a second sketch that's more detailed but still rough, further developing the concept without jumping into fine-tuning details just yet. Do this by expanding the thumbnail, lowering its opacity, and sketching on a new layer above it. Keep pushing the abstract shape elements, due to the fantastical nature of the character – it will be a spirit-like, mystical creature. At this stage, you can even add some quick, temporary values or colours under the drawing to see how the silhouette holds up at this larger size.

Here you can see how the character's head is inspired by the pitcher plant's flower, which is noticeably different from the rest of the plant. The flower almost looks like a pendant or jewel, appropriate for adorning the character's head like a mane or crown. Perhaps the older and wiser you are in this character's world, the more glorious your flower mane becomes.

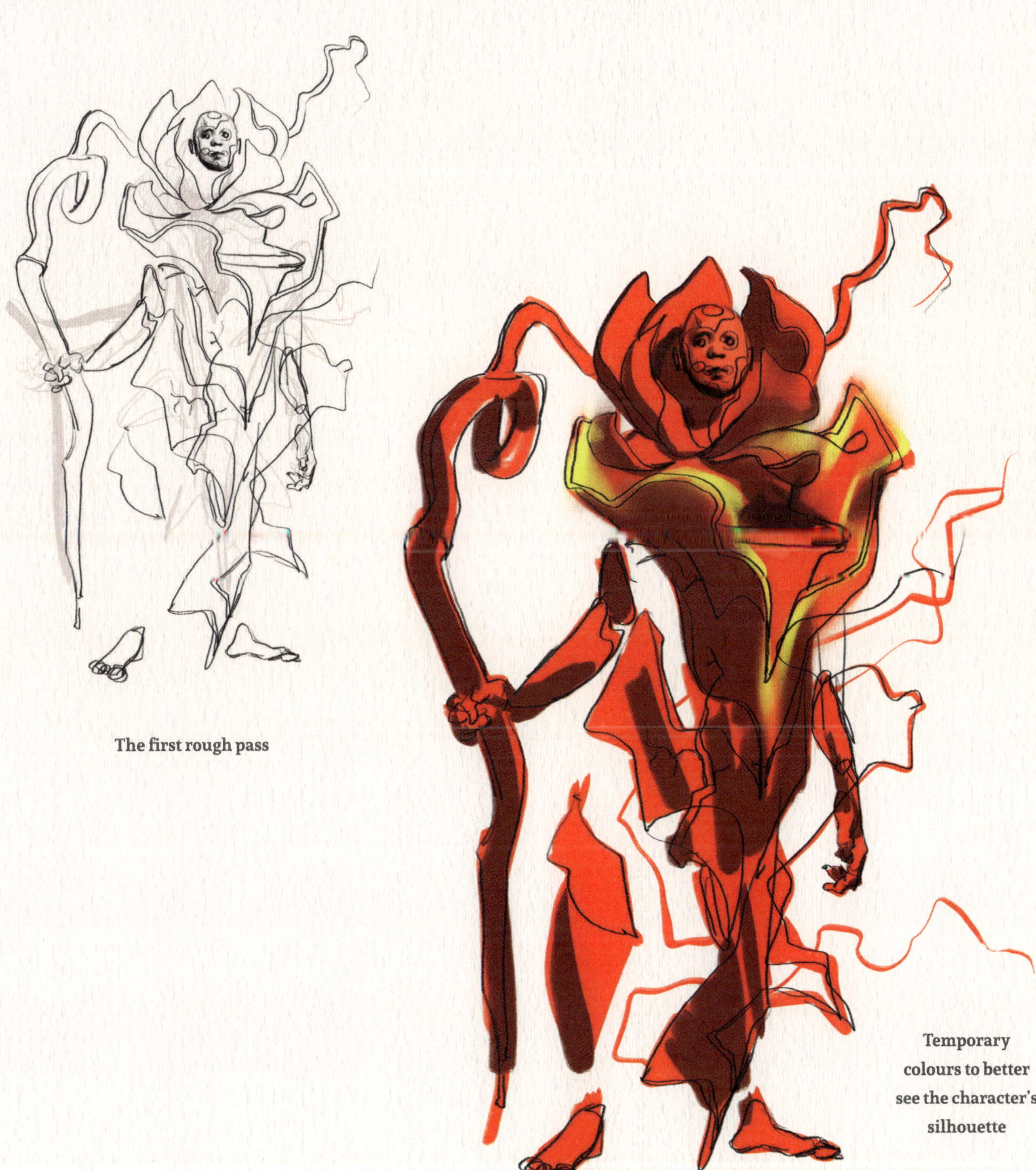

The first rough pass

Temporary colours to better see the character's silhouette

REFINING SHAPES AND LINES

Now, with the under-sketch figured out, you can lower the layer's opacity, create a new layer on top, and begin drawing clean lines that streamline the shapes and simplify the silhouette. Use a textured ink brush that is both precise and not too digital-looking. Take the loose, random shapes of the rough drawing and turn them into functional parts of the character; the arm, for example, now has an armour-like feel thanks to the stacked nature of the pitcher plant's petals and leaves, almost like an onion bulb. Segment the character's face to match the pitcher flower's petals and make it blend nicely with the more abstracted shapes. Try to capture the thickness and rounded-off corners of the pitcher's leaves as you go along. The feet in the previous step make the character a little too humanoid; returning to the thumbnails for inspiration leads to a more magical, stylized look without feet. You can develop that in the next step, so for now, just focus on lining the character's head and upper body.

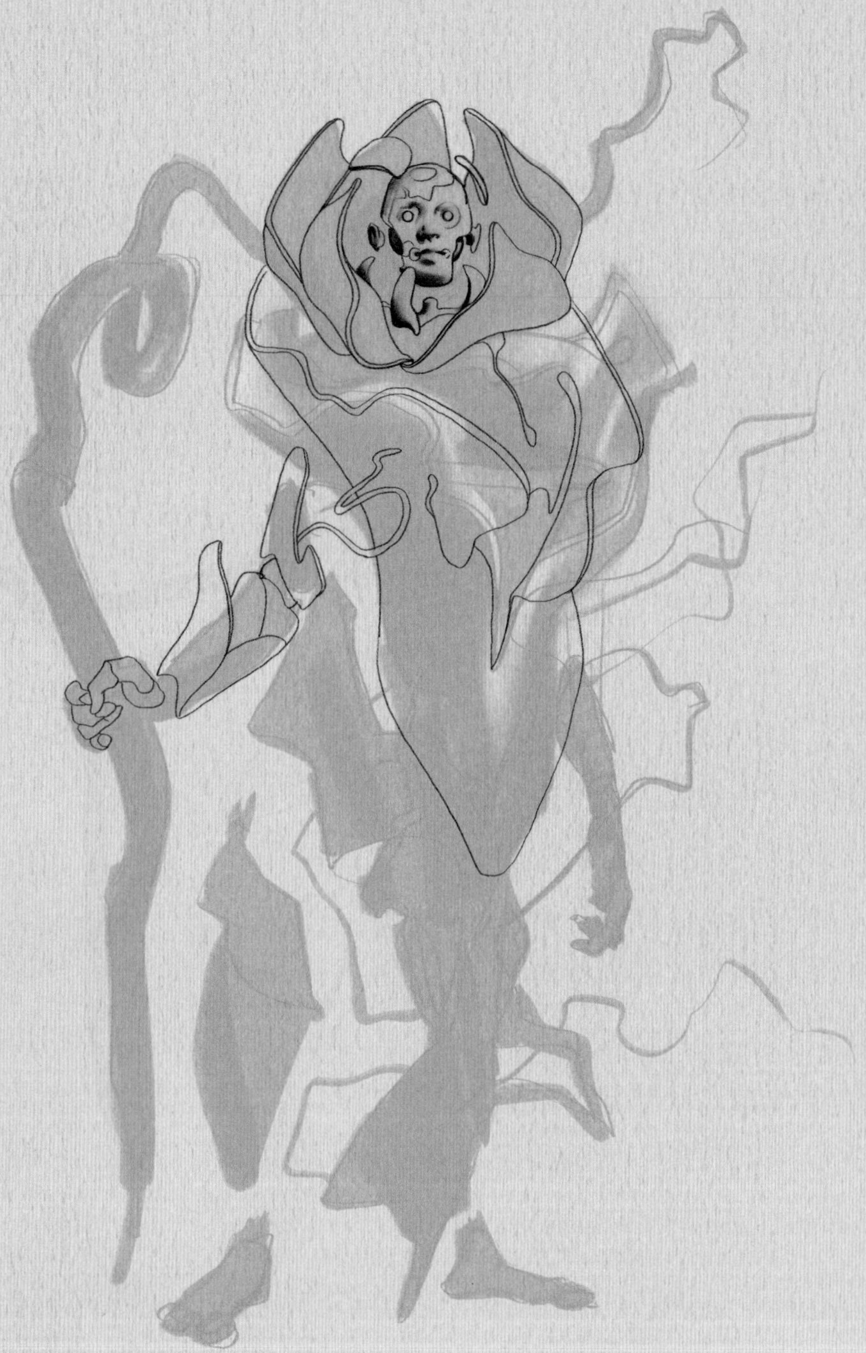

The beginning of the refined line work

CHECK FOR FLOW

More often than not, characters will lose flow and rhythm once details are added. To minimize this, pay close attention to what makes a thumbnail powerful; in most cases, it's a strong silhouette that has a bold flow from the speed and confidence of the line marks. Try to emulate that feeling and keep it in the final version of the drawing, even if that means making major silhouette and flow changes during the refinement stages.

BUILDING UP THE LINE WORK

The line work is heading in a good direction, so continue pushing and defining the shapes while keeping functionality and design in mind. Refine the character's lower body, remembering that you are substituting legs and feet with more abstract shapes. Try drawing stylized roots as floating, rope-like shapes below the character – they add variation that balances the rest of the design, since the torso and upper body have simpler, rounder forms. They are also visually similar to the character's staff – perhaps they are even part of the same magical root formation.

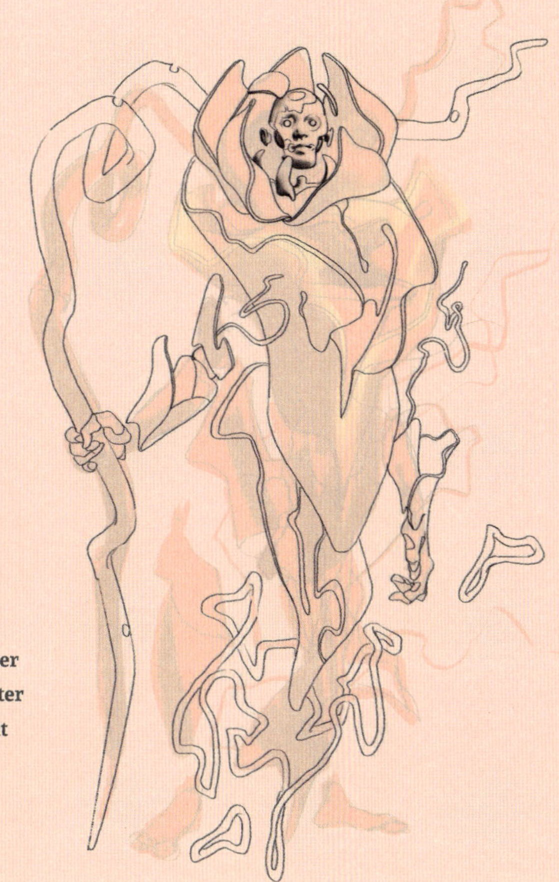

The character line work after refinement

STARTING THE SHADING

Once the line work is complete, begin shading by loosely cross-hatching and then using a textured brush for blending. This suggests a soft, paper-like texture that prevents the image from looking too digital, making it more like traditional pencil shading. Keep in mind that you're not really defining a specific light source yet – instead, focus more on the general volume and how the shapes are stacked over one another. This keeps the image in line with a stylized botanical illustration look.

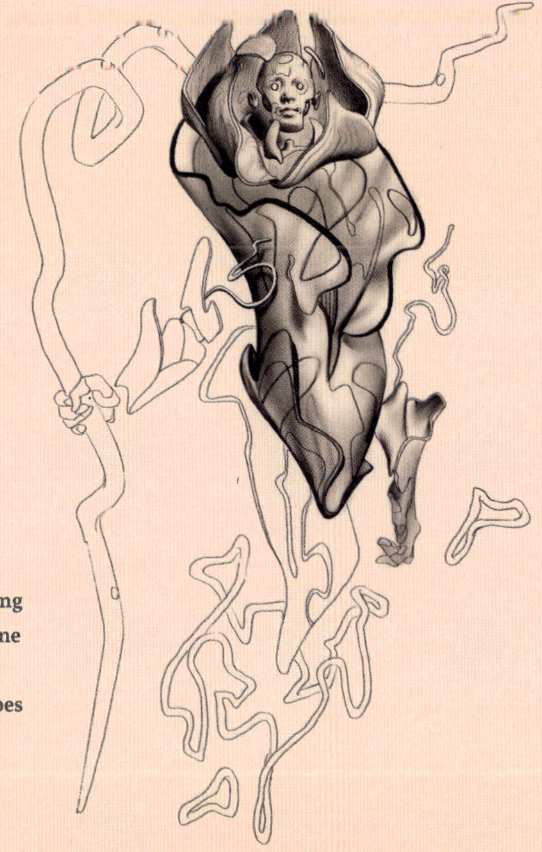

An initial shading pass to determine volumes and layering of shapes

THE FINISHED SHADING

Once the volumetric shading is complete, add a layer of flowy texture lines to break up the monotony. This suggests some topography, texture, and surface material, while also being inspired by the beautiful marbling on the purple pitcher plant. These visible veins could show the character's vitality – you can imagine them pulsating with colours and lights in a heartbeat-like rhythm.

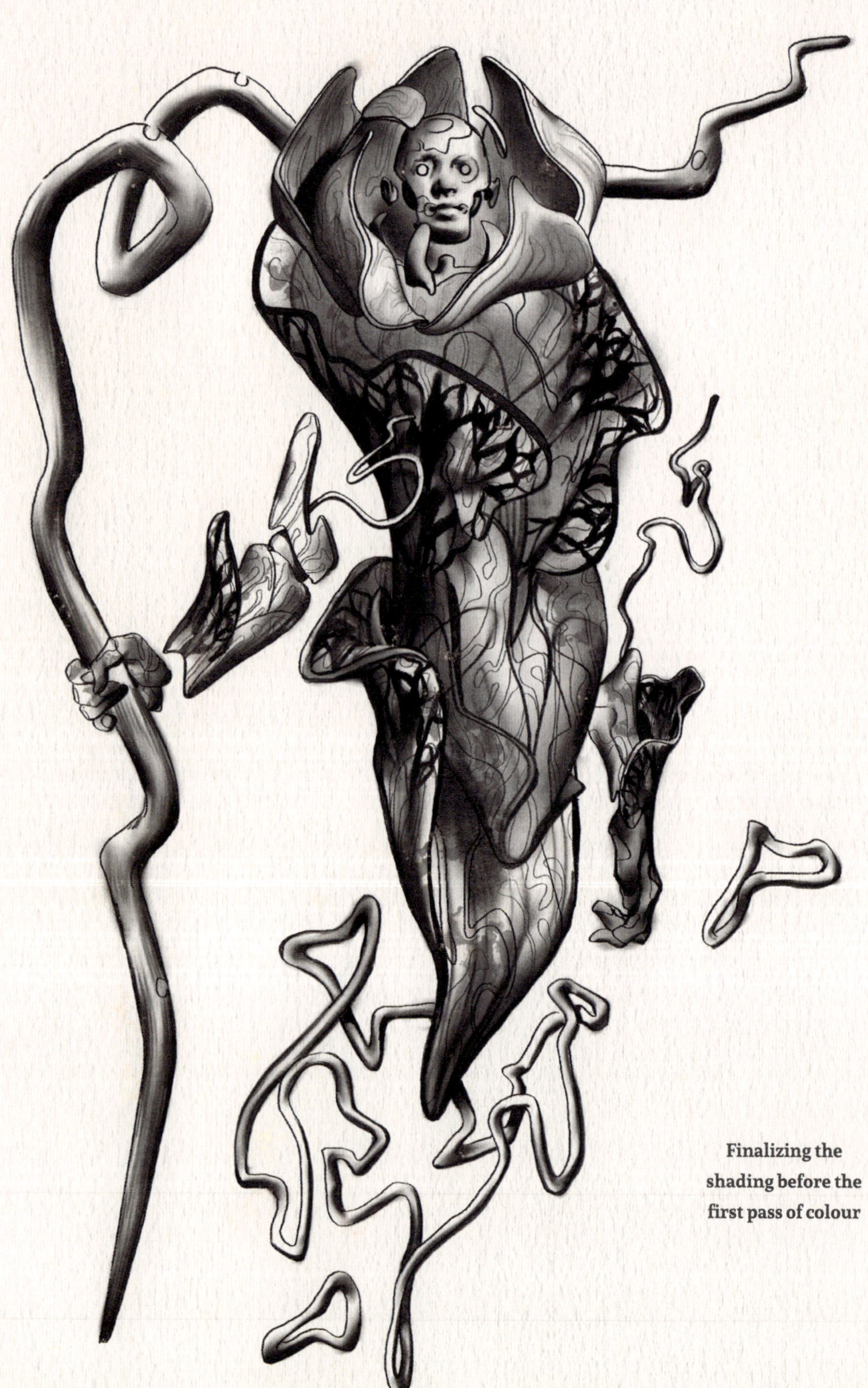

Finalizing the shading before the first pass of colour

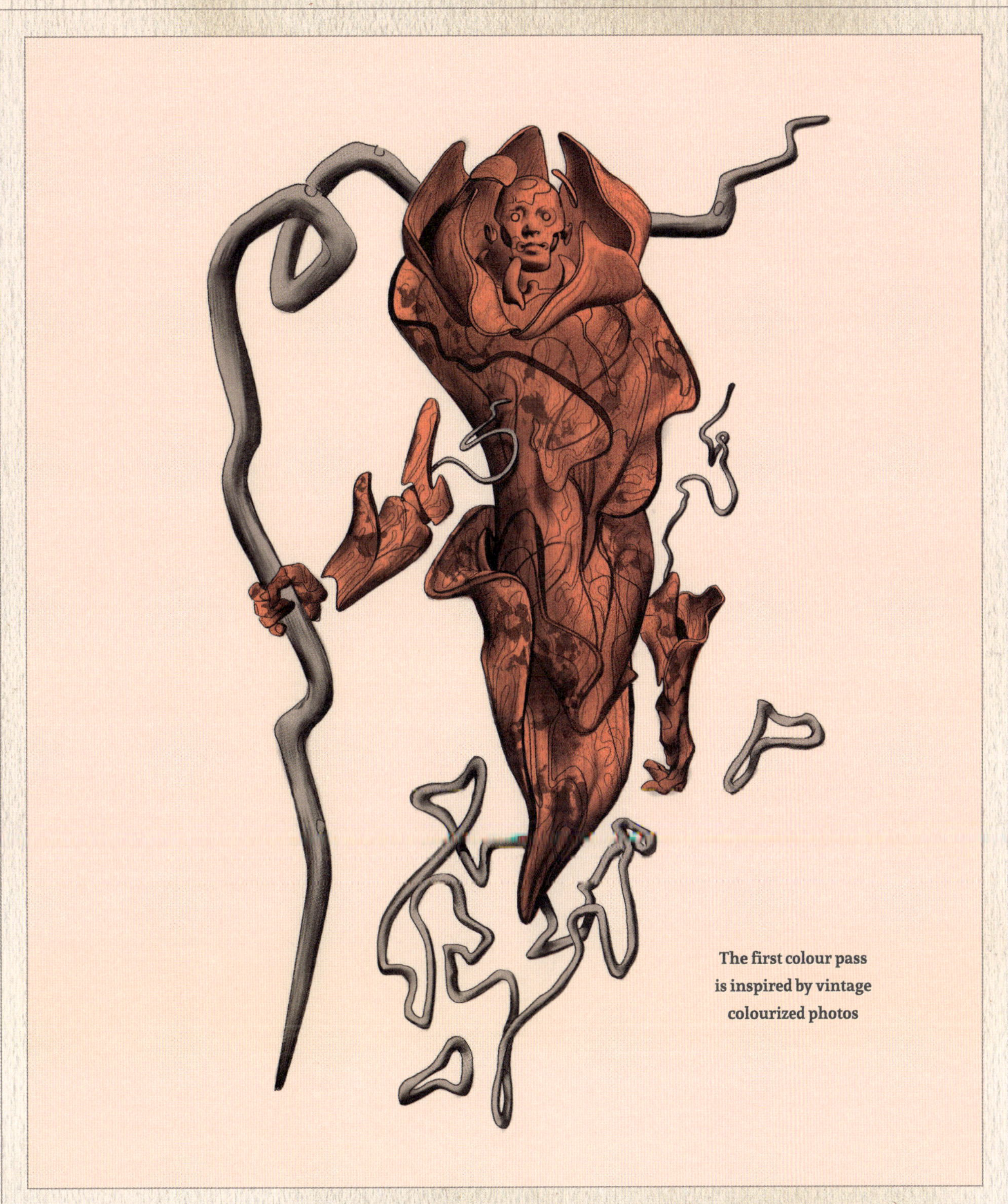

The first colour pass is inspired by vintage colourized photos

THE COLOUR BASE

Use a monochrome base for the colour, choosing shades that are reminiscent of old colourized photos: a red-brick sienna tone for the figure and a flat grey for the staff and abstracted roots. You can also experiment with using texture brushes on the body to distinguish it from the flower-bulb head. The monochrome look is a great way to suggest colour while letting the line work dictate volume, tone, and mood.

A STRONG, CLEAR SILHOUETTE

Be aware of the character's silhouette at all times and correct any tangents (lines or edges touching in a confusing, unclear way) or overlapping elements that muddy the silhouette from afar. This helps you push for a more convincing drawing, even in the early stages of developing a concept or a character.

BOTANICAL ELEMENTS

Before diving into the main colouring stage of the character, you can add one more texture pass that's less about brushes and more about drawing inspiration from the original pitcher plant. On a separate layer, add veins to the character's leaf-like skin to give it a translucent feel. You can do this with a fairly dense, heavy line quality, using an inky brush, such as Procreate's Calligraphy Blotchy brush, to add more variety to the shading. Having these additional texture elements on their own layer will allow you play around with colouring them independently.

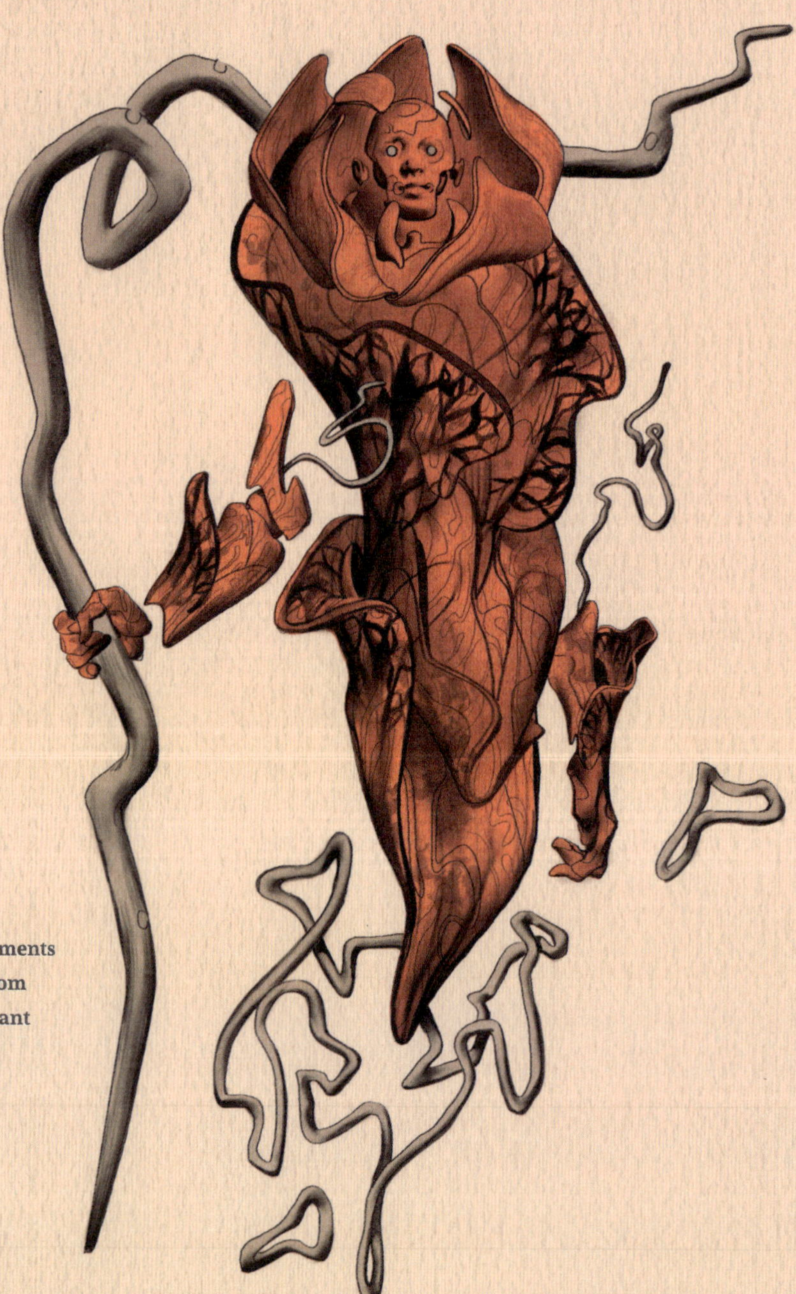

Adding botanical elements drawn directly from the real pitcher plant

MAIN BODY COLOURS

Now it's time for the most involved colouring stage, where you lay out the colours for every element of the character to determine the palette, materials, and translucency. Again, keep all the elements on separate layers, so you can easily experiment with colours and blending modes. Colour the body with yellow and green hues to contrast with the red flower-bulb head and the leaf veins. Leave the lower body darker, so the upper body and collar area stand out more. Add an extra pass of colour and highlights to the head and flower petals, making them shinier and more opaque than the body. The leaf veins have no sheen to help push the body's translucent look.

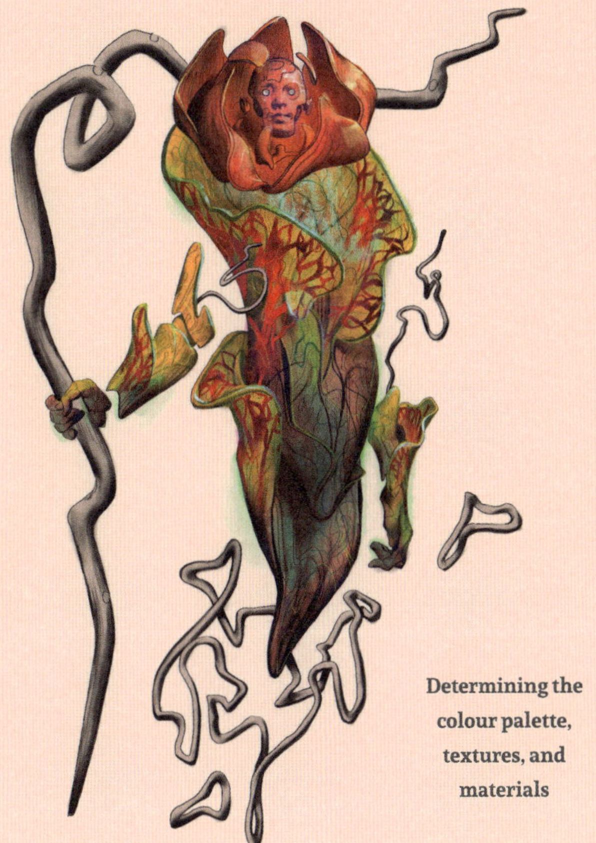

Determining the colour palette, textures, and materials

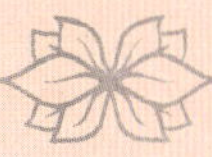

ADDITIONAL COLOURS

After colouring the body, colour the staff and roots with brown gradients to keep them simpler than the character itself. While painting, you can use many layers in order to experiment with different colour variations or blending mode interactions. However, always keep an eye on what's going on 'under the hood' and structure the layers into groups. Otherwise, you may run into a problem with a layer and be unable to easily find the culprit. Pay attention to the layer hierarchy and try grouping the layers that work together but sometimes may need to be isolated from the others; for example, the root and staff colours are less complex and less important, so can be kept together on one layer or in one layer group that can easily be turned on and off.

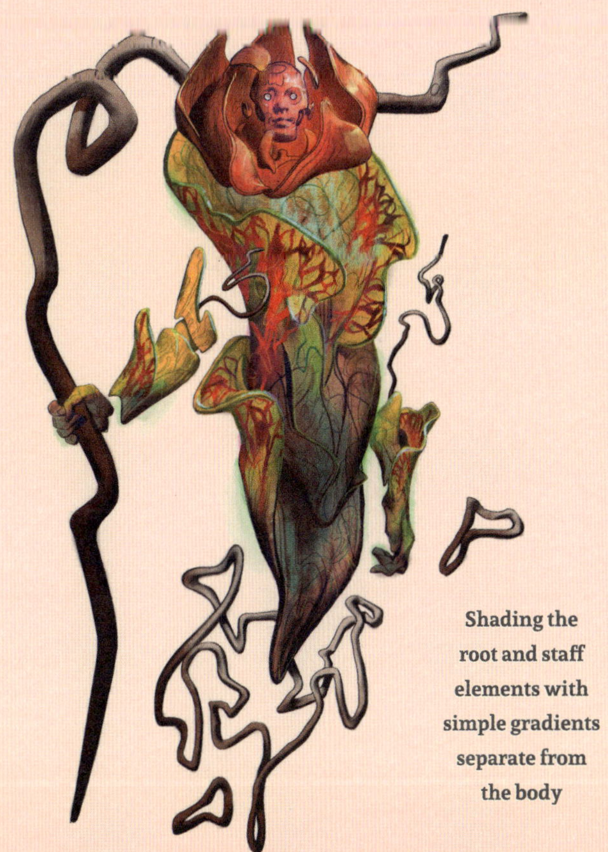

Shading the root and staff elements with simple gradients separate from the body

COLOUR ADJUSTMENTS

Now that the colours and details are all in place, you can make further refinements to tie everything together. The saturation currently feels too strong, without much commonality between the character's elements; the head, body, and staff appear too segmented. Try bringing the character's saturation down to match the staff a little more. Pull colours from the body and use them to add some shimmer to the head and petals, helping bridge the stark contrast between the two. Add some of the brown from the staff to the leaf veins, bringing them closer in value to achieve better overall flow.

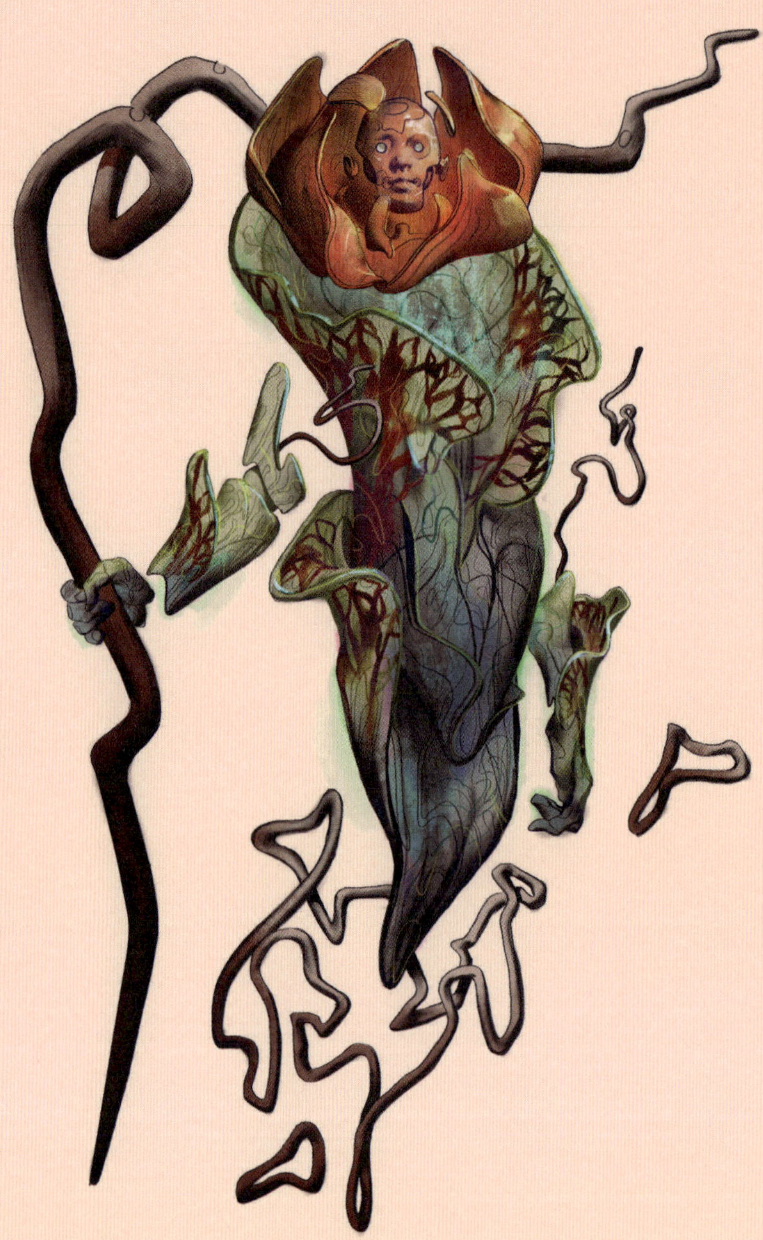

Decreasing saturation and tying the pieces of the character together

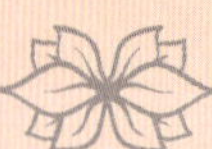

TOO MUCH, TOO LATE!

You will often see characters that are overly saturated, to the point where there is no colour cohesion and they feel overworked. This actually works against appeal, showing a rookie's overcompensation with no clear direction in mind. To avoid that, make a point of keeping your colours in check at all times; pay attention to the overall look of the design and whether it appears too visually messy. Too many elements may be fighting for attention, or the colours may not go together and have no flow into one another. Remind yourself of the original visual goal of the piece (which, in this case, is to be reminiscent of a vintage botanical illustration). This focus will help you to avoid creating a discombobulating character – unless that's your desired look!

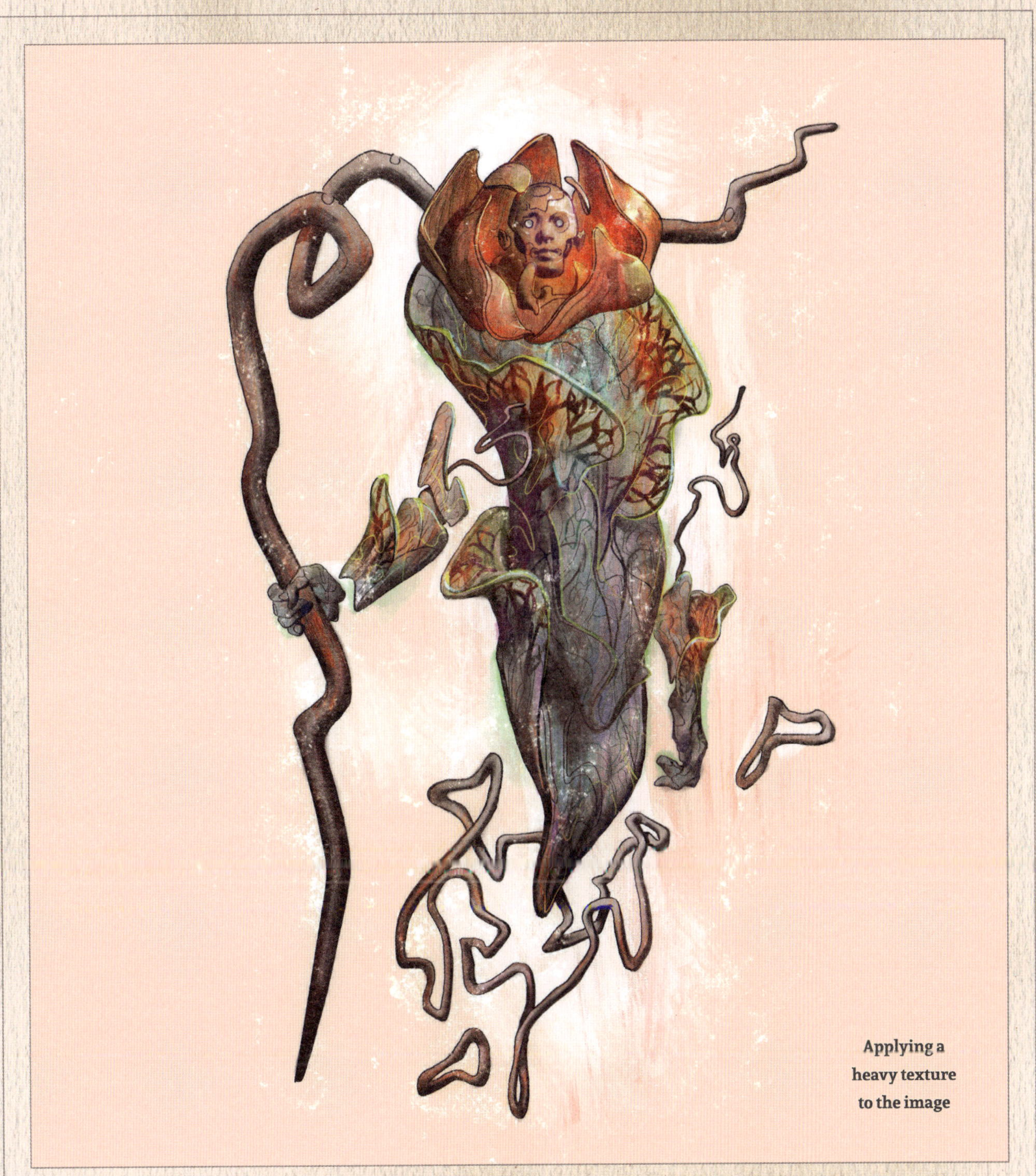

Applying a heavy texture to the image

TEXTURE PASS

Once you're happy with the colours, you can venture into texturizing the character by adding layers of various textured brushstrokes. To avoid monotony and repeating texture patterns, you can use the same texture brushes to erase parts of the strokes. Aim to brighten the overall look of the figure while simultaneously involving the background and creating atmosphere. A brighter tone behind the figure brings the character to the forefront and creates the illusion of space and a light source. The spotty texture over the entire sketch ties everything together, covering the background, staff, and abstract floating roots. Finally, add a light grey wash over the character's empty hand, as it's further away from the viewer and needs to 'sink into' the background ever so lightly.

FINAL DETAILS

At this point, return to the original thumbnails and evaluate your design in comparison, seeing if there are any last enhancements you can make to finalize the image. Try to intensify the glowing elements, such as the inside of the pitcher-like body, right under the petals, and the sheen on the petals themselves. Add some leaks of greenish colour around some of the edges for a fun, alien feel that will add to the mysterious look of this otherworldly spirit character. For example, a few floating leafy or flame-like wisps help to bring the final illustration closer to the original thumbnail's flow.

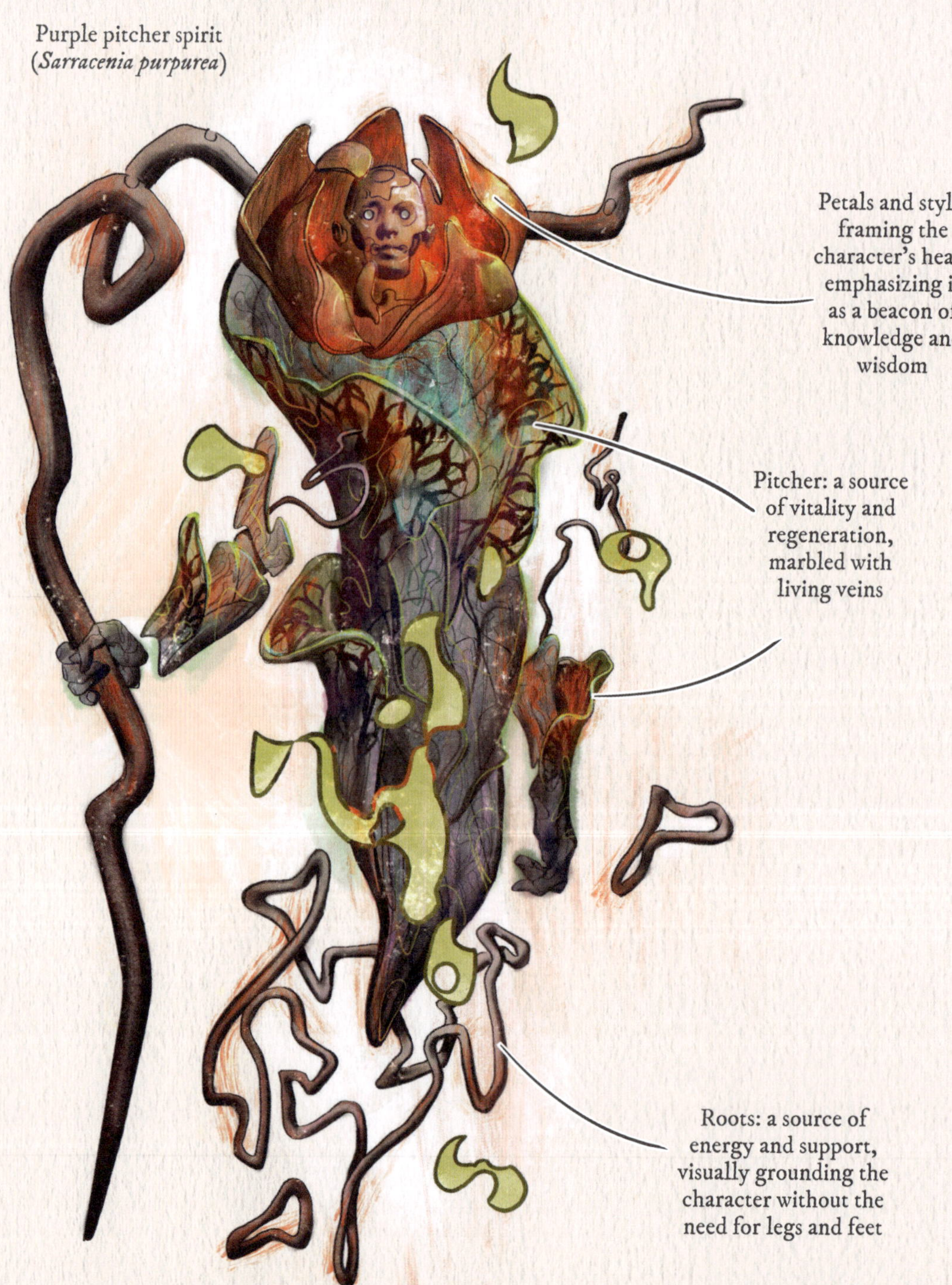

Bringing the final image together coherently with a few visually pleasing adjustments

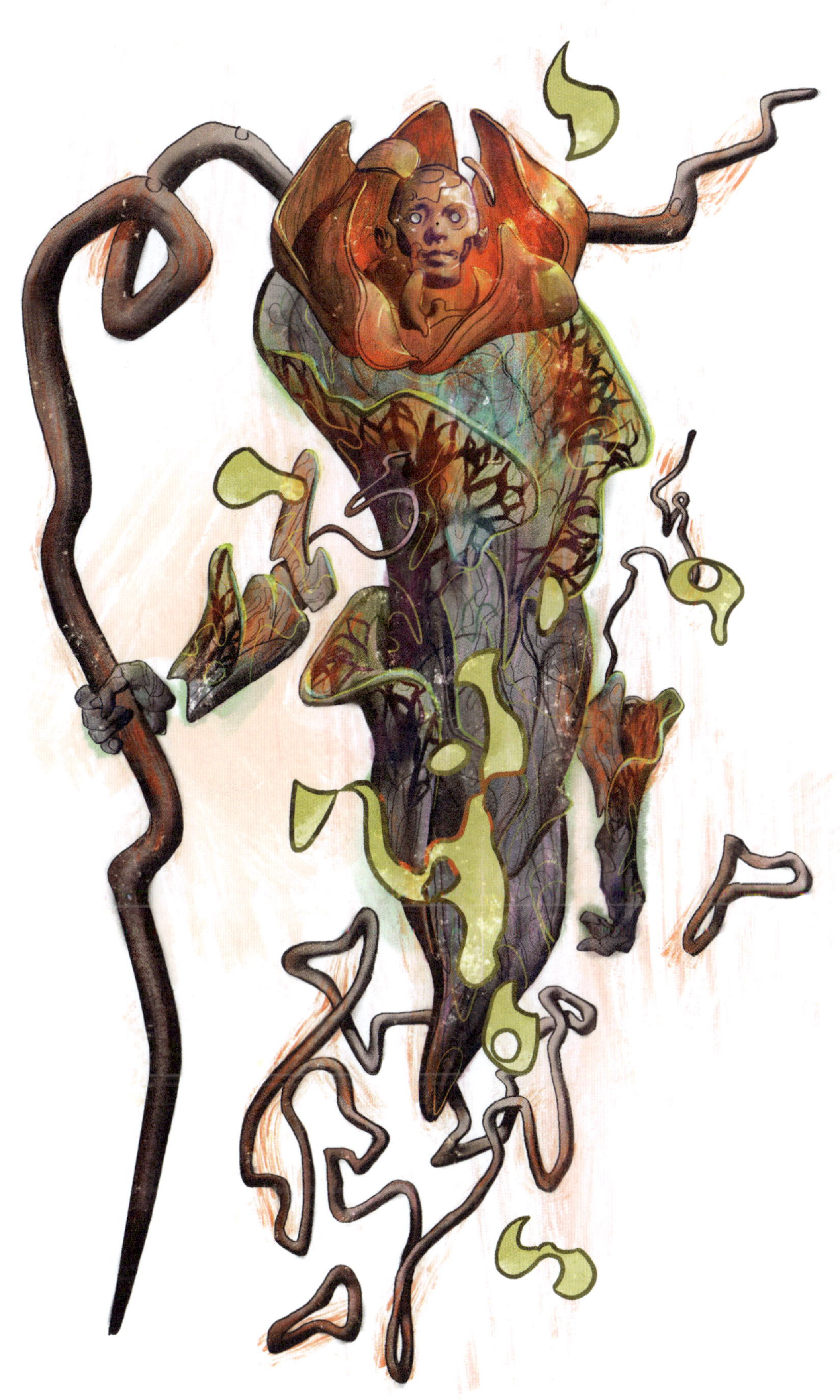

PURPLE PITCHER SPIRIT

Final image © Eliza Ivanova

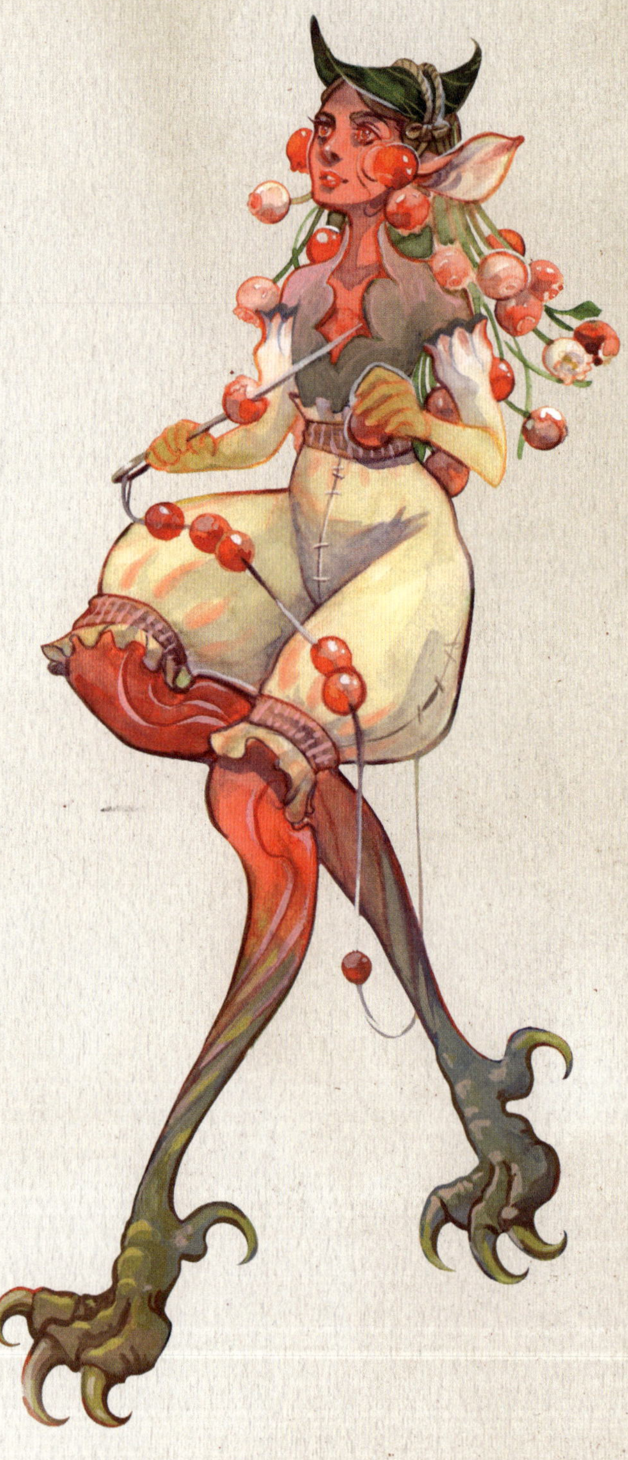

Found on the west coast of Canada and North America, the red huckleberry's bright crimson berries, delicate branches, and attractive bell-shaped flowers provide ample inspiration to draw from. Peeking through the canopy, there's an almost luminous, glass-like effect as the sun shines through them, giving the berries an enchanting look.

This tutorial will be completed with traditional media – including pencil, watercolour, watered-down gouache, and coloured pencils – but you can follow along using the materials you have to hand.

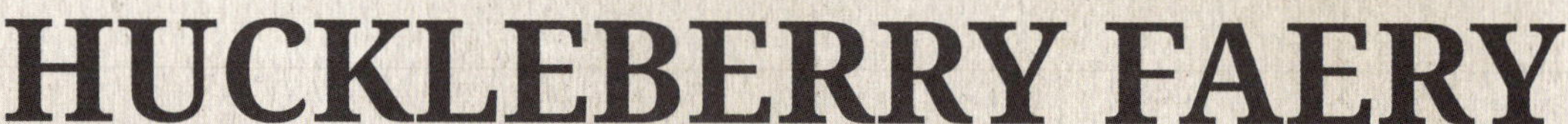

fruit

HUCKLEBERRY FAERY

AUDRA AUCLAIR

RESEARCHING YOUR SUBJECT

In order to recreate the look of a plant accurately, it's a good idea to start by studying it. Spend some time looking at the different life stages and elements that make up the red huckleberry plant and familiarize yourself with its various parts. You might find that a specific season or section of the plant inspires unique ideas. This is a great way to add structure, shapes, and colours to your mental library that you can draw from later. Assuming you've never drawn a red huckleberry before, begin observing it closely and sketch its various forms.

The huckleberry is a summer berry. The berries themselves are semi-translucent and range in colour from red to pink. The stem has flat planes and sharp corners, and the overall shrub is quite spindly. When blooming, it has white bell flowers with pink details. The flowers appear to have roughly five points, which become around five points on the bottom of the berry when it's formed.

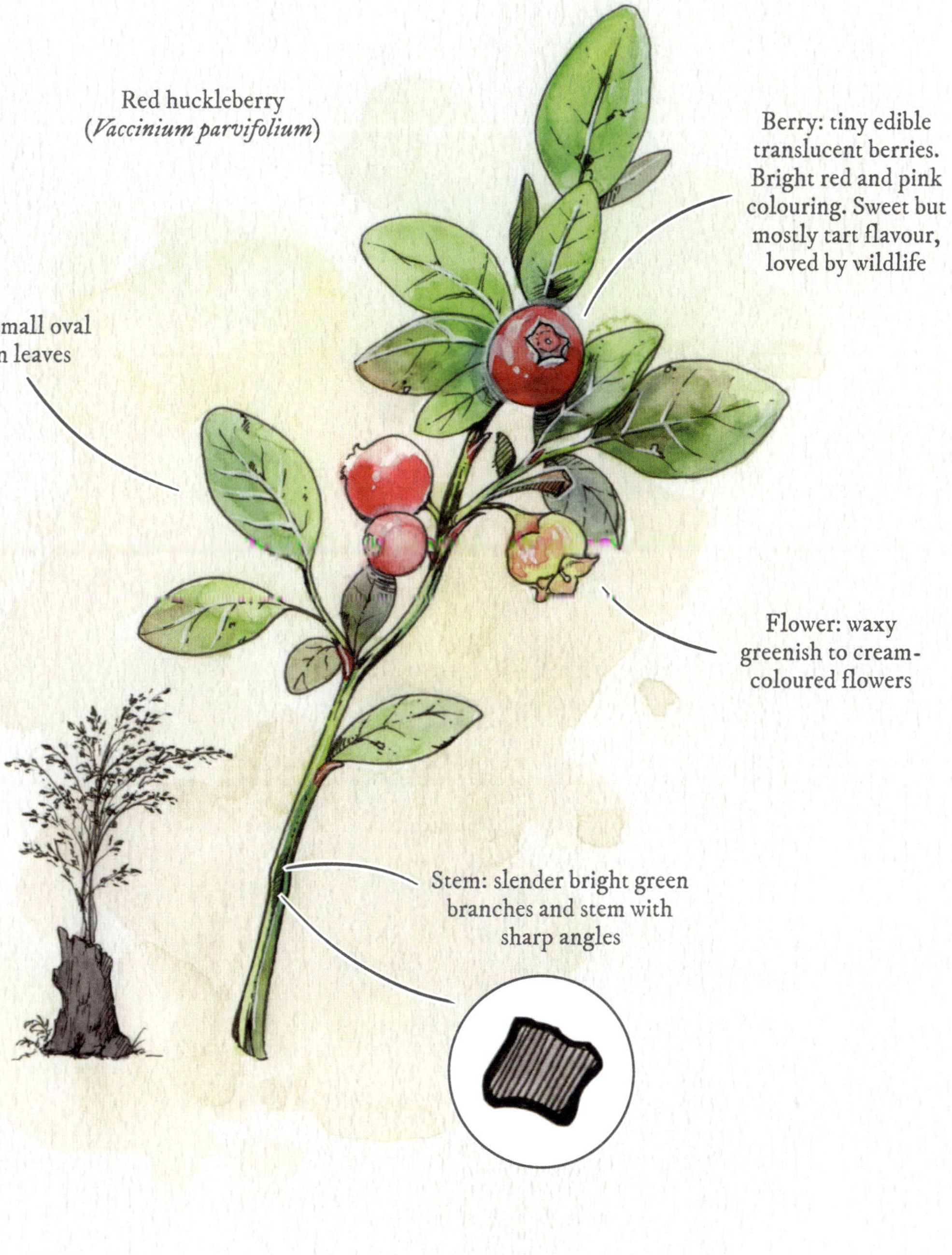

A basic scientific illustration, using watercolour and ink

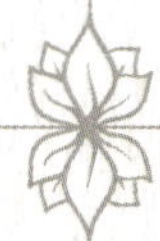

CONCEPT SKETCHES

The journey to producing a creative illustration starts with creating a collection of concept sketches. The purpose of this step is to find an idea that really inspires you. That inspiration will be the fuel you need to complete your artwork. Think about the size of your character and how you could incorporate the huckleberry plant into their design. For example, you could use the berries to form the character's hair. On this page of sketches, the character is slim like the stem of the huckleberry plant, which balances against the roundness of the berries and leaves.

Use a drawing tool that you're comfortable with, as this will allow you to focus on the experimentation and idea creation. Try to keep a quick and loose creative flow to enable your mind to notice any ideas you like, which you can then develop later.

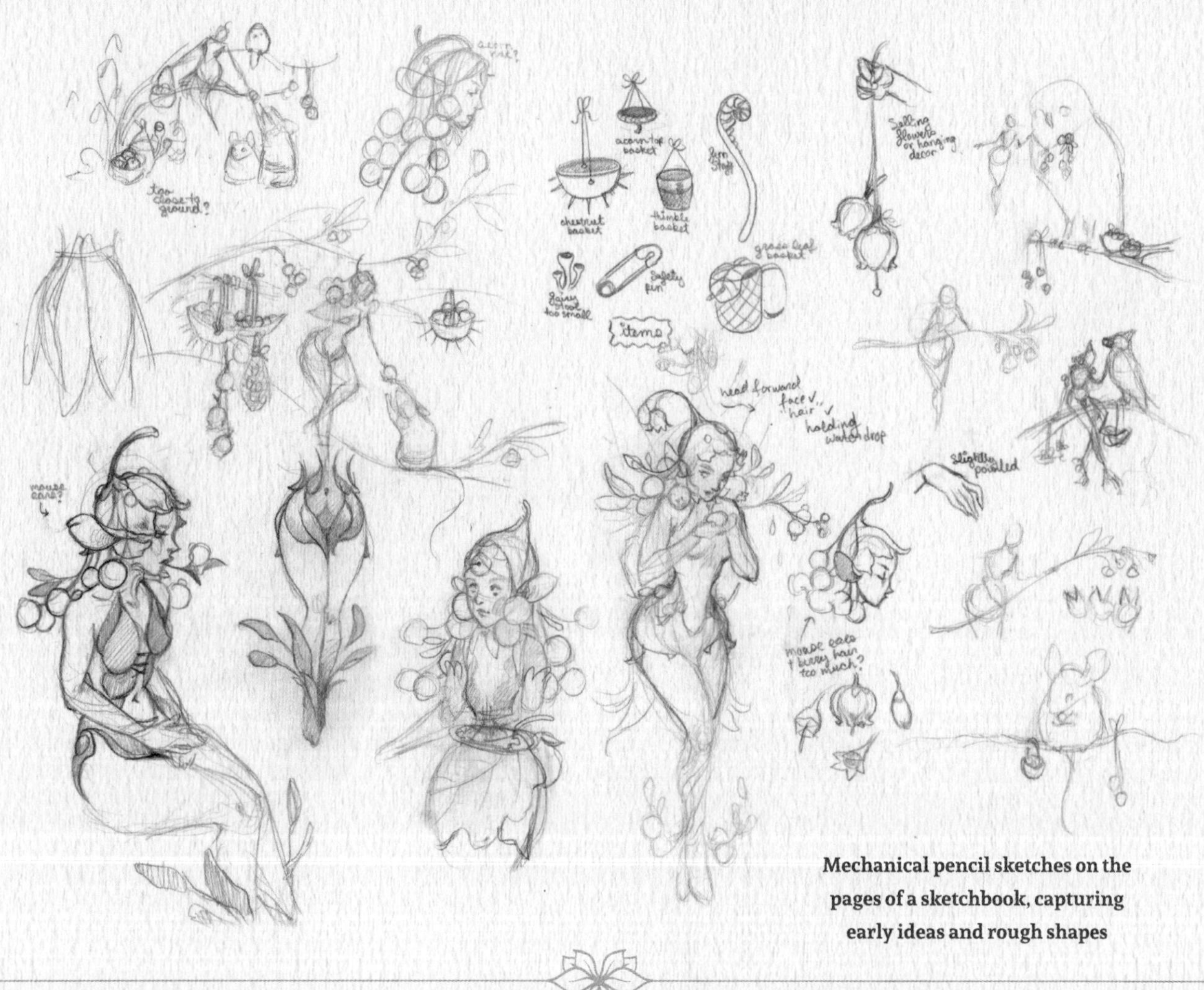

Mechanical pencil sketches on the pages of a sketchbook, capturing early ideas and rough shapes

HYPNAGOGIA

If you're really struggling for ideas, try to brainstorm just as you're falling asleep. When you're in a half-sleep state, it's possible to come up with some truly wild concepts. This state is called hypnagogia, which Salvador Dalí is known to have used to inspire his surreal paintings. He would lie down on his couch with a key in his hand and a metal pan placed strategically underneath it. If he started to fall asleep, he would drop the key in the pan and wake up. He'd then repeat this process of remaining in this half-sleep state until he came up with an idea.

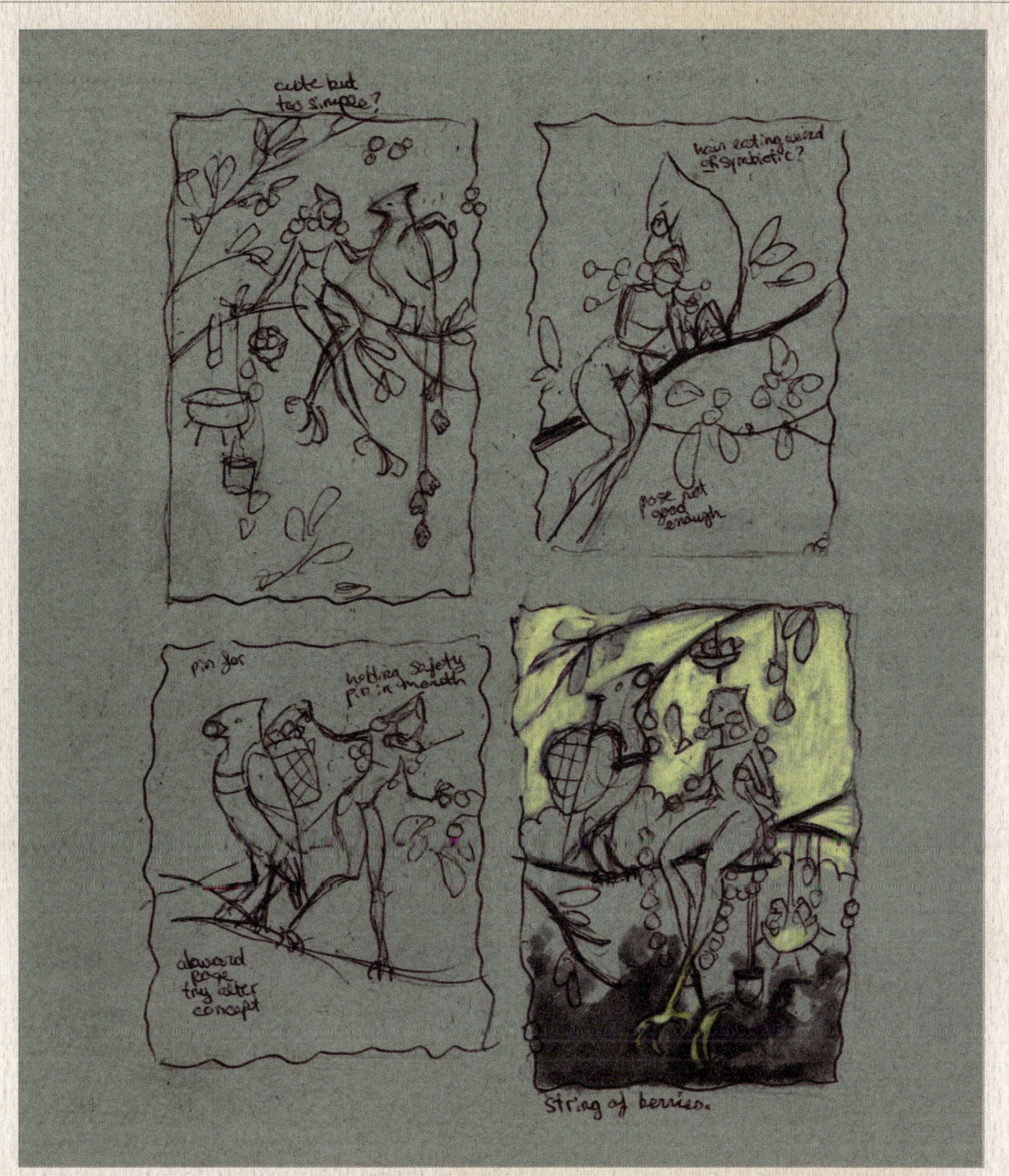

These thumbnails are drawn on grey-toned paper, as this allows you to add light and dark tones easily

THUMBNAILS

Now that you have a concept, you can tighten up your idea by creating a series of thumbnails. This step allows you to spend more time conveying your story by trying out different angles and layouts. Thumbnails are useful because they enable you to envision your idea on your canvas. Going forward, you can use them to create a compelling composition. You can also use your thumbnails to make sure your painting has a good balance of light tones, dark tones, and midtones. Avoid going into too much detail with your thumbnails, as they're meant to be rough and quick, almost like squinting your eyes at a finished painting.

COLOURS

Once you've chosen your concept and thumbnail, it's time to select a colour palette. Keep in mind the colours of the red huckleberry plant as you take out your tubes of paint – in this case, gouache – and arrange a colour palette by grouping the tubes of colours together. If you don't have a wide selection of colours, you can mix unique hues from primary colours and create swatches on paper to cut out and move around on your work surface to create various palettes. Alternatively, you can look on sites such as Pinterest, which has a huge selection of colour swatches to provide inspiration. Additionally, if you have access to a drawing tablet, you can take a photo of your thumbnail and plot out your colours on there.

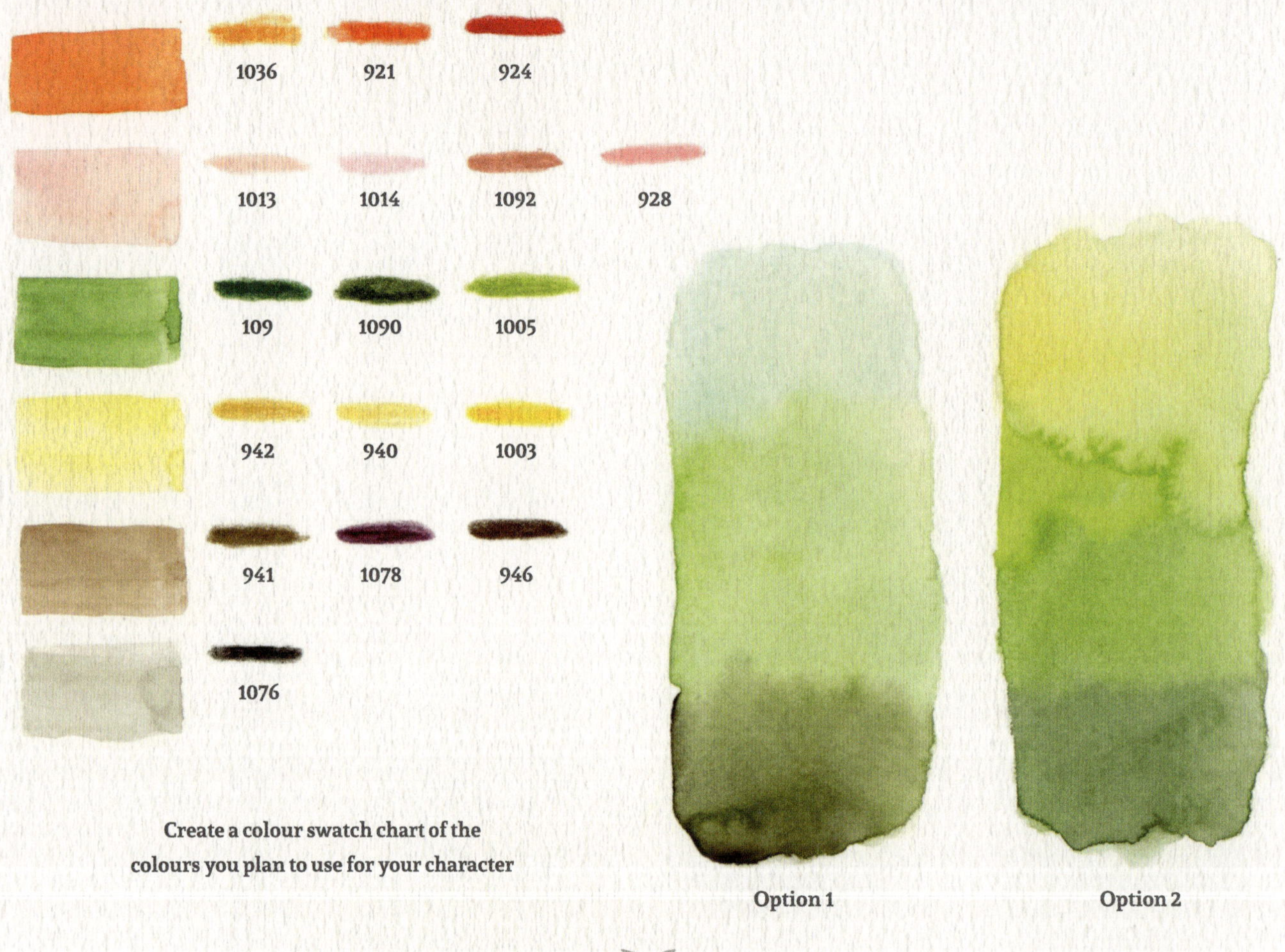

Create a colour swatch chart of the colours you plan to use for your character

Option 1

Option 2

CHOOSING COLOURS

Don't worry if you struggle to decide on a colour palette or if it takes you a while to work out which colours pair well together. This is a skill that takes practice. Try limiting your colours, as limitation inspires creativity and can lead to some beautiful colour palettes. Consider using colours in the same colour group, such as yellow, orange, and brown, or complementary colours, such as red and green. You could try sticking to three main colours, with one colour being the brightest and the others slightly more muted. This can prevent your painting from feeling too chaotic and bright, unless chaotic and bright is the effect you're after!

FRAMEWORK

The next step is to get your first marks down on paper. These marks will be the framework of your sketch. Start with lighter lines to explore and hint at some of the key subjects, thinking about how you can make the character's form and shape dynamic. The key here is to focus on creating shapes. Use your thumbnail as a reference, but know that you are free to change it if you need to. If you keep things loose from the beginning, it will create some breathing room for creativity and keep the final product from appearing stiff and lifeless.

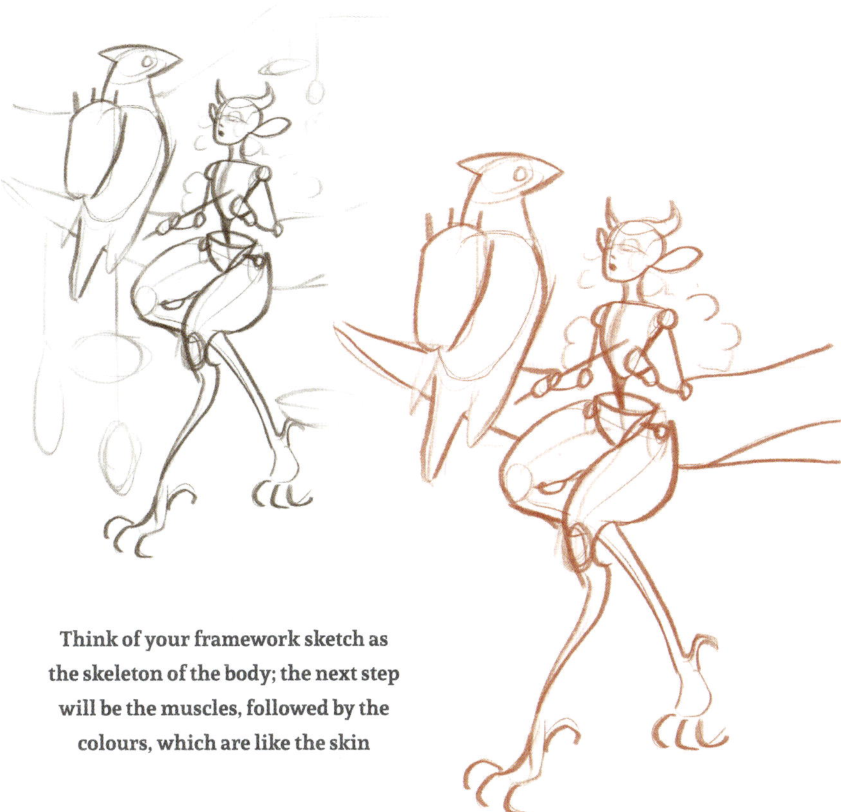

Think of your framework sketch as the skeleton of the body; the next step will be the muscles, followed by the colours, which are like the skin

FINAL SKETCH

Once you have a light pencil sketch of the framework, use a kneaded eraser to dab at the lines until they are barely visible. These will act as your guidelines. Next, begin to sketch in details with a heavier hand than in the previous step. Use darker, heavier lines for the more important, definitive lines. Make use of your kneaded eraser as you work to dab away any lines you don't need. Take the time to really solidify the concept by drawing long gloves and puffy pantaloons that mimic the shape of huckleberry blossoms. You could also add a small twist to this character by giving them some features that mimic the fauna that eat the berries.

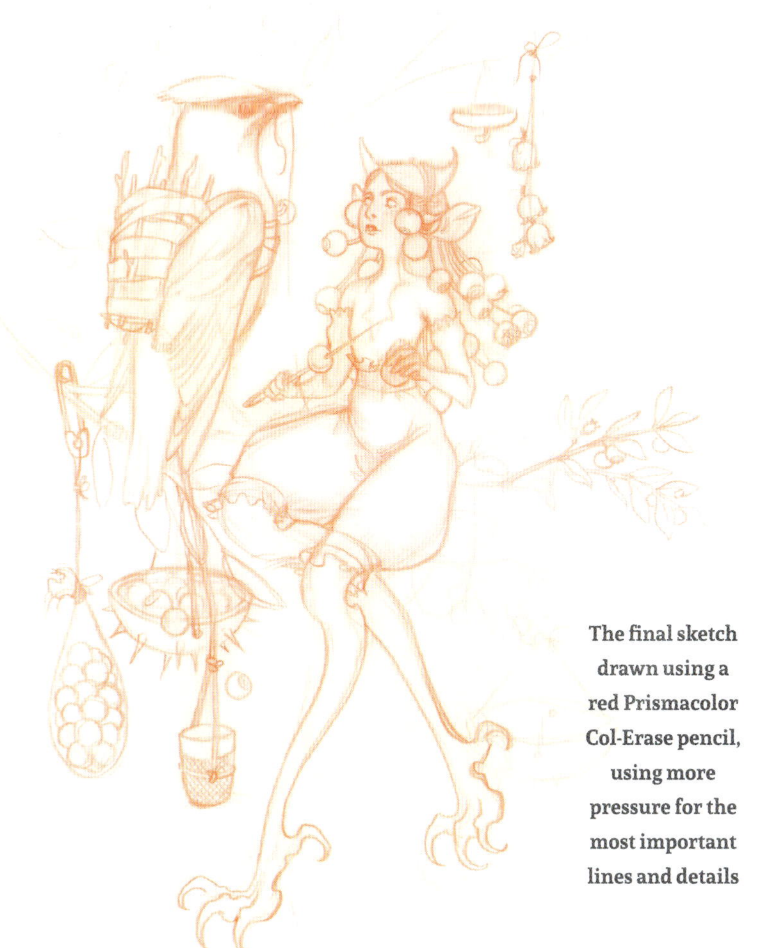

The final sketch drawn using a red Prismacolor Col-Erase pencil, using more pressure for the most important lines and details

BACKGROUND BASE

For the base layer, use colour swatch option 2 that was created on page 244. This palette is similar to the colours of the huckleberry leaves. You can use watercolour or watered-down gouache for your base, paired with a very fluffy brush that can hold a decent amount of paint. Watercolour can create natural textures that can inspire new focal points in your painting. It helps to pre-mix your colours in wells, as this will allow you to work quickly while the paper is wet. One approach is to let this base layer be a little messy, while still loosely adding small strokes to hint at the foliage in the distance. As you're going to add layers on top of this that are cleaner and more detailed, letting this base layer be slightly untidy will create contrast and interest.

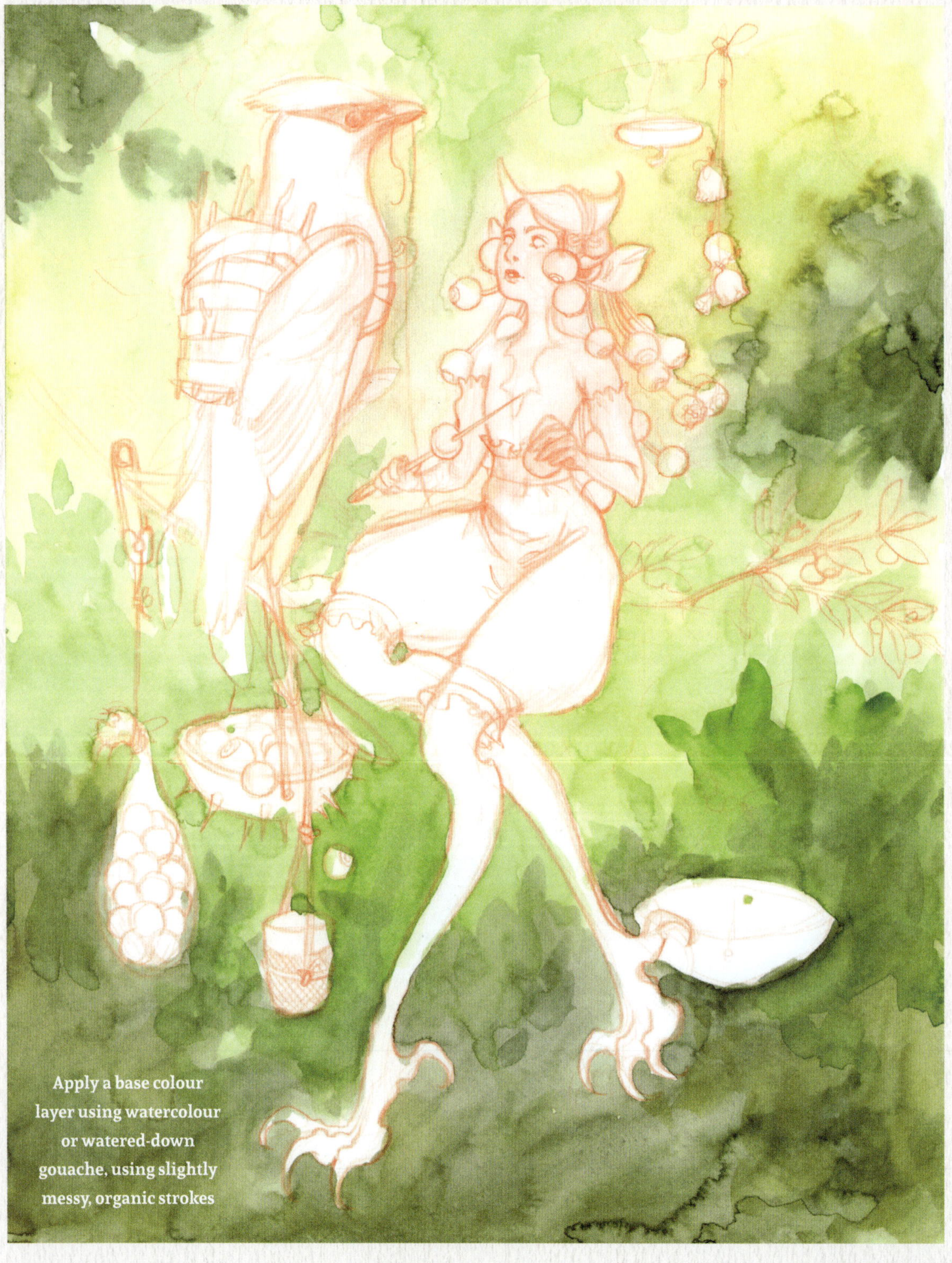

Apply a base colour layer using watercolour or watered-down gouache, using slightly messy, organic strokes

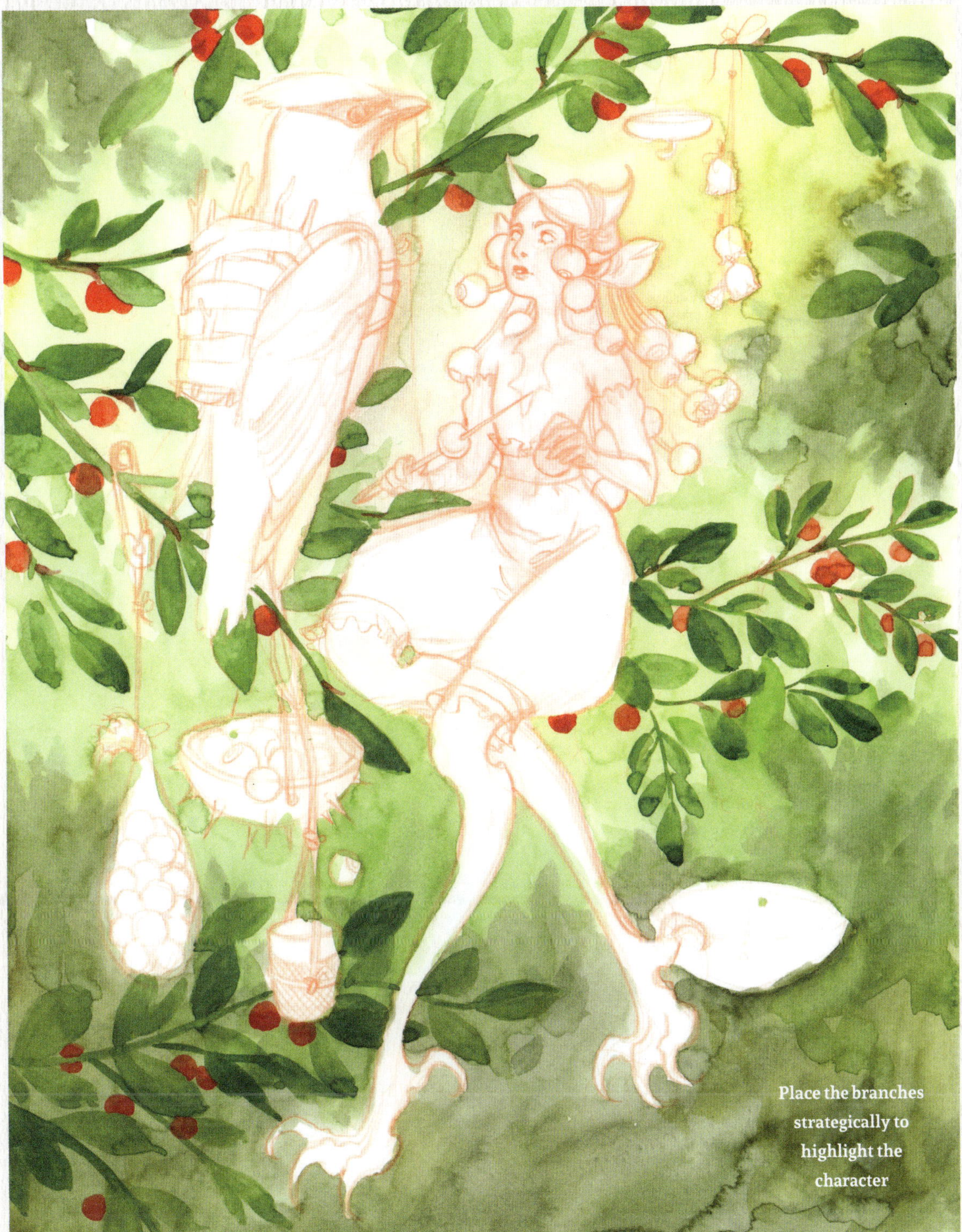

Place the branches strategically to highlight the character

FOLIAGE BASE LAYER

Once you've created a loose background and it's dried, it's time to paint on the first layer of foliage. It can be helpful to wait and see what the dried base layer looks like before placing the branches. As the base layer is light, you can paint directly on top of it with ease. This is much simpler than painting around the sketches of the leaves, which would be much more time-consuming. Watercolour is wonderful for painting plants, because its natural gradients so easily duplicate the look of organic subjects. Using a round brush will enable you to focus on creating the oval-shaped leaves of the plant. Remember to position the leaves at different angles to make the foliage look natural.

BASKET & BIRD BASE

Using washes of watercolour, lay down the first layer of the baskets and bird. Cedar waxwings are beautiful birds that love red huckleberries. They have colourful yet muted plumage, meaning their colours won't draw any attention away from the huckleberry character. Combining muted colours with more saturated colours can provide a pleasing balance in a painting, so consider using the waxwing's muted tones to provide some breathing room in this bright painting. An added bonus is that this bird has tiny red wax tips on their secondary feathers.

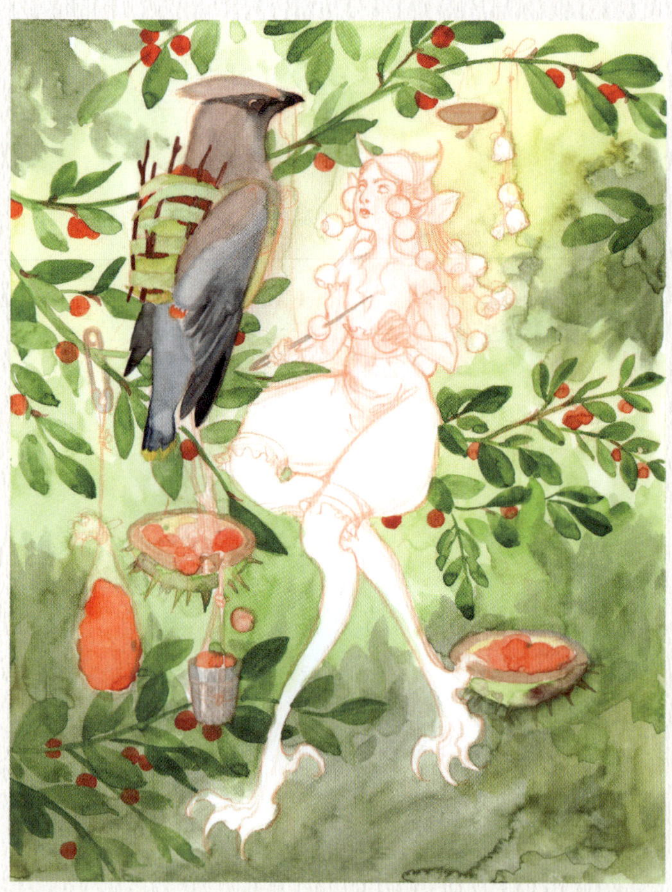

Use a wet-on-wet technique to create smooth gradients and convincing bruising on chestnut shells

CHARACTER BASE

Now you have the base laid down everywhere else, you can begin the first layer of the character. Select a mid-light pink skin tone that mimics the berries enough that they match, but not dark enough that the skin blends in too much with the colour of the berries in the character's hair. Bring in some yellows to hint at the yellow stamen of the blossoms. The shirt colour is too dark and doesn't match the theme, so that will be changed in a future step. If you keep the base layers light, you can build them up to darker colours. If you're unsure what colour to paint an item, simply leave it blank and paint it later.

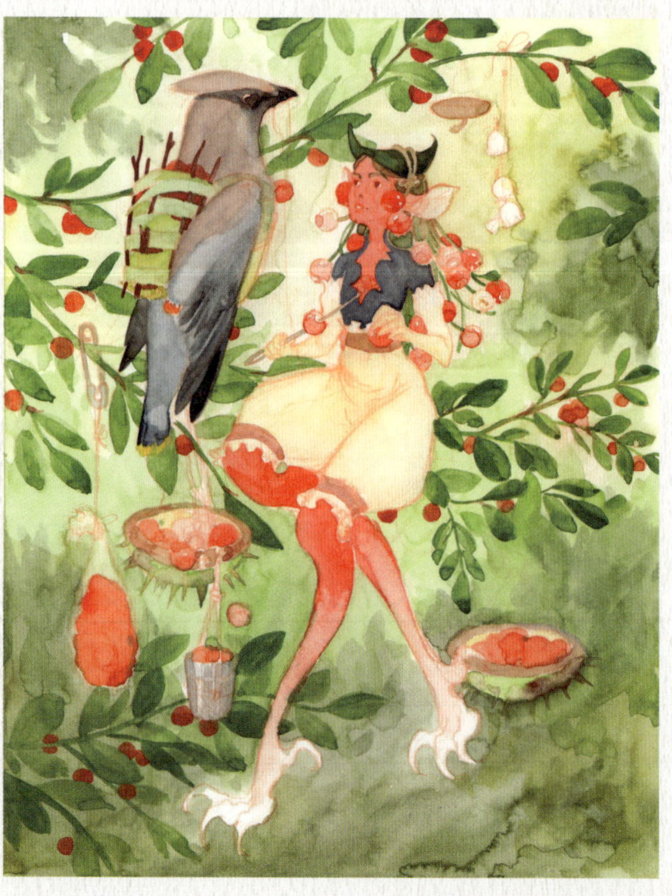

Things might look a little weird at this stage, but have faith in the process!

CASTING SHADOWS

Now that you have a good base laid out, you can begin to introduce shadows. Start by deciding on the direction of the light source. Since this character is in a forest, the light will be sunlight filtering through the canopy above. Take some time to add shadows to all of the subjects in the painting, including the foliage. You might think it would be best to use a watered-down black for the shadows, but the best shadows are made from a light wash of colour. The most common shadow colour is purple, but you could use a watered-down magenta, blue, or something else entirely, depending on the scene you're creating. After painting in the shadows, use the purple to darken some of the foliage near the base to create more dark tones in the painting.

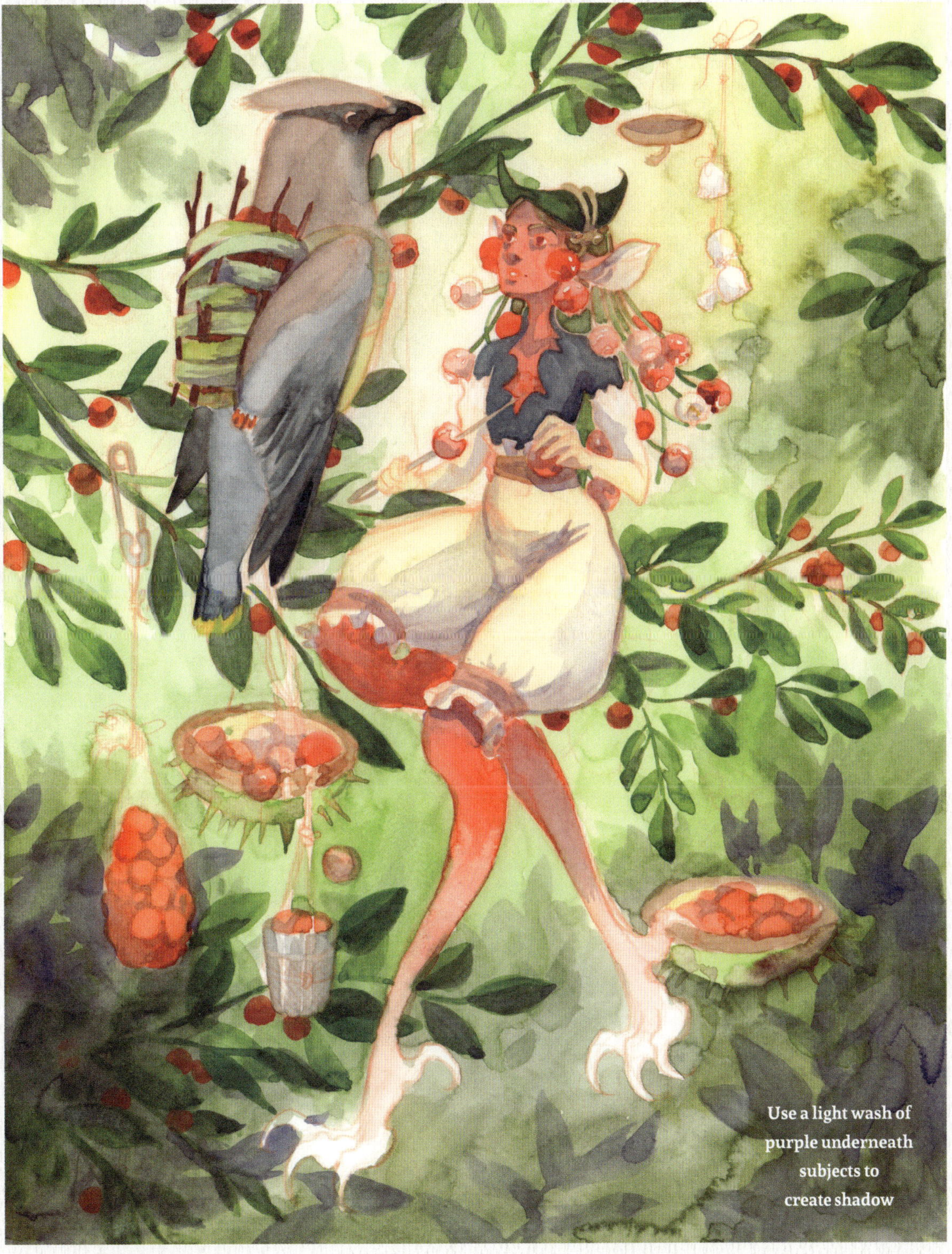

Use a light wash of purple underneath subjects to create shadow

ADDING DETAILS

You can now begin to add detail to your painting, using gouache to increase vibrancy and define shapes. Start texturizing the berries with shine and add more depth to your colours. Work on painting some detail into the character's face, such as detailing their eyes and lips in red to keep their face looking as close to the huckleberry as possible. Paint some highlights and details onto the leaves and begin to string together any loose parts. Add little pink stripes at the end of the character's ears to mimic the pink stripes on the tips of huckleberry blossoms. It can be helpful to leave the berry beads until this step in case you decide you want to drape the berries over something. This step comes down to what feels right to you, so trust your gut and have fun with it.

ERASING PAINT

When you're painting with gouache or watercolour, it's possible to erase if you make a mistake or there's something you don't like. If watercolour is still wet, you can lightly dab up the water with a paper towel to remove the pigment. Even if gouache is dry, you can add water and pick up the pigment with a brush or paper towel. This is why it's best to invest in good quality thick paper, as it will stand up better to being dabbed. Blue paper towel works best, as its fibres don't stick to the paper and it lasts a long time.

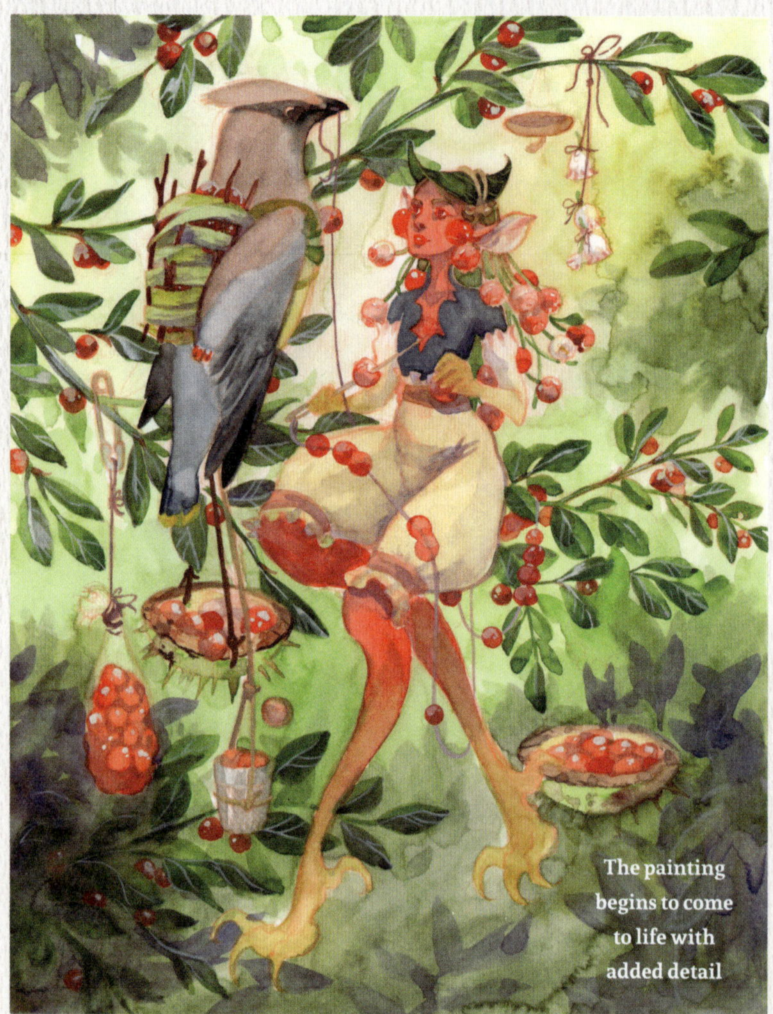

The painting begins to come to life with added detail

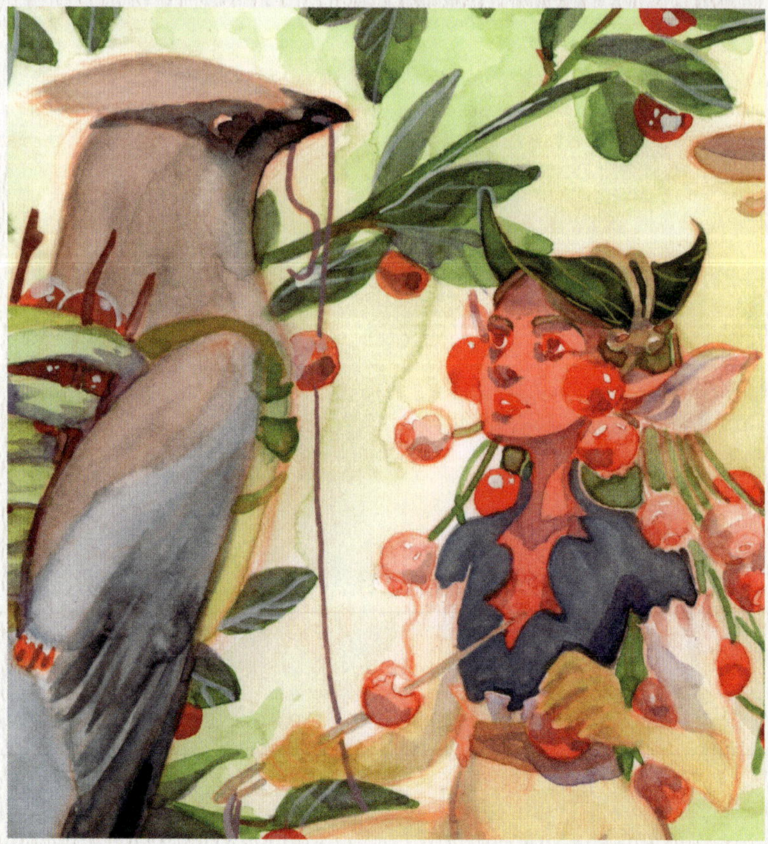

LINES

The next step is to define your characters and really make the objects stand out using line work. This step is optional, but it will help to bring your character to life! You can use pens, gouache, or coloured pencils; this example will use coloured pencils. Try using various colours for your lines instead of just one colour or black. If you look at the trousers and gloves of this character, you can see the colours have been swapped in different areas to give more life to the lines. Next, exaggerate the spindly nature of the character's legs by creating twisting lines running along them. The long legs hint at the long, thin features of the huckleberry stems.

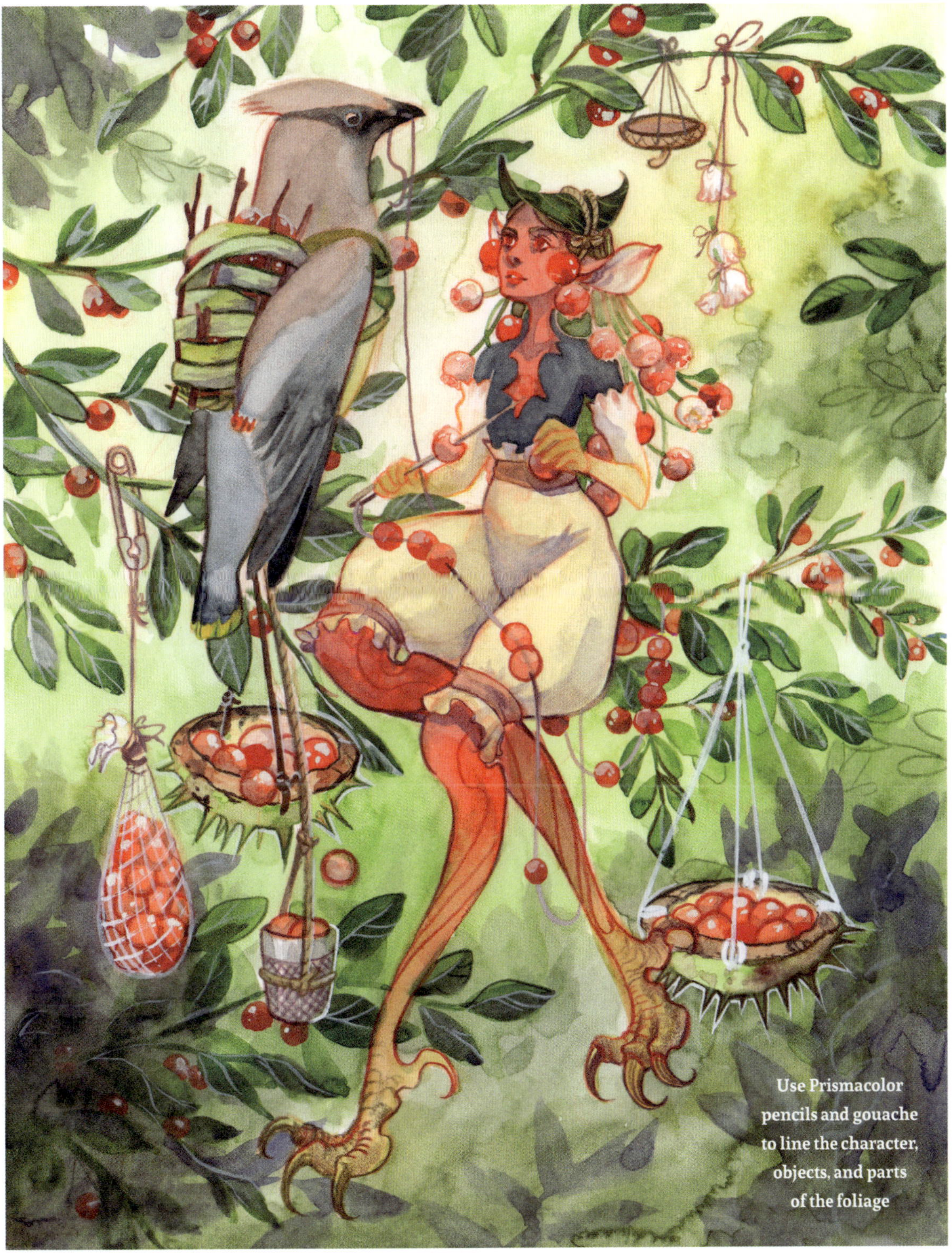

Use Prismacolor pencils and gouache to line the character, objects, and parts of the foliage

FINAL DETAILS

Use this step to add highlights and make any final edits. For example, clean up lines, check for tangents, and make sure you didn't miss or skip over anything important earlier. If you painted over any areas that you want to appear as shiny, simply add some white gouache straight out of the tube to make it fully opaque. The translucent quality of the red huckleberries captured in the hair is one element that works particularly well. The surrounding foliage and background elements all help to tell her story. The character's design was inspired by more than just the look of the plant, but by the whole ecosystem it lives in. Brainstorming the character's design and surroundings is always a fun challenge and can lead to boundless unique designs.

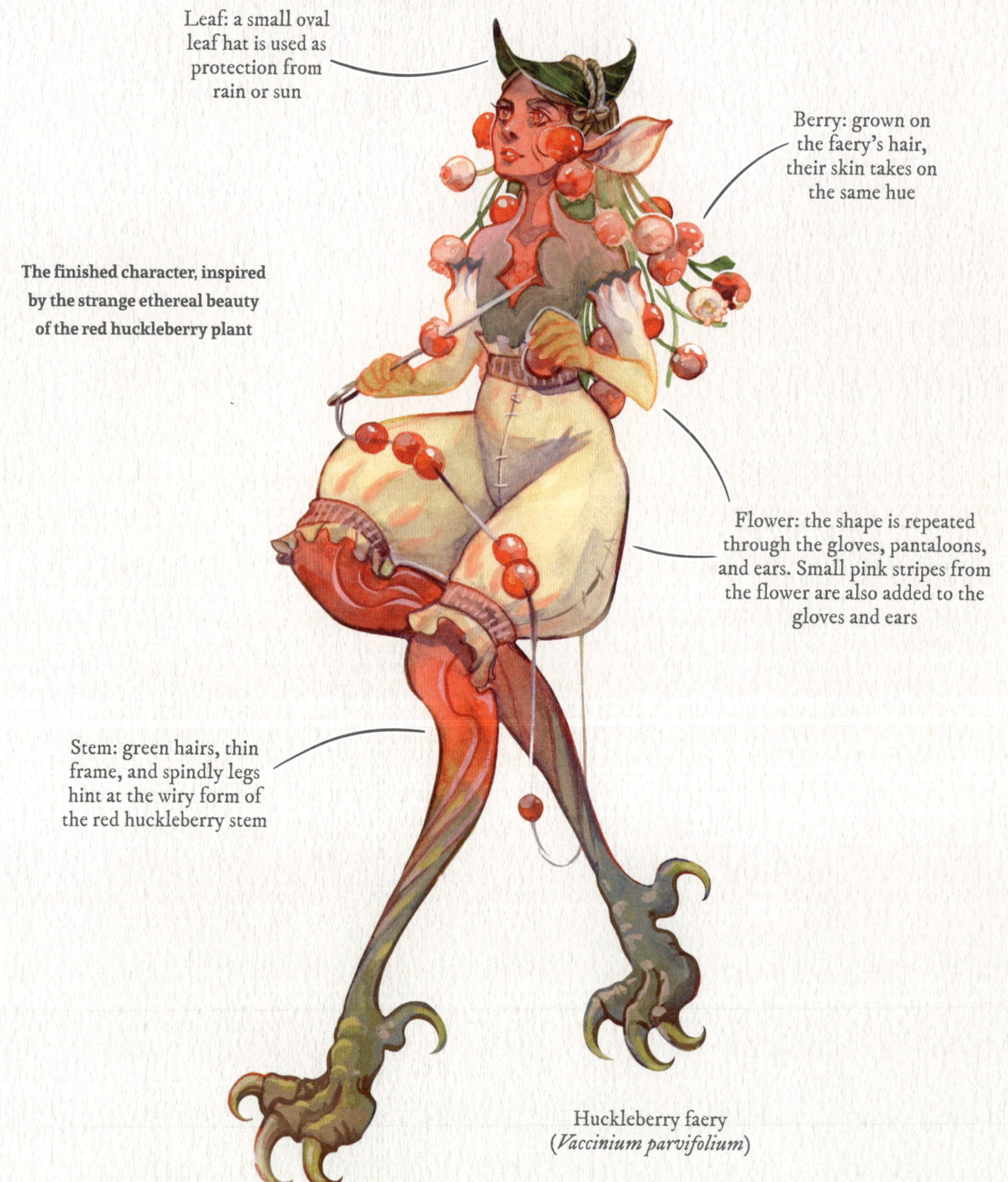

The finished character, inspired by the strange ethereal beauty of the red huckleberry plant

Huckleberry faery (*Vaccinium parvifolium*)

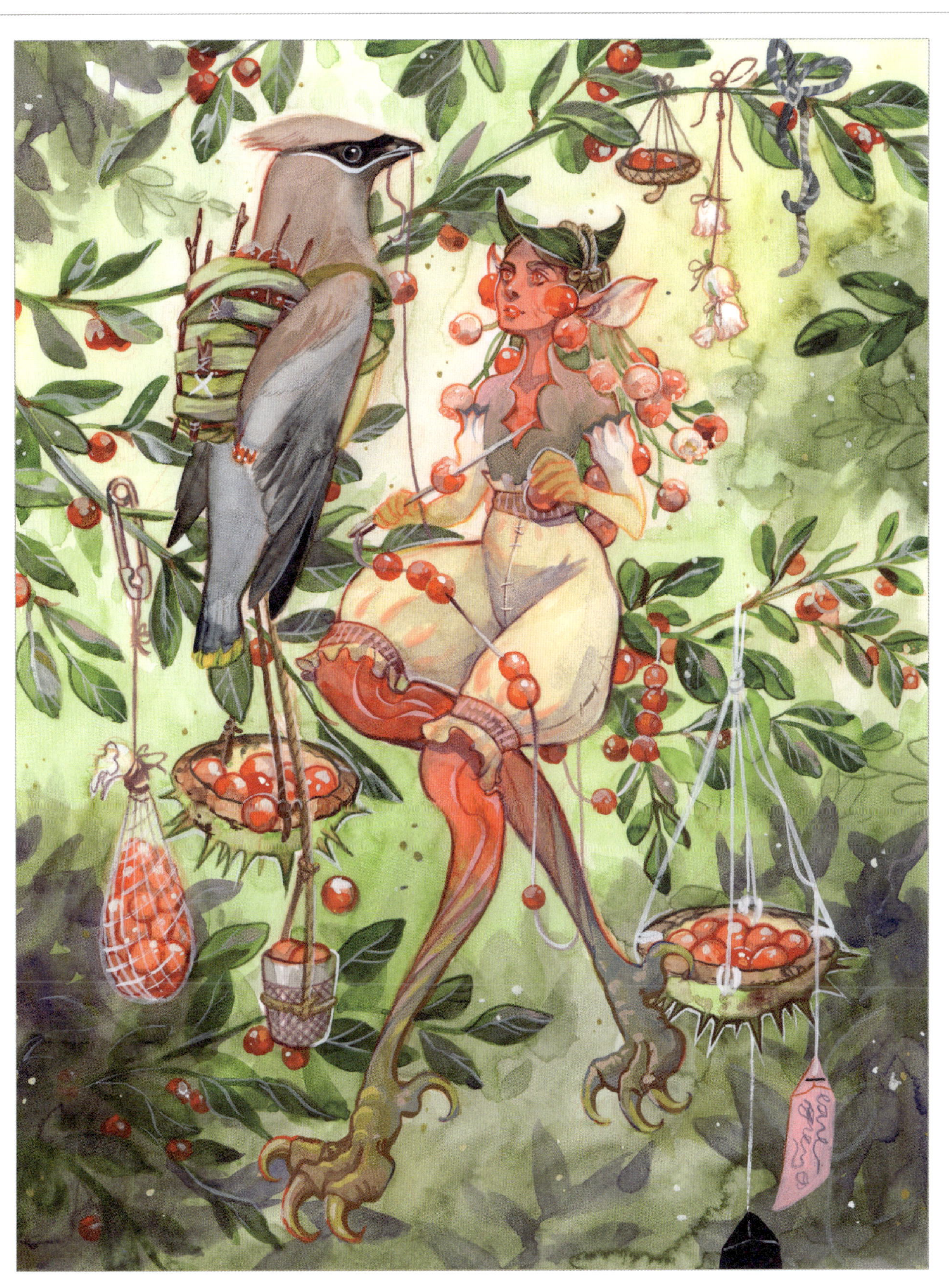

HUCKLEBERRY FAERY

Final image © Audra Auclair

GALLERY

256
KACEY LYNN BROWN

258
NORA POTWORA

260
SIMONE GRÜNEWALD

262
KIRI LEONARD

264
CHRIS HONG

266
CORAH LOUISE

268
OGNJEN SPORIN

270
IRIS COMPIET

272
SIBYLLINE MEYNET

274
ESTER CONCEICAO

276
FEEFAL

278
LARA GEORGIA CARSON

280
ROMA GEWSKA

282
DAVID NAVARRO

284
DOMINIQUE VASSIE

286
ELIZA IVANOVA

288
AUDRA AUCLAIR

KACEY LYNN BROWN

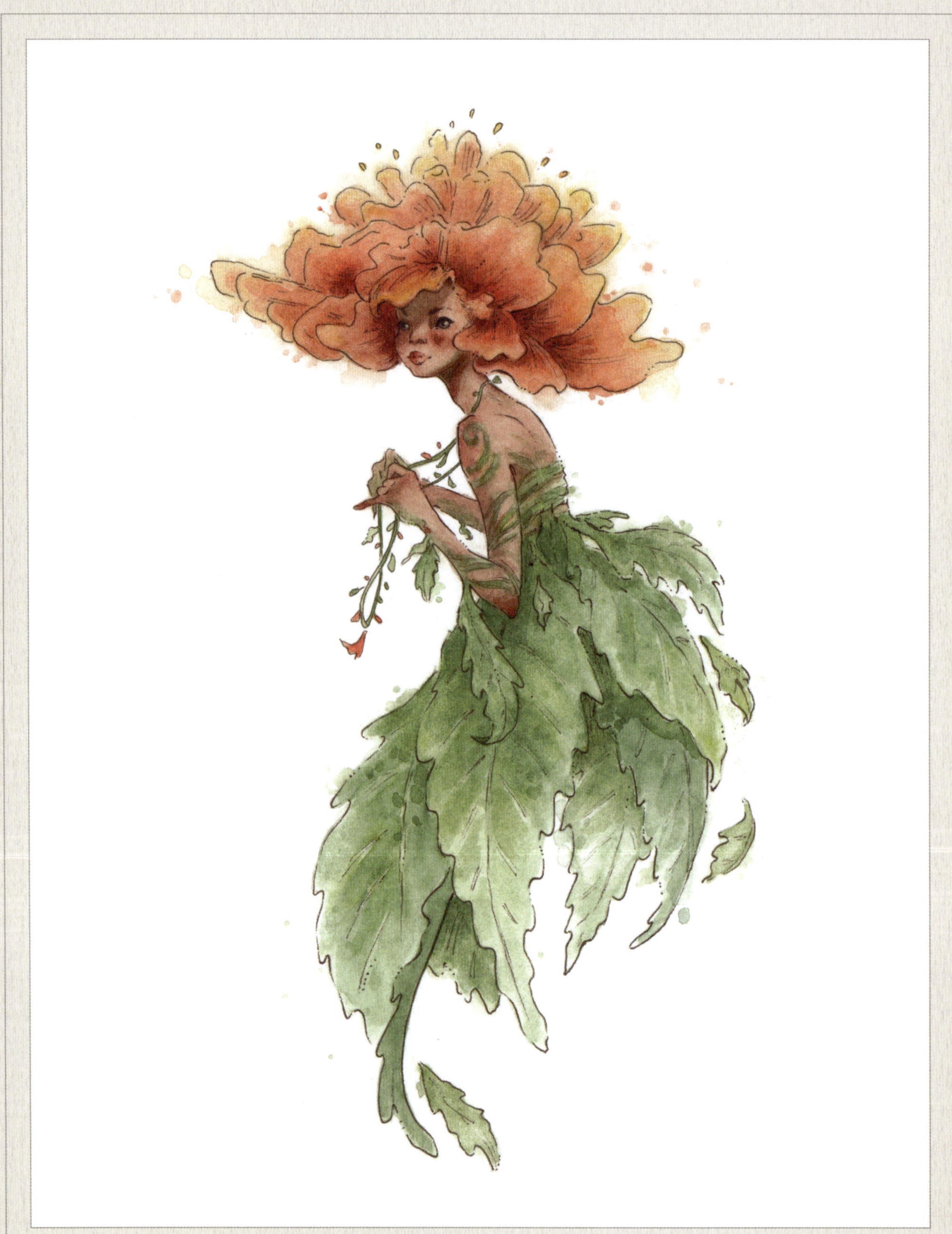

Marigold Flower Fae

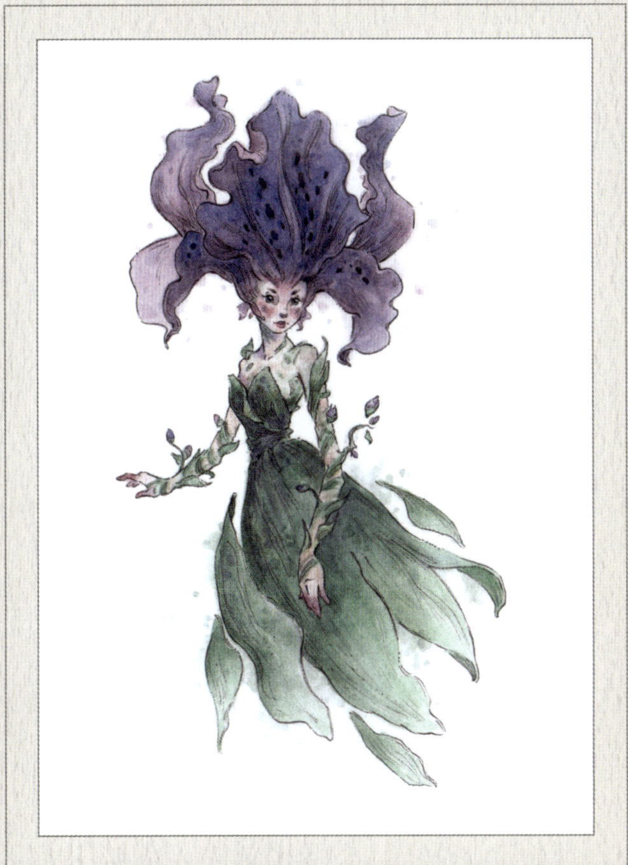

Iris Flower Fae

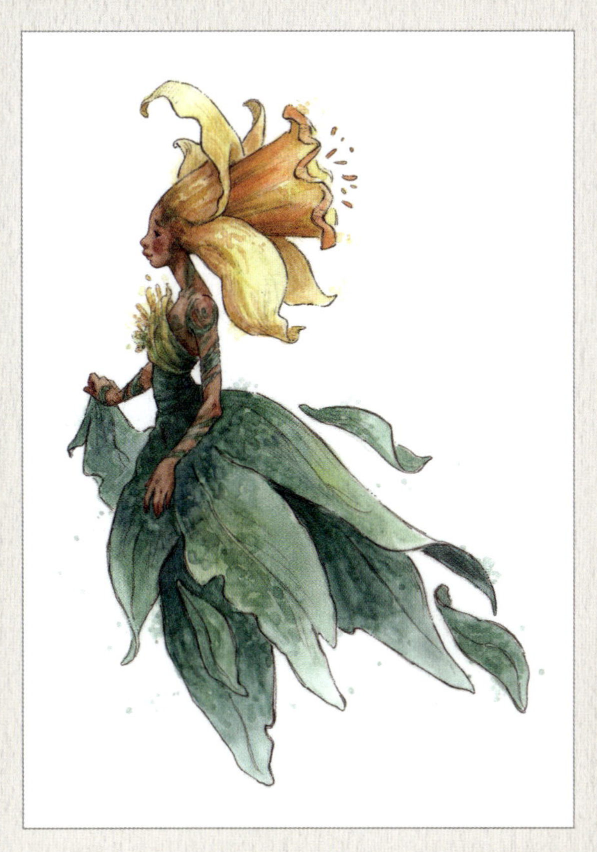

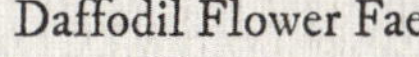

Daffodil Flower Fae

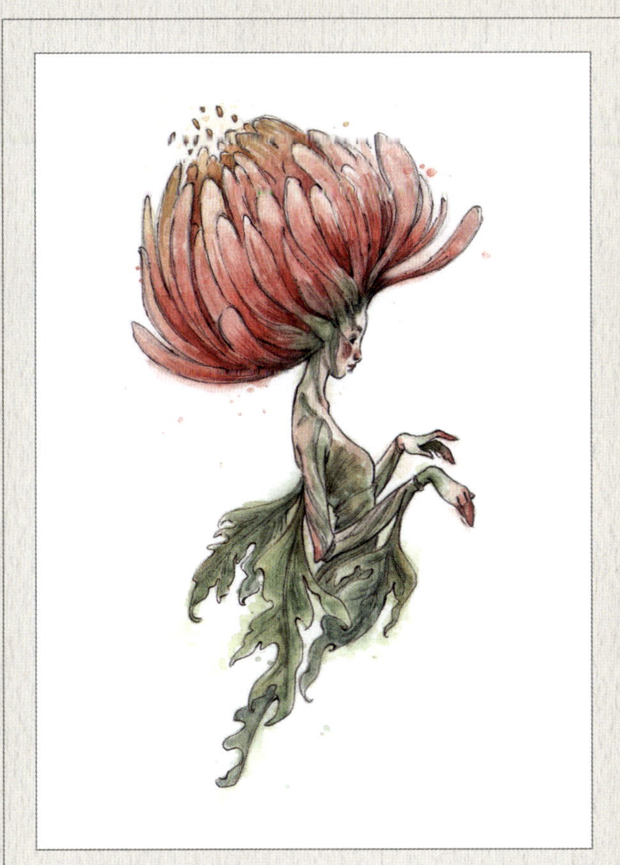

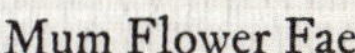

Mum Flower Fae

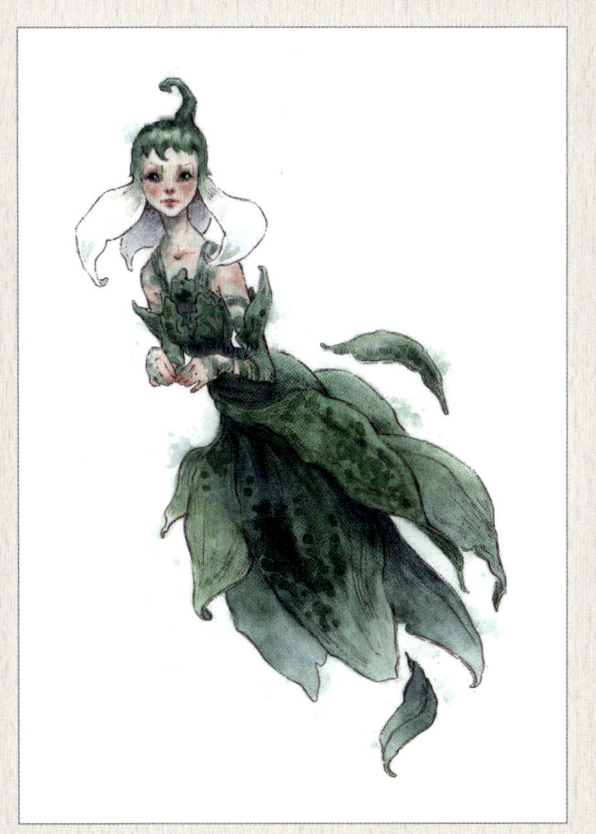

Snowdrop Flower Fae

NORA POTWORA

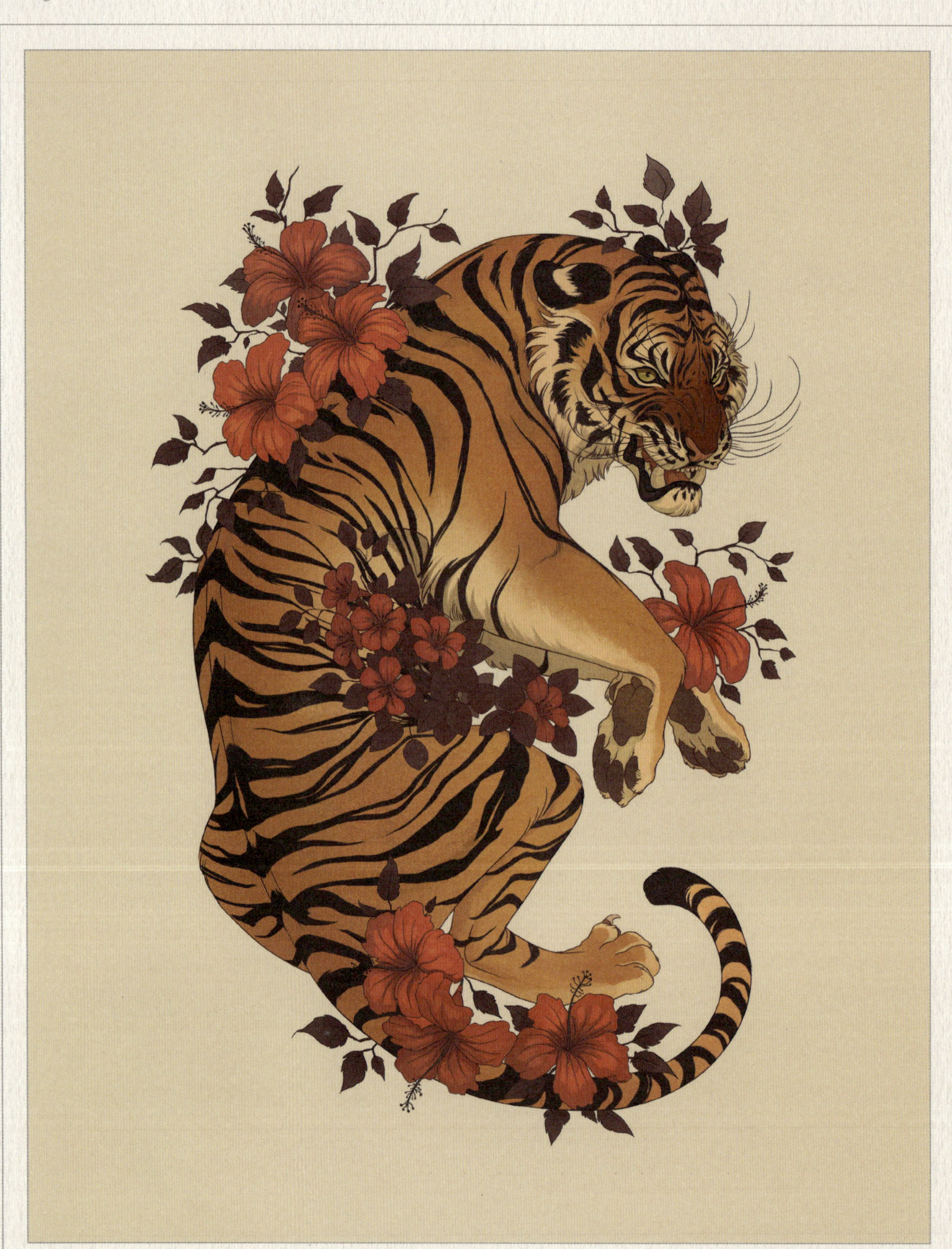

Hibiscus Tiger

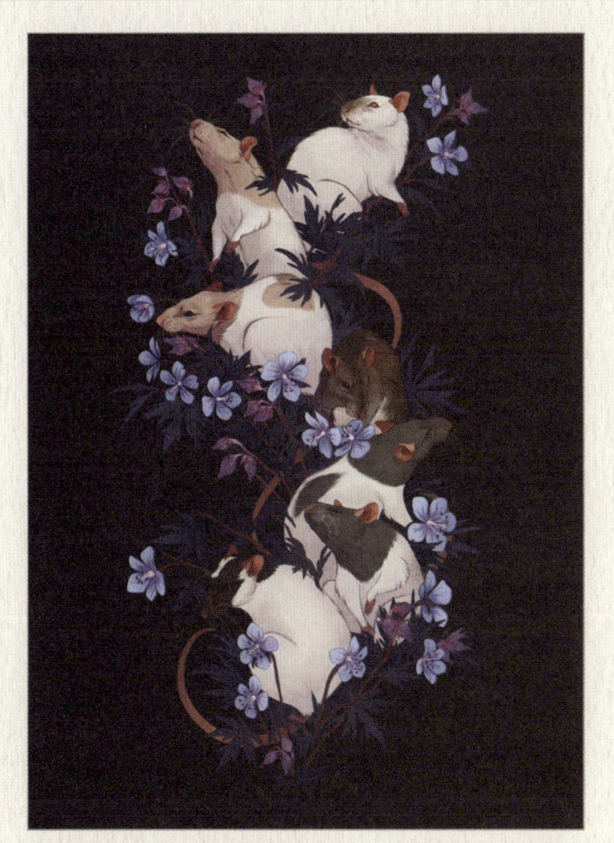

Harmony

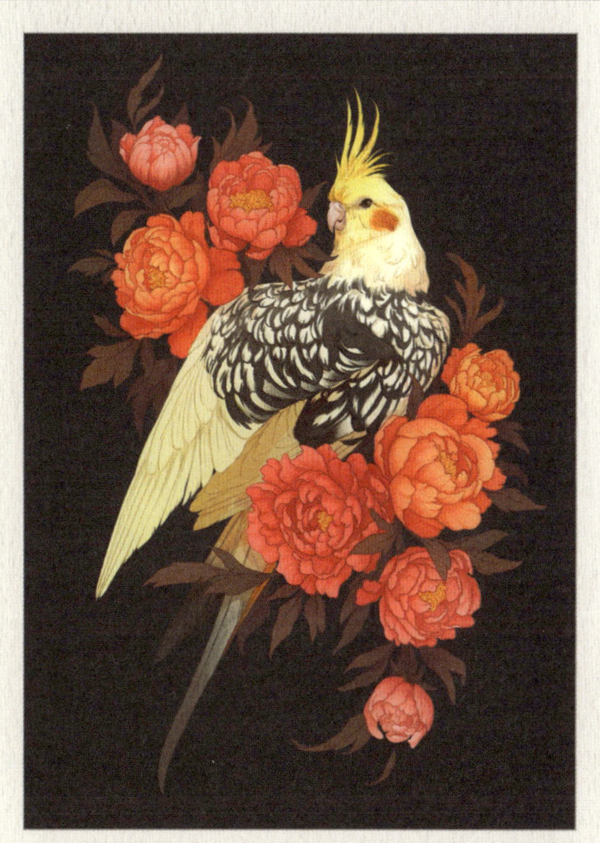

Peony Cockatiel

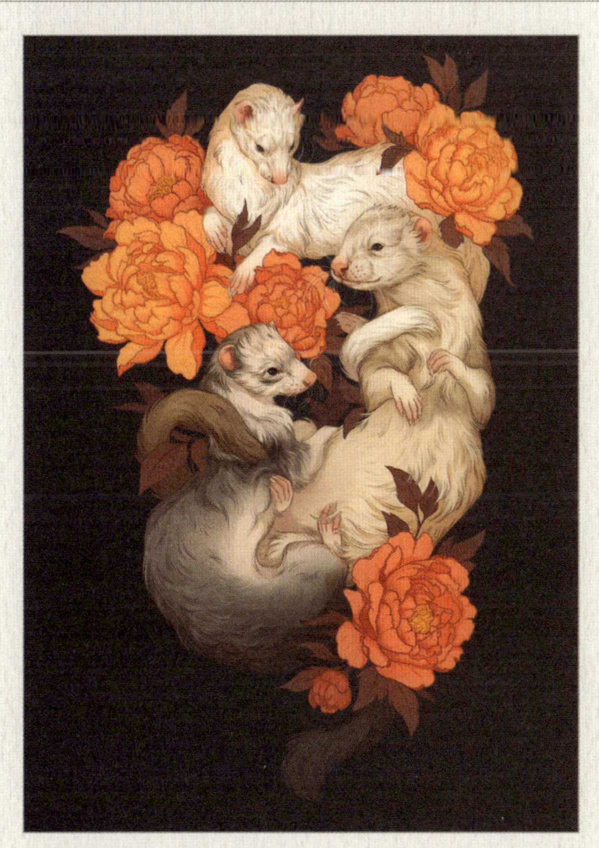

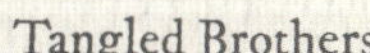

Tangled Brothers

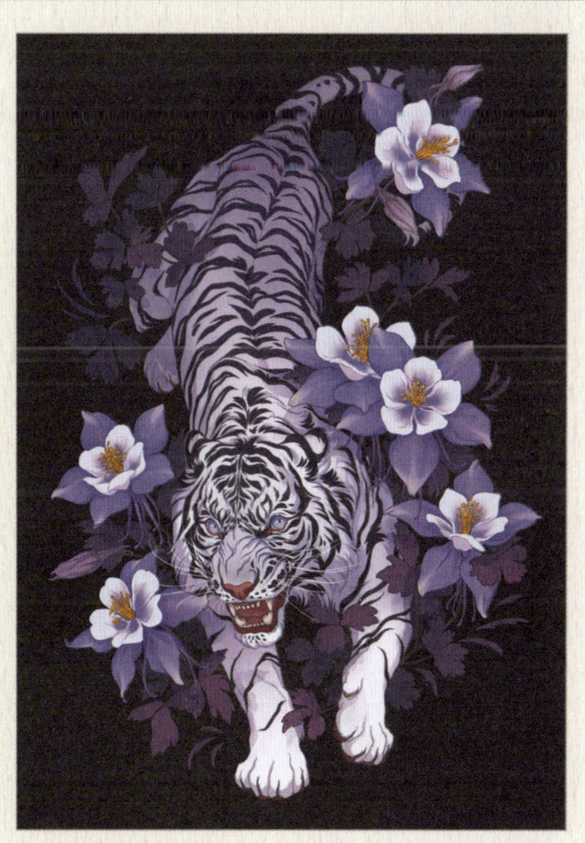

Shades of Purple

SIMONE GRÜNEWALD

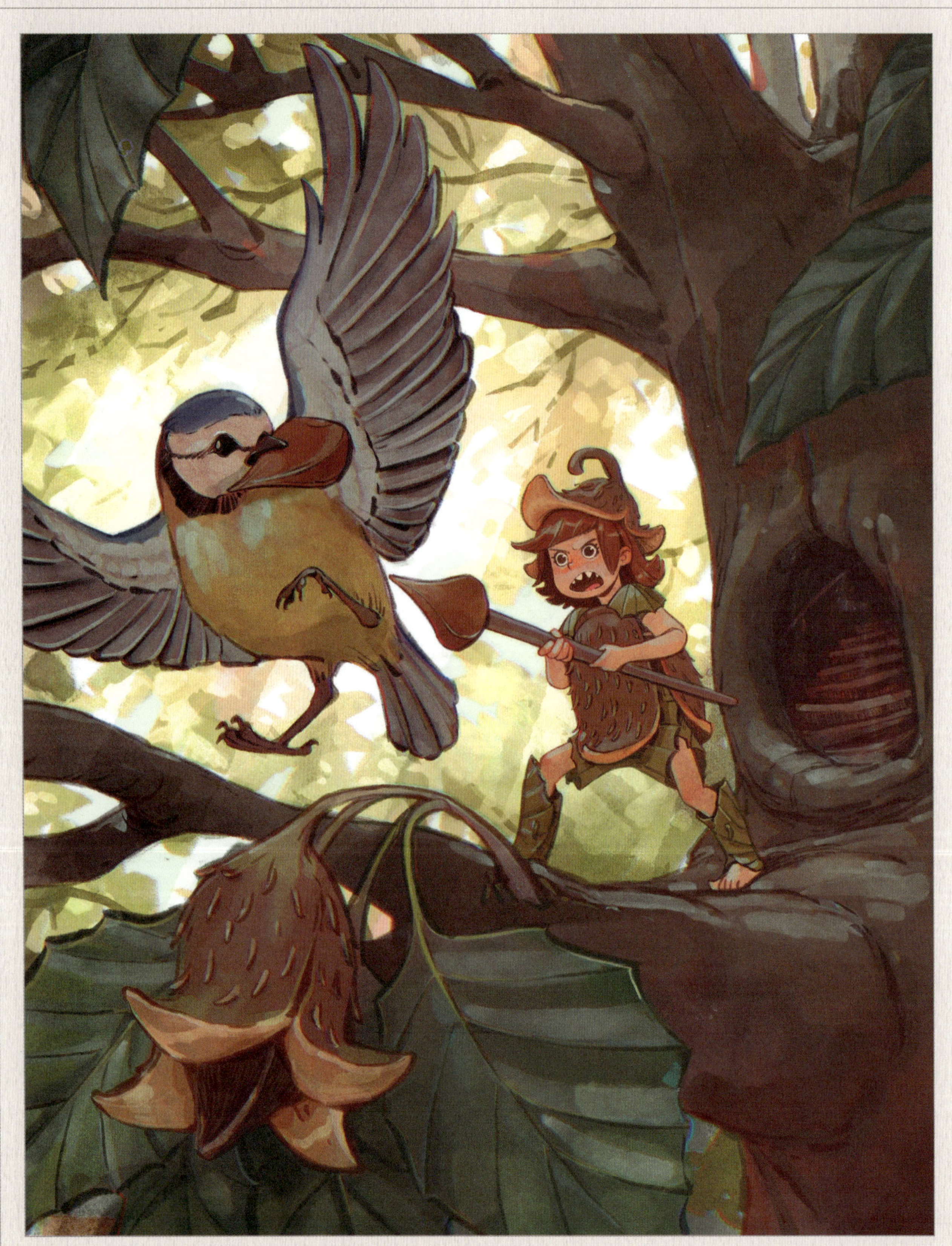

Thieving Bluetit

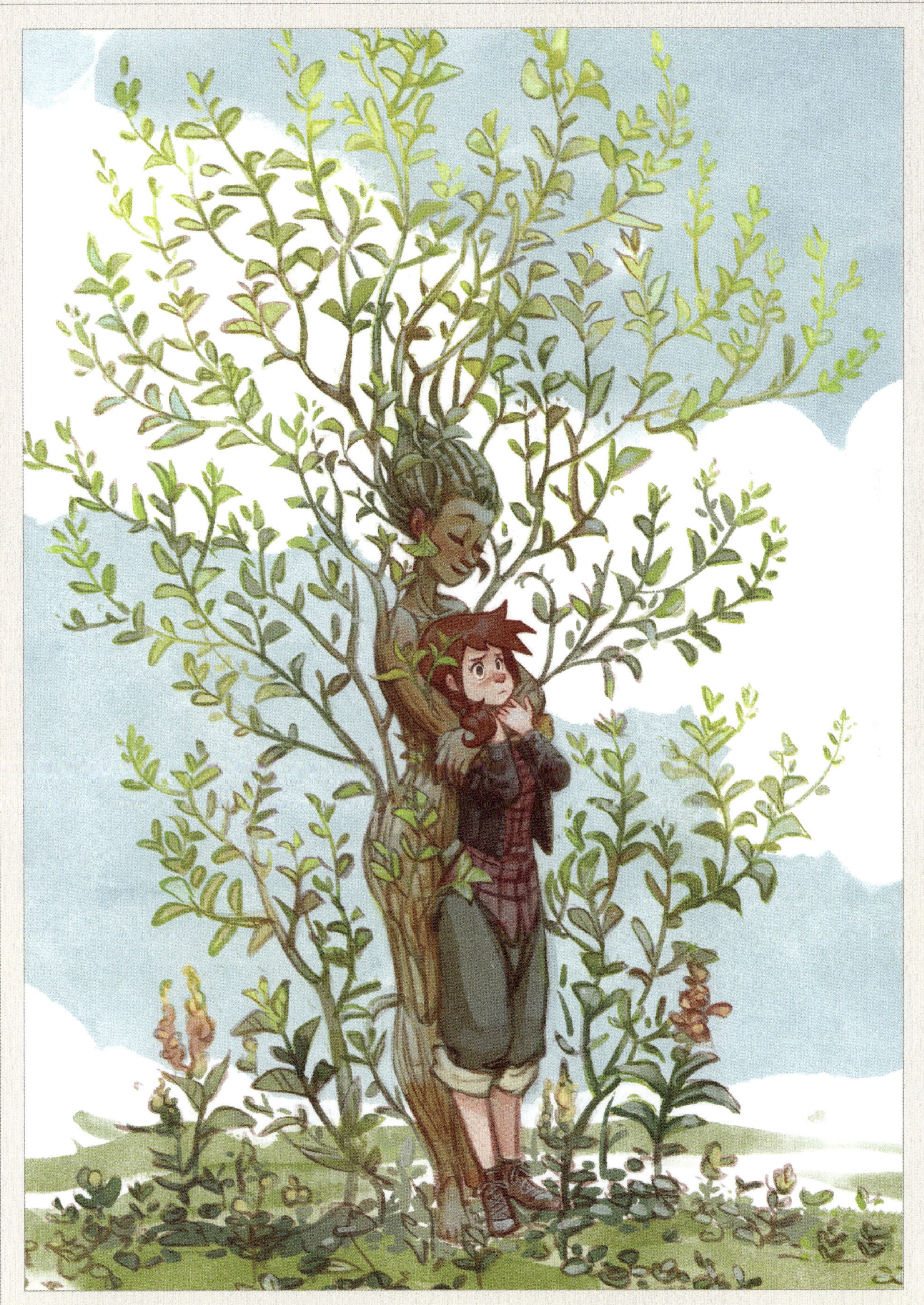

Mother Nature

KIRI LEONARD

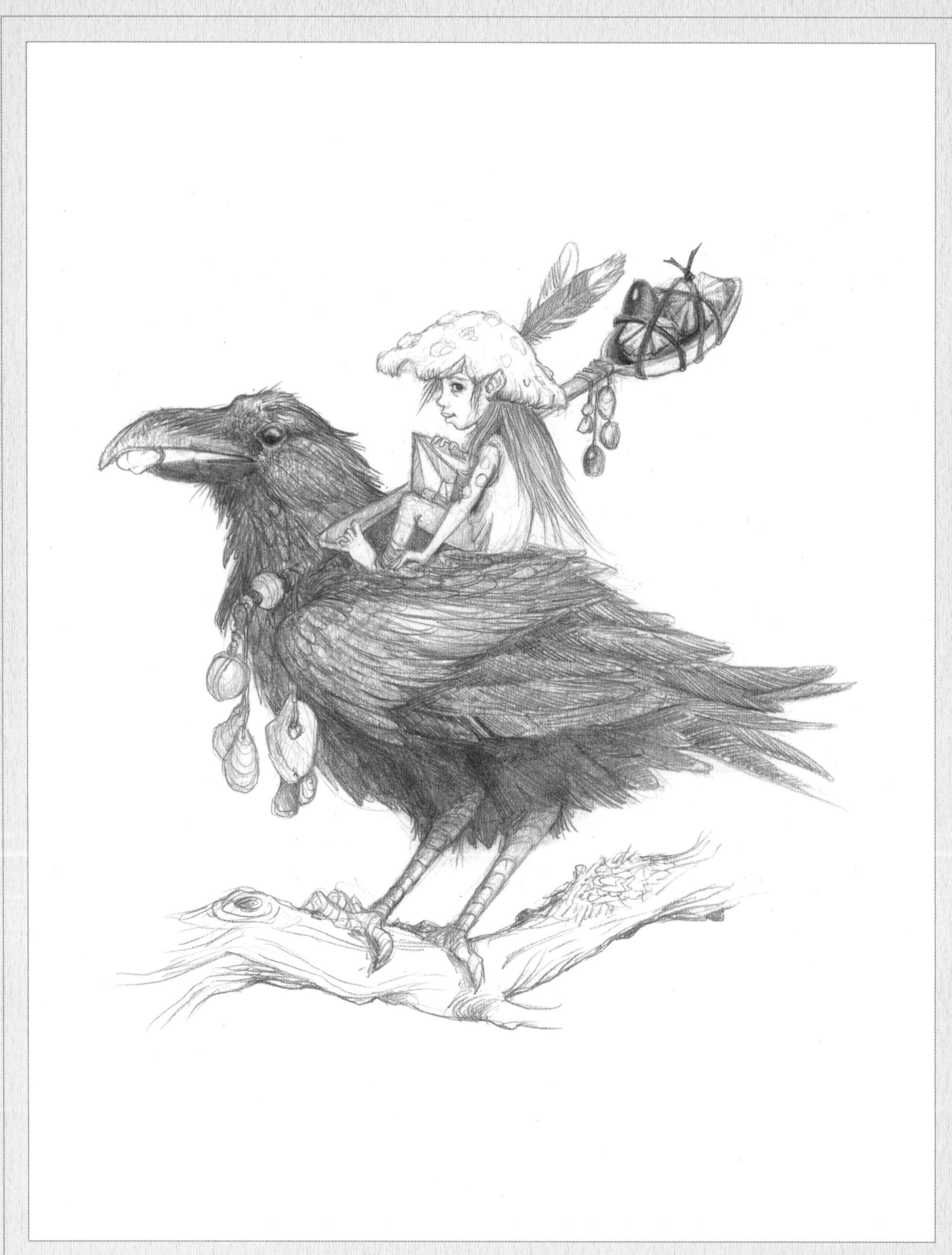

Oarika and Giberdyflibbert

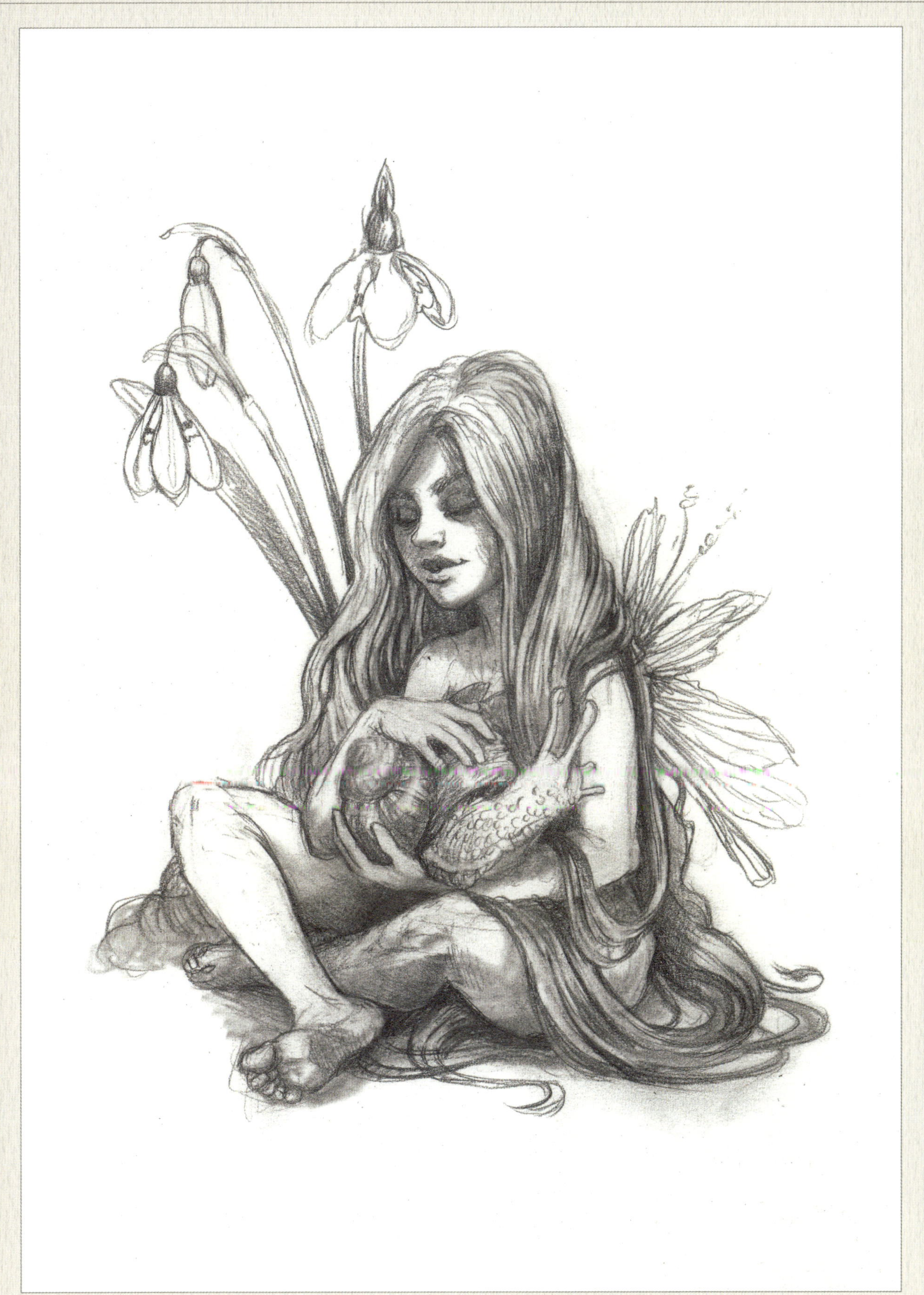

Fairy Rest

CHRIS HONG

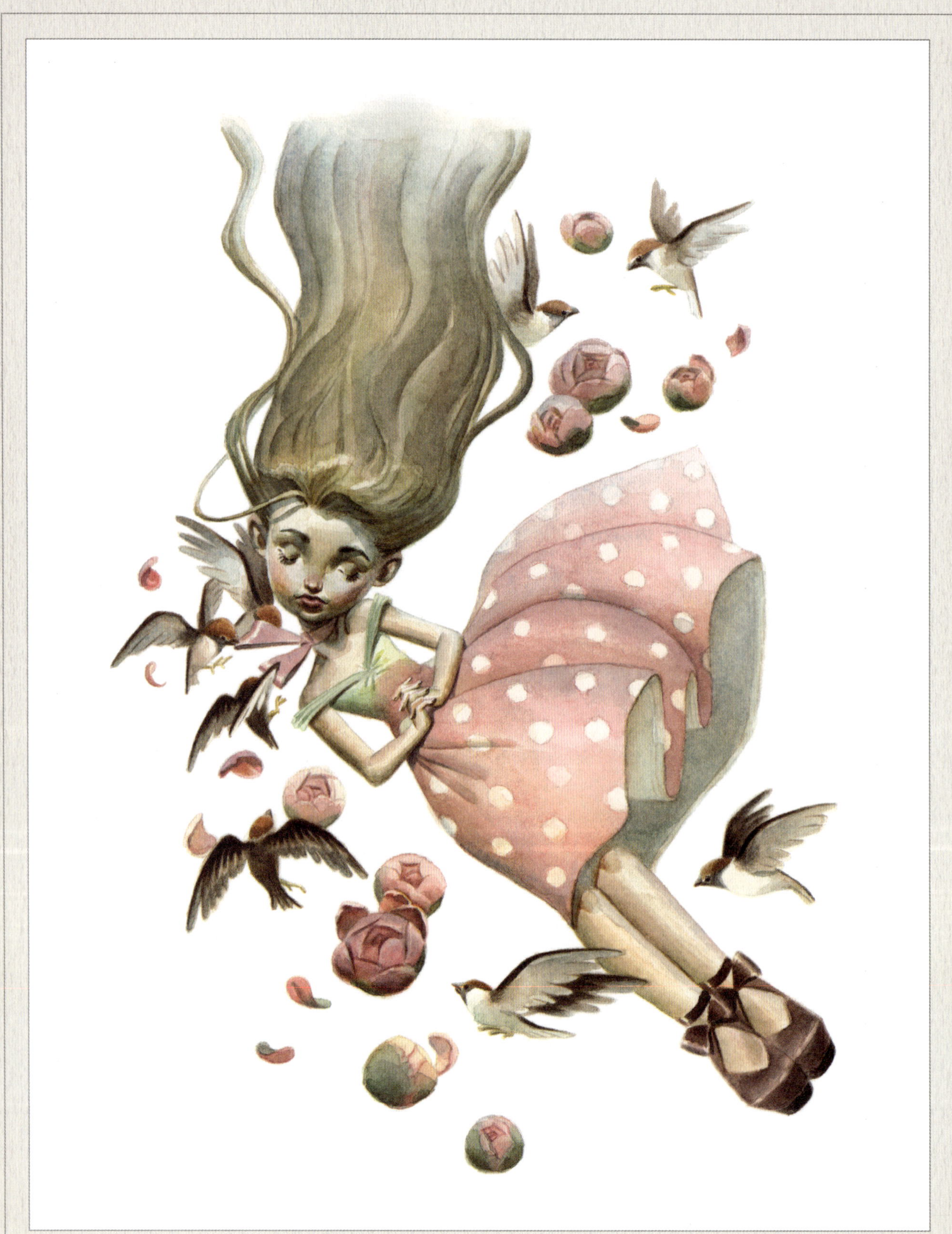

Sparrow

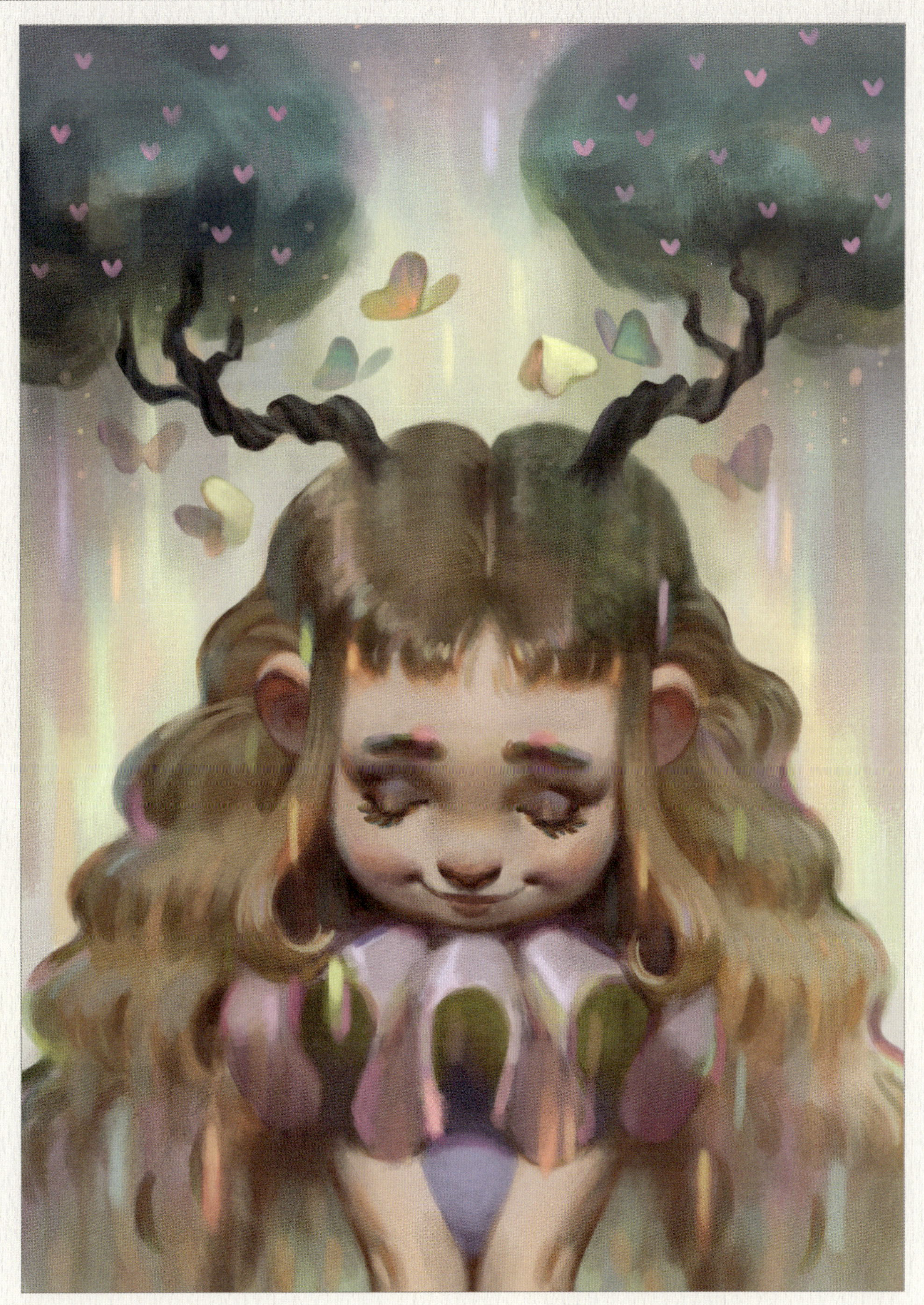

Bonsai Girl

CORAH LOUISE

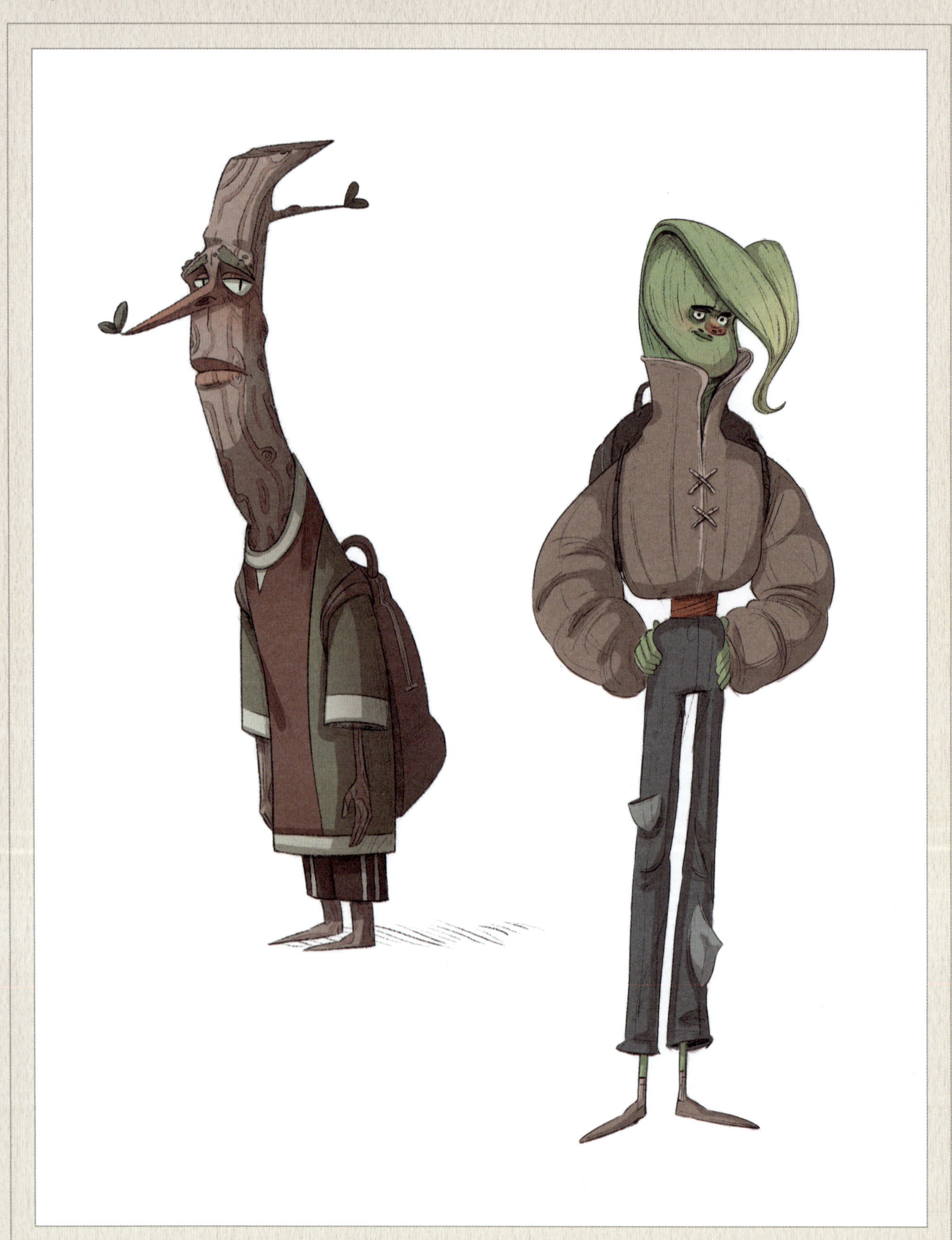

Ent & Leaf

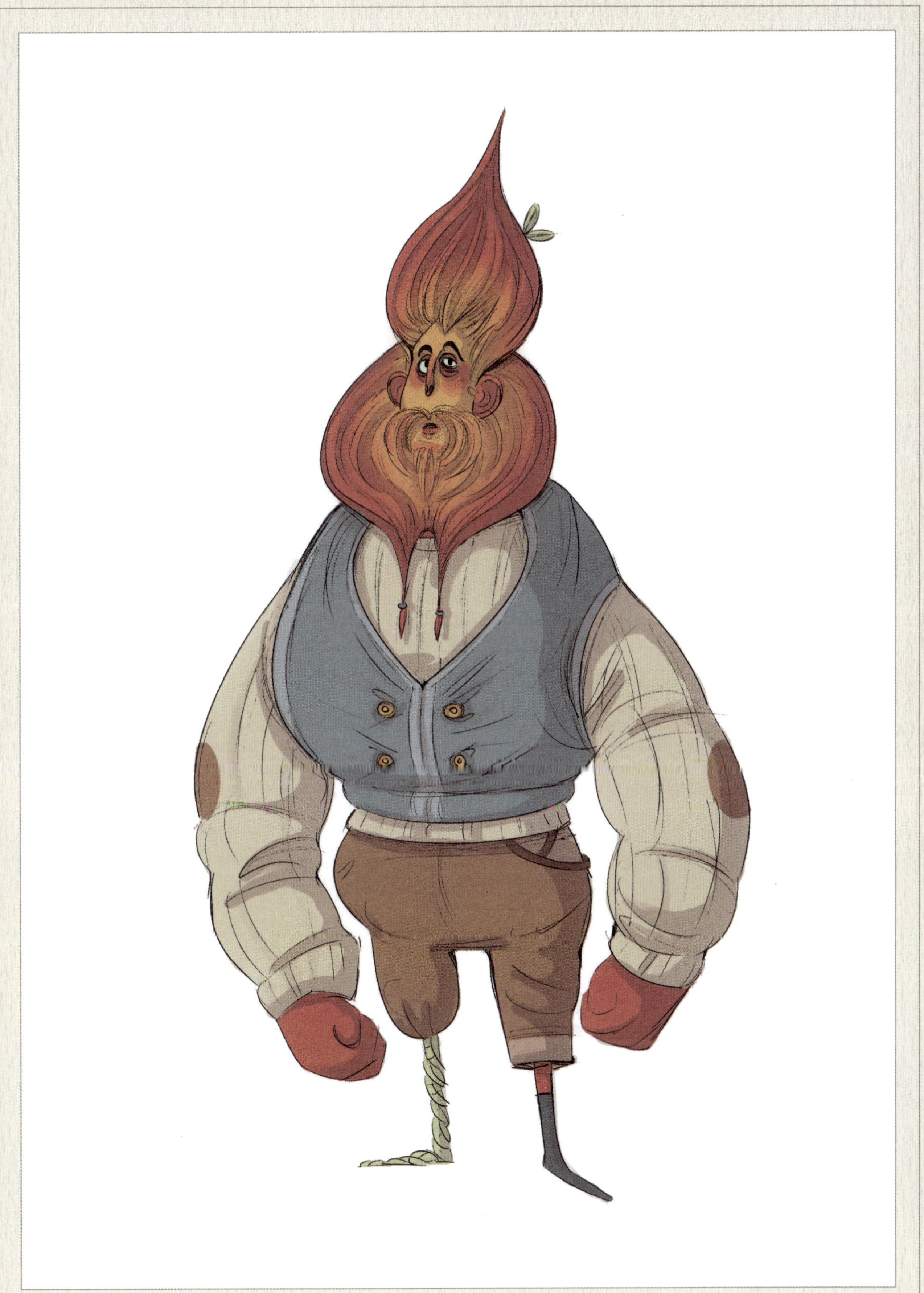

Petal

OGNJEN SPORIN

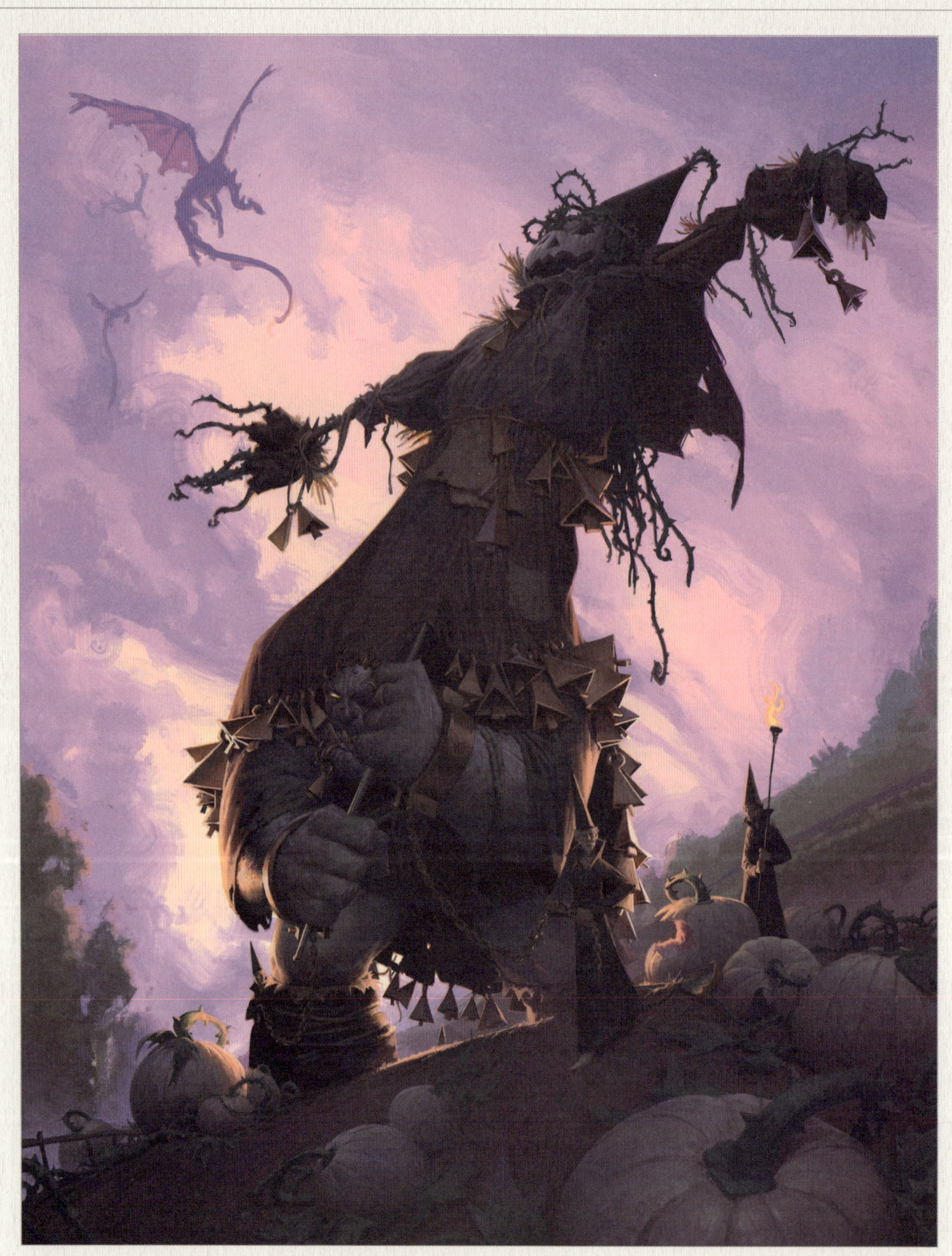

Scarecrow Carrier

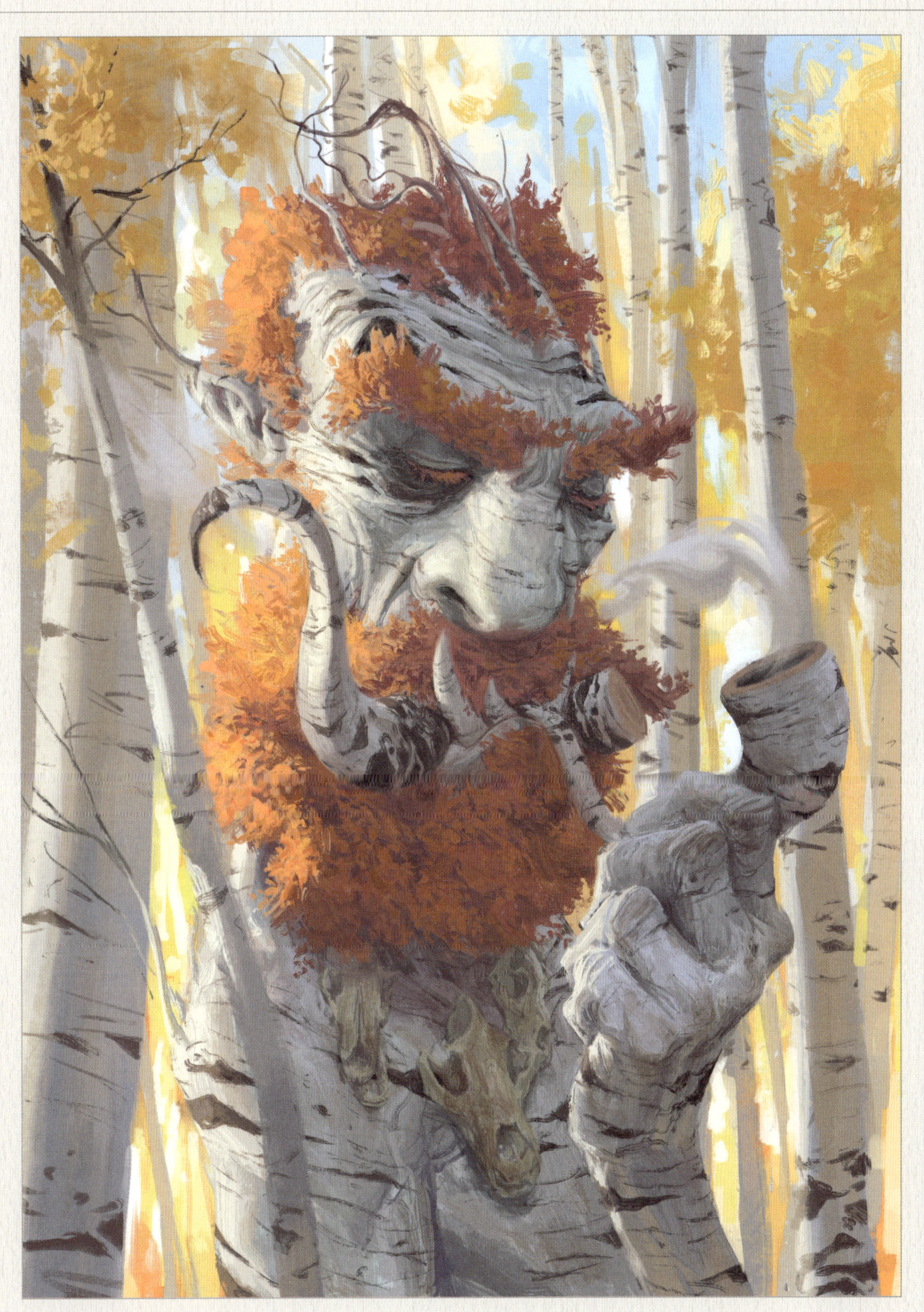

Birch Treeant

IRIS COMPIET

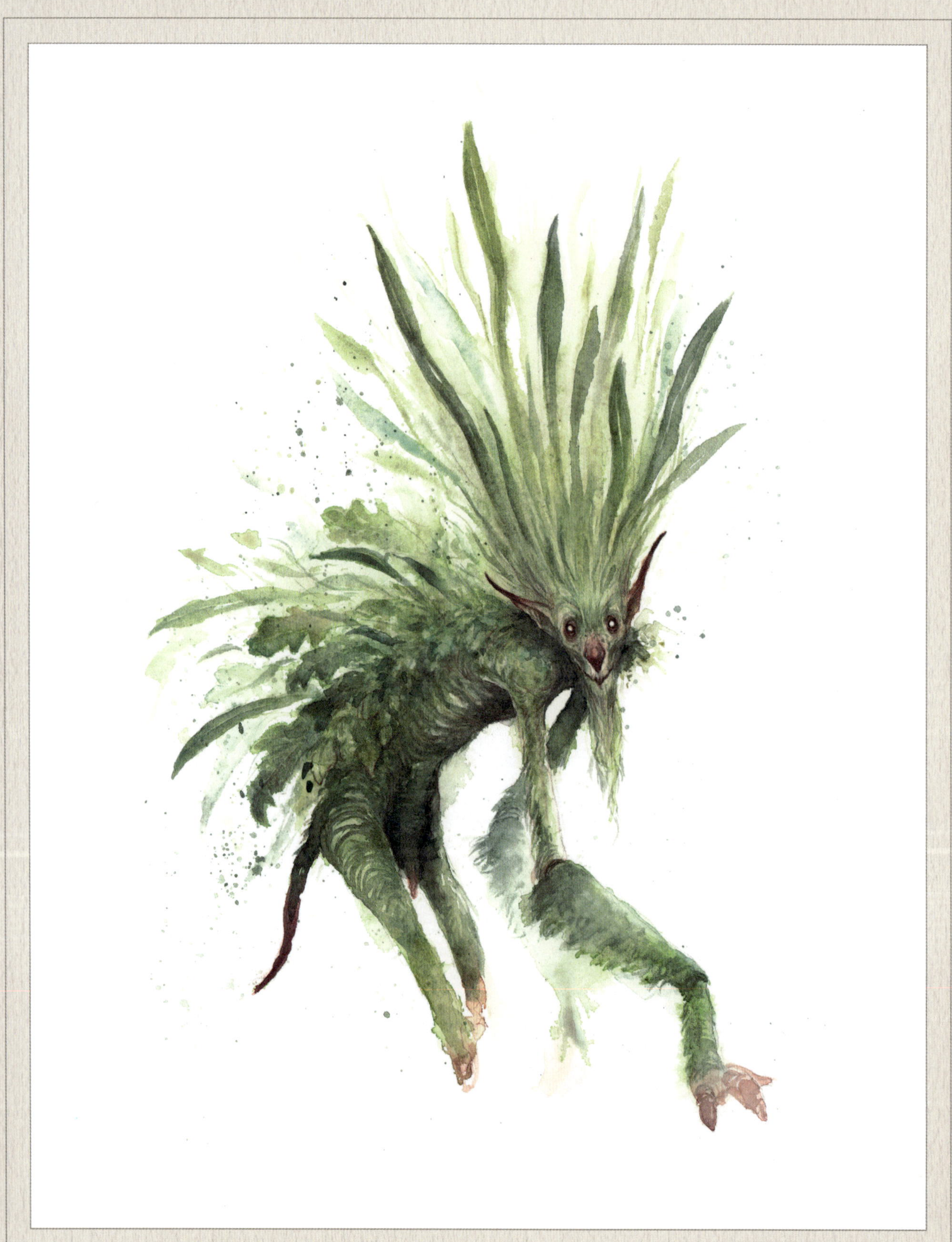

Tuft

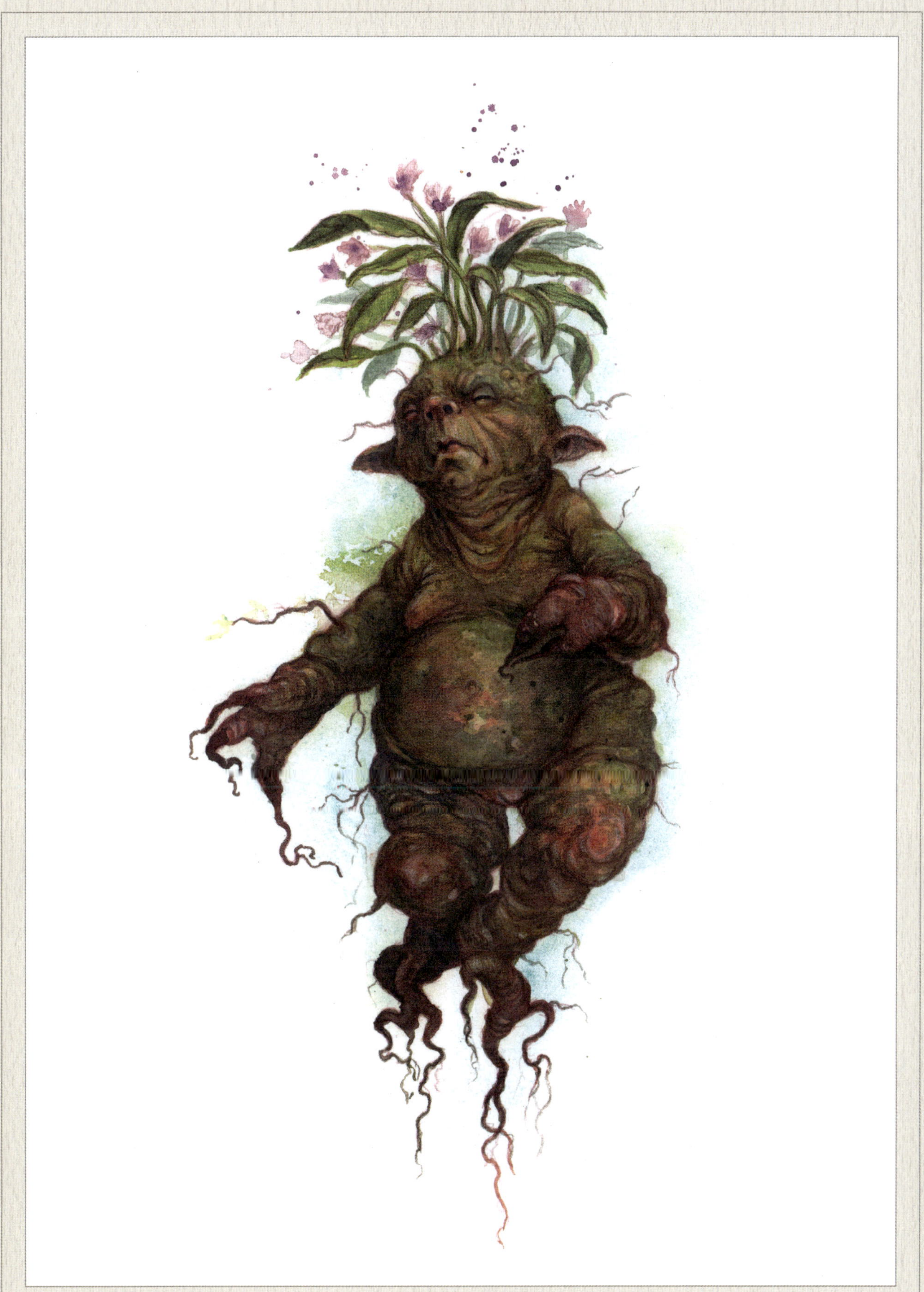

Mandrake Baby

SIBYLLINE MEYNET

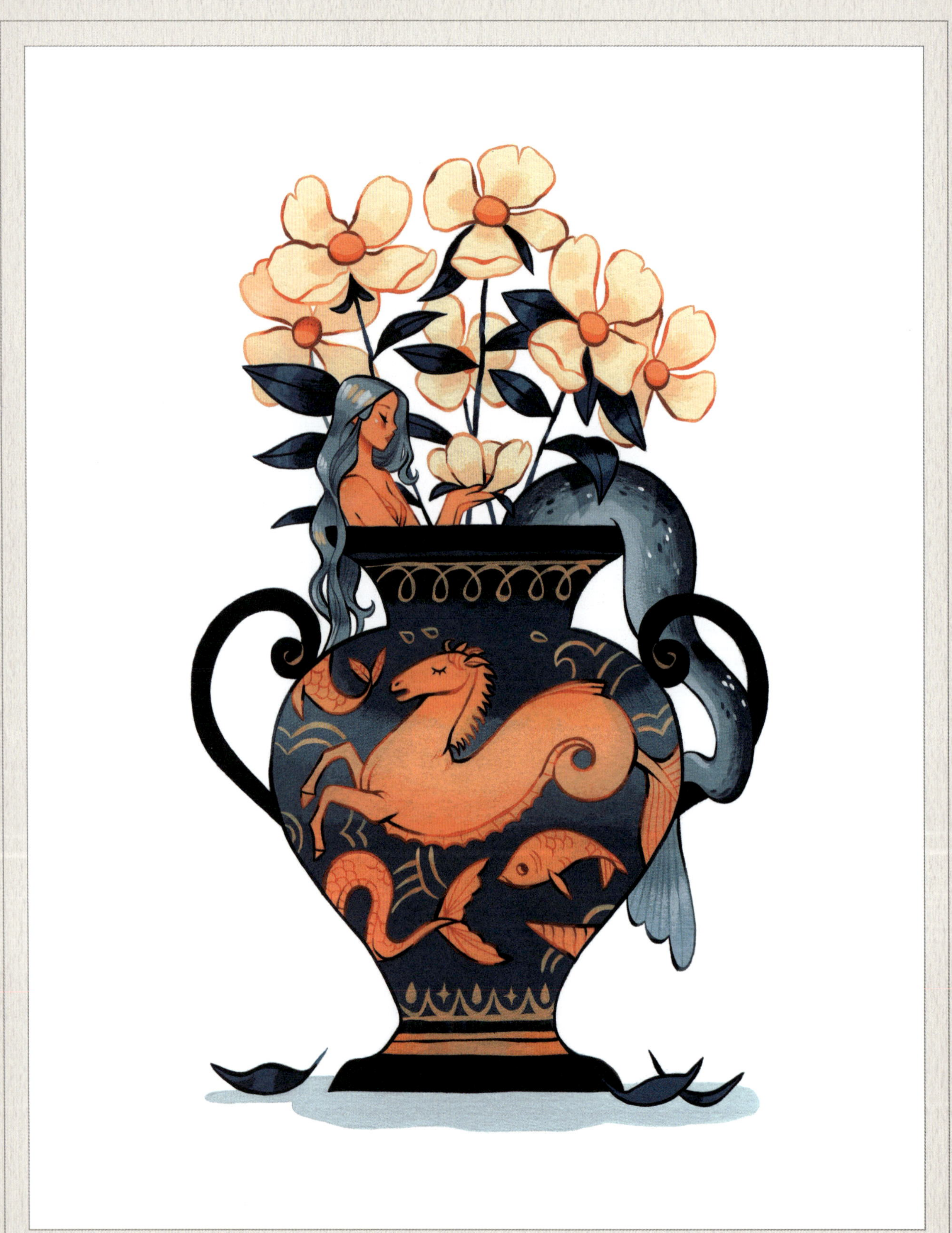

Safe Place

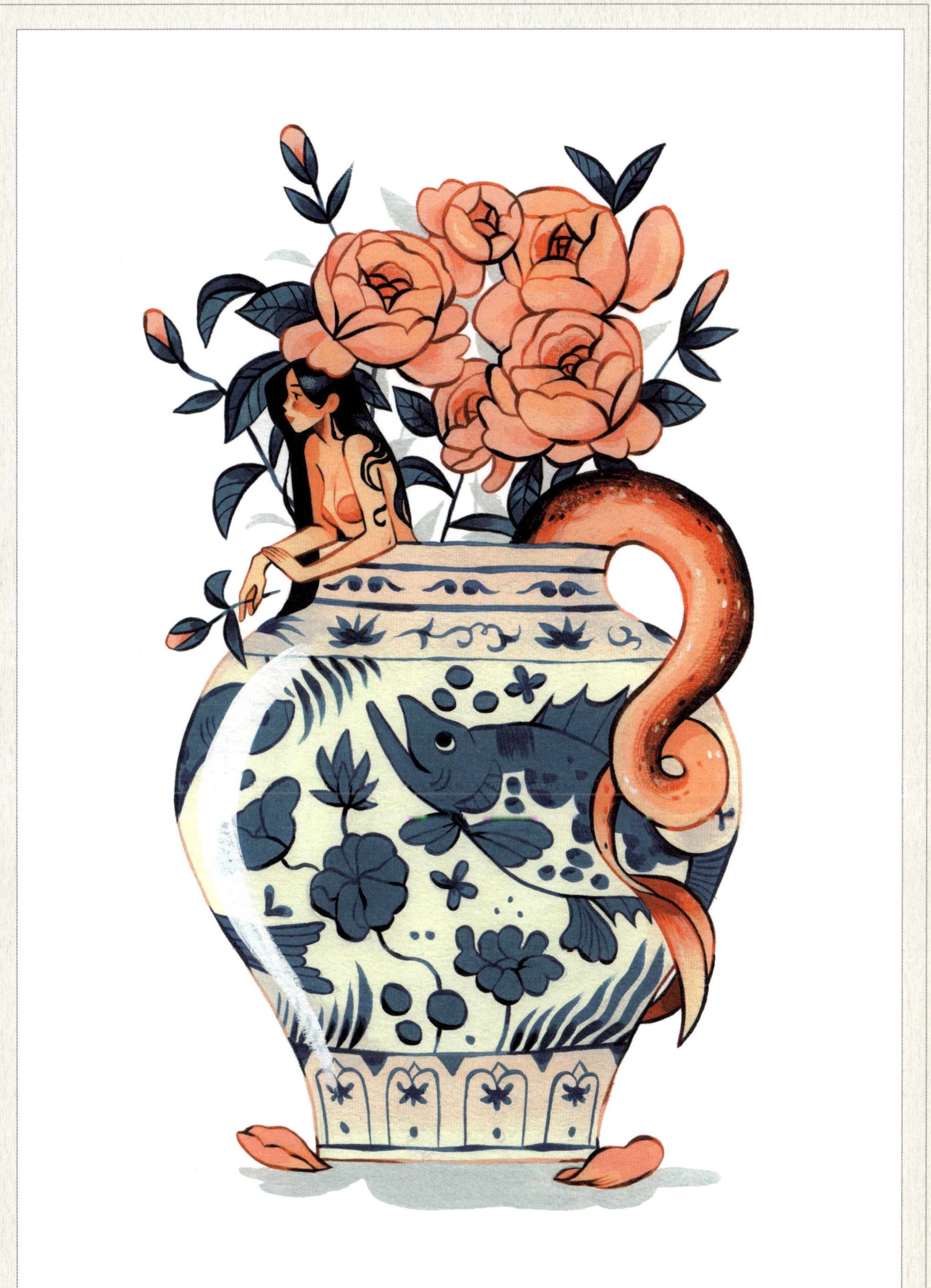

Haven

ESTER CONCEICAO

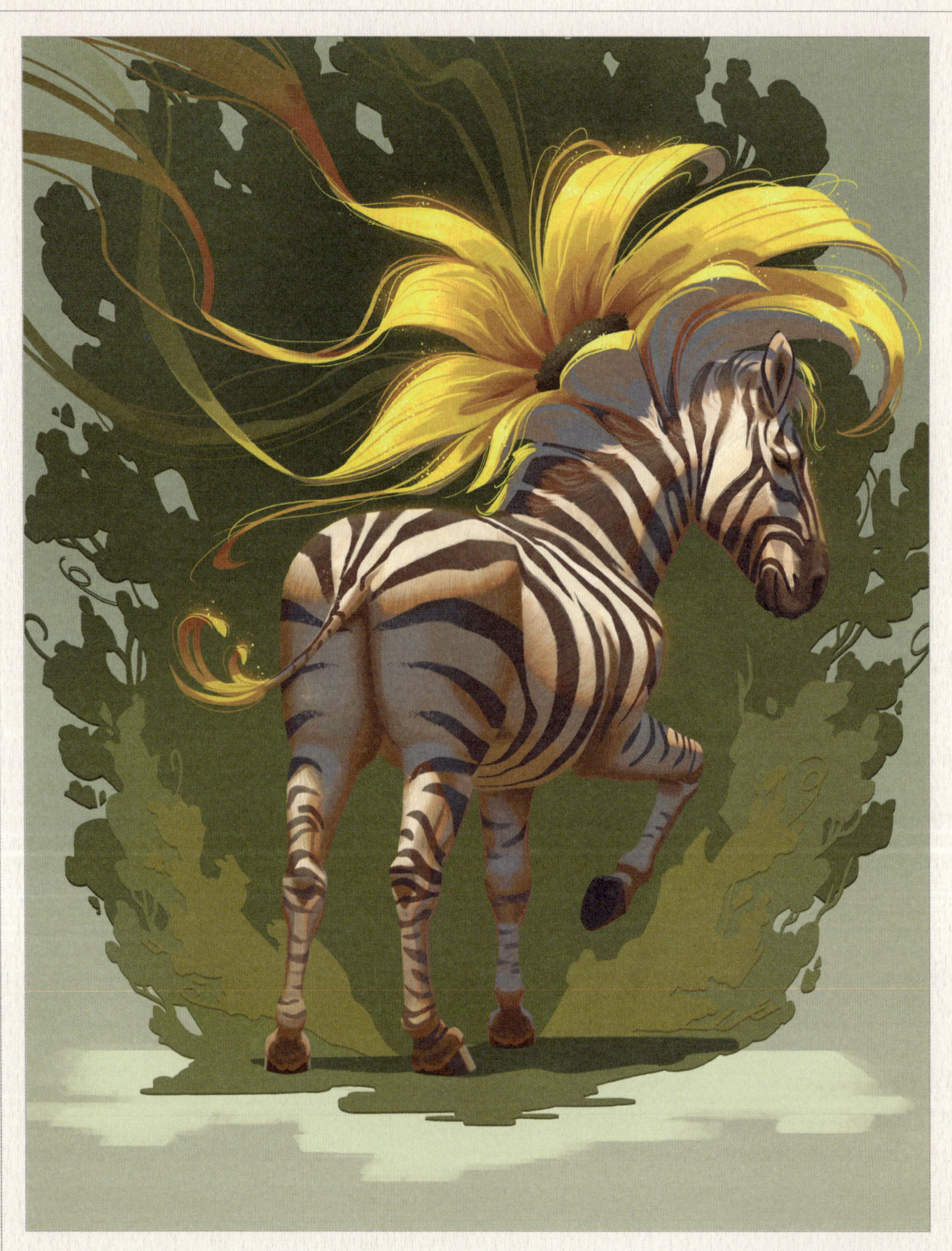

Zebra and Daisies

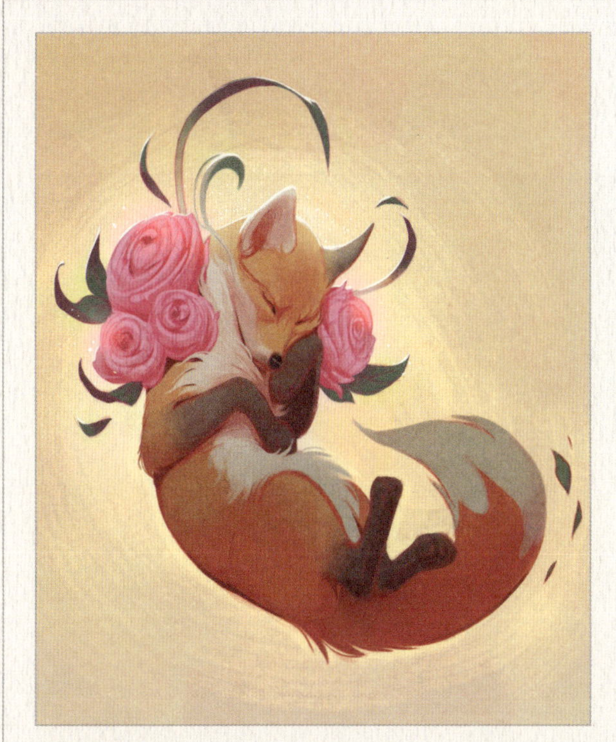

Fox and Roses

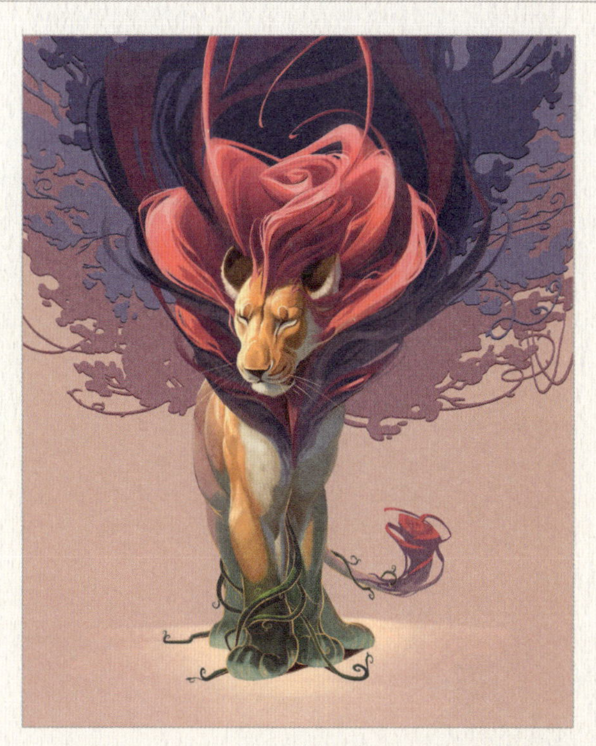

Lion and Roses

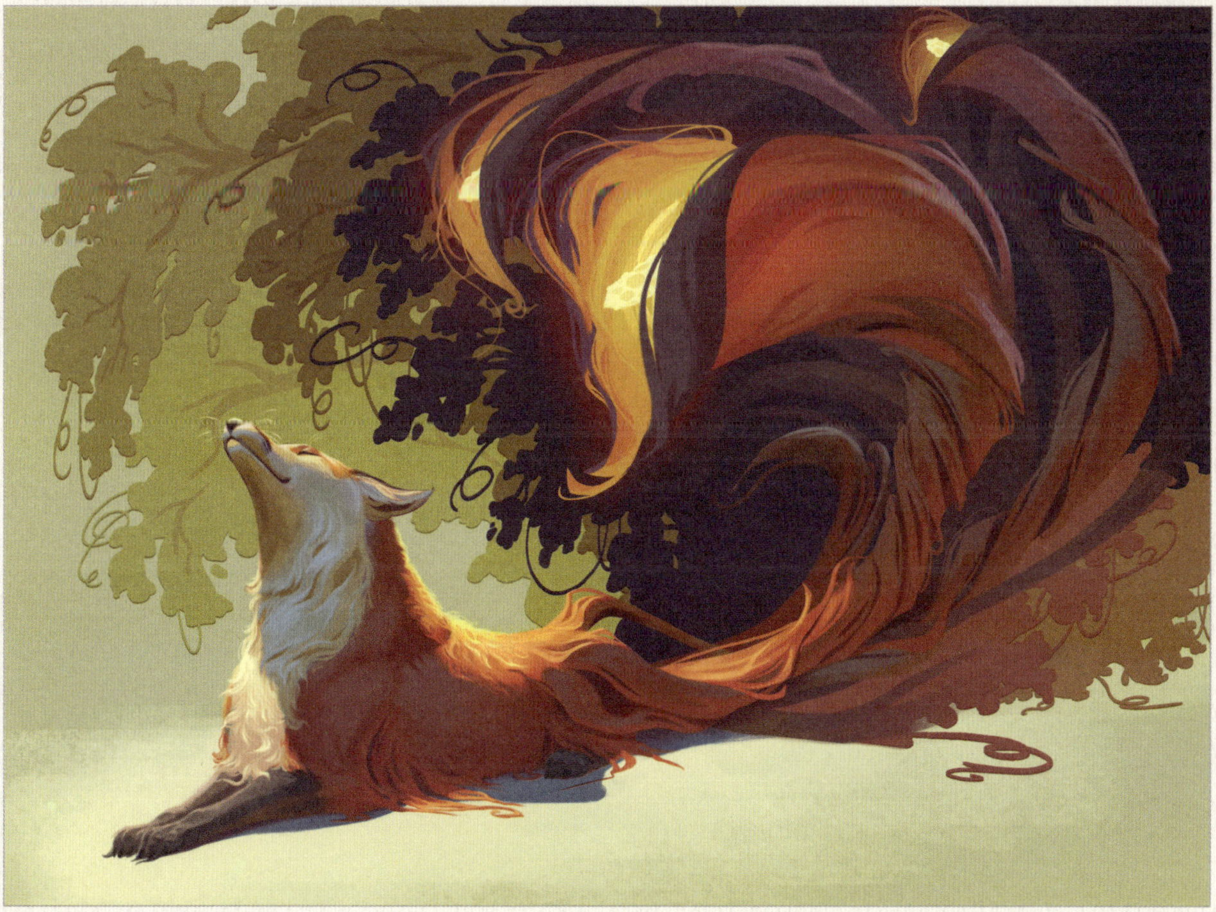

Fox and Lilies

FEEFAL

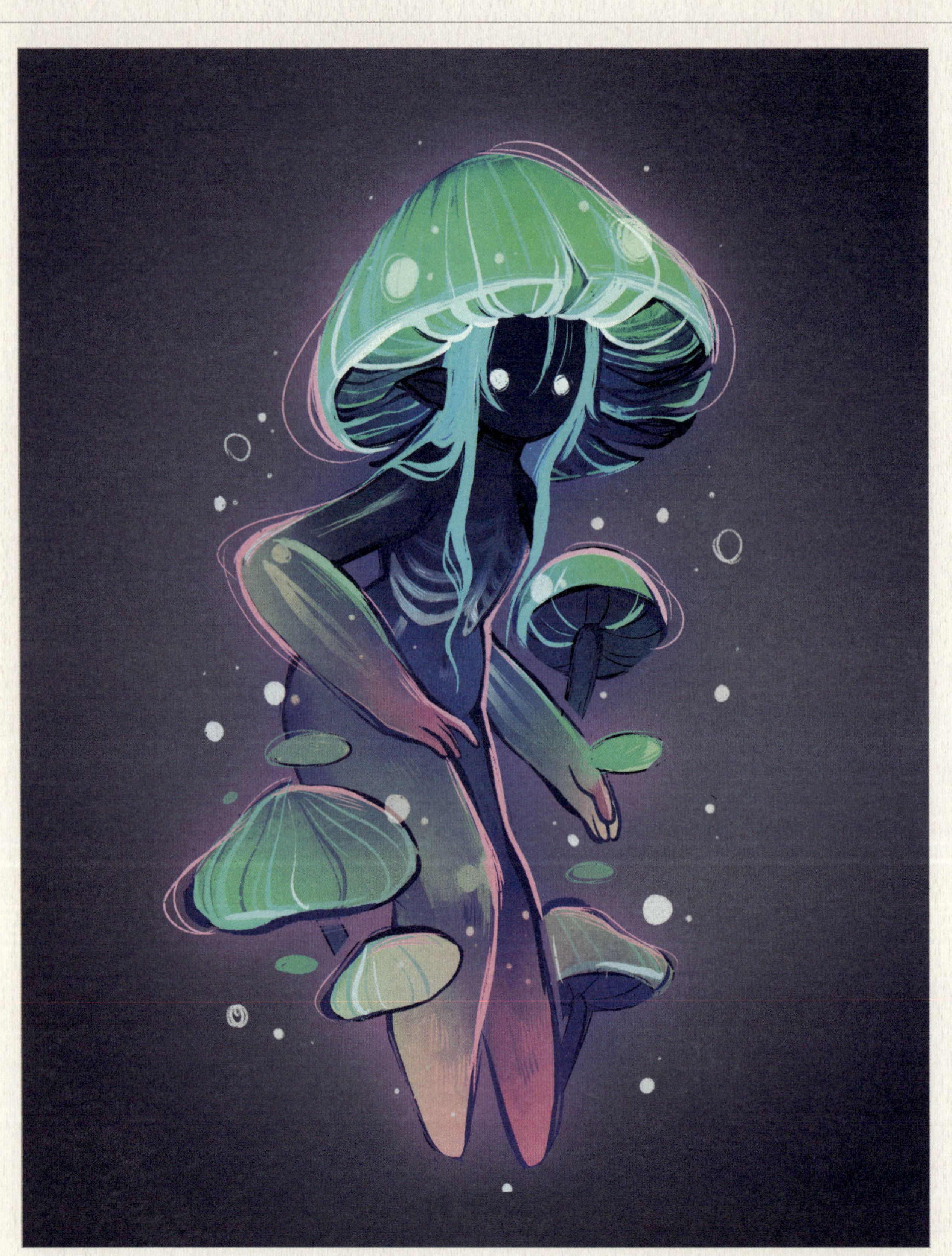

Mycena Chlorophos

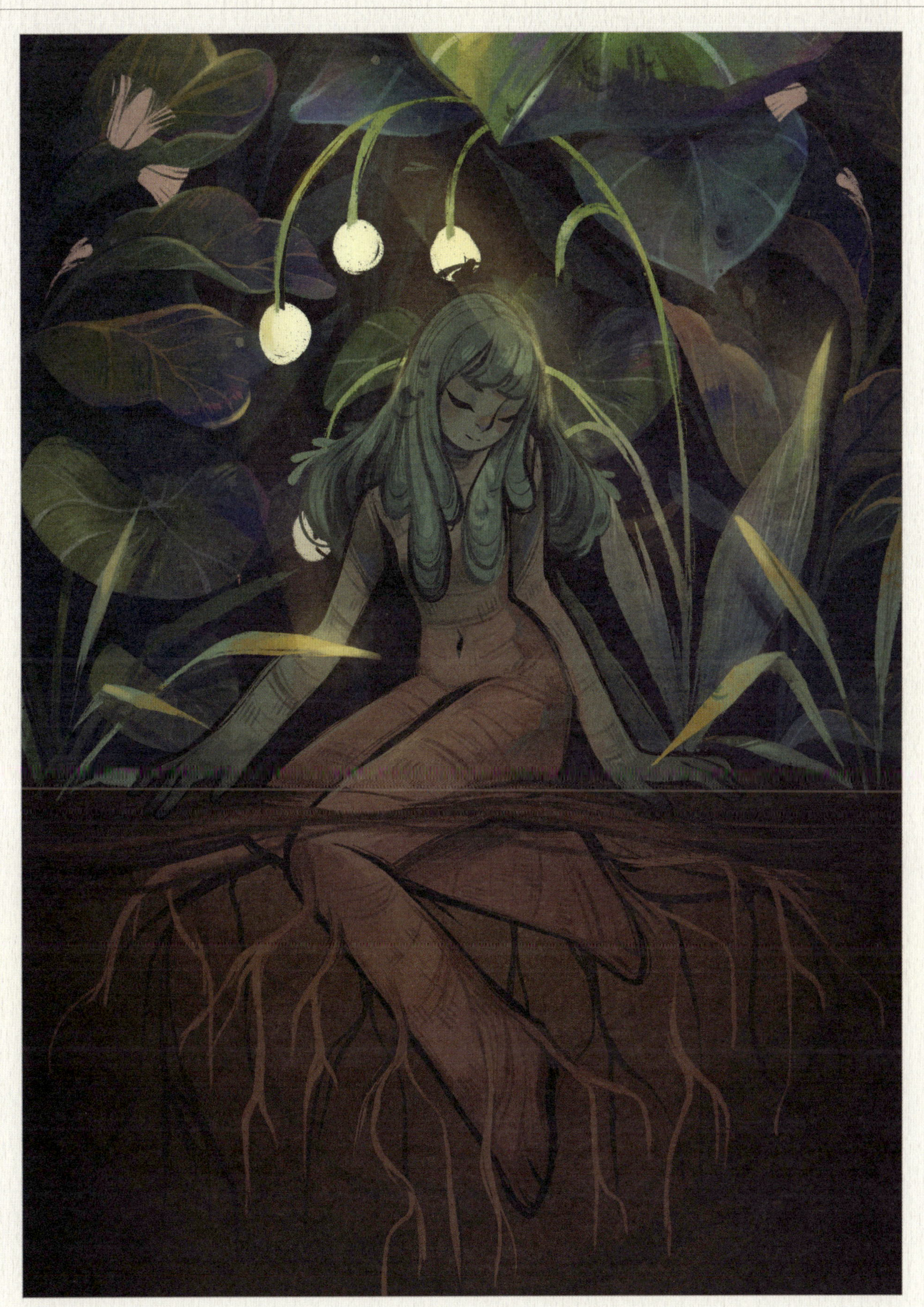

Plantling

LARA GEORGIA CARSON

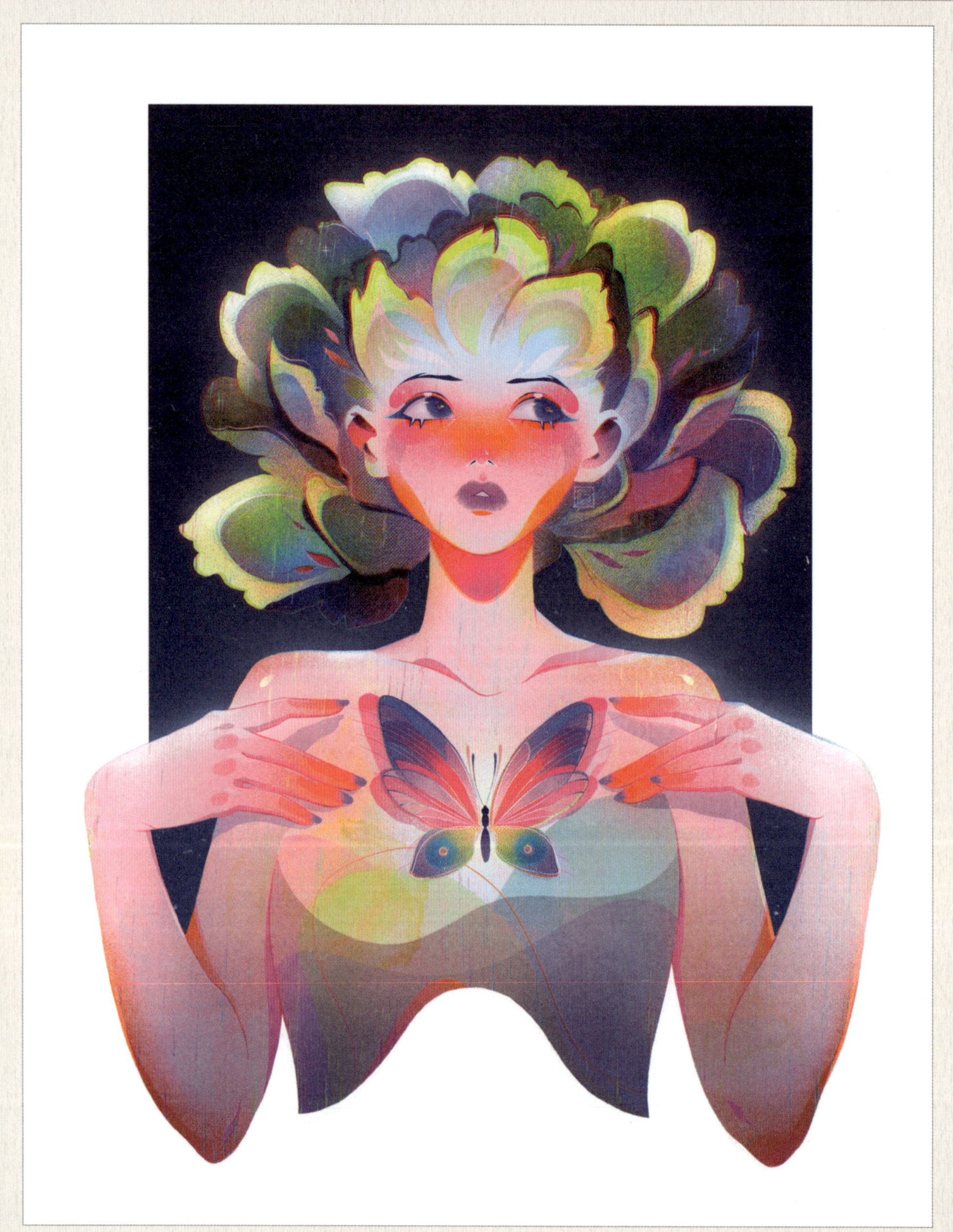

Pollinator

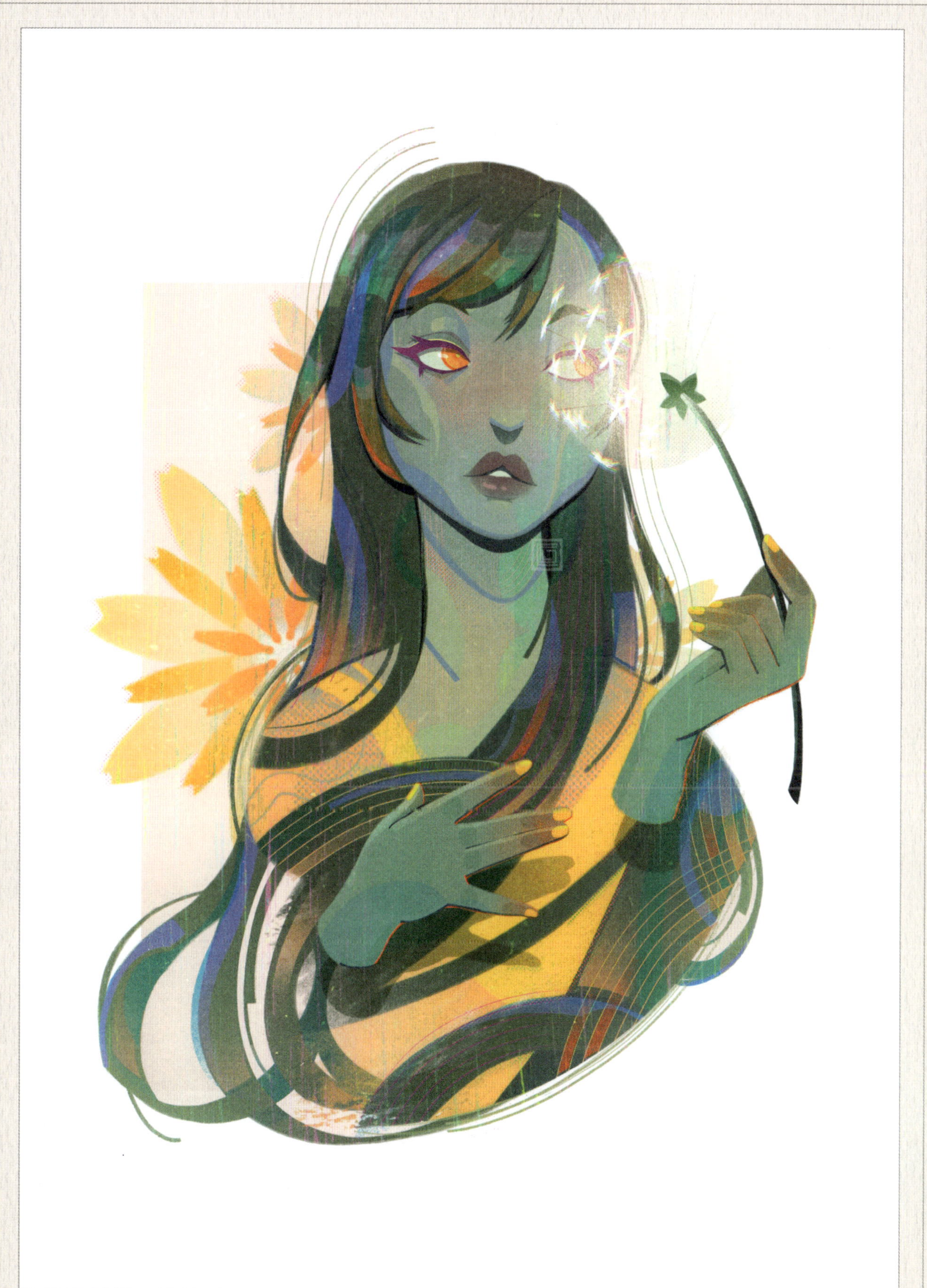

Dandelion

ROMA GEWSKA

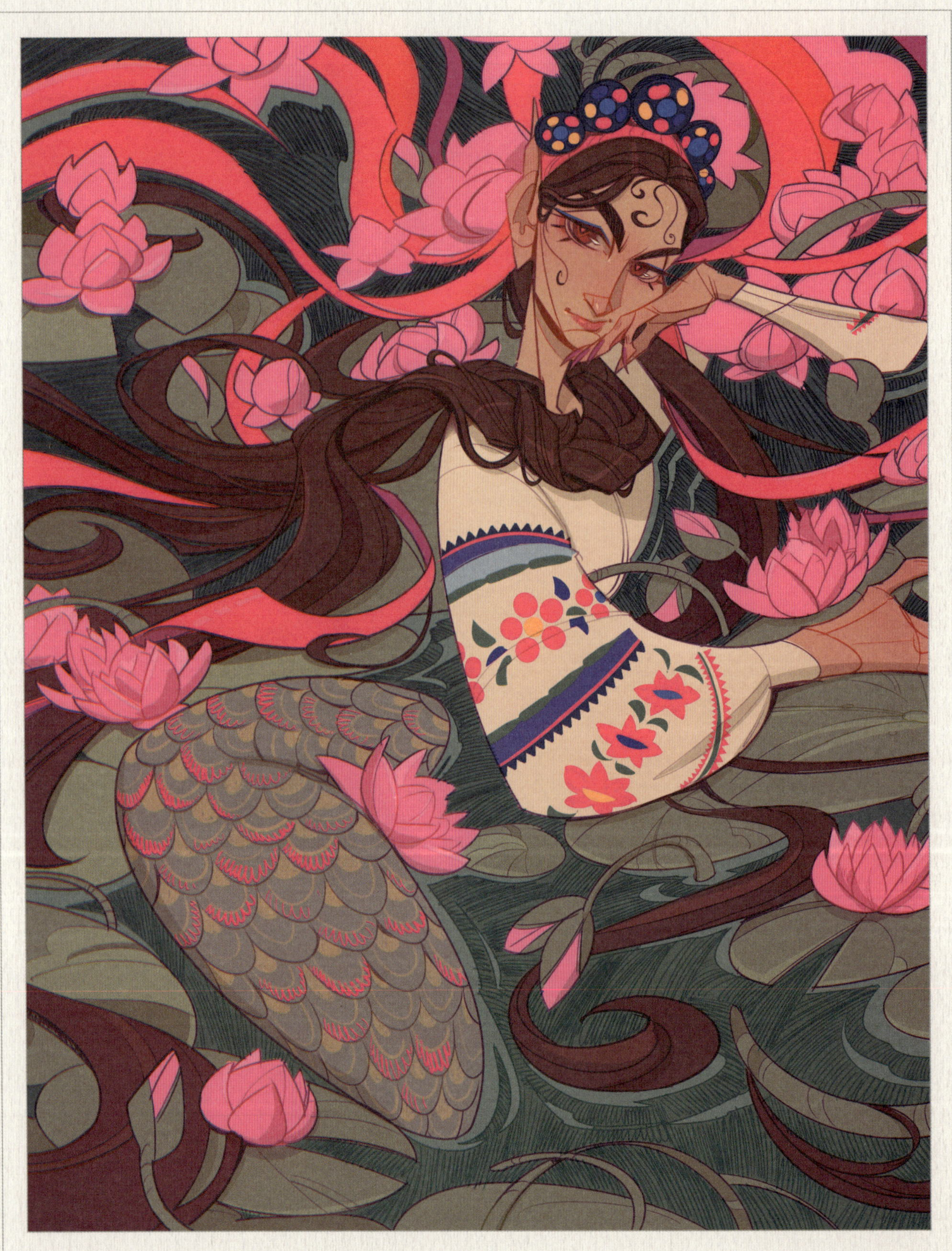

Mermaid

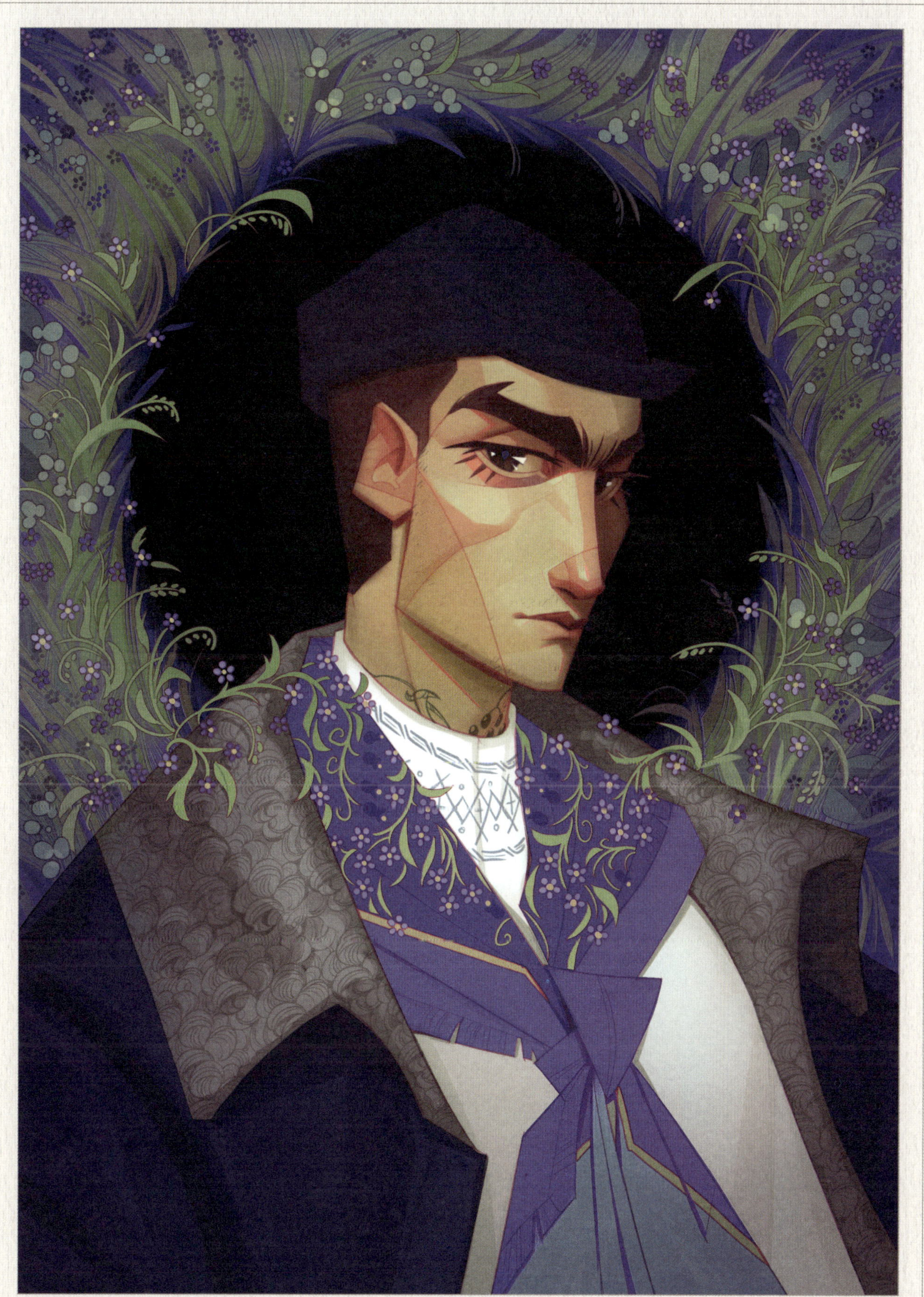

Forget-Me-Nots

DAVID NAVARRO

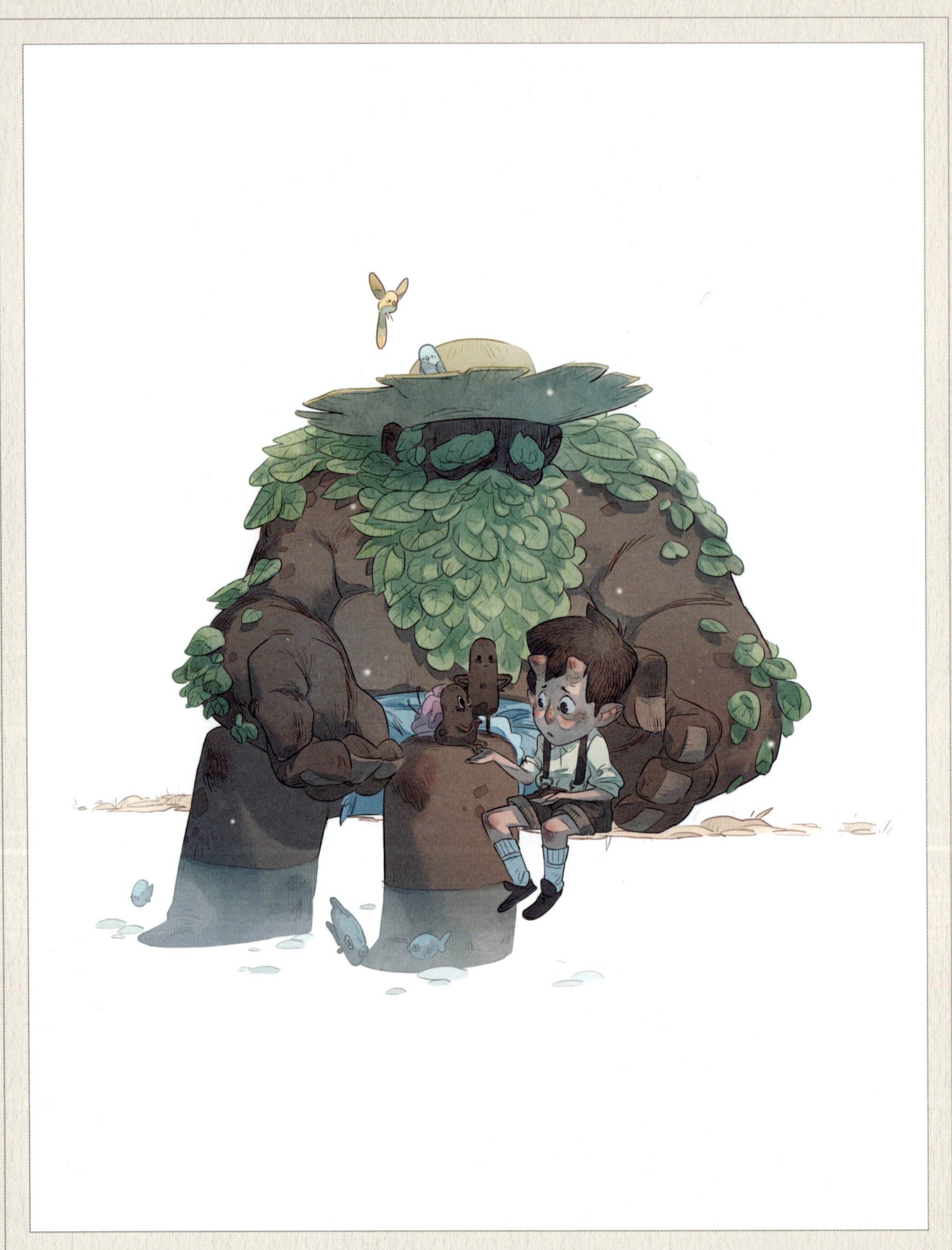

You're Not Alone

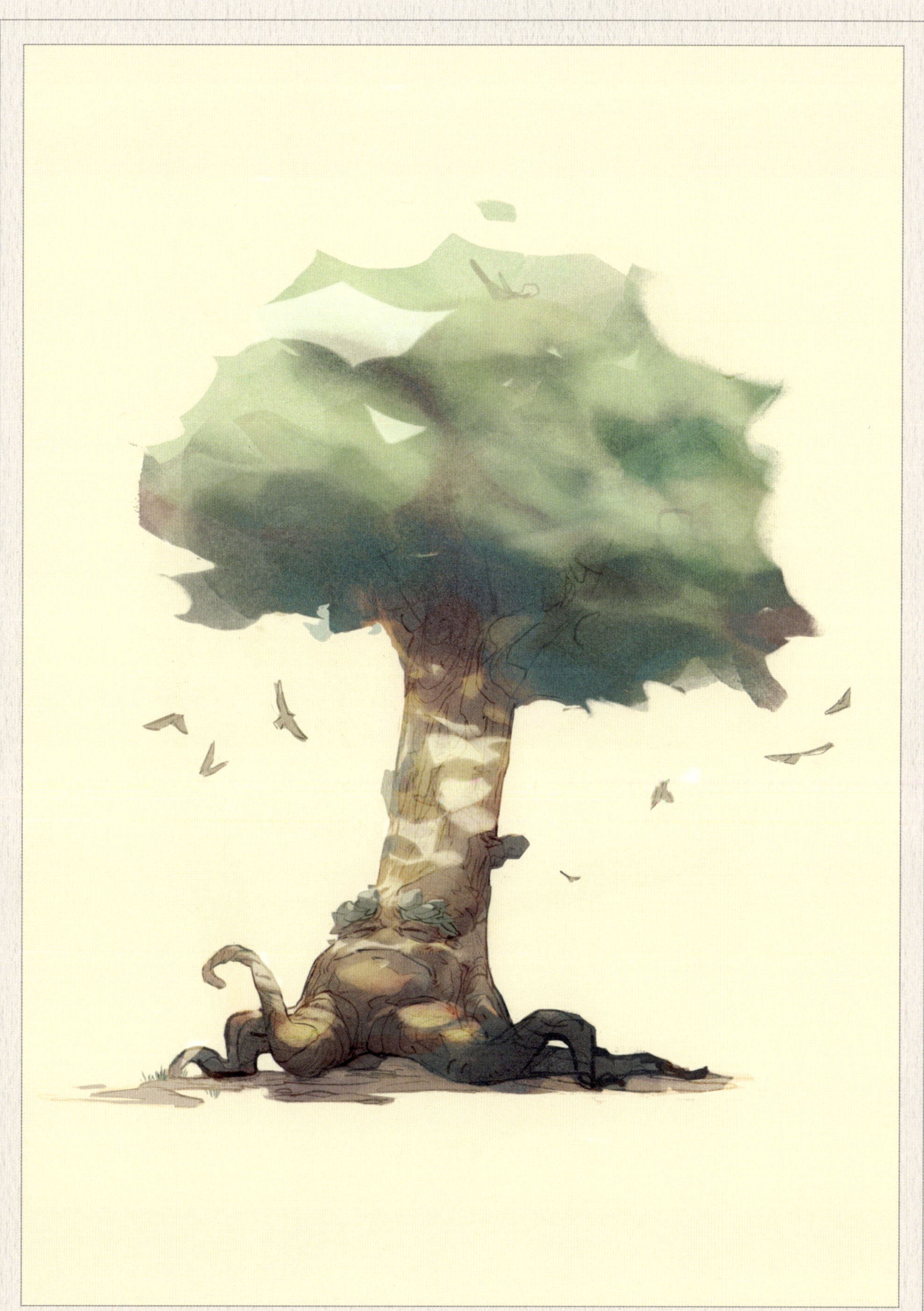

The Old Tree

DOMINIQUE VASSIE

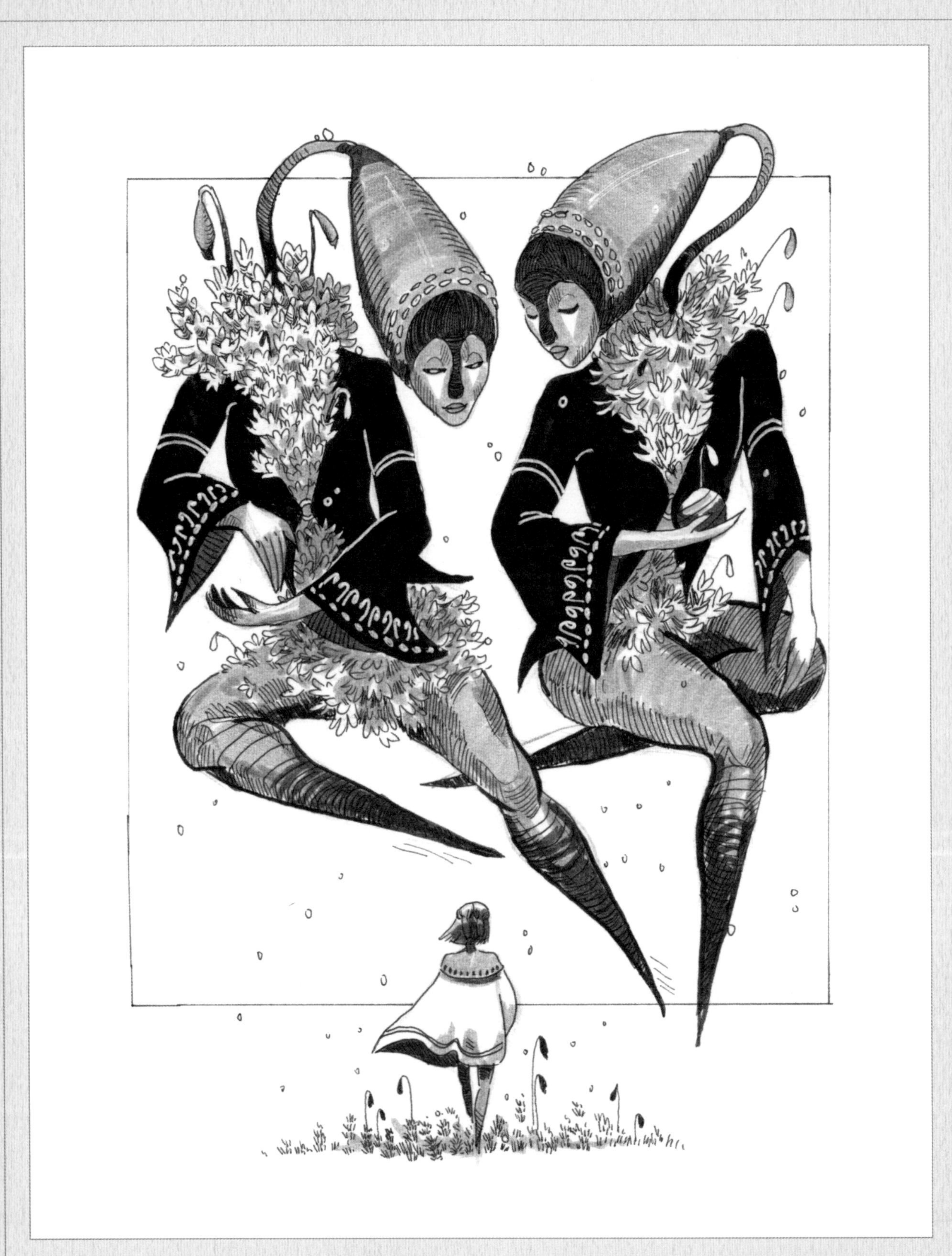

Sisters in the Moss

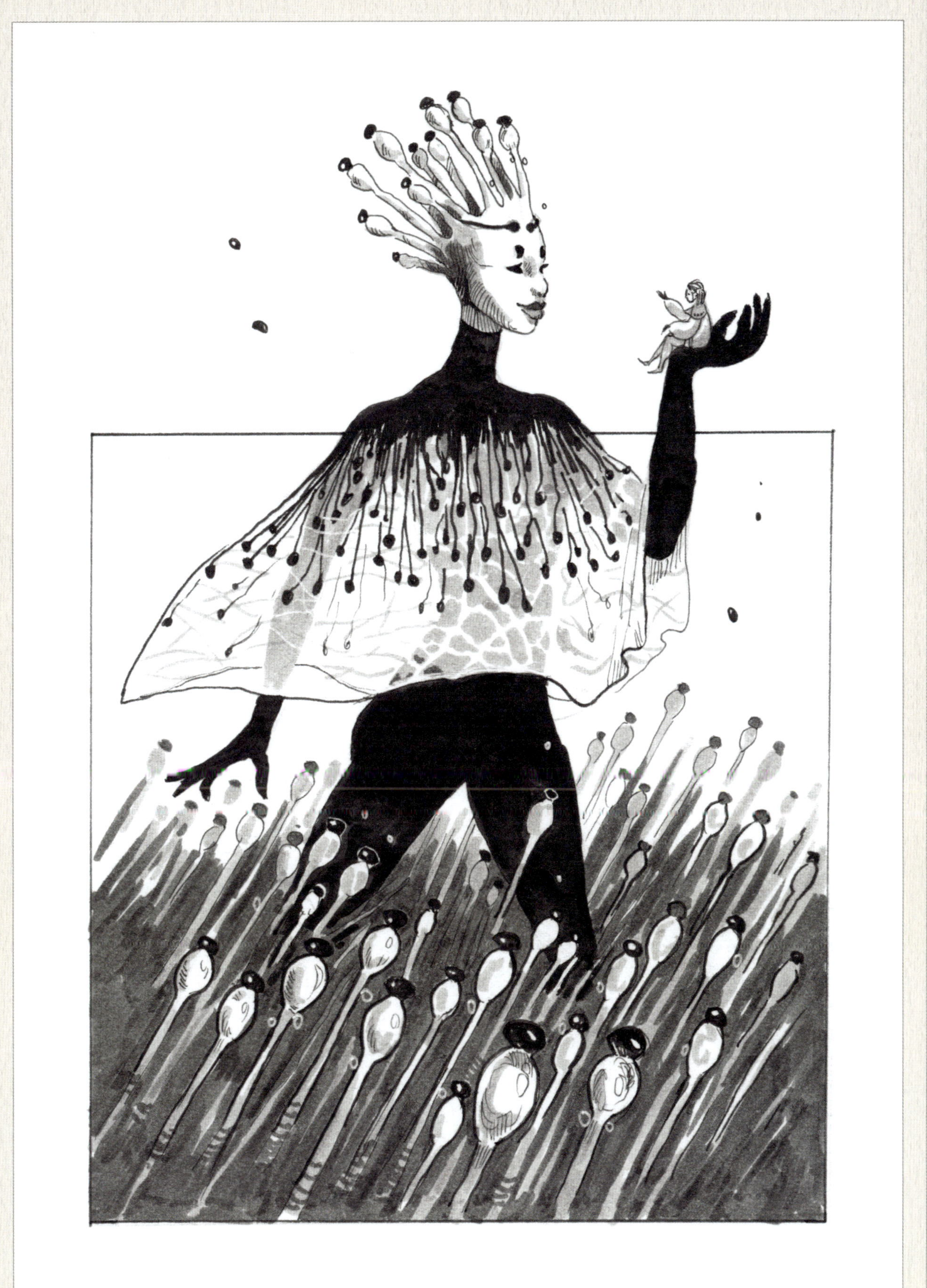

The Zygomycota Queen

ELIZA IVANOVA

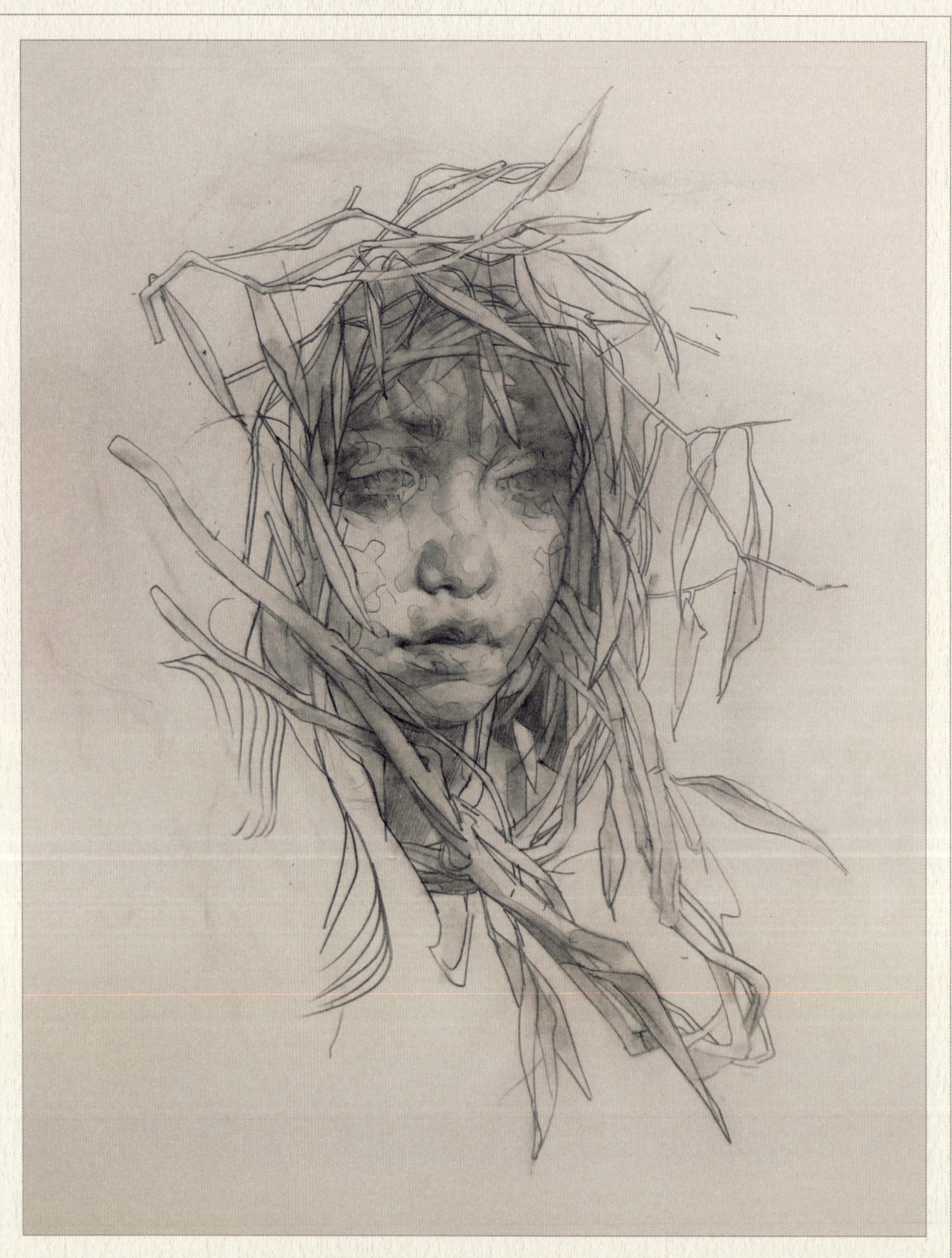

Bamboo

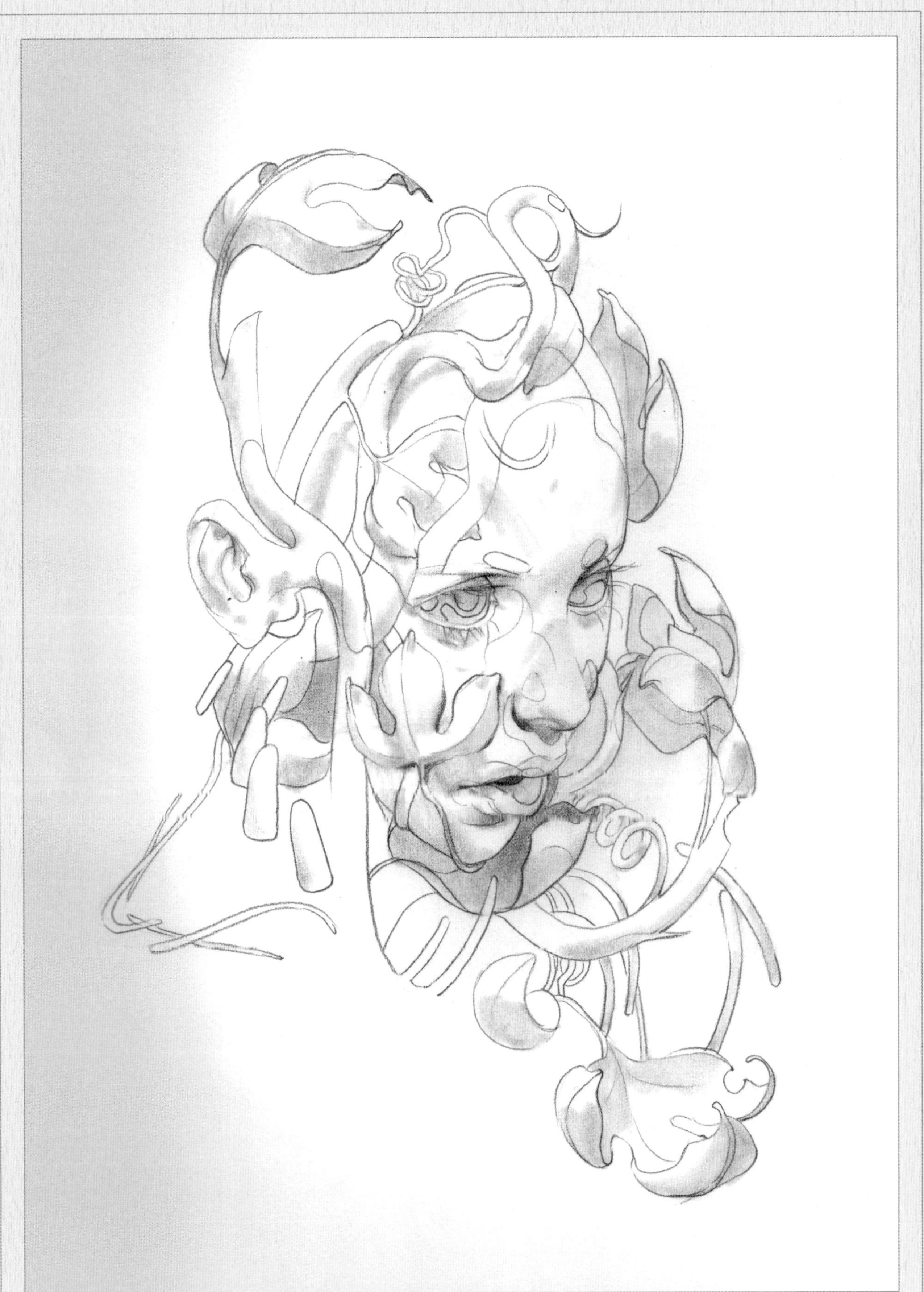

Ivy

AUDRA AUCLAIR

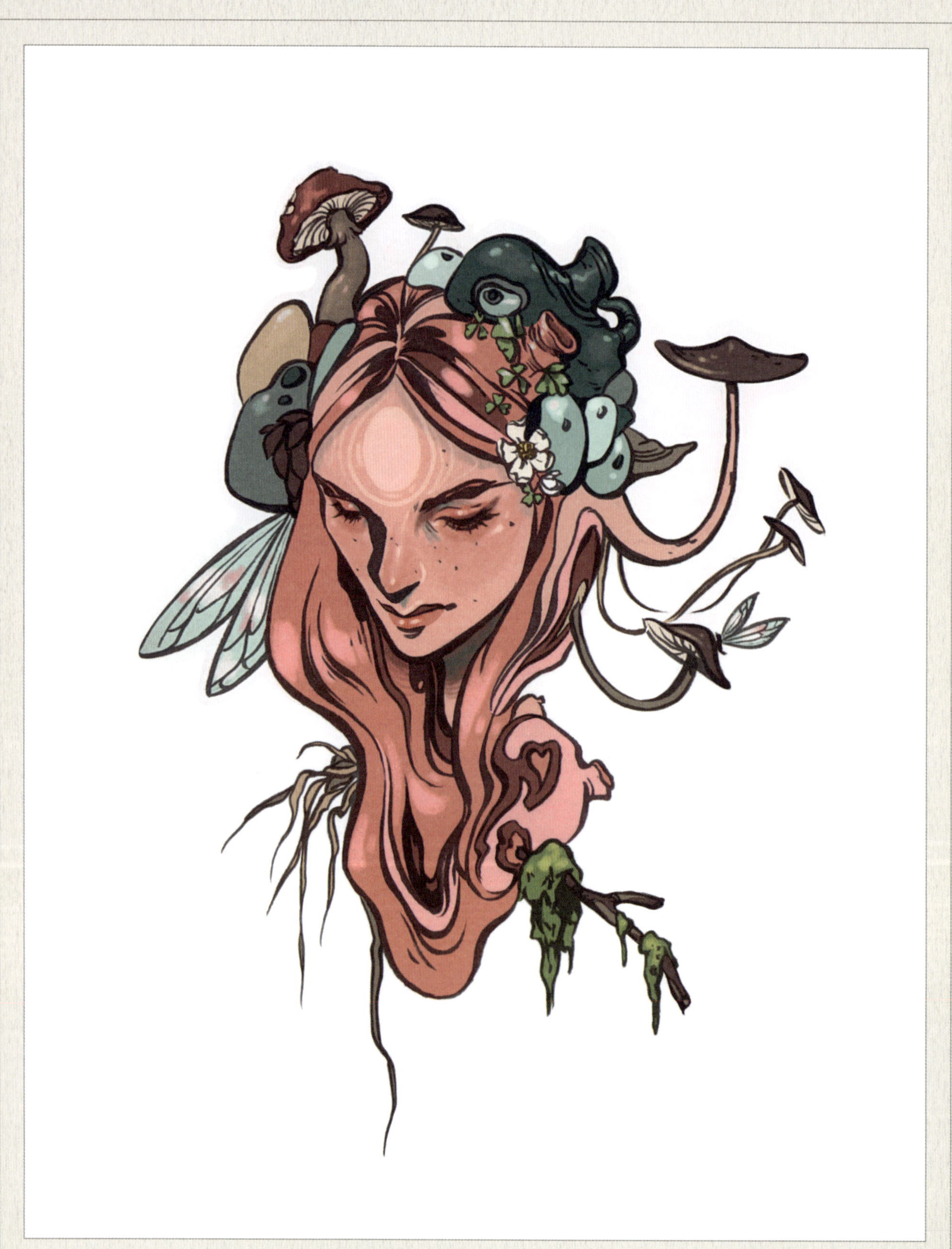

Growing

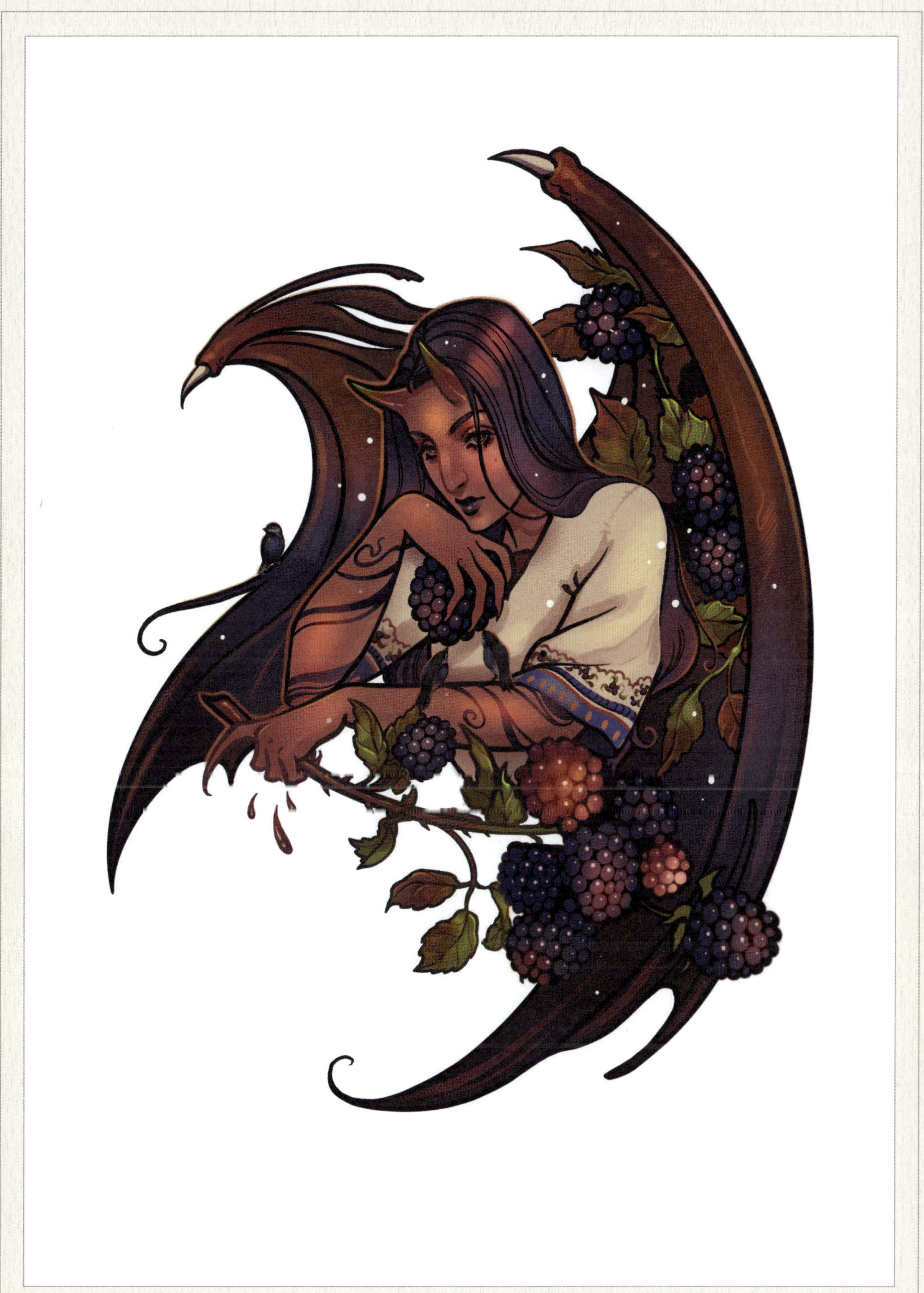

Blackberry Demon

CONTRIBUTORS

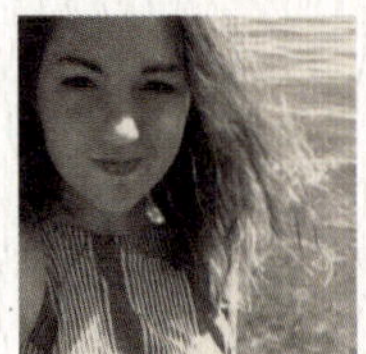
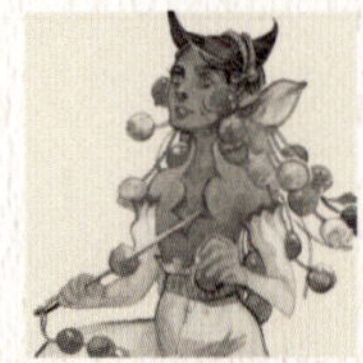

AUDRA AUCLAIR

Artist

audraauclair.com

Audra is a Canadian artist who specializes in surrealist art with a taste for expressing the complexities of mental illness with her transcendent fusion of fine art and illustration.

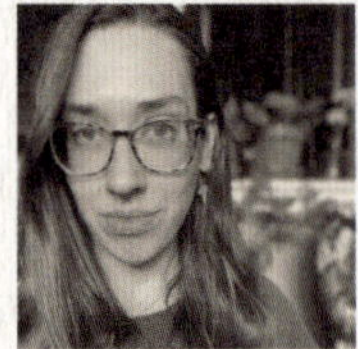
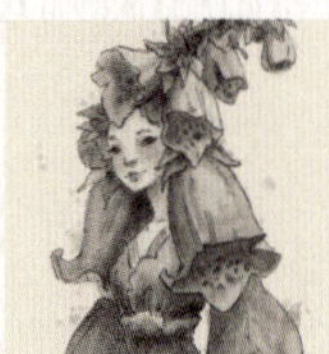

KACEY LYNN BROWN

Illustrator

instagram.com/untroubledheart

Kacey is an illustrator with a fondness for all things fairy-tale and fantastical. She is greatly inspired by the natural world and seeks to bring its beauty into each of her imaginative creatures.

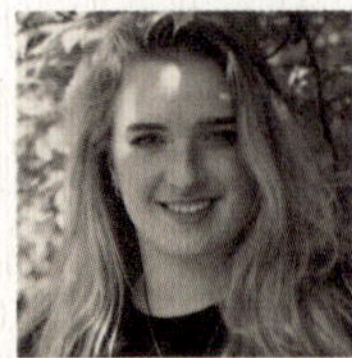
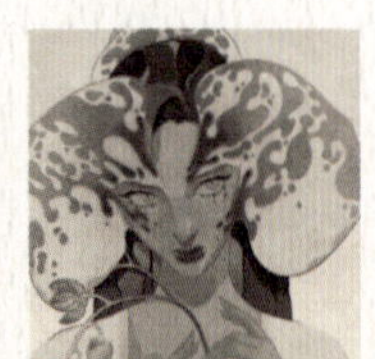

LARA GEORGIA CARSON

2D Designer & freelance illustrator

larageorgiacarson.com

Lara is an illustrator and 2D designer who has been working in the animation industry since receiving her BFA in Illustration. She's a first-generation Canadian living in Vancouver.

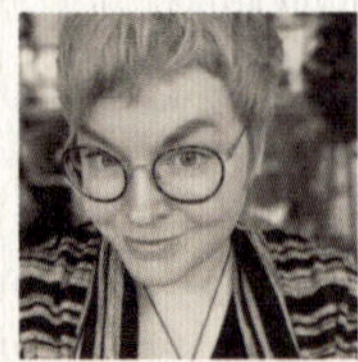
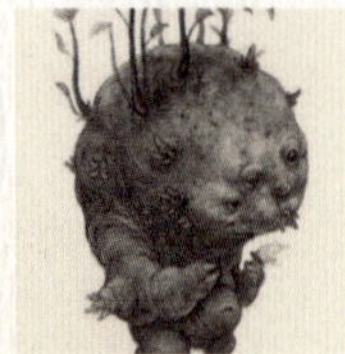

IRIS COMPIET

Artist & illustrator

iriscompiet.art

Iris is an award-winning traditional artist working for international clients in the fields of publishing, concept art, gaming, and galleries. She is the creator of *Faeries of the Faultlines.*

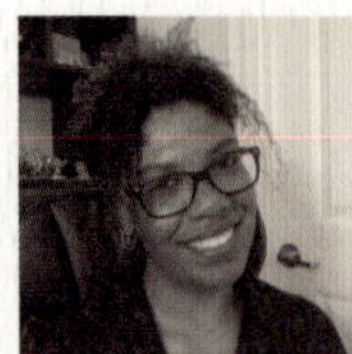
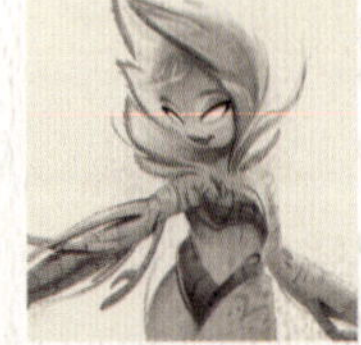

ESTER CONCEICAO

Visual development & character design

esterconceicao.com

Ester is a visual development and character design artist living in Florida. She's currently working as a freelance visual development artist for Warner Bros. Animation.

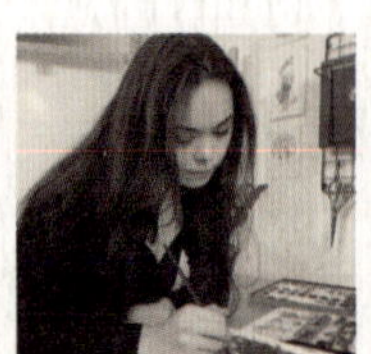
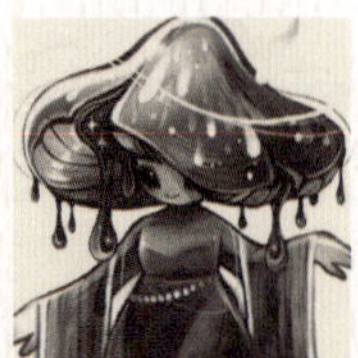

FEEFAL

Illustrator & artist

feefal.com

Feefal is an illustrator from Sweden. She takes lots of inspiration from nature in her work and has a particular soft spot for all things fungi.

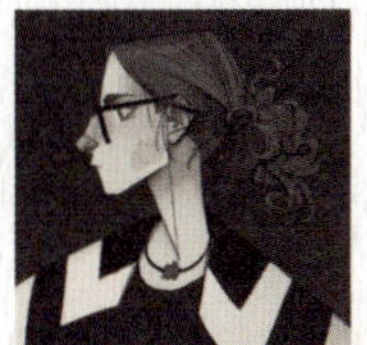
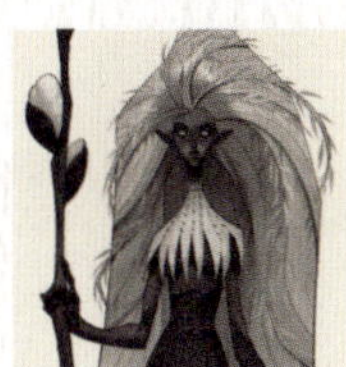

ROMA GEWSKA

2D Illustrator

instagram.com/gewska

Roma is a 2D illustrator and comic maker from Kyiv, Ukraine.

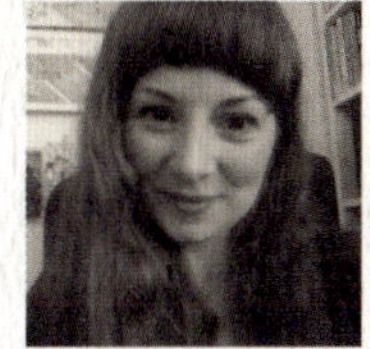
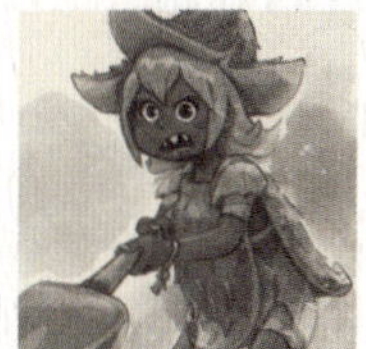

SIMONE GRÜNEWALD

Freelance artist

instagram.com/schmoedraws

Simone, aka 'Schmoedraws', is a visual development artist from Germany. After working in the game industry for over ten years, she is now a freelance artist and creates tutorials on her Patreon.

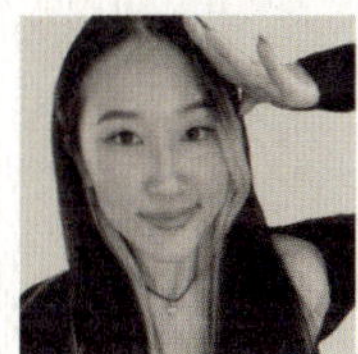
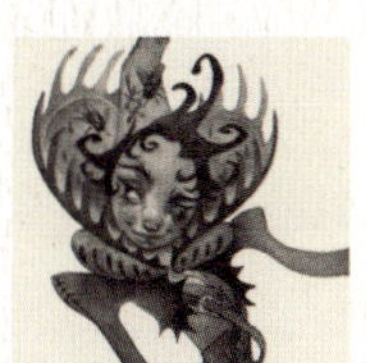

CHRIS HONG

Artist & content creator

chrishongart.com

Chris is a full-time artist and content creator based in Toronto, Canada. She has a strange affinity for clowns, and anything a little quirky and whimsical.

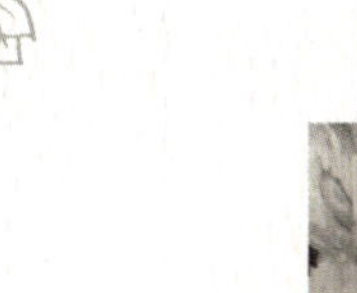
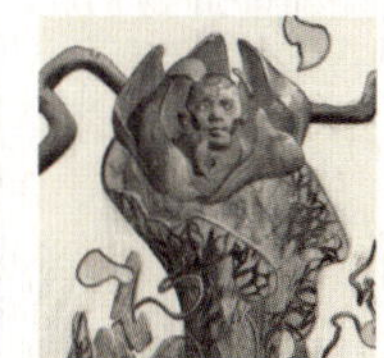

ELIZA IVANOVA

Fine artist

elizaivanova.com

Eliza is a fine artist and illustrator living and working in the Bay Area, California, USA. She is also a veteran in the animation industry with over ten years' experience in 2D and 3D character animation.

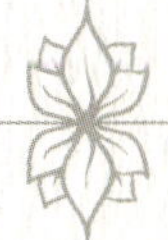

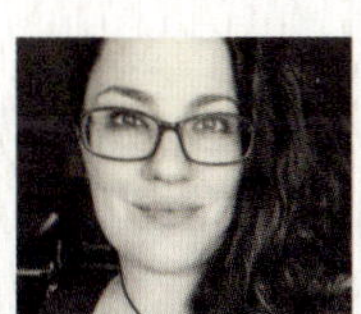
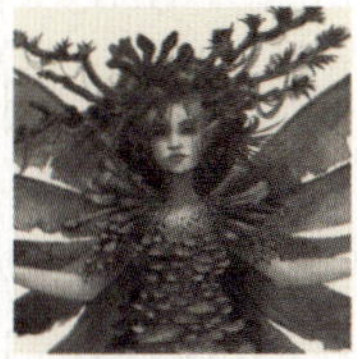

KIRI LEONARD

Artist & small-business owner

valkiri.llc

Kiri is an award-winning fantasy artist and illustrator from Denmark. She currently lives in Austin, Texas, USA, and specializes in whimsical art with a fairy-tale twist.

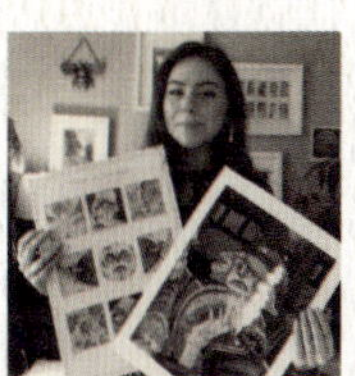
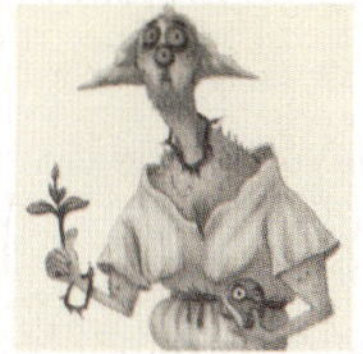

CORAH LOUISE

Freelance artist & character designer

corahlouise.com

Corah is a freelance artist and character designer from the UK. Her work combines traditional with digital tools to create vibrant, textured pieces full of story, character, and magic.

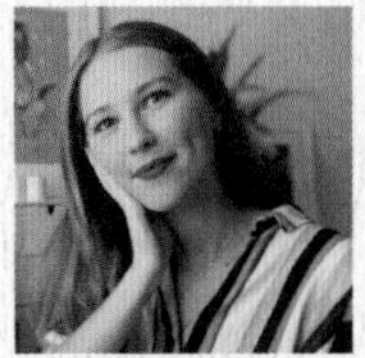
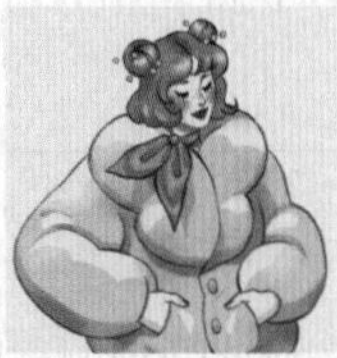

SIBYLLINE MEYNET

Illustrator

sibyllinemeynet.com

Sibylline is a freelance illustrator from France. She creates cover work for comics, character design for animation, and illustration for magazines and books.

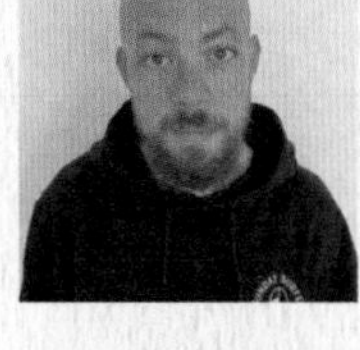
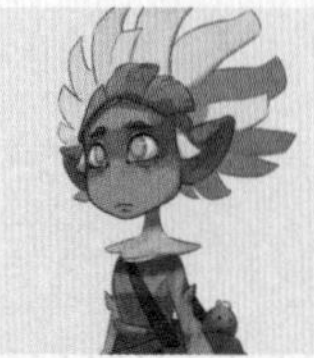

DAVID NAVARRO

Character designer

instagram.com/danavarrow

Always glued to a pencil, David has drawn for as long as he can remember. He's a chilled guy who loves telling stories through his characters and tries to improve every day.

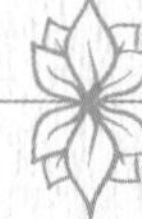
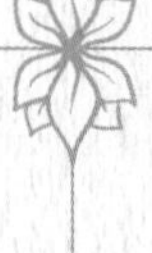

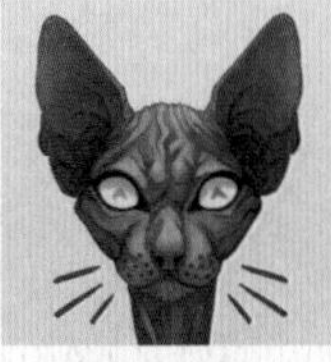
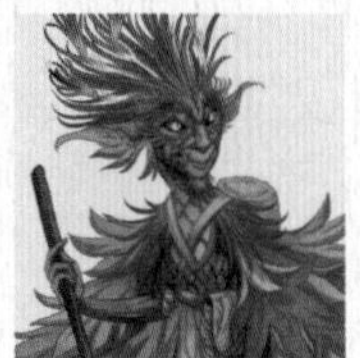

NORA POTWORA

2D artist & illustrator

behance.net/norapotwora

Nora is a full-time artist based in Poland. She translates her love of nature into her artwork, the themes of which revolve around the world of animals and plants.

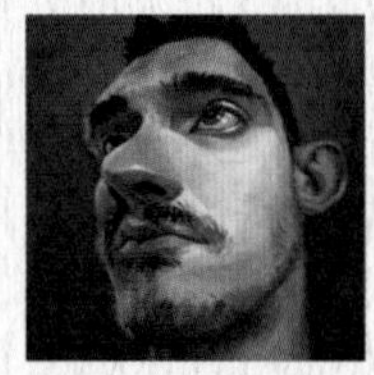
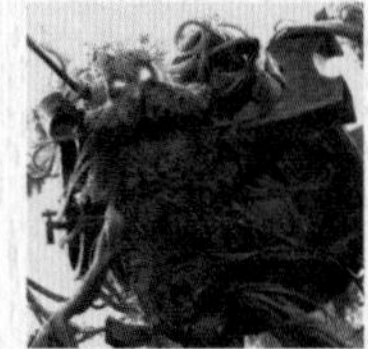

OGNJEN SPORIN

Freelance illustrator, concept artist, & teacher

artstation.com/ognjensporin

Ognjen is a freelance illustrator and concept artist who has created art for video games, animated movies, books, and tabletop games. Notable past clients include Netflix, Blizzard, Marvel, and NetEase.

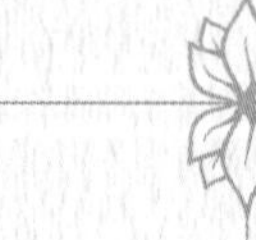

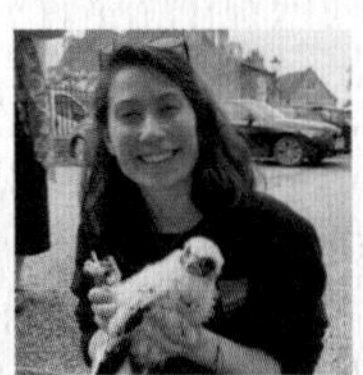
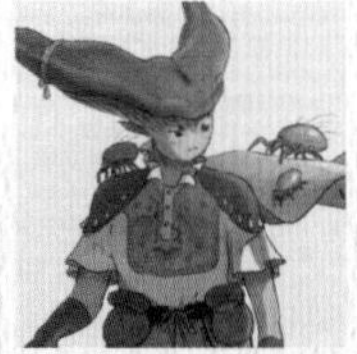

DOMINIQUE VASSIE

Artist & designer

dominiquevassie.com

Dominique is an artist and designer from the UK with an academic background in biology.

'In the vastness of the various plant types and species, you can find a limitless supply of inspiration for your own creative endeavours'

Ognjen Sporin

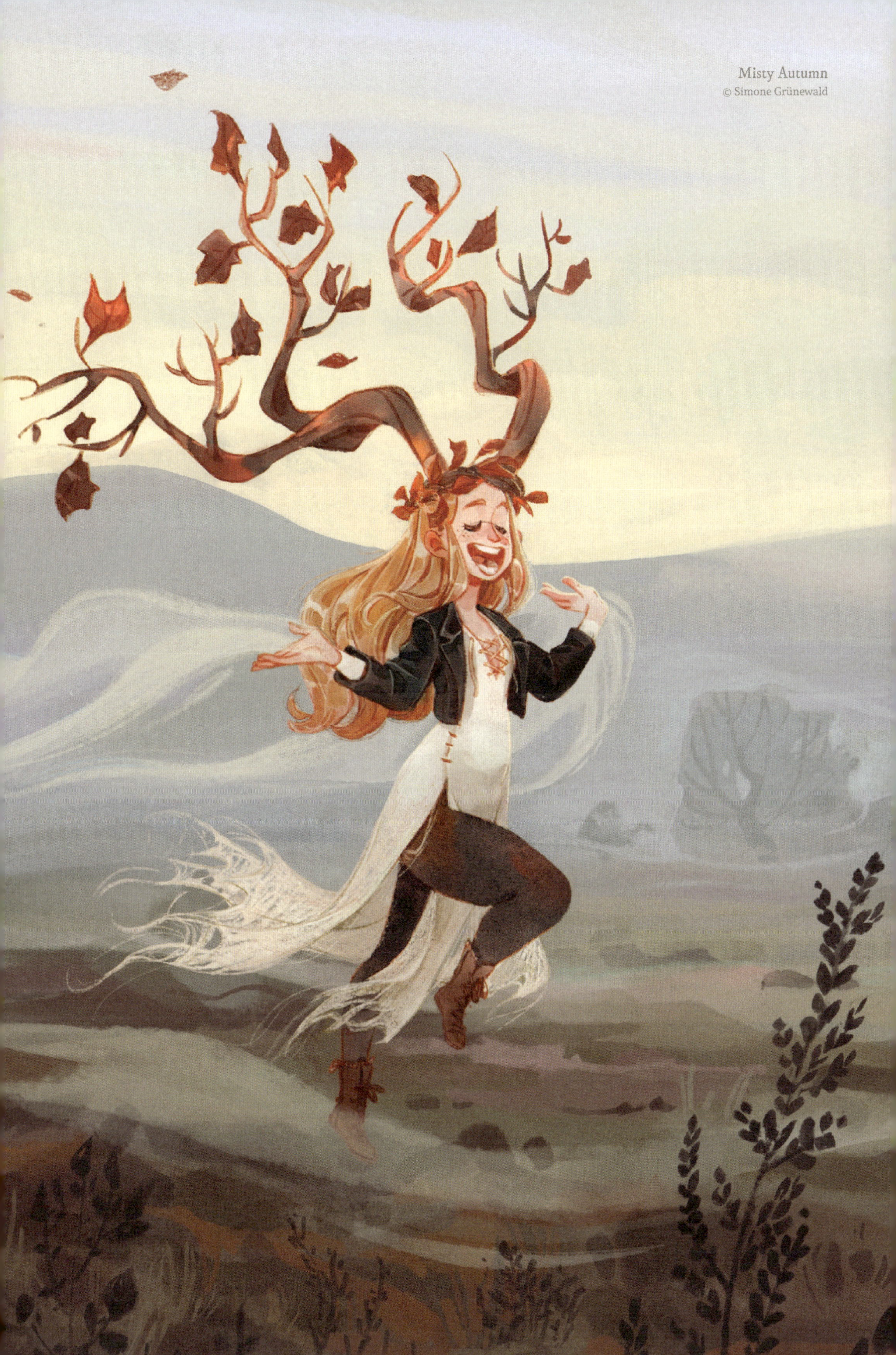

Misty Autumn

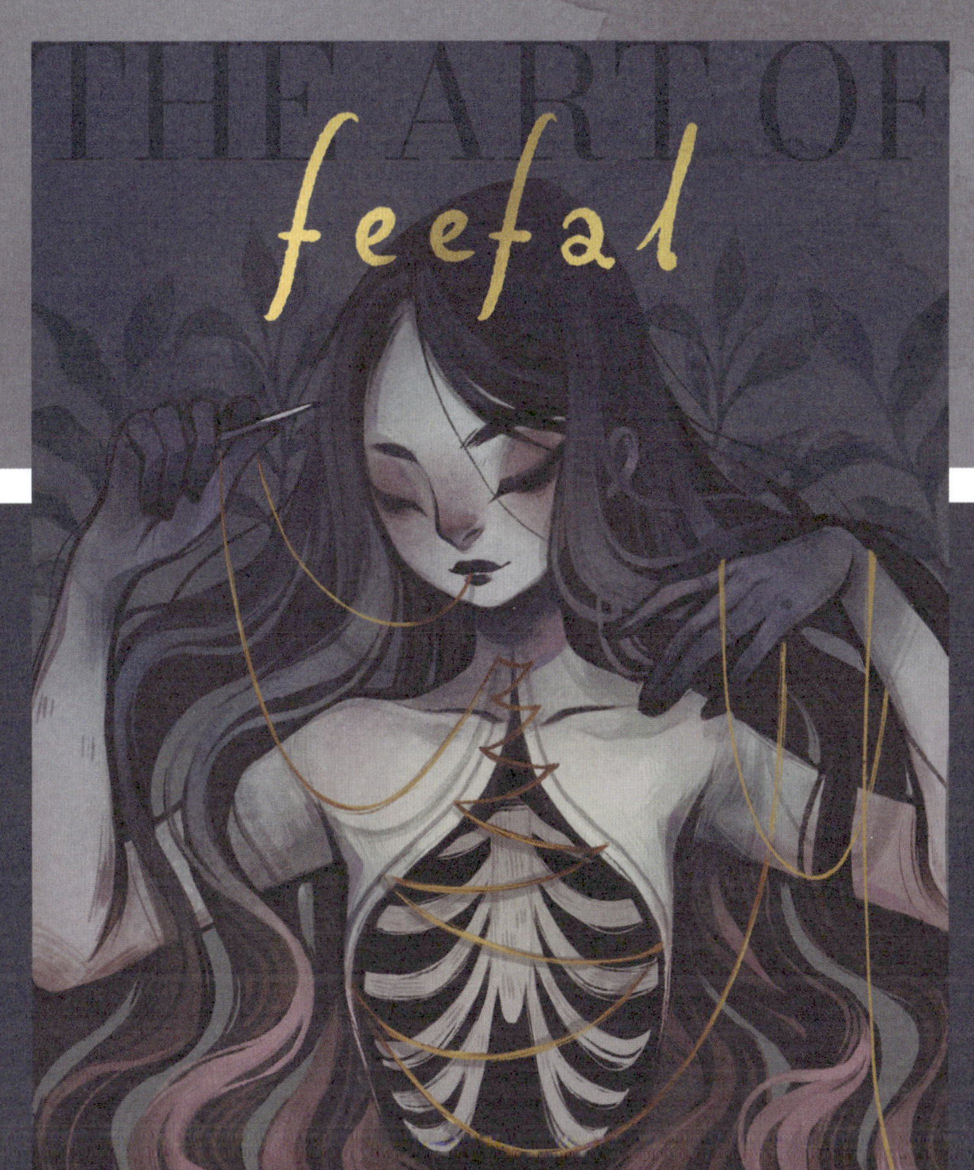
THE ART OF
feefal

3dtotalPublishing

3dtotal Publishing is a trailblazing, creative publisher specializing in inspirational and educational resources for artists.

Our titles feature top industry professionals from around the globe who share their experience in skilfully written step-by-step tutorials and fascinating, detailed guides. Illustrated throughout with stunning artwork, these best-selling publications offer creative insight, expert advice, and essential motivation. Fans of digital art will enjoy our comprehensive volumes covering Adobe Photoshop, Procreate, and Blender, as well as our superb titles based around character design, including *Fundamentals of Character Design* and *Creating Characters for the Entertainment Industry*. The dedicated, high-quality blend of instruction and inspiration also extends to traditional art. Titles covering a range of techniques, genres, and abilities allow your creativity to flourish while building essential skills.

Well-established within the industry, we now offer over 100 titles and counting, many of which have been translated into multiple languages around the world. With something for every artist, we are proud to say that our books offer the 3dtotal package:

LEARN • CREATE • SHARE

Visit us at store.3dtotal.com

3dtotal Publishing is part of 3dtotal.com, a leading website for CG artists founded by Tom Greenway in 1999.